OPINIONS '90

ISSN: 1050-0383

OPINIONS '90

Extracts from Public Opinion Surveys and Polls Conducted
by Business, Government, Professional
and News Organizations

CUMULATION

Cumulates Opinions '90, Issues 1, 2, and 3,
which may be discarded. Also includes 150 new surveys.

Chris John Miko & Edward Weilant

Editors

 **Gale Research Inc.** · *DETROIT* · *LONDON*

Editors: Chris John Miko and Edward Weilant

Gale Research Inc. Staff

Senior Editor: Linda Metzger
Coordinating Editor: Susan L. Stetler

Production Manager: Mary Beth Trimper
External Production Assistant: Shanna Philpott

Art Director: Arthur Chartow
Graphic Designer: Kathleen A. Mouzakis

Contents

Introduction

Opinion polls are conducted constantly on every conceivable topic. Because a democratic society is guided by the will of the people, knowing what the people "think" becomes an essential part of the decision making process.

Although opinion polls are numerous, the results of these polls are scattered among hundreds of sources, making it difficult to locate this information. Yet, this information is a crucial aid for such diverse activities as developing an understanding of current trends, generating new ideas in many fields of endeavor, and studying the ebb and flow of opinion on a topic. *Opinions '90* brings together extracts of the most important polls from a variety of sources, covering the most interesting and timely issues of the day.

Current Surveys in an Accessible Format

Readers involved in such varied activities as business and marketing decisions, government policy, student research papers, and news reports will find *Opinions '90* an essential tool that meets their needs for:

• **One-stop reference.** The editors have searched general interest and subject specific databases and indexes covering more than 1,700 magazines and journals as well as the most prominent U.S. newspapers. From these searches, they have selected general interest and topical surveys for inclusion in *Opinions '90*. Entries in *Opinions '90* allow the user to gain an impression of the survey and its results and determine if further research is desirable.

• **Broad scope.** Unlike other compilations of opinion polls, *Opinions '90* includes information from a number of different and diverse polls and surveys.

• **Timeliness.** This cumulation contains polls and surveys published between January 1, 1990 and December 31, 1990. Three serial issues are published each year. These issues, plus an additional 150 polls, are cumulated annually in this hardbound edition which covers an entire year of published opinions. While the serial issues offer the timeliness of opinions published in each quarter of the year, the cumulation allows the user to track the opinions and trends of the entire year.

• **Convenient arrangement.** *Opinions '90* entries are arranged alphabetically under the main subject of the poll or survey. If the poll covers a double subject (e.g., women engineers) or if the content of the poll covers two or more subjects, a cross reference directs readers to the appropriate listing in both the Outline of Contents and Index.

Clear Presentation of Information

• **Easy retrieval.** Each *Opinions '90* entry contains a description of the poll or survey; results of the poll; extracts from the poll, highlighting a specific question or result; details of the poll itself—who conducted it, when it was conducted, sampling error, etc.; other information provided in the poll not included in the entry; and a bibliographic citation listing the original published source(s) of the poll.

• **Graphic interpretation.** In addition to providing an extract from the poll, the results are often presented graphically, through the use of pie charts, bar graphs, or other visual forms, to provide the user with another representation of the poll results.

Alternate Search Strategies

• **Appendix provides additional information.** *Opinions '90* includes an appendix listing the organizations, centers, or firms (with address and telephone number) that have conducted the polls and surveys included within this edition for the user who wishes to make additional inquiries.

• **Outline of Contents, comprehensive Index provide flexible access.** The Outline of Contents allows users to easily search the subject areas covered in a particular issue. Additionally, users may access *Opinions '90* entries through a keyword index. The Index includes citations for subjects, polling and sponsoring organizations, and groups in a single alphabetical sequence. Indexes from the three issues are cumulated in this hardbound edition.

Acknowledgments

The editors thank the organization officials who generously responded to our requests for information. We would also like to thank Sue Stetler and Floris Wood for their editorial suggestions and technical assistance. For providing their time, patience, and understanding, we extend special thanks to Ben, Mom Weilant, Susan, and Ulla.

Suggestions Are Welcome

The editors welcome any comments regarding the scope and coverage of this publication. Please address correspondence to: Editors, *Opinions '90*, Gale Research Inc., 835 Penobscot Bldg., Detroit, Michigan 48226-4094; or call toll-free 1-800-347-4253.

Outline of Contents

OPINIONS '90

ARGUMENTS FOR AND AGAINST ABORTION

Description: Describes the public's attitude toward each side's position in the abortion debate.

Results: The majority of Americans support a woman's right to abortion. Americans don't approve of abortion as a method of birth control. Slightly more men than women support the right of choice. Significant numbers on both sides of the abortion debate recognize the validity of the opposing points of view.

Poll Extracts:

MOST CONVINCING ARGUMENTS AGAINST ABORTION, AS SEEN BY THE PEOPLE AGAINST ABORTION:

Abortion is against God's law 82%
A pregnant woman who doesn't want a child
  can give it up for adoption 80%
Abortion is the same as murdering a human being 75%
The availability of legal abortions results in
  people's abusing abortion and using it
  as a means of birth control 73%

MOST CONVINCING ARGUMENTS IN SUPPORT OF ABORTION, AS SEEN BY THE PEOPLE IN FAVOR OF ABORTION:

Restricting the right to abortion will mean
  that more women will die from illegal abortions ... 77%
Every women has the right to control her own body ... 77%
Restricting choice is unnecessary government
  intrusion in our personal life 67%
Restrictions will result in more children
  growing up in poverty 65%
In the first few months after conception
  a fetus is so undeveloped it's hardly
  recognizable as a human being 39%

Also in Source: The percentage of those surveyed who favor or are opposed to abortion. Arguments on both sides of the issue which are recognized as being valid by their opponents. Catholic versus Protestant opinion. Opinions as to morally acceptable methods of family planning.

Poll Details: The survey was commissioned by *Parents* Magazine.

Availability: Published in *Parents*, March 1990 (volume 65, number 3), p. 30.

CATHOLICS AND ABORTION

Description: Presents the results of a survey concerning Catholics' views on the legality of abortion.

Results: Almost 60% of the Catholics surveyed think that abortion should not be illegal.

Poll Extracts:

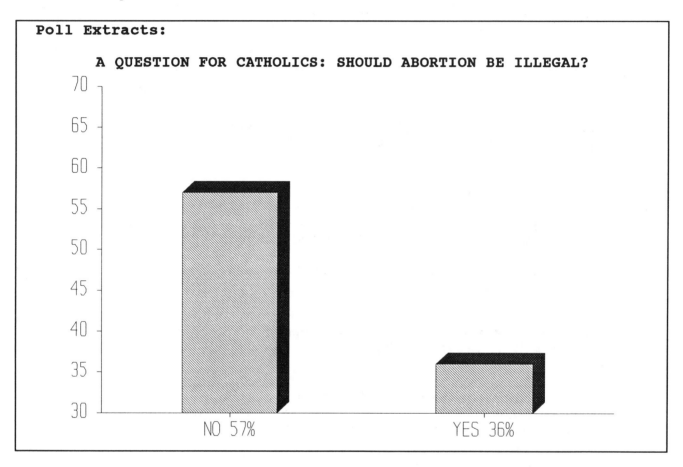

A QUESTION FOR CATHOLICS: SHOULD ABORTION BE ILLEGAL?

NO 57%   YES 36%

Also in Source: 32% of the respondents representing all voters thought abortion should be illegal, while 60% thought it should be legal.

Poll Details: The results are taken from a *Wall Street Journal*/NBC News Poll on June 10, 1990.

Availability: Published in *The Wall Street Journal*, October 16, 1990, p. A26.

GEORGIANS' VIEWS ON ABORTION

Description: Presents the results of a survey of the citizens of the State of Georgia concerning their views on abortion.

Results: Almost half of the respondents think abortion should be legal under certain circumstances.

Poll Extracts:

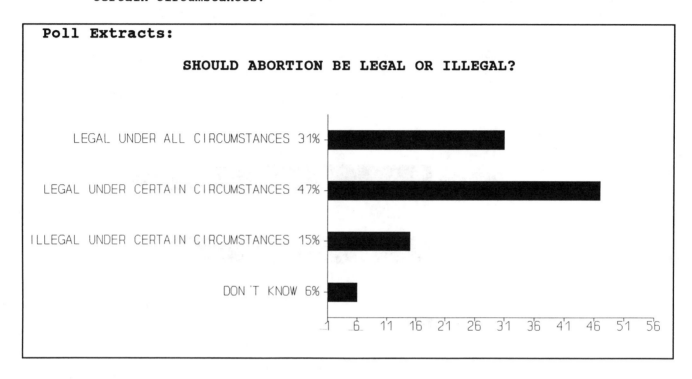

SHOULD ABORTION BE LEGAL OR ILLEGAL?

Also in Source: The article includes a number of surveys concerning a wide range of topics including the death penalty, the state lottery, crime, politics, and the general condition of the State of Georgia.

Poll Details: The poll was based on telephone interviews of 652 adults, 18 years or older, who were identified as likely voters. The survey was conducted from April 13 through April 24, 1990 with the exception of Easter Sunday.

Availability: Published in *The Atlanta Journal and Constitution*, April 29, 1990, p. A1, A14.

GOVERNORS' VIEWS ON ABORTION

Description: Presents the results of a survey of governors concerning their official support of a woman's right to an abortion. The survey also included the governors' personal views on abortion.

Results: Approximately half of the governors support a woman's right to an abortion. However, half of those governors who support abortion rights as a matter of public policy personally oppose abortion.

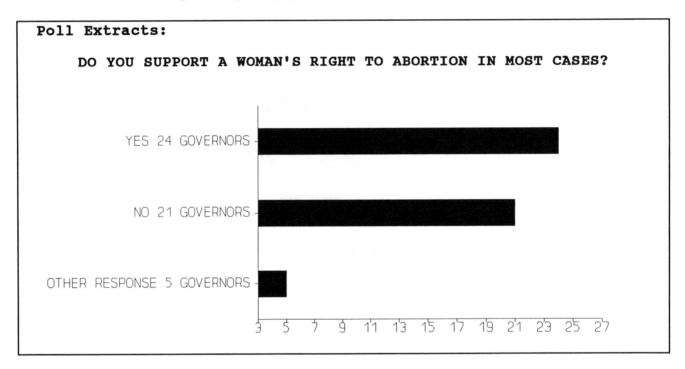

Poll Extracts:

DO YOU SUPPORT A WOMAN'S RIGHT TO ABORTION IN MOST CASES?

YES 24 GOVERNORS

NO 21 GOVERNORS

OTHER RESPONSE 5 GOVERNORS

3 5 7 9 11 13 15 17 19 21 23 25 27

Also in Source: A number of governors oppose abortion rights but say it should be available in certain cases such as incest or rape.

Poll Details: *USA Today* surveyed each governor during the week of March 22, 1990.

Availability: Published in *USA Today*, April 2, 1990, p. 1A.

NORTHEASTERN SUPPORT FOR ABORTION

Description: Respondents were asked if "in general" a woman ought to be able
to obtain an abortion.

Results: The majority of respondents supported a woman being able to obtain an
abortion. Abortion rights were supported by 80% of the Independents, 77%
of the Democrats, and 60% of the Republicans.

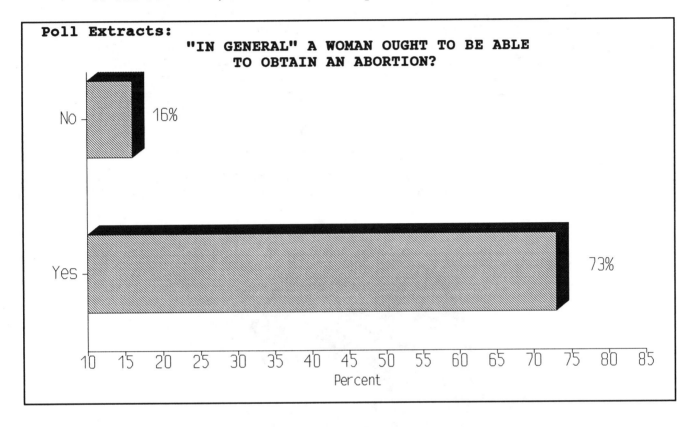

Poll Extracts:

**"IN GENERAL" A WOMAN OUGHT TO BE ABLE
TO OBTAIN AN ABORTION?**

No — 16%

Yes — 73%

Percent

Also in Source: Responses to questions on a variety of areas such as taxes,
general issues facing Massachusetts, and voter confidence in the local,
state, and federal government.

Poll Details: This *Boston Globe* and WBZ-TV poll surveyed 436 "likely general
election voters" during August 26-30, 1990. The poll has a margin of error
of 5%.

Availability: Published in *The Boston Globe*, September 3, 1990, p. 1, 8, 9.

PARENTAL ADVICE AND CONSENT

Description: This poll queried adult Americans about the advice they would give their teenage sons or daughters if they were involved in a pregnancy. Poll includes actions that teenagers should or should not be able to take without parental consent.

Results: Respondents thought that if their teenage daughter became pregnant, they would advise her to: raise the child alone - 22%, give the child up for adoption - 15%, get an abortion - 11%. Respondents thought that if their teenage son made someone pregnant they would advise him to: help pay for medical expenses and child support - 52%, marry the mother - 20%, help pay for an abortion - 7%, try to get out of the situation - 1%. Respondents also thought that teenagers should be able to do the following without parental consent: have a tooth pulled - 63%, donate blood - 59%, obtain birth control - 53%, have an abortion - 38%.

Poll Extracts:

DO YOU FAVOR OR OPPOSE A LAW REQUIRING A TEENAGER TO HAVE HER PARENTS' CONSENT BEFORE AN ABORTION?

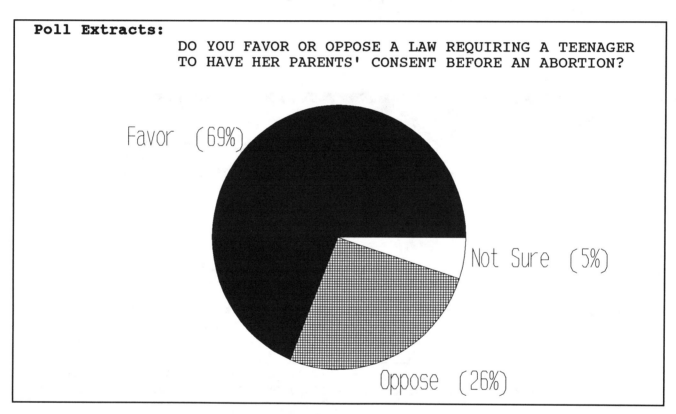

Favor (69%)

Not Sure (5%)

Oppose (26%)

Also in Source: The percentage of respondents who felt that the government should pay for an abortion when a rape victim becomes pregnant and cannot afford an abortion.

Poll Details: This *Time*/CNN telephone poll was conducted May 8-9, 1990 by Yankelovich Clancy Shulman. 1,000 adult Americans were polled. The sampling error is 3%.

Availability: Published in *Time*, July 9, 1990 (volume 136, number 2), p. 22-26.

POLITICAL PARTIES AND ABORTION

Description: Ohio voters were surveyed as to the Republican and Democratic parties' positions regarding abortion.

Results: Most Ohio voters do not associate either major political party with a specific position on the issue of abortion.

Poll Extracts:

DOES THE POSITION A CANDIDATE TAKES ON ABORTION EFFECT HOW YOU WILL VOTE ?

No 37%

IS ABORTION THE MOST IMPORTANT POLITICAL ISSUE ?

Yes 10%

The Democratic Party is for
     abortion rights 26%
Don't know where the Democratic
     Party stands on abortion 60%
The Republican Party is against
     abortion rights 30%
Don't identify the Republican
     Party with a position on abortion 55%

Also in Source: The only group having a majority that say the Republican Party is anti-abortion, and the Democratic Party favors abortion rights, is among college graduates.

Poll Details: The Ohio Poll was conducted by the Institute for Policy Research at the University of Cincinnati. It was conducted for the *Dayton Daily News*, and the *Cincinnati Post*. A random sample of 544 registered voters were interviewed from February 2 through 12. The margin for error is plus or minus 4%.

Availability: Published in the *Dayton Daily News*, March 19, 1990, p. 3-A.

PSYCHOLOGICAL EFFECTS OF ABORTION

Description: Presents the results of a survey concerning the psychological response of women after a first-trimester abortion.

Results: Over three-fourths of the women surveyed reported feeling relief two weeks after a first-trimester abortion.

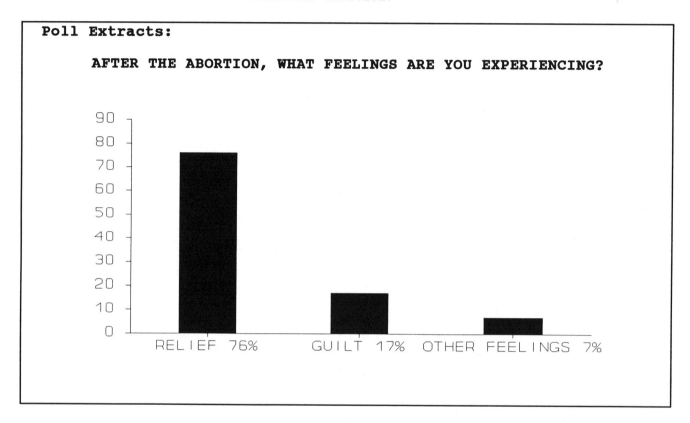

Poll Extracts:

AFTER THE ABORTION, WHAT FEELINGS ARE YOU EXPERIENCING?

RELIEF 76%   GUILT 17%   OTHER FEELINGS 7%

Also in Source: Most women do not find the decision to abort difficult. The decision, however, is more difficult later in pregnancy. 7% of 100 first-trimester patients reported initial indecision and 12% reported difficulty in deciding about abortion. Corresponding figures among 200 second-trimester patients were 36% and 51%.

Poll Details: Women were interviewed two weeks after a first-trimester abortion.

Availability: Published in *Science*, April 6, 1990 (volume 248, number 4951), p. 41-43.

REGIONAL AND CLASS ATTITUDES TOWARD ABORTION

Description: This poll attempted to measure how Americans feel about the quality of their lives, their standard of living, and the state of their nation.

Results: Abortion is opposed across America by 5 to 4, with women much more opposed than men. But in California, abortion is supported by 3 to 2.

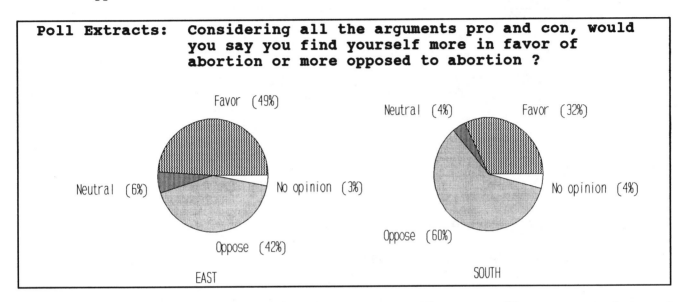

Poll Extracts: **Considering all the arguments pro and con, would you say you find yourself more in favor of abortion or more opposed to abortion ?**

EAST

SOUTH

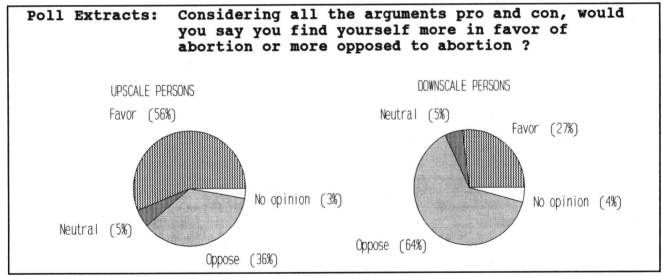

Poll Extracts: **Considering all the arguments pro and con, would you say you find yourself more in favor of abortion or more opposed to abortion ?**

UPSCALE PERSONS

DOWNSCALE PERSONS

Also in Source: Responses from other segments of the country (Midwest & West), and also from "Midscale" people. A broad number of other issues.

Poll Details: This *Los Angeles Times* Poll consisted of a nationwide telephone poll of 2,095 adults, conducted on the five days ending December 20. The poll has a sampling tolerance of 3% in either direction. The poll was directed by I.A. Lewis.

Availability: Published in the *Los Angeles Times*, January 1, 1990, p. A1.

VOTER RESPONSE TO CANDIDATES' POSITIONS

Description: Results were presented regarding voter reaction to candidates' positions on abortion, and the availability of the abortion procedure.

Results: Almost half the people in the poll say that abortion is a key factor in deciding who they vote for.

Poll Extracts:

**WOULD YOU VOTE FOR OR AGAINST CANDIDATES
PRIMARILY ON THEIR ABORTION VIEWS?**

Yes 48%

SHOULD ABORTION:

Always be left to a woman and her doctor? 37%

Be left to a woman and her doctor
in the first three months? 21%

Be allowed only in cases of rape, incest, or where the
woman's life is in danger? 33%

Never be allowed? 7%

Also in Source: The overall percentage of adults who would vote for or against candidates has increased from a similar poll taken July 6, 1989.

Poll Details: The poll of 811 adults was taken December 20 and 26, 1989 by the Gordon S. Black Corp., and has a 3.5% sampling error.

Availability: Published in *USA TODAY*, January 2, 1990, p. 1A.

ADVERTISING FOR ALCOHOL

Description: This poll queried respondents on their attitudes toward placing
health warnings on advertisements for alcoholic beverages. They were also
asked about placing a ban on all alcoholic advertising.

Results: The majority of respondents favor placing health warnings on
advertising for alcoholic beverages, but 36% of the respondents believe
that if warning labels are placed on advertising for alcoholic beverages it
will have no effect on alcoholic beverage consumption. 42.2% of the
respondents favor a ban on all beer, wine, and liquor advertising.

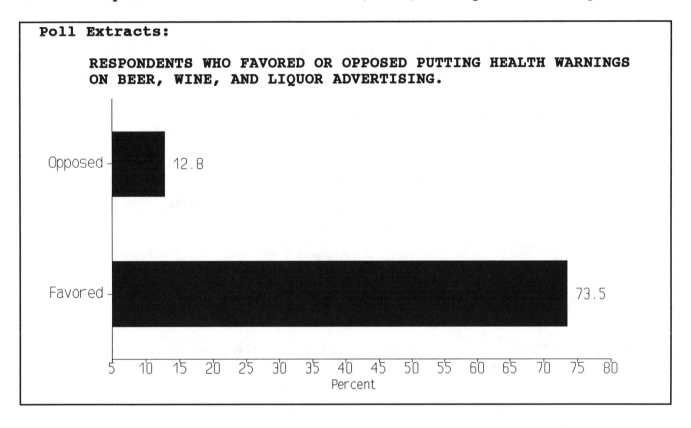

Poll Extracts:

**RESPONDENTS WHO FAVORED OR OPPOSED PUTTING HEALTH WARNINGS
ON BEER, WINE, AND LIQUOR ADVERTISING.**

Opposed — 12.8

Favored — 73.5

Percent

Also in Source: A majority of the respondents were aware of the proposed plan
to put health warnings on beer, wine, and liquor advertising, similar to
the ones currently in place on cigarette advertising and packaging.

Poll Details: This *Advertising Age* / Gallup Organization poll interviewed 823
adults by telephone on April 5, 1990. The margin of error is plus or minus
3.5%.

Availability: Published in *Advertising Age*, April 9, 1990 (volume 61,
number 15), p. 1, 64.

ADVERTISING RECALL

Description: This survey measured advertising awareness by asking a nationally
projectable sample to name the first advertising that comes to mind from
all seen, heard or read in the previous 30 days.

Results: Ford and Pepsi-Cola tied for the position of number one best recalled
advertiser in January 1990.

Poll Extracts:

TOP 10 ADVERTISERS WHO HAD THE BEST CONSUMER RECALL IN JANUARY:

```
            Tied for 1st Place - Ford
                                 Pepsi-Cola
                           3rd - Budweiser/Bud Light
                           4th - Coca-Cola
            Tied for 5th Place - McDonald's
                                 Infiniti
                           7th - Chevrolet
                           8th - Miller
                           9th - Diet Coke
                          10th - Toyota
```

Also in Source: In soft-drink advertising, the top five products in
advertising awareness for January.

Poll Details: This "Adwatch" survey is a joint project of *Advertising Age* and
the Gallup Organization. In January 1,000 adults were polled by phone.
The margin of error is plus or minus 3.1%.

Availability: Published in *Advertising Age,* February 26, 1990 (volume 61,
number 9), p. 28.

APPLIANCE STORE ADVERTISING

Description: This survey asked which retailers or types of retailers are guilty of abuses in their advertising.

Results: Appliance stores, more than any other retail store, lack credibility with consumers.

Poll Extracts:

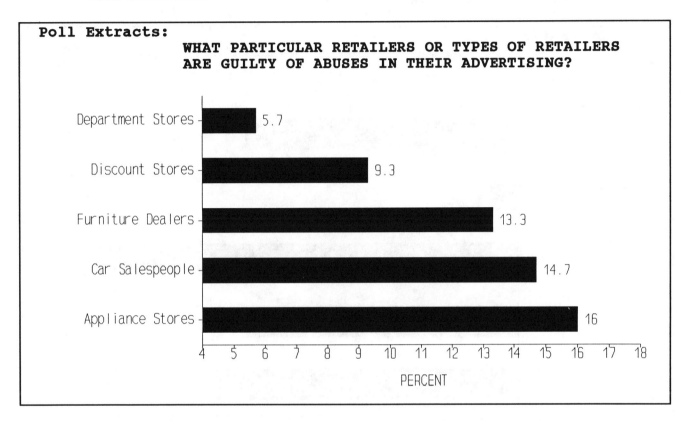

WHAT PARTICULAR RETAILERS OR TYPES OF RETAILERS
ARE GUILTY OF ABUSES IN THEIR ADVERTISING?

Retailer	Percent
Department Stores	5.7
Discount Stores	9.3
Furniture Dealers	13.3
Car Salespeople	14.7
Appliance Stores	16

PERCENT

Also in Source: The percentage of respondents who thought that advertising was "very truthful" or "somewhat truthful." The percentage of respondents who "frequently," "often" or "sometimes" shop a store only when it is having a sale. The percentage of respondents who found comedy/humor/entertainment as the factor that appealed to them most, in their favorite advertisements.

Poll Details: The survey of 300 consumers was conducted by the Better Business Bureau and the Advertising Club of St. Louis.

Availability: Published in *HFD*, February 26, 1990 (volume 64, number 9), p. 113.

BANNING ADVERTISING IN MOVIE THEATERS

Description: Respondents were queried about banning commercials in movie
theaters.

Results: More respondents support a ban on commercials than oppose a ban on
commercials in movie theaters.

Poll Extracts:

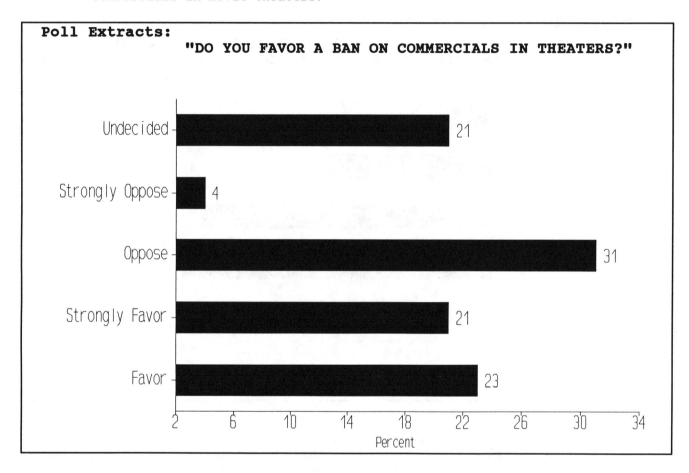

"DO YOU FAVOR A BAN ON COMMERCIALS IN THEATERS?"

Also in Source: The percentage of moviegoers who would continue to favor a
ban on commercials in movie theaters, if it meant the price of a movie
would increase 50 cents, or $1, or $2. The results from a poll sponsored
by Walt Disney Co., on whether moviegoers want commercials shown in movie
theaters, that was released earlier in the month. Cinema advertisers that
moviegoers thought of first.

Poll Details: This *Advertising Age* / Gallup Organization poll was conducted by
telephone with 1,000 persons in March 1990. These people were asked if
they had seen a movie in a movie theater in the last three months. 435
persons had seen a movie in a movie theater during the last three months,
and these people were asked questions about advertising shown before
movies.

Availability: Published in *Advertising Age*, April 23, 1990 (volume 61,
number 17), p. 4.

COMMERCIALS AT THE MOVIES

Description: Presents the results of a survey concerning the showing of
commercials at movie theaters.

Results: 90% of the respondents indicated that they do not want commercials
shown in movie theaters.

Poll Extracts:

ADS OR PREVIEWS?

SHOULD COMMERCIALS BE SHOWN AT MOVIE THEATERS?

NO...90%

SHOULD MOVIE PREVIEWS BE SHOWN AT MOVIE THEATERS?

YES...95%

Also in Source: The Walt Disney Company commissioned the survey to support
their ban on advertising in movie theaters.

Poll Details: 18,772 moviegoers were surveyed by National Research Group Inc.
The poll was conducted on March 31, 1990 in Chicago, Boston, New York, and
seven other communities by the research unit of Saatchi & Saatchi Company.

Availability: Published in *The Wall Street Journal*, April 11, 1990, p. B3.

CONSUMERS AND HEALTH/NUTRITION LABELS

Description: Presents the results of a survey of consumers concerning the importance and believability of health and nutrition labels on product packaging.

Results: Over 40% of the respondents read the health and nutrition labels either most or all the time.

Poll Extracts:

DO YOU READ HEALTH & NUTRITION LABELS?

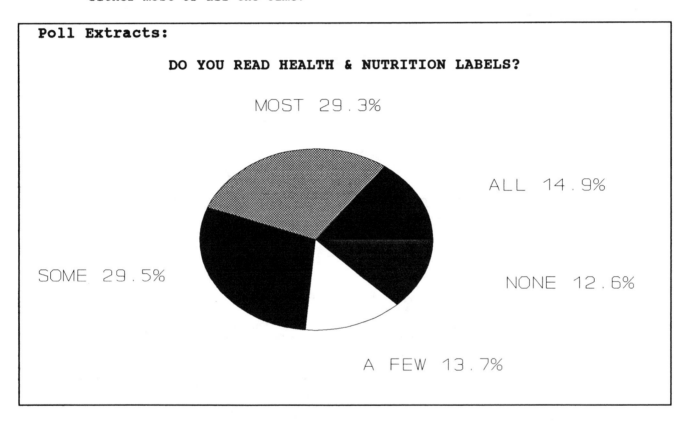

MOST 29.3%

ALL 14.9%

SOME 29.5%

NONE 12.6%

A FEW 13.7%

Also in Source: The survey also showed that 50.5% of the respondents do not believe the "reduce cholesterol" claim; 50% do not believe "reduce the risk of colon cancer"; and 36.2% are skeptical of the "low fat" claim.

Poll Details: The Gallup survey was based on telephone interviews with 972 people. Margin of error is 3.2%,

Availability: Published in *Advertising Age,* May 7, 1990 (volume 61, number 19), p. S-2.

MOST POPULAR ADS ON TV

Description: This survey asked consumers to pick the best commercials of 1989.

Results: Ads with surprise endings or unusual twists did well.

Poll Extracts:

PRODUCTS WITH THE MOST POPULAR TELEVISION ADVERTISEMENTS

         1.   McDonald's
         2.   Pepsi/Diet Pepsi
         3.   California Raisins
         4.   Energizer batteries
         5.   Isuzu
         6.   Bud Light
         7.   Coca-Cola
         8.   Miller Lite
         9.   Infiniti
        10.   Nike

Also in Source: Products having the most popular TV ads that were ranked eleventh through fifteenth.

Poll Details: The 1989 survey results were based on interviews with 24,000 consumers across the country. The survey was conducted by Video Storyboard Tests Inc.

Availability: Published in *The Atlanta Journal and Constitution*, February 17, 1990, p. F-1.

RECALL FOR ADVERTISING WITH CARTOON CHARACTERS

Description: This survey asked respondents to name the first ads that came to mind among those featuring cartoon/licensed characters.

Results: The top recall for advertisers featuring a cartoon/licensed character was Holiday Inn, which ran a summer promotion tied to Bugs Bunny's 50th Birthday.

Poll Extracts:

THE CARTOON/LICENSED CHARACTERS USED IN ADVERTISING THAT WERE BEST REMEMBERED:

Rank	Advertiser	Character
1.	Holiday Inn	Bugs Bunny
2.	Walt Disney World	Mickey Mouse, etc.
3.	Metropolitan Life	Snoopy
4.	Nestle's Butterfinger	Bart Simpson
4.	McDonald's	Dick Tracy
6.	Burger King	Ninja Turtles
6.	Embassy Suites	Garfield
8.	California Raisins	California Raisins
8.	Disneyland	Mickey Mouse, etc.
8.	Ralston's Teenage Mutant Ninja Turtles Cereal	Ninja Turtles

---

Also in Source: Respondents favorite and least favorite cartoon characters. The agencies that are connected to the advertising with the best remembered cartoon/licensed characters.

Poll Details: This survey was conducted for *Advertising Age* by the Gallup Organization. 1,000 adults were randomly surveyed by telephone in July 1990. The margin of error is plus or minus 3.1%.

Availability: Published in *Advertising Age*, September 17, 1990 (volume 61, number 38), p. 3, 73.

VIDEO ADS: PRO & CON

Description: Presents the results of a survey concerning people's approval of videotapes which include advertising.

Results: Over two-thirds of the respondents found the ads annoying.

Poll Extracts:

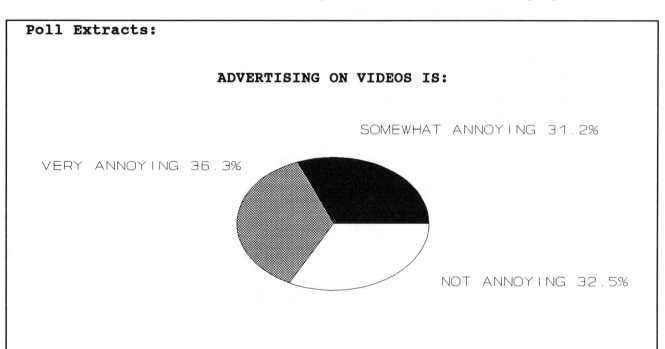

ADVERTISING ON VIDEOS IS:

SOMEWHAT ANNOYING 31.2%

VERY ANNOYING 36.3%

NOT ANNOYING 32.5%

Also in Source: Overall, 57% of the respondents watched the ads, while 42% fast-forwarded past the advertising. Advertisers had the best chance of getting persons age 18 to 34 to watch their videocassette commercial. 60% of survey respondents in this age group left the fast-forward button alone. Among those age 35 to 54, 54% watched the commercial, while 59% of those 55 and older kept their seats during the ad.

Poll Details: The Gallup survey was conducted by telephone using a randomly selected but nationally projectable sample. Margin of error is plus or minus 3.1%.

Availability: Published in *Advertising Age*, May 28, 1990, (volume 61, number 22) p. 8.

WHICH ADS DO YOU REMEMBER?

Description: Presents the results of an AdWatch survey identifying the top ten best-recalled advertisers from the month of October 1990.

Results: McDonald's advertising was identified as the best-recalled from the month of October 1990. The advertising is produced by the Leo Burnett USA agency.

Poll Extracts:

    FROM THE MONTH OF OCTOBER, WHICH ADS COME TO MIND FIRST?

	Advertiser	Agency
1.	McDonald's	Leo Burnett USA
2.	Political ads (general)	Various
3.	Automobiles (general)	Various
4.	Chevrolet	Lintas: Campbell-Ewald
5. (tie)	Budweiser/Bud Light	D'Arcy Masius Benton & Bowles/ DDB Needham Worldwide
5. (tie)	Pepsi-Cola	BBDO Worldwide
7.	Ford	J. Walter Thompson USA
8.	AT&T	NW Ayer/Ogilvy & Mather/ Young & Rubicam
9.	Coke/Coca-Cola	McCann-Erickson Worldwide
10.	Nike	Wieden & Kennedy

Also in Source: A general overview of the advertising business is included in the article.

Poll Details: AdWatch is a joint project of *Advertising Age* and the Gallup Organization. Advertising awareness is measured by asking a nationally projectable sample to name the first advertising that comes to mind from all seen, heard, or read in the previous 30 days. 1,000 adults were polled by telephone. The survey's margin of error is plus or minus 3.1%.

Availability: Published in *Advertising Age*, November 26, 1990 (volume 61, number 49), p. 28.

ELDERLY PARENTS

Description: National survey on attitudes and opinions about middle age.

Results: Children have an obligation to care for aging parents until they die.

Poll Extracts:

SHOULD KIDS CARE FOR ELDERLY PARENTS?

Middle-aged ....Yes................. 62%
Seniors ....Yes................. 61%

(Middle-aged being defined by most respondents
 as age 46-66)

**ARE MIDDLE-AGED PARENTS OFTEN UNDER SEVERE
FINANCIAL STRAIN BECAUSE THEY CARE FOR BOTH
THEIR CHILDREN AND THEIR AGING PARENTS?**

Yes 71%

Also in Source: The percentage who want to die before becoming "too old."
    The best thing about middle age, and also the worst part.

Poll Details: The national survey was commissioned by the American Board of
    Family Practice and conducted by New World Decisions Inc. About 1,200
    adults aged 18-76 were questioned.

Availability: Published in *USA Today,* January 23, 1990, p. 1D.

LIFE AS A SENIOR CITIZEN

Description: This poll asked the respondents about their attitudes toward their life as senior citizens.

Results: 96.3% of the respondents were "basically happy," and more than 50% were excited about the future. 83.6% of the respondents said that they consider themselves useful members of society. 67% of the respondents thought that the environment in retirement communities was "safe and comfortable."

Poll Extracts:

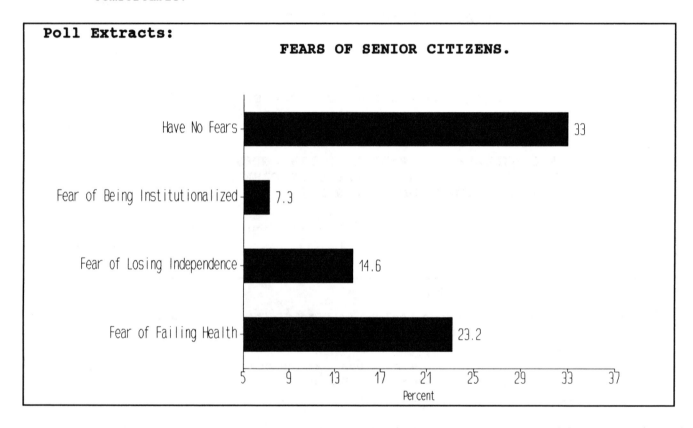

FEARS OF SENIOR CITIZENS.

Also in Source: Respondents felt they were younger than their actual chronological age by an average of 12 years. On the average, respondents "realistically" expected to live to the age of 86. The way men and women spend their leisure time.

Poll Details: This national survey was conducted by the ICR Survey Research Group for the Marriott Corp. 1,004 adults, age 65 and older, were interviewed by telephone from May 11, 1990 to June 11, 1990.

Availability: Published in *The Atlanta Journal and Constitution*, June 23, 1990, p. A-3.

MIDDLE AGE

Description: National survey on attitudes and opinions about middle age.

Results: Beliefs about the meaning of middle age are presented. The majority of respondents agreed that middle age begins at 46 and ends at 65.

Poll Extracts:

BEING MIDDLE-AGED MEANS:

You think more about past events than the future 47%

You don't recognize the names of music groups
on the radio 46%

It takes a day or two longer to recover
from strenuous exercise 44%

You worry about having enough money for
health care concerns 41%

THE BEST PART ABOUT BEING MIDDLE-AGED IS:

That the children are grown 23%

Also in Source: The best thing about middle age, and also the worst part.

Poll Details: The national survey was commissioned by the American Board of Family Practice.

Availability: Published in the *Chicago Tribune*, March 11, 1990, section 5, p. 9.

TAPPING HOME EQUITY

Description: Presents the results of a survey identifying the motivations of
senior citizens who apply for reverse mortages, thus tapping the equity in
their homes. A reverse mortgage provides those eligible with tax-free
monthly payments for the rest of their lives while they continue to own and
live in their homes.

Results: Almost half of the respondents said they would use the money for
luxury items and discretionary activities. Of those, most ranked
travel/vacation as the number one expenditure they would make. Other
respondents would utilize it to enjoy life more, citing "going out to
dinner more often" as an example.

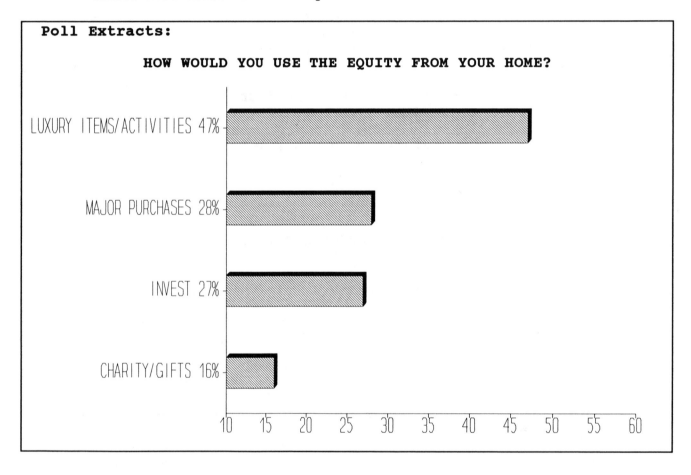

Poll Extracts:

HOW WOULD YOU USE THE EQUITY FROM YOUR HOME?

LUXURY ITEMS/ACTIVITIES 47%
MAJOR PURCHASES 28%
INVEST 27%
CHARITY/GIFTS 16%

Also in Source: Prior to these findings, the prevailing industry view had
been that potential reverse mortgage customers were motivated by dire
financial conditions leading to servere hardships, possibly necessitating
the sale of their dwellings.

Poll Details: This national study was conducted by Capital Holding
Coorporation of San Francisco, California.

Availability: Published in *USA Today Special Newsletter Edition*, December 1990
(volume 119, number 2547), p. 12, 13.

CALIFORNIA MALATHION SPRAYING

Description: This poll presents views on malathion spraying in California against the Mediterranean fruit fly.

Results: A moratorium on malathion spraying is supported by 57% of the respondents. Only 32% of the respondents are in favor of continuing the spraying. There is widespread concern over the potential health risks posed by the use of the pesticide. In those neighborhoods which had been sprayed, 20% believe they and their families have suffered from problems related to malathion, or have increased their chances of problems.

Poll Extracts:

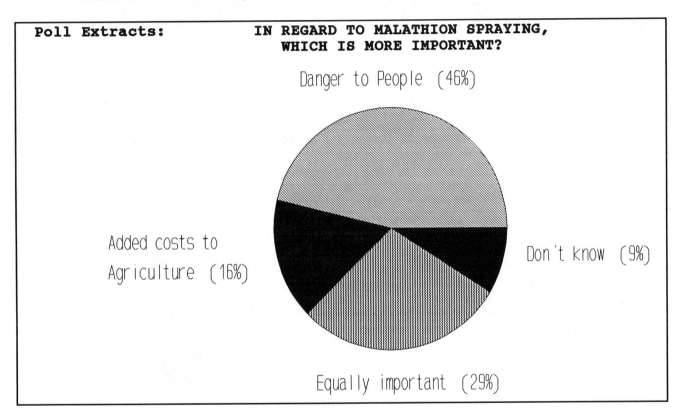

IN REGARD TO MALATHION SPRAYING, WHICH IS MORE IMPORTANT?

Danger to People (46%)

Added costs to Agriculture (16%)

Don't know (9%)

Equally important (29%)

Also in Source: The percentage of respondents who: said they live in areas that had been sprayed, thought people had been given enough warning, worry about malathion spraying, felt that their pets and wild animals were at risk, said automobiles in their neighborhoods had been damaged by the aerial spraying.

Poll Details: The Times Poll questioned 1,901 residents of Los Angeles and Orange counties between February 4 and February 7, 1990. The poll has a margin of error of 3%.

Availability: Published in the *Los Angeles Times*, February 11, 1990, p. A1, A42.

CATTLE PRODUCTION

Description: Measured consumers' opinions on beef cattle production in regards to animal welfare concerns.

Results: Two-thirds of consumers do not think the beef cattle industry needs animal welfare groups or governmental units to have a "watchdog role" over cattle production, or the impact of production on natural resources. In consumers' decisions to eat beef, issues such as environmental impact or animal husbandry are much less important to consumers than beef nutrition, price, and safety. Almost half of the public would support government regulations on cattle treatment, but many would withdraw their support if those regulations would cost millions in taxes, increase beef prices 15%, or drive producers out of business.

Poll Extracts:

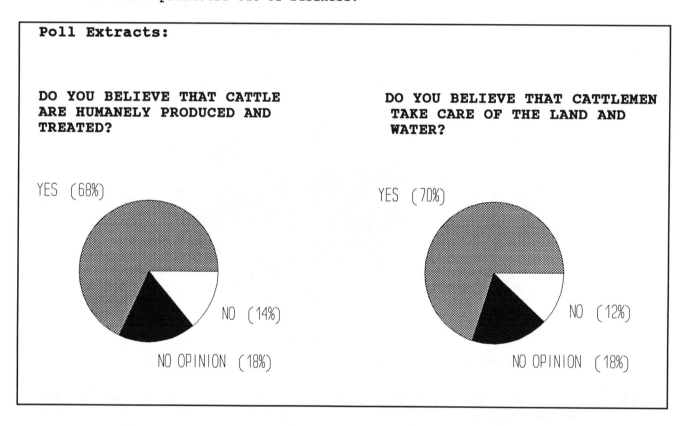

DO YOU BELIEVE THAT CATTLE ARE HUMANELY PRODUCED AND TREATED?

YES (68%) NO (14%) NO OPINION (18%)

DO YOU BELIEVE THAT CATTLEMEN TAKE CARE OF THE LAND AND WATER?

YES (70%) NO (12%) NO OPINION (18%)

Also in Source: The percentage of consumers who: say that animals have rights, say cattle should not be produced for food, believe that private control and ownership of agricultural land is better than government ownership, say cattle grazing is a good use of public rangeland, say cattle production is not using up natural resources.

Poll Details: The poll was commissioned by The Beef Board and conducted by The Wirthlin Group and included companion surveys of allied industry and producers.

Availability: Published in *Feedstuffs*, January 22, 1990 (volume 62, number 4), p. 20.

INCREASED TAXES VERSUS MORE TREES

Description: Presents the results of a survey measuring support among Georgia
voters for providing tax breaks for timber growers as an inducement to
replant trees.

Results: Over 60% of the respondents favor a tax reduction for timber growers
to encourage them to plant trees.

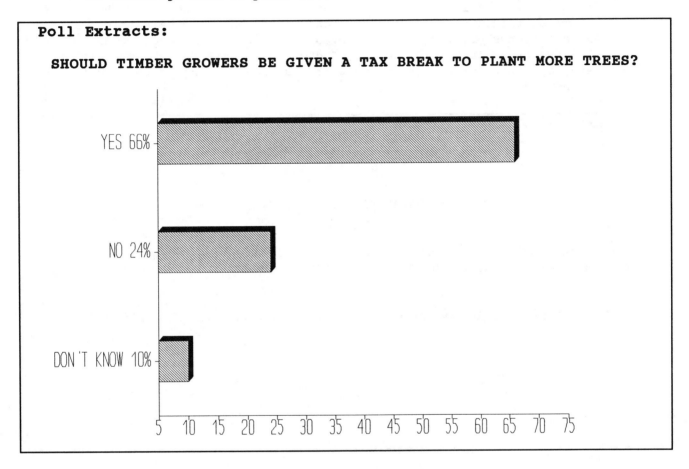

Poll Extracts:

SHOULD TIMBER GROWERS BE GIVEN A TAX BREAK TO PLANT MORE TREES?

YES 66%

NO 24%

DON'T KNOW 10%

5 10 15 20 25 30 35 40 45 50 55 60 65 70 75

Also in Source: If the timber growers were granted a tax break, 55% of the
respondents would be willing to pay more property taxes to support the tax
reduction. 41% would not support the tax increase and 4% didn't know.

Poll Details: This poll of 691 likely voters was conducted by *The Atlanta
Journal and Constitution* October 25 through 28, 1990.

Availability: Published in *The Atlanta Journal and Constitution*, November 1,
1990, p. A1, A14.

PESTICIDE LIMITATIONS, NOT BANS

Description: This poll queried respondents about the use of agricultural chemicals.

Results: The majority of respondents did not support a ban on pesticides, but believed that farmers should reduce their use of agricultural chemicals or continue usage at current levels. 79% of the respondents believed that farmers are reducing their use of chemicals by adopting new methods, while 73% thought that farmers used more chemicals than necessary in order to achieve higher profits. 56% believed that few farmers had extensive training or education in the use of chemicals. 78% thought that it was very important for farmers to support research leading to the reduced use of chemicals.

Poll Extracts:

RESPONDENTS FELT THAT:

Farmers should reduce their use of agricultural
chemicals or continue usage at current levels .... Nearly 80%

Pesticides should be banned 21%

Also in Source: The percentage of all farms owned by corporations, and also the percentage of farmland owned by absentee owners. The percentage of the respondents who were "very concerned" about pesticides, growth hormones given to livestock, and antibiotics given to livestock.

Poll Details: This nationwide poll of 1,000 adults was commissioned by the American Farm Bureau.

Availability: Published in *Chemical Marketing Reporter,* August 6, 1990 (volume 238, issue 6), p. 4, 25.

PROTECTING PRODUCE FROM CHEMICALS

Description: The poll questioned whether the presence of organic foods and the publicity surrounding organic foods has had much of an effect on American consumers.

Results: Americans' perceptions on food are changing.

Poll Extracts:

IS THE FEDERAL GOVERNMENT DOING A GOOD OR POOR JOB OF PROTECTING THE PUBLIC FROM POTENTIALLY HARMFUL CHEMICALS?

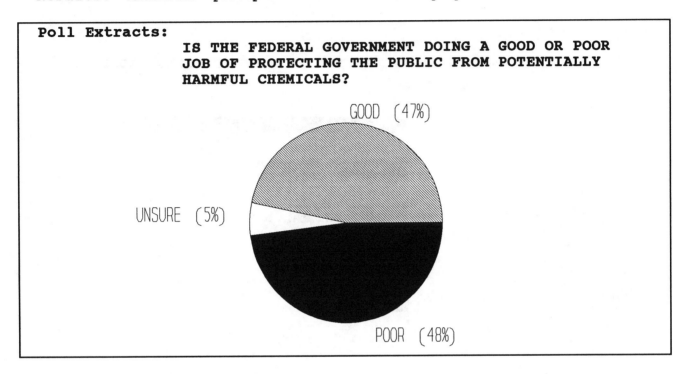

Also in Source: The percentage of respondents who perceive organically grown produce to have long-term health benefits. The percentage of respondents who have eaten organically grown produce and listed taste as an important reason to eat it. The percentage of Americans who have changed their eating habits due to reports of pesticides and other chemicals in the food supply.

Poll Details: The poll was conducted by Louis Harris and Associates Inc. during November and early December 1989, and bases its findings on 1,250 random telephone interviews of adults throughout the United States.

Availability: Published in the *Chicago Tribune*, March 22, 1990, section 7, p. 10.

A ROSE IS A ROSE

Description: Presents the results of a survey concerning the popularity of different types and hybrids of roses.

Results: Almost half of the respondents say that flower color and form are the most important features in selecting roses.

Poll Extracts:

WHAT ARE THE MOST IMPORTANT FEATURES IN SELECTING ROSES?

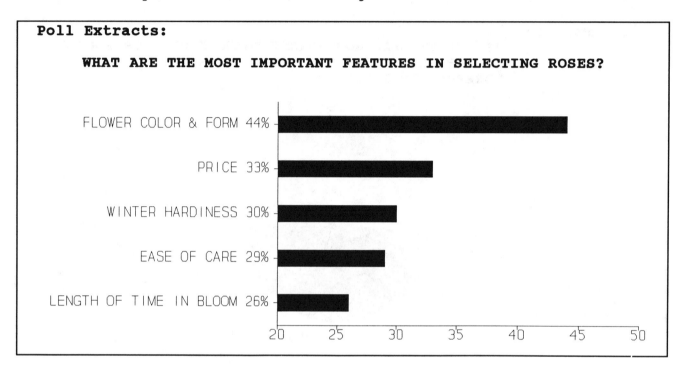

Also in Source: About one in four U.S. households - an estimated 23 million - have rose bushes. Each year an estimated 10 million households buy rose bushes. Each household spends approximately $36 per year on roses. Retail and mail order sales of roses total approximately $350 million annually. Fragrant Cloud, Fragrant Memory, Intrigue, Angel Face, and Tropicana are among the most fragrant varieties. However, there are many opinions about fragrances.

Poll Details: The Gallup poll was conducted for the National Gardening Association and All-America Rose Selections.

Availability: Published in *The Columbus Dispatch*, April 20, 1990, p. 2F.

AIDS AND BLACK GAY MEN

Description: Presents the results of a survey of black gay and bisexual men concerning their knowledge of safer sex and unsafe sex. The survey also addressed the probable sexual behavior of the respondents.

Results: While almost 100% of the respondents claimed knowledge of what constitutes safer or unsafe sex, only 54% "always or nearly always" practice safer sex.

Poll Extracts:

SEXUAL ATTITUDES AND BEHAVIORS:

Do you know what constitutes safer and unsafe sex?

Yes...97%

Do you always or almost always practice safer sex?

Yes...54%

Would you engage in unsafe sex if you had AIDS or were infected with the human immunodeficiency virus?

Yes...20%

Also in Source: Half of the men who engaged in anal intercourse, the sexual activity most likely to transmit the virus, said that they always or almost always used a condom. One-third of the men said they have vaginal intercourse; of those, only 30% always or almost always use a condom.

Poll Details: The survey of 952 men was funded by the U.S. Centers for Disease Control and conducted by the National Task Force on AIDS Prevention, a project of the National Association of Black and White Men Together. The men who participated were interviewed in 25 medium and large urban areas by specially trained workers through organizations and in private homes, bars, and other gay meeting places.

Availability: Published in the *Los Angeles Times*, June 14, 1990, p. A25.

AIDS MISCONCEPTIONS AMONG TEENS

Description: Presents the results of several surveys concerning the level of
          AIDS information and knowledge among American teenagers. The surveys also
          include information on the sexual behavior of the respondents.

Results: The surveys revealed a wide range of AIDS information among teenagers.
          Sexual behavior and drug use also varies depending upon the individual
          survey.

Poll Extracts:

DID YOU KNOW THAT-

AIDS cannot be acquired by giving blood?

YES...58%

AIDS does not come from mosquito bites?

Yes...48%

Public toilets do not spread AIDS?

Yes...73%

Also in Source: Depending on the location of the survey, between 7% and 40%
          of the respondents reported having four or more sex partners. The median
          was 21%. Between 2% and 5% said they injected cocaine, heroin, or other
          intravenous drugs. Between 93% and 100% of the students in the survey knew
          that AIDS can be transmitted by drug needles, and between 74% and 98% knew
          that it can be spread by sex without the use of condoms.

Poll Details: The surveys were sponsored by the U.S. Centers for Disease
          Control. The 1989 surveys were conducted in 30 states, 10 cities, and two
          U.S. territories. The surveys from the participating cities and states do
          not represent a national sampling. State-by-state comparisons are not
          relevant because different locations reported different response rates and
          the same questions were not asked of all students.

Availability: Published in the *Chicago Tribune*, June 15, 1990, p. 16.

CONDOMS

Description: The survey results deal with condom usage and teenagers' knowledge of AIDS.

Results: The majority of teenagers do not use a condom during intercourse. The survey found 48% of the teenagers reported having had intercourse. Although 88% of the students said that it wasn't possible to become infected by being in the same classroom with someone having the HIV infection, only 59% said that they would be willing to attend classes with someone having the HIV infection.

Poll Extracts:

	YES
Are you aware the use of condoms can reduce the risk of HIV infection?	91%
Do you always use a condom during intercourse?	17%

Also in Source: The percentage of students who say they received most of their AIDS information from teachers, or from their family. The percentage of students who knew that they could not become HIV-infected from a mosquito bite.

Poll Details: The survey by the Indiana Department of Education, was based on one developed by the U.S. Center for Disease Control, and given to 2,307 students at 26 randomly selected high schools in the State of Indiana.

Availability: Published in *CDC Aids Weekly*, February 5, 1990, p. 11.

DOCTORS' ATTITUDES TOWARD AIDS

Description: This study measured physician contact with HIV-seropositive
patients and their attitudes toward HIV-seropositive patients.

Results: "Nearly 50% of the nonfederal patient care physicians in our
nationally representative sample have treated at least one HIV patient,
with an average of 6.7 such patients being treated per physician." The
majority of physicians perceived a responsibility to treat HIV-seropositive
patients.

Poll Extracts:

PHYSICIAN IS OBLIGATED TO TREAT HIV-SEROPOSITIVES

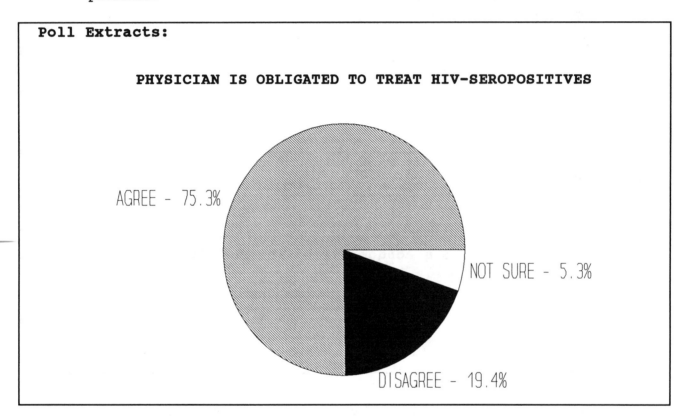

AGREE - 75.3%

NOT SURE - 5.3%

DISAGREE - 19.4%

Also in Source: The responses of those surveyed, regarding the number of
physicians who have treated HIV-seropositive patients, and those who
perceive a responsibility to treat HIV-seropositive patients, are broken
down by selected characteristics. These characteristics include: the
medical specialty, the type of practice, years of experience, place of
graduation (U.S. or foreign), board certification status, area size, in top
20 AIDS SMSA (standard metropolitan statistical area), sex, and marital
status (with or without children).

Poll Details: "The study was conducted as part of the Spring 1988
Socioeconomic Monitoring System (SMS) survey (a periodic telephone survey
program conducted for the American Medical Association by Mathematica
Policy Research, Inc.). 3,506 physicians were asked about their
experiences with HIV-seropositive patients." Further details on the
interview and survey procedure are also given in the article.

Availability: Published in *Medical Care,* March 1990 (volume 28, number 3),
p. 251-260.

FUNDING FOR AIDS RESEARCH

Description: This poll queried respondents about the amount of research
dollars that AIDS has received compared to other diseases.

Results: The majority of respondents do not believe that funding for AIDS
research is too great when compared to the research dollars provided for
other diseases.

Poll Extracts:
"DO YOU THINK THAT AIDS HAS RECEIVED A DISPROPOR-TIONATE SHARE OF RESEARCH DOLLARS COMPARED WITH OTHER DISEASES?"

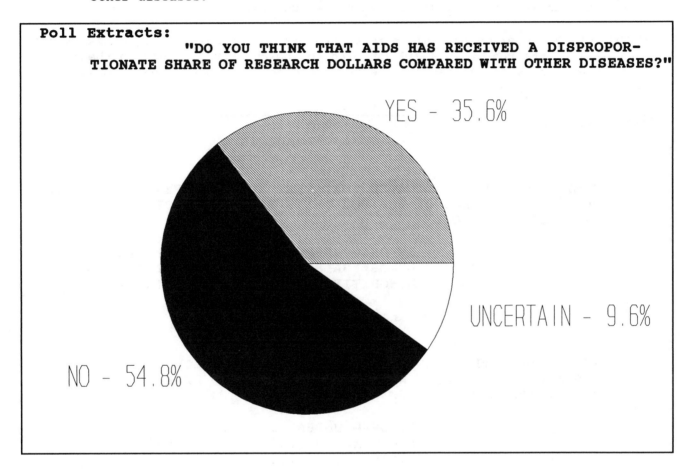

Also in Source: The percentage of respondents who thought that the political
nature of funding medical research damages long-term research programs.

Poll Details: The results are based on responses from 250 hospital CEOs.
Professional Research Consultants provided the survey results.

Availability: Published in *Hospitals*, August 20, 1990 (volume 64, number 16),
p. 22.

PHYSICIANS' ATTITUDES TOWARD HIGH-RISK PATIENTS

Description: This survey queried internal medicine residents about their attitudes toward homosexuals, intravenous drug users, and ethnic patients. "Researchers also asked respondents about their perceived risk of contracting HIV from an occupational exposure, attitudes about professional duty, career plans for future medical practice, and experience with AIDS patients." Residents were also asked questions from the "Index of Homophobia," by W.A. Ricketts and W.W. Hudson.

Results: A number of medical trainees are prejudiced against high-risk groups. 63% of the respondents did not plan to include HIV patients in their practice. 66% of the respondents were concerned about occupational exposure to HIV.

Poll Extracts:

RESPONDENTS WHO INDICATED THAT THEY WOULD PREFER
NOT TO HAVE A LOT OF THE FOLLOWING TYPES OF PEOPLE
IN THEIR PRACTICE:

IV DRUG USERS .... 92% Yes
HOMOSEXUALS .... 59% Yes
MINORITIES .... 24% Yes

RESPONDENTS WHO AGREED THAT MOST OF THE FOLLOWING
TYPES OF PEOPLE WITH AIDS HAVE BROUGHT THE DISEASE
UPON THEMSELVES:

IV DRUG USERS .... 85% Yes
HOMOSEXUALS .... 60% Yes
MINORITIES .... 42% Yes

Also in Source: Three other surveys dealing with HIV, that were presented at the Sixth International Conference on AIDS (June 1990, San Francisco), were mentioned.

Poll Details: 1,045 internal medicine residents from 41 U.S. training programs were surveyed.

Availability: Published in *AIDS Alert*, August 1990 (volume 5, number 8), p. 155-156.

RESCUE WORKERS AND AIDS

Description: This survey asked CPR (cardiopulmonary resuscitation) teachers
about the impact of AIDS and other infectious diseases on their life-
saving skills.

Results: The fear of AIDS and other infectious diseases makes CPR teachers
hesitant about using their life-saving skills. "When asked to respond to
hypothetical scenarios, nearly all would rescue a drowning 4-year-old, but
almost half would hesitate to assist a female college student." Teachers
were most reluctant about saving adult "high-risk" victims.

Poll Extracts:

> **RESPONDENTS SAID FEAR MADE THEM HESITATE TO USE
> MOUTH-TO-MOUTH RESCUE BREATHING IN AN EMERGENCY ... 40% Yes**

Poll Details: A Virginia survey of 1,794 CPR teachers. The majority of the
teachers surveyed were health care workers -- doctors, nurses, emergency
medical technicians. Police, firefighters, and others made up about 10% of
the teachers.

Availability: Published in *The Cincinnati Enquirer*, March 8, 1990, p. A-9.

TEENS, SEX, AND AIDS

Description: Presents the results of a survey of teenagers concerning the affect of AIDS on their own sexual attitudes and behavior.

Results: Because of AIDS, 96% of the male respondents and 94% of the female respondents said they were more selective of sexual partners. 12% of both male and female respondents have stopped having intercourse. 52% of the male respondents and 67% of the female respondents talk about AIDS with their partners. 71% of the male respondents and 64% of the female respondents use condoms.

Poll Extracts:

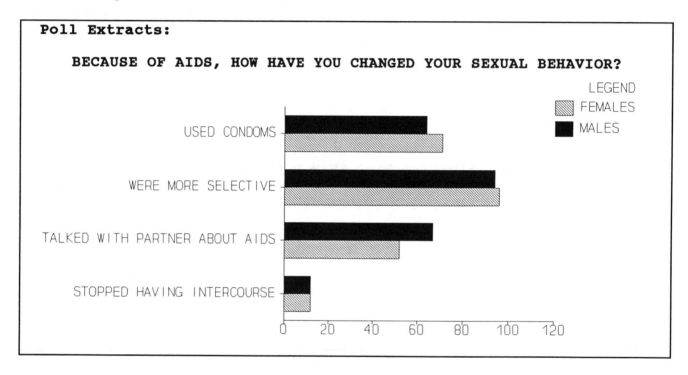

Also in Source: A discussion of the various issues concerning AIDS and changing sexual attitudes and behaviors is included in the article.

Poll Details: The results are taken from a survey of 1,200 Philadelphia youth, ages 14 through 18.

Availability: Published in *The Atlanta Journal and Constitution*, April 2, 1990 p. A1, A7.

AMERICANS AT REST

Description: Presents the results of a survey measuring the amount of leisure
time Americans currenty enjoy and identifying some of their favorite
leisure activites.

Results: Over half of the respondents feel they have less free time today
compared to five years ago.

Poll Extracts:

COMPARED TO FIVE YEARS AGO, HOW MUCH FREE TIME DO YOU HAVE?

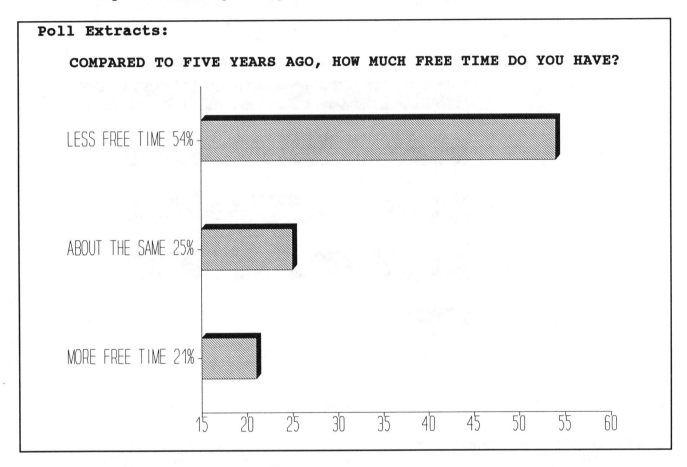

Also in Source: When asked which activities they enjoy doing the most in
their free time, 36% of the respondents said just relaxing at home, 23%
said spending time with the family, 23% said outdoor activities, 7% said
watching television, 6% said shopping, and 3% weren't sure.

Poll Details: The survey of 1,255 adults was conducted November 9 through 13,
1990, for *Business Week* by Louis Harris & Associates Inc. Results should
be accurate to within 3%.

Availability: Published in *Business Week*, November 26, 1990 (number 3189),
p. 144.

BARBECUING

Description: This poll asked Americans why they like to barbecue so much.

Results: The taste of food cooked on the grill was the answer given most often.

Poll Extracts:

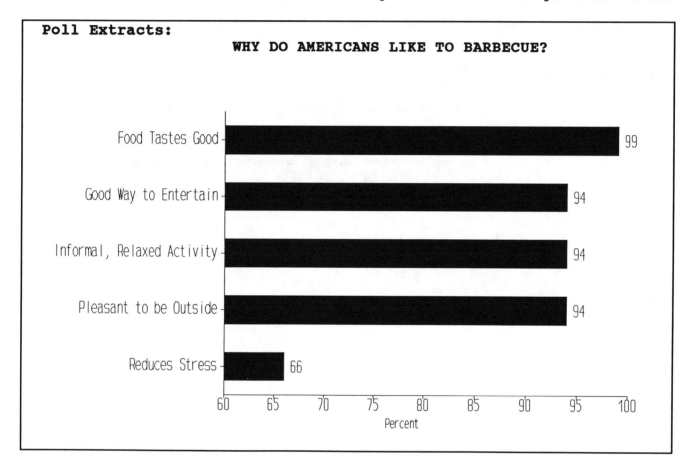

WHY DO AMERICANS LIKE TO BARBECUE?

Also in Source: More Americans barbecue on the Fourth of July, than any other
day of the year. 36% of the respondents wear bathing suits while they are
barbecuing their food.

Poll Details: "The survey was commisssioned by Weber-Stephen Products Co. of
Palatine, Ill., makers of the Weber charcoal kettle grill and Genesis gas
barbecue grill."

Availability: Published in *Washington Home (The Washington Post)*,
July 5, 1990, p. 7.

CATS, DOGS, AND OTHER PETS

Description: Americans were questioned about the types of pets they own, their attitudes toward their pets, the names given to their pets, and other aspects of pet ownership.

Results: 58% of American households have pets. In households with animals, 88% of owners regard their pets as family members. More households have dogs as pets than have cats. The most popular name for a dog is Lady, while the most popular name for a cat is Baby. 81% of pet owners who talk to their pet, believe that the animal seems to respond through sounds, facial expressions, or body movements. 82% of pet owners believe that their pets can sense their moods. 44% of Americans think that dog owners often look like their pets.

```
+-----------------------------------------------------------------------+
| Poll Extracts:                                                        |
|                                                                       |
|                                                                       |
|                   RESPONDENTS DID THE FOLLOWING:                      |
|                                                                       |
|                                                                       |
|   Gave Christmas gifts to their pets ............. 65%               |
|                                                                       |
|   Turned on the TV, radio, etc., when leaving                        |
|   their pet alone ................................. 30%              |
|                                                                       |
|   Celebrated their pet's birthday ................ 24%               |
|                                                                       |
|   Kept their pet's picture in their                                  |
|   wallet or purse ................................. 17%              |
|                                                                       |
|   Displayed their pet's picture at work .......... 8%                |
|                                                                       |
+-----------------------------------------------------------------------+
```

Also in Source: The amount of time owners spend per day to feed, exercise, and clean up after their pets. The approximate cost of a pet per year. The percentage of households having a dog, cat, bird, or fish as a pet. The most common breeds of dogs and cats in the United States. Popular names given to cats and dogs. The percentage of Americans who do not like animals and who think that pets detract from life. The percentage of households where dogs and cats are allowed to sit on the furniture.

Poll Details: The responses provided in the poll extracts were taken from a population of 740 adults who own pets. Other findings were based on the 1990 Gallup Mirror of America Survey, which interviewed a random sample of 1,242 Americans on July 19-22, 1990.

Availability: Published in the *Dayton Daily News*, September 9, 1990, p. 1-E, 3-E.

A CLEAN HOME: WHO & HOW

Description: Presents the results of a survey concerning the attitudes, practices, and responsibilities involved in cleaning around the house.

Results: While over 80% of the respondents report feeling positive after cleaning their home, only 20% said they actually enjoy performing the chore.

Poll Extracts:

HOW DO YOU FEEL ABOUT CLEANING YOUR HOUSE?

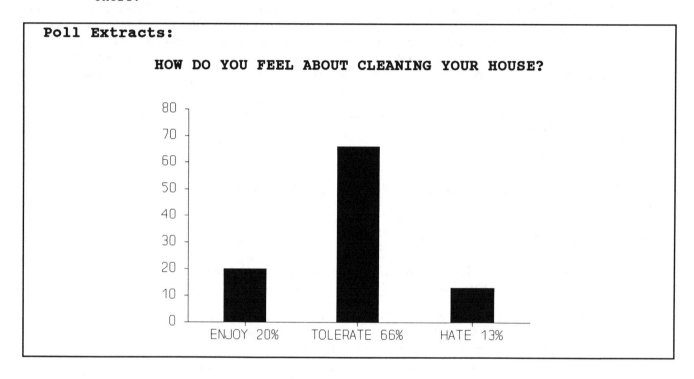

Also in Source: 58% of the respondents make the job less painful by doing a major cleaning once a week while 15% tidy up continuously. 61% of the respondents agree that the appearance of their home improves when their lives are less busy. 40% predicted they would clean more often if they had more time or if cleaning were easier. 41% said that having fewer supplies would make the job easier. Overall, 86% of women said they do the housecleaning compared with 24% of the men. 58% of those households polled with children report cleaning everyday compared with 42% of childless households. Only 5% of households surveyed with children said that everyone shares responsibility for cleaning. Only 1% said a son or daughter is primarily responsible for housecleaning.

Poll Details: 1,000 people were surveyed in a national poll by a manufacturer of cleaning towels.

Availability: Published in the *Chicago Tribune*, June 15, 1990, "Your Place," p. 16.

DREAM HOMES

Description: Presents the results of a survey concerning the types of homes
Americans would like to own.

Results: The most popular type of home, cited by over one-third of the
respondents, is an ocean front home.

Poll Extracts:

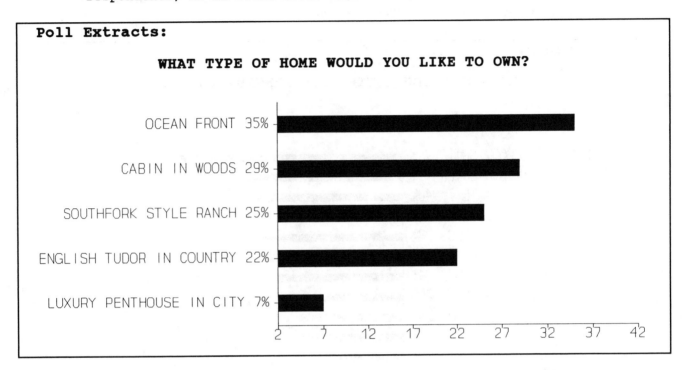

Also in Source: The source only includes a graph illustrating the results of
the survey.

Poll Details: The telephone survey of 1,000 adults was conducted by Bruskin
Associates Market Research.

Availability: Published in *USA Today*, April 30, 1990, p. 1D.

FANTASY HOMES

Description: Presents the results of a survey concerning how Americans would equip their fantasy home.

Results: Almost three-fourths of the respondents would like a master bedroom suite in their fantasy home. Fewer than 10% of the respondents would include a tennis court in the back yard.

Poll Extracts:

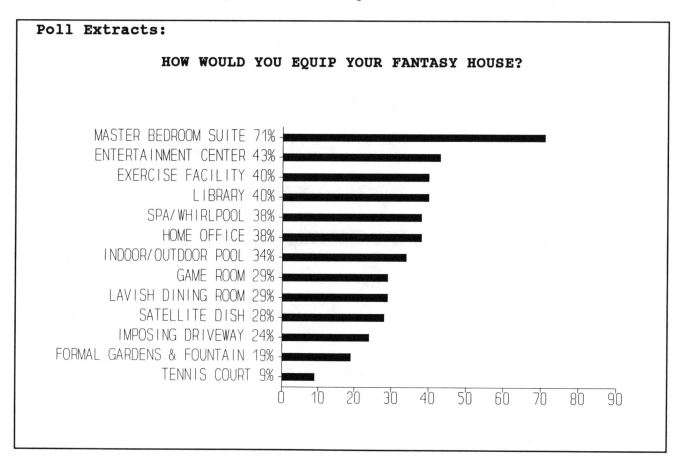

HOW WOULD YOU EQUIP YOUR FANTASY HOUSE?

Also in Source: The American fantasy home would include four bedrooms, three bathrooms, two fireplaces, seven closets, three TVs, and four telephones. Approximately half dreamed of owning a gourmet kitchen but only 29% would equip their dream kitchen with servants. 37% of those polled found their inspiration for the dream house in a magazine or catalogue. 21% found their inspiration from television shows and movies. For one in ten Americans, owning their dream home would enable them to escape from neighbors they hate.

Poll Details: The survey was conducted by the *Spiegel Home Fashion Monitor*. 1,000 males and females over the age of 18 completed the telephone survey.

Availability: Published in *The Detroit News*, May 26, 1990, p. 1D.

FAVORITE AND LEAST FAVORITE HOBBIES

Description: Presents the results of a survey concerning Americans favorite hobbies.

Results: Americans enjoy a wide range hobbies. The most popular and least popular hobbies vary by location across the country.

Poll Extracts:

FAVORITE AND LEAST FAVORITE HOBBIES

	Most Popular	Least Popular
Knitting	Presque Isle, ME	Miami, FL
Reading books	Charlottesville, VA	Laredo, TX
Hunting/shooting	Casper, WY	Sarasota, FL
Bicycling	Fort Myers, FL	Springfield, MT
Crossword puzzles	Steubenville, OH	Salt Lake City, UT
Following fashion	New York, NY	Durango, CO
Gourmet cooking	San Francisco, CA	Sioux City, IA
Pets	Medford. OR	Palm Beach, FL
Running/jogging	El Paso, TX	Glendive, MT
VCR viewing	Las Vegas, NV	Sioux Falls, SD
Watching TV sports	Indianapolis, IN	Presque, Isle, ME
Real estate	Santa Barbara, CA	Clarksburg, WV
Personal computers	Charlottesville, VA	Greenwood, MS

Also in Source: The article includes a brief description of the survey.

Poll Details: The survey is based on *The Lifestyle Market Analyst*, a report by National Demographics & Lifestyles Inc. The report is from a survey of 7.4 million households in 212 cities.

Availability: Published in *USA Today*, June 1-3, 1990, p. 1A.

GIFTS FOR GROOMS

Description: This survey queried newly married or about-to-be married men on gifts for the kitchen.

Results: 63% of the men wanted a microwave oven as a gift. But if given a fondue pot, 24% of the men would probably return it.

Poll Extracts:

GIFTS THAT MEN WANT:

Microwave Oven	63%
Food Processor	52%
Knife Set	42%
Blender	38%
Coffee Maker	33%
Wok	31%
Toaster	30%
Ice Cream Maker	28%
Espresso/Cappuccino Machine	20%
Coffee Grinder	16%

GIFTS THAT MEN WOULD PROBABLY RETURN:

Fondue Pot	24%
Electric Bread Maker	18%
Waffle Iron	12%
Electric Knife	11%
Popcorn Popper	8%
Electric Can Opener	5.5%
Electric Frying Pan	5.4%
Pressure Cooker	4%
Mixer	1.4%
Slow Cooker	1%

Poll Details: The survey was sponsored by Robert Krups, a small-appliance manufacturer.

Availability: Originally published in *The Boston Globe*. The information provided is based on an article printed in *The Atlanta Journal and Constitution*, August 16, 1990, p. W-1.

MORNING HABITS

Description: This survey asked respondents about the activities they do at home every morning.

Results: Making love came in last place at 7%. Only 4% of the respondents said that they felt "sexy" in the morning.

Poll Extracts:

THE TOP TEN MORNING ACTIVITIES ARE:

1. Personal Hygiene 84%
2. Listen to the Radio 55%
3. Drink Coffee 53%
4. Make my Bed 53%
5. Make Breakfast 50%
6. Kiss my Spouse/Partner 49%
7. Read the Newspaper 35%
8. Watch Television 30%
9. Exercise 22%
10. Iron my Clothes 11%

Also in Source: Twice as many people on the West Coast than on the East Coast are morning lovers. For some of the top ten activities, the responses are broken down according to age groups and gender. Least popular morning habits are also included.

Poll Details: Robert Krups, North America, commissioned this national survey "Morning Habits of America."

Availability: Published in *USA TODAY* (magazine), July 1990 (volume 119, number 2542), p. 8.

REDECORATING THE HOUSE

Description: Presents the results of a survey concerning the reasons why people redecorate their homes.

Results: Boredom is the top motivator for redecorating the house. Women, at 58%, seem to get bored sooner than men.

Poll Extracts:

TOP 10 MOTIVATIONS FOR REDECORATING:

1. Got bored with the way my home looked.

2. Just wanted to make my home more fashionable.

3. Moved into a new place. The perfect opportunity to redecorate.

4. Had to make more space.

5. Wanted to express my personality in my surroundings.

6. Had a irresistible urge to redecorate.

7. Wanted to improve the appearance of a home before selling.

8. Got married or moved in with someone.

9. Had a baby.

10. Wanted to change my lifestyle.

Also in Source: A brief description of the survey is included in the article.

Poll Details: The survey of 1,000 people was conducted for *Spiegel* by R.H. Bruskin Associates.

Availability: Published in the *Dayton Daily News*, April 22, 1990, p. 4-G.

TELEVISION AND REAL LIFE

Description: This survey asked questions regarding opinions about families on television. Which is the funniest? What character is the biggest brat? Who's most like you?

Results: The Bundys of Fox's *Married With Children* would be the family 40% of the respondents would hate to have living next door.

Poll Extracts:

We asked if the following TV scenarios mirror life in your home. Percentages reflect the number of "yes" answers.

Always have milk in the refrigerator 82%

Eat dinner together a lot 67%

Always have whatever tool is needed for the job 36%

Never go to fast-food restaurant for dinner 25%

Find all family problems can be solved in 22 minutes ... 11%

Also in Source: The television family that would be the preferred dinner guests, son/brother most like my own, daughter/sister most like my own, the squarest dad, the best mom, TV remarks heard in my house, and the top five all-time favorite shows.

Poll Details: The answers were from 4,700 readers of *USA WEEKEND*.

Availability: Published in *USA WEEKEND*, February 16-18, 1990, p. 10, 11.

TOILET PAPER

Description: This survey asked questions about daily life that the U.S. Census
did not ask.

Results: When telephoning someone, 54% of the respondents were more aggravated
by hearing the phone ring endlessly, while the remainder of the respondents
were more aggravated by getting the answering machine. The results did not
seem to establish any trends, as each question seemed to be independent of
each of the other questions.

Poll Extracts: **HOW MANY ROLLS OF TOILET PAPER DO YOU HAVE
STASHED AWAY?**

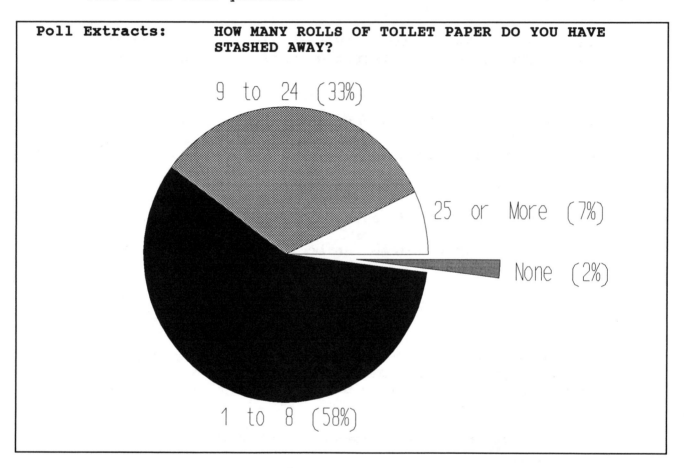

9 to 24 (33%)

25 or More (7%)

None (2%)

1 to 8 (58%)

Also in Source: The number of shoes that people own/need, how many times
respondents had called their mothers that week, respondents who own a
microwave, how many frozen dinners are in the respondent's freezer, the
amount of the work-week that is fun, methods of getting out of bed, what do
respondents expect to earn in the year 2000, how many plants live with the
respondents.

Poll Details: The answers were from 38,465 readers of *USA WEEKEND*.

Availability: Published in *USA WEEKEND*, March 16-18, 1990, p. 4, 5.

WEEKENDS

Description: This poll asked Americans what they did last weekend.

Results: More than half of the respondents used their weekend for household
        chores, among other responses.

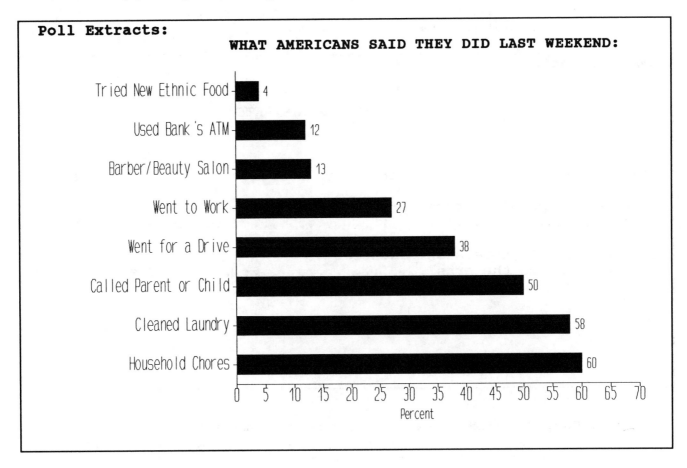

Poll Details: The poll was conducted by the Roper Organization.

Availability: Published in *The Atlanta Journal and Constitution*, August 14,
        1990, p. C-2.

ATTITUDES TOWARD ART

Description: Presents the results of a survey concerning importance of the arts in people's lives.

Results: Over three-fourths of the respondents said the arts are an important part of their lives. Over half of the respondents said there are not enough cultural programs in their community.

Poll Extracts:

ISSUES INVOLVING THE ARTS:

Are the arts an important part of your life?.........Yes...76%

Are there enough cultural programs in
your community?......................................No....60%

Is freedom of expression essential
to artists and the arts?.............................Yes...93%

Also in Source: Nine out of ten people believe that even if they find a piece of art offensive others have the right to see it. 80% disagree with the statement "nudity in art is usually pornographic."

Poll Details: The poll of 1,200 people was commissioned by People for the American Way Action Fund.

Availability: Published in *USA Today*, April 20, 1990, p. 1D.

CENSORSHIP AND ARTISTIC FREEDOM

Description: Respondents were asked several questions relating to the issue of offensive or obscene works of art.

Results: While the majority thought that the government has no business telling them what to say, nearly 59% of the respondents thought that the government should have some power of censorship. 74% of the respondents backed artists' rights to display works that could be considered offensive. Spending tax money for "objectionable" art, films, or plays was opposed by 72% of the respondents.

Poll Extracts:

RESPONDENTS THOUGHT THAT:

The First Amendment's guarantees of free speech
did not cover art works, films, music, radio,
cable and network television, plays, newspapers, or
photographs .... between 25% and 30%

The government has the right to ban the sale of
recordings that favor drug use or the broadcasting
of sexually explicit lyrics .... more than 50%

Recorded songs that contain lyrics favoring drug
use or that are sexually explicit should have
mandatory labeling 84%

Poll Details: This survey was sponsored by the Thomas Jefferson Center for the Protection of Free Expression, a nonprofit institute associated with the University of Virginia. 1,500 adults were interviewed in a nationwide telephone survey conducted in June 1990.

Availability: Published in *The Boston Globe*, September 15, 1990, p. 4.

CENSORSHIP AND THE ARTS

> **Description:** Presents the results of a survey concerning issues involved with
> government-funded art. Questions included the future of government-funded
> art, content responsibility, and the popularity of art events.

> **Results:** Almost 70% of the respondents endorse the concept of the government
> funding the arts.

Poll Extracts:

DO YOU ENDORSE THE CONCEPT OF GOVERNMENT FUNDED ART?

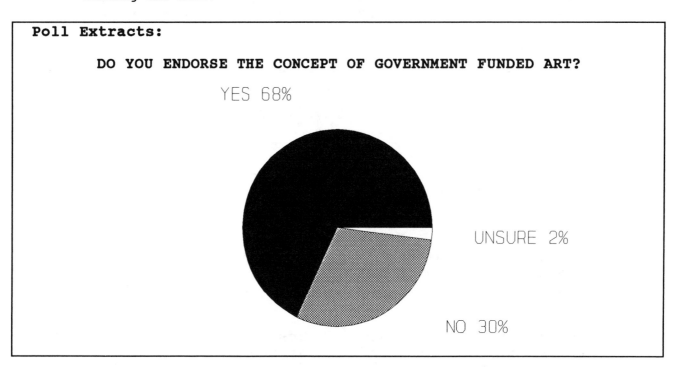

YES 68%

UNSURE 2%

NO 30%

> **Also in Source:** 30% of the respondents believe government funding for *avant
> garde* art should be stopped because some of it is controversial and 66%
> disagreed with the contention that Congress should cut off funding for
> controversial art projects or shows. Attendance at arts events is more
> popular than going to live sporting events nationwide. 72% of the
> respondents reported attending arts events in the last year compared to 53%
> who went to sportng events. 60% agreed that the National Endowment for the
> Arts should be held responsible for the content of the artwork it supports.
> 51% agreed that artists who receive government grants should "sign an oath
> regarding the content of the art." 83% of the respondents agreed with the
> statement that the National Endowment for the Arts "serves a very useful
> purpose for American society." Nearly a quarter of the respondents favor
> increasing the NEA budget, 56% favor keeping the budget the same, and 13%
> advocate cutting NEA funding.

> **Poll Details:** The telephone survey of 1,200 was conducted by Research &
> Forecasts Inc. for People for the American Way. The poll sample had an
> average age of 40. It was 52% female and 48% male. Margin of error is
> plus or minus 3%.

> **Availability:** Published in the *Los Angeles Times*, April 20, 1990, p. F12, 13.

CINCINNATI SPEAKS OUT TO CENSORS

Description: Presents the results of a survey concerning the views of the residents of Hamilton County, Ohio, which includes Cincinnati, toward the Robert Mapplethorpe exhibit at the Contemporary Arts Center.

Results: Approximately 85% of the respondents agree that it is important for Cincinnati's national image to offer a variety of arts, including contemporary arts.

Poll Extracts:

VOICES OF CINCINNATI:

Is it important for Cincinnati's national image to offer a variety of arts, including contemporary arts?................................Yes...84%

Are you aware of the Mapplethorpe exhibit at the Contemporary Arts Center?.....................Yes...93%

Among those aware: Are you in favor of prosecuting the Contemporary Arts Center?...........Yes...26%

Would the image of Cincinnati be hurt if the Contemporary Arts Center was found guilty?.......Yes...59%

Also in Source: A general discussion of the issue of censorship is included in the article.

Poll Details: The results are taken from a telephone survey of 424 adults in Hamilton County, Ohio, which includes Cincinnati, on September 12-15, 1990. The survey was conducted by Assistance Marketing Inc. and commissioned by the Cincinnati Contemporary Arts Center.

Availability: Published in *The Wall Street Journal*, October 8, 1990, p. B1, B3.

FEDERAL FUNDS AND ARTS PROJECTS

Description: This poll asked Americans about federal funds being used to
support selected arts projects and about censorship of the arts.

Results: 75% of the respondents felt that it was more important that adults
like themselves have the right to determine what they should see and hear,
rather than society having laws to prohibit material that might be
offensive to some segments of the community. When asked about federally
funded arts projects, and who should make judgements to ensure that the
works of art produced don't offend the public -- federal officials or
independent panels of established arts experts in each field -- 63% of the
respondents wanted the experts to judge.

Poll Extracts:

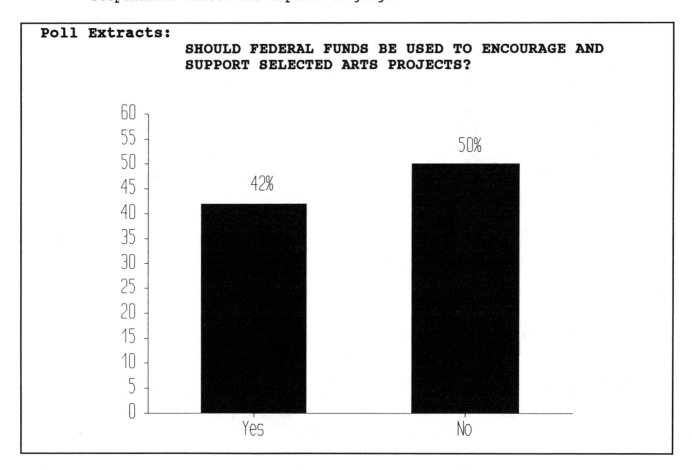

SHOULD FEDERAL FUNDS BE USED TO ENCOURAGE AND
SUPPORT SELECTED ARTS PROJECTS?

Also in Source: Responses from a 1989 poll that asked the same questions.

Poll Details: This *Newsweek* Poll was conducted by the Gallup Organization
during June 20-21, 1990. A random national sample of 605 adults were
interviewed by telephone. Some responses, such as "Don't Know," were not
provided. The margin of error is 4%.

Availability: Published in *Newsweek*, July 2, 1990 (volume 116, number 1),
p. 50.

AUTOMOBILE SALES AND SAFETY CONCERNS

Description: Presents the results of a survey concerning the popularity of automobile models and manufacturers. Specific questions concerning quality and safety are also included in the survey.

Results: The Ford Taurus and Honda Accord were selected as the top models most respondents would buy. Ford was ranked as the favorite manufacturer and the Honda Accord was cited as the model of car most people would buy again.

Poll Extracts:

THE NEW MODEL CAR I WOULD BUY TODAY:

1.   Ford Taurus

1.   Honda Accord

3.   Toyota Camry

4.   Ford Thunderbird

5.   Acura Legend

6.   Dodge Caravan

7.   Lincoln Town Car

8.   Acura Integra

8.   Chevrolet Blazer

8.   Pontiac Bonneville

Also in Source: 76.7% of the respondents identified antiskid brakes as the most preferred safety option. 46.6% selected airbags. 35.2% of the respondents thought Volvo was the safest production car and 56.5% cited drunk drivers as their biggest safety worry. The Mercedes-Benz is the number one dream car. 58.5% identified power windows and locks as favorite accessories. The Ford Escort was selected as the best car under $9,000. Germany was picked as the country producing the best cars.

Poll Details: The results are taken from a readers' survey of *Design News*. This is the 11th annual survey conducted by the magazine. The readership of the magazine is primarily automotive engineers.

Availability: Published in *Design News*, October 1, 1990 (volume 46, number 19), p. 84-88, 90.

AUTOMOTIVE PERFORMANCE

Description: This survey examined automotive performance features and asked buyers of new cars to rate their auto's producer on various characteristics.

Results: Men consider the most important aspect of automotive performance to be "brake response," and the least important aspect of automotive performance to be "acceleration." "A majority of respondents in each class gave high marks to styling and warranties of American cars; styling, performance, engineering, quality, fuel efficiency and value per dollar to Asian cars; and styling, performance, engineering and quality to European cars." Vehicles manufactured over the last two years were thought to have improved by a minority of domestic and import truck buyers.

Poll Extracts:

What is the most important aspect of automotive performance?

BRAKE RESPONSE ... 72.8%

ACCELERATION ... 24%   (Ranked Last)

When asking performance car owners, what is the most important aspect of automotive performance?

HANDLING/MANEUVERING ... Ranked First.

Also in Source: The source also mentions that criteria such as handling/maneuvering, steering response, fuel economy, passing power, smooth ride, and cornering were also ranked, but fails to give the actual rankings. The percentage of domestic and import truck buyers who gave high marks to styling. The percentage of: import buyers who praised their factory warranties, domestic buyers who praised their truck's performance and engineering.

Poll Details: The survey was commissioned by *Motor Trend* magazine and had 1,419 male respondents.

Availability: Published in *The Cincinnati Enquirer*, March 3, 1990, p. E-1, E-3.

CAR DEPENDABILITY

Description: Presents the results of a survey concerning vehicle dependability after four years of ownership.

Results: Mercedes-Benz was ranked as the most dependable automobile after four years of ownership.

Poll Extracts:

THE 12 MOST DEPENDABLE AUTOMOBILES:

1. Mercedes-Benz
2. Toyota
3. Honda
4. Buick
5. Cadillac
6. BMW(tie)
6. Porsche(tie)
8. Lincoln
9. Oldsmobile
10. Mercury
11. Mazda
12. Pontiac

Also in Source: A discussion of the survey is included in the article.

Poll Details: This owners survey was conducted by J.D. Power and Associates. The dependability rating survey involved 1985 model year cars.

Availability: Published in the *Detroit Free Press*, April 3, 1990, p. 1E.

DRIVING SKILLS AND SPEED

Description: This poll asked Americans about their driving skills, other drivers' skills, and 10 questions regarding auto safety.

Results: 81% of Americans love or like to drive, while 16% dislike driving. 54% of the respondents thought that they were better at driving than other drivers in their communities. 30% of the respondents thought that drivers in New York City were the worst. 32% of the respondents did not think that either men or women made better drivers. For the 10 questions dealing with auto safety, not one of the respondents answered all of the questions correctly.

Poll Extracts:

RESPONDENTS SAID THEY OBSERVED POSTED SPEED LIMITS:

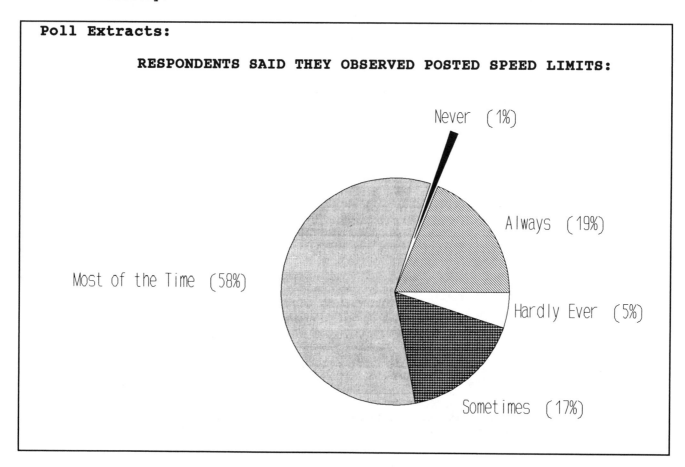

Never (1%)

Always (19%)

Most of the Time (58%)

Hardly Ever (5%)

Sometimes (17%)

Also in Source: The 10 true-or-false questions dealing with auto safety and the correct answers.

Poll Details: 500 licensed drivers were interviewed in this nationwide telephone poll that was conducted during June 1990. The results were issued by Valvoline, a subsidiary of Ashland Oil Inc.

Availability: Published in the *Dayton Daily News*, August 20, 1990, p. 1-A.

FUEL ECONOMY - MILES PER GALLON

Description: This survey was part of a larger survey on environmental factors causing the greenhouse effect and global warming. Voters were asked their attitudes about raising the corporate average fuel economy (CAFE) standards.

Results: Raising the CAFE standards from the current 27.5 mpg to 45 mpg by the year 2000 is supported by 80% of the voting public. Also, "83% said they would be willing to pay $500 more for a 45-mpg car, knowing that they would recoup this money in gas savings." Another 83% of respondents "strongly agreed" or "somewhat agreed," that automakers could make available a car averaging 45 mpg well before the year 2000.

Poll Extracts:

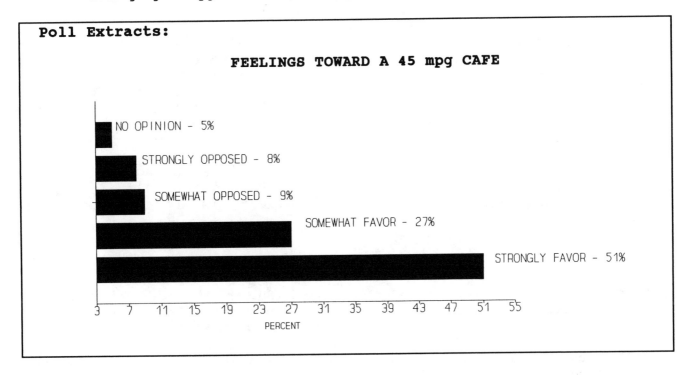

Poll Details: The survey was released by the Union of Concerned Scientists. The answers presented in the Poll Extracts are based on 1,200 voters polled by telephone.

Availability: Published in *Motor Trend*, March 1990 (volume 42, number 3), p. 36.

NEW CAR EVALUATIONS

Description: Presents the results of a survey concerning owners' satisfaction with their cars after three months of ownership.

Results: The car with the least number of problems is the Toyota Cressida and the car with the most number of problems is the Chevrolet Camaro.

Poll Extracts:

THE BEST AND WORST NEW CARS

The Best	The Worst
1990 Model	1990 Model
1. Toyota Cressida	1. Chevrolet Camaro
2. Mercedes-Benz E-Series	2. Pontiac Firebird
3. Toyota Camry	3. Oldsmobile Custom Cruiser
4. Lexus LS400	4. Buick Reatta
5. Mercedes-Benz S-Class	5. Buick Estate Wagon
6. Buick LeSabre	6. Subaru Justy
7. Nissan Maxima	7. Hyundai Excel
8. Infiniti Q45	8. Cadillac Brougham
9. Toyota Corolla	9. Volkswagen Golf
10. Mazda Miata	10. Chrysler LeBaron Coupe

Also in Source: The article also includes a table ranking the automobile divisions by number of problems in the first three months of ownership. Lexus had the fewest problems while Hyundai had the most.

Poll Details: This owners survey was conducted by J.D. Power and Associates. 1990 model year cars were used in the survey.

Availability: Published in *The Detroit News and Free Press*, June 9, 1990, p. 1A, 13A.

POSSIBLE ALTERNATE-FUEL USE

Description: Presents the results of a survey concerning consumers'
willingness to use alternate-fuels to help solve the problems of air
pollution and limited petroleum reserves.

Results: Nationally, 4% of the respondents said they would buy an alternate-
fuel vehicle as their next car.

Poll Extracts:

WHAT DO YOU THINK ABOUT ALTERNATE FUELS?

Nationally:

Would you buy an alternate-fuel vehicle as your next car?

Yes...4%

In Chicago:

Should the government and large businesses test alternate-fuels
in their own vehicle fleets before their use is mandated?

Yes...79%

Would you rather use reformulated gasoline than alternate-fuels?

Yes...86%

Also in Source: Those polled generally agreed that alternate-fuel vehicles
are a good idea and would help solve the problems of air pollution and
limited petroleum resources. However, they said the inconveniences and
operating limitations of such fuels - including poor cold-weather starting,
low resale value, and trouble finding refueling stations - would make them
reluctant to buy. The survey shows buyers would resist any car that burns
methanol, ethanol, natural gas, or that runs on battery power.

Poll Details: The poll of 900 consumers in Chicago, Baltimore, Houston,
Milwaukee, New York, and Philadelphia was conducted for the Motor Vehicle
Manufacturers Association by the Wirthlin Group.

Availability: Published in the *Chicago Tribune*, May 8, 1990, Section 3, p. 6.

SACRIFICE TO CURB POLLUTION

Description: Presents the results of a survey concerning the level of support for lifestyle sacrifices among Americans in the name of a cleaner environment.

Results: In most cases, Americans are willing to modify their lifestyle to ensure a cleaner environment. However, only a third of the respondents are willing to close pollution-producing factories which would result in a loss of jobs.

Poll Extracts:

FOR A CLEANER ENVIRONMENT, WHAT WOULD YOU BE WILLING TO DO?

Require testing and repairs of your car
each year for air pollution emissions......Yes..80%..No..19%

Require pollution control equipment that
would add $600 to the cost of a new car....Yes..68%..No..28%

In metropolitan areas, require people
who drive to work to take public
transportation one day a week.............Yes..57%..No..41%

Limit the number of large
cars produced.............................Yes..51%..No..44%

A 20 cent per gallon increase in
the price of gasoline for cleaner fuels....Yes..48%..No..50%

Also in Source: Over 90% of the respondents would favor a requirement to separate garbage and solid waste for recycling. 84% would favor a ban on foam containers used by fast food chains and other packaging that adds to the solid waste problem. Approximately three-fourths of the respondents would favor a ban on disposable diapers. Almost 60% would favor the enforcement of stricter air quality regulations increasing utility bills $10.00 per month.

Poll Details: The *Wall Street Journal*/NBC News poll was based on nationwide telephone interviews of 1,001 registered voters conducted April 11, 12, 14, and 16, 1990 by the polling organization of Peter Hart and Robert Teeter. Margin of error is plus or minus 3.2%

Availability: Published in *The Wall Street Journal*, April 20, 1990, p. A1, A12.

WOULD JAPANESE BUY AMERICAN?

Description: Presents the results of a survey measuring Japanese willingness to buy American cars.

Results: Over 85% of the respondents said they would not buy an American automobile.

Poll Extracts:

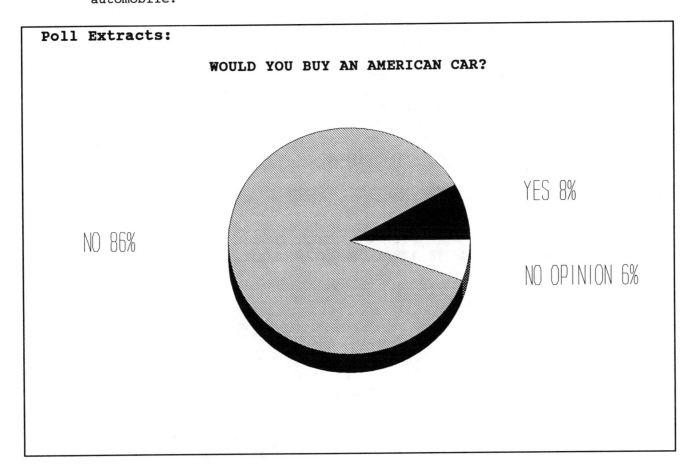

WOULD YOU BUY AN AMERICAN CAR?

YES 8%

NO 86%

NO OPINION 6%

Also in Source: 11% of the respondents said their respect for the United States has increased over the past five years, 33% said it decreased, and 56% had no opinion. 71% of the respondents consider Japanese products superior to American products, 11% don't think they are superior, and 18% have no oponion.

Poll Details: The survey of Japanese citizens was conducted for *Fortune* by Chuo Chosa Sha, a Tokyo research organization.

Availability: Published in *Fortune, Pacific Rim Special Issue*, Fall 1990 (volume 122, number 8), p. 17.

ADVANCED MANUFACTURING TECHNOLOGY

Description: This survey measured senior executives' opinions on the utilization of advanced technology.

Results: The majority of respondents believe advanced technologies yield only moderate or minor benefits. Assessing their own application of technology in five areas (product and process design, production process, expert systems, manufacturing planning and control, and information technology), seven industry groups rated themselves as "D" or "D-plus", with only aircraft/aerospace obtaining a "C-minus." Assessing their actual performance relative to six criteria for success (quality, flexibility, technological leadership, product price/cost, customer service, and marketing), firms felt they rated a "B-minus." Fewer than 10% of the executives surveyed thought their firms have applied state-of-the-art systems. Fewer than 25% of the manufacturers were applying either CAD (Computer Aided Design) or CNC (Computer Numerical Control) at state-of-the-art levels.

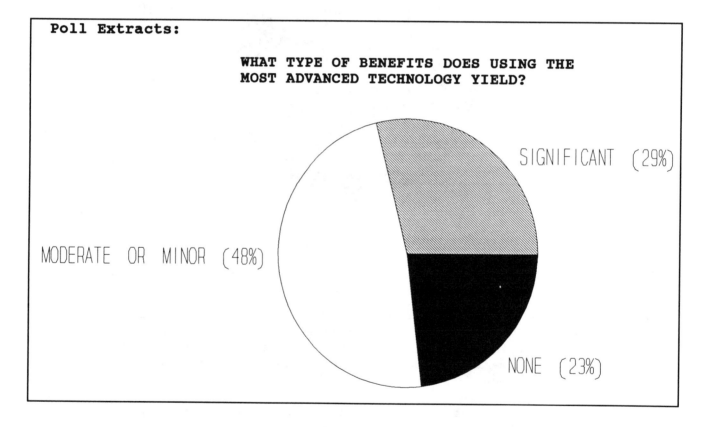

Poll Extracts:

WHAT TYPE OF BENEFITS DOES USING THE MOST ADVANCED TECHNOLOGY YIELD?

SIGNIFICANT (29%)

MODERATE OR MINOR (48%)

NONE (23%)

Also in Source: A chart which presents the grades that industry gave itself regarding the application of advanced technology to five areas, and industry's actual performance relative to six critical success factors.

Poll Details: The survey was conducted by manufacturing consultants in the Cleveland office of Deloitte & Touche. This office polled 759 senior executives of North American manufacturing firms.

Availability: Published in *Industry Week*, February 19, 1990 (volume 239, number 4), p. 62-63.

ATTITUDES TOWARD FOREIGN INVESTMENT

Description: Respondents were asked about their attitudes toward European and Japanese investments in the U.S.

Results: More Americans believe Japanese investments in the U.S. pose a threat to U.S. economic independence than European investments, even though Europeans invest more in the U.S. than do the Japanese. 61% of the respondents favor restricting foreign investments in American real estate.

Poll Extracts:

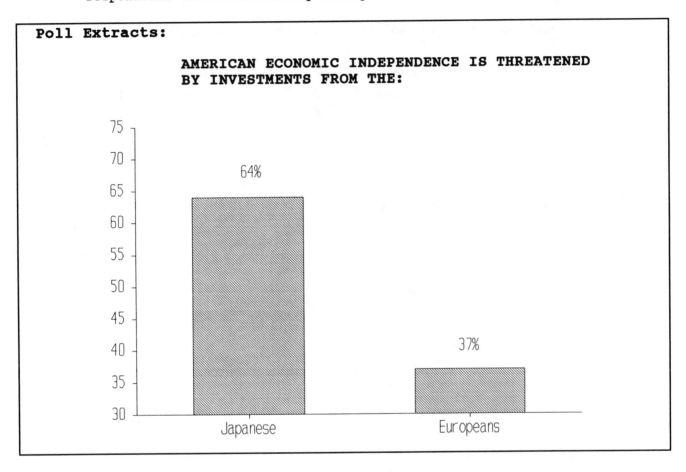

AMERICAN ECONOMIC INDEPENDENCE IS THREATENED BY INVESTMENTS FROM THE:

Also in Source: In a matched public opinion poll conducted in Japan by the Tokyo Broadcasting System, 70% of the Japanese respondents thought that Americans looked down on the Japanese. U.S. and Japanese responses to questions dealing with economic competition, trade restrictions, and overall feelings toward the other country.

Poll Details: The U.S. component of this *New York Times*/CBS News/Tokyo Broadcasting System poll was based on telephone interviews with 1,084 adults, conducted during June 5-8, 1990. The margin of sampling error is 3%.

Availability: Published in *The New York Times*, July 10, 1990, p. A11.

ATTITIDES TOWARD MERGERS

Description: Presents the results of a survey concerning chief financial
  officers' views on business mergers and acquisitions.

Results: 85% of the respondents are not interested in merging or being
  acquired.

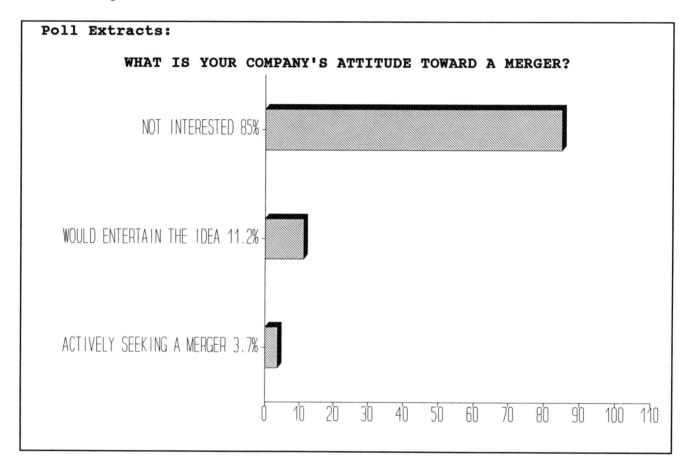

Poll Extracts:

WHAT IS YOUR COMPANY'S ATTITUDE TOWARD A MERGER?

NOT INTERESTED 85%

WOULD ENTERTAIN THE IDEA 11.2%

ACTIVELY SEEKING A MERGER 3.7%

0 10 20 30 40 50 60 70 80 90 100 110

Also in Source: 100% of the respondents would be interested in a business
  similar closely related to their own if they were considering or planning
  to make an acquisition. 30.1% of the respondents are considering launching
  one or more joint ventures, 21.4% are definitely planning to launch one or
  more joint ventures in the next year, while 48.5% are not considering any
  joint ventures. For those companies who are not interested in
  acquisitions, 39.1% say it is because they are satisfied with the present
  structure of business, 43.5% say they plan to grow through operations,
  17.4% say the climate toward leverage is less friendly, 34.8% are not
  willing to take on more debt at this time, 30.4% say the economic climate
  is uncertain, 23.9% say there are fewer attractive opportunities, and 30.4%
  say prices are too high.

Poll Details: *Institutional Investor* surveyed chief financial officers.

Availability: Published in *Institutional Investor*, December 1990 (volume XXIV,
  number 16), p. 175.

BEST BUSINESS LOCATIONS

Description: Presents the results of a survey identifying the most attractive United States cities to locate a business.

Results: Seattle was selected as the best city in the United States to locate a business. It received the highest percentage of "excellent" rankings of all American cities.

Poll Extracts:

WHICH CITIES ARE THE BEST TO LOCATE A BUSINESS?

1. Seattle

2. Sacramento

3. Portland

4. Norfolk

5   San Diego

6. Atlanta

7. Columbus

8. Dallas-Fort Worth

9. Minneapolis-St. Paul

10. Tampa

Also in Source: The most unattractive cities to locate a business are Detroit by Philadelphia, Miami, New York, and Baltimore. The cities in which conditions are expected to improve are led by Houston, followed by Dallas-Fort Worth, Denver, Sacramento, and San Antonio. The cities which gained in favor from 1989 are Sacramento, Portland, Norfolk, Dallas-Fort Worth, and San Antonio. The cities that fell from favor are New York, Washington, D.C., Los Angeles, San Francisco, and Chicago.

Poll Details: The results are based on interviews with 400 chief executives by Louis Harris & Associates Inc. The source is Cushman & Wakefield Inc.'s *Business America Real Estate Monitor: Best Business Cities.*

Availability: Published in *The Dallas Morning News*, October 3, 1990, p. 1D, 2D.

BUSINESS BUYING PLANS INVOLVING COMPUTERS

Description: Presents the results of a survey concerning business executives'
plans and expectations for computer hardware and software purchases during
the coming year.

Results: Despite the slow-down in United States economy, almost half of the
respondents expect their company's budget for computer and office systems
to increase in 1991.

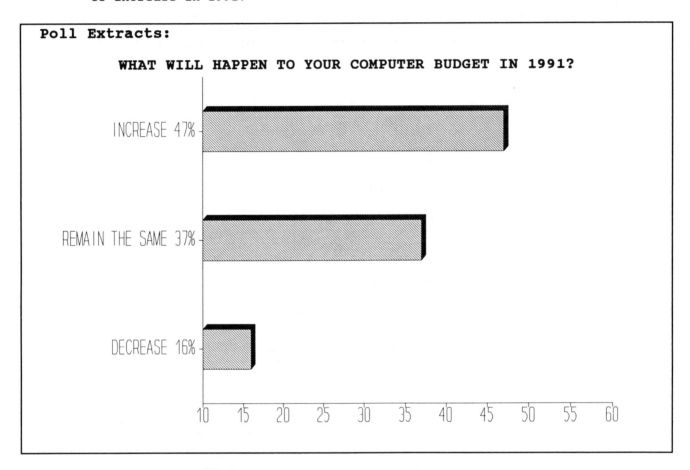

Poll Extracts:

WHAT WILL HAPPEN TO YOUR COMPUTER BUDGET IN 1991?

INCREASE 47%

REMAIN THE SAME 37%

DECREASE 16%

10   15   20   25   30   35   40   45   50   55   60

Also in Source: 55% of the respondents said their company plans to acquire
personal computers with a higher level of computing power during this
coming year, while 21% said they buy the same type of personal computer,
20% said they will upgrade exisiting personal computers, 11% said they will
retain current personal computers with no additional purchases, and 3% said
they will acquire their first personal computers. 54% of the respondents
said their company's budget will increase 11% to 25% over 1990's budget.
65% of the respondents believe that purchases of computer and office
systems by American businesses will increase in 1991, 30% said they will
stay the same, and 5% said they will decrease.

Poll Details: *Today's Office* surveyed business executives who are readers of
the magazine.

Availability: Published in *Today's Office*, December 1990 (volume 25, number
7), p. 42-47.

COMPLAINTS OF SMALL BUSINESS OWNERS

Description: Presents the results of survey which studied the attitudes and spending patterns of small business owners.

Results: Coping with "Uncle Sam" is the small business owner's biggest nuisance -- especially stronger environmental regulations.

Poll Extracts:

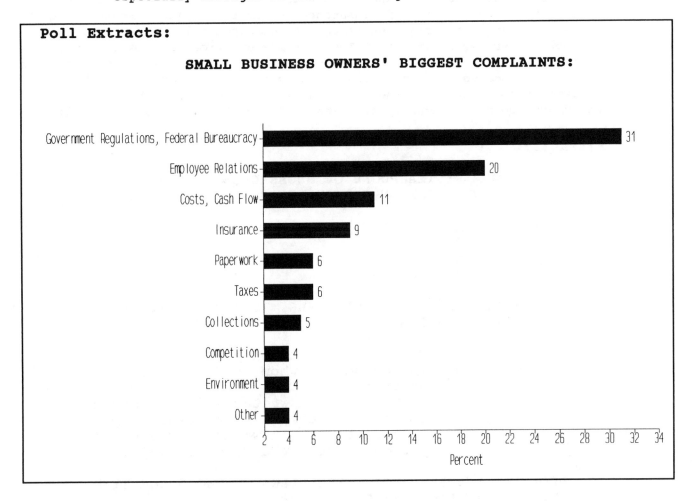

SMALL BUSINESS OWNERS' BIGGEST COMPLAINTS:

Also in Source: The percentage of respondents who felt that Congress is more sympathetic to big than to small business. The average number of travel trips and average expense per trip that small business employees make per month. The percent who hired new people in the last year and who say they will in the next 12 months.

Poll Details: The source of the study is MasterCard Businesscard. 414 small business owners participated in the study.

Availability: Published in *The Atlanta Journal and Constitution*, September 4, 1990, p. D-2.

CONSUMER KNOWLEDGE

Description: Presents some of the results from a comprehensive test on consumer knowledge, including areas such as banking; insurance; product safety; and buying a house, car, and food.

Results: "Most Americans don't know that auto insurance rates vary widely from company to company, that life insurance is considered less important as one grows older, and that real estate agents represent only the seller." Correct answers were given to 54% of the 249 questions on the consumer test. Hispanics and blacks, combined, scored lower than whites. Consumers with lower incomes and less education also had lower scores. The best-educated respondents averaged only 62%. (It was estimated that a person could get about 25% right by guessing at the multiple choice questions.)

Poll Extracts:

1. **HOW MANY TEASPOONS OF SUGAR DOES A TYPICAL 12-OUNCE CAN OF CARBONATED SOFT DRINK CONTAIN?**

   A. 1
   B. 5
   C. 10
   D. 20

2. **WHEN A CHECK BOUNCES, WHO, IF ANYONE, IS USUALLY CHARGED A FEE?**

   A. The check writer only.
   B. The person to whom the check is written only.
   C. Both the check writer and the person to whom the check is written.
   D. Neither the check writer nor the person to whom the check is written.

   CORRECT ANSWERS, WITH PERCENTAGE OF THOSE SURVEYED WHO GOT IT RIGHT IN PARENTHESES:

   1. C (23%); 2. C (29%)

Also in Source: 25 questions from the test, along with the correct answers, and the percentage of the respondents who answered that question correctly.

Poll Details: The test was sponsored by the Consumer Federation of America, a coalition of 240 consumer groups. The consumer test was developed by the Educational Testing Service, along with experts from a number of areas. TRW Information Systems and Services Foundation paid for the test.

Availability: Published in the *Detroit Free Press*, September 25, 1990, p. 1A, 10A.

CONSUMER SATISFACTION

Description: Presents the results of a survey concerning consumer satisfaction
and executives' priorities involving consumer service.

Results: Half of the consumer respondents said service is improving, the
highest mark in the 19 years of the survey. The survey also found that 95%
of the executives surveyed put a premium on quality customer service and
91% had taken steps to monitor and improve service.

Poll Extracts:

HOW SATISFIED ARE CONSUMERS?

Has service improved?...............................Yes...50%

Is quality declining?...............................Yes...45%

Is personal attention from service-providers
declining?..Yes...51%

Do you perceive declining value for the
money you spend?....................................Yes...60%

Also in Source: Service idustries were ranked from top to bottom based on
response to complaints: retailers, leisure-entertainment-hospitality,
banks, telecommunications, utilities, health care, other financial
institutions, and - coming in last - insurance companies.

Poll Details: The poll, commissioned by John Hancock Financial Services and
conducted by the Harris Survey, questioned 1,250 consumers and 500
executives from service-oriented businesses such as retailers, utilities,
and financial services companies. The survey was conducted in July and
August 1990, and had a margin of error of plus or minus 3%.

Availability: Published in *The Atlanta Journal and Constitution*, November 19,
1990, p. C-3.

CORPORATE TRAVEL

Description: A survey on corporate travel and entertainment.

Results: Top executives say too much is spent on travel and entertainment (approximately $115 billion in 1990). The percentage of firms that added a travel manager to their staff last year is 29%, up from 8% in 1982, and up from 16% in 1986. Only 42% of the executives surveyed say their companies control expenses successfully. The percentage of companies that update their travel policies annually is at 36%.

Poll Extracts:

IS EMPLOYEE TRAVEL OCCASIONALLY ABUSED? .... 62% Yes

DO COMPANIES NEED A CENTRALLY CONTROLLED TRAVEL BUDGET? .... 66% Yes

DOES YOUR COMPANY HAVE A WRITTEN POLICY? ... 42% No

Also in Source: The percentage of those surveyed who gave cash advances, and the percentage who did so in 1986 when a similar survey was taken.

Poll Details: The survey questioned 1,600 executives by American Express Co.

Availability: Published in *USA Today,* March 19, 1990, p. 1E.

COURTING INVESTORS

Description: Presents the results of a survey of investor relations officers concerning their attitudes and activities toward improving communication with institutional investors.

Results: Almost 85% of the respondents consider setting up small meetings with key institutions the best technique in communicating with institutional investors.

Poll Extracts:

WHICH TECHNIQUE WORKS BEST IN COMMUNICATING WITH INVESTORS?

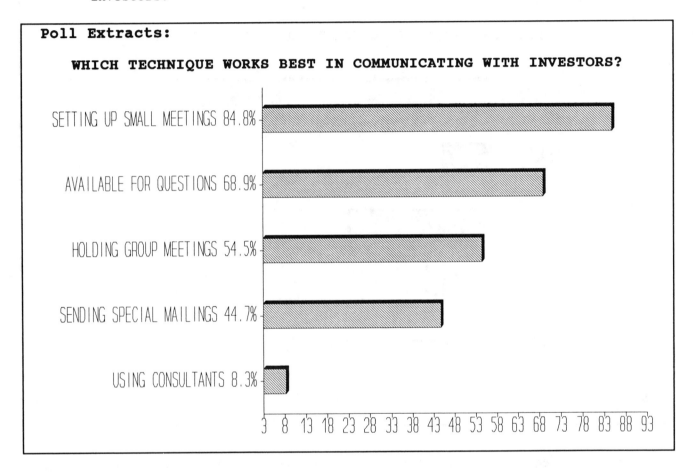

Also in Source: 78% of the respondents are increasing their efforts to directly communicate with institutional investors. 61.4% of the respondents rate the ability of Wall Street analysts to convey information about their companies as good, 20.4% rate it as fair, 17.4% rate it as very good, and 0.8% rate it as poor.

Poll Details: *Institutional Investor* surveyed 700 investor relations officers.

Availability: Published in *Institutional Investor*, November 1990 (volume XXIV, number 15), p. 175, 176.

CREDIT AVAILABILITY FOR SMALL BUSINESSES

Description: Presents the results of a survey concerning the availability of credit loans for small businesses.

Results: 91% of the respondents feel that small businesses are facing a "credit crunch."

Poll Extracts:

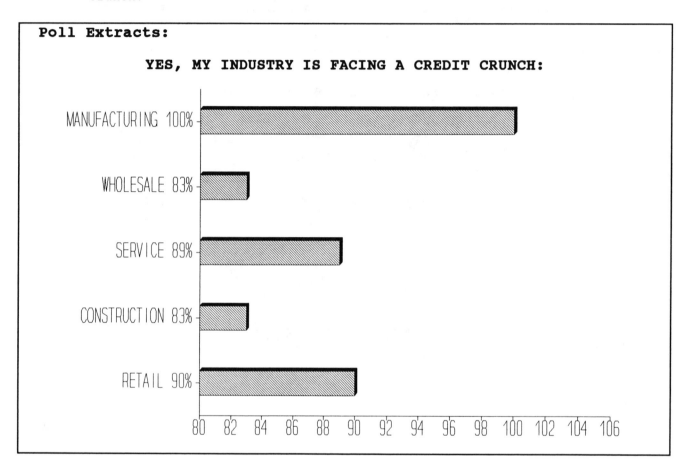

YES, MY INDUSTRY IS FACING A CREDIT CRUNCH:

Also in Source: Among those businesses who recently tried to borrow a large sum for business expansion or development, 55% were turned down. Of those who were denied the loans, 33% cited lender hesitance and 42% cited lack of assets or collateral as reasons for the denial.

Poll Details: The results were taken from a survey of 200 members by National Small Business United, a national business association.

Availability: Published in *USA Today*, December 13, 1990, p. 8B.

DECIDING HOW TO INVEST

Description: Respondents were queried as to what they relied on when making an investment.

Results: The majority of the respondents relied on personal research the most when making an investment decision. For respondents who had a full-service broker, the broker's advice was followed: always -- 7%; frequently -- 27%; sometimes -- 52%; and rarely/never -- 14%.

Poll Extracts:

WHAT RESPONDENTS RELY ON MOST IN MAKING AN INVESTMENT DECISION:

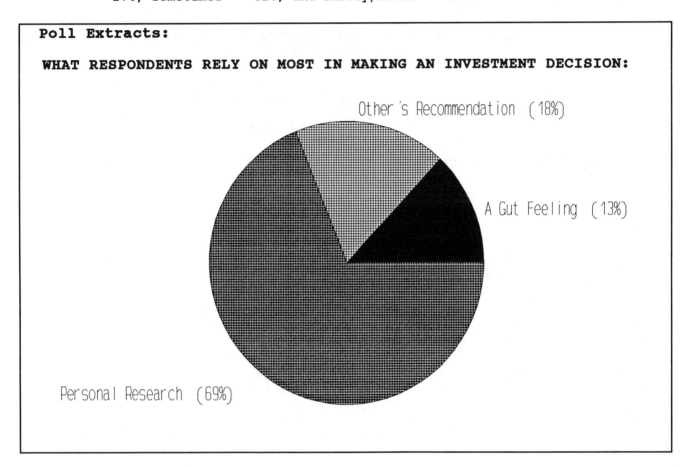

Also in Source: Demographic characteristics and expectations of the special investor panel formed by *USA Today*. Statistics regarding how members of the panel manage and monitor their investments.

Poll Details: The survey involved the 442-member panel of active, but non-professional investors formed by *USA Today*. 75% of the members on the panel are male, 90% work full-time, and 76% are married.

Availability: Published in *USA Today*, July 16, 1990, p. 3B.

DIFFERENCES CONCERNING PROMOTION REQUIREMENTS

Description: Presents the results of a survey concerning what women believe is important for promotion and what their organizations actually require.

Results: Corporations and their women managers differ significantly in their perceptions of what it takes to get promoted.

Poll Extracts:

WHAT ARE THE MINIMUM REQUIREMENTS FOR PROMOTIOM TO UPPER MANAGEMENT?

	Women Mangers	Companies
Lateral job rotation within company	21.7%	24.3%
Relocation out of city	16.7%	35.5%
Additional technical training	28.3%	40.1%
Additional on-the-job training	55.0%	62.2%
Additional or more specific leadership skills	73.3%	75.7%
Additional or more specific interpersonal skills	53.3%	81.1%
Additional or specific communication skills	55.0%	83.3%
Additional or specific administrative skills	67.0%	81.1%
Additional or more specific cognitive skills	51.7%	75.5%

Also in Source: Similar differences in perception were identified for promotion to middle management. For example, 3.3% of women mangers believe lateral job rotation within the company is required, while 28.6% of the companies surveyed view it as required. 1.6% of women mangers feel relocation out of the city as a requirement compared to 25% of the companies.

Poll Details: The results are taken from the study *Moving Up...Moving On* conducted by Drs. Griffin and Connie Grant of Texas Women's University and Women's Center of Dallas. 28 Dallas area companies in 13 industries responded. 60 women in first-line and middle-management jobs in these companies responded.

Availability: Published in *The Dallas Morning News*, October 30, 1990, p. 1D, 9D.

DREXEL BURNHAM LAMBERT

Description: This poll questioned senior executives regarding their opinions
           on the Drexel affair.

Results: The majority of those polled think: the government should not have
           bailed Drexel out (95%), Drexel Burnham was not driven out of business by
           overzealous government prosecutors (86%), the junk bond market would have
           collapsed even if Michael Milken had not been forced out of the company
           (75%), the ethical standards of similar Wall Street firms are about the
           same (74%), Drexel's activities left many firms with far more debt than can
           be safely handled (85%), the takeover wave of the 1980s will now subside
           (76%), and the financial excesses of the 1980s will create problems in the
           1990s (59%).

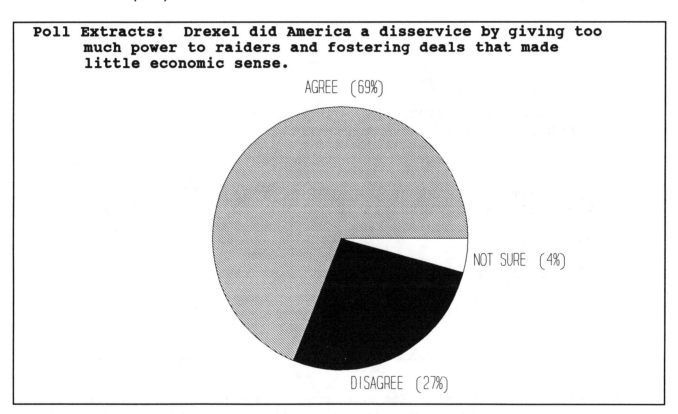

Poll Extracts: **Drexel did America a disservice by giving too
        much power to raiders and fostering deals that made
        little economic sense.**

AGREE (69%)

NOT SURE (4%)

DISAGREE (27%)

Also in Source: The percentage of respondents who felt the past decade of
           buyouts and takeovers has made Corporate America more or less competitive.
           The percentage of respondents who felt that Drexel did Corporate America a
           great service by making capital available to small or high-risk companies
           that might not otherwise have been able to find financing.

Poll Details: This Business Week/Harris Poll was conducted February 20-27,
           1990 by Louis Harris & Associates for *Business Week*. This survey of 404
           senior executives was drawn from the Business Week Top 1000.

Availability: Published in *Business Week*, March 12, 1990 (number 3149),
           p. 41.

ELECTRONICS INDUSTRY

Description: This survey of 750 chief executives questioned their beliefs
about the electronics industry in the 1990s.

Results: Chief executives of U.S. electronics companies say the U.S.
technological edge is declining, and more than 60% expect the decline to
continue over the next five years. The theme of the 1990s in the
electronics industry will be the globalization of markets, manufacturing
and business strategies. By mid-decade 27% of the capital needs of U.S.
electronics companies are expected to be supplied by foreign sources.
Although only 12% of executives now believe that the Pacific Rim is an
essential market, the number who believe it will be an essential market in
1995 is about 25%.

Poll Extracts:

**WILL FOREIGN COMPANIES BE YOUR PRIMARY
COMPETITORS BY 1995** .... 30%   Yes

**WILL WESTERN EUROPE BE CRITICAL TO YOUR
BUSINESS STRATEGY BY 1995** .... 26%   Yes

WILL JAPAN BE AN ESSENTIAL MARKET BY 1995 .... 31%   Yes

Also in Source: The percentage of respondents who believe that foreign
companies are their primary competitors today. The percentage of
respondents who believe Western Europe is critical to their business
strategy today.

Poll Details: The survey of 750 chief executives of computer and electronics
companies was conducted by the accounting and consulting firm Ernst & Young
and *Electronic Business* Magazine.

Availability: Published in *The Atlanta Journal and Constitution*, March 15,
1990, p. D-10.

FEMALE EXECUTIVES' ATTITUDES TOWARD CORPORATE AMERICA

Description: This survey of women executives queried respondents about the
corporate environment in which they work.

Results: 10% of the respondents rate large corporations as an "excellent" place
for women executives to work. 63% think that large corporations are
"pretty good" places for women executives to work. 60% of the respondents
thought that "a male-dominated corporate culture" is an obstacle to success
for women executives at their company. When asked to rate their company on
"the absence of a boys' club culture," respondents replied: excellent –
13%, pretty good – 32%, only fair – 34%, poor – 16%, and not sure – 5%.

Poll Extracts:

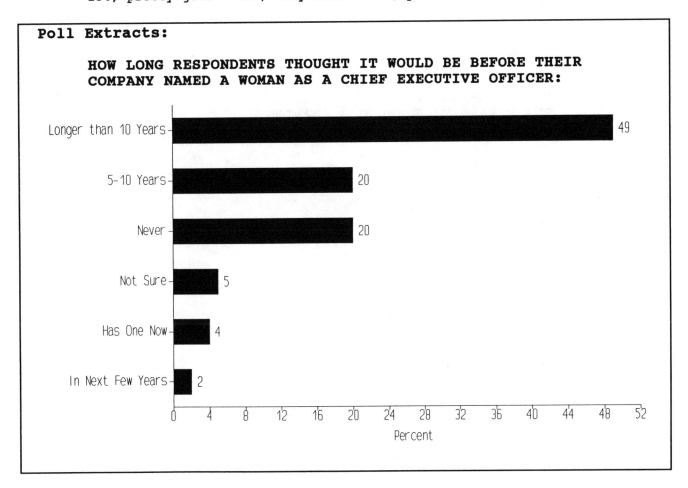

**HOW LONG RESPONDENTS THOUGHT IT WOULD BE BEFORE THEIR
COMPANY NAMED A WOMAN AS A CHIEF EXECUTIVE OFFICER:**

Also in Source: Things which companies have or have not done to improve
conditions for women executives during the past five years.

Poll Details: 450 women executives at corporations with at least $100 million
in annual sales or at least 1,500 employees participated in the survey.
Louis Harris & Associates Inc. conducted the survey from June 20-27, 1990,
for *Business Week*.

Availability: Published in *Business Week*, August 6, 1990 (number 3172), p. 54.

FLEXTIME WORKERS

Description: A survey of 521 firms regarding work scheduling policies.

Results: The majority of personnel chiefs say part-time, job-sharing, and flextime employees are good producers and high performers. From the firms surveyed, 93% say they offer at least one of the following options: part-time, flextime, job-sharing, or home-based work. Clerical and support staff are more likely to choose flexible schedules than professionals (with home-based work the exception).

Poll Extracts:

**PERSONNEL CHIEFS THAT SAY
THEIR PART-TIME AND JOB-SHARING
EMPLOYEES ARE GOOD PRODUCERS** .... 90% Yes

**PERSONNEL CHIEFS THAT SAY
THEIR FLEXTIMERS ARE HIGH
PERFORMERS** .... More than 80% Yes

Poll Details: A study of 521 firms by The Conference Board; survey director – Kathleen Christensen, a City University of New York psychologist.

Availability: Published in *USA Today*, January 8, 1990, p. 1A.

GASOLINE AND DRIVING BEHAVIOR

Description: Respondents were queried about the recent oil price increases
after the Iraqi invasion of Kuwait, and how the price of oil will effect
their driving behavior.

Results: 91% of the respondents thought that the oil companies were taking
advantage of the Iraqi situation in order to increase profits, and that the
price increase for oil was unnecessary. About 20% of the respondents say
that they have already reduced their driving since the Iraqi crisis began.

Poll Extracts:

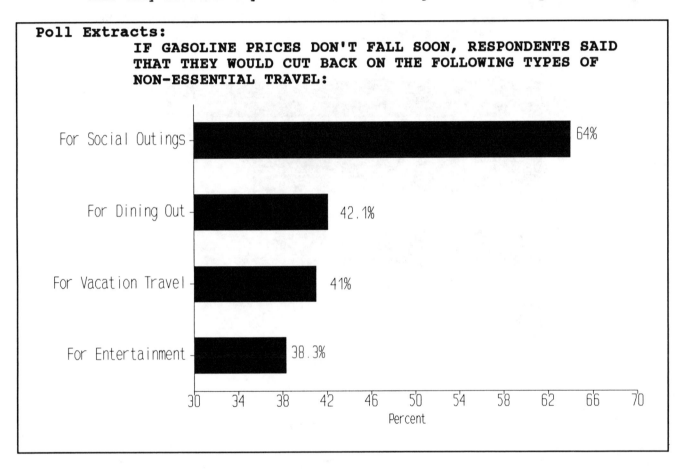

**IF GASOLINE PRICES DON'T FALL SOON, RESPONDENTS SAID
THAT THEY WOULD CUT BACK ON THE FOLLOWING TYPES OF
NON-ESSENTIAL TRAVEL:**

Also in Source: The percentage of those surveyed who say that they've already
cut travel for entertainment, dining out, and social outings.

Poll Details: The Gallup Organization conducted this poll for *Advertising Age*
on August 15, 1990. 515 adults were interviewed by telephone nationwide.
The margin of error is 4.4%.

Availability: Published in *Advertising Age*, August 20, 1990 (volume 61,
number 34), p. 1, 63.

GUILT FROM IMPORT PURCHASES

Description: Respondents were asked if they felt at least somewhat guilty about purchasing foreign goods.

Results: 51% of the respondents feel somewhat guilty when buying non-American-made products. 62% of the respondents agreed that, "It's not worth it for me to pay more for a product just because it is American-made."

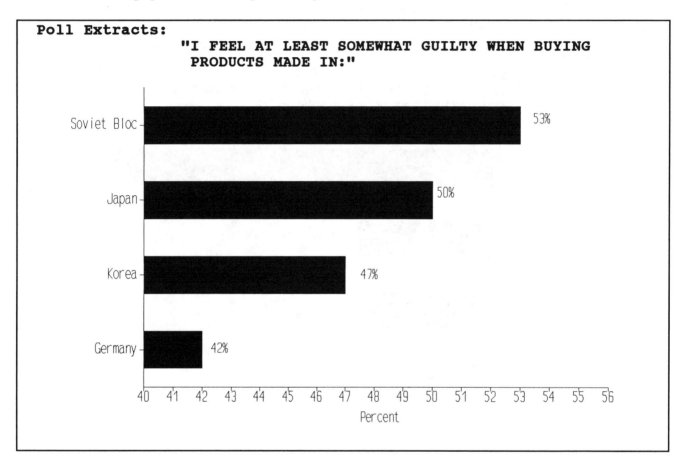

Poll Extracts:
"I FEEL AT LEAST SOMEWHAT GUILTY WHEN BUYING PRODUCTS MADE IN:"

Also in Source: The percentage of consumers who felt guilty about purchasing foreign goods in 1988 and 1989.

Poll Details: Yankelovich Clancy Shulman surveyed 2,500 consumers.

Availability: Published in *The Washington Post*, November 18, 1990, p. H3.

INSTITUTIONAL INVESTORS

Description: CEOs were polled on their attitudes toward institutional ownership (institutional shareholders) of corporations.

Results: CEOs thought that state and public pension funds were the most activist shareholders (57%). 50% of the respondents thought that significant institutional ownership decreases a company's stability. 43% of the respondents thought that the growing activism of institutional investors was good, with 20% saying that because it provides better communication between shareholders and management. 34% of the respondents thought that the growing activism of institutional investors was bad, with 34% saying that because it focuses too much on the short term.

Poll Extracts:

"HAVE THE INSTITUTIONS THAT OWN STOCK IN YOUR COMPANY TAKEN A MORE ACTIVE ROLE IN THE PAST FEW YEARS?"

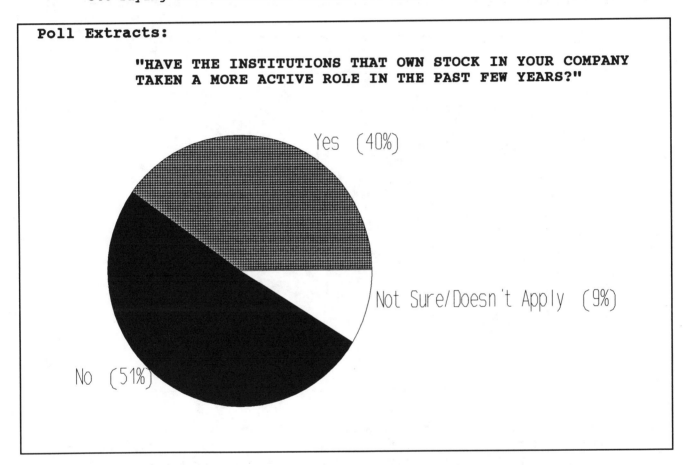

Also in Source: The percentage of respondents who say that their companies evaluate the performance of its pension fund managers on a quarterly basis, or more frequently, or less frequently. The percentages found in the results sometimes total over 100% because of multiple responses.

Poll Details: 200 CEOs of Fortune 500 and Service 500 companies were polled by the public opinion research firm of Clark Martire & Bartolomeo. The poll was conducted from June 5-16, 1990.

Availability: Published in *Fortune*, July 30, 1990, p. 95, 98.

INTERNATIONAL BUSINESS ACQUISITIONS

Description: Presents the results of a survey concerning regions of the world companies would be most interested in if they were to consider an international merger or acquisition.

Results: Almost 90% of the respondents would be most interested in an acquisition in Western Contintental Europe. They are least interested in Africa and the Middle East.

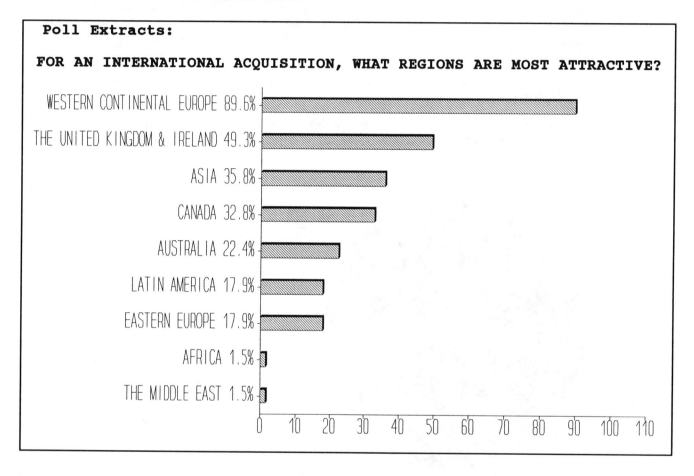

Poll Extracts:

FOR AN INTERNATIONAL ACQUISITION, WHAT REGIONS ARE MOST ATTRACTIVE?

WESTERN CONTINENTAL EUROPE 89.6%
THE UNITED KINGDOM & IRELAND 49.3%
ASIA 35.8%
CANADA 32.8%
AUSTRALIA 22.4%
LATIN AMERICA 17.9%
EASTERN EUROPE 17.9%
AFRICA 1.5%
THE MIDDLE EAST 1.5%

0 10 20 30 40 50 60 70 80 90 100 110

Also in Source: 14.7% of the respondents would consider a joint venture in Eastern Europe, 6.3% in China, and 5.5% in the Soviet Union. 73.5% of the respondents would not consider a joint venture in these countries or regions.

Poll Details: *Institutional Investor* surveyed chief financial officers.

Availability: Published in *Institutional Investor*, December 1990 (volume XXIV, number 16), p. 175.

INTERNATIONAL IMAGE OF THE U.S.

Description: This survey of 1,800 business leaders in 34 countries ranked the world's most "unfair players" in international markets.

Results: The U.S. was ranked as the world's third most unfair player. Respondents also ranked Japan, the U.S., and West Germany, respectively as first, second, and third at being the best able to turn innovations into competitive products.

Poll Extracts:

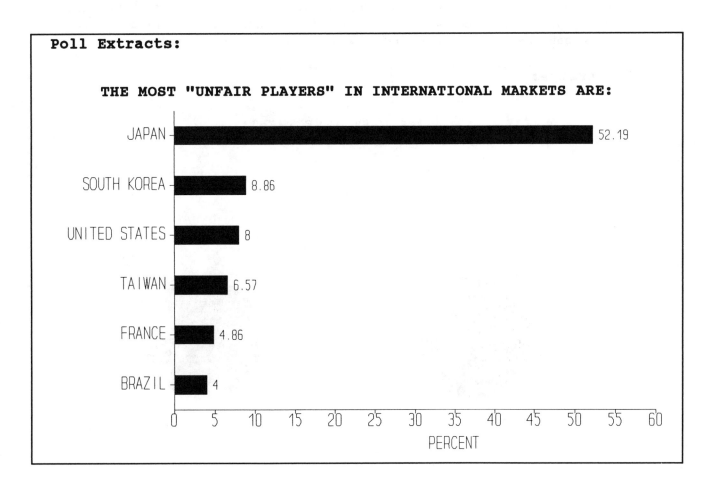

THE MOST "UNFAIR PLAYERS" IN INTERNATIONAL MARKETS ARE:

Also in Source: Countries which were seen as the "brightest rising stars" of international business. Countries which were seen as "resting on their laurels."

Poll Details: "The survey was conducted by the International Institute for Management Development, a Lausanne, Switzerland-based business school, and the World Economic Forum, which runs an annual businessmen's meeting in Davos."

Availability: Published in the *Los Angeles Times*, March 14, 1990, p. D5.

INVEST IN STOCKS

Description: Respondents were asked which investments they expect to give the best returns in one year and in three years. Respondents were also asked if they had considered or had bought international investments since the fall of the Iron Curtain.

Results: Respondents expected stocks to be the best investment over the next one-year and three-year period. Since the fall of the Iron Curtain: 25% of the respondents have bought international investments; 4% have thought about buying and decided against it; 25% are still considering international investments; and 46% haven't even considered it.

Poll Extracts:

THE BEST INVESTMENT:

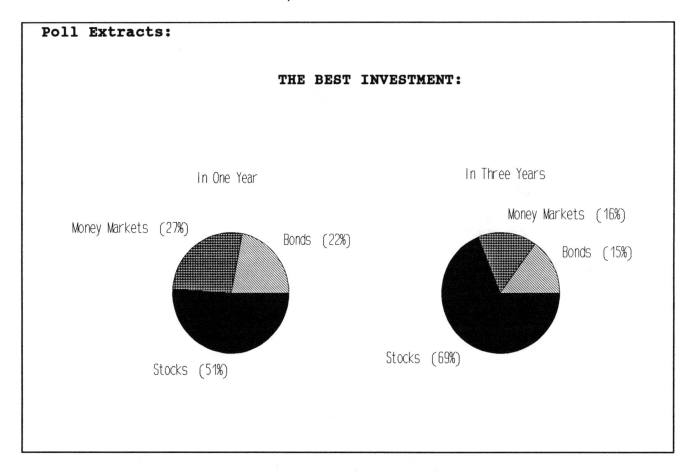

Also in Source: The respondents outlook toward interest rates and the Dow Jones industrial average.

Poll Details: Participants in this telephone poll were members of the *USA Today* Investor Panel -- "a group of regular *Money* Section readers who are serious investors." 90% of the members were reached for the survey.

Availability: Published in *USA Today*, July 17, 1990, p. 1B.

JAPANESE INVESTMENTS IN THE UNITED STATES

Description: Presents the results of a survey concerning the appropriate level of Japanese investments in the United States.

Results: Almost 70% of the Americans surveyed felt that Japan has invested too much in the United States while 45% of the Japanese surveyed share the same opinion. 23% of the Americans and 44% of the Japanese surveyed felt that the level of investment was appropriate. 5% of Americans and 6% Japanese surveyed felt that Japan has invested too little in the United States.

Poll Extracts:

THE LEVEL OF JAPANESE INVESTMENTS IN THE U.S. IS:

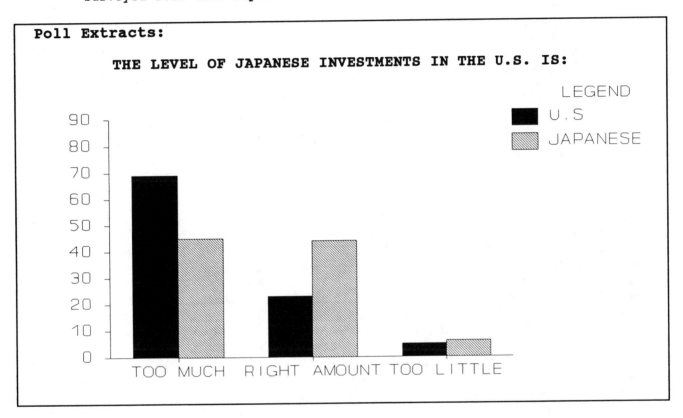

Also in Source: The article includes a discussion of the issues surrounding the economic interrelationship between the United States and Japan.

Poll Details: The survey was conducted by *Wall Street Journal*/Nippon Research and *Wall Street Journal*/NBC News poll.

Availability: Published in *The Wall Street Journal*, June 19, 1990, p. A1, A12.

LOBBYING IN CONGRESS

Description: This poll asked Congressional aides about the industries that do
the most effective job of lobbying in Congress, and also asked the
Congressional staffers to name the business executives that are most
effective in representing their interests to Congress.

Results: The top ten industries that do the most effective job of lobbying in
Congress are: Banking (18%), NRA (16%), Defense (16%), Agriculture (14%),
Automotive (14%), Insurance (14%), Oil companies (14%), Elderly/AARP (10%),
Tobacco (10%), and Health care (9%). The top ten industries that do the
least effective job of lobbying in Congress are: Oil companies (9%),
Utilities (7%), Agriculture (7%), Human-service advocates:
poor/homeless/children (7%), Automotive (7%), Tobacco (6%), Banking (6%),
Teachers/NEA (6%), Environmentalists (6%), and Health care (5%).

Poll Extracts:
"IN YOUR EXPERIENCE, WHICH TWO OR THREE INDIVIDUAL TOP BUSINESS EXECUTIVES ARE THE MOST EFFECTIVE IN REPRESENTING THEIR INTERESTS IN CONGRESS?"

Lee A. Iacocca, chairman, Chrysler Corp.	49%
T. Boone Pickens Jr., chairman, United Shareholders Assn.	5%
Jack Valenti, president, Motion Picture Assn. of America	4%
H. Ross Perot, chairman, Perot Systems Inc.	4%
Frank A. Lorenzo, chairman, Texas Int. Airlines Inc.	3%
James A. Robinson III, chairman, American Express Co.	3%
John S. Reed, chairman, Citicorp	3%
Richard Lesher, president, U.S. Chamber of Commerce	2%
Roger Smith, chairman, General Motors Corp.	2%
Lane Kirkland, president, AFL-CIO	2%
Stanley C. Pace, chairman, General Dynamics Corp.	2%
Norman R. Augustine, chairman, Martin Marietta Corp.	2%
All other mentions	38%
Don't know	21%
Refused	2%

Also in Source: The most effective and ineffective members of Congress. The
top Congressional staff members in influencing the course of major
legislation.

Poll Details: This *Business Week*/Harris Poll surveyed 304 of the most senior
Congressional staffers (177 Democrats and 127 Republicans) from the House
and Senate. Approximately two-thirds of the Congressional aides work in
members' offices, with the rest of the aides on committees.

Availability: Published in *Business Week*, April 16, 1990 (number 3155),
p. 58-59.

LOWER DEBT RATIOS

Description: Presents the results of a survey of CFOs on corporate debt.

Results: 76% of CFOs believe that changes in economic conditions have made
lower debt ratios more desirable now than one year ago. 45% of the CFOs
have seen their debt-equity ratio increase in the last two years. The
percentage of CFOs who, ideally, would like their debt-to-total-capital
ratio reduced is: 10.1% --"greatly reduced," and 33.9% -- "slightly
reduced." 63.7% of the CFOs felt that their company has unused borrowing
capacity and could afford to borrow more.

Poll Extracts:

**HOW THE CFOs PLAN TO REDUCE THEIR
DEBT-EQUITY RATIOS:**

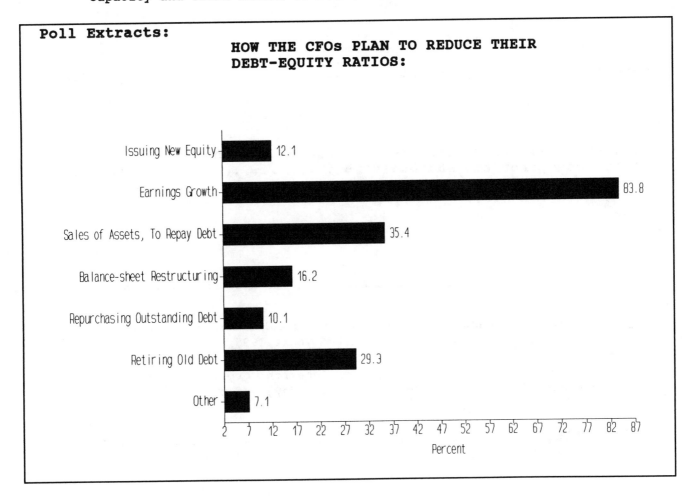

Also in Source: Responses to several other questions dealing with debt.

Poll Details: This respondents in this survey were CFOs.

Availability: Published in *Institutional Investor*, September 1990 (volume 24,
number 11), p. 241.

MERGERS AND TAKEOVERS

Description: The poll measured public attitudes toward unfriendly takeovers, leveraged buyouts, and other mergers that have changed the corporate world.

Results: Almost half of Americans believe that mergers hold back economic growth. Just over 33% said that mergers hurt productivity.

Poll Extracts:

Mergers decrease employment .... 75% said Yes

Corporate executives are the real winners in the merger game, not the shareholders .... 48% said Yes

---

Also in Source: Chart showing Americans who believe mergers "benefit" or "hinder" U.S. economic growth, in the years 1983, 1985, 1986, and 1990.

Poll Details: This poll was by Opinion Research Corp., and the opinions were tabulated from February 1-4, 1990 (nine days before Drexel Burnham Lambert filed for bankruptcy).

Availability: Published in *The Atlanta Journal and Constitution*, March 15, 1990, p. D-2.

MERGERS AND WALL STREET

Description: This poll asked adults about their attitudes toward corporate mergers and Wall Street.

Results: Thirty percent of adults did "not at all" trust Wall Street bankers to do what was best for the economy. Sixty-eight percent thought that if they had $1,000 to spend, investing it in the stock market would be a bad idea. An equal percentage (68%) thought mergers and takeovers were not good for the nation's economy. Heavy corporate debt was thought to be a serious or very serious problem for the economy in the 1990s by 74% of those polled.

Poll Extracts:

DO MERGERS AND TAKEOVERS HELP OR HURT THE FOLLOWING:

	HELP	HURT
The lawyers and bankers who arrange them	80%	13%
The top management of the companies involved	52%	36%
Employees of the companies	26%	62%
American consumers	25%	60%

Also in Source: A pie chart describing "who owns junk bonds," and a brief history of Michael Milken and Drexel Burnham Lambert, from 1969 to February 1990.

Poll Details: Yankelovich Clancy Shulman conducted the telephone poll of 500 adult Americans for *Time*/CNN on February 14, 1990. The sampling error is plus or minus 4.5%.

Availability: Published in *Time*, February 26, 1990 (volume 135, number 9), p. 46-50, 52.

OHIOANS WANT UNION PROTECTION

Description: Presents the results of a poll of Ohioans on labor unions.

Results: 69% of the respondents felt that labor unions are necessary. 54% of the respondents thought that labor unions have been "very important" in helping to achieve this country's standard of living.

Poll Extracts:

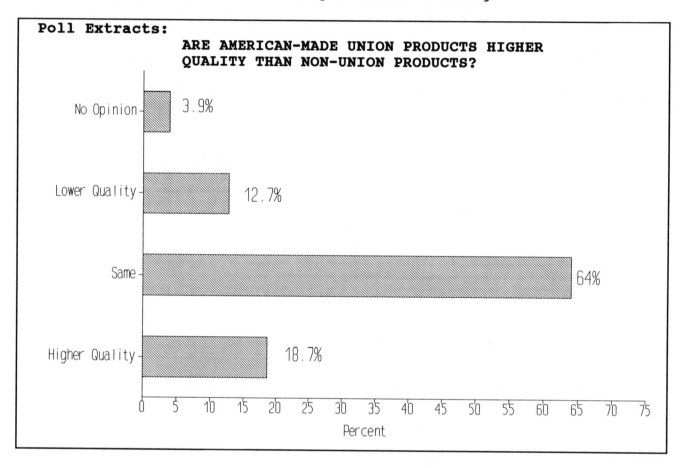

ARE AMERICAN-MADE UNION PRODUCTS HIGHER QUALITY THAN NON-UNION PRODUCTS?

Also in Source: Union membership has dropped 15% in the last 10 years to 16.9 million in 1989. In the 1980s, union representation of the work force decreased from 25% to 17%.

Poll Details: This Ohio Poll was conducted by the University of Cincinnati from April 27 - May 4, 1990, for the *Dayton Daily News* and *Cincinnati Post*. 628 adults in Ohio were interviewed by telephone in this random poll.

Availability: Published in the *Dayton Daily News*, July 2, 1990 (Dayton, Inc. section), p. 8-9.

PERFORMANCE REVIEWS

Description: Respondents were asked about their attitudes toward the
    performance review process.

Results: Employee dissatisfaction with the performance review process is higher
    now than it was in a similar survey conducted in 1987. 52.4% of the
    respondents preferred semiannual reviews. When compared to the similar
    survey conducted in 1987, the percentage of respondents who felt that
    reviews are a waste of time has risen from 6% to 9%. 48.8% of the
    respondents said that reviews often crumble into second-guessing sessions.

Poll Extracts:

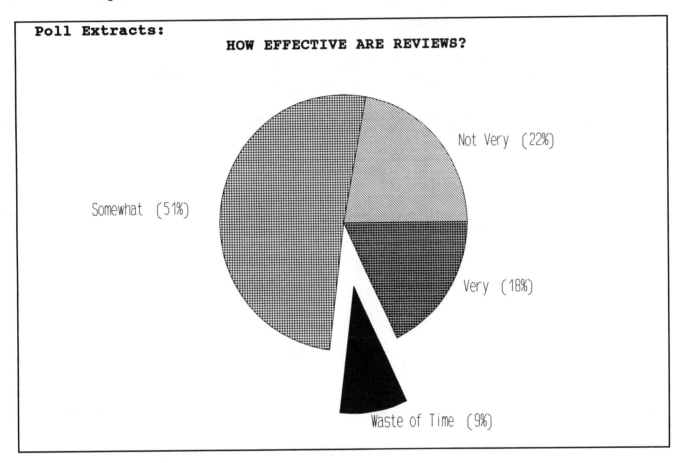

HOW EFFECTIVE ARE REVIEWS?

Not Very (22%)

Somewhat (51%)

Very (18%)

Waste of Time (9%)

Also in Source: The percentage of respondents who thought that companies
    should insist that managers review all employees.

Poll Details: The survey was conducted by *Industry Week* of *Industry Week*
    readers.

Availability: Published in *Industry Week*, August 20, 1990 (volume 239,
    number 16), p. 49, 53-54.

PROS ANS CONS OF MERGERS

Description: Presents the results of a survey concerning the effects of
corporate mergers and acquisitions on the growth of the United States
economy. The survey also sought to identify who benefits and suffers most
from mergers.

Results: Half of the respondents feel executives benefits most from a merger.
Only 4% think the employees benefits most.

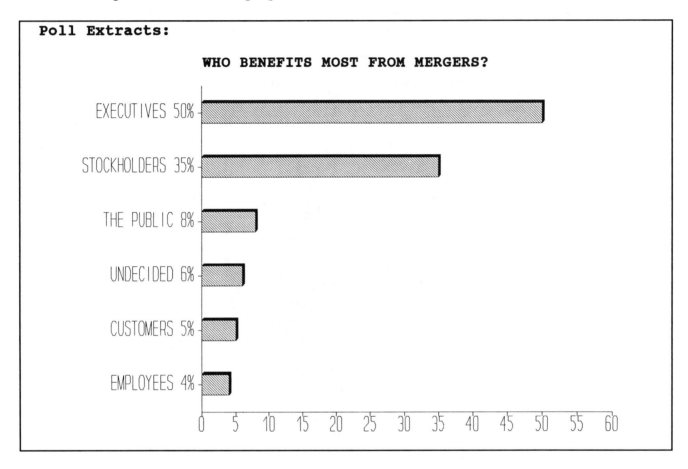

Also in Source: 49% of the respondents think corporate mergers hinder the
United States economy, 23% think they are beneficial, 19% don't know, and
9% think mergers will have no effect. 56% of the respondents said
employees suffer most from mergers, 19% said the public, 8% said customers,
8% were undecided, and 6% said stockholders.

Poll Details: This survey was conducted by Opinion Research Corporation.

Availability: Published in *The Atlanta Journal and Constitution*, October 6,
1990, p. B-2.

SCIENTIFIC FRAUD

Description: This reader's survey asked respondents about their knowledge of
fraud in industrial research.

Results: 56% of the respondents said that they had witnessed or had knowledge
of research fraud (alteration of data in order to produce more favorable
results). 42% of the respondents felt increased pressure to produce
research results supporting predetermined outcomes.

Poll Extracts:

**"ARE CURRENT REGULATIONS AND CHECKING SYSTEMS
SUFFICIENT TO PREVENT FRAUD IN INDUSTRIAL
RESEARCH?"**

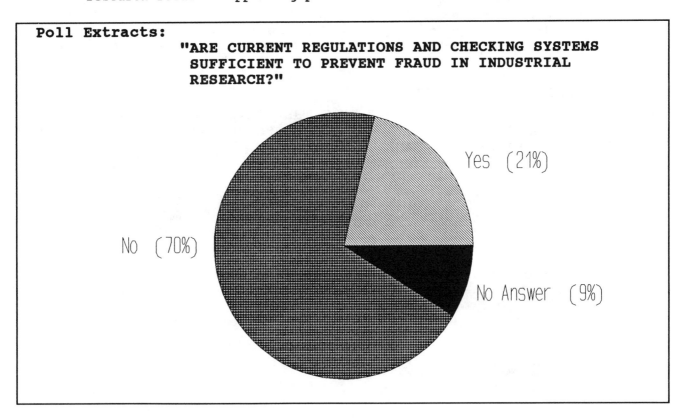

Poll Details: This *Research & Development* reader's poll was presented in the
May 1990 issue. 99 readers responded to the poll questions.

Availability: Published in *Research & Development*, October 1990 (volume 32,
number 10), p. 146.

SERVICE QUALITY IN AMERICA

Description: Presents the results of a survey asking about the overall quality
of service in the U.S., and which companies offer the best service.

Results: Just over half of the respondents felt that the quality of service in
America has decreased over the last 10 years. Respondents also thought
that, regarding service, the telephone companies were at the top of the
list while the auto companies were at the bottom of the list. For the best
service among Fortune 500 companies, IBM was listed as number one, followed
by Nordstrom's, American Express, AT&T, McDonald's, Federal Express, Walt
Disney, General Electric, Marriott, American Airlines, Delta, Xerox, and
Wal-Mart.

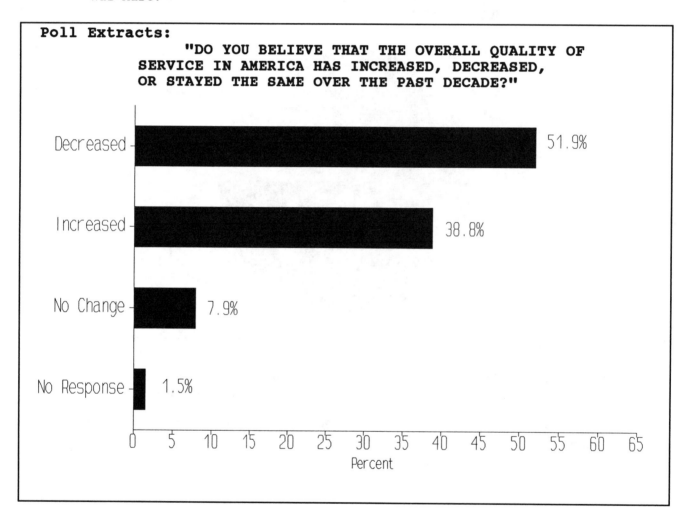

Poll Extracts:

**"DO YOU BELIEVE THAT THE OVERALL QUALITY OF
SERVICE IN AMERICA HAS INCREASED, DECREASED,
OR STAYED THE SAME OVER THE PAST DECADE?"**

Poll Details: 534 managers were interviewed by Paul R. Ray & Co., an executive
search consulting firm.

Availability: Published in the *The Atlanta Journal and Constitution*,
September 6, 1990, p. F-2.

SHOPPERS SPEAK OUT

Description: Presents the results of a survey concerning the opinions and
activities of American shoppers.

Results: Almost half of the respondents said they shop less today compared to
five years ago.

Poll Extracts:

COMPARED TO FIVE YEARS AGO, HOW MUCH TIME DO YOU SPEND SHOPPING?

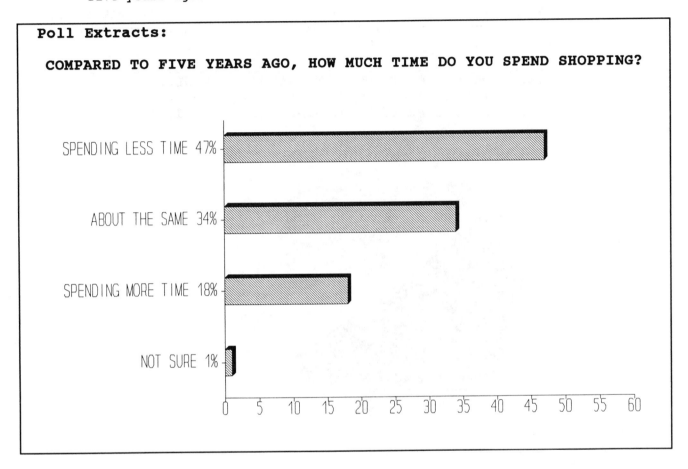

Also in Source: 48% of the respondents said that even though shopping is a
pleasure from time to time, it is something they do because they have to.
33% of the repondents said that large department stores which are
experiencing financial trouble are in that situation because of poor
management, 26% cited high prices, 23% said they opened too many stores,
and 14% said they lost touch with their customers. 54% of the respondents
will buy less this holiday season compared to a year ago, 29% will buy as
much, and 17% will buy more.

Poll Details: This survey of 1,255 adults was conducted November 9 through 13,
1990 for *Business Week* by Louis Harris & Associates Inc. Results should be
accurate to within 3%.

Availability: Published in *Business Week*, November 26, 1990 (number 3189),
p. 144.

SOCIAL RESPONSIBILITY

Description: Respondents were queried about the boycott of Nike athletic
  products called for by PUSH, a Chicago-based activist group founded by the
  Rev. Jesse Jackson. PUSH had criticized Nike for its business relations
  with blacks, as up to one-third of Nike's sales are to black consumers.

Results: 31% of the respondents were aware of the boycott call. 64% of the
  respondents thought that they would buy about the same amount of Nike
  products as before the boycott call.

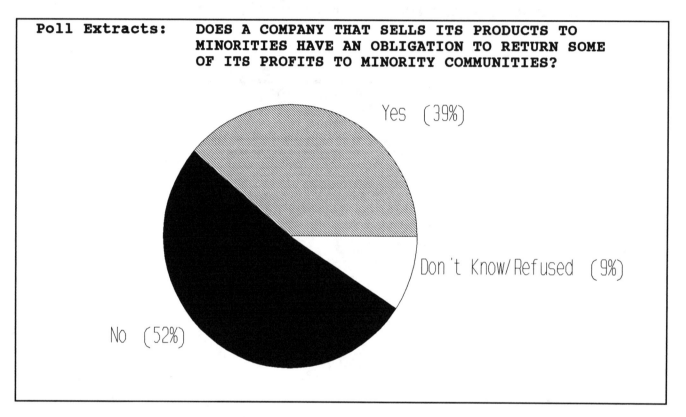

Poll Extracts: **DOES A COMPANY THAT SELLS ITS PRODUCTS TO
                       MINORITIES HAVE AN OBLIGATION TO RETURN SOME
                       OF ITS PROFITS TO MINORITY COMMUNITIES?**

Yes (39%)

Don't Know/Refused (9%)

No (52%)

Also in Source: The percentage of respondents planning to buy fewer Nike
  products. Awareness of the boycott call among: men, women, whites, and
  non-whites.

Poll Details: This *Advertising Age* survey was conducted by the Gallup
  Organization during September 1990. 1,050 adults were interviewed by
  telephone. The margin of error is 3.1%.

Availability: Published in *Advertising Age*, October 29, 1990 (volume 61,
  number 45), p. 59.

STOCK BUYBACKS

Description: Presents the results of a survey measuring the scope of corporate
stock repurchasing activity as well as identifying the rationale for the
buybacks.

Results: 69.5% of the respondents said their company either definitely plans or
would consider repurchasing some of its stock next year. Almost 70% of the
respondents agree that corporations are using buybacks more frequently than
in the past to discourage takeovers.

Poll Extracts:

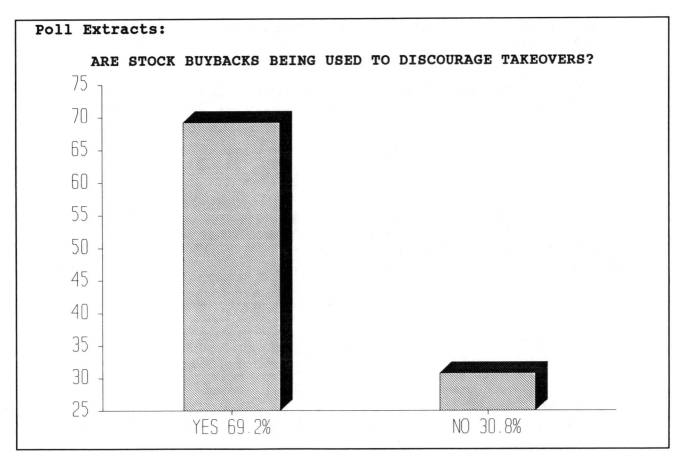

ARE STOCK BUYBACKS BEING USED TO DISCOURAGE TAKEOVERS?

YES 69.2%   NO 30.8%

Also in Source: 58.2% of the respondents whose companies repurchased stock in
the last 18 months did so to obtain shares to use for employee purchase
plans, stock options, and conversions; 46.4% of these respondents did so to
take advantage of underevaluation of stock; 43.6% to enhance stockholders'
investment; 27.3% to make an investment with a return comparing favorably
with alternatives; and 24.5% to send a message to Wall Street that
management believes in the company and its prospects.

Poll Details: *Institutional Investor* surveyed chief financial officers.

Availability: Published in *Institutional Investor*, November, 1990 (volume
XXIV, nmuber 15), p. 169, 170.

TIGHTENING CREDIT

Description: Respondents were queried about a supposed credit crunch within New England.

Results: More than one-third of the respondents thought that their banks had tightened their credit recently.

Poll Extracts:

HAS YOUR BANK RENEGOTIATED, CAPPED, OR SUSPENDED
LINES OF CREDIT? .... 37% said Yes

HAVE ANY OF YOUR LOANS BEEN MONITORED MORE CLOSELY
DURING THE PAST SIX MONTHS? .... 38% said Yes

HAVE LENDERS REAPPRAISED THE VALUE OF COLLATERAL
ON ONE OR MORE OF YOUR LOANS? .... 24% said Yes

HAVE LENDERS CHANGED COVENANTS OR OTHER ASPECTS
OF YOUR LOAN AGREEMENT, OR HAVE THEY CHANGED THE
WAY THEY INTERPRET AND ENFORCE EXISTING
COVENANTS? .... 22% said Yes

Also in Source: An informal straw poll during April 1990 found that 80% of the Smaller Business Association of New England members felt that there had been a definite tightening of credit.

Poll Details: The poll consisted of a 10-point questionnaire that was mailed to 2,400 members of the Smaller Business Association of New England during August 1990. 168 of the members responded.

Availability: Published in *The Boston Globe*, September 20, 1990, p. 57-58.

WILL HIRING INCREASE OR DECREASE?

Description: Presents the results of a survey forcasting companies' hiring
plans for 1991.

Results: Based on the results of the survey, there will be a net decrease in
hiring of 1% in 1991.

Poll Extracts:

WHAT WILL HAPPEN TO YOUR WORK FORCE IN 1991?

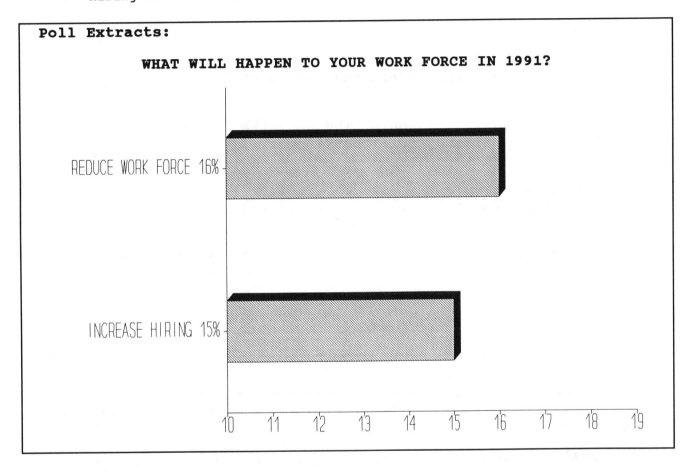

Also in Source: The 15% of firms intending to hire compares with 20% for the
same period in 1990. The 16% planning work force cuts compares to 12% a
year earlier. By industry, the survey showed the steepest declines in
hiring plans were in the construction and retail trade sectors. The survey
showed a 9% advance in hiring plans in the service category, which suggests
service jobs will account for much of the total increase in United States
job activity through early 1991.

Poll Details: Manpower Inc. surveyed 15,000 American businesses.

Availability: Published in *The Detroit Free Press*, December 4, 1990, p. 1E.

CALIFORNIA HOMES

Description: This annual survey of California home shoppers asked what items
buyers would like to see in their new homes.

Results: The average Californian is willing to pay $199,430 for a new home.
The average homebuyer also desires 1,942 square feet of space.

Poll Extracts:

CALIFORNIA HOMEBUYERS WANT:

"The flexibility of converting an extra bedroom
into a den, office, or library." 68%

Tile Roofs 75%
Wood Shake Roofs 17%

A three-car garage .... for homebuyers outside
                                  of Northern California

Also in Source: The median annual household income of consumers looking for
new homes in California. The percentage of homebuyers who own security
systems.

Poll Details: The survey was conducted by the real estate brokerage subsidiary
of Great Western Financial Corp. 2,700 home shoppers were interviewed at
146 new developments throughout the State of California.

Availability: Originally published in the *San Francisco Chronicle*. The
information provided is based on an article printed in the
Chicago Tribune, July 21, 1990, Section 4, p. 2.

CLOTHES FOR WOMEN

Description: This survey queried respondents on women's career clothing buying
intentions.

Results: "The findings reveal a profile of a working woman who is just as apt
to wear casual sportswear to work as she is a tailored suit." 62% of the
respondents usually shop for a special piece of clothing to wear with an
item that is already owned, rather than shopping for a complete outfit.
Women prefer tailored fit and classic styling in the clothes that they wear
to work. More than 50% of the respondents prefer clothes that can be worn
to work and also on the weekend. More than 21% of the respondents said
they shop for career clothing once a month. The majority of women (57%)
said that during the next 12 months, they intend to shop for career
clothing in a department store.

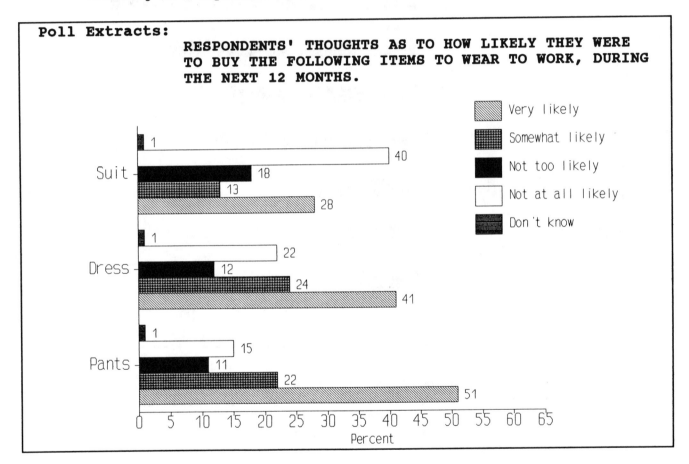

Poll Extracts:

RESPONDENTS' THOUGHTS AS TO HOW LIKELY THEY WERE
TO BUY THE FOLLOWING ITEMS TO WEAR TO WORK, DURING
THE NEXT 12 MONTHS.

Very likely
Somewhat likely
Not too likely
Not at all likely
Don't know

Also in Source: Responses as to buying expectations for three items of
clothing that were not listed in the poll extracts: a skirt, jacket or
blazer, and coordinated top and bottom. Some of the responses are broken
down according to the characteristics of the respondents: age, income, and
occupation.

Poll Details: This study was conducted by the Gallup Organization for *Apparel
Merchandising*. The study involved a sample of women across the nation who
are employed.

Availability: Published in *Apparel Merchandising*, April 1990, p. 25-27.

FOOD LABELS AND FOOD SHOPPING

Description: Presents the results of a survey concerning the relationship
between reading food labels and eating and buying habits of consumers.

Results: Almost 90% of the respondents said that taste is the most important
factor in food selection. Three-fourths of the respondents said nutrition
was the most important factor.

Poll Extracts:

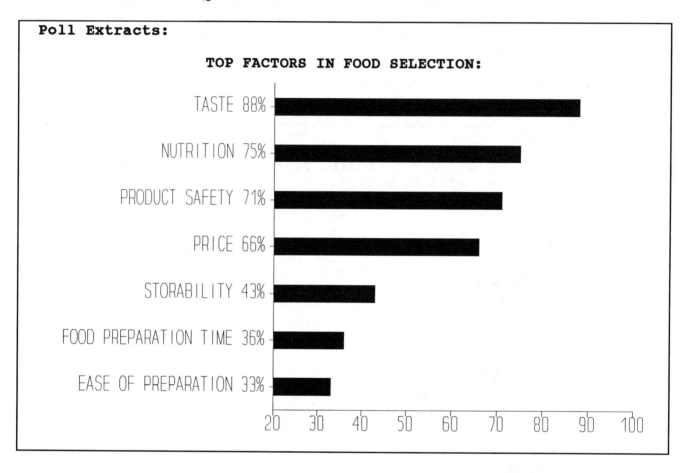

TOP FACTORS IN FOOD SELECTION:

TASTE 88%
NUTRITION 75%
PRODUCT SAFETY 71%
PRICE 66%
STORABILITY 43%
FOOD PREPARATION TIME 36%
EASE OF PREPARATION 33%

20 30 40 50 60 70 80 90 100

Also in Source: An average of 53% of all shoppers always read the ingredients
list when making a first time purchase. 48% of men read the list compared
to 49% of working women, 59% of non working women; households with
children, 46%; childless households, 59%; medically restricted diets, 64%;
and unrestricted diets, 50%,

Poll Details: The poll was conducted by the Food Marketing Institute.

Availability: Published in the *Chicago Tribune*, June 18, 1990, p. C1, C4.

FRESH FISH

Description: This survey queried extension homemakers within the State of Oregon about their: frequency of fresh fish consumption, reasons for not consuming fresh fish, place of purchase, factors influencing purchase, knowledge regarding preparation and storage, and attitudes regarding fresh fish quality.

Results: 60% of the respondents served fresh fish at home two or three times per month. Respondents thought that cost was the major reason they did not serve fresh fish more often. 46% of the respondents were often disappointed in the quality of the fresh fish that they purchased. 67% of the respondents thought that they would buy fish more often if they knew it was really fresh.

Poll Extracts:

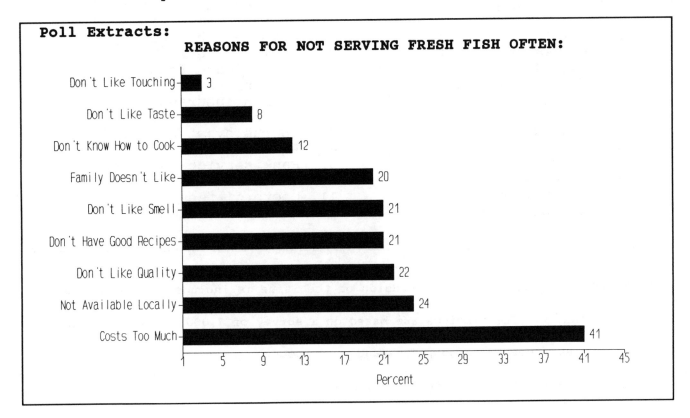

REASONS FOR NOT SERVING FRESH FISH OFTEN:

- Don't Like Touching — 3
- Don't Like Taste — 8
- Don't Know How to Cook — 12
- Family Doesn't Like — 20
- Don't Like Smell — 21
- Don't Have Good Recipes — 21
- Don't Like Quality — 22
- Not Available Locally — 24
- Costs Too Much — 41

Percent

Also in Source: The percentage of respondents who correctly agreed or disagreed with three knowledge statements about fresh fish storage and preparation.

Poll Details: "After pilot testing, the questionnaire was distributed to extension homemakers in two areas of Oregon, the urban west (about 75 miles from coastal waters), and the rural east (about 300 miles inland). Questionnaires were completed at extension group meetings during the Spring of 1987 and returned to the researcher for data analysis using SPSS. All tests were conducted at the 0.05 significance level. 398 completed questionnaires were returned.

Availability: Published in the *Journal of the American Dietetic Association*, August 1990 (volume 90, number 8), p. 1109-1111.

GOOD BUYS, BAD BUYS

Description: Presents the results of a survey concerning consumer satisfaction or disappointment with specific goods and services.

Results: Poultry was given the highest rating for consumer satisfaction while hospital charges were rated the lowest.

Poll Extracts:

AMERICA RATES PRODUCTS AND SERVICES:

Dozen Best Buys

1. Poultry
2. Videotape rental
3. TV set
4. Fruits, vegetables
5. Appliances
6. Meat
7. Pet food
8. Haircuts
9. Fish
10. Electricity
11. Restaurant meals
12. Telephone service

Dozen Worst Buys

1. Hospital charges
2. Lawyers' fees
3. Credit card fees
4. Premium pay TV
5. Health insurance
6. Movies & theaters
7. Sports event tickets
8. Auto insurance
9. Bank service charges
10. Used cars
11. Doctors' fees
12. College tuition

Also in Source: A brief discussion of the issue is included in the article.

Poll Details: The findings are based on a survey of 7,000 families by the Conference Board. Participants were asked to rate the value of 50 products and services as "good", "average", or "poor."

Availability: Published in *The Atlantal Journal & Constitution*, June 7, 1990, p. D-2.

THE IMPORTANCE OF PRICES

Description: Presents the results of a survey concerning the importance of prices to consumers.

Results: Almost half of the respondents said that price is extremely important when deciding where to shop for groceries. Almost 40% said they shop at another supermarket if it offers good specials or a lot of items on special during a particular week.

Poll Extracts:

HOW IMPORTANT ARE GROCERY PRICES TO YOU?

SOMEWHAT IMPORTANT 35%

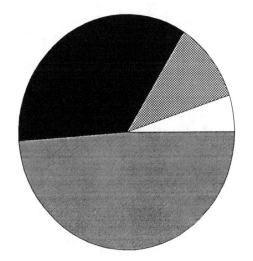

NOT VERY IMPORTANT 11%

NOT AT ALL IMPORTANT 5%

EXTREMELY IMPORTANT 49%

Also in Source: There is a wide discrepancy between shoppers' knowledge of prices and the actual prices. For example, 98% of the respondents from Phoenix thought they knew the price of a gallon of whole milk. In reality, only 35% knew the correct price. Accordingly, 98% thought they knew the price of white bread but only 24% knew the actual price, 94% thought they knew the price of ten pounds of dry dog food while only 28% knew the real price, and 96% thought they knew the price of a one pound can of Maxwell House coffee but only 36% knew the actual price.

Poll Details: Telephone interviews with the principal shopper in a total of 480 households in Phoenix, Arizona, and Birmingham, Alabama, for *Supermarket Business* by two local independent market research firms.

Availability: Published in *Supermarket Business*, June, 1990, (volume 45, number 6) p. 15, 19, 21.

MADE IN AMERICA

Description: Presents the results from several surveys on consumer attitudes toward products made inside or outside of the United States.

Results: The majority of American consumers say they believe the quality of American-made goods has, generally, improved in recent years.

Poll Extracts:

U.S. CONSUMERS FEELINGS ABOUT U.S.-MADE AND FOREIGN PRODUCTS.

AMERICANS WHO:

won't buy foreign products 39%

wouldn't buy foreign products
five years ago 21%

say U.S. products are very good 38%

say Japanese products are very good 42%

say quality is more important than price ... 80%

opted for quality over price 12 years ago .. 30%

Also in Source: The majority of Americans still believe that foreign-made cars are better made than American cars. The number of Americans who say they refuse to buy products because they're foreign made has increased from 1985 to 1989. The percentage of Americans who buy American out of patriotism, with quality being a secondary consideration.

Poll Details: The surveys were conducted by Research & Forecasts Inc., Cambridge Reports, and Yankelovich Clancy Shulman.

Availability: Published in *The Atlanta Journal and Constitution*, February 17, 1990, p. F-1, F-9.

MOST POPULAR RECREATIONAL PROPERTY

Description: Presents the results of a survey identifying those states where people would like to own recreational property.

Results: Most people would want to own recreational property in Florida followed by California.

Poll Extracts:

IN WHICH STATE WOULD YOU LIKE TO OWN RECREATIONAL PROPERTY?

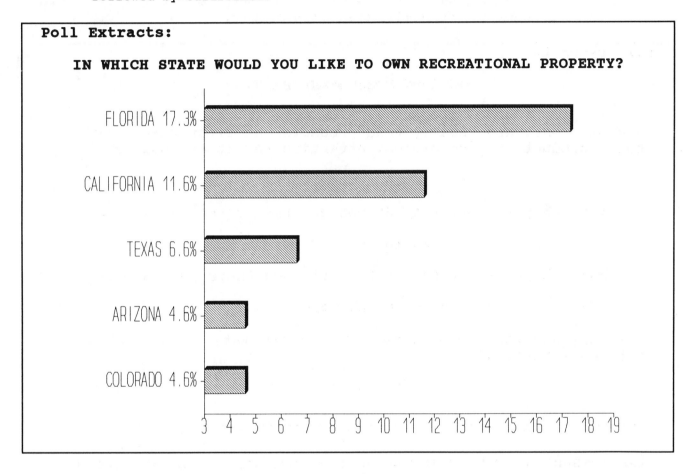

Also in Source: The types of recreational property Americans own include detached home or cabin: 41.5%; attached condominium or townhouse: 15.9%; vacant land: 15.1%; time-sharing: 12.7%; campsite: 8.3%; and other: 6.5%.

Poll Details: The survey was conducted by the American Resort and Residential Development Association.

Availability: Published in *The Columbus Dispatch*, November 11, 1990, p. 1I.

READING FOOD LABELS

Description: Presents the results of a survey concerning the level of food and nutritional labeling information attention and understanding among consumers.

Results: Approximately 80% of the respondents surveyed said they usually read product labels the first time they buy a product.

Poll Extracts:

SHOPPERS AND FOOD LABELS:

How many shoppers usually read products the first time they buy a product, paying closest attention to fat and sodium?

8 in 10 shoppers

How many shoppers say they do not understand the labels?

1 in 10 shoppers

How many shoppers say the facts influence their purchase decision?

8 in 10 shoppers

How many shoppers favor more details: Are fats saturated? Are key nutrients missing?

8 in 10 shoppers

Also in Source: A brief discussion of the food and nutritional information labeling issue is included in the article.

Poll Details: The nationally representative poll of 1,006 households was conducted by Opinions Research Corporation for the National Food Processors Association.

Availability: Published in *USA Today*, May 10, 1990, p. 1D.

SERVICES FOR CUSTOMERS

Description: This poll asked consumers about which shopping amenities they desire.

Results: A majority of respondents want restroom access while shopping. "A large number are willing to pay extra to have money refunded at any time (43%), for delivery (42%), for an information booth (39%) and to have the store open 24 hours (38%). Thirty-one percent would absorb additional charges to have in-store babysitting, while others would pay for such services as contests (15%), valet parking (12%) and instore entertainment (10%)."

Poll Extracts:

DO YOU WANT RESTROOM ACCESS WHILE SHOPPING? ..... 93% Yes

WOULD YOU PAY EXTRA FOR ACCESS TO A RESTROOM WHILE SHOPPING?
      MEN .... 44% Yes
      WOMEN .... 49% Yes

Also in Source: Two charts which describe the "Extras Shoppers Want," and "What They'll Pay For," regarding six amenities (restrooms, places to sit down, delivery, ability to shop by phone, coffee or tea, valet parking), broken down according to male and female responses.

Poll Details: This poll was an *Adweek's Marketing Week*/Warwick Baker & Fiore poll.

Availability: Published in *Adweek's Marketing Week*, January 15, 1990 (volume 31, number 3), p. 4-5.

TIME SPENT AT MALLS

Description: This survey asked Americans about the time they spend, per trip, at shopping malls.

Results: More people have decreased rather than increased their use of malls. Broken down by sex, the people shopping "less" at malls are almost 40% of the women, and 25% of the men surveyed. The majority of those polled say they spend one to two hours in the mall, with 40% shopping at least once or twice a month.

Poll Extracts:

DO YOU USE SHOPPING MALLS LESS FREQUENTLY
THAN A YEAR AGO? .... 32% Yes

DO YOU USE SHOPPING MALLS MORE FREQUENTLY
THAN A YEAR AGO? .... 14% Yes

Also in Source: The number of hours that Americans say they spend, per trip, at shopping malls, broken down by male and female respondent. Also the percentage of those people who shop at a mall: once or twice a month, three or four times a month, five to eight times a month, and eight or more times a month.

Poll Details: A nationwide telephone poll of 1,000 adults by Maritz AmeriPoll of St. Louis.

Availability: Published in *The Atlanta Journal and Constitution*, March 10, 1990, p. F-2.

WHAT BOYS THINK OF THEIR MOMS

Description: Presents the results of a survey concerning sons' opinions of
their mothers on a number of topics, including fashion.

Results: Almost half of the sons surveyed looked to their mothers for fashion
decisions.

Poll Extracts:

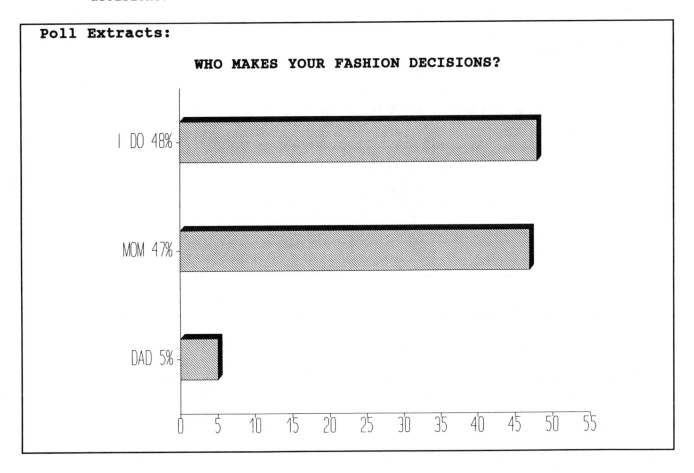

WHO MAKES YOUR FASHION DECISIONS?

Also in Source: 65% of the sons gave their moms top honors in the "cool"
category, ranking her above television "moms" Claire Huxtable and Marge
Simpson. Their mothers even topped Barbara Bush and Paula Abdul. 36% of
sons and 42% of moms rated surfer/beach-style clothing "awesome" (or No.
1). The next choice for sons was the "skater look" at 31%. The second
choice for moms was "preppy" at 40%. 74% of the sons surveyed gave their
mothers' fashion sense a B-plus, the same grade that 76% of mothers gave
their sons. 38% rated mom as "pretty cool"; 7% even admitted to having a
mother who was a "babe" in her junior years. More than 80% of the boys
surveyed opted for short, close-cropped hair, styled as either a flat-top
or a more spiky version; the look was favored by 71% of moms.

Poll Details: The results are taken for "The Levi Cool Quiz." The survey,
commissioned by Levi Strauss and Company, polled mothers and their 7-11-
year-old sons.

Availability: Published in *The Columbus Dispatch*, December 2, 1990, p. 3G.

ATTRIBUTES OF HIGHLY PAID EXECUTIVES

Description: This survey asked senior executives earning more than $250,000 a year to describe themselves and list those characteristics which contributed to their success.

Results: The most important attribute, according to these executives, is the ability to communicate well.

Poll Extracts:

THE TOP FIVE ATTRIBUTES OF A SUCCESSFUL EXECUTIVE:

1. Ability to communicate well
2. Intelligence
3. Integrity
4. Experience
5. Positive attitude

Also in Source: Executives disagree that corporate loyality and morality are less important today. On average, executives had been promoted three times in 10 years but changed companies only once.

Poll Details: Lamalie Associates surveyed 204 executives of Fortune 500 midsize and small firms. More than 40% were CEOs, chief operating officers, or presidents. About 43% lived in the Midwest, 24% in the South, 2% in the northwest, and 11% in the west, 2% lived abroad.

Availability: Published in *The Atlanta Journal and Constitution*, March 6, 1990, p. B-2.

CAREERS VS. FAMILY NEEDS

Description: Presents the results of a survey concerning future job related benefits in the context of personal and family needs.

Results: 59% of the human resources executives surveyed feel that the availability of a flexible schedule will be a highly important recruitment feature in the future.   Only 15% of the respondents feel that it is important today. On the other hand, the respondents feel that the recruitment incentive of advancement opportunities will decline in popularity. Currently, 68% of the respondents feel it is highly important. 48% of the respondents feel it will be as important in the future.

Poll Extracts:

POPULARITY OF CURRENT AND FUTURE RECRUITMENT INCENTIVES:

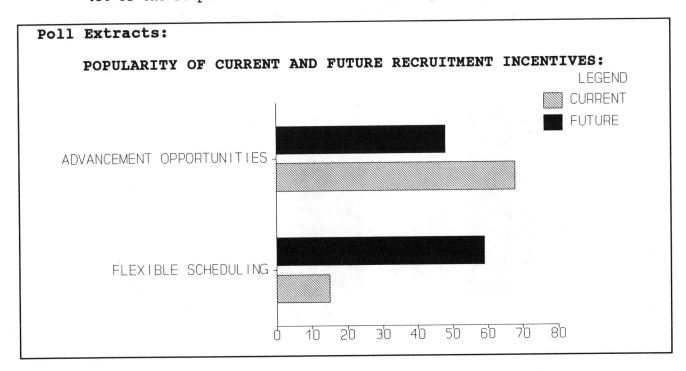

Also in Source: Currently, 44% of the companies surveyed provide no flexible scheduling, 42% provide flextime, 36% provide part-time employment, 17% provide job sharing, 13% provide compressed work schedules, 9% provide work at home schedules, and 3% provide some other kind of flexible scheduling. More than half of 500 men polled recently by Robert Half International said they would be willing to cut their salaries as much as 25% to have more family time or personal time. 45% said they would likely turn down a promotion if it meant spending less time with their families.

Poll Details: The source includes surveys by the Conference Board, the Hewitt Association, Yankelovich Clancy Shulman, and Robert Half International.

Availability: Published in *The Wall Street Journal*, June 18, 1990, p. B1, B5.

CHILDREN AND CAREERS

Description: Presents the results of a survey concerning the affect of having
children on a woman's ability or opportunity to compete in a career on an
equal footing with men.

Results: Almost half of the women surveyed said that they could compete equally
with men regardless of whether they had children. Almost 40% said they
could compete equally but only if they did not have children.

Poll Extracts:

IS A WOMAN ABLE TO COMPETE IN A CAREER EQUALLY WITH MEN?

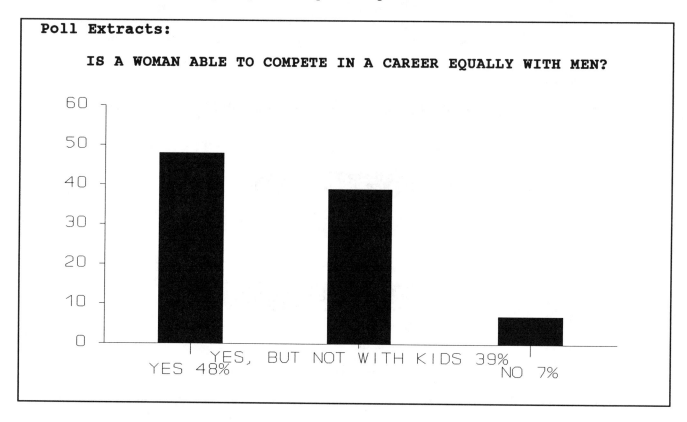

YES 48%   YES, BUT NOT WITH KIDS 39%   NO 7%

Also in Source: Concerning the issue of working, when women were asked if
they could do whatever they wanted, 62% would work part-time, 25% would
stay home, and 6% said they would work full-time. The source also includes
a number of questions concerning the broad issue of the increasing role of
women, especially women with children, in the workplace.

Poll Details: The results are taken from a readers' poll by *Parents* magazine.
30,000 readers responded to a questionnaire.

Availability: Published in *Parents*, June, 1990 (volume 65, number 6),
p. 107, 108, 110, 112, 114.

ENGINEERS' FAVORITE PASTIMES

Description: Presents the results of a survey of engineers concerning their personal characteristics and tastes.

Results: While engineers enjoy a diverse range of after-work activities, reading is the favorite.

Poll Extracts:

ENGINEERS' FAVORITE AFTER-WORK ACTIVITIES:

1. Reading
2. Golf
3. Spending time with the family
4. Travel
5. Music

Also in Source: When asked their choice of automobiles, Fords and Chevys were the most popular choices. Of the 3,000 engineers surveyed, seven of the respondents cited drinking as a cherished pastime, one said "cross-dressing," and four said sex.

Poll Details: The survey was conducted by Karakas, Van Sickle and Ouellette of Beaverton, Oregon. It surveyed 3,000 engineers across the United States. The response rate was 43%.

Availability: Published in *The Cincinnati Enquirer*, March 22, 1990, p. D-4.

JOB SEARCHING FOR EXECUTIVES

Description: Presents the results of a study concerning the most effective
methods used by hospital executives to find new positions.

Results: Over 55% of the respondents said that networking with colleagues was
the best way to find a new job. Over 33% said employing executive
recruitment firms was best.

Poll Extracts:

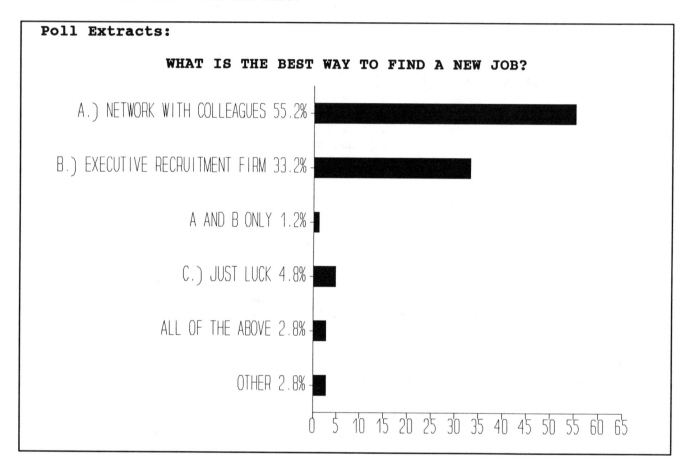

WHAT IS THE BEST WAY TO FIND A NEW JOB?

A.) NETWORK WITH COLLEAGUES 55.2%

B.) EXECUTIVE RECRUITMENT FIRM 33.2%

A AND B ONLY 1.2%

C.) JUST LUCK 4.8%

ALL OF THE ABOVE 2.8%

OTHER 2.8%

0 5 10 15 20 25 30 35 40 45 50 55 60 65

Also in Source: 6% of the respondents rated the reputations of the health
care executive recruitment firms as excellent, 54.4% rated them as good,
30.8% as fair, 1.6% poor, and 7.2% were uncertain.

Poll Details: The survey was based on responses from 250 hospital chief
executive officers. It was conducted by Professional Research Consultants.

Availability: Published in *Hospitals*, April 5, 1990 (volume 64, number 7),
p. 46.

LAWYERS ARE MISERABLE

Description: This survey of lawyers asked lawyers about their job
satisfaction, and other factors relating to their satisfaction.

Results: Lawyers report they are: "less fulfilled, more fatigued, more
stressed, more caught up in office politics, more likely to be in unhappy
marriages, and more likely to drink excessively than they once did."

Poll Extracts:

**LAWYERS WHO SAID THEY WERE VERY SATISFIED WITH
THEIR CURRENT JOB** 33%

LAWYERS WHO SAID THEY WERE DISSATISFIED

SOLO PRACTICE--MEN--43%
WOMEN--55%

PRIVATE PRACTICE--MALE PARTNERS--22%
FEMALE PARTNERS--42%

Also in Source: The percentage of lawyers who worked 240 hours or more per
month, and the percentage of lawyers who consume six or more drinks a day.
Figures from a similar survey in 1984, which show the negative results
reported in 1990 have increased from 1984.

Poll Details: Based on a survey by the American Bar Association in which 2,289
lawyers participated.

Availability: Published in *The Atlanta Journal and Constitution*, August 17,
1990, p. C-4.

PHARMACY GRADUATES

Description: Pharmacists were surveyed about their job satisfaction, and also queried about the adequacy of their education.

Results: 98% of the respondents were "very satisfied" or "somewhat satisfied" with their career choice. "On the whole, pharmacists are very positive about their education. On a scale of 1 to 10 (1=poor, 10=excellent), pharmacists in the survey gave their education an average mark of 8 when it came to preparing them for their current positions."

Poll Extracts:

PHARMACISTS THOUGHT THAT THEIR EDUCATION WAS INADEQUATE OR INSUFFICIENT IN THE FOLLOWING AREAS:

Computer education 57%

Accounting 53%

Marketing 50%

Nuclear Pharmacy 48%

Management 46%

Parenteral preparation 39%

High-technology/biotechnology 38%

Nutritional training 31%

Also in Source: The percentage of pharmacists who had little trouble finding employment after graduation. The percentage of respondents who had jobs waiting for them, or were employed within two months. Areas in which the respondents felt their education was sufficient or more than sufficient.

Poll Details: Pharmacists in both community and hospital settings were surveyed, with recent graduates (1980-1989) being targeted for the survey. Questionnaires were sent out on February 26, 1990, with responses being accepted until April 3, 1990. 317 responses were received giving the survey a response rate of 26%. Details are provided as to when the respondents graduated, and in what area of the country the respondents attended school and now reside. Details are also provided as to the type of pharmacy in which the respondents are employed.

Availability: Published in *Drug Topics*, July 23, 1990 (volume 134, number 14), p. 36-37.

SATISFACTION OF COMPUTER PROFESSIONALS

Description: Provides information on the career satisfaction of information systems professionals who are also executives.

Results: Three out of four information systems professionals are happy in their current positions and say if they could start over, they would likely or definitely select the same field.

Poll Extracts:

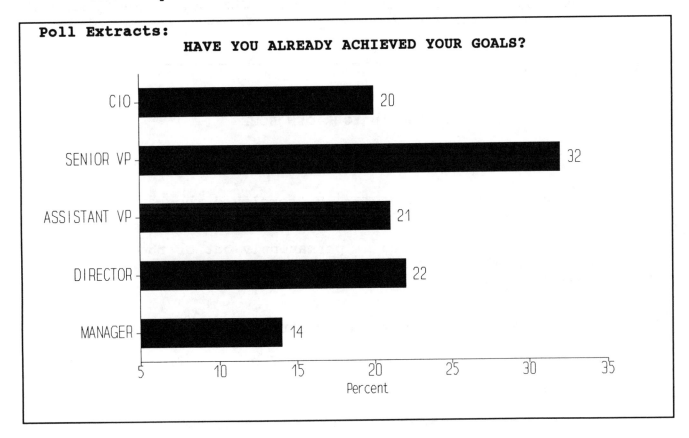

HAVE YOU ALREADY ACHIEVED YOUR GOALS?

Also in Source: The survey also includes salary ranges for the survey respondents and the percentage of executives who think they will meet their career goals at their present firm.

Poll Details: The survey results were compiled by the Society for Information Management (SIM), after a 1989 survey of 420 SIM members.

Availability: Published in *Computerworld*, February 12, 1990 (volume 24, number 7), p. 4.

SELF-EMPLOYMENT AND HOME BUSINESS

Description: Respondents were asked about the idea of being their own boss and about working at home.

Results: When respondents were divided into three age groups (18-34, 35-54, 55+), the percentage of the respondents who wanted to be their own boss declined with age. Also, the percentage of women who wanted to be their own boss was less than the percentage of males who wanted to be their own boss in each of the three age groups. Overall, 58% of the respondents wanted to be self-employed.

Poll Extracts:

WORKING IN YOUR OWN HOME

Respondents who are currently employed who would rather work mainly in their own home 38%

Respondents who are temporarily unemployed who would prefer to work in their own home 57%

Respondents who claim to be permanently out of the workforce, who would rethink that decision if they could work from their own home 41%

WHY RESPONDENTS WANT TO BE SELF-EMPLOYED

To control their own time 23%

To make their own decisions 21%

To collect the financial rewards if successful 19%

Poll Details: This survey was conducted for the Shaklee Corporation, San Francisco.

Availability: Published in *USA TODAY* (magazine--special newsletter edition), August 1990 (volume 119, number 2543), p. 6.

WOMEN ENGINEERS

Description: Presents the the results of a survey of female engineers concerning sexual harassment and discrimination on the job.

Results: While the majority of women feel their work is important, many have experienced sexual harassment and discrimination within their profession.

Poll Extracts:

WOMEN ENGINEERS EXPERIENCE SEXUAL HARASSMENT ON THE JOB:

Do you feel your work is important?............Yes..........90%

Do you work harder than your male colleagues?...Yes..........33%

Are merit raises gender-blind?..................Yes..........60%

Are men promoted faster?......................Yes..........35%

Have you suffered on-the-job harassment?.......Yes..........50%

Has your work created marital conflicts?.......Yes...........5%

Also in Source: Many women claim that young women seeking to enter the engineering profession receive inadequate support from teachers and counselors.

Poll Details: The survey was conducted by Eleanor Baum of Cooper Union; 4,000 women engineers responded to the survey.

Availability: Published in *Technology Review*, February/March, 1990, p. 80.

DONALD TRUMP: HERO OR VILLAIN

Description: Presents the results of a survey concerning whether Donald Trump
symbolizes what makes the United States a great country or whether he
symbolizes the things that are wrong with this country.

Results: Over 80% of the respondents feel he symbolizes what makes the United
States a great country.

Poll Extracts:

DOES DONALD TRUMP SYMBOLIZE WHAT IS GREAT OR WRONG WITH THE USA?

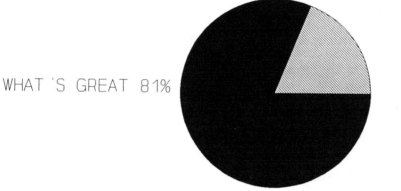

WHAT 'S WRONG 19%

WHAT 'S GREAT 81%

Also in Source: The article includes a discussion of the results of the poll.

Poll Details: *USA Today* conducted a telephone call-in poll. 6,406 readers
responded.

Availability: Published in *USA Today*, June 11, 1990, p. 1B, 2B.

MOST POPULAR WAITERS AND WAITRESSES

Description: Respondents were also asked to name which celebrity they would
most want as a guest waitress or waiter.

Results: For male diners the top vote-getter was Jane Pauley, for female diners
the top vote-getter was Harrison Ford.

Poll Extracts:

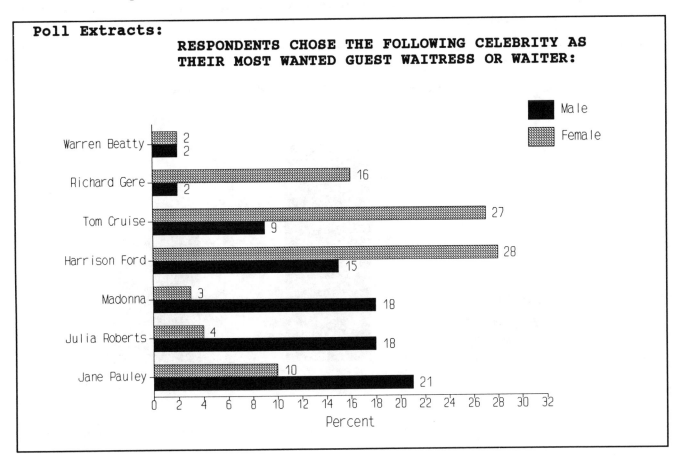

Also in Source: Preferences toward various aspects of restaurant service:
knowing the server's name, having the waitstaff sing "Happy Birthday,"
being able to read the specials, and knowing the price of the specials
before ordering. For respondents who dined out at least once a month, male
and female opinion on the quality of the service received in the last six
months.

Poll Details: The findings were revealed in a survey conducted by American
Express Travel Related Services as part of its "Salute to Restaurant
Service" poll.

Availability: Published in *Restaurant Hospitality*, November 1990 (volume 74,
no. 11), p. 25.

PRINCESS DIANA AND PRINCE CHARLES

Description: This survey asked *People Weekly* readers whether or not Princess
Diana should have an extramartial affair.

Results: 58% of the respondents felt that Princess Diana should not have an
affair. However, 59% of the people within the 18-24 age range were in
favor of an affair. 49% of the male readers polled agreed that she should
have the affair.

Poll Extracts:

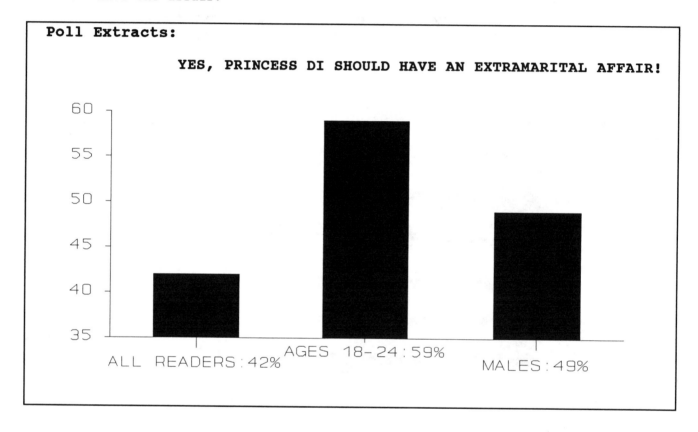

YES, PRINCESS DI SHOULD HAVE AN EXTRAMARITAL AFFAIR!

ALL READERS:42%   AGES 18-24:59%   MALES:49%

Also in Source: The article includes a number of questions concerning a wide
variety of celebrities.

Poll Details: The poll was conducted by Audits & Surveys Inc. for *People
Weekly*. They contacted 1,000 *People Weekly* readers. This is the
magazine's 11th annual poll.

Availability: Published in *People Weekly*, January 8, 1990, p. 58-68.

RISING BODY TEMPERATURES

Description: This poll asked respondents which celebrities and normal people, in a love or hate reaction, raise their body temperatures.

Results: The overall favorites for raising body temperatures were Cher and Tom Cruise. "In the everyday people category, those surveyed had the biggest surge of happy heat for their romantic partners." "But on a personal level, the strongest negative reaction was reserved for the boss. Supervisory types managed to take the dubious honor of being more disliked than the in-laws."

Poll Extracts:

CELEBRITIES WHO BOOSTED THE RESPONDENTS' BODY HEAT, IN EITHER A POSITIVE OR A NEGATIVE REACTION:

Leona Helmsley .... the most negative reaction.

Roseanne Barr .... a close second to Leona Helmsley in the negative reaction category.

Morton Downey Jr. .... generated a negative reaction in 90% of the respondents.

Oprah Winfrey .... among women, generated the top positive reaction.

Poll Details: This survey was conducted with 1,000 adults nationwide. The survey was commissioned by Degree deodorant.

Availability: Published in *The Columbus Dispatch*, April 8, 1990, p. 8F.

TRUMP MEDIA COVERAGE OVERKILL

Description: This survey asked Americans whether they thought the media had overcovered the story of Donald Trump's dissolving marriage to former model Ivana.

Results: Over half of the respondents said that the media had devoted too much coverage to the Trump's marital dispute.

Poll Extracts:

LEVEL OF INTEREST IN DONALD TRUMP:

Has the Trump story been overcovered? .... Yes .. 55%

Do you pay "very close attention" to the story? ..... Yes .. 12%

Are you able to identify Trump's girlfriend,
Marla Maples? .... Yes .. 40%

Also in Source: This survey also includes information on the publics knowledge of a wide range of national and international public events and news stories.

Poll Details: This survey is included in the Times Mirror News Interest Index, a monthly survey of public attitudes towards the news.

Availability: Published in the *Los Angeles Times*, March 9, 1990, p. 26.

THE FATE OF JUVENILE RAPISTS

Description: Presents the results of a survey concerning the appropriate
punishment and/or treatment of juvenile rape offenders.

Results: Over 55% of the respondents favor prison terms over treatment for
juvenile rapists.

Poll Extracts:

WHAT IS THE APPROPRIATE FATE FOR JUVENILE RAPISTS?

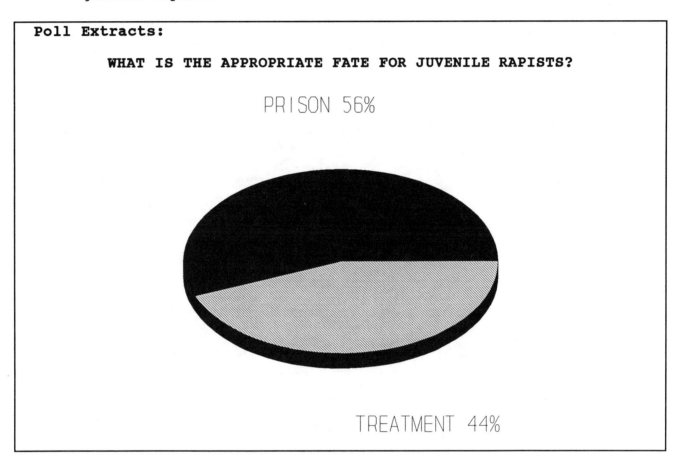

PRISON 56%

TREATMENT 44%

Also in Source: 99% of the respondents feel we should be tougher on juvenile
rapists than we currently are. 94% said that juvenile rapists who were
themselves victims of abuse should not be given a lighter sentence.

Poll Details: Nearly 3,000 readers of *Redbook* magazine responded to a
questionnaire in the April 1990 issue.

Availability: Published in *Redbook*, October, 1990 (volume CLXXV, number 6),
p. 160.

FEELING SAFE IN DETROIT

Description: Presents the results of a survey concerning safety in the city of
Detroit.

Results: Approximately 85% of the respondents feel safe in downtown Detroit in
the daytime.

Poll Extracts:

DURING THE DAY, HOW DO YOU FEEL IN DOWNTOWN DETROIT?

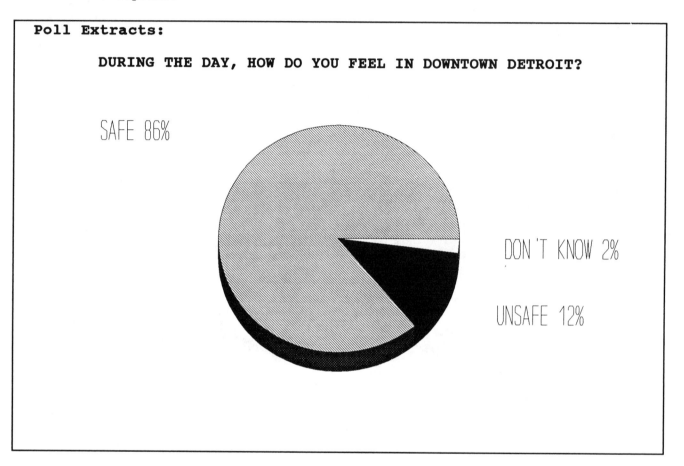

SAFE 86%

DON'T KNOW 2%

UNSAFE 12%

Also in Source: 51% of the respondents feel safe in downtown Detroit at
night, while 44% feel unsafe. 60% feel safe out alone in their
neighborhood at night and 39% feel unsafe.

Poll Details: The results are taken from a *Detroit Free Press*/Market Opinion
Research poll of 700 Detroiters interviewed on November 28 through 30,
1990. The margin of error is plus or minus 3.8%.

Availability: Published in *The Detroit News and Free Press*, December 15, 1990,
p. 1A, 8A, 9A.

THE FUTURE OF THE CRIMINAL JUSTICE SYSTEM

Description: Presents the results of a survey concerning the future of the criminal justice system over the next ten years.

Results: Approximately one-half of the municipal judges surveyed think the criminal justice system will improve in its ability to administer justice that is "swift and sure." Approximately one-third of the police surveyed share the same opinion.

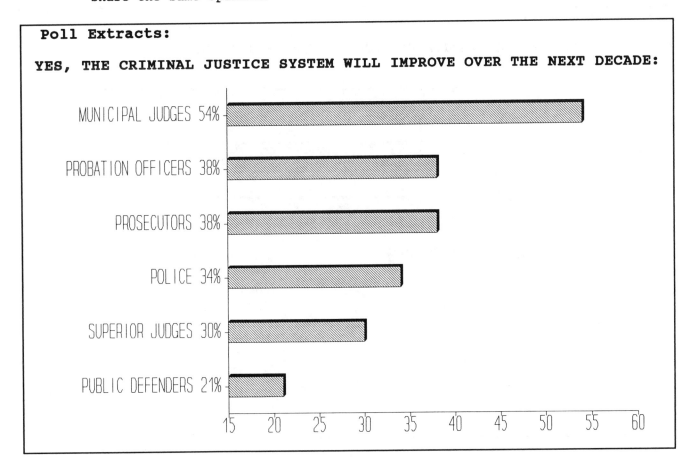

Poll Extracts:

YES, THE CRIMINAL JUSTICE SYSTEM WILL IMPROVE OVER THE NEXT DECADE:

MUNICIPAL JUDGES 54%
PROBATION OFFICERS 38%
PROSECUTORS 38%
POLICE 34%
SUPERIOR JUDGES 30%
PUBLIC DEFENDERS 21%

15 20 25 30 35 40 45 50 55 60

Also in Source: 90% of the municipal judges surveyed are satisfied with their work, superior judges, 87%; public defenders, 81%; prosecutors, 89%; probation officers, 79%; and police, 88%. 71% of the municipal judges surveyed think that more courts and judges would help solve the problems of the criminal justice system, superior judges, 78%; public defenders, 63%; prosecutors, 77%; probation officers, 49%; and police, 56%.

Poll Details: The results are taken from a telephone survey of 2,211 judges, prosecutors, public defenders, probation officers, and police. This *Los Angeles Times* poll was conducted from July 30 through September 25, 1990, and has a margin of error of plus or minus four to eight percentage points.

Availability: Published in the *Los Angeles Times*, December 22, 1990, p. A31.

HOW SOUND IS THE CRIMINAL JUSTICE SYSTEM?

Description: Presents the results of a survey concerning the condition of the
criminal justice system in the United States.

Results: While over 80% of the municipal judges responding to the poll feel the
criminal justice system is sound, only half of the police surveyed share
the same opinion.

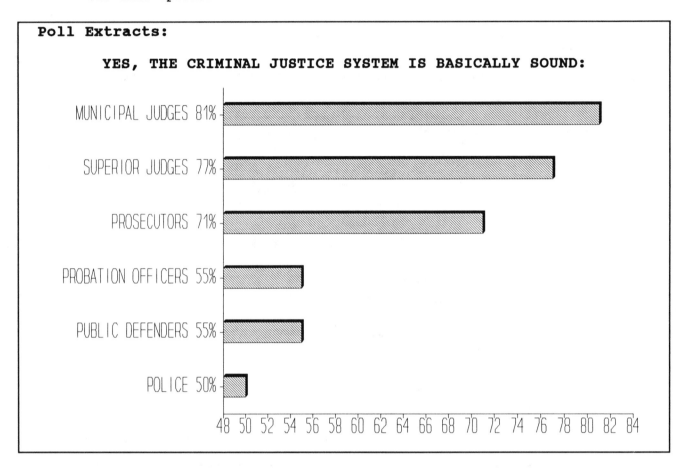

Poll Extracts:

YES, THE CRIMINAL JUSTICE SYSTEM IS BASICALLY SOUND:

MUNICIPAL JUDGES 81%

SUPERIOR JUDGES 77%

PROSECUTORS 71%

PROBATION OFFICERS 55%

PUBLIC DEFENDERS 55%

POLICE 50%

48 50 52 54 56 58 60 62 64 66 68 70 72 74 76 78 80 82 84

Also in Source: 32% of the municipal judges surveyed think the criminal
justice system has improved over the past 10 years, superior judges, 30%;
public defenders, 5%; prosecutors, 19%; probation officers, 23%; and
police, 18%. 27% of the municipal judges surveyed say the quality of
justice in Los Angeles has improved, superior judges, 25%; public
defenders, 5%; prosecutors, 14%; probation officers, 16%; and police, 16%.
60% of the municipal judges and superior judges surveyed feel the criminal
justice system has some effect in deterring crime, public defenders, 31%;
prosecutors, 55%; probation officers, 51%; and police, 38%.

Poll Details: The results are taken from a telephone survey of 2,211 judges,
prosecutors, public defenders, probation officers, and police. This *Los
Angeles Times* poll was conducted from July 30 through September 25, 1990,
and has a margin of error of plus or minus four to eight percentage points.

Availability: Published in the *Los Angeles Times*, December 16, 1990, p. A45.

PLEA BARGAINING IN THE CRIMINAL JUSTICE SYSTEM

Description: Presents the results of a survey concerning a wide number of
criminal justice issues in Los Angeles, California.

Results: Almost 80% of the police surveyed feel there is too much plea
bargaining, while only 11% of superior judges agree.

Poll Extracts:

YES, THERE IS TOO MUCH PLEA BARGAINING:

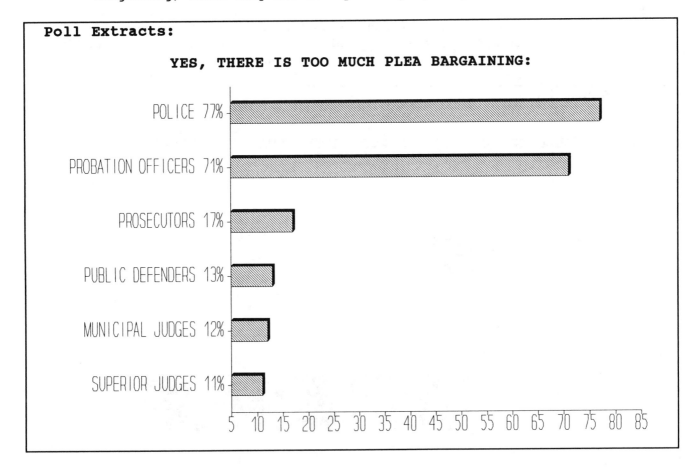

Also in Source: 55% of the municipal judges surveyed feel defendants receive
longer sentences today compared to 10 years ago, superior judges, 51%;
public defenders, 66%; prosecutors, 29%; probation officers, 17%; and
police, 14%. 76% of the municipal judges surveyed feel that increasing
caseloads have encouraged more plea bargaining, superior judges, 63%;
public defenders, 63%; prosecutors, 67%; probation officers, 79%; and
police 81%. 26% of the municipal judges surveyed agree that defendants
released on probation today are more dangerous than 10 years ago, superior
judges, 24%; public defenders, 9%; prosecutors, 48%; probation officers,
73%; and police, 68%.

Poll Details: The results are taken from a *Los Angeles Times* poll.

Availability: Published in the *Los Angeles Times*, December 20, 1990, p. A1,
A42, A43.

POLICE PROTECTION SATISFACTION IN THE DETROIT AREA

Description: Presents the results of a survey of metropolitan Detroit
    residents concernng their satisfaction with police protection in their
    area. They were also asked if they would be willing to pay more taxes for
    more police protection.

Results: The results of the survey indicate that residents of Detroit are less
    satisfied with their police protection than suburban Detroit residents.
    Also, a greater percentage of Detroiters are willing to pay more taxes for
    better police protection compared to suburbanites.

Poll Extracts:

YES, I WOULD PAY MORE TAXES FOR BETTER POLICE PROTECTION.

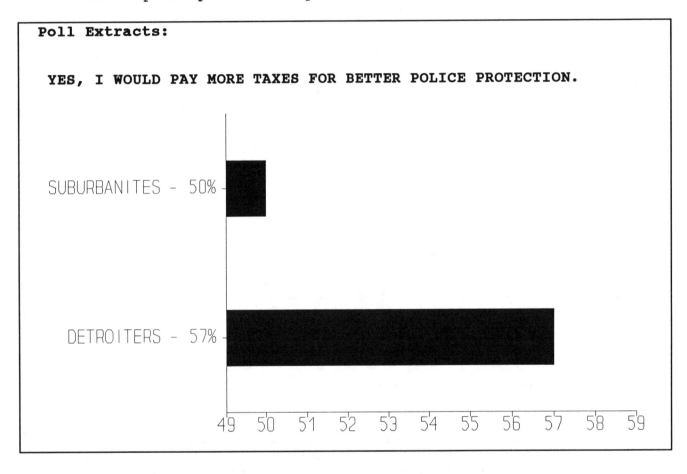

Also in Source: A discussion of the causes and implications of the results of
    the survey is included in the article.

Poll Details: Wayne State University's Center for Urban Studies conducted a
    telephone survey of 1,500 people. Of the 1,500 people contacted, 436 were
    Detroit residents. The survey was done between January 17 and February 13,
    1990.

Availability: Published in the *Detroit Free Press*, March 6, 1990, p. 1B.

SHOPLIFTERS' "SUCCESS" RATE

Description: Presents the results of a survey of shoplifters concerning how often they were caught in the act of shoplifting and how often they were prosecuted.

Results: Of the 4,000 shoplifters surveyed, a very small percentage are caught and even fewer are prosecuted.

Poll Extracts:

HOW OFTEN HAVE YOU BEEN CAUGHT OR PROSECUTED FOR SHOPLIFTING?

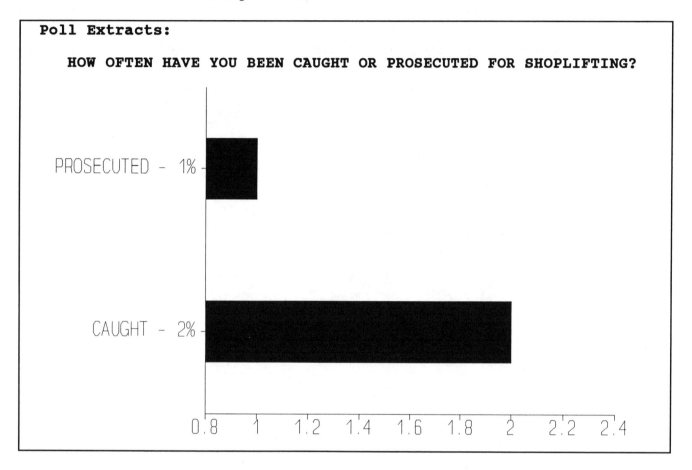

Also in Source: The article also includes other statistical information concerning shoplifting. For example, items most frequently shoplifted by men are cosmetics, beer, and cigarettes. Items most frequently shoplifted by women are cosmetics, women's clothing, and jewelry. The most frequently shoplifted item in United States drug stores is Preparation H.

Poll Details: The article only states that 4,000 shoplifters were surveyed.

Availability: Published in *The Columbus Dispatch*, March 15, 1990, p. 3G.

THE SUPERVISION OF PROBATIONERS

Description: Presents the results of a survey concerning the state of the probation system.

Results: Over 50% of the probation officers surveyed describe the level of supervision given probationers as good.

Poll Extracts:

DESCRIBE THE SUPERVISION OF PROBATIONERS TODAY:

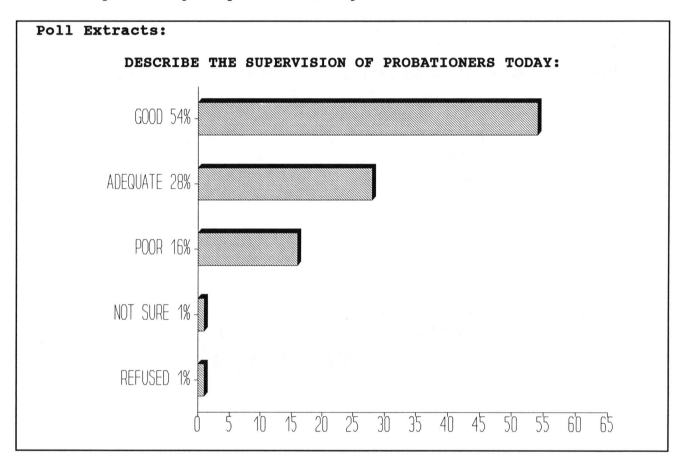

Also in Source: 68% of the probation officers surveyed are somewhat confident, given the Probation Department's present caseload and resources, that it can protect the community and prevent recidivism among criminals; 29% are not confident; and 3% are not sure. 81% of the respondents say if criminals on probation were more closely supervised, they would occasionally be deterred from committing new crimes; 14% say they would rarely be deterred; and 5% are not sure.

Poll Details: 798 probation officers were surveyed for this *Los Angeles Times* poll.

Availability: Published in the *Los Angeles Times*, December 21, 1990, p. A29.

DEATH PENALTY ISSUES

Description: This survey asked the citizens of the State of California their
opinions concerning the death penalty issue.

Results: When asked if a life sentence could be guaranteed, 67% of the
respondents favored that option as opposed to the death penalty. However,
a clear majority would still favor the existence of the death penalty.

Poll Extracts:

ISSUES INVOLVING THE DEATH PENALTY:

Do you favor the existence of the death penalty?.....Yes...80%

Do you strongly favor the death penalty?............Yes...50%

Should the mentally retarded be given the
death penalty?......................................Yes...35%

Should juveniles be given the death penalty?........Yes...50%

Also in Source: A discussion of the death penalty issue is included in the
article.

Poll Details: The telephone poll was conducted by the San Francisco-based
Field Institute in December 1989. The poll has an error margin of plus or
minus 4.5%.

Availability: Published in the *Los Angeles Times*, March 1, 1990, p. A3, A31.

DEATH PENALTY: PRO AND CON

Description: Presents the results of a survey of California residents
measuring the level of support for capital punishment.

Results: The survey found that 77% of the respondents favor the death penalty
for persons convicted of murder. Only 15% oppose the death penalty.

Poll Extracts:

ARE YOU FOR OR AGAINST THE DEATH-PENALTY?

Do you favor the death penalty for persons
convicted of murder?....................................Yes......77%

Do you strongly favor the death penalty
for persons convicted of murder?........................Yes......56%

Do you oppose capital punishment?.......................Yes......15%

Do you have an opinion concerning capital punishment...No........8%

Also in Source: In this poll, virtually every socioeconomic, political,
religious, and racial group favored capital punishment by at least 2 to 1,
and usually by more than 3 to 1.

Poll Details: The telephone survey, conducted by the *Los Angeles Times*,
contacted 2,058 California residents. The margin of error of this survey,
conducted over a six day period in late February and early March 1990, is
three percentage points in either direction.

Availability: Published in the *Los Angeles Times*, March 5, 1990, p. A18.

GEORGIANS' VIEWS ON THE DEATH PENALTY

Description: Presents the results of the survey concerning the penalty for
first-degree murder in the State of Georgia.

Results: Over 64% of the respondents favor the death penalty as the punishment
for first-degree murder.

Poll Extracts:

WHAT SHOULD BE THE MAXIMUM PUNISHMENT FOR FIRST-DEGREE MURDER?

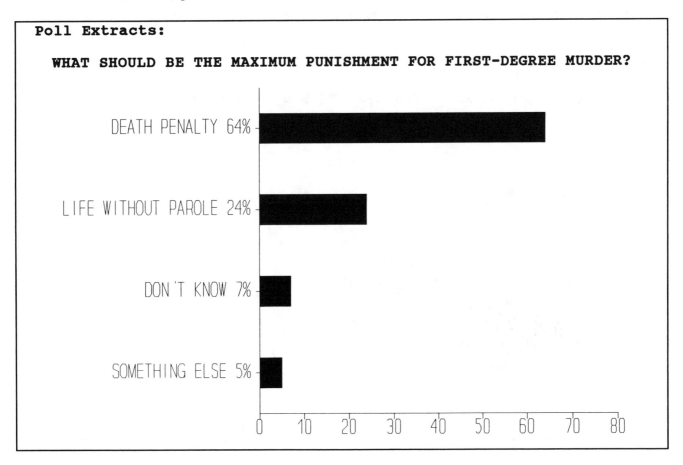

Also in Source: The article includes a number of surveys concerning a wide
range of topics including abortion, the state lottery, crime, politics, and
the general condition of the State of Georgia.

Poll Details: The poll was based on telephone interviews of 652 adults, 18
years or older, who were identified as likely voters. The survey was
conducted from April 13 through April 24, 1990 with the exception of Easter
Sunday.

Availability: Published in *The Atlanta Journal and Constitution*, April 29,
1990, p. A1, A14.

SHOULD ROBERT ALTON HARRIS DIE?

Description: Presents the results of a survey concerning whether Robert Alton Harris, sentenced to death in California for killing two San Diego teenagers, should be executed. He would be the first person executed in the gas chamber in California since 1967.

Results: 60% of the respondents were in favor of the execution. 16% opposed the execution.

Poll Extracts:

ARE YOU IN FAVOR OF THE EXECUTION OF ROBERT ALTON HARRIS?

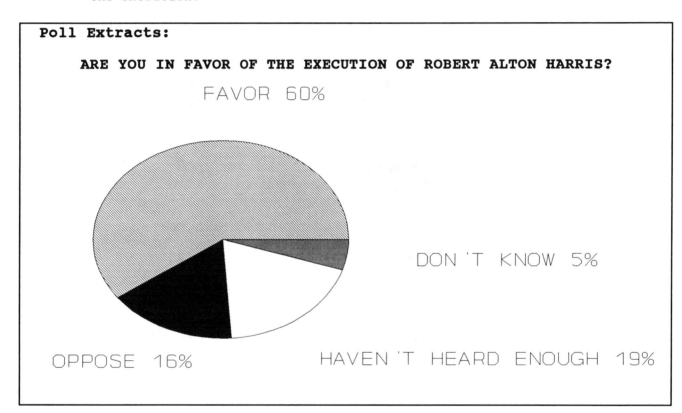

FAVOR 60%

DON 'T KNOW 5%

OPPOSE 16%   HAVEN 'T HEARD ENOUGH 19%

Also in Source: Almost 80% of the respondents favor the death penalty for persons convicted of murder. 31% feel that it is always morally wrong to take a life. 76% feel it is wrong to execute prisoners in order to save money. 70% feel the state should not execute murderers as revenge for their victims. 80% feel that innocent persons are sometimes executed. 36% feel that minority groups are often more likely to receive the death penalty than whites who commit the same kind of crime.

Poll Details: The survey was conducted by I.A. Lewis for the *Los Angeles Times*. 1,667 registered voters were interviewed by telephone over a six day period. Margin of error is plus or minus 3%.

Availability: Published in the *Los Angeles Times*, April 2, 1990, p. A1, A19.

ARMS CONTROL NEGOTIATIONS

Description: Presents the results of a survey concerning the approach
President Bush should take towards arms control with Mikhail Gorbachev.

Results: Almost 70% of the respondents feel President Bush should bargain
cautiously on arms control with Mikhail Gorbachev.

Poll Extracts:

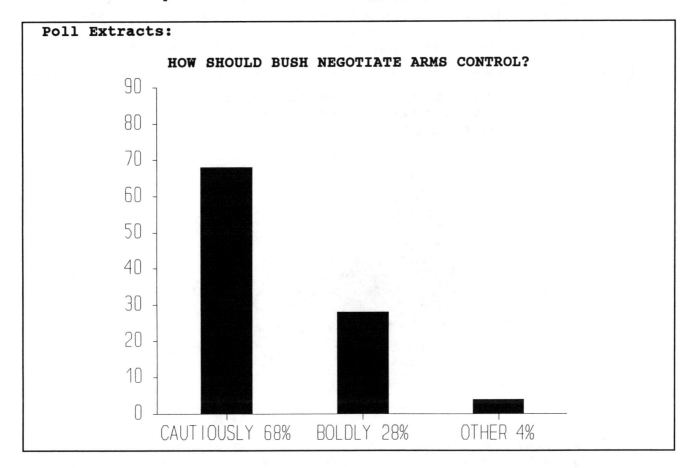

Also in Source: 55% of the respondents feel that the United States should
pull all or most of its troops out of Europe. 56% of the respondents agree
that the United States should recognize Lithuanian independence. Only 18%
believe the purpose of superpower summits is to make agreements while 46%
believe their purpose is to set groundwork. In negotiations, 35% said
President Bush would get a better deal and 31% said Mikhail Gorbachev would
do better.

Poll Details: The poll is based on telephone interviews with 800 Michigan
residents on May 20 through May 22, 1990. The survey was designed and
analyzed with the Gannett Co. Inc. research department. Margin of error is
plus or minus 3.5%.

Availability: Published in *The Detroit News and Free Press*, May 27, 1990,
p. 1A, 6A.

CONVENTIONAL WARFARE

Description: Respondents were queried about the U.S. defense strategy and the
next year's defense budget.

Results: The majority of respondents (80%) saw the U.S. defense posture
changing toward preparation for more conventional warfare. Half of the
respondents saw the next year's defense budget as remaining the same, 33%
thought that the defense budget should be drastically reduced, and 17%
thought that the defense budget should be drastically increased.

Poll Extracts:

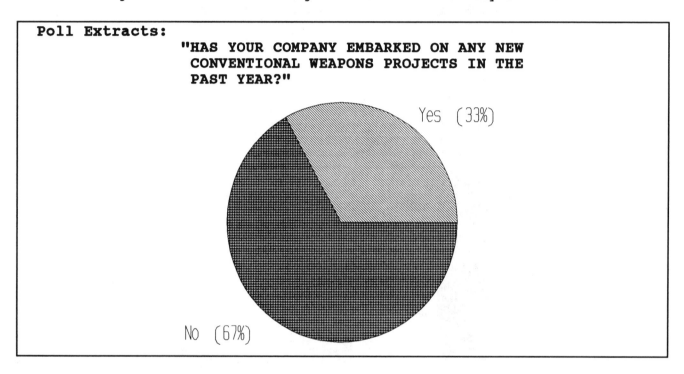

"HAS YOUR COMPANY EMBARKED ON ANY NEW
CONVENTIONAL WEAPONS PROJECTS IN THE
PAST YEAR?"

Yes (33%)

No (67%)

Also in Source: Respondents who had been personally affected by defense
budget cuts. Respondents who thought that their employer would begin more
commercial projects.

Poll Details: This October 15, 1990, *Electronic Engineering Times* Career
Opinion Poll is an engineer's equivalent of a man-on-the-street random
survey. About 80% of the respondents work on defense projects.

Availability: Published in *Electronic Engineering Times*, November 26, 1990
(number 618), p. 87, 89.

THE DIMINISHING MILITARY

Description: Presents the results of a survey concerning any adjustments that could be made to the level of military presence worldwide in light of the domestic challenges which confront the United States, as well as the international shift towards democracy.

Results: The majority of those polled feel that the American military presence around the world could be reduced. A large majority favor an increased cooperative relationship with the Soviet Union.

Poll Extracts:

NEW LEVELS AND TYPES OF MILITARY COMMITMENTS:

Should Europe and Japan be responsible
for a greater share of their own defense?.................Yes...80%

Would you strongly like to see a nuclear free Europe?.....Yes...68%

Would you prefer to see an expanded
and more cooperative relationship with the Soviet Union?..Yes...83%

Should the United States shift military spending
to domestic investment?...................................Yes...75%

Also in Source: The article includes a number of other questions concerning national priorities. The topics asked range from defense to economics to the environment.

Poll Details: This telephone survey of 1,003 registered voters was sponsored by the World Policy Institute of New York.

Availability: Published in the magazine, *USA TODAY*, January, 1990, p. 18-20.

PEACE DIVIDEND SPENDING PRIORITIES

Description: This survey asked Americans how the money saved, if any, through defense cuts caused by the end of the cold war, should be spent.

Results: Most Americans feel that any money saved should be spent at home fighting such problems as drugs, homelessness, cutting taxes, and reducing the federal deficit.

Poll Extracts:

HOW TO SPEND THE PEACE DIVIDEND:

DRUGS & HOMELESSNESS - 62%

NO ANSWER - 2%
OTHER - 5%

CUT TAXES - 10%

REDUCE DEFICIT - 21%

Also in Source: Approximately half of the respondents felt that federal spending on military and defense should be kept the same. Roughly 60% of Americans hold the opinion that the United States should not increase aid to Eastern European countries that are now becoming more independent of the Soviet Union. Also, nearly 60% feel that federal spending on the environment should be increased.

Poll Details: This *New York Times*/CBS News Poll was based on telephone interviews conducted January 13 through Janaury 15, 1990 with 1,557 adults around the United States. Margin of error is no more than three percentage points in either direction.

Availability: Published in *The New York Times*, January 25, 1990, p. B9.

REUNIFIED GERMANY AND NATO

Description: Presents the results of a survey concerning the future alignment
of a reunified Germany.

Results: Over 50% of the American respondents prefer to see a reunified Germany
as a part of NATO.

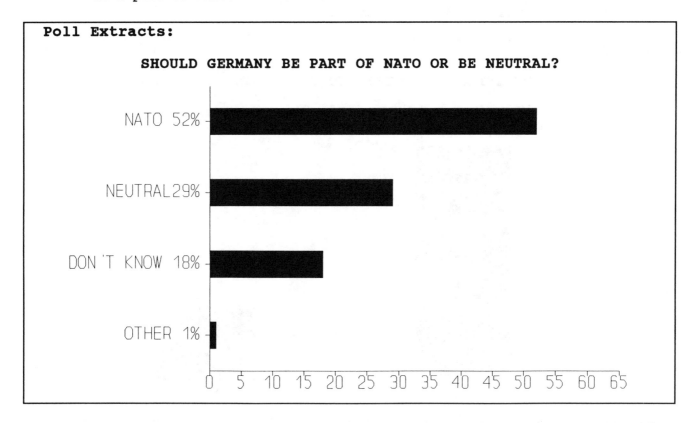

Poll Extracts:

SHOULD GERMANY BE PART OF NATO OR BE NEUTRAL?

Also in Source: 73% of the Soviet respondents would rather see a neutral
Germany. 68% of the American respondents and 53% of the Soviet respondents
would describe the relationship between the United States and the Soviet
Union as friendly. As far as the Baltic Republics are concerned, people in
the Soviet Union agree by four to three that they should be "allowed to
leave the Soviet Union." Overall, Soviet citizens approve of Gorbachev's
handling of the Lithuania situation by three to two. Americans approve of
Bush's handling of it by two to one. Roughly half of the people in both
countries believe the Cold War continues.

Poll Details: The questions for both countries were written by the Times Poll.
In the Soviet Union, door-to-door interviews of 1,485 people were conducted
on May 9 through May 24, 1990 by the Soviet Academy of Sciences in Moscow.
Those interviewed were selected randomly. In the United States, the Times
Poll interviewed 2,144 randomly selected Americans by telephone from May 10
to May 14, 1990. Margin of error for both polls is plus or minus 3%.

Availability: Published in the *Los Angeles Times*, May 31, 1990, p. A1, A14.

ATTITUDES TOWARD DRUG USE

Description: This survey asked students to rank the risk level of occasional
use of cocaine and marijuana.

Results: Approximately 70% of high school seniors said that occasional cocaine
use is very risky. Approximately one-third of high school seniors felt
that occasional marijuana use is very risky.

Poll Extracts:

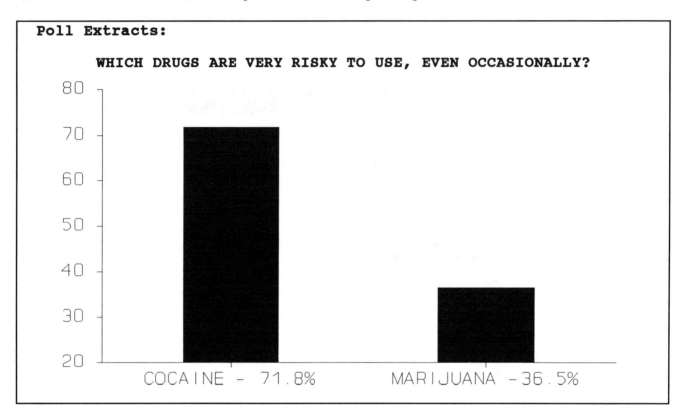

WHICH DRUGS ARE VERY RISKY TO USE, EVEN OCCASIONALLY?

COCAINE - 71.8%   MARIJUANA - 36.5%

Also in Source: The survey showed that 19.7% of high school seniors used an
illicit drug at least once during the previous month compared to 21.3% in
1988. Cocaine use was 2.8% in 1989 versus 3.4% in 1988. Marijuana use was
16.7% in 1989 versus 18% in 1988. 77.2% disapproved of occasional use of
marijuana and 90.5% disapproved of those who tried cocaine once or twice.
18.9% were daily cigarette smokers, up from 18.1% in 1988.

Poll Details: The survey, conducted by the National Institute on Drug Abuse in
1989, contacted 17,142 high school seniors.

Availability: Published in *USA Today*, February 14, 1990, p. 1D.

COLOMBIAN AND AMERICAN RELATIONS

Description: Presents the results of a survey of Americans and Colombians concerning their views as to how best fight the war on drugs.

Results: The citizens of the two countries hold very different views concerning possible solutions and methods proposed for fighting the drug war.

Poll Extracts:

YES, THE US SHOULD SEND TROOPS TO COLOMBIA TO FIGHT THE DRUG WAR

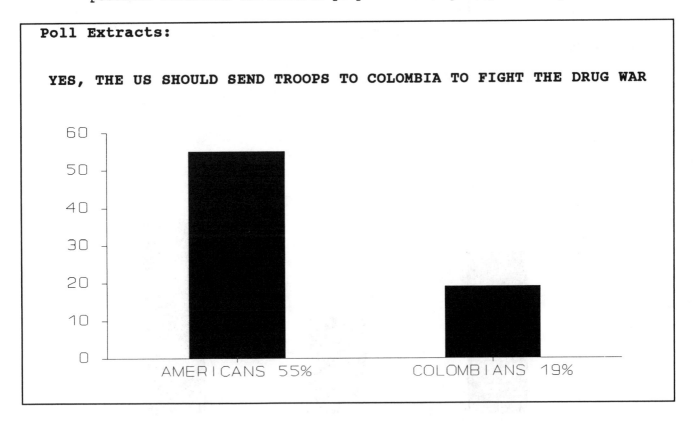

Also in Source: Approximately 80% of Americans and Colombians think that the drug crisis is caused mainly by the demand for drugs in the United States. 70% of Americans feel that Colombia is losing its fight against drugs while 19% of Colombians share that opinion. 51% of Americans favor U.S. financial aid to Colombia to strengthen their police and judicial system. 57% of Colombians favor this measure as well.

Poll Details: Surveys were conducted by *The Washington Post* and ABC News. 1,002 randomly selected adults were surveyed in Colombia and 1,008 randomly selected adults were surveyed in the United States. Margin of error for both surveys is plus or minus 4%.

Availability: Published in *The Washington Post*, February 9, 1990, p. A20, A24.

DRUGS IN SCHOOL

Description: Presents the results of a wide ranging survey concerning
students' views on the presence and use of drugs in school.

Results: One third of the students said that drugs could easily be bought in
their school. Approximately the same number of students replied negatively
to the same question.

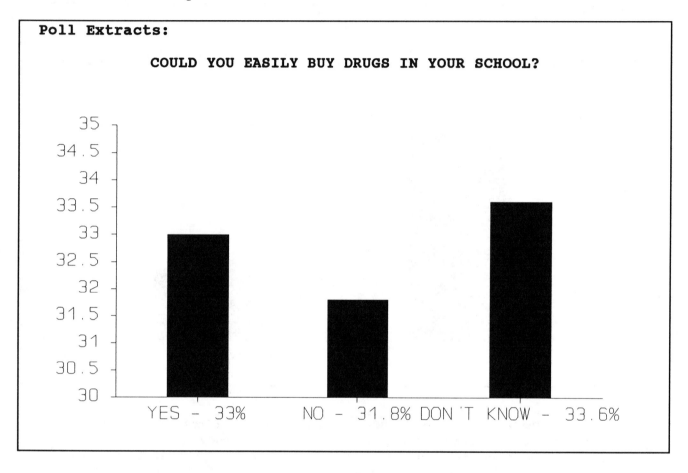

Poll Extracts:

COULD YOU EASILY BUY DRUGS IN YOUR SCHOOL?

YES - 33%   NO - 31.8% DON'T KNOW - 33.6%

Also in Source: The survey includes 15 questions concerning attitudes toward
drug use, drug education, and drug testing in the schools.

Poll Details: This *Scholastic*/CNN Newsroom survey received responses from over
150,000 students. The poll was conducted in December 1989 and was funded
in part by the Armour Food Company.

Availability: Published in *Scholastic Update*, March 9, 1990 (volume 122,
number 13), p. A1-A4.

DRUGS IN THE WORKPLACE

Description: Presents the results of a poll concerning the attitudes, practices, and policies involving drug use in the office and workplace.

Results: Almost 70% of the respondents thought that the company should pay rehabilitation costs on a case-by-case basis for employees.

Poll Extracts:

HOW OFTEN SHOULD A COMPANY PAY FOR EMPLOYEE DRUG REHABILITATION?

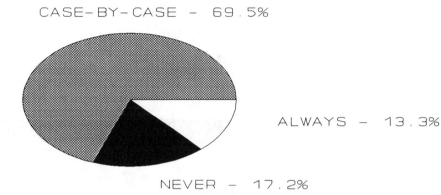

CASE-BY-CASE - 69.5%

ALWAYS - 13.3%

NEVER - 17.2%

Also in Source: Approximately 77% said that if they discovered a trusted subordinate was an addict they would convince the individual to seek counseling. Nearly 70% strongly disagreed with the idea that casual drug use outside the office is acceptable. Almost half would not support a surtax to help fight the war against drugs, while 59.8% approved drug testing.

Poll Details: The answers to the poll were telefaxed to *Business Month* in response to a set of questions in an earlier issue. The margin of error is plus or minus 3.3 percentage points.

Availability: Published in *Business Month*, January, 1990 (volume 135, number 1), p. 9.

EXPERIMENTING WITH DRUGS

Description: This survey included a number of questions involving the presence
and use of drugs in school. This specific question asked students if they
could try a drug once or a few times without slipping into drug abuse.

Results: Approximately one-fourth of the students said they could try a drug
once or twice without becoming an addict. Nearly 30% said they did not
know.

Poll Extracts:

COULD YOU TRY A DRUG A FEW TIMES WITHOUT BECOMING AN ADDICT?

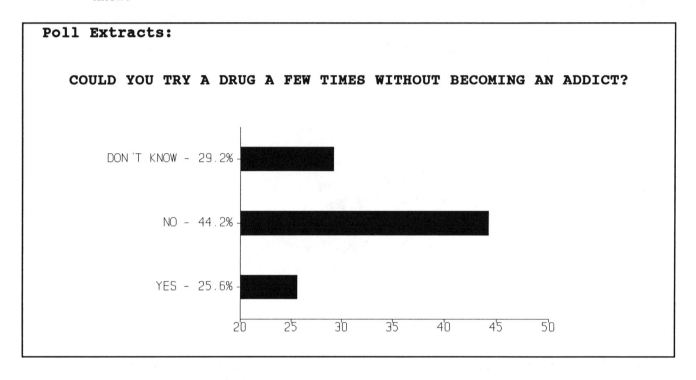

Also in Source: This survey includes 15 questions concerning attitudes toward
drug use, drug abuse, and drug testing in the schools.

Poll Details: This *Scholastic*/CNN Newsroom survey received reponses from over
150,000 students. The poll was conducted in December, 1989 and was funded
in part by Armour Food Company.

Availability: Published in *Scholastic Update*, March 9, 1990 (volume 122,
number 13), p. A1-A4.

PERSPECTIVES ON LEGALIZED DRUGS

Description: This survey attempted to measure, given the solutions forwarded
by the Bush administration, the level of support for the legalization of
drugs.

Results: Giving the respondents' two choices - the Bush administration's policy
of "more prison sentences for casual drug use, the use of the
military...and more tax dollars spent on prisons" or making drugs legally
available to adults while "providing more drug treatment and better
education" - the poll found 36% supporting the legalization option.

Poll Extracts:

VIEWS ON DRUG RELATED ISSUES:

Would you use cocaine if it were made legal?..........Yes....2%

Is all drug use immoral?.............................Yes...65%

Do you support using the military
to aid local police efforts?.........................Yes...81%

Do you support the U.S. invasion of Panama?..........Yes...79%

Also in Source: Most recent polls have shown support for drug legalization at
about 10% of the public.

Poll Details: The telephone poll of 1,401 adults was conducted by Targeting
Systems Inc. and was commissioned by the Drug Policy Foundation.

Availability: Published in the *Washington Post*, March 1, 1990, p. A23.

PROBABLE DRUG USE BY TEENS

Description: Presents the results of a survey concerning probable future drug
   use among teenagers. Students in the sixth grade were asked whether they
   would have tried alcohol, drugs, or cigarettes by the time they enter high
   school.

Results: Over a third of the respondents said they will probably try alcohol by
   the time they enter high school. Approximately one-fourth will try
   cigarettes and less than 10% will experiment with drugs.

Poll Extracts:

BY THE TIME I ENTER HIGH SCHOOL, I WILL PROBABLY HAVE TRIED:

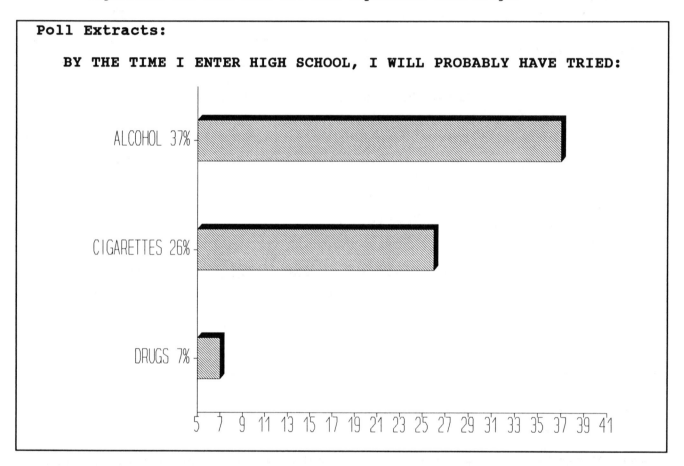

Also in Source: 4% of the sixth grade respondents have been offered drugs and
   14% have been offered alcohol. Curiosity was the main reason given for
   trying beer if it were offered by a friend.

Poll Details: This attitude survey of children ages 10 to 12 was conducted on
   behalf of the Kids for Change Drug Education Mission, a two-day conference
   promoting Drug Abuse Resistance Education (D.A.R.E.) program. The survey,
   conducted by NFO Research Inc. of Chicago, consisted of telephone
   interviews with 500 children selected from a nationally representative
   sampling of 250,000 households. Adult members of the households were
   contacted for permission to have their children interviewed. The margin of
   error was plus or minus 5%.

Availability: Published in *The Atlanta Journal and Constitution*, October 24,
   1990, p. A-3.

TREATMENT OR JAIL?

Description: Presents the results of a survey concerning whether drug addicts
should be treated as people in need of medical care or treated as criminals
who should be arrested and prosecuted.

Results: Two-thirds of the respondents say that drug addiction should be viewed
as a medical illness.

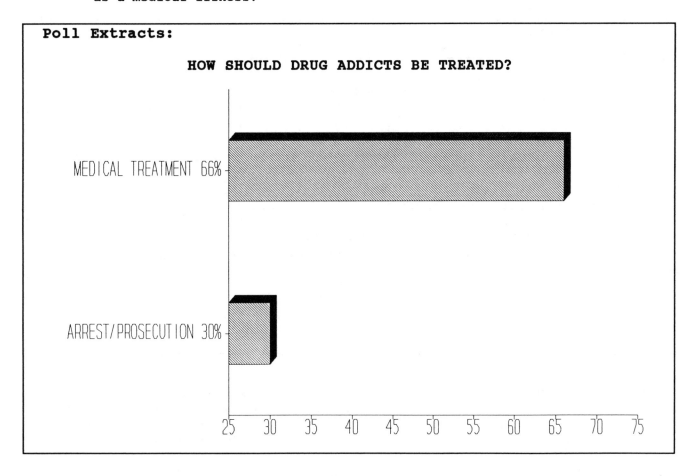

Poll Extracts:

HOW SHOULD DRUG ADDICTS BE TREATED?

Also in Source: When it comes to spending money for anti-drug programs, 10%
called for new jails, while 38% said they want more drug treatment centers,
and 46% chose job-training centers. Although half of those polled said
they felt illegal drug activity was at a crisis level in their
neighborhoods, 65% said they were willing to have a drug treatment center
built in their community. 70% disapproved of legalization of any illicit
drugs. On the idea of an additional tax to fight drug abuse, 39% said they
would volunteer to pay $50 more a year.

Poll Details: 601 residents of the District of Columbia were surveyed by
telephone. The poll was conducted by the District's Office of Criminal
Justice Plans and Analysis.

Availability: Published in *The Washington Post*, October 11, 1990, p. D7.

THE WAR ON DRUGS

Description: Presents the results of a survey measuring attitudes toward combatting the war on drugs.

Results: Almost 90% of the respondents would provide information about a drug dealer to police, while only less than 65% would support a halfway house or corrections facility in their neighborhood.

Poll Extracts:

ATTITUDES ON THE WAR ON DRUGS:

Would you provide information about a drug
dealer to police?.................................Yes...89%

Would you hire a qualified person who had
completed drug or alcohol treatment?................Yes...88%

Would you petition for removal of a drug
dealer from your neighborhood?.....................Yes...80%

Would you support a residential drug
treatment center in your neighborhood?.............Yes...74%

Would you support a halfway house or
corrections facility in your neighborhood?..........Yes...64%

Also in Source: 4% of the respondents agree that all drugs should be sold legally, while 8% would agree that all drugs except for the two or three of the most dangerous should be sold legally. 15% say that only marijuana should be legalized. 72% say no illegal drugs should be legalized.

Poll Details: The results are taken from the Governor's Office of Criminal Justice Services. The survey, conducted by the University of Akron, contacted 804 Ohioans by telephone between October 11 and November 5, 1990. The survey has a margin of error of 4%.

Availability: Published in *The Columbus Dispatch*, December 4, 1990, p. 7B.

DIETING SENSIBLY

Description: This survey asked successful dieters to list their most effective ways to lose weight.

Results: Cutting out snacks and desserts, eating less, exercising, eating less fat, stop eating at night, eating more fruits and vegetables, and counting calories were reported as the most effective ways of losing weight.

Poll Extracts:

AS A SUCCESSFUL DIETER, HOW DO YOU LOSE WEIGHT?

Cut out Snacks and Desserts.................................42%

Eat Less...37%

Exercise...32%

Eat Less Fat...32%

Stop Eating at Night.......................................29%

Eat More Fruits and Vegetables.............................20%

Count Calories...19%

Also in Source: 59% eat differently in cold weather and 42% eat differently when depressed. Sweets are the top comfort foods: candy, 22%; ice cream, 20%; chocolate, 16%. 3% found special diet foods like protein powders helpful and 1% credit books for weight loss, though 20% tried them. The top foods for staying thin are vegetables at 36%, fruit at 27%, fish at 16%, and chicken at 11%.

Poll Details: The poll was co-sponsored by *American Health* magazine, Gallup, and Campbell Soup. Gallup polled 1,026 people and found 117 successful dieters.

Availability: Published in *USA Today*, March 15, 1990, p. 1D.

EATING AND HEALTH

Description: Presents the results of a survey concerning the healthy eating
habits of Americans.

Results: 96% of the respondents are either quite concerned or somewhat
concerned about what they eat.

Poll Extracts:

THINKING ABOUT NUTRITION:

Are you quite concerned about what you eat?...........Yes...51%

Are you somewhat concerned about what you eat?........Yes...45%

Are you eating a less healthy diet today
compared to five years ago?...........................Yes....6%

Do you give any thought to nutrition?..................No....4%

Also in Source: Most respondents had cut back on fat, cholesterol, and salt.
Despite the emphasis on healthy eating, most had refused to give up
snacking. Nearly eight out of ten said the increased focus on nutrition is
here to stay. 75% of the respondents admit they eat late-night snacks an
average of three times a week. 41% occasionally or often hide a favorite
food from the family. 24% of the women reported chocolate as the vice they
wouldn't give up. 27% of the men reported they would not relinquish red
meat. 53% of the men surveyed said they maintain a healthy diet to live
longer, while 60% of the women surveyed do so to look better. 61% of
the respondents aged 30-45 chose a healthy diet to look better.

Poll Details: This unscientific survey, conducted by *USA Weekend*, is skewed to
an older, more health conscious audience than the public at large. 61% of
the respondents were aged 30-60 and 82% were female.

Availability: Published in *USA Weekend*, November 30-December 2, 1990, p. 8, 9.

FAST-FOODS AND CHOLESTEROL

Description: This survey asked respondents about their fast-food eating-
habits following Phil Sokolof's full-page newspaper ads in April, which
charged McDonald's with contributing to the nation's high rate of heart
disease.

Results: 68% of the respondents were unaware of any claims about a fast-food
hamburger restaurant cooking its products in animal fat. For the 31% of
the respondents who were aware of the charges, the majority of that group
had not changed their eating-habits.

Poll Extracts: **WHAT CONSUMERS WHO WERE AWARE OF THE CHARGES
AGAINST McDONALD'S SAID ABOUT THEIR RECENT USAGE OF FAST-FOOD
HAMBURGER CHAINS.**

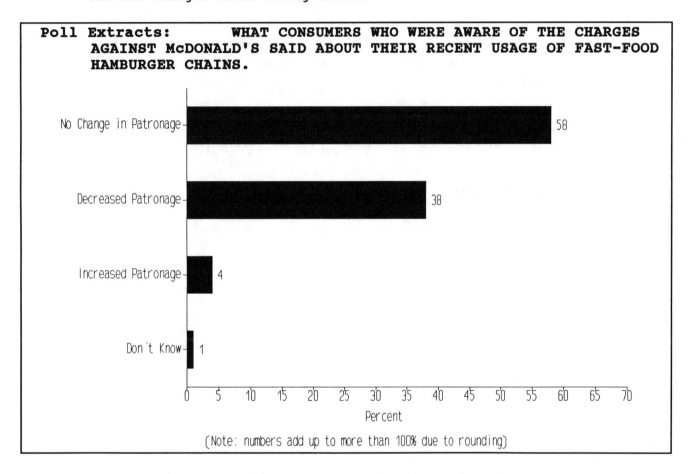

(Note: numbers add up to more than 100% due to rounding)

Also in Source: Awareness of the saturated fat and cholesterol charges among
several age groups. The mean number of times that several age groups had
eaten at or bought food for takeout from McDonald's in the previous month.

Poll Details: This *Advertising Age*/Gallup Organization survey was conducted
with a nationally projectable sample of 1,001 adults in May 1990.

Availability: Published in *Advertising Age*, July 2, 1990 (volume 61,
number 27), p. 1, 32.

ORGANIC PRODUCE

Description: The poll questioned whether the presence of organic foods and the publicity surrounding organic foods has had much of an effect on American consumers.

Results: Americans' perceptions on food are changing.

Poll Extracts:

ALMOST 31% OF AMERICANS HAVE CHANGED THEIR EATING HABITS DUE TO REPORTS OF PESTICIDES AND OTHER CHEMICALS IN THE FOOD SUPPLY.

28% HAVE TRIED TO OBTAIN ORGANICALLY GROWN PRODUCE OR PRODUCE GROWN WITH LIMITED USE OF CHEMICALS.

ABOUT 57% OF THOSE POLLED SAID THEY HAVE EATEN ORGANICALLY GROWN PRODUCE.

Also in Source: The percentage of respondents who perceive organically grown produce to have long-term health benefits. The percentage of respondents who have eaten organically grown produce and listed taste as an important reason to eat it. The results of the question of whether the federal government was doing a good or poor job of protecting the public from potentially harmful chemicals.

Poll Details: The poll was conducted by Louis Harris and Associates Inc. during November and early December 1989, and bases its findings on 1,250 random telephone interviews of adults throughout the United States.

Availability: Published in the *Chicago Tribune*, March 22, 1990, section 7, p. 10.

PERSPECTIVES ON BEING OVERWEIGHT

Description: Presents the results of a poll measuring peoples attitudes toward their own weight and problems concerning the battle against being overweight.

Results: Over 60% of the respondents considered themselves overweight.

Poll Extracts:

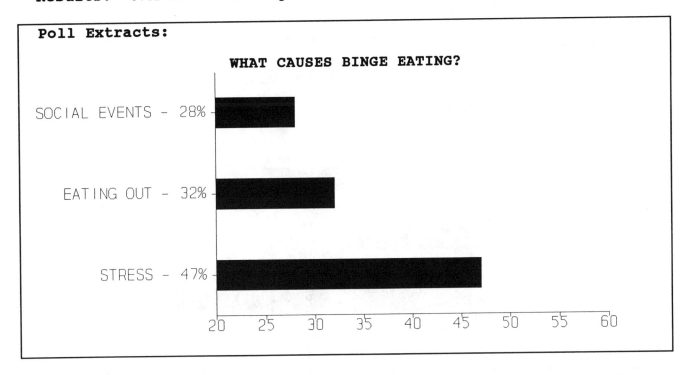

WHAT CAUSES BINGE EATING?

Also in Source: 66% of those surveyed have difficulty choosing a sensible way to lose weight. 63% said they found reports about cholesterol confusing. Almost 80% feel that support from others is important to successful weight loss.

Poll Details: Weight Watchers International conducted the poll. 1,003 people were contacted.

Availability: Published in *USA Today*, January 4, 1990, 1D.

SNACKING ATTITUDES AND BEHAVIORS

Description: Presents the results of a survey concerning the importance of snacking relative to other activities.   It also attempted to measure the level of guilt associated with snacking.

Results: One in three feel guilty when they snack. Among other findings, 10% of the respondents would rather snack than make love.

Poll Extracts:

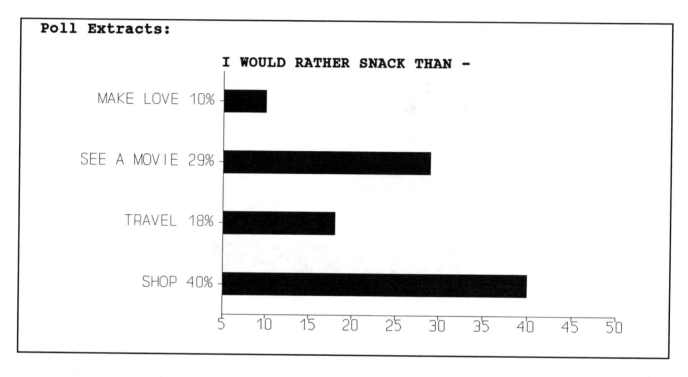

Also in Source: 11% of the respondents said they felt guiltier snacking than cheating on their taxes. Also, 10% felt more guilt snacking than lying to their spouse about how much money they spend and 18% said they would feel less guilt lying about their weight than grabbing a snack.

Poll Details: The survey was conducted by Continental Baking Company. A random sample of 1,000 people over the age of 18 was contacted the weekend of February 2, 1990.

Availability: Published in *The Cincinnati Enquirer*, March 8, 1990, p. A-9.

TRYING TO CONTROL WEIGHT

Description: Presents the results of a survey concerning weight loss and
weight control among Americans.

Results: Over 60% of the respondents are overweight and only one in three get
regular strenuous exercise.

Poll Extracts:

SOME WEIGHTY CONCERNS:

Percentage of respondents overweight..................60%

How many perform regular strenuous exercise?.........33%

Do you "try a lot" to avoid high
cholesterol food?............................Yes.......50%

Do you avoid eating too much fat?.........Yes.......58%

Also in Source: Some areas improved when compared to polls taken in previous
years. In 1983 only 42% said they "tried a lot" to avoid eating high-
cholesterol foods. 55% said they avoided eating too much fat. Among those
who are overweight, more than half are at least 10% over the recommended
weight range for their height and build. A quarter those polled were
within their recommended range and 15% were underweight. Men were more
likely to exercise strenuously while women were found to be more nutrition
conscious.

Poll Details: The survey was conducted by Louis Harris and Associates for
Prevention magazine.

Availability: Published in the *Los Angeles Times*, June 5, 1990, p. A23.

ATLANTA'S ECONOMY

Description: Presents the results of a survey concerning the present state of
the economy of Atlanta, Georgia.

Results: Over 60% of the respondents feel Atlanta's economic condition is good.

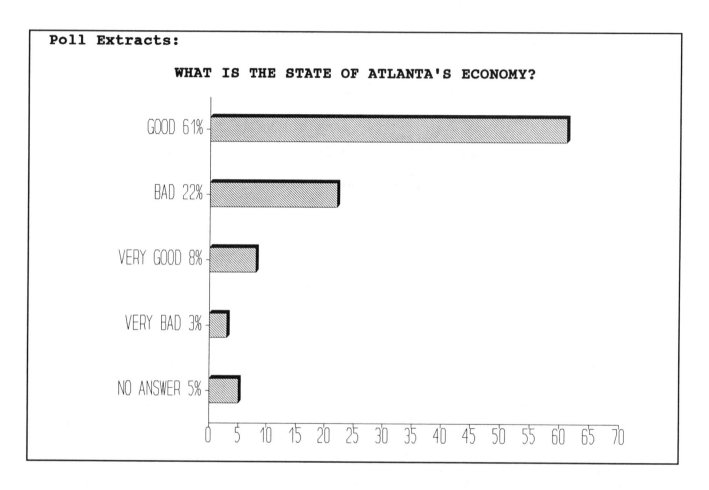

Poll Extracts:

WHAT IS THE STATE OF ATLANTA'S ECONOMY?

Also in Source: 44% of the respondents will spend the same this year on
holiday shopping as last year, 35% will spend less, and 19% will spend
more. When whites were asked what they thought their household financial
situation would be by next spring compared to today 57% said it would get
better, 26% said it would stay the same, 14% said it would get worse, and
3% had no opinion. When blacks were asked the same question, 69% said it
would get better, 14% said it would stay the same, 9% said it would get
worse, and 8% had no opinion.

Poll Details: Results of *The Atlanta Journal and Constitution* Confidence Poll
are based on telephone interviews with 889 adults in Clyton, Cobb, DeKalb,
Fulton, and Gwinnett counties in Georgia. The margin of error is plus or
minus 3%. The poll was conducted by Voice Information Services Inc., an
operating unit of *The Atlanta Journal and Constitution*.

Availability: Published in *The Atlanta Journal and Constitution*, November 21,
1990, p. A1, A4.

THE BEST INVESTMENTS IN THE NEAR FURTURE

Description: Presents the results of a survey concerning the types of
investments expected to give the best return in the next 12 months.

Results: Over 40% of the respondents favored money markets as a safe investment
over the next 12 months.

Poll Extracts:

WHICH ARE THE BEST INVESTMENTS OVER THE NEXT 12 MONTHS?

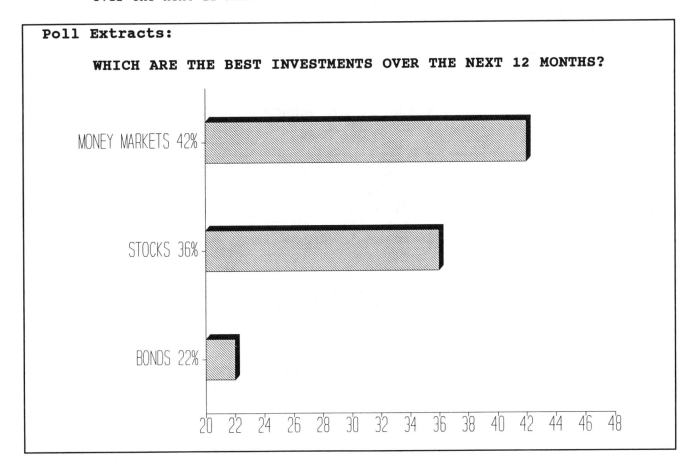

Also in Source: In response to the dramatic stock market decline since mid-
July 1990, 49% said they would do nothing, 8% said they would sell stock
and stock mutual funds, 25% said they would buy stock and stock mutual
funds, and 18% said they would buy and sell stock and stock mutual funds.

Poll Details: This survey of *USA Today*'s Investor Panel was conducted in early
October 1990. The panel is comprised of 700 regular *USA Today* readers who
are active investors.

Availability: Published in *USA Today*, October 15, 1990, p. 3B.

BURDENS ON THE ECONOMY

Description: Presents the results of a survey of chief executive officers
   identifying issues and problems which will adversely affect the United
   States economy as we move through the 1990s.

Results: Health-care costs was identified as the most serious burden on the
   economy in the 1990s. Child-care for working parents was considered the
   least burdensome.

Poll Extracts:

BURDENS ON THE ECONOMY:

   1. Health-care costs
   2. Federal budget deficit
   3. Savings and loan crisis
   4. Inadequately educated work force
   5. Foreign trade deficit
   6. Environmental protection
   7. Aging U.S. infrastructure
   8. Asian competition
   9. Slow productivity growth
   10. U.S. lag in technology
   11. Low savings rate
   12. High cost of capital
   13. European competition
   14. Aging labor force
   15. Labor shortage
   16. Child-care for working parents

Also in Source: Executives from nearly 600 corporations indicated that
   economic problems will prevent the gross national product from matching its
   2.9% growth rate of the 1980s in the 1990s.

Poll Details: The poll was conducted by the Conference Board in late July
   1990. The survey was mailed to approximately 600 chief executive officers
   about a week before the Iraqi invasion of Kuwait. 25% of the surveys were
   completed prior to the invasion. Almost half of the 600 companies
   participating in the survey have sales of more than one billion dollars.
   47% of them are in manufacturing. Finance, insurance, and real estate
   companies accounted for 18% of the respondents and retail trade accounted
   for 7%. All other categories accounted for 16%.

Availability: Published in *The Dallas Morning News*, October 27, 1990,
   p. 1F, 3F.

CHANCES OF A RECESSION

Description: Presents the results of a poll of adult Americans concerning the
          future of the economy.

Results: 60% of those surveyed feel that a recession in the next 3 months is
          unlikely. Over 60% feel that economic conditions will not change during
          the next 3 months.

Poll Extracts:

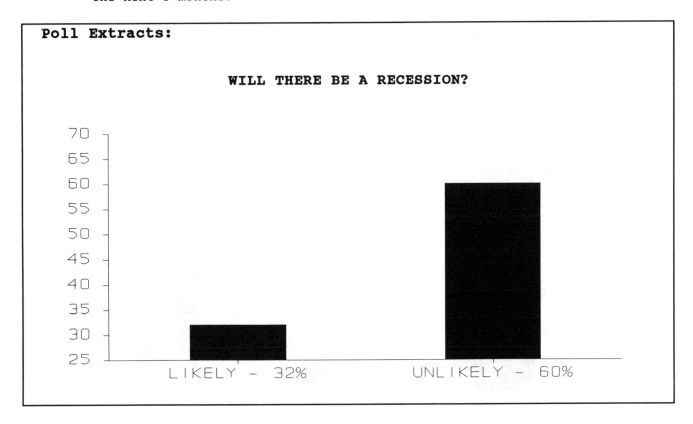

WILL THERE BE A RECESSION?

Also in Source: Approximately half of the respondents expect the government
          to raise taxes next year. Over 70% favor allowing depositors to earn tax-
          free interest on savings accounts. Nearly 30% favor reducing Social
          Security payroll taxes and 36% favor reducing the capital-gains tax.

Poll Details: This telephone poll of 1,000 adult Americans was conducted for
          TIME/CNN on January 31 through February 1, 1990 by Yankelovich Clancy
          Shulman. Sampling erorr was plus or minus 3%.

Availability: Published in *Time*, February 12, 1990 (volume 135, number 7),
          p.48-50.

CONSUMER CONFIDENCE

Description: This survey asked consumers to predict the health of the economy over the short term future.

Results: Consumers are predicting a healthier economy but they are not planning to increase their spending levels.

Poll Extracts:

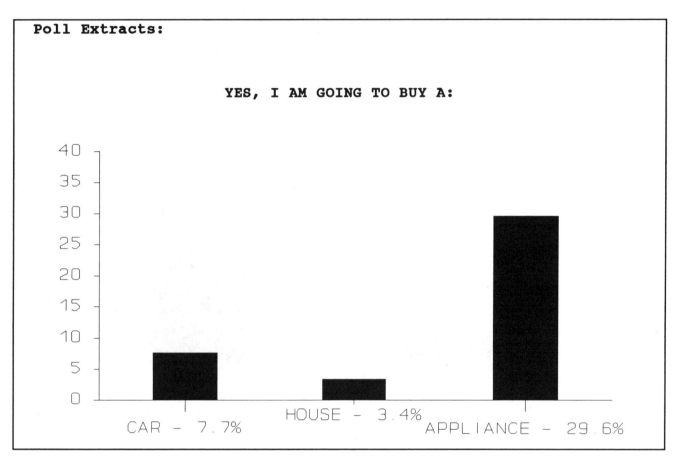

YES, I AM GOING TO BUY A:

CAR - 7.7%   HOUSE - 3.4%   APPLIANCE - 29.6%

Also in Source: 18.7% of the respondents expected business conditions to improve. 71.5% of the respondents expected no change in the economy.

Poll Details: The poll was conducted by The Conference Board. 5,000 people were surveyed.

Availability: Published in *USA TODAY*, March 29, 1990, p. 1B.

DISTRICT OF COLUMBIA RESIDENTS ARE OPTIMISTIC

Description: Presents the results of a poll which attempted to measure the economic conditions around the Washington, D.C. area.

Results: 86% of the respondents believe that they will remain about the same or be better off financially one year from now. 82% of the respondents believe that they are better off or about the same financially than they were one year ago. 58% of the respondents think that now is a good time for people to buy major household items. 59% think that now is a good time to buy a home in their area.

Poll Extracts: **COULD YOU, PERSONALLY, AFFORD TO BUY YOUR HOME FOR WHAT IT WOULD SELL FOR IN TODAY'S HOUSING MARKET? (ASKED ONLY OF HOME OWNERS.)**

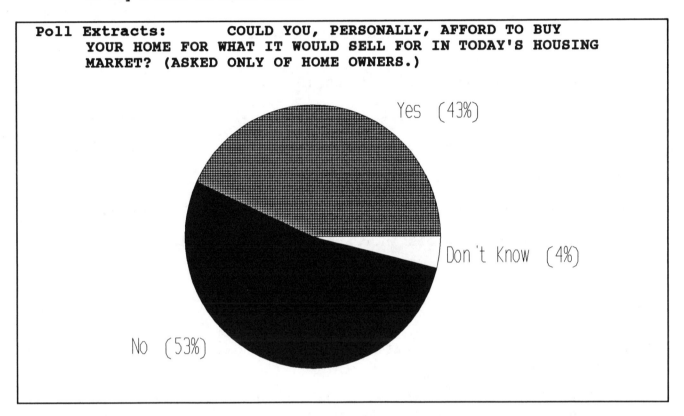

Also in Source: Some similar questions which were posed during a national survey conducted during May 1990. "The survey found surprisingly few significant differences in the attitudes toward the local economy as expressed by blacks and whites, men and women, rich and poor, or by where in the Washington area the respondent lived." The one exception was the responses regarding the improvement of business conditions during the next year.

Poll Details: "*Washington Post* figures are based on a telephone survey of a random sample of 1,232 adults 18 years of age and older living in the Washington, D.C. Metropolitan Statistical Area. The survey was conducted from May 31–June 8, 1990. Margin of sampling error for the overall results is plus or minus three percentage points." The survey was conducted by ARRO Research of Hyattsville.

Availability: Published in *The Washington Post* (Washington Business section), July 2, 1990, p. 1, 12.

ECONOMIC PROJECTIONS

Description: Presents the results of a survey of the nation's top business
economists concerning the state of the economy over the next three years.

Results: Approximately 60% of the respondents believe that the economy will
avoid a recession through 1993. 72% of the respondents felt the Federal
Reserve's policies were appropriate.

Poll Extracts:

ECONOMIC PROJECTIONS:

Will there be a recession through 1993........No......60.6%

The Federal Reserve is acting appropriately...Yes.......72%

At what rate will the economy grow in 1990?............1.7%

At what rate will the economy grow in 1991?...........2.5%

At what rate will prices increase in 1990?............4.2%

At what rate will prices increase in 1991?............4.2%

Also in Source: The article also includes a discussion of the implications of
this survey.

Poll Details: The poll, conducted by the National Association of Business
Economists, contacted 65 of the nation's top business executives.

Availability: Published in *The Atlanta Journal and Constitution*,
February 27, 1990, E-1.

THE EFFECTS OF A RECESSION

Description: Presents the results of a survey identifying the effects of a recession on the nation's economy as well as steps which could be taken to avoid the recession.

Results: Almost 90% of the respondents said their companies' business plans have been affected by "recession talk."

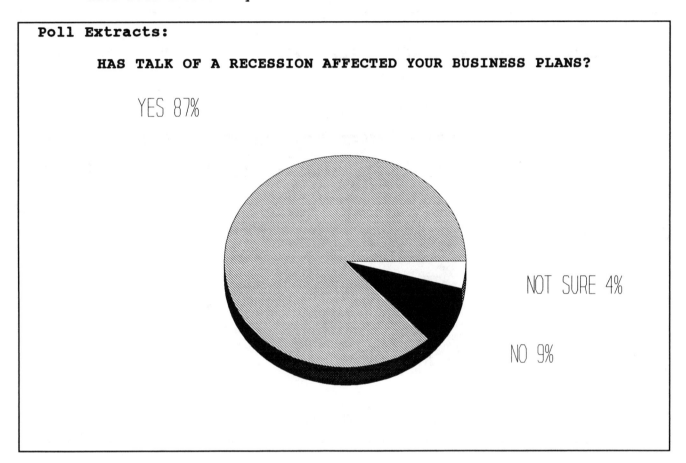

Poll Extracts:

HAS TALK OF A RECESSION AFFECTED YOUR BUSINESS PLANS?

YES 87%

NOT SURE 4%

NO 9%

Also in Source: When asked what one or two things the federal government should be doing to keep the nation out of a recession, 67% of the respondents said deal with the federal deficit/balance the budget/reduce government spending; 63% said lower interest rates/ease the money supply; 10% said avoid new taxes; 7% said solve the Iraq problem; 5% said impose an oil tax; 4% said reduce government interference with business; and 1% said encourage more research and development.

Poll Details: The independent opinion research firm Clark Martire & Bartolomeo spoke by telephone with 221 chief executives of Fortune 500 and Service 500 companies between August 29 and September 6, 1990.

Availability: Published in *Fortune*, October 8, 1990 (volume 122, number 9), P. 73, 76, 80, 81.

EMPLOYMENT OUTLOOK FOR 1991 COLLEGE GRADUATES

Description: Presents the results of a survey of private and public sector
employers concerning near future hiring plans.

Results: On average, employers plan to hire 9.8% fewer college graduates in
1990-1991 compared to 1989-1990.

Poll Extracts:

COMPARED TO 1989/1990, HIRING PLANS FOR 1990/1991 WILL BE LESS:

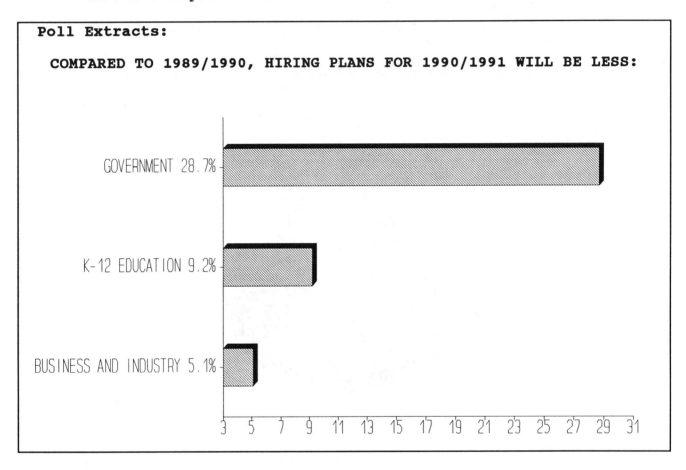

Also in Source: The employers surveyed said the uncertainty of war and the
slumping economy has produced the lowered hiring expectations. The south-
central region of the United States is the only area where empolyers plan
to increase hiring.

Poll Details: The results of the survey were taken from Michigan State
University's Career Development and Placement Services Office 20th annual
college-graduate hiring survey. 549 private and public sector employers
were surveyed.

Availability: Published in *USA Today*, December 10, 1990, p. 1B.

EXECUTIVES LOOK AT THE ECONOMY

Description: Presents the results of a survey concerning the views of Fortune 1000 executives toward the United States economy.

Results: The most serious threat to the United States economy is the quality of public education, followed closely by the size of the federal deficit.

Poll Extracts:

WHAT ARE THE MOST SERIOUS THREATS TO THE U.S. ECONOMY?

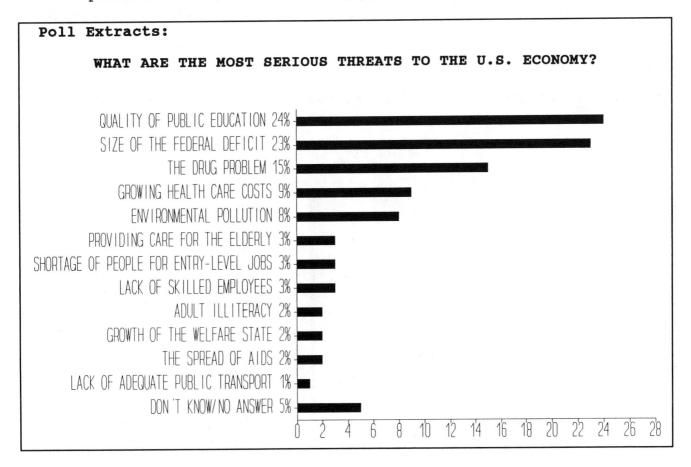

Also in Source: 29% of the respondents think a united Germany is a greater threat to United States business than a united European Community. 76% believe the U.S. can afford a defense budget cut as a result of the collapse of communism in Eastern Europe. 89% of the executives surveyed are distressed about the federal deficit and 57% are very distressed. Half of the resondents predict the deficit will grow, 20% predict a decrease, and 28% think it will remain at the current level. 41% believe the Bush Administration's S&L bailout will fail and 64% predict that a national program will be established by the end of the decade to address the spiraling cost of health care.

Poll Details: The results are taken from *The Chivas Regal Report on American Business Leaders: Executives in a Time of Upheaval*. Interviews were conducted in late spring of 1990 with 251 executives at Fortune 1000 companies.

Availability: Published in *USA Today Special Newsletter Edition*, December 1990 (volume 119, number 2547), p. 1, 2.

GRADING THE PRESIDENT AND CONGRESS

Description: Presents the results of a survey concerning the performance of
President George Bush and Congress and their attempts to create a budget-
deficit plan.

Results: 55% of the respondents gave President Bush and Congress either a C or
a D grade for their performance in attempting to create a budget-deficit
plan.

Poll Extracts:

CONCERNING THE BUDGET-DEFICIT PLAN, HOW DO YOU GRADE BUSH & CONGRESS?

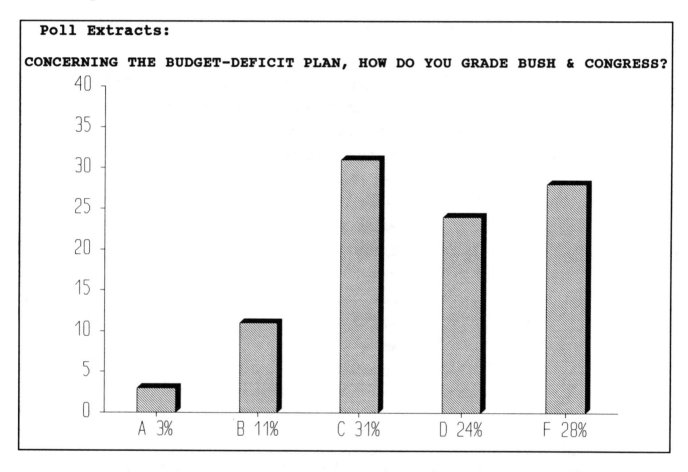

Also in Source: 61% of the respondents feel Congress is more responsible for
the budget formulation difficulties, while 23% blame President Bush. 34%
of the respondents said the Democratic Party was more responsible for the
budget situation, 33% blame the Republican Party, and 18% said both parties
are equally to blame.

Poll Details: The results were taken from a telephone poll of 500 adult
Americans for *Time*/CNN by Yankelovich Clancy Shulman. Sampling error is
plus or minus 4.5%.

Availability: Published in *Time*, October 22, 1990 (volume 136, number 17),
p. 31.

HAS THE ECONOMY AFFECTED SPENDING PLANS?

Description: Presents the results of a survey concerning future spending plans
in light of worsening economic conditions.

Results: Over 60% of the respondents expect to alter their future spending
plans due to the slowdown in the economy.

Poll Extracts:

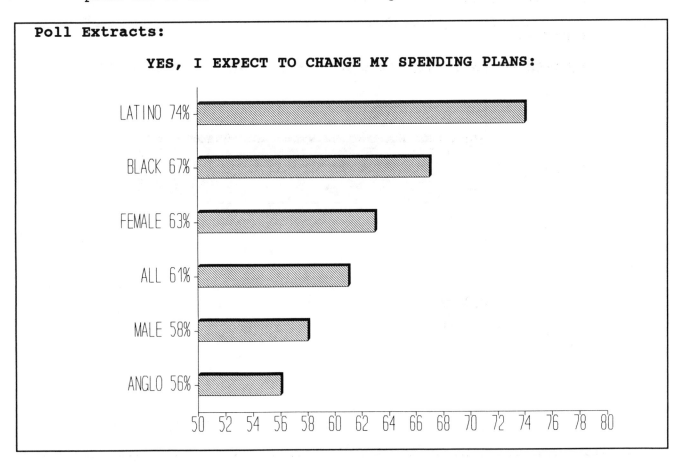

YES, I EXPECT TO CHANGE MY SPENDING PLANS:

Also in Source: 51% of the respondents believe the United States economy is
now in a recession, 21% predict a recession in one year, and 17% feel there
is no recession at this time or in the next year. 27% of the respondents
will change their spending plans on the purchase of a house, 31% on a car,
28% on Christmas presents, 22% on major appliances, 32% on vacations, and
32% on dining and entertainment.

Poll Details: This *Los Angeles Times* poll interviewed 2,564 residents in
California, asking about their plans for coping with the economic slowdown
and their overall assessments of the problems facing the economy.

Availability: Published in the *Los Angeles Times*, October 28, 1990, p. A1,
A16, A17.

HOLIDAY SPENDING

Description: Presents the results of a survey concerning the expected level of shopping and spending during the 1990 holiday season.

Results: Compared to last year, approximately three-fourths of the respondents will spend the same or less this year on gifts.

Poll Extracts:

COMPARED TO LAST YEAR, HOW MUCH WILL YOU SPEND ON GIFTS?

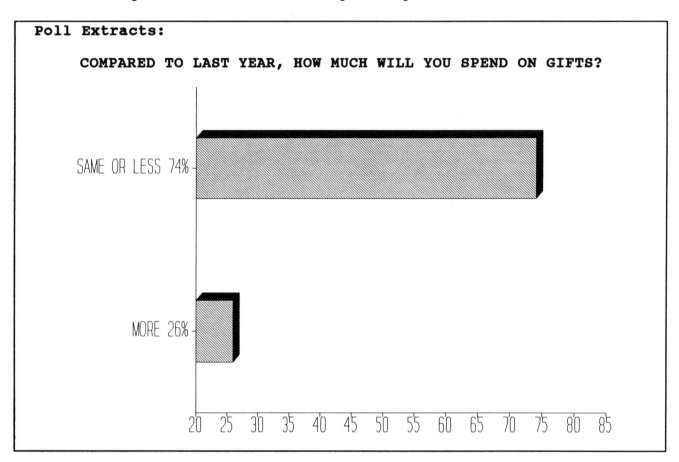

Also in Source: Many in the 26% group that will spend more this year on gifts say it's because prices are up, not because they have more money to spend. The poll found consumers expect to spend about 8% less this holiday season. Almost 60% of the respondents say they will pay for most or all gifts with cash and 35% say they will use credit cards less than last year. For shoppers who rate the economy as poor or fairly poor, 41% say they will pay entirely in cash. To cut costs, 65% of the respondents will try to shop at stores with the lowest prices and 34% will give homemade gifts.

Poll Details: The *USA Today* poll was conducted before the 1990 holiday season.

Availability: Published in *USA Today,* November 12, 1990, p. 1B, 2B.

THE HOUSING INDUSTRY

Description: Presents the results of a survey concerning the future of housing real estate.

Results: Except for the northeast, a house that sells today for $100,000 will sell for more in 12 months.

Poll Extracts:

HOW MUCH WILL A $100,000 HOUSE SELL FOR IN 12 MONTHS?

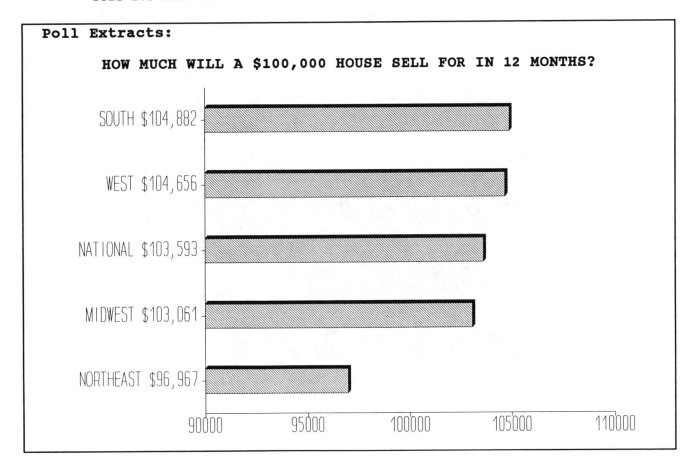

Also in Source: 27% of the respondents said the number of people looking for houses has increased, 39% said they have decreased, and 34% said the number has stayed the same. The respondents said the typical percentage drop between the original listing price and the final sales price in 1990 is 15.2%. 67% of the respondents said they occasionally refused a listing because of unrealistic price expectations, 18% said frequently, and 15% said never.

Poll Details: *USA Today* asked realtors at the National Association of Realtors Conference in New Orleans to complete a survey about the real estate market. Although the 1,015 responses are not a scientific sample, they do give a wide geographical representation.

Availability: Published in *USA Today*, November 21, 1990, p. 4B.

INTEREST RATES TO FALL

Description: Respondents were asked if they expect lower interest rates within
        the next year, and also if they expect the Dow Jones industrial average to
        rise at least 10% within the next two years.

Results: Nearly half of the respondents expected lower interest rates over the
        next year, with dramatic changes not anticipated. Nearly two-thirds of the
        respondents expected the Dow Jones industrial average to rise at least 10%
        in the next two years.

Poll Extracts:

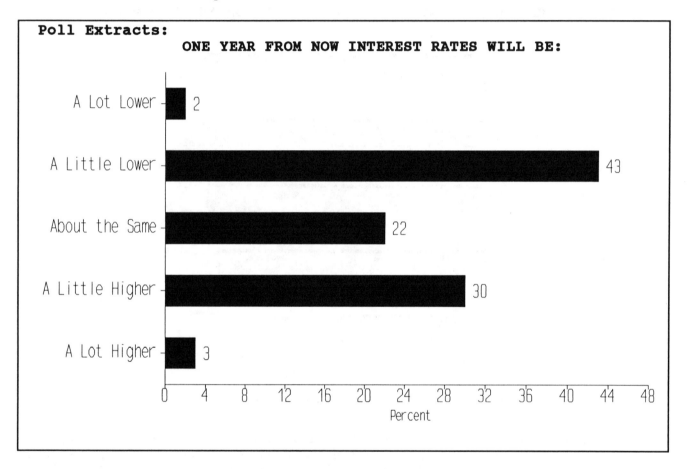

ONE YEAR FROM NOW INTEREST RATES WILL BE:

Also in Source: Predictions as to the which investments will give the best
        returns in the near future. The percentage of respondents who have
        purchased international investments in connection with the recent downfall
        of the Iron Curtain.

Poll Details: Participants in this telephone poll were members of the *USA
        Today* Investor Panel -- "a group of regular *Money* Section readers who are
        serious investors." 90% of the members were reached for the survey.

Availability: Published in *USA Today*, July 17, 1990, p. 1B.

JOB SECURITY

Description: Presents the results of a survey concerning employment issues and
trends in the United States economy.

Results: 20% of the respondents worry about losing their jobs.

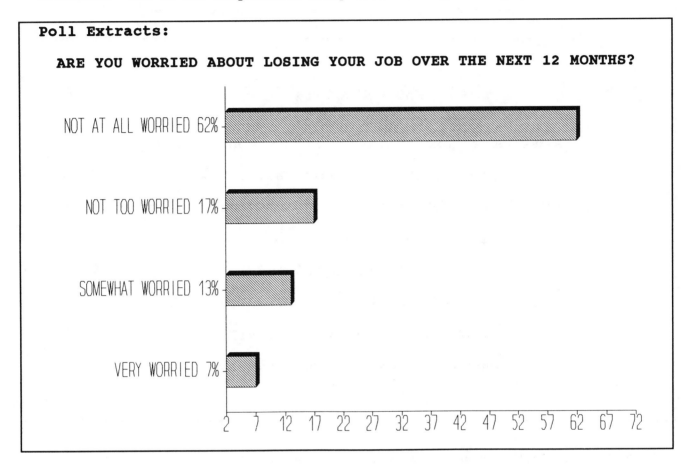

Poll Extracts:

ARE YOU WORRIED ABOUT LOSING YOUR JOB OVER THE NEXT 12 MONTHS?

Also in Source: 37% of the respondents could go without work, if they lost
their job, for one month; 20% could go for three months; 17% for six
months; 8% for one year; and 14% could go without work for more than a
year. 42% of the respondents, if they lost they job, would move to a new
location; 62% would change their line of work; 17% would sell their car;
19% would sell their home; 28% would ask their spouse to get a job or a
second job; 20% would seek financial aid from their parents; and 14% would
live with their parents.

Poll Details: This *Newsweek* poll was conducted on October 25 and 26, 1990.

Availability: Published in *Newsweek*, November 5, 1990 (volume CXVI, number
19), p. 44-47.

MANAGERS ECONOMIC PROJECTIONS

Description: Presents the results of a survey of business managers concerning the economic trends in the second quarter of 1990.

Results: Most managers are optimistic about second quarter sales and profits, but they do not expect to see an increase in employment levels.

Poll Extracts:

DO YOU EXPECT:

Revenues to exceed last year's second quarter?

Yes.....65%   A Decline.....8%

A higher net income than last year's second quarter?

Yes.....60%   A Decline.....6%

No change in prices?

Yes.....38%   No.....57%

A change in employment levels?

No change.....74%   Increase.....21%

Also in Source: A discussion of the implications of the survey is included in the article.

Poll Details: The survey, conducted by Dun & Bradstreet Corp., asked 1,500 manufacturing, wholesale and retail executives to predict business conditions in the April through June quarter of 1990.

Availability: Published in *USA Today*, March 28, 1B.

MASSACHUSETTS VOTERS GLOOMY ABOUT THE STATE'S ECONOMY

Description: Presents the results of a poll on the economic confidence within the State of Massachusetts.

Results: 47% of the residents of the State of Massachusetts would consider moving out of the state if the economy gets any worse. One-third of the respondents are cutting back on groceries because of the economy. 30% of the respondents worry about losing their jobs. 42% of the respondents blame the current state of the economy in Massachusetts on state policymakers.

Poll Extracts:

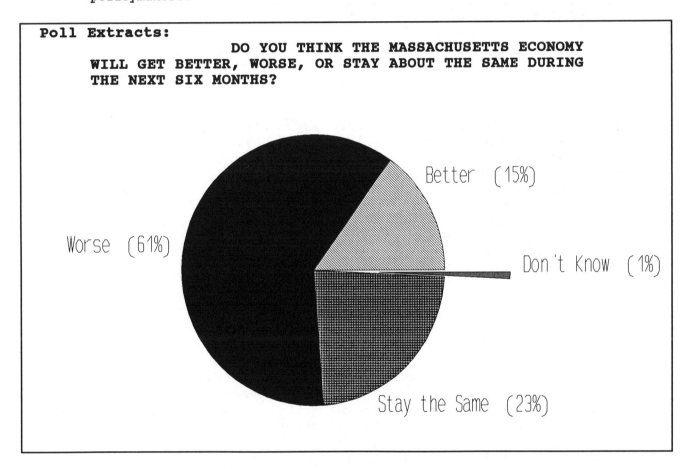

DO YOU THINK THE MASSACHUSETTS ECONOMY WILL GET BETTER, WORSE, OR STAY ABOUT THE SAME DURING THE NEXT SIX MONTHS?

Better (15%)

Worse (61%)

Don't Know (1%)

Stay the Same (23%)

Also in Source: Other questions less directly tied to the Massachussetts economy, such as respondents who thought they would be better off living someplace else (quality of life).

Poll Details: The poll was conducted by KRC Communications Research for *The Boston Globe*/WBZ-TV during August 26-30, 1990. 436 Massachusetts voters were interviewed by telephone for the poll. The margin of error is 5%.

Availability: Published in *The Boston Globe*, September 4, 1990, p. 1, 12.

PREDICTING THE ECONOMIC FUTURE

Description: Presents the results of a survey of corporate executives
        concerning their economic projections. They were asked whether they
        expected a recession in the next two years and what indicators and actions
        signal a recession or a change in the economy.

Results: Less than half of the respondents expect a recession in the next two
        years. Almost a quarter of the respondents named rising interest rates as
        the most important indicator of a coming recession.

Poll Extracts:

HOW DO YOU TELL IF A RECESSION IS COMING?

1. Interest rates...................................22%
2. Unemployment rates.............................14%
3. Stock market...................................10%
4. Financial press.................................9%
5. Sales...9%
6. Construction starts.............................8%
7. Newspapers & magazines..........................8%
8. Clients & customers.............................7%
9. Real estate market..............................7%
10. Auto sales......................................6%

Also in Source: 48% of the respondents from the Northeast expect a national
        recession compared to only 31% of the respondents from the Southeast. 41%
        of the respondents from the service sector expect a national recession
        compared to 30% from the manufacturing industry.

Poll Details: In December 1989, a two-page questionnaire was sent to 3,072
        companies that have appeared on either the *Inc.* 500 or the *Inc.* 100, as
        well as to another 720 growth companies. Response rate was 26%. Survey
        results were tabulated by Harrison & Goldberg in Cambridge, MA.

Availability: Published in *Inc.*, April, 1990, (volume 12, number 4)
        p. 52-54, 56.

PRESIDENT BUSH AND THE ECONOMY

Description: Presents the results of a survey concerning President Bush's handling of the economy.

Results: 60% of the respondents said the country has "gotten pretty seriously off on the wrong track." 70% of the respondents approve of the job Bush is doing as president compared to 79% in January, 1990.

Poll Extracts:

VIEWS ON ECONOMIC ISSUES:

Do you approve of the job George Bush
is doing as president?..........................Yes...70%

Has the country "gotten seriously
off on the wrong track?"........................Yes...60%

Do you approve of the way President Bush
is handling the nation's economy?...............Yes...52%

The nation's economy is:
                      Getting better...7%
                      Getting worse...46%
                      Staying the same...46%

Should President Bush abandon his no-new-taxes pledge
and "consider raising some taxes in order to reduce
the budget deficit?"
                    Yes...49%
                    No....49%

Also in Source: 68% of the respondents said they approve of the way Bush is handling foreign affairs, a level unchanged since a March poll.

Poll Details: A total of 1,526 adults were interviewed on May 17-21, 1990 for *The Washington Post*-ABC News Poll. The margin of error is plus or minus 3%.

Availability: Published in *The Washington Post*, May 23, 1990, p. A4.

THE PUBLIC IS PESSIMISTIC

Description: Presents the results of a nationwide survey which asked
     respondents for their perception of the condition of the local and national
     economy, and the overall state of the country.

Results: About 60% of the respondents felt that the national economy is getting
     worse, and also that the country has gotten off on the wrong track.

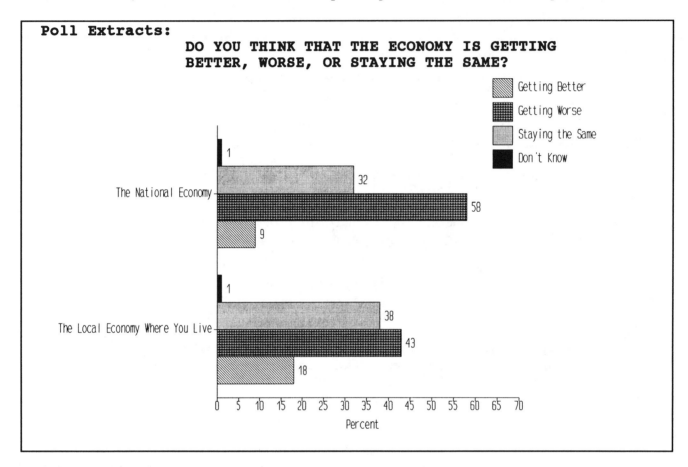

Poll Extracts:

DO YOU THINK THAT THE ECONOMY IS GETTING BETTER, WORSE, OR STAYING THE SAME?

Also in Source: The percentage of respondents who approve/disapprove of the
     way President Bush is handling: his job as president; foreign affairs; the
     nation's economy; the federal budget deficit.

Poll Details: This *Washington Post*/ABC News poll was conducted on July 19-24,
     1990. 1,509 adults were interviewed across the nation by Chilton Research
     Services. The margin of error is 3%.

Availability: Published in *The Washington Post*, July 26, 1990, p. A10.

REAL ESTATE RECOVERY

Description: Presents the results of a survey concerning the future of real estate markets in the United States.

Results: Almost 80% of the respondents predict that America's property markets will not recover until the mid-1990s or later. Less than 5% anticipate that the current drop in commercial building and investment will be a short-term decline.

Poll Extracts:

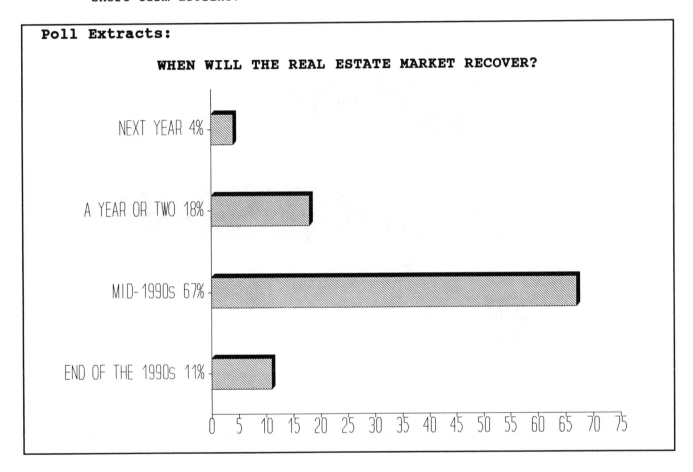

WHEN WILL THE REAL ESTATE MARKET RECOVER?

Also in Source: *Emerging Trends* asked developers, lenders, and real estate brokers to rank the following cities from best to worst on overall real estate investment, lending, and development prospects for the coming year. The ranking is Seattle, San Francisco, Los Angeles, Washington D.C., Chicago, San Diego, Dallas, Houston, Philadelphia, Atlanta, St. Louis, New York, Detroit, Miami, Boston, Phoenix, and Denver.

Poll Details: The results are taken from a report published by Real Estate Research Corporation titled *Emerging Trends in Real Estate*. The annual survey of developers, lenders, and real estate brokers is sponsored by Equitable Investment Management Inc.

Availability: Published in *The Dallas Morning News*, October 30, 1990, p. 1D, 12D.

RECESSION JITTERS

Description: Presents the results of a poll on the economy, and the financial
situation of the respondents as compared to a year ago.

Results: "Consumers are more nervous about the economy than at any time since
the last recession ended in October 1982." 21% of the respondents feel
worse off financially than they were a year ago.

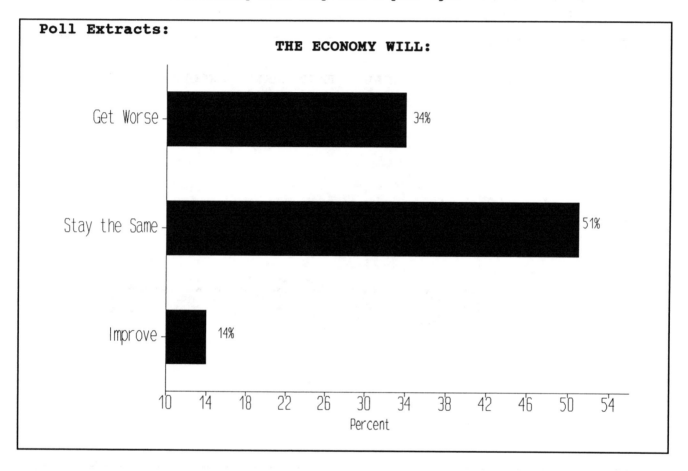

Poll Extracts:

THE ECONOMY WILL:

Also in Source: 41% of the respondents have postponed or soon will be
postponing major purchases due to the current economy. Only 14% of the
respondents in a similar survey conducted after the October 1987 stock
market crash expected the economy to get worse.

Poll Details: This *USA Today* Poll was conducted by the Gordon S. Black Corp.
813 consumers were interviewed by telephone on July 16-17, 1990. The
margin of sampling error is 3.5%.

Availability: Published in *USA Today*, July 25, 1990, p. 1A, 2A.

STRONGER ECONOMIC POWER: JAPAN OR UNITED STATES

Description: Presents the results of a survey focusing on the economy but also including general questions concerning the state of the union.

Results: Nearly half of the registered voters polled agree that the country is headed in the right direction. But over 73% believe that Japan is in a stronger economic position than the United States.

Poll Extracts:

WHICH COUNTRY IS IN A STRONGER ECONOMIC POSITION?

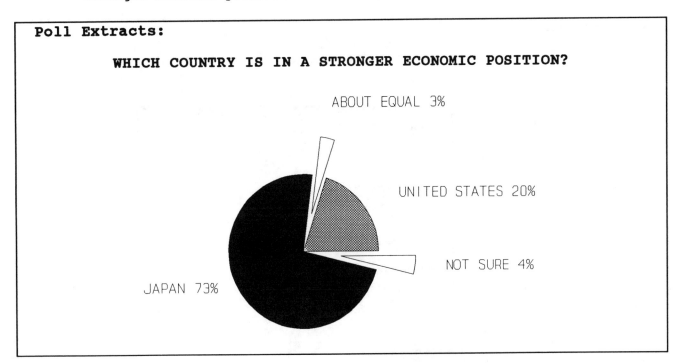

ABOUT EQUAL 3%

UNITED STATES 20%

NOT SURE 4%

JAPAN 73%

Also in Source: 54% want President Bush and Congress to "shake things up" while only 36% want a "steady-as-you-go" approach. Over 70% of the respondents approve President Bush's performance. However, by 55% to 28%, they trust Congress more than they trust the president to make the right decisions about where the budget deficit should be cut. 40% think the peace dividend should be used to reduce the budget.

Poll Details: The *Wall Street Journal*/NBC News poll was based on nationwide telephone interviews of 1,510 registered voters. It was conducted by the polling organizations of Peter Hart and Robert Teeter. Margin of erorr is 2.6% in either direction.

Availability: Published in *The Wall Street Journal*, January 19, 1990, p. A1-A4.

WHO DO YOU TRUST?

Description: Presents the results of a survey concerning the course of the nation's economic policy as well as those responsible for its implementation.

Results: Most of the respondents, 36%, trust Congressional Democrats to set the course for the nation's economic policy.

Poll Extracts:

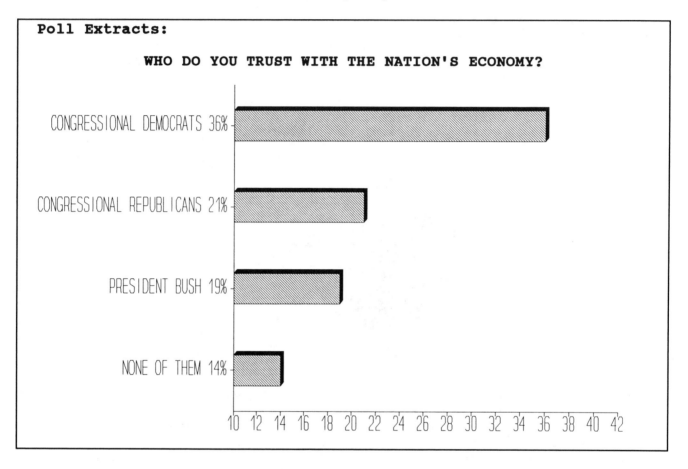

WHO DO YOU TRUST WITH THE NATION'S ECONOMY?

CONGRESSIONAL DEMOCRATS 36%

CONGRESSIONAL REPUBLICANS 21%

PRESIDENT BUSH 19%

NONE OF THEM 14%

10 12 14 16 18 20 22 24 26 28 30 32 34 36 38 40 42

Also in Source: 33% of the respondents think economic conditions in the United States will improve, while 56% think they will not improve.

Poll Details: For this *Newsweek* poll, the Gallup Organization interviewed a national sample of 753 adults by telephone on October 25-26, 1990. The margin of error is plus or minus 4%.

Availability: Published in *Newsweek*, November 5, 1990 (volume CXVI, number 19), p. 20-22.

WHO'S STRONGEST: JAPAN, USA, OR GERMANY?

Description: Presents the results of a survey concerning the relative economic
strengths of Japan, the United States, and Germany.

Results: 69% of the American respondents said that Japan had the strongest
overall economy while 43% of the Japanese respondents agreed. 17% of the
American respondents said the United States was strongest and 50% of the
Japanese agreed. 9% of the Americans and 2% of the Japanese said Germany
had the strongest economy.

Poll Extracts:

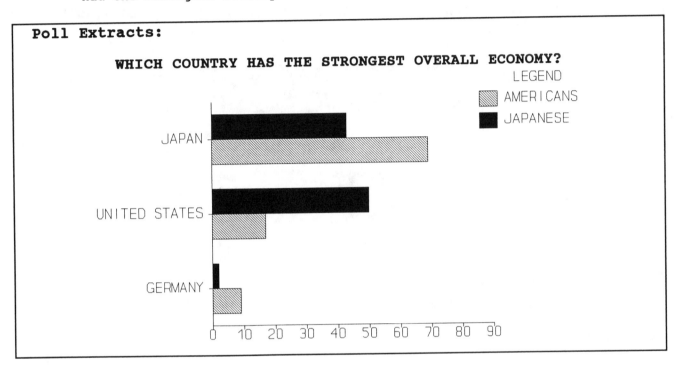

Also in Source: 41% of the American respondents think that Japan will have
the strongest economy ten years from now. 41% of the Japanese respondents
think that the United States will have the strongest economy. 63% of the
American respondents said it is very important that their country try to be
the world's leading economic power. 51% of the Japanese replied similarly.

Poll Details: The results of the poll are taken from *The Wall Street
Journal*/NBC News Poll. Japanese responses are taken from *Wall Street
Journal*/Nippon Research.

Availability: Published in *The Wall Street Journal*, June 13, 1990, p. A1, A8.

WILL THERE BE A RECESSION?

Description: Presents the results of a survey concerning the future of the
United States economy.

Results: Over 60% of the respondents believe the economy is presently in a
recession.

Poll Extracts:

WILL THE U.S. EXPERIENCE A RECESSION IN THE NEXT TWO YEARS?

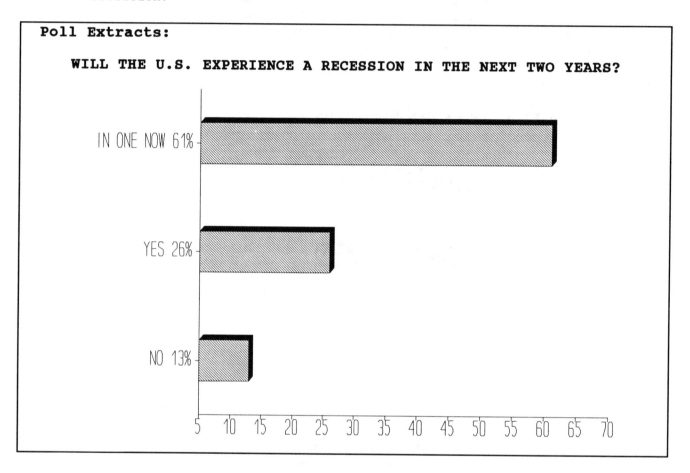

Also in Source: 54% of the respondents expect the economy to decline somewhat
in the next six months and 8% expect it to decline dramatically. 16%
predict the economy will stay about the same and 21% expect it to improve
somewhat. Only 1% expect the economy to improve dramatically in the next
six months. Because of the weak economy, 42% have postponed or plan to
postpone major consumer purchases in the next six months. 8% of the
respondents have dropped stocks or stock funds.

Poll Details: The results are taken from a survey of *USA Today*'s Investor
Panel during early October 1990. The panel is not a representative sample
of U.S. consumers. The 308 panelists have been hand-picked for being
serious investors.

Availability: Published in *USA Today*, October 15, 1990, p. 1B.

ACHIEVING OUR NATIONAL GOALS

Description: Respondents were asked to prioritize and state the likelihood of attainment for the six national educational goals which were adopted last February by President Bush and the nation's governors.

Results: 75% of the respondents assigned a high priority to all six of the national educational goals. The percentage of respondents who thought that it was likely or very likely that any of these goals would be achieved in the next 10 years ranged from 19% to 50%. 50% of the respondents thought that it was likely or very likely that by the year 2000, all children in America would start school ready to learn.

Poll Extracts:
  STATED GOAL: BY THE YEAR 2000, EVERY SCHOOL IN AMERICA WILL BE FREE OF DRUGS AND VIOLENCE AND WILL OFFER A DISCIPLINED ENVIRONMENT CONDUCIVE TO LEARNING.

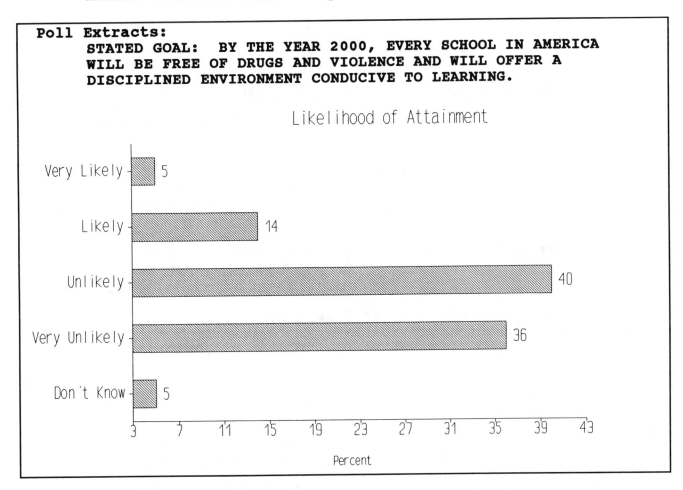

Likelihood of Attainment

Very Likely — 5
Likely — 14
Unlikely — 40
Very Unlikely — 36
Don't Know — 5

Percent

Also in Source: The percentage of the respondents who thought that the public schools in their community had gotten better, worse, or stayed about the same, in the last five years. The percentage of white respondents and nonwhite respondents who said that the racial or ethnic composition of the student body would influence their choice of school. Information on how to order copies of the poll.

Poll Details: This poll was the 22nd annual Gallup/Phi Delta Kappa poll of the Public's Attitudes Toward the Public Schools. 1,594 adults were interviewed in April-May 1990.

Availability: Published in *Education Week*, September 5, 1990 (volume 10, number 1), p. 12.

AMERICAN STUDENTS ARE OPTIMISTIC

Description: This international survey polled American and Japanese junior and senior high school students about their attitudes toward money, schools, businesses, and other institutions.

Results: When compared to Japanese students, American students are: taking more business, computer, and economics classes; more optimistic about their schools; and more optimistic about themselves.

```
┌──────────────────────────────────────────────────────────────────────────┐
│  Poll Extracts:                                                            │
│                                                                            │
│                                                                            │
│                             STUDENTS WHO:                                  │
│                                                                            │
│                                                                            │
│  Say they have a "great deal" or "quite a lot"                             │
│  of confidence in public schools ............... U.S. -- 56% -- Yes        │
│                                                   Japan -- 44% -- Yes       │
│                                                                            │
│                                                                            │
│  Think that their high schools do a good job of                            │
│  teaching math .................................. U.S. -- 90% -- Yes        │
│                                                   Japan -- 70% -- Yes       │
│                                                                            │
│                                                                            │
│  Plan to attend College ......................... U.S. -- 81% -- Yes        │
│                                                   Japan -- 68% -- Yes       │
│                                                                            │
│                                                                            │
│  See themselves winding up in professional or                              │
│  managerial careers ............................. U.S. -- 65% -- Yes        │
│                                                   Japan -- 26% -- Yes       │
│                                                                            │
└──────────────────────────────────────────────────────────────────────────┘
```

Also in Source: The percentage of students who have taken or plan to take business or economics courses and computer science courses. The percentage of students who plan to look for employment straight out of high school. High school completion rates for Japanese and American students.

Poll Details: This Junior Achievement-Gallup International Youth Survey of 750 American and 790 Japanese junior and senior high school students was completed by telephone in February 1990. The margin of sampling error ranged from 2% to 4%, depending on the number of respondents per question.

Availability: Published in the *Chicago Tribune*, September 22, 1990 (Section 1), p. 1, 10.

ATTITUDES OF NEW TEACHERS

Description: This poll of beginning teachers queried respondents about their attitudes and expectations.

Results: Teachers entering the classroom as teachers for the first time are optimistic about their career choice, but are not naive about the problems they will face. Respondents thought that: their training adequately prepared them to teach students from various ethnic backgrounds -- 80% agreed; most teachers are dedicated to their work -- 90% agreed; a school's only job is to teach children, and responsibility for health and social problems falls outside of the school -- 19% agreed; children have so many problems that it is often difficult for them to be good students -- 75% agreed; even the best teachers will have problems in teaching more than two-thirds of their students -- nearly 50% agreed; teachers are respected in today's society -- 60% agreed.

Poll Extracts:

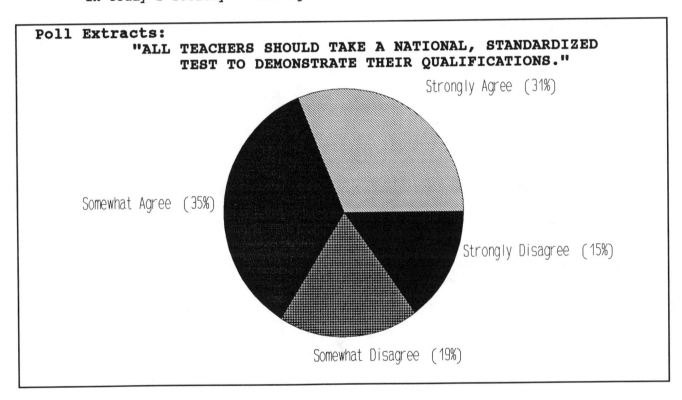

"ALL TEACHERS SHOULD TAKE A NATIONAL, STANDARDIZED TEST TO DEMONSTRATE THEIR QUALIFICATIONS."

Strongly Agree (31%)

Somewhat Agree (35%)

Strongly Disagree (15%)

Somewhat Disagree (19%)

Also in Source: The percentage of respondents who: expect that their principal will create an environment to assist their students in learning; view teaching as a long-term career choice; think that parents treat teachers as adversaries.

Poll Details: This poll, "The Metropolitan Life Survey of New Teachers: Expectations and Ideals," involved 1,002 beginning teachers. All of the respondents were 1990 college graduates, and had accepted a teaching position or expected to obtain a position for the 1990-91 academic year. Respondents were interviewed by telephone during July-August, 1990.

Availability: Published in *Education Week*, September 26, 1990 (volume 10, number 4), p. 6.

A BETTER WORK FORCE THROUGH EDUCATION

Description: Presents the results of a survey concerning what the federal government and business can do to improve the quality of the United States work force.

Results: Over 60% of the respondents said improving education is the most important step American government and business can take to improve the quality of the U.S. work force.

Poll Extracts:

THE MOST IMPORTANT FACTOR WHICH WOULD IMPROVE THE WORK FORCE IS:

Improve education...64%

Raise educational standards................................16%

Other suggestions regarding education......................14%

Expand training programs for employees.....................11%

Improve incentives for workers..............................7%

Manage better...6%

Reduce government intervention..............................5%

Give families more responsibility
for education...5%

Give localities more control
of education..5%

Pay teachers more...5%

Address the dissolution of the family.......................3%

Also in Source: 39% of the respondents said the quality of the U.S. work force has improved in the past 10 years, 34% said it has grown worse, 26% said it has stayed the same, and 1% weren't sure. 64% of the respondents said colleges and universities improve the quality of the work force, 57% said the managerial styles of U.S. companies improves the work force, 13% said the public education system improves the work force, and 6% said labor unions are responsible for improvement in the work force.

Poll Details: The opinion research firm of Clark Martire & Bartolomeo interviewed 206 chief executives of Fortune 500 and Service 500 corporations between July 31 and August 8, 1990.

Availability: Published in *Fortune*, October 22, 1990 (volume 122, number 10), p. 75-77.

CENSORED TEXTS

> **Description:** Presents the results of a survey concerning materials which have been challenged as objectionable by parents and organized groups in California.

> **Results:** The most cited challenge of educational texts is the alleged satanic/witchcraft nature of the material.

Poll Extracts:

REASONS FOR CHALLENGING EDUCATIONAL MATERIALS:

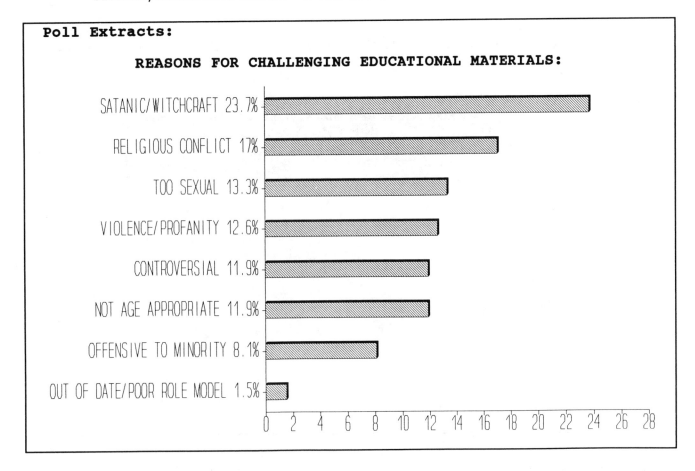

> **Also in Source:** The most frequently challenged materials include *Catcher in the Rye*, J.D. Salinger; *Death of a Salesman*, Arthur Miller; *ET*, Steven Spielberg; *Grapes of Wrath*, John Steinbeck; *Halloween ABC*, Eve Merriam; *Huckleberry Finn*, Mark Twain; *Little Red Riding Hood*, a fairy tale; *The Lorax*, Dr. Seuss; *Macbeth*, William Shakespeare; *Of Mice and Men*, John Steinbeck; *Snow White*, The brothers Grimm; *Sports Illustrated*'s swimsuit issue, *Where the Sidewalk Ends*, Shel Silverstein; *The Wizard of Oz*, Frank L. Baum; and *1984*, George Orwell.

> **Poll Details:** The results are taken from a survey of 421 California school districts by education professor Louise Adler of California State Fullerton.

> **Availability:** Published in the *Los Angeles Times*, December 7, 1990, p. A3, A24.

CEOs GRADE THE SCHOOLS

Description: Presents the results of a survey concerning chief executive
officers' opinions of the American educational system.

Results: Over three-fourths of the respondents claim that the schools have
worsened the quality of the United States work force.

Poll Extracts:

HAVE THE PUBLIC SCHOOLS IMPROVED OR WORSENED THE U.S. WORK FORCE?

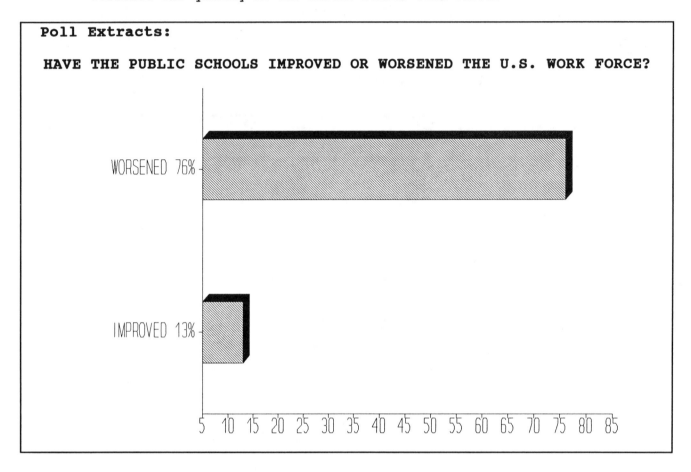

Also in Source: 64% of the respondents think higher education has improved
the quality of the work force, while 36% think higher education has
worsened it. 39% of the respondents say the quality of the work force has
improved in the last decade, 34% say it has worsened, 26% see no
difference, and 1% were not sure.

Poll Details: Opinion researchers Clark Martire and Bartolomeo asked 206 chief
executive officers of Fortune 500 and Fortune 500 Service firms what they
thought of the American school system.

Availability: Published in *The Atlanta Journal and Constitution,* October 6,
1990, p. B-2.

COLLEGE SCHOLARSHIPS

Description: Presents the results of a survey concerning high school students'
comparative scholarship eligibility between athletics and academics.

Results: Approximately 16% of the respondents felt that they would most likely
be eligible for an athletic scholarship while approximately 14% thought
academics were their best chance.

Poll Extracts:

MY COLLEGE SCHOLARSHIP WILL MOST LIKELY BE IN:

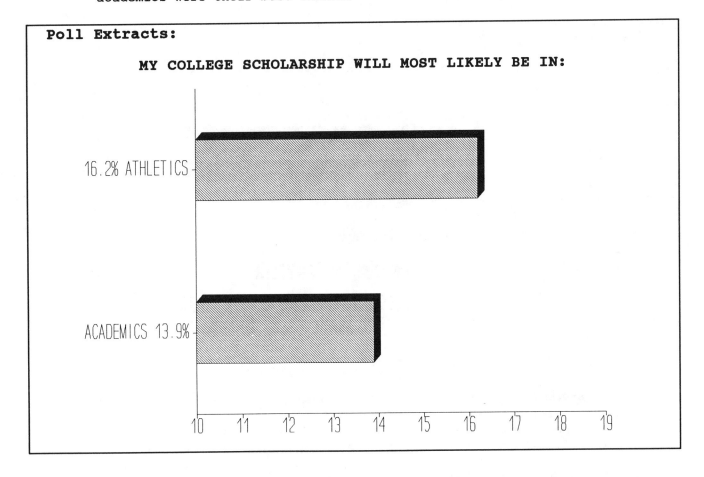

Also in Source: In 1980, the results of the survey were reversed. 19.2%
thought they would most likely be eligible for an academic scholarship
compared to 13% who cited sports as the more likely route.

Poll Details: The results were taken from an annual survey conducted by the
National Research Center for College and University Admissions. The
754,000 high school juniors and seniors surveyed were asked to pick from 14
scholarships, including academics, athletics, music, math, art, debate,
writing, and leadership.

Availability: Published in *USA Today*, November 26, 1990, p. 1A.

EDUCATIONAL REFORMS

Description: Presents the results of a survey concerning the level of support
for various educational reform initiatives in Fairfax County, Virginia.

Results: Over 70% of the respondents favor the concept of merit pay for
teachers. Less than half of the respondents favored a longer school day in
the elementary grades.

Poll Extracts:

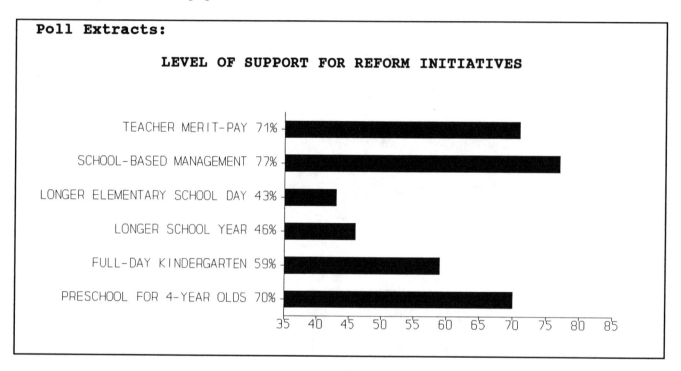

LEVEL OF SUPPORT FOR REFORM INITIATIVES

Also in Source: The schools' biggest problems were identified as student
abuse of drugs and alcohol, 40%; student attitudes/behavior/discipline,
23%; poor administrators and teachers, 12%; lack of parental involvement,
11%; fiscal concerns, 11% and; lack of emphasis on basic skills, 10%.

Poll Details: The school-sponsored survey contacted 1,033 parents and other
adults from March 28 to April 9, 1990. The survey was conducted by Market
Opinion Research Inc. and Forecasting International Ltd.

Availability: Published in *The Washington Post*, May 25, 1990, p. C7.

FACULTY RECRUITMENT

Description: Presents the results of a survey on how institutions are responding to the changing academic labor market.

Results: 59% of the respondents said that faculty staffing was among their top three concerns. "To deepen their pools of applicants, some colleges reported they were re-examining their traditional criteria for new faculty appointments. Some institutions, including more than one-third of the two-year colleges surveyed, said they were considering whether to accept candidates who did not have teaching experience." Increased competition for professors has led some institutions to offer higher salaries than normal, job assistance for candidates' spouses, and hiring of personnel in advance of actual vacancies.

Poll Extracts:

IT HAS TAKEN LONGER TO FIND QUALIFIED PEOPLE:

        Yes, generally 20%
        Yes, in a few fields 45%
        No 34%

INSTITUTION HAS HAD GREATER DIFFICULTY IN GETTING TOP APPLICANTS TO ACCEPT POSITIONS:

        Yes, generally 22%
        Yes, in a few fields 41%
        No 37%

Also in Source: The turnover rate for full-time faculty members in the academic year 1988-1989. Other poll questions and responses dealing with faculty recruitment. Information on how to order copies of the report.

Poll Details: This report, "Campus Trends, 1990," is based on a survey of senior administrators at 364 colleges and universities that was conducted in the Spring of 1990.

Availability: Published in *The Chronicle of Higher Education*, July 25, 1990, p. A3, A11-A12.

GEOGRAPHY KNOWLEDGE

Description: This survey asked teachers if they favored requiring high school students to pass a geography course before they graduate. They were also asked if they wanted state governments to increase geography requirements.

Results: Almost 90% of the respondents favored requiring a geography course for high school graduation and nearly the same number favored increased state geography requirements.

Poll Extracts:

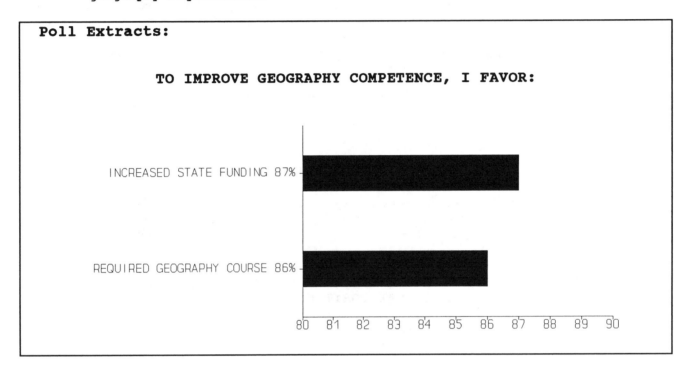

TO IMPROVE GEOGRAPHY COMPETENCE, I FAVOR:

INCREASED STATE FUNDING 87%

REQUIRED GEOGRAPHY COURSE 86%

80 81 82 83 84 85 86 87 88 89 90

Also in Source: *The Rand McNally Report on Geography Education in America* reported that high school seniors have a serious gap in their knowledge of geography, with only 37% able to find Southeast Asia on a world map. The average student could answer 57% of the questions.

Poll Details: These results were taken from a nationwide survey of 852 elementary and secondary school social studies and geography teachers.

Availability: Published in *The Cincinnati Enquirer*, February 27, 1990, A-3.

GRADING THE SCHOOLS

Description: Presents the results of a survey of school administrators which
   asked them to rate the quality of public education in the United States.

Results: The average grade given public education by these school
   administrators is a "B-".

Poll Extracts:

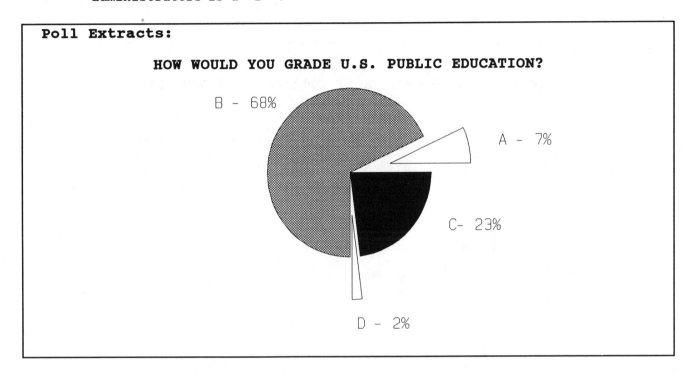

HOW WOULD YOU GRADE U.S. PUBLIC EDUCATION?

B - 68%

A - 7%

C- 23%

D - 2%

Also in Source: 73% said that public education is better now than a decade
   ago, 19% felt it is about the same, and 8% ranked public education today as
   worse. 51% rated U.S. public schools as better than England's schools.
   70% thought U.S. schools were better than schools in the Soviet Union while
   only 36% rated U.S. schools better than Japan's.

Poll Details: The survey, which contacted 385 school administrators, was
   conducted by Allstate Insurance Company and the American Association of
   School Administrators.

Availability: Published in *USA Today*, February 8, 1990, p. 1D.

HOW TO PAY FOR COLLEGE

Description: Presents the results of a survey concerning the expense of a college education and the relative necessity of some form of financial assistance.

Results: 60% of the respondents say the loan burden for most students is too high.

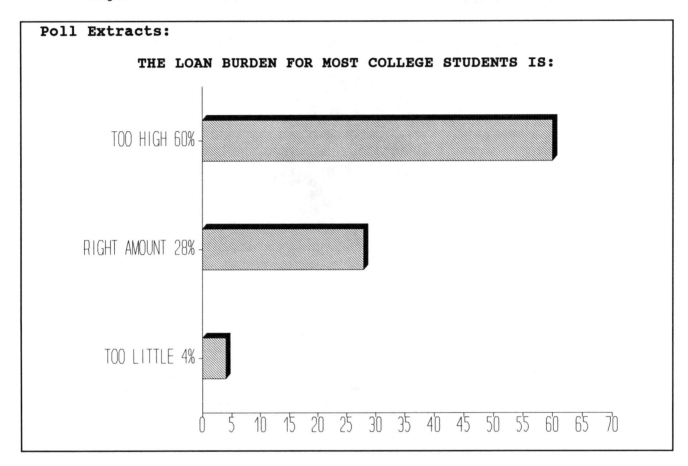

Poll Extracts:

THE LOAN BURDEN FOR MOST COLLEGE STUDENTS IS:

TOO HIGH 60%

RIGHT AMOUNT 28%

TOO LITTLE 4%

0 5 10 15 20 25 30 35 40 45 50 55 60 65 70

Also in Source: 91% of the respondents believe it is not possible for most people to go to college without receiving some form of financial aid. 66% of the respondents said if the federal government is to give out financial aid it should be based on both academic ability and financial need. 20% prefer the current system, which is based solely on financial need, with 11% preferring that additional aid be based strictly on academic potential.

Poll Details: The telephone survey of 1,014 adults in June 1990 was conducted by the Gallup Organization.

Availability: Published in the *Chicago Tribune*, October 14, 1990, section 1, p. 6.

IS COLLEGE AFFORDABLE?

Description: Presents the results of a survey concerning the cost of a college education and the appropriate level of financial suuport provided by the federal government.

Results: Nine out of ten Americans think most people can't afford to go to college without financial aid.

Poll Extracts:

THE COST OF A COLLEGE EDUCATION:

Do you think most people can afford
to go to college without financial aid?..............No....90%

Do most students rely too much on loans
while attending college?............................Yes...60%

If the federal government were to give out
additional financial aid, would you support
changing federal policy to include academic
ability as a criterion for eligibility, in
addition to financial need?........................Yes...66%

Also in Source: About 75% of the respondents said the United States would see major advancements in science, medicine, and technology if more Americans were able to get a college education. Nearly 60% of the respondents said that having more college-educated Americans would significantly improve the nation's ability to solve social problems such as crime and homelessness. About half of the respondents think that if colleges receive additional money, most of the funds should be put toward financial aid programs. About 45% believe most of the money should go for research on medical, scientific, social, and other national problems.

Poll Details: The survey was commissioned by the Council for Advancement and Support of Education. The Gallup Organization conducted the survey, in which 1,014 American adults were questioned about their perceptions of higher education.

Availability: Published in *The Chronicle of Higher Education* (volume XXXVII, number 7), p. A2.

A LONGER SCHOOL YEAR

Description: Presents the results of a survey concering the need for a longer
school year.

Results: Two-thirds of the elementary school principals surveyed said they
would want the school year lengthened from the existing 175-180 days to 200
days. 40% said they would want a year-round schedule with vacation time
offered throughout the year.

Poll Extracts:

SCHOOL YEAR LONG?

Would you like the school year to be
lengthened to 200 days?.....................Yes...........66%

Would you like a year-round schedule?......Yes......about 40%

Do you prefer the current 6 hour
school day?...............................Yes.....about 50%

Also in Source: The survey also asked the principals what they thought of
Carnegie Foundation President Ernest L. Boyer's "basic school" concept
which suggests reorganizing the first five years of elementary school,
perhaps by merging some of the grades. 47% agreed with the idea but had
different views on how it should be accomplished.

Poll Details: 479 elementary school principals were surveyed by the National
Association of Elementary School Principals.

Availability: Published in *NSTA Reports*, April/May, 1990, p. 8.

MEDICAL STUDENT MISTREATMENT

Description: Presents the results of a survey concerning medical student perceptions of mistreatment and professional misconduct in medical school training.

Results: The survey indicates that medical students perceive mistreatment to be pervasive and professional misconduct quite common.

Poll Extracts:

EFFECTS OF STUDENT MISTREATMENT:

Did mistreatment interfere with your emotional health?...Yes...67%

Did mistreatment affect your family life?.................Yes...40%

Did mistreatment affect your physical health?...........Yes...40%

Did you avoid assignments because of mistreatment?.......Yes...33%

Because of mistreatment, did you seriously consider dropping out of medical school?........................Yes...37%

Because of mistreatment, are you more cynical about academic life and the medical profession?...............Yes...77%

Also in Source: 85% of the respondents reported verbal abuse; 24% reported being theatened with physical harm; 47% perceived they had been treated unfairly; 55% of the female respondents reported sexual harassment; 50% of those who gave their race as nonwhite or Hispanic reported experiencing racial or ethnic slurs; 85% experienced sleep deprivation; 41% reported observing residents or interns cover up mistreatment of patients.

Poll Details: Questionnaires were returned by 75 of the 93 students surveyed, a response rate of 81%. 84% of the respondents were white. The sex distribution was 59% male and 41% female. The mean age of the sample was approximately 26 years.

Availability: Published in *JAMA*, January 26, 1990, (volume 263, number 4), p. 533-537.

OBSTACLES TO EFFECTIVE TEACHING

Description: Presents the results of a survey concerning the main obstacles
that get in the way of effective teaching. Respondents were also asked
what were the key things teachers needed to help them do their jobs.

Results: 40% of the respondents said insufficient funds for supplies and
materials was the major barrier in the way of effective teaching.

Poll Extracts:

WHAT ARE THE MAJOR BARRIERS IN THE WAY OF EFFECTIVE TEACHING?

Discipline problems in your classroom?......................10%

Too many children in your classes?.........................33%

Non-teaching duties such as lunchroom
duty, study halls, etc....................................20%

Administrative bureaucracy.................................29%

Not having enough time to
prepare for classes.......................................39%

Not being allowed to design your
own courses and pick your own curriculum..................11%

Lack of parental involvement...............................25%

Insufficient funds for supplies and materials.............40%

Lack of technology equipment...............................28%

Lack of technology training................................22%

Standardized tests for students............................19%

Also in Source: What would help a great deal toward doing their job? 86% of
the respondents said having their own computer, 84% said meeting with other
teachers and colleagues, 83% said access to a copying machine, 79% said
attending professional conferences, 73% said more support staff to help
with clerical duties, 70% said release time, 66% said a budget for
supplies, 52% said their own phone, 51% said a television and VCR in their
classroom, 44% said their own office, and 19% said access to a fax machine.

Poll Details: The results are taken from a Gallup Organization survey of 231
semifinalists in the Thanks to Teachers competition. The poll was
conducted for the National Education Association's National Foundation for
the Improvement of Education and was sponsored by Apple Computer.

Availability: Published in *NEA Today*, December, 1990 (volume 9, number 4),
p. 24.

ON-THE-JOB EDUCATION

Description: Presents the results of a survey concerning the type and amount of basic on-site education they will need to provide their employees.

Results: Over 90% of the nation's largest companies will be providing basic educational skills to their employees over the next three years.

Poll Extracts:

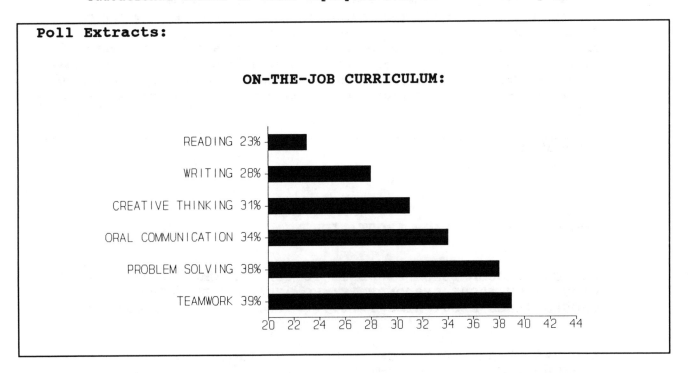

ON-THE-JOB CURRICULUM:

READING 23%
WRITING 28%
CREATIVE THINKING 31%
ORAL COMMUNICATION 34%
PROBLEM SOLVING 38%
TEAMWORK 39%

Also in Source: Currently, 22% of 2000 Fortune 500 and large private companies surveyed teach employees reading, 41% teach writing, and 31% offer training in computation.

Poll Details: The survey was conducted by the American Society for Training and Development.

Availability: Published in *The Wall Street Journal*, March 1, 1990, p. B1.

OPINIONS ON PUBLIC SCHOOLS

Description: Presents some of the results from the eighth annual State of Michigan survey of public opinion on education.

Results: Respondents rated Michigan public schools as deserving: an "A" or "B" grade -- 51%; a "C" grade -- 30%; a "D" or Failing grade -- 6%; and 13% didn't know. 26% of the respondents said their schools have improved. Respondents thought that: the mandatory attendance age should be raised from 16 to 18 -- 72%; there should be year-round schools with varying vacation schedules -- 51%; drivers licenses should be withheld or taken away from dropouts -- 65%; parents should be able to choose the school their children attend without consideration of where the family resides -- 60%.

Poll Extracts:

SCHOOLS SHOULD TEACH ABOUT AIDS .... 90% Yes

SCHOOLS SHOULD TEACH STUDENTS TO USE CONDOMS TO PREVENT AIDS -- OF THOSE RESPONDENTS WHO AGREED THAT SCHOOLS SHOULD TEACH ABOUT AIDS .... 88% Yes

APPROVE OF SEX EDUCATION IN SCHOOLS, INCLUDING INSTRUCTION ON BIRTH CONTROL .... 86% Yes

---

Also in Source: The percentage of respondents who thought that the differences in the financial conditions among school districts is a serious problem.

Poll Details: The Michigan State Department of Education conducted this random telephone survey of 650 adults. The survey was taken from June 18-21, 1990. The margin of error is 4%.

Availability: Published in the *Detroit Free Press*, September 12, 1990, p. 1B, 2B.

PARENTS' PRIORITIES

Description: Presents the results of a survey of parents and corporation officials concerning school selection criteria for families relocating in specific areas.

Results: Expenditures related to pupil instruction ranks as the most important selection criterion.

Poll Extracts:

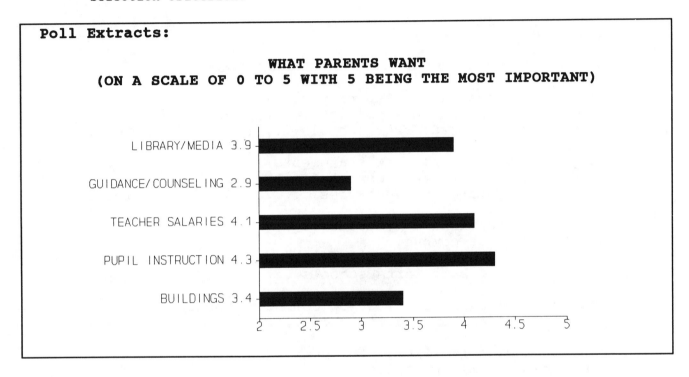

WHAT PARENTS WANT
(ON A SCALE OF 0 TO 5 WITH 5 BEING THE MOST IMPORTANT)

Also in Source: The education level of the community ranks high as does student test scores as an indication of academic rigor. Parents avoid very large or very small school systems. Less than 1% prefer very small systems and only 1.6% look for very large systems.

Poll Details: SchoolMatch, a data-based information and counseling service in Columbus, Ohio, surveyed parents and corporation officials involved in personnel relocation.

Availability: Published in *The American School Board Journal*, May, 1990, (volume 177, number 5) p. 32, 33.

QUALITY OF LIFE ON CAMPUS

Description: Presents the results of a survey of university presidents
concerning the quality of life on college campuses in the United States.

Results: More than half of the presidents surveyed said they were now more
concerned about the quality of campus life than they were a few years ago.

Poll Extracts:

QUALITY OF LIFE ISSUES ON CAMPUS:

Is alcohol abuse a problem on your campus?
        Large universities.....................Yes...80%
        Liberal arts schools..................Yes...75%

Do you favor devising new statements
stressing civility and respect for others?
        Large universities....................Yes...86%

Are racial tensions a moderate to major
problem on your campus?
        Research institutions.................Yes...68%
        Liberal arts schools..................Yes...28%

Are you increasing services to commuter students?
        All presidents........................Yes...45%

Are inadequate facilities for campus gatherings
a moderate to major problem?
        All presidents........................Yes...55%

Are thefts a moderate to major problem
on your campus?
        All presidents........................Yes...50%

Also in Source: A discussion of the issues and possible causes and solutions
are included in the article.

Poll Details: The American Council on Education conducted the survey in
conjunction with a year-long study by the Carnegie Foundation for the
Advancement of Teaching. 380 college presidents responded representing all
types of institutions.

Availability: Published in *The Chronicle of Higher Education,* May 2, 1990,
p. A1, A32.

QUALITY OF PUBLIC EDUCATION

Description: Presents the results of a poll which questioned respondents about the quality of public education in America.

Results: 91% of all respondents, and 96% of respondents who were parents with children in public schools, were "somewhat or very concerned" about the quality of their local public schools. Respondents rated public schools with an "A" or "B" grade as follows: the national school system -- 30%; the statewide school system -- 41%; and the local school system -- 53%. Respondents thought public schools are doing a fair or poor job of: preparing students to go directly to a job -- 58%; and to college -- 48%.

Poll Extracts:

THE QUALITY OF PUBLIC EDUCATION IN THE PAST FEW YEARS HAS:

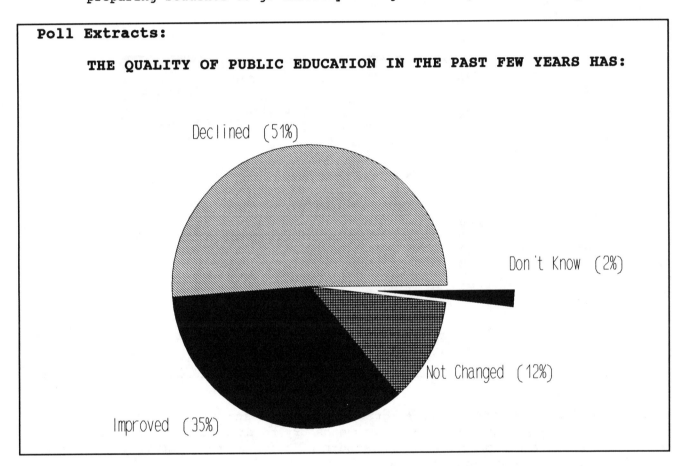

Also in Source: The percentage of respondents who thought education was the key to the economic success of Europe and Asia.

Poll Details: The Roper Organization conducted this nationwide survey for the Center for Workforce Preparation and Quality Education (an affiliate of the U.S. Chamber of Commerce). 1,003 adults were interviewed between August 6-12, 1990.

Availability: Published in the *Dayton Daily News*, September 5, 1990, p. 6-A.

RESPECT FOR STANDARDIZED TESTS

Description: Presents the results of a survey concerning students' attitudes towards standardized tests.

Results: Three-fourths of the second-grade respondents but only 5% of the 11th-grade respondents agree "test scores show how intelligent you are."

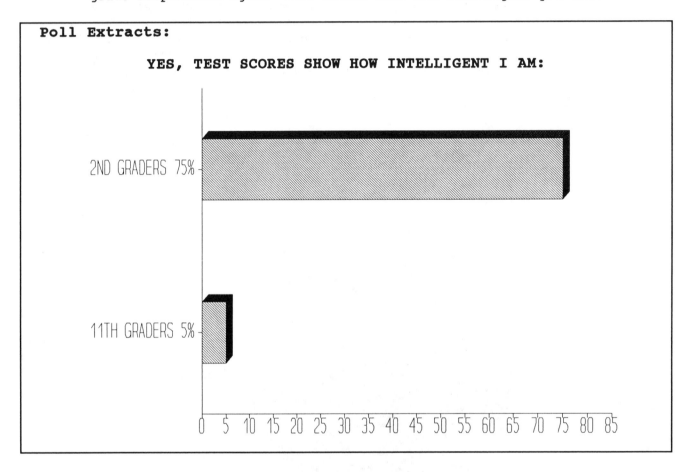

Poll Extracts:

YES, TEST SCORES SHOW HOW INTELLIGENT I AM:

Also in Source: 95% of second-grade respondents and 40% of 11th-grade respondents agree that "most students try to do their best on tests." Low achievers are more likely than their high-achieving counterparts to give up and fill in answers at random.

Poll Details: Scott Paris of the University of Michigan surveyed 900 Michigan, Arizona, California, and Florida students, grades 2 and 11.

Availability: Published in *USA Today*, November 20, 1990, 1D.

SAFETY IN THE SCHOOLS

Description: Presents the results of a survey concerning safety and discipline
in the Cincinnati Public Schools.

Results: Less than half of the children in grades seven through 12 feel safe in
neighborhood schools.

Poll Extracts:

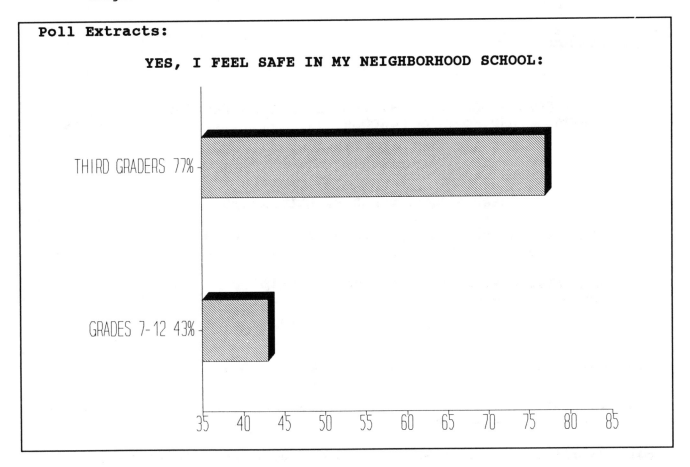

YES, I FEEL SAFE IN MY NEIGHBORHOOD SCHOOL:

THIRD GRADERS 77%

GRADES 7-12 43%

35 40 45 50 55 60 65 70 75 80 85

Also in Source: Of those respondents in alternative programs, 49% feel safe
in school. 47% of the respondents from alternative schools said there
was good discipline at their school. 85% of third graders in alternative
schools feel safe. In grades four through six, 37% said students at their
schools were well-behaved.

Poll Details: The Cincinnati Public School District surveyed more than 27,000
students in grades three through 12, together with parents snd teachers in
neighborhood and alternative schools.

Availability: Published in *The Cincinnati Enquirer*, December 8, 1990, p. C2.

SCHOOLS AND TAXES

Description: This CBS News poll queried respondents about the financing of education.

Results: Respondents were willing to pay more taxes for better schools. Respondents also felt that President George Bush is all talk and no action as the "education president."

Poll Extracts:

RESPONDENTS BELIEVE THAT THE FEDERAL GOVERNMENT SHOULD SPEND MORE ON SCHOOLS .... 69% -- Yes

RESPONDENTS WOULD BE WILLING TO:

Pay $100 a year more in taxes if it went to their local schools .... 71% -- Yes

Pay $100 a year more in taxes to help schools anywhere .... 49% -- Yes

---

Also in Source: The percentage of respondents who felt that Japanese schools are doing a better job at educating children.

Poll Details: This CBS News poll of 1,107 adults was conducted during the Spring of 1990. The key findings were presented in a television special on September 6, 1990, called *"America's Toughest Assignment: Solving the Education Crisis."*

Availability: Published in *USA Today,* September 6, 1990, p. 1D.

STUDENT ATTITUDES

Description: Presents the results of a survey concerning the academic
interests, social attitudes and goals of university and college students.

Results: The survey indicates that an increasing number of college freshman are
concerned about improving the environment and are willing to work for that
and a variety of other social changes.

Poll Extracts:

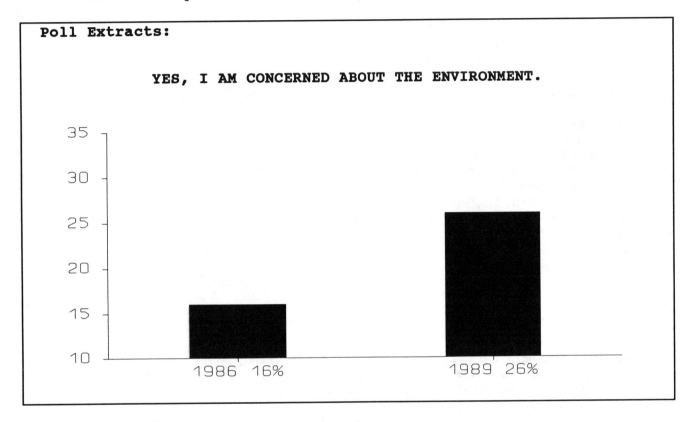

YES, I AM CONCERNED ABOUT THE ENVIRONMENT.

Also in Source: The survey included questions concerning student beer, wine,
and liquor consumption, student depression, the need for remedial work,
cultural interests, and future educational plans.

Poll Details: The survey was conducted jointly during the fall of 1989 by the
Higher Education Research Institute at the University of California at Los
Angeles and by the American Council on Education. The survey, which is in
its 24th year, questioned more than 200,000 students at 403 colleges and
universities.

Availability: Published in *The Chronicle of Higher Education*, January 24,
1990, A31-32.

STUDENTS' KNOWLEDGE OF HISTORY

Description: Presents the results of a survey concerning the level of United
    States history and civics knowledge among students.

Results: Depending of the particular idea or subject, the level of knowledge
    varies widely.

Poll Extracts:

WHAT DO STUDENTS KNOW?

Idea or subject	Percentage correct
Western trail	94.9
Rights of slaves	83.9
First atomic bomb	79.8
"Give me liberty or give me death"	53.4
Teddy Roosevelt	42.8
Area acquired in Mexican War	32.0
Intent of Emancipation Proclamation	28.0
Leaders of women's movement	25.4
Reconstruction	20.3

Also in Source: During the 1988 presidential race, when the survey was
    taken, less than 40% of seniors knew that the candidates are chosen at
    national conventions. Almost all 12th-graders knew that it is illegal not
    to pay taxes but less than two-thirds knew it is legal to organize a recall
    election, take part in a boycott or hunger strike or impeach legislators.

Poll Details: The results are based on scores from multiple-choice tests of
    16,000 12th-graders in about 1,000 public and private schools. The surveys
    are conducted by the United States Department of Education.

Availability: Published in the *Los Angeles Times*, April 3, 1990, p. A18.

STUDENTS' VIEWS

Description: Presents the results of a survey of high school juniors and seniors concerning a wide range of topics.

Results: 80% of the students want television or video programs in their classrooms, even if they include commercials.

Poll Extracts:

STUDENTS ADDRESS ISSUES OF THE DAY:

Do you want television and video programs
in your classroom, even if they include
commercials?..Yes...80%

Are you concerned about eating a proper diet,
including eating less fat?............................Yes...69%

Would you pay more for a book if it were
printed on recycled paper to conserve trees?.........Yes...65%

Do you favor a ban on cigarette advertising?.........Yes...61%

Do you favor labels to caution consumers when
video-cassettes and recordings contain
"objectionable material," such as profanity?.........Yes...57%

Also in Source: There was an even split among respondents on whether beer and tobacco companies should be allowed to sponsor sports events or rock concerts.

Poll Details: The survey of 5,000 "high achiever" juniors and seniors was conducted by *Who's Who Among American High School Students*.

Availability: Published in *The Wall Street Journal*, October 25, 1990, p. B1.

TEACHERS' MORALE LOW

Description: Some of the results from a survey on teachers' attitudes are presented.

Results: Teachers are increasingly unhappy with their lack of authority, their working conditions, and with the school reform movement.

Poll Extracts:

TEACHERS SAID:

They are unhappy with the amount of control
they have over their professional lives 45%

They are only slightly or not at all
involved in setting policies for student
promotion and retention .... About 70%

Their classes are too large .... Nearly 40%

They don't have enough time to prepare
their lessons with only one hour or
less set aside for class preparation 60%

They graded school reform with a grade of
"B" or "A" 18%

They graded school reform with a failing grade .. 28%

Also in Source: Inconsistencies that exist within the survey.

Poll Details: This survey by the Carnegie Foundation for the Advancement of Teaching involved 21,000 elementary and secondary public school teachers.

Availability: Published in the *Chicago Tribune*, September 2, 1990 (section 1), p. 22.

WHAT STUDENTS LIKE

Description: Presents the results of a survey concerning students' attitudes toward school and various educational issues.

Results: Almost 70% of fourth and sixth grade students surveyed like their teachers a lot.

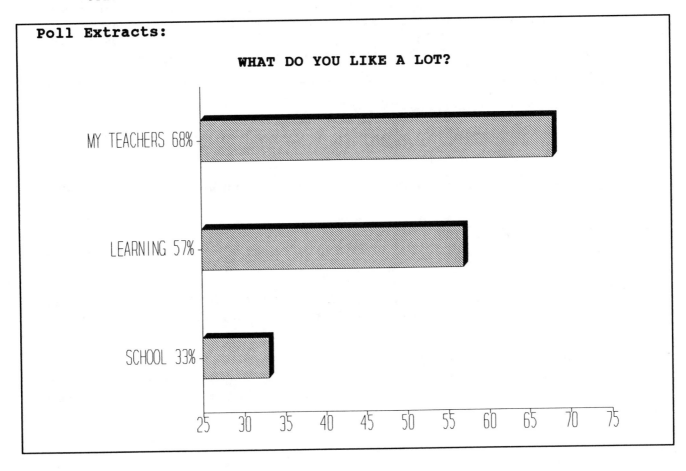

Poll Extracts:

WHAT DO YOU LIKE A LOT?

Also in Source: 39% of the students surveyed call math their favorite subject, with science second at 19%, and reading third at 13%. 73% of the fourth graders see a need for drug and alcohol education, up from 57% in 1985. 29% of the students think disabled kids should be "mainstreamed" - kept in regular classes. That figure is up from 23% in 1985.

Poll Details: The results are taken from a school news publication, *Weekly Reader*. 100,000 fourth and sixth graders were surveyed.

Availability: Published in *USA Today*, November 23, 1990, p. 1D.

WHAT'S IMPORTANT IN COLLEGE

Description: College students in the U.S. and Japan were questioned about their student lifestyles.

Results: The amount of time that students spend on studying varies greatly from Japan to the United States. Students who said they spend two hours or less per day on studying: Japanese students -- Yes -- 52.5%, American students -- Yes -- 26%. Students who said they do not study at all: Japanese students -- Yes -- 35.7%, American students -- Yes -- 0.5%. 30% of the American students said they study seven hours a day or longer.

Poll Extracts:

WHAT'S IMPORTANT IN YOUR COLLEGIATE LIFE?

Keeping company with friends .... Japanese students -- 48% -- Yes

Lectures, seminars, and
experiments .... American students -- About 50% -- Yes

Club Activities .... Japanese students -- 10% -- Yes
.... American students -- 6.3% -- Yes

The company of friends of
the opposite sex .... Japanese students -- 11% -- Yes
.... American students -- 8% -- Yes

Also in Source: The amount of time that Japanese and American students say they spend in the classroom or lab. "Employment opportunities for young Japanese are based primarily on what university they attended, while in the United States opportunities are based primarily on a student's performance in college."

Poll Details: This survey was conducted between October and December 1989, by Gakusei Engo-kai, a Tokyo-based publisher of a job-placement information magazine. 1,200 students from 31 colleges in Japan and 1,000 students at 12 colleges in the U.S. were interviewed for the survey.

Availability: Published in the *Dayton Daily News*, July 25, 1990, p. 1-D.

DISPOSABLE DIAPERS

Description: Presents the results of a survey concerning the taxing or banning of disposable diapers.

Results: Over 40% of the respondents favor a ban on disposable diapers while 47% are opposed to the ban.

Poll Extracts:

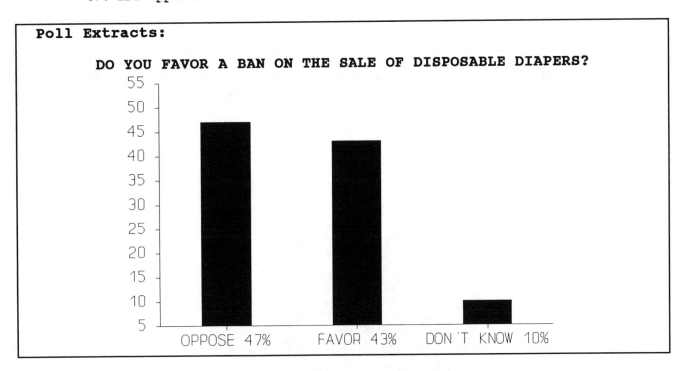

DO YOU FAVOR A BAN ON THE SALE OF DISPOSABLE DIAPERS?

OPPOSE 47%   FAVOR 43%   DON'T KNOW 10%

Also in Source: Overall, 52% of the respondents are opposed to a special tax on disposable diapers while 38% are in favor. Of people with annual household incomes of $75,000 or more, 50% favor a special tax while 43% do not. Only 39% of those earning less than $20,000 annually back a tax while 50% do not. Of those respondents age 18 to 34, 50% oppose a tax and 42% support the idea. Those age 35 to 54 represented the largest opposition group in terms of age, with 57% against a tax and 38% in favor. More men than women favor the tax concept, 45% to 34%.

Poll Details: This Gallup survey was conducted for *Advertising Age*. The sample of 1,029 was contacted by telephone on June 6, 1990.

Availability: Published in *Advertising Age*, June 11, 1990, (volume 61, number 24) p. 3, 57.

DRILLING FOR OIL

Description: This poll asked respondents if they are concerned that the crisis
in the Persian Gulf will result in an oil shortage, and if they would
support offshore drilling to decrease dependence on Arab oil supplies.

Results: Nearly two-thirds of the respondents were "concerned" that the Middle
East crisis could lead to a gasoline shortage. Respondents opposed
drilling for oil off of the California coastline.

Poll Extracts: DO YOU FAVOR DRILLING TO SUPPORT LESS DEPENDENCE
ON ARAB OIL SUPPLIES, OR OPPOSE DRILLING IN ORDER TO PROTECT
THE SCENIC BEAUTY OF CALIFORNIA, AND THE ENVIRONMENT?

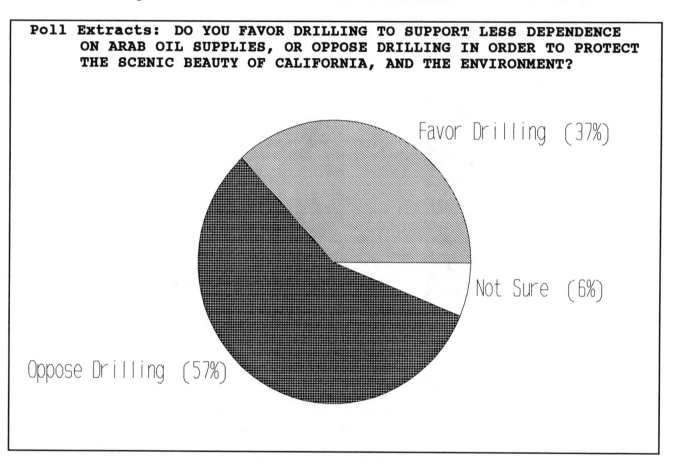

Also in Source: Questions dealing with the Middle East crisis in Kuwait.

Poll Details: This *Los Angeles Times* poll was conducted by telephone during
August 17-22, 1990. 1,586 registered voters in California were polled with
the margin of error being 3%.

Availability: Published in the *Los Angeles Times*, August 26, 1990, p. A7.

THE ENVIRONMENTALLY ACTIVE

Description: This national study queried respondents about their environmental attitudes and behavior.

Results: "The survey found almost 80% of Americans say more should be done to improve the environment, but less than 25% say they are actually doing something about it. Women say they are generally more environmentally aware than men, and people with higher incomes say they tend to be more involved than those who earn less."

Poll Extracts:

FIVE DISTINCT CATEGORIES OF AMERICANS WERE IDENTIFIED:

1. **True-blue greens** -- typically involved in pro-environmental practices

2. **Greenback greens** -- willing to spend up to 22% more money on environmentally safe products

3. **Sprouts** -- concerned, but not actively committed

4. **Grousers** -- often feel that since others aren't doing much, why should they

5. **Basic browns** -- indifferent, sometimes to the point of opposition

---

Also in Source: Generalizations about the income, sex, and education of the five categories of Americans.

Poll Details: 1,413 adults were interviewed in February-March, 1990 by the Roper Organization.

Availability: Originally published in *The Baltimore Sun*. The information provided is based on an article printed in *The Cincinnati Enquirer*, August 5, 1990, p. A-14.

INCREASED SPENDING ON THE ENVIRONMENT

Description: Presents the answers to a question from a survey which asked
Americans if more money should be spent on improving and protecting the
environment.

Results: Nearly 60% of the respondents felt that federal spending on the
environment should be increased.

Poll Extracts:

FEDERAL SPENDING ON THE ENVIRONMENT SHOULD BE:

INCREASED - 57%

NO OPINION - 4%

DECREASED - 4%

KEPT THE SAME - 35%

Also in Source: Most of the questions included in this survey deal with the
possibility of increased federal monies because of the apparent end of the
cold war. Approximately half of the respondents felt that federal spending
on military and defense should not be changed. Most Americans believe that
any money saved should be shifted to solving such domestic problems as drug
abuse and homelessness.

Poll Details: This *New York Times*/CBS News Poll was based on telephone
interviews conducted January 13 through January 15, 1990 with 1,557 adults
around the United States. Margin of error is plus or minus 3%.

Availability: Published in *The New York Times*, January 25, 1990, p. B9.

INDUSTRY AND THE ENVIRONMENT

Description: This study attempted to determine where leaders in a wide variety of professions stand on the environment as a policy issue.

Results: About 70% of American decision makers are skeptical of private industry acting voluntarily to protect the environment.

Poll Extracts:

SHOULD INDUSTRY BE HELD LIABLE FOR
ENVIRONMENTAL DAMAGE CAUSED BY THEIR
ACTIONS, AND THE CLEANUP? .... 80% Yes

DO YOU THINK THE PUBLIC WOULD BE
WILLING TO PAY MORE FOR ENVIRONMENTALLY
SAFE PRODUCTS? .... 77.7% Yes

DO YOU THINK THE FEDERAL GOVERNMENT
SHOULD TAKE THE LEAD OVER STATES IN
SETTING ENVIRONMENTAL STANDARDS? .... 85% Yes

DO YOU SEE THE PUBLIC'S AWARENESS OF
ENVIRONMENTAL ISSUES GROWING "VERY
RAPIDLY" IN THE NEXT FEW YEARS? .... 90% Yes

Poll Details: This information is from a study commissioned in 1989 by the Ford Motor Co.; some 7,000 leaders in business, education, the media, government, and environmental advocacy took part.

Availability: Published in *The Atlanta Journal and Constitution*, March 10, 1990, p. F-2.

OIL SPILL DISASTERS

Description: Respondents were queried about oil spill disasters; who should pay the cleanup costs, should there be stricter regulations on oil tankers, and should Texas start an oil-barrel tax on tankers to create an emergency response fund.

Results: 91% of the respondents thought that industry rather than government should pay for the cleanup of an oil spill. 79% of the respondents favored the government enforcing stricter regulations on oil tankers, even if it would increase the cost of oil for consumers.

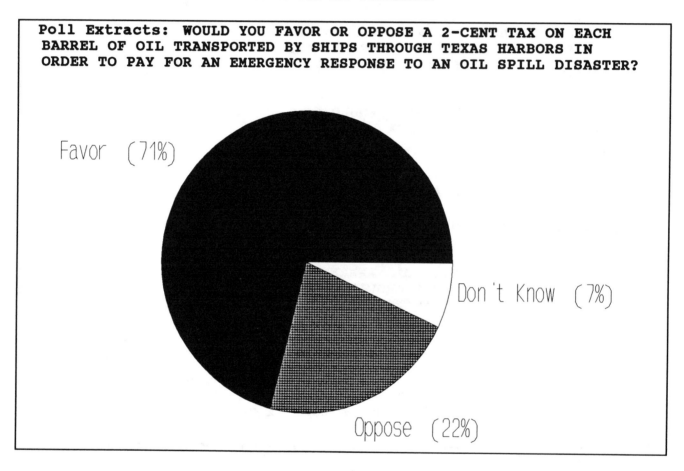

Poll Extracts: WOULD YOU FAVOR OR OPPOSE A 2-CENT TAX ON EACH BARREL OF OIL TRANSPORTED BY SHIPS THROUGH TEXAS HARBORS IN ORDER TO PAY FOR AN EMERGENCY RESPONSE TO AN OIL SPILL DISASTER?

Favor (71%)

Don't Know (7%)

Oppose (22%)

Also in Source: The plan to levy one or two cents on each barrel of oil shipped in or out of Texas ports is expected to raise between $8 and $16 million annually. The current taxpayer-supported Texas Spill Response Fund is capped at $5 million.

Poll Details: This telephone poll of 1,021 adult Texans was conducted by the Public Policy Resources Laboratory at Texas A&M University for Harte-Hanks Communications Inc. The survey was taken between August 4, 1990 and August 19, 1990, after two major oil spills this summer in waters off Texas.

Availability: Published in *The Dallas Morning News*, August 27, 1990, p. 1A, 7A.

POLLUTION ISSUES

Description: Presents the results of a survey concerning the seriousness of environmental pollution and possible solutions and remedies.

Results: Over two-thirds of the respondents feel that pollution has increased in the last ten years. Only 13% feel that pollution has decreased in that time period.

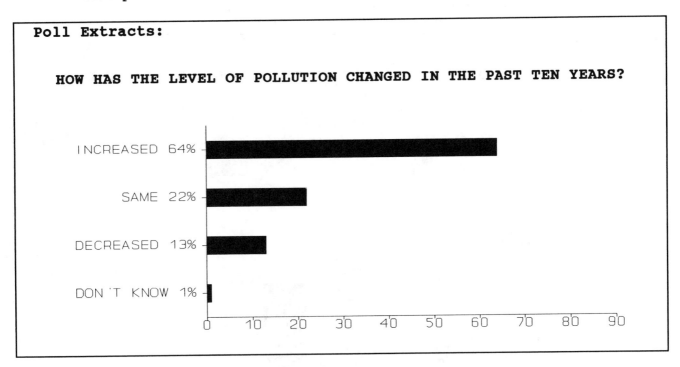

Poll Extracts:

HOW HAS THE LEVEL OF POLLUTION CHANGED IN THE PAST TEN YEARS?

Also in Source: Over three-fourths of the respondents said their communities did not require residents to separate and recycle household glass, cans, and paper refuse. The same percentage felt that anti-pollution laws are too weak. Only one-third of the respondents expect pollution to decrease during the next three years. Toxic waste disposal is the greatest priority with 65% saying it required "urgent government action no matter what the cost." 88% favored restrictions on product packaging to reduce trash. 84% favored a ban on foam plastic containers. 71% support a ban on disposable diapers.

Poll Details: The poll was conducted by Media General-Associated Press. The figures are based on a telephone survey of 1,143 adults conducted on May 11-20, 1990. The margin of error is plus or minus 3%.

Availability: Published in *The Atlanta Constitution*, June 12, 1990, p. F-4.

SACRIFICE FOR THE ENVIRONMENT

Description: Presents the results of a survey concerning the willingness of
    Americans to sacrifice in order to improve the environment.

Results: 80% of the respondents believe it is more important to protect the
    environment than to keep prices down. Only 13% believe keeping prices down
    is more important. In 1981, 51% believed protecting the environment was
    more important compared to 38% for keeping prices down.

Poll Extracts:

WHAT'S MORE IMPORTANT: THE ENVIRONMENT OR KEEPING PRICES DOWN?

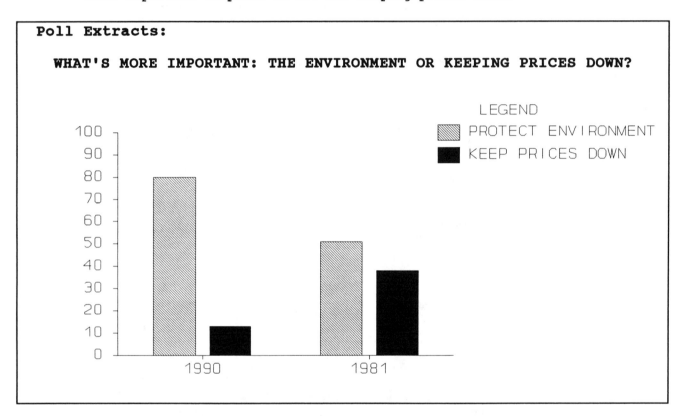

Also in Source: 93% of the repondents favor requiring people to separate
    garbage and solid waste for recycling. 84% favor banning foam containers.
    74% favor banning disposable diapers. 57% favor enforcing stricter air
    quality regulations increasing utility bills $10.00 a month. 33% favor
    closing pollution-producing factories resulting in a loss of jobs. 80%
    favor annual auto air pollution emission tests and repairs. 48% favor a 20
    cent per gallon increase in the price of gasoline for cleaner fuels.

Poll Details: *The Wall Street Journal*/NBC News Poll was based on nationwide
    interviews by telephone of 1,001 registered voters conducted on April 11,
    12, 14, and 16, 1990 by the polling organizations of Peter Hart and Robert
    Teeter. Margin of error is plus or minus 3.2%.

Availability: Published in *The Wall Street Journal*, April 20, 1990, p. A1,
    A12.

THE STATE OF THE ENVIRONMENT

Description: Presents the results of a survey concerning the progress or lack of progress made towards improving the environment.

Results: Three-fourths of the respondents believe that environmental conditions have worsened over the last decade. 55% feel that during the next ten years, global environmental conditions will improve or at least stay the same.

Poll Extracts:

EDUCATION AND THE ENVIRONMENT:

Have environmental conditions worsened
over the last decade?.........................Yes.........75%

Will environmental conditions improve
or stay the same during the next ten years?..Yes.........55%

Is corporate America doing enough to
support environmental education in schools?..No..........80%

Has your school increased support for
environmental education?......................Yes...about 50%

Will student interest in environmental
subjects increase?............................Yes.........90%

Also in Source: The article includes a discussion concerning education's role in improving the environment.

Poll Details: The survey was sponsored by the Monsanto Company in cooperation with the National Science Teachers Association. The study consisted of 500 "intercept" interviews in the registration and publications areas on the opening day, April 5, 1990, of the association's meeting in Atlanta, Georgia.

Availability: Published in *NSTA Reports*, April/May, 1990, p. 8.

AIDING SUICIDE

Description: Presents the results of a survey concerning the general issue of the right to die and specifically the role of Michigan doctor Jack Kevorkian in aiding the death of a woman with Alzheimer's disease.

Results: Almost half of the respondents said that Dr. Kevorkian should face criminal charges or lose his medical license.

Poll Extracts:

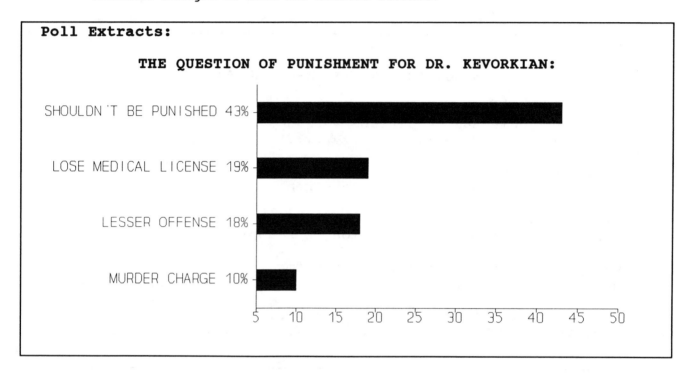

THE QUESTION OF PUNISHMENT FOR DR. KEVORKIAN:

SHOULDN'T BE PUNISHED 43%

LOSE MEDICAL LICENSE 19%

LESSER OFFENSE 18%

MURDER CHARGE 10%

Also in Source: 52% of those over 55 think a person should be allowed to commit suicide compared with 74% of those younger than 55. 68% say there are circumstances in which a person with a terminal illness should be allowed to commit suicide; 26% disagree; 6% don't know. 65% say medical facilities should be available for the terminally ill to end their lives; 25% disagree; 10% don't know.

Poll Details: The *USA Today* poll was conducted by Gordon S. Black Corporation. 724 people were surveyed. Margin of error was 3.5%.

Availability: Published in *USA Today*, June 8-10, 1990, p. 1A.

ANIMAL RIGHTS

Description: Presents the results of a survey concerning the various questions surounding the issue of animal rights.

Results: 80% of the respondents agreed that animals have rights that should limit how humans use them.

Poll Extracts:

ARE THERE LIMITS TO HOW HUMANS SHOULD USE ANIMALS?

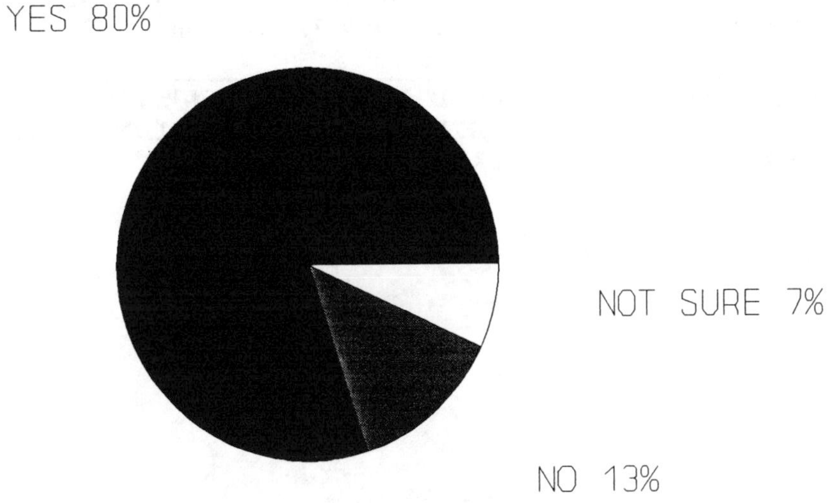

YES 80%

NOT SURE 7%

NO 13%

Also in Source: 63% said that killing animals to make fur coats should be prohibited by law and 58% agreed that using animals for cosmetics research should be illegal. 85% said it's acceptable to kill animals for food, 66% to capture and exhibit them in zoos, 63% to train them to perform for humans, and 58% to use them for medical research. 78% of the respondents were in favor of using animals for AIDS research while 15% were opposed to the idea.

Poll Details: The results are taken from a national opinion poll commissioned by *Parents* magazine.

Availability: Published in *Parents*, May, 1990 (volume 65, number 5), p. 33.

CASINO GAMBLING

Description: This poll asked Ohio registered voters, "Should the Ohio
Constitution be amended to authorize the establishment of an entertainment-
hotel resort in which games of chance for profit are conducted, in the city
of Lorain, Ohio? Subject to approval by a majority of voters of Lorain, it
would be part of a pilot project to determine the impact of such a facility
on economic development and travel and tourism in Ohio."

Results: The percentage of voters supporting the amendment to allow legalized
casino gambling has increased from 41% in May 1990 to 47% in this poll.
The latest poll found that the amendment was supported by Catholics --60%,
Democrats --53%, non-whites --53%, and men --50%.

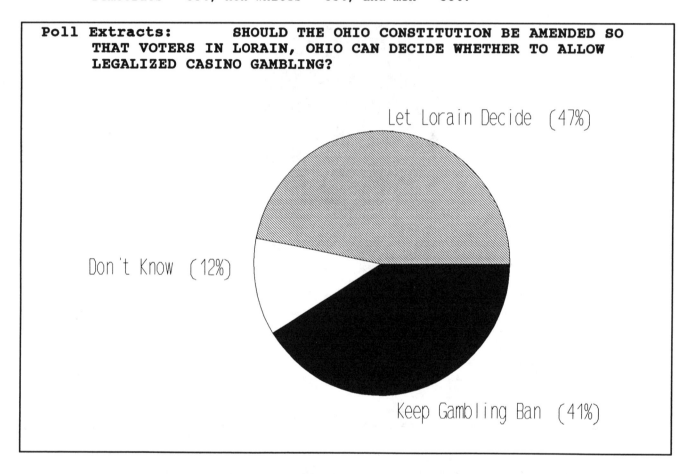

Poll Extracts: **SHOULD THE OHIO CONSTITUTION BE AMENDED SO
THAT VOTERS IN LORAIN, OHIO CAN DECIDE WHETHER TO ALLOW
LEGALIZED CASINO GAMBLING?**

Let Lorain Decide (47%)

Don't Know (12%)

Keep Gambling Ban (41%)

Also in Source: Should casino gambling be allowed in Lorain, Ohio, a Lorain
developer proposes to build a $400 million hotel-entertainment complex. A
demographic breakdown of the respondents into various categories.

Poll Details: The results are based on responses from 1,581 registered Ohio
voters who responded from August 30 - September 6, 1990 to a *Columbus
Dispatch* poll. The response rate in the poll was 21%, with the margin of
error being 2.2%.

Availability: Published in *The Columbus Dispatch*, September 14, 1990,
p. 1A, 9C.

CHEATING AT COLLEGE

Description: Presents the results of a survey concerning the amount of
cheating taking place at the college level.

Results: The study found that a high percentage of students cheat on their
written assignments.

Poll Extracts:

PLAGIARISM ON CAMPUS:

Have you engaged in different types of plagiarism?..Yes...91.2%

Have you failed to cite a reference for
paraphrased or quoted material?......................Yes...74.2%

Have you submited assignments completed by
others as your own?..................................Yes...44.2%

Have you included purposefully misleading
references to hide plagiarism?......................Yes...39.9%

Also in Source: A general discussion of this problem is included in the
article.

Poll Details: The survey was conducted by Jerold L. Hale, Delores Young and
Paul Mongeau of Miami University in Oxford, Ohio. 284 Miami University
students were contacted.

Availability: Published in *The Columbus Dispatch*, March 22, 1990, p. 5E.

CORPORATE FRAUD

Description: Presents the results of a survey concerning attitudes toward fraud in the corporate world.

Results: A significant percentage of the respondents would commit fraud.

Poll Extracts:

HOW COMMON IS FRAUD?

Would you commit fraud?...........................Yes....87%

Would you be willing to overstate assets?.........Yes...50+%

Would you establish insufficient return
reserves for defective products?...................Yes....48%

Would you pad a government contract?...............Yes....38%

Also in Source: A survey of 443 industrial salespeople found highly supervised employees at bureaucratic firms more likely to act ethically than those at less structured , less supervised firms. There was no correlation with age or gender but ethical behavior increased with experience.

Poll Details: The National Association of Accountants was surveyed.

Availability: Published in *The Wall Street Journal*, March 1, 1990, p. A1.

FETAL TISSUE RESEARCH

Description: This reader's survey queried respondents about the utilization of fetal tissue from aborted fetuses in medical research.

Results: 61% of the respondents thought that it was wrong to use tissue taken from aborted fetuses for medical research. 58% of the respondents thought that, "some women who are ambivalent about having an abortion would decide to do so if they knew that they could donate the fetal tissue." 73% of the respondents thought that "publicizing the benefits of fetal tissue would lead to a "black market," in which women and/or doctors are paid for aborted fetuses."

Poll Extracts: **"WOULD IT BE WRONG FOR A WOMAN TO BECOME PREGNANT IN ORDER TO DONATE THE TISSUE TO SAVE THE LIFE OF A CLOSE RELATIVE WHO HAD NO OTHER HOPE?"**

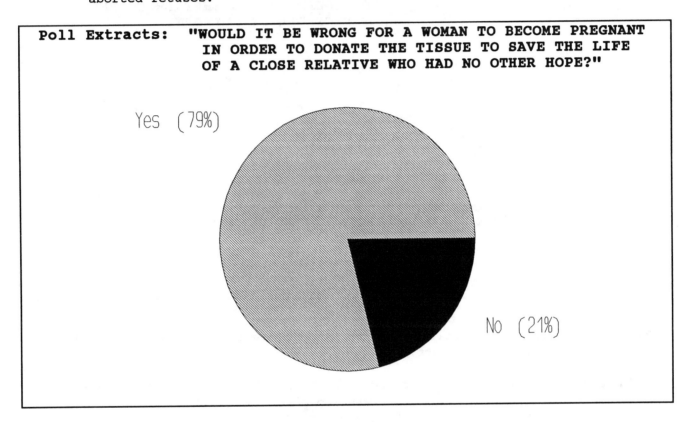

Yes (79%)

No (21%)

Poll Details: This *Redbook* reader's survey appeared in the September 1990 issue. Nearly 1,300 readers responded.

Availability: Published in *Redbook*, December 1990 (volume 176, number 2), p. 170.

LIFE AND DEATH DECISIONS

Description: The survey asked who should make the decision to end artificial
life support.

Results: Almost 90% said the family should decide whether to end artificial
life support when an individual is in a coma without hope of recovery and
has left no instructions on personal wishes.

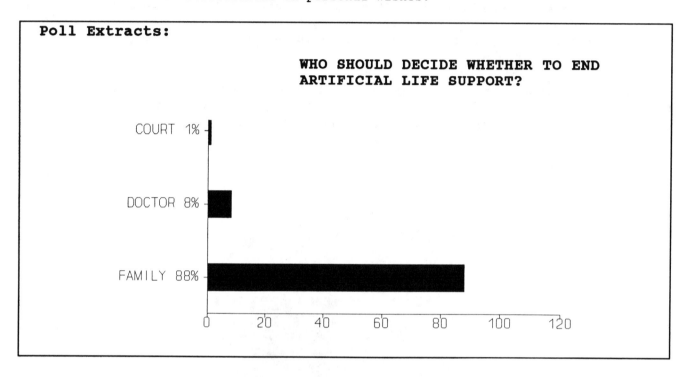

Poll Extracts:

WHO SHOULD DECIDE WHETHER TO END
ARTIFICIAL LIFE SUPPORT?

Also in Source: The article includes several questions concerning issues
facing the Supreme Court.

Poll Details: The poll was conducted by Penn & Schoen Associates for *National
Law Journal*/Lexis. 805 Americans above the age of 18 were interviewed on
January 27 and 28, 1990. Margin of error was 3.4%

Availability: Published in *The National Law Journal*, February 26, 1990, p. 1,
36-37.

PERCEPTIONS IN BUSINESS

Description: This readers survey asked respondents about their perceptions of
the legality or ethics of various business situations.

Results: 56% of the respondents believe that American business ethics have
deteriorated in the last 10 years. A majority of the respondents felt that
the following situations were illegal or unethical: boss treating clients
to cocaine --99%; a real estate agent not mentioning that the basement of a
house floods --92%; a public relations officer withholding critical
information in order to make the company's financial outlook appear
brighter --84%. 66% of the readers thought that government was a "hotbed"
of unethical behavior, and 62% of government workers thought that the
government is most unethical. More than 60% of the respondents would use a
stolen secret report from a competitor's company. For the respondents
whose workplaces do not have a formal code of ethics, almost 60% think it
would be helpful to have one.

Poll Extracts:

PERCEPTIONS OF THE FOLLOWING SITUATIONS:

"A job applicant finds out the morning before her job interview
that she is pregnant. She decides not to say anything rather
than jeopardize her chances." illegal/unethical--24%
no problem--76%

"A manager has accumulated sick days. She takes a few days off
and calls in sick." illegal/unethical--34%
no problem--66%

"After a year of poor sales, a sales representative convinces
her boss to let her give expensive gifts to prospective clients.
The tactic works and sales increase." ... illegal/unethical--46%
no problem--54%

"An administrative assistant routinely makes up excuses for her
boss when he takes long lunches with his secretary."
... illegal/unethical--56%
no problem--44%

Also in Source: Responses to several other questions on ethical situations.
The percentage of respondents who had personally observed "Fairness
Violations," "Dishonesty," "Stealing," and "Sexual Trading" (flirting to
make a sale, sexual intimacy with boss, sex with a co-worker on company
time, and sex with client to make a sale).

Poll Details: More than 1,400 readers of *Working Woman* responded to the poll
published in the February 1990 issue, "Business Ethics: What Are Your
Personal Standards?"

Availability: Published in *Working Woman*, September 1990, p. 113-114, 116.

PRO BONO WORK BY LAWYERS

Description: Presents the results of a survey identifying reasons why
          Washington, D.C. lawyers perform limited pro bono work.

Results: Over 50% cite their amount of billable workload as the main reason why
          they perform limited pro bono legal services for the poor.

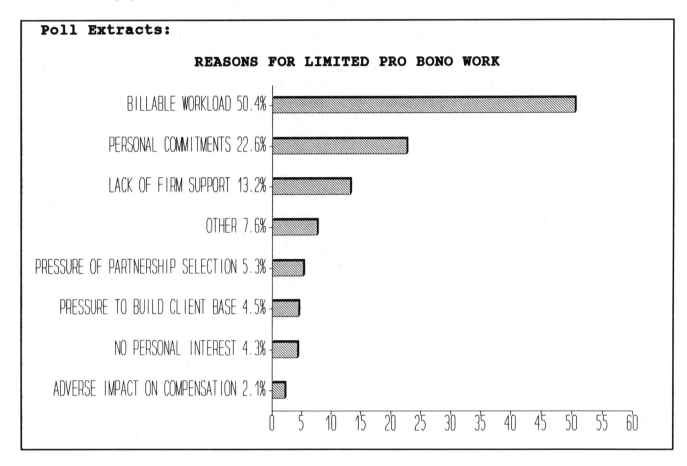

Poll Extracts:

REASONS FOR LIMITED PRO BONO WORK

BILLABLE WORKLOAD 50.4%
PERSONAL COMMITMENTS 22.6%
LACK OF FIRM SUPPORT 13.2%
OTHER 7.6%
PRESSURE OF PARTNERSHIP SELECTION 5.3%
PRESSURE TO BUILD CLIENT BASE 4.5%
NO PERSONAL INTEREST 4.3%
ADVERSE IMPACT ON COMPENSATION 2.1%

0 5 10 15 20 25 30 35 40 45 50 55 60

Also in Source: More than 40% of the approximately 800 lawyers surveyed did
          20 or fewer hours of free work each year, even though local judges'
          voluntary guidelines call on them to put 40 hours a year into what the
          legal profession calls "pro bono" work.

Poll Details: The Washington Council of Lawyers interviewed 806 lawyers.

Availability: Published in *The Washington Post*, October 1, 1990, p. D1, D5.

RIGHT TO DIE

Description: Presents the results of a survey measuring attitudes toward
euthanasia.

Results: Approximately 80% of the respondents felt that if a patient is
terminally ill and unconscious but has left instructions in a living will,
the doctor should be allowed to withdraw life sustaining treatment.

Poll Extracts:

ARE THERE CASES IN WHICH DOCTORS MAY ADMINISTER LETHAL DRUGS?

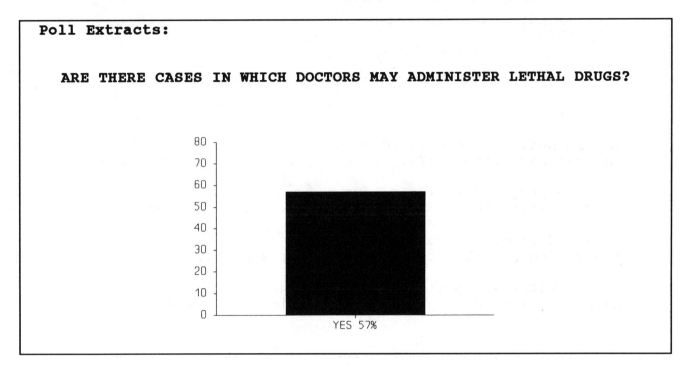

Also in Source: The article includes a general discussion of the right to die
issue.

Poll Details: The poll was conducted by *Time*/CNN during February, 1990.

Availability: Published in *Time*, March 19, 1990 (volume 135, number 12),
p. 62-71.

RIGHT TO DIE

Description: Presents the results of a survey concerning the moral right of
incurably ill patients to commit suicide.

Results: 80% of the respondents believe patients should be allowed to die in
some circumstances and about one-half say some incurably ill patients have
a moral right to commit suicide.

Poll Extracts:

RIGHT TO DIE ISSUES AND QUESTIONS

Should patients be allowed to die
in some circumstances?.........................Yes...80%

Do incurably ill patients have
a moral right to commit suicide?................Yes...49%

Should doctors and nurses always do
everything possible to save a patient's life?...Yes...15%

Do incurably ill patients suffering great
pain have a moral right to commit suicide?......Yes...55%

Also in Source: A short discussion of the issues involved is included in the
article.

Poll Details: The poll, by the Times Mirror Center for the People and the
Press, was conducted before Dr. Jack Kervorkian, a retired pathologist in
Pontiac, MI, aided the June 4 suicide of Janet Adkins who had been
diagnosed as having early Alzheimer's disease.

Availability: Published in *The Columbus Dispatch,* June 13, 1990, p. 7A.

SALES OF NATURAL FURS

Description: Presents the results of a survey measuring the level of support
for the banning of natural fur sales.

Results: Approximately three quarters of the respondents feel that the sales of
natural furs should not be banned.

Poll Extracts:

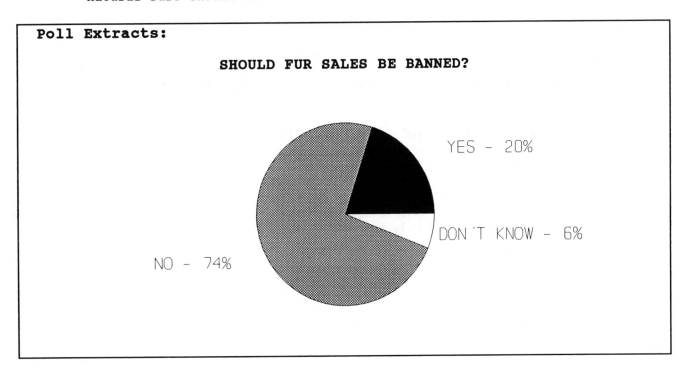

SHOULD FUR SALES BE BANNED?

YES - 20%

DON'T KNOW - 6%

NO - 74%

Also in Source: A discussion of legal and ethical issues concerning the
banning of wild animal fur sales is including in the article.

Poll Details: The poll was conducted by *USA Today.* 1020 adults were contacted
and the margin of error was plus or minus 3%.

Availability: Published in *USA Today,* February 8, 1990, p. 1A.

STUDENTS MORALITY VIEWS

Description: Presents the results of a survey concerning the moral views of young people.

Results: The results includes reponses to a wide range of questions involving a number of moral and ethical issues.

Poll Extracts:

IF YOUR ARE UNSURE, HOW DO YOU DECIDE WHAT TO DO?

Do what was best for everyone involved...................23%

Follow the advice of authority..........................20%

Do what would make them happy...........................18%

Do what God or the Scriptures say is right..............16%

Do what would improve their own situation...............10%

Don't know...9%

Follow their conscience..................................3%

Also in Source: 65% of the high school students surveyed said they would probably cheat on a test. A little over a third of the junior and senior high school students said they would have sexual intercourse if asked by a steady boyfriend or girlfriend.

Poll Details: The survey was conducted by Louis Harris & Associates for the Girl Scouts of America. A 90 item questionnaire was distributed to 5,012 students in October and November, 1989.

Availability: Published in *The Atlanta Journal and Constitution,* March 19, 1990, p. B-2.

TURNING OFF LIFE-SUPPORT

Description: Presents the results of a survey concerning the various issues surrounding the life-and-death decisions for critically ill relatives.

Results: Over half of the respondents said that the family members should have the right to decide whether to take a comatose relative off a life-support system.

Poll Extracts:

DECIDING WHETHER TO TAKE A COMATOSE RELATIVE OFF LIFE-SUPPORT:

Family has the right to remove
life-support.................................Yes...50.8%

Remove life-support only if patient
previously indicated such a preference......Yes...25.6%

Decision should be left to doctors.........Yes....8.6%

Machines should continue operating
until patient dies or recovers.............Yes....7.2%

Also in Source: 62.3% said they could decide to end life-support from a comatose relative with virtually no chance of recovery, 22.5% said they could not, and 14.8% did not know. 50.7% felt euthanasia is a "purely personal choice." 25.7% said it was acceptable only in cases of terminal illness or irreversible coma. 12.9% said it was always morally wrong.

Poll Details: The survey of 1,000 persons aged 18 to 80 was commissioned by Maturity News Service. The telephone poll conducted by International Communications Research of Media has a margin of error of 3%.

Availability: Published in the *Detroit Free Press*, June 5, 1990, p. 3F.

CHANGING FAMILY STRUCTURE

Description: This poll questioned the American public about the impact of various changes upon the family structure (high divorce rates, more single parent households, increasing numbers of working mothers with young children), and the acceptability of these changes.

Results: 50% of respondents say the changes point to a different kind of society and are not necessarily bad. 40% of respondents believe these changes are bad, and will lead to weaknesses in society. 57% believe the trends taking place in society will continue regardless of what we try to do about them. 35% believe the current trends in society can be reversed.

Poll Extracts:

WHAT RESPONDENTS SAY ABOUT THE CHANGES IN AMERICAN FAMILY STRUCTURE:

It's acceptable for mothers of preschool
children to work outside of the home Yes--65%

It's acceptable to have families with young
children in which only one parent, usually
the mother, lives in the household Yes--61%

It's acceptable for parents with young
children to divorce Yes--46%

It's acceptable for women to have
children out of wedlock Yes--27%

Also in Source: The percentage of respondents who in order to help families cope with changes in society favor the following proposals: leave of absence for new working mothers, employers providing child care, flex-time or job sharing, a minimum wage high enough so that a family of four can live above the poverty line if the father works and the mother stays home, higher income tax deductions for children, leaves of absence for new working fathers, greater government provision of child care.

Poll Details: The poll was commissioned by *Parents* Magazine.

Availability: Published in *Parents,* January 1990 (volume 65, number 1), p. 31.

CHANGING YOUR SPOUSE

Description: This poll asked respondents about their views on marriage and
their spouse.

Results: 14% of the wives polled said they would change nothing about their
husbands, and 10% of the men said they would change nothing about their
wives. 45% of the men and 21% of the women agreed with the statement,
"Fidelity is difficult." 75% of the men and 65% of the women were
"certain" that their spouses would never cheat on them.

Poll Extracts:

**WHAT MEN AND WOMEN WOULD, IF GIVEN THE CHOICE, CHANGE
IN THEIR WIVES AND HUSBANDS:**

WIVES WOULD IMPROVE THEIR HUSBANDS':

Personal Habits 23%
Temper 21%
Salary 20%
Family 17%
Hobbies 10%
Friends 7%

HUSBANDS WOULD IMPROVE THEIR WIVES':

Self-confidence 35%
Sexual attitudes 31%
Sexual performance ... 20%
Appearance 15%
Willpower 11%
Sense of humor 10%
Voice 4%

Also in Source: When wives and husbands feel closest to one another. What
wives and husbands fight about.

Poll Details: This *Esquire* readers' survey included no postage or incentive
for completion, but was returned by the respondents, in the "thousands."
Two out of three of the respondents were husbands, and most of the other
people who replied were wives. "Typically, a respondent was around 36
years old, a college graduate earning up to $50,000, and married--for about
nine years--to a spouse of similar characteristics."

Availability: Published in *Esquire*, June 1990 (volume 113, number 6),
p. 39-40.

THE FAMILY MEAL

Description: Presents the results of a survey concerning the frequency and characterics of today's family dinner.

Results: Approximately 75% of the respondents said it is very important for the family to eat dinner together.

Poll Extracts:

HOW IMPORTANT TO YOU IS EATING DINNER WITH YOUR FAMILY?

VERY 74%

NOT VERY 4%

SOMEWHAT 22%

Also in Source: 46% of the respondents said the family ate dinner together every day for the past week. 81% of the respondents said when the family eats together, they eat the same basic meal. 32% said their children prepare their own meals. 80% said their family ate dinner together last night. 56% of the respondents said they talk during dinner, 15% said they watch television, and 27% said they do both. 48% said dinner usually lasts a half hour when the family eats together.

Poll Details: The results are based on a *New York Times*/CBS News Poll conducted by telephone November 13-15, 1990, with 555 adults who said they have children under 18 living with them.

Availability: Published in *The New York Times*, December 5, 1990, p.A1, C6.

ISSUES FACING TODAY'S FAMILIES

Description: Presents the results of a wide-ranging survey concerning marriage
and the family.

Results: More than 80% of the respondents, aged 18 to 24, feel that couples in
their generation are more likely to get divorced than those in their
parents' generation.

Poll Extracts:

COMPARED TO YOUR PARANTS' GENERATION, IS DIVORCE MORE LIKELY?

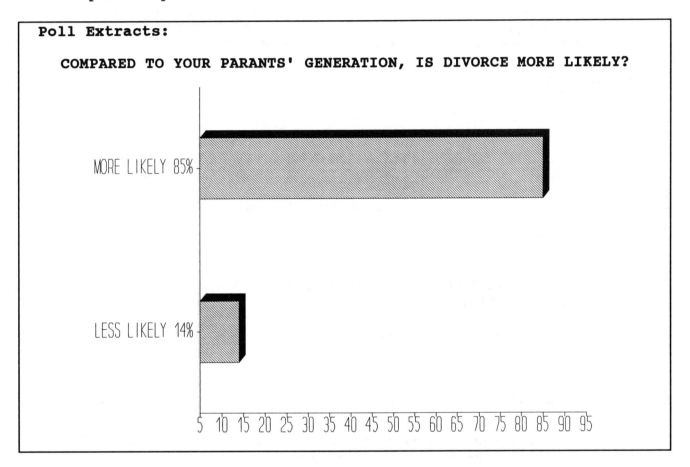

Also in Source: 56% of the female respondents said it is difficult to have a
good marriage today, while 55% of the male respondents share the same
opinion. 56% of the respondents said they would raise their own children
the same way they were raised, while 43% said they would raise them
differently. 66% of the female respondents said that they would, if they
had the opportunity, stay home and raise the children. 48% of the male
respondents would do the same.

Poll Details: The results are taken from a telephone survey of 505 Americans
aged 18 to 24 conducted for *Time* on September 5-11, 1990, by Yanklovich
Clancy Shulman. Sampling error is plus or minus 4.5%.

Availability: Published in *Time*, Special Fall Issue, 1990 (volume 136, number
19), p. 10-14.

MARITAL FIDELITY

Description: This survey of adult Americans queried respondents about marital fidelity and other aspects of modern marriage.

Results: The overwhelming majority of married Americans are more monogamous than most people believe. According to the survey, fewer than one in 10 currently married people have been unfaithful to their spouse. 91% of married people say they "talk privately and intimately" as a couple. 61% of married people say they pray together. 21% of married people say they "watch X-rated videos" as a couple, at least sometimes.

Poll Extracts:

WHEN RESPONDENTS WERE ASKED ABOUT THE PROPOSITION THAT, "MOST COUPLES ARE FAITHFUL TO ONE ANOTHER"

----- A quarter of the respondents strongly agreed.

WHEN RESPONDENTS WERE ASKED IF THEY WOULD MARRY THE SAME PERSON AGAIN

----- Four out of five married people said yes.

Also in Source: The percentage of respondents who: take baths or showers together, have bought erotic underclothes, work out or play sports, and swim in the nude.

Poll Details: The poll is based on telephone interviews with 657 adults in "intact marriages." The poll was conducted in November 1989, by the Gallup Organization. The findings are reported in "Faithful Attraction," written by the Rev. Andrew M. Greeley, the Chicago priest, sociologist, and novelist.

Availability: Published in *The New York Times*, February 12, 1990, p. A18.

MEN AND MARRIAGE

Description: Men were asked what was most important to them and to society.
They were queried about the importance of fidelity to a marriage, and
whether they would marry their wives again.

Results: 62.5% of the respondents, and 75% of the married men, chose marriage
(above money, sex, fame, or career) as being most important in their lives.
32% of the respondents thought that a strong family structure was most
important to society (above an excellent educational system, healthy
economy, strong religious institutions, and law and order). Respondents
thought that marital fidelity was about equally important for the man (79%)
and the woman (82%). The majority of men would marry their wives again.

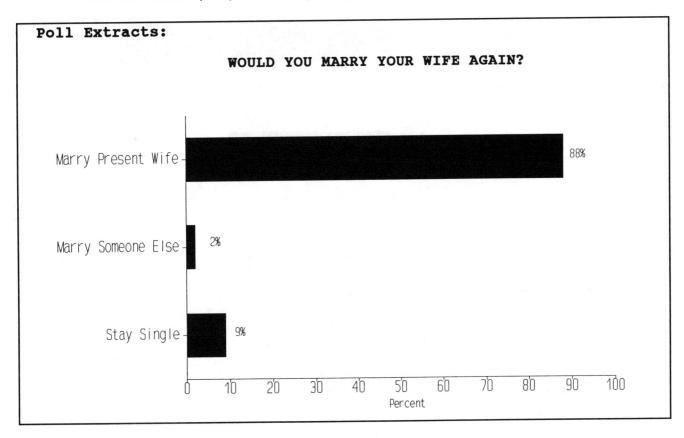

Poll Extracts:

WOULD YOU MARRY YOUR WIFE AGAIN?

Also in Source: Responses to questions dealing with work, sex, values, and
sports.

Poll Details: Peter D. Hart Associates of Washington, D.C., interviewed 815
American men from age 18 through retirement. The margin of error was 4%.

Availability: Published in *Men's Life*, Fall Issue 1990 (volume 1, number 1),
p. 64-70.

MOTHERS

Description: Presents the results of a survey of mothers concerning their family related problems and frustrations.

Results: Finding time for themselves was cited as the biggest problem facing mothers' followed by feeling tired all the time.

Poll Extracts:

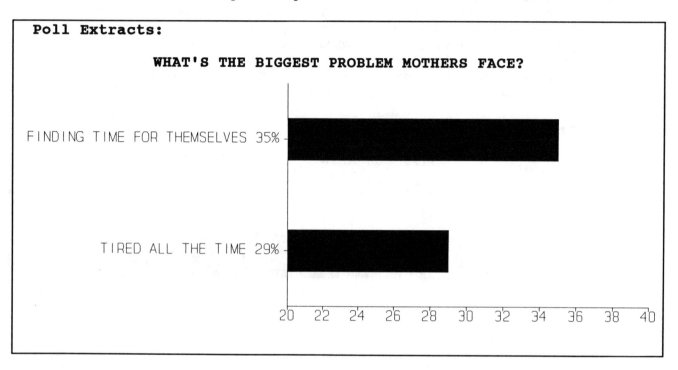

Also in Source: 59% of mothers agree the teen years are the most trying years. If they could make some changes, 74% wish they could control their temper better. 85% believe that while there are some things about their children they can never alter, they struggle with different forms of discipline. Though fewer than 5% believe they have psychologically or physically abused their child, 16% admit they worry that the stresses of their lives might so overwhelm them that they would inflict harm.

Poll Details: The results of the survey are taken from a readers poll by *Ladies Home Journal*. Over 22,000 readers responded.

Availability: Published in *Ladies Home Journal*, May, 1990 (volume VII, number 5), p. 132, 134, 136.

RAISING KIDS

Description: Presents the results of a survey relating to the various issues concerning child raising.

Results: Over 80% of the respondents said that it is harder to raise children today compared to a generation ago.

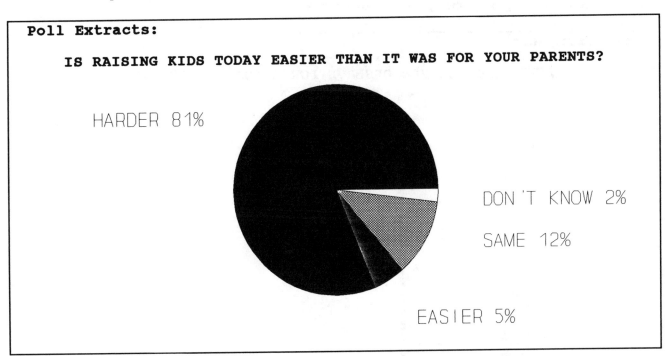

Poll Extracts:

IS RAISING KIDS TODAY EASIER THAN IT WAS FOR YOUR PARENTS?

HARDER 81%

DON'T KNOW 2%

SAME 12%

EASIER 5%

Also in Source: 22% of the respondents said that cost was the greatest child related problem. 81% said that parents are not strict enough. According to the respondents, the ideal child is an eight year-old boy. The most difficult child is a 14 year-old girl. When asked to talk about the "greatest plus or the thing you gain most from having children," 12% said the love and affection children bring, 11% said having the pleasure of watching them grow, 10% said the joy, happiness, and fun they bring, 7% said the sense of family they create, and 6% said the fulfillment and satisfaction they bring.

Poll Details: The Gallup survey results are based on telephone interviews with a randomly selected national sample of 1,239 adults, 18 and older conducted on April 19 through April 22, 1990. Sampling error is plus or minus 4%.

Availability: Published in the *Dayton Daily News*, June 3, 1990, p. 1E, 2E.

RAISING KIDS

Description: Presents the results of a survey concerning parents' perceptions of how well they are raising their children.

Results: Over half of the respondents with children under the age of 18 gave themselves a grade of B for the job they are doing bringing up their kids, followed by 31% who gave themselves an A.

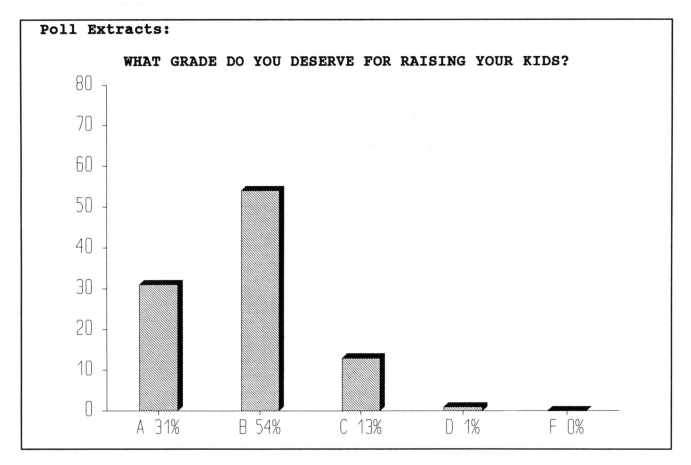

Poll Extracts:

WHAT GRADE DO YOU DESERVE FOR RAISING YOUR KIDS?

A 31%   B 54%   C 13%   D 1%   F 0%

Also in Source: 81% of the respondents say it is more difficult to raise children now than it was when their parents raised them. 12% think it's about the same and 5% think it's easier. 2% have no opinion. 43% of adults felt that boys were easier to rear than girls, while 27% said girls were easier, and 23% said there was no difference.

Poll Details: The results are taken from a recent Gallup survey.

Availability: Published in *The Wall Street Journal*, October 2, 1990, p. B1.

THE STATE OF THE FAMILY

Description: This poll queried respondents about their attitudes toward family life, parenthood, and careers.

Results: 79% of the mothers and 39% of the fathers surveyed would quit their jobs, if they could, to stay at home to raise their children. "Altogether, about eight in 10 said the most important things in their lives are family and children, marriage and love, and financial security -- more important than work and career or leisure time." More than half of the respondents said that they often feel guilty for spending too little time with their children. 64% of the fathers and 72% of the mothers often worry about whether they are doing a good job as a parent. Many parents cannot even maintain the simplest family traditions, such as eating dinner together. 65% of the respondents felt that it was important to attend church services, but only 48% said that they actually attended services.

Poll Extracts:

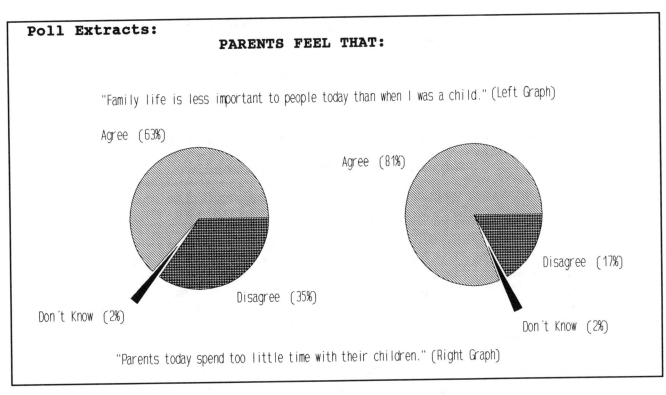

PARENTS FEEL THAT:

"Family life is less important to people today than when I was a child." (Left Graph)

Agree (63%)

Agree (81%)

Disagree (17%)

Disagree (35%)

Don't Know (2%)

Don't Know (2%)

"Parents today spend too little time with their children." (Right Graph)

Also in Source: That according to a study by the Ford Foundation, only 10% of the homes in America today are traditional breadwinner models -- father going off to work and mother staying home to take care of the children. The percentage of fathers and mothers who feel that: the job they're doing as a parent has suffered as a result of their work career, their work career has suffered because of the demands of raising children and having a family. The biggest problems for parents in Orange and Los Angeles County.

Poll Details: The *Los Angeles Times* commissioned this telephone survey by Irvine-based Mark Baldassare & Associates. 1,000 households were surveyed; 500 in Orange County, and 500 in Los Angeles County. The margin of error is 3% for the total sample. Further details provided in the source.

Availability: Published in the *Los Angeles Times*, August 12, 1990, p. A1, A32, A34.

STEREOTYPICAL ATTITUDES

Description: Presents the results of a survey concerning attitudes towards men, women, and work in a family relationship.

Results: Almost 80% of the respondents said that raising a child is as rewarding as having a career. Over 60% agreed that raising a family is the most important experience in a woman's life.

Poll Extracts:

SOME THINGS NEVER CHANGE:

Raising a child is as rewarding for a women as having a career.
                  Agree...78%   Disagree...16%

Raising a child is as rewarding for a man as having a career.
                  Agree...45%   Disagree...42%

Raising a family is the most important experience
in a woman's life.
                  Agree...63%   Disagree...29%

Raising a family is the most important experience
in a man's life.
                  Agree...43%   Disagree...42%

Also in Source: 30% said a child is most likely to become self-reliant and independent if a mother works. 22% said the child of a working mother is most likely to develop serious behavior problems. 38% said a child is most likely to have a close relationship with his or her mother if the mother does not work. 31% feel a child of a mother who stays home most likely will be secure and well adjusted. 26% believe a child is most likely to have a happy childhood if she or he has a nonworking mother. 21% feel the child most likely will be a better spouse and 20% believe the child most likely will be happy later in life if the mother stays home.

Poll Details: The results of the survey were taken from a readers poll of *Parents* magazine. 30,000 readers answered a questionnaire.

Availability: Published in *Parents*, June, 1990, (volume 65, number 6) p. 107, 108, 110, 112, 114.

TRENDS IN CHILD SPANKING

Description: Presents the results of a survey concerning the frequency of
disciplinary spanking and hitting directed at children.

Results: Half of the parents of children under the age of 18 reported that they
had spanked or hit their kids at least once during the previous year.

Poll Extracts:

PARENTS WHO SPANKED THEIR KIDS AT LEAST ONCE IN THE PAST YEAR:

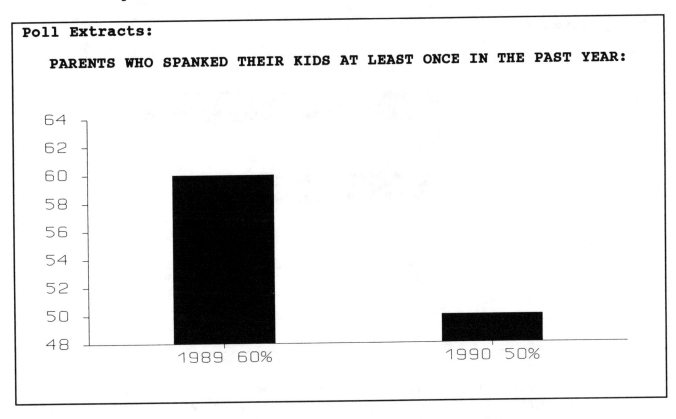

Also in Source: A discussion of the issue of violent discipline is included
in the article.

Poll Details: The poll was taken for the National Committee for the Prevention
of Child Abuse. The poll has a margin of error of plus or minus 5%.

Availability: Published in the *Chicago Tribune*, April 8, 1990, Section 1,
p. 5.

WORKING MOMS AND THEIR KIDS

Description: Presents the results of a survey concerning the effects of
    mothers' working full time on their young children.

Results: A majority of the pediatricians surveyed said children up to the age
    of three may be hurt by their mothers' working full time.

Poll Extracts:

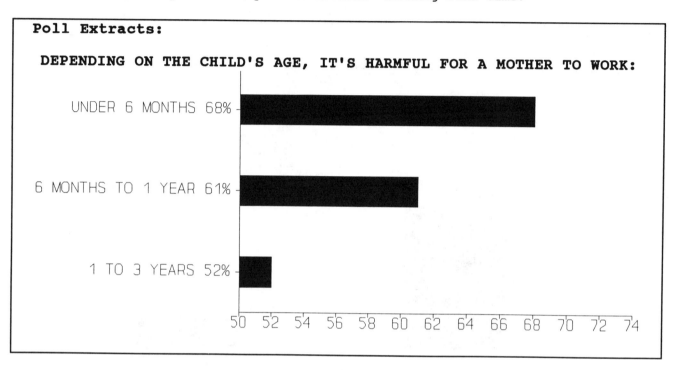

DEPENDING ON THE CHILD'S AGE, IT'S HARMFUL FOR A MOTHER TO WORK:

UNDER 6 MONTHS 68%

6 MONTHS TO 1 YEAR 61%

1 TO 3 YEARS 52%

50 52 54 56 58 60 62 64 66 68 70 72 74

Also in Source: The poll also reflected the age and sex of the respondents.
    Female pediatricians and younger doctors tended to be less concerned about
    mothers working full time. Half of the female doctors but 77% of the males
    thought it might be harmful under age six months. For ages one to three,
    concern dropped to 29% for female doctors and 63% for males. Nearly three-
    fourths of the pediatricians said that financial necessity is an
    appropriate reason for a mother to work.

Poll Details: 1,100 pediatricians were surveyed by the American Academy of
    Pediatrics and *Working Mother* magazine.

Availability: Published in *The Atlanta Constitution,* May 2, 1990, p. E1, E4.

WORRYING PARENTS

Description: Presents the results of a survey concerning parents' fears regarding their children.

Results: It appears that parents worry more about immediate events over which they have little realistic control and have less concern in areas in which parents can have influence.

Poll Extracts:

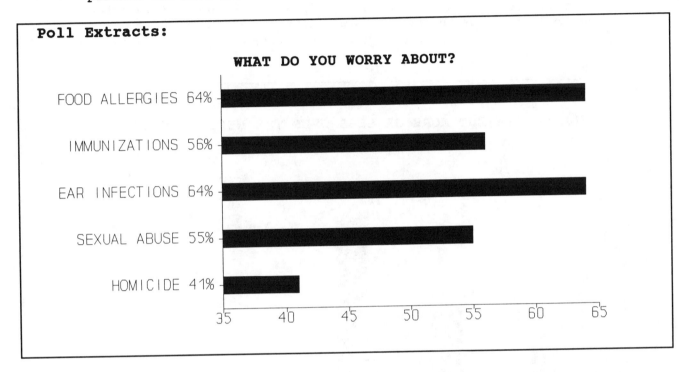

Also in Source: Parents worry more about homicide and sexual abuse than about drugs, depression, too much TV, poor school performance, sexual promiscuity, or delinquency. Almost three-quarters of the mothers surveyed expressed fear that their children would be kidnapped by a stranger although the chances of that happening are 1.5 in 1 million. Half of the mothers were very concerned that their children would get cancer. But cancer-related deaths in children under age 15 occur in three of every 100,000 people. The survey showed that parents worry excessively about health care issues that rarely lead to serious problems such as ear infections, reactions to immunizations, and food allergies.

Poll Details: Pediatricians from the Mayo Clinic in Rochester, MN and Rhode Island Hospital in Providence, RI polled 400 mothers.

Availability: Published in the *Los Angeles Times*, May 21, 1990, p. B2.

BABY-BOOMER INVESTORS

Description: Presents the results of a survey concerning baby-boomer investing
patterns and behavior.

Results: When asked whether they will be investing more or less over the next
five years versus the last five years, 45% of the respondents in the 35 to
54 age group said they would invest more compared to 20% in the 55 and over
age group. 9% of the younger age group said they would invest less
compared to 30% of the older group. 46% of the baby-boomers and 47% of the
55+ group said they invest at the same level. 3% of the the later group
didn't know.

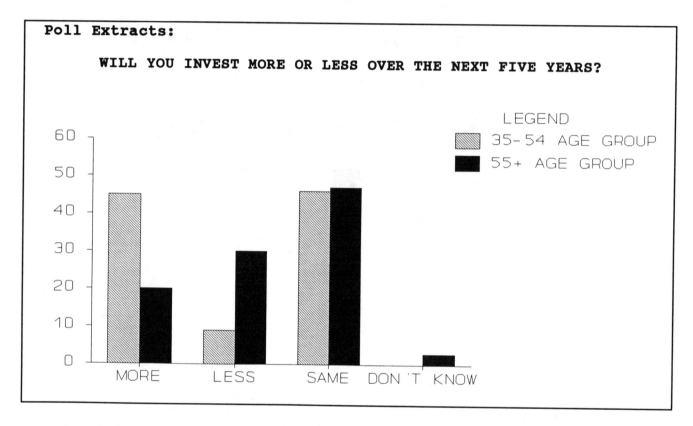

Poll Extracts:

WILL YOU INVEST MORE OR LESS OVER THE NEXT FIVE YEARS?

LEGEND
35-54 AGE GROUP
55+ AGE GROUP

Also in Source: 33% of the 35 to 54 age group and 47% of the 55 and over age
group identified stockbrokers as their primary financial advisor. 30% of
the baby-boomers and 42% of the 55+ age group rated the service from their
financial advisor as excellent. Approximately half of each group rated the
service as good.

Poll Details: The poll was conducted for John Nuveen & Company by Hal Riney &
Partners. 400 affluent investors were surveyed in summer, 1989.

Availability: Published in the *Los Angeles Times*, June 11, 1990, p. D5, D8.

PESSIMISTIC FINANCIAL FUTURE

Description: Presents the results of a survey concerning the personal economic
future and the ability of Americans to cope with future financial
responsibilities.

Results: Americans, particularly aging baby boomers, are increasingly
pessimistic about their financial future and, consequently, are beginning
to save more than ever before. 75% of this group said they are currently
saving or planning to save more in 1990 because they feel they will likely
have to pay for a child's education, support an aging parent, and save for
their own retirement at the same time.

```
Poll Extracts:

                         FINANCIAL FEARS:


   Yes, we are currently saving or planning to save more in 1990?
                  Aging baby-boomers...75%
                  General population...62%

   Do you have any real financial worries?............No...8%

   Is the cost of child-care a worry?................Yes...4%

   Do you worry about outliving your retirement savings?
                  Aging baby-boomers.......Yes...62%
                  General population.......Yes...52%

   Do you believe that college costs have
   risen beyond the means of most Americans?..........Yes...86%

   Is severe inflation likely to be a problem?........Yes...86%
```

Also in Source: In reponse to the question, "What are your top two or three
long-term financial goals", 30% of the general population and 52% of the
wealthy category said saving for retirement, 17% of the general population
and 23% of the wealthy category said saving for a child's education, 16% of
the general population and 16% of the wealthy category said buying/making
payments on a home, and 7% of the general population and 8% of the wealthy
category said increased savings.

Poll Details: The Gallup Organization conducted the poll for the International
Association for Financial Planning with a random telephone sample of 1,058
households. It also called 600 additional families with incomes above
$50,000 to determine the concerns of affluent Americans. The margin of
error was plus or minus 3%.

Availability: Published in the *Los Angeles Times*, June 14, 1990, p. D3.

VALUED CHARACTERISTICS OF FINANCIAL ADVISORS

Description: Presents the results of a survey concerning what consumers look for in their financial advisors.

Results: Trust and honesty are held in high regard. Over 50% of the consumers who use financial advisors said they believe "trust and ethics" are the most important components of their relationship, more important than either compensation or investment returns.

Poll Extracts:

CONSUMERS AND FINANCIAL PLANNERS:

Would you want to be informed, in writing, about how your financial advisor is paid, including a range of fees and commissions?..........Yes...95%

Are "trust and ethics" the most important components in your relationship with your financial planner?.................................Yes...51%

Should financial planners be licensed and regulated by the government?........................Yes...76%

Also in Source: A discussion of the issues related to the survey is included in the article.

Poll Details: 1,058 Americans were surveyed by the Gallup Organization for the International Association for Financial Planning.

Availability: Published in *The Atlanta Journal and Constitution*, May 28, 1990, p. B-11.

WHAT INVESTORS WORRY ABOUT

Description: Presents the results of a survey concerning the issues, conditions, and trends which investors find most troublesome.

Results: The issue which concerns investors the most, approximately 60% of the respondents, is the ethics of stock brokers. The percentage of various kinds of investors who say they are "very concerned" with particular economic conditions and investment trends are listed below. (**Key:** D - Direct shareholders; M - Stock mutual fund owners; I - Indirect shareholders; N - Non-owners of shares)

Poll Extracts:

CONDITIONS OF WHICH INVESTORS ARE VERY CONCERNED:

Condition/trend	D	M	I	N
Ethics of stock brokers	58	66	58	65
Interest rates	47	54	49	61
Inflation	41	51	52	67
Insider trading	39	31	28	29
Recession	37	39	46	51
Bankruptcies of business	35	36	44	45
Junk bonds	28	18	23	20
Leveraged buyouts	27	20	18	24
Unrest around the world	25	29	28	31
Mergers and acquisitions	21	20	17	19
Volatility	18	11	6	10
Program trading	11	13	11	13
Index futures/options	9	5	3	9

Also in Source: More than half of the investors surveyed had never heard of program trading and 79% of people who directly own stock had never heard of index arbitrage, the most common form of program trading. Those who own stock directly said they considered 76 points a "large drop" in the Dow Industrials. Also 41% of direct shareholders and more than half of the other groups believe - wrongly - that the New York Stock Exchange can control prices.

Poll Details: 560 investors were contacted by telephone in February, 1990 for a New York Stock Exchange panel on "Market Volatility and Investor Confidence."

Availability: Published in the *Chicago Tribune*, June 18, 1990, Section 4 p. 1, 2.

IOWANS' EXPECTATIONS FOR THE 1990s

Description: This Iowa Poll asked respondents about their expectations for the
        1990s.

Results: 80% of Iowans expect to still be living in the state at the end of the
        1990s. 71% of Iowans say that by the year 2000, "Iowa and the rest of the
        Midwest will become a popular, mellow haven for those stress-ridden
        urbanites on the East and West coasts." 46% of the respondents expect that
        there will be more job opportunities for college graduates in Iowa, in the
        year 2000.

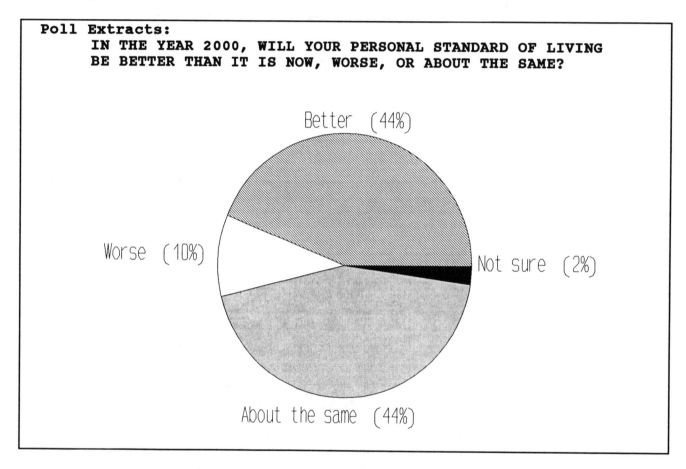

Poll Extracts:
**IN THE YEAR 2000, WILL YOUR PERSONAL STANDARD OF LIVING
BE BETTER THAN IT IS NOW, WORSE, OR ABOUT THE SAME?**

Better (44%)

Worse (10%)

Not sure (2%)

About the same (44%)

Also in Source: A brief discussion of how people in small towns responded
        compared to urbanites, in regards to the standard of living question, and
        the migration question.

Poll Details: The Iowa Poll is based on interviews with 814 Iowans, age 18 and
        older. Randomly selected telephone numbers were used to contact the
        respondents, from November 27 - December 5, 1989. The margin of error is
        3.4%.

Availability: Published in *The Des Moines Register*, January 1, 1990,
        p. 1A, 4A.

LOOKING TOWARD 2000 A.D.

Description: The poll queried respondents about what they anticipate the future to hold for their own lives, and the nation's social and economic problems.

Results: Respondents were optimistic about their own lives in the future but thought many of the nation's social and economic problems would be getting worse. 77% of the respondents expected the quality of their life and their family life to be better by 2000. 74% thought their financial situation would be better, and 82% of those working thought their job situation would be better.

Poll Extracts:

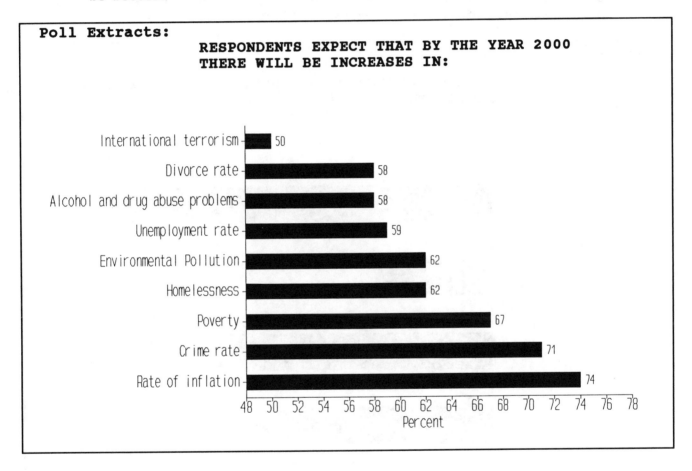

RESPONDENTS EXPECT THAT BY THE YEAR 2000 THERE WILL BE INCREASES IN:

Also in Source: The percentage of respondents who thought by the year 2000: people will be spending more time on leisure and recreation or work or household duties, tensions between racial and ethnic groups will decrease, a cure for cancer will be found, a cure for AIDS will be found, Soviet Communism will have disappeared, there will be a nuclear war, there will be an ecological disaster, it will be harder to afford college, it will be harder to buy a house, it will be harder to afford retirement, and it will be harder to afford medical care.

Poll Details: This telephone poll of 1,234 adults on November 16-19, 1989, was conducted by the Gallup Organization. The margin of sampling error is 4%.

Availability: Published in *The New York Times*, January 1, 1990, p. 10.

STUDENTS' VIEWS OF THE 22ND CENTURY

Description: Junior and senior high school students were questioned about their views of the 22nd century.

Results: 83% of the respondents said that most shopping will be done from the home. 68% think people will still go to schools. 63% believe Americans will be living in space by 2100. 24% believe people will be able to control the weather. 51% believe people will be able to buy artificial body parts -- "off the shelf." 33% of the respondents think the average life span will be 100 years. 51% think there will be communication with extraterrestrial beings. 16% think that nuclear power will be the main energy source. 55% think the average work week will be shorter.

Poll Extracts:

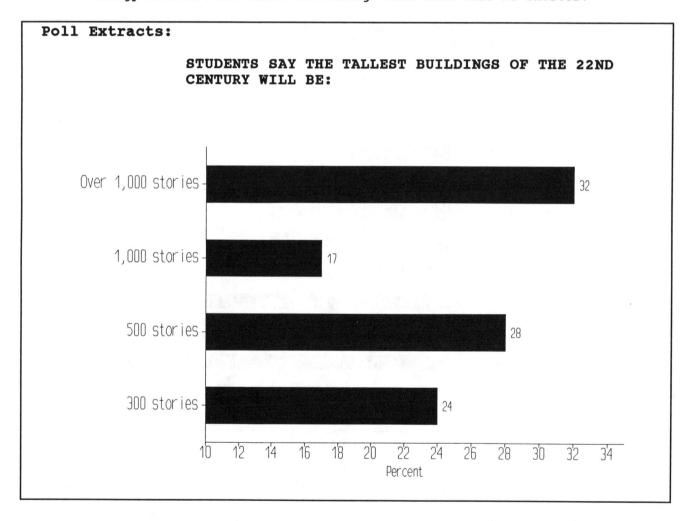

STUDENTS SAY THE TALLEST BUILDINGS OF THE 22ND CENTURY WILL BE:

Poll Details: The results of the survey were announced by the National Society of Professional Engineers. 12,300 junior and senior high school students were surveyed. The survey was conducted in December 1989, by the society's National Engineers Week committee and *Science World.*

Availability: Published in the *Dayton Daily News,* February 25, 1990, p. 2-E.

TAKING IT WITH YOU

Description: This poll asked Iowans, "If you could take one thing with you after you die, what would it be?"

Results: Some of the more unusual items which respondents wanted to take with them were: a 12-pack of beer, a book, "all my guns," and for three Iowans -- their sense of humor.

Poll Extracts:

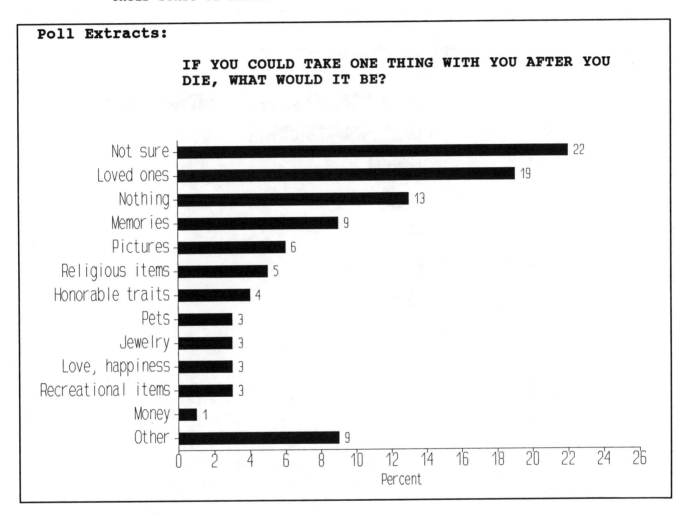

IF YOU COULD TAKE ONE THING WITH YOU AFTER YOU DIE, WHAT WOULD IT BE?

Poll Details: The Iowa Poll is based on interviews with 814 Iowans, age 18 and older. Randomly selected telephone numbers were used to contact the respondents, from November 27 - December 5, 1989. The margin of error is 3.4%.

Availability: Published in *The Des Moines Register*, January 21, 1990, p. 1B.

ATTITUDES TOWARD THE CENSUS

Description: Presents the results of a survey concerning various census-
          related issues.

Results: Over half of the people who had not returned the census forms said they
          were too busy or forgot.

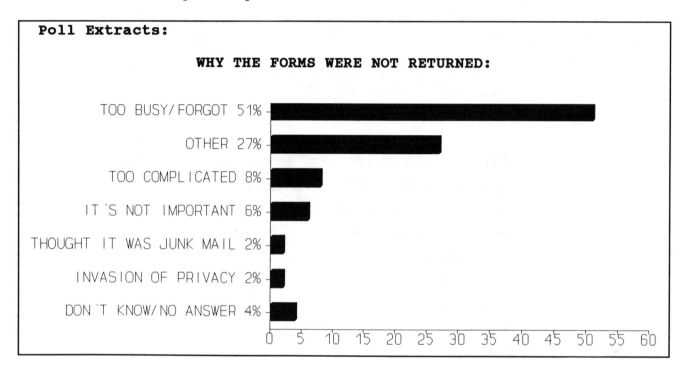

Poll Extracts:

WHY THE FORMS WERE NOT RETURNED:

TOO BUSY/FORGOT 51%

OTHER 27%

TOO COMPLICATED 8%

IT'S NOT IMPORTANT 6%

THOUGHT IT WAS JUNK MAIL 2%

INVASION OF PRIVACY 2%

DON'T KNOW/NO ANSWER 4%

0   5   10 15 20 25 30 35 40 45 50 55 60

Also in Source: Among the adults who had not completed a census form or had
          not yet received one, 56% were very willing to talk personally with a
          census taker, 32% were somewhat willing, 6% not too willing, 4% not willing
          at all, and 2% didn't know or had no answer. Among those adults who
          received but not returned the census form, 40% said the census form is too
          long, 51% said the government asks for more information than it needs to
          know, 52% said they believe the Census Bureau shares information with
          agencies like the I.R.S., 49% said they think it is very important to be
          counted in the census, and 55% said they heard advertisements about the
          census.

Poll Details: This *New York Times* Poll was based on telephone interviews with
          1,462 adults nationwide on April 18 through April 22, 1990.

Availability: Published in *The New York Times*, April 26, 1990, p. A1, B13.

BELIEFS OF NON-VOTERS

Description: This poll asked adults who vote rarely or never about their views on government.

Results: "Almost half of non-voters say they don't know enough about candidates and issues to participate."

Poll Extracts:

VIEWS ON GOVERNMENT HELD BY THE NON-VOTING PUBLIC

"Politicians have lost touch with the people" 79%--Yes

"Special interest groups have too much control" ... 69%--Yes

"Government is corrupt" 62%--Yes

Poll Details: This Gannett News Service/Gordon S. Black poll was conducted with 607 adults who vote rarely or never.

Availability: Published in *USA Today*, September 5, 1990, p. 1A.

CALIFORNIA LEGISLATURE AND BRIBES

Description: This poll was a series of questions regarding opinions on the California Legislature and state government.

Results: The majority of respondents believe that taking bribes is a relatively common practice for their state legislators. Respondents agreed with the statement "most state legislators are for sale to their largest campaign contributors" by two to one. Respondents agreed with the statement "state government is pretty much run by a few big interests" rather than "for the benefit of all the people" by 2.5 to 1. Almost half of the respondents thought that the state government did not pay much attention to the wishes of the citizens, when deciding what to do. Respondents also estimated that about a third of the California Legislature and executive branch obtained office by using unethical or illegal methods. 75% of the respondents were in favor of banning every private campaign contribution and instead providing campaign funds for legislative campaigns through tax support. In order to finance all political campaigns in California and eliminate private donations, two-thirds said they would be willing to have a dollar or two added to their state income tax.

Poll Extracts:

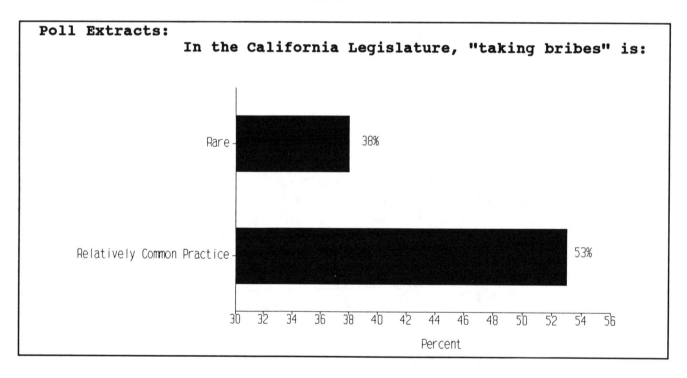

In the California Legislature, "taking bribes" is:

Also in Source: Voter approval of the way Governor George Deukmejian is handling his job. The most important problem facing California today (crime and drugs).

Poll Details: The Times poll queried 2,046 California adults, including 1,594 registered voters, by telephone during December 2-6, 1989. The margin of error for the survey is 3%.

Availability: Published in the *Los Angeles Times*, January 3, 1990, p. A1, A15.

CEOs LOOK AT WASHINGTON

Description: Presents the results of a survey concerning the confidence chief executives in business have in the federal government.

Results: Over 60% of the respondents have less confidence today compared with 10 years ago in the federal government's ability to identify and deal with the major problems America will face in the decade ahead.

Poll Extracts:

**COMPARED TO TEN YEARS AGO,
HOW MUCH CONFIDENCE DO YOU HAVE IN THE FEDERAL GOVERNMENT?**

LESS CONFIDENCE 62%

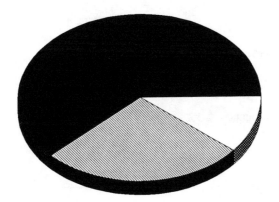

MORE CONFIDENCE 11%

ABOUT THE SAME 27%

Also in Source: 56% of the respondents said that more power should be shifted from the federal government to state and local governments. 50% of the respondents said Congress has become less responsive to business's concerns during the past decade, 27% said more responsive, 21% said there has been no change, and 2% were not sure. The most cited specific reform of the federal government which would help most to make it more effective was to change the length or limit the number of legislators' terms.

Poll Details: The opinion research firm of Clark Martire & Bartolomeo surveyed 201 chief executives of Fortune 500 and Service 500 companies on their attitudes toward government in July 1990.

Availability: Published in *Fortune*, November 5, 1990 (volume 122, number 12), p. 83, 87, 89.

CIVICS KNOWLEDGE

Description: Presents the results of a survey concerning the level of United States civics and history knowledge among 12th grade students.

Results: Depending on the particular idea or subject, the level of knowledge varies widely.

Poll Extracts:

HIGH SCHOOL SENIORS AND CIVICS

Idea or subject	Percentage correct
Right to a lawyer	97.6
Name of president	93.7
Voting age is 18	92.4
Brown vs. Board of Education	68.1
Difference between U.S & U.S.S.R.	60.8
Congress can double income tax	38.7
Supreme Court can strike down laws	14.5

Also in Source: During the 1988 presidential race, when the survey was taken, less than 40% of seniors knew that the candidates are chosen at national conventions. Almost all 12th-graders knew that it is illegal to not pay taxes but less than two-thirds knew it is legal to organize a recall election, take part in a boycott or hunger strike, or impeach legislators.

Poll Details: The results are based on scores from multiple-choice tests of 16,000 12th-graders in about 1,000 public and private schools. The surveys were conducted by the United States Department of Education.

Availability: Published in the *Los Angeles Times*, April 3, 1990, p. A18.

CONSTITUTIONAL BELIEFS AND FLAG BURNING

Description: This poll asked respondents about adding various amendments to the Constitution, if the Constitution guarantees the "right of privacy," and if flag burning is constitutionally protected.

Results: 69% believe there should be a constitutional amendment to balance the budget. 70% believe there should be a constitutional amendment to add an equal rights amendment. 73% believe the Constitution guarantees a right of privacy, and 51% say the right is written in the Constitution. 46% of the respondents disagree with the Supreme Court ruling that flag burning during political demonstrations is constitutionally protected.

Poll Extracts:

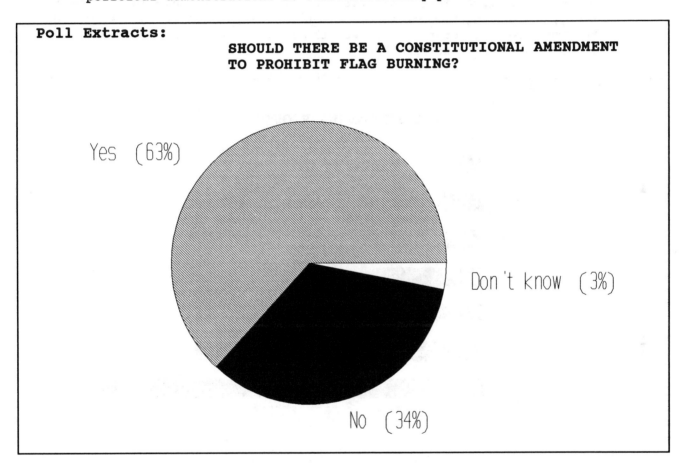

SHOULD THERE BE A CONSTITUTIONAL AMENDMENT TO PROHIBIT FLAG BURNING?

Yes (63%)

Don't know (3%)

No (34%)

Also in Source: Questions about cameras, politics, and sentencing in the courts.

Poll Details: The poll was conducted by Penn & Schoen Associates for *National Law Journal*/Lexis. 805 Americans above the age of 18 were interviewed on January 27 and 28, 1990. Margin of error was 3.4%.

Availability: Published in *The National Law Journal*, February 26, 1990, p. 1, 36-37.

DEMOCRATIC VALUES

Description: The poll attempted to determine what are today's prevailing
political values.

Results: Fewer young people (age 18-34) believe that civic duties such as
displaying the flag, serving in the military, serving on a jury, answering
the census, and paying all taxes are as important as their elders.
Respondents felt that the following were "very important" to being a good
citizen: obeying the law (94%), voting (86%), paying all taxes (79%),
answering the census (69%), serving on a jury (63%), serving in the
military (61%), following politics in the news (56%), displaying the flag
(44%), and giving time or money to causes (21%). 64% of the respondents
thought that low voter turnout was the biggest threat to democracy, with
women being more concerned than men

Poll Extracts:

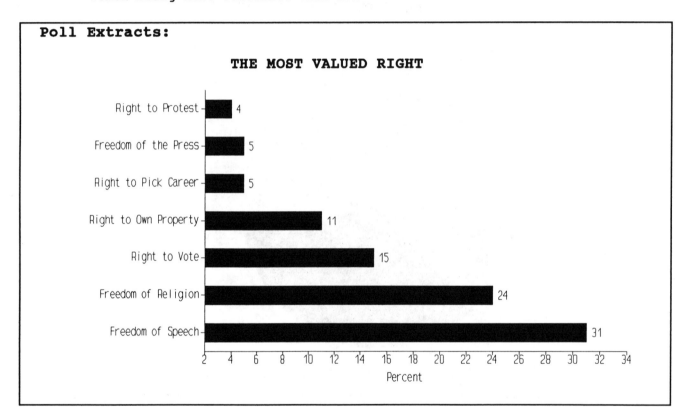

THE MOST VALUED RIGHT

Also in Source: The percentage of respondents who believe democracy is valued
more in Eastern Europe than in the U.S. Reasons for why other people don't
vote. Respondent's attitudes toward banning rap music.

Poll Details: Gordon S. Black Corp. conducted this *USA Today* poll on June 25-
26, 1990. 811 adults were interviewed in this nationwide telephone poll.
The sampling error is 3.5%.

Availability: Published in *USA Today*, July 3-4, 1990, p. 1A, 11A.

EXECUTIVES RATE U.S. AGENCIES

Description: Presents the results of a survey identifying those federal
     agencies which are most respected and least respected among former
     government executives.

Results: The National Security is the most respected federal agency, while the
     Bureau of Indian Affairs is the least respected.

Poll Extracts:

MOST RESPECTED FEDERAL AGENCIES

1. National Security Council

2. Federal Reserve

3. National Institutes of Health

4. Council on Economic Affairs

5. Office of the Treasury Secretary

6. Office of Trade Representative

7. Defense Advanced Research Projects Agency

8. Federal Bureau of Investigation

9. Central Intelligence Agency

10. Securities and Exchange Commission

Also in Source: The least respected federal agencies in rank order are:
     Bureau of Indian Affairs, Small Business Administration, Indian Health
     Service, Department of Education, Office of Thrift Supervision, Commission
     on Civil Rights, Department of Housing and Urban Development, Equal
     Employment Opportunity Commission, Consumer Product Safety Commission, and
     Employment and Training Administration.

Poll Details: Members of the Washington-based Council for Excellence in
     Government were asked to rate federal agencies on a scale of 1 to 5, with 5
     being the strongest. 250 members returned the survey.

Availability: Published in *The Washington Post*, November 1, 1990, p. A21.

LIMITED POLITICAL TERMS

Description: Presents the results of a survey concerning the limitation on the number of terms federal or state elected officials can serve.

Results: Approximately 75% of the respondents favor a limit on the number of terms an elected federal or state official can serve.

Poll Extracts:

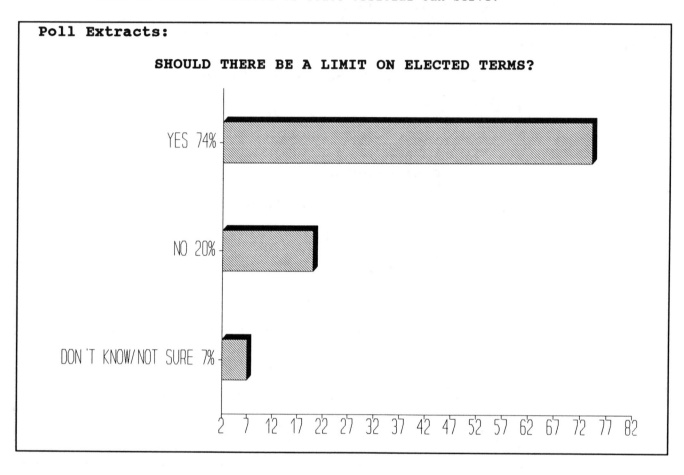

SHOULD THERE BE A LIMIT ON ELECTED TERMS?

YES 74%

NO 20%

DON'T KNOW/NOT SURE 7%

2 7 12 17 22 27 32 37 42 47 52 57 62 67 72 77 82

Also in Source: 82% of the respondents said federal and state elected officials generally are more responsive to special interest groups, 9% said the voters, 4% said both equally, and 4% didn't know.

Poll Details: Market Opinion Research conducted a poll between October 26 through 28, 1990.

Availability: Published in *The Detroit Free Press*, November 4, 1990, p. 1A, 9A.

POWER IN GOVERNMENT

Description: This poll dealt with power in government and defense funds.

Results: The majority of those polled believe Congress is the most powerful branch of government. 56% of the respondents believe military spending should not be cut.

Poll Extracts:

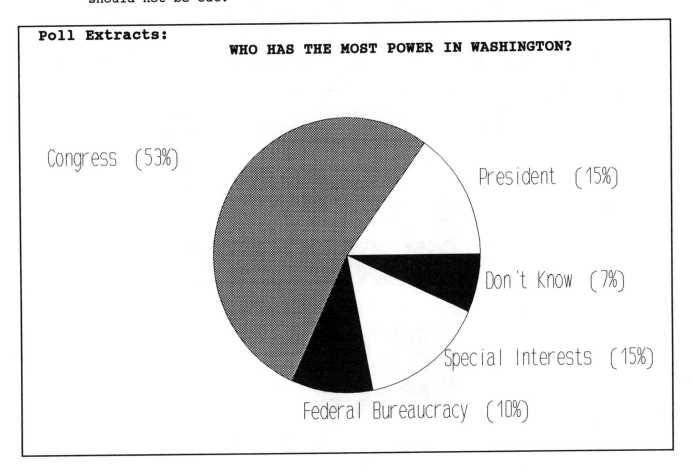

WHO HAS THE MOST POWER IN WASHINGTON?

Also in Source: Respondents were asked to assume the defense budget was being reduced; given ten choices, the percentages were listed as to what respondents would most like to see the money (that was taken from defense) spent on. The results from a separate poll on national problems, and the outlook for solving them in the next decade.

Poll Details: A *Washington Post* telephone survey of 1,004 randomly selected adults, conducted by ICR Survey Research Group of Media, Pennsylvania, on January 12-15, 1990. The margin of sampling error is 3%.

Availability: Published in *The Washington Post*, January 21, 1990, p. A1, A24.

PUBLIC PERCEPTIONS OF CONGRESS

Description: This poll asked respondents about the way Congress is handling its job, and Congressional attempts to reduce the budget.

Results: More respondents disapproved than approved of the way Congress is handling its job. When respondents were asked about their own representative, the majority of respondents did approve of their representative's handling of his or her job. 59% of the respondents did not think that President Bush and the leaders of Congress are making a serious effort to reduce the Federal budget deficit.

Poll Extracts:

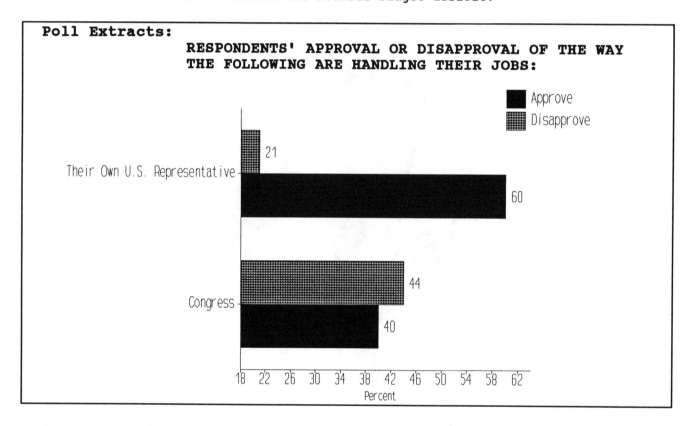

Also in Source: The percentage of respondents who: feel that their U.S. Representative deserves to be re-elected; would pay higher taxes to help protect Saudi Arabia against Iraqi aggression; would be less likely to vote for their member of Congress if he or she voted for a raise, took contributions from a savings and loan institution, or opposed capital punishment; have not yet formed an opinion on U.S. Supreme Court nominee David Souter; and believe that there is financial corruption in Congress.

Poll Details: This *New York Times*/CBS News poll was conducted with 1,422 adults from the U.S., excluding Alaska and Hawaii, from August 16-19, 1990. The interviews were conducted by telephone, with further details as to how the telephone numbers were selected provided in the source. The sampling error is 3%, with the potential sampling error being larger for smaller subgroups.

Availability: Published in *The New York Times*, September 4, 1990, p. A1, A13.

REASONS FOR NOT VOTING

Description: Presents the results of a survey of Californians as to why
citizens don't register to vote and why citizens don't vote.

Results: The most popular reasons given by the respondents as to why they had
not registered to vote were: too busy (22%); not interested in politics
(21%); not in current home long enough (18%); forgot to register (10%);
didn't like the candidates (9%); voting doesn't matter (9%). The top four
reasons that registered voters gave for not voting were: too busy (35%);
not interested in politics (8%); didn't like the candidates (6%); voting
doesn't matter (5%).

Poll Extracts:

**THE TOP FIVE CHANGES THAT RESPONDENTS SAID
WOULD ENCOURAGE THEM TO VOTE:**

1. If issues were less confusing 35%

2. Higher quality candidates 13%

3. If it were easier to vote 9%

4. Elections on Sunday 8%

5. Shorter ballots 7%

Also in Source: Characteristics of the citizens who did not register to vote,
or did not vote in the June 5, 1990 California primary, such as age,
income, race, sex, education, and ideology.

Poll Details: This *Los Angeles Times* poll was conducted from June 15-20, 1990.
2,260 U.S. citizens living in California were interviewed by telephone.
The margin of error is 3%.

Availability: Published in the *Los Angeles Times*, July 8, 1990, p. A1, A28.

SAVINGS AND LOAN CRISIS

Description: Presents the results of a survery concerning the government's
handling of the thrift industry crisis.

Results: Almost 60% of the respondents gave the Bush administration negative
marks in handling the crisis, which could cost the taxpayers $325 billion
to $500 billion, according to estimates by the General Accounting Office.

Poll Extracts:

ADMINISTRATION'S RATING ON THE S & L CRISIS:

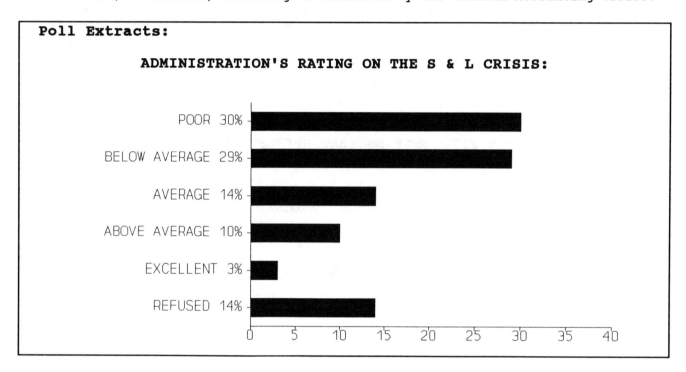

Also in Source: 47% of the Republicans gave the administration negative
marks. 66% of the independent voters and 64% of the Democrats did
likewise. 64% gave Congress negative marks on handling the crisis. 64% of
the Democrats marked Congress negatively. 67% of independent voters and
72% of the Republicans responding to the survey gave Congress poor marks.
27% said the White House was likely to do a good job resolving the thrift
debacle. 36% said the Democrats were more likely to provide leadership.
President Bush's favorability rating was 79%.

Poll Details: The *Boston Globe*-WBZ-TV poll was conducted by KRC Communications
Research Inc. 1,002 registered voters were interviewed by telephone on
June 10 through June 12, 1990. Margin of error is 3%.

Availability: Published in *The Boston Globe*, June 14, 1990, p. 4.

SHOULD THE PENNY BE PITCHED?

Description: Presents the results of a survey concerning a proposal to limit the use of the penny as legal tender. The House Banking subcommittee considered a bill to round off cash transactions to the nearest five cents. The proposal would keep pennies only in groups of five and no more than 25 at one time. Under the bill, the Treasury would still make pennies, but only for collectors.

Results: Over 60% of the respondents disapprove of the proposal.

Poll Extracts:

A PENNY FOR YOUR THOUGHTS?

Do you agree with this proposal?...............No....62%

Are you concerned that merchants will
raise prices to compensate for losses
due to rounding?................................Yes...77%

Is the penny a longstanding tradition
in the United States?..........................Yes...92%

Also in Source: The most common use of pennies is to help pay for items priced at levels not divisible by five.

Poll Details: This Gallup survey of 750 adults, conducted by telephone between April 23 and April 26, 1990, has a margin of error of 4%. It was sponsored by Americans for Common Cents.

Availability: Published in the *Dayton Daily News*, May 24, 1990, p. 6-B.

THE U.S. SUPREME COURT

Description: Respondents were questioned on their knowledge of the U.S.
        Supreme Court.

Results: "Less than one-fourth of the respondents knew how many justices there
        are, and nearly two-thirds of them could not name a single member of the
        court."

Poll Extracts:

RESPONDENTS THINK OR BELIEVE:

The present Supreme Court in recent decisions
has not done enough to help women and minorities
fight discrimination 53%

It is "very important" that women, blacks,
other minorities and people of different
religions sit on the high court 55%

Non-lawyers, as well as lawyers, should sit
as justices 57%

Justices act on other factors than the facts
and the law in deciding cases 47%

Also in Source: Respondents' beliefs about the Constitution, and reactions to
        issues facing the Supreme Court.

Poll Details: The poll was conducted by Penn & Schoen Associates for *National
        Law Journal*/Lexis. 805 Americans above the age of 18 were interviewed on
        January 27 and 28, 1990. Margin of error was 3.4%.

Availability: Published in *The National Law Journal,* February 26, 1990,
        p. 1, 36-37.

VOTER CONFIDENCE IN MASSACHUSETTS

Description: Respondents were queried about their attitudes toward state
government.

Results: "The poll shows a widespread distrust of, and alienation from, state
government and widespread cynicism about elected officials." 81% of the
respondents think Massachusetts state government is out of touch with the
state's residents. 62% of the respondents think Massachusetts state
government serves them worse than they would expect. 65% of the
respondents are not very confident about the ability of state government to
solve the problems facing Massachusetts. Only 6% of the respondents felt
that they had more confidence in state government than local or federal
government.

Poll Extracts:

WHO DO YOU THINK STATE GOVERNMENT SERVES?

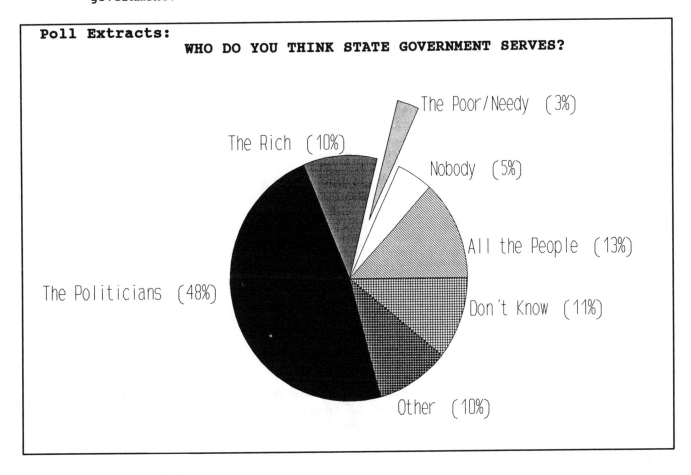

Also in Source: Questions dealing with a tax roll-back petition, the state
budget, and issues considered by respondents when evaluating candidates for
governor.

Poll Details: KRC Communications Research conducted the poll for *The Boston
Globe* and WBZ-TV during August 26-30, 1990. Telephone interviews were
conducted with 173 registered Democrats, 183 Independents, and 71
Republicans.

Availability: Published in *The Boston Globe*, September 3, 1990, p. 1, 8-9.

WHO DOES CONGRESS SERVE?

Description: Presents the results of a survey concerning which constituency
Congress better serves: the people or special interests.

Results: Over 70% of the respondents feel members of Congress are more
interested in serving the needs of special interest groups than they are in
serving the needs of the people they represent.

Poll Extracts:

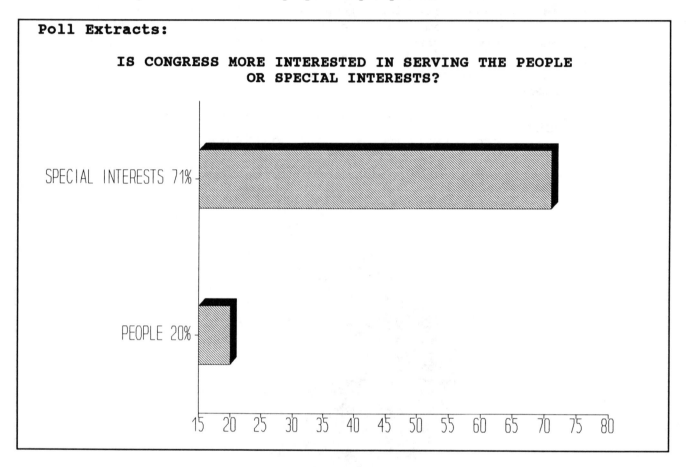

IS CONGRESS MORE INTERESTED IN SERVING THE PEOPLE
OR SPECIAL INTERESTS?

Also in Source: 56% of the respondents said members of Congress should be
limited to a total of 12 years of service, while 37% said they should serve
as long as they are able to be re-elected.

Poll Details: The results of this *New York Times*/CBS News Poll are based on
interviews with 960 adults nationwide conducted by telephone between
October 8 and 10, 1990.

Availability: Published in *The New York Times*, October 12, 1990, p. A21.

YOUTHS AND DEMOCRATIC BELIEFS

Description: This poll questioned attitudes toward the democratic process.

Results: Youths valued "Freedom of Speech" the most. It was the right they would fight hardest to keep, and be least willing to give up, when choosing from a list of seven rights and freedoms.

Poll Extracts:

WHEN IT COMES TO READING THE NEWSPAPER OR WATCHING THE NEWS ON TV, HOW MUCH INTEREST DO YOU HAVE IN POLITICS AND GOVERNMENT?

A great deal	16%
Quite a bit	26%
Just some	39%
Very little	18%

THE ONLY RESPONSIBILITIES OF BEING A GOOD CITIZEN ARE PAYING YOUR TAXES AND OBEYING THE LAW:

Agree strongly	13%
Agree slightly	15%
Disagree slightly	28%
Disagree strongly	43%

GOVERNMENT OFFICIALS DON'T CARE MUCH ABOUT WHAT AVERAGE PEOPLE THINK:

Agree strongly	19%
Agree slightly	31%
Disagree slightly	31%
Disagree strongly	15%

Also in Source: Responses to the following questions: "How much do you feel you know about the way the government works?", "How likely are you to register and vote in the first election after you turn 18?", and "How often can you trust the government in Washington to do what is right?" Respondents were also asked to respond to the following statements: "America is the best country in the world to live in.", "Sometimes politics and government seem so complicated that a person like me can't really understand what's going on.", "If a person doesn't care how an election comes out, that person shouldn't vote in it.", "So many people vote in the national election that it doesn't matter much whether I vote or not."

Poll Details: This poll questioned 15-to-23-year-olds. The poll is from the People for the American Way, a constitutional-liberties organization.

Availability: Published in *Scholastic Update*, March 9, 1990 (volume 122, number 13), p. 14-15, 17.

THE AFFECT OF THE S&L SCANDAL ON SENATOR GLENN

Description: Presents the results of a survey concerning United States Senator John Glenn's political future as a result of his alleged participation in the savings and loan investigation.

Results: Approximately one-third of the respondents said John Glenn should run for re-election for the United States Senate from the State of Ohio.

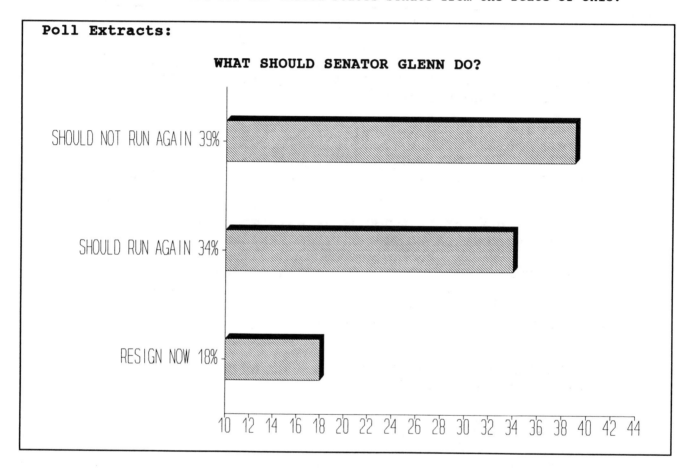

Poll Extracts:

WHAT SHOULD SENATOR GLENN DO?

SHOULD NOT RUN AGAIN 39%

SHOULD RUN AGAIN 34%

RESIGN NOW 18%

10 12 14 16 18 20 22 24 26 28 30 32 34 36 38 40 42 44

Also in Source: On whether Senator Glenn should run for re-election, 44% of Democrats and 24% of Republicans surveyed said he should run, while 34% of Democrats and 44% of Republicans said he should not. 46% of the respondents said Ohio's financial condition has not changed, while the rest were split about whether the state's economy had improved or worsened.

Poll Details: Voter Research & Surveys asked 1,957 Ohio voters to fill out questionnaires on a variety of topics, including whether Senator John Glenn should run for office again in 1992. The margin of error is about 2.8%.

Availability: Published in *The Cincinnati Enquirer*, November 8, 1990, p. B4.

DAVID SOUTER'S SENATE TESTIMONY

Description: Presents the results of a survey concerning Supreme Court nominee
David Souter's testimony before the Senate Judiciary Committee.

Results: 65% of the Republicans thought David Souter was right not to tell the
Senate what he thinks about abortion. 52% of the Independents and 36% of
the Democrats have similar positions.

Poll Extracts:

SOUTER WAS RIGHT NOT TO TELL HIS VIEWS ON ABORTION:

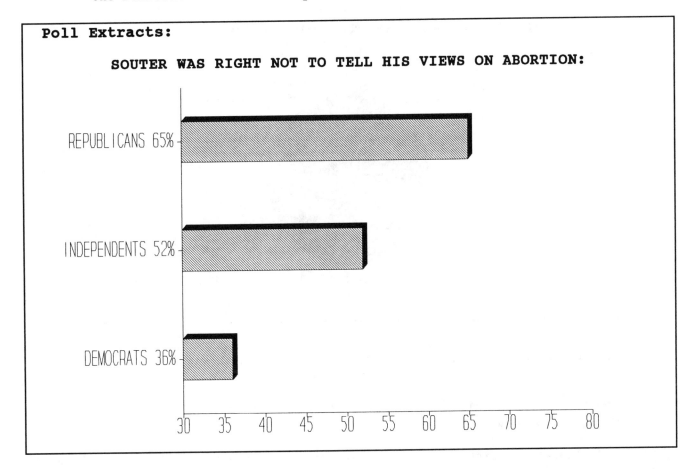

Also in Source: 48% of the respondents aged 18-39 think Souter was right not
to give his views, while 45% said he was wrong. In the 40-64 age bracket,
that split was 51% to 40%. Among voters aged 65 and up, 53% thought Souter
was right in withholding his views, only 34% disagreed. 46% of the
respondents said they did not know if Souter is in favor of a
constitutional right to an abortion. A total of 33% said they believed
Souter is opposed to a constitutional right to an abortion, while 22% said
they believed Souter favors such a right.

Poll Details: The *Boston Globe*-WBZ-TV poll was conducted by KRC Communications
Research. 1,006 registered voters were interviewed nationwide by telephone
on September 16-18, 1990. The margin of error is 3%.

Availability: Published in *The Boston Globe*, September 20, 1990, p. 20.

DETROIT POLITICS

Description: The survey asked Detroiters for their opinion of Mayor Young.

Results: Only one-third of those Detroiters who had voted for Mayor Young in November, 1989 would vote for him in February, 1990.

Poll Extracts:

HOW DO YOU FEEL ABOUT MAYOR COLEMAN YOUNG?

SOMEWHAT NEGATIVE 19.9%

VERY NEGATIVE 31.4%

NO RESPONSE 3.8%

NEUTRAL 9.7%

VERY POSITIVE 16.6%

SOMEWHAT POSITIVE 18.6%

Also in Source: A general discussion of the causes and implications of the results of the poll are included in the article.

Poll Details: The poll was conducted through a scientific telephone survey of 501 registered voters.

Availability: Published in *The Detroit News and Free Press*, February 25, 1990 p. 1A,12A.

JAMES A. BAKER III

Description: Presents the results of a survey on the popularity of U.S.
Secretary of State James A. Baker III, following his participation in
obtaining the United Nations Security Council resolution which authorized
the use of force against Iraq, and his participation in negotiations with
Iraq.

Results: U.S. Secretary of State Baker was found to evoke a more positive
reaction in this poll than the 43% favorable rating he received in a
similar survey conducted three weeks earlier.

Poll Extracts:

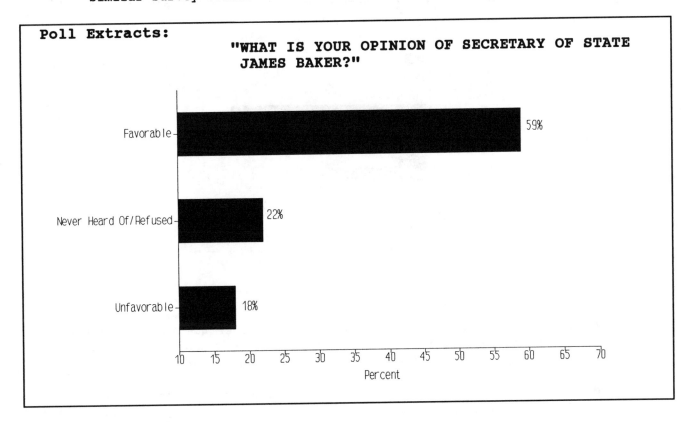

**"WHAT IS YOUR OPINION OF SECRETARY OF STATE
JAMES BAKER?"**

Also in Source: The popularity rating of President George Bush and Vice
President Dan Quayle. Respondents who thought that talks with Iraq would
bring about a peaceful solution to the Iraqi crisis. The percentage of
respondents who had heard of the "Keating Five" compared to the results of
a survey conducted in December 1989. The percentage of respondents who
thought that the five senators in the "Keating Five" should not run for
reelection. Support for public financing of congressional elections.

Poll Details: This nationwide *Boston Globe*/WBZ-TV poll surveyed 1,006
registered voters during December 2-4, 1990. KRC Communications Research
conducted the survey. The margin of error is 3%.

Availability: Published in *The Boston Globe*, December 7, 1990, p. 3.

MARION BARRY'S ARREST

Description: Presents the results of a survey of Washington D.C. residents
concerning the issues surrounding the arrest of Mayor Marion Barry.

Results: Almost half of the respondents felt that race was not a factor in the
investigation which led to Barry's arrest.

Poll Extracts:

IF MAYOR BARRY WAS WHITE, WOULD THE INVESTIGATIVE EFFORTS DIFFER?

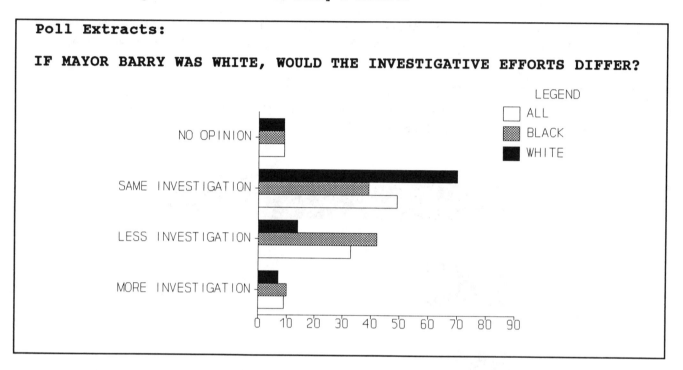

Also in Source: The survey contains a number of other questions involving
the investigation and arrest of Marion Barry. Questions also cover the
political implications of the current situation.

Poll Details: The results of the survey, sponsored by *The Washington Post*, are
based on telephone interviews of a randomly selected sample of 661 District
of Columbia residents. Sampling error is plus or minus 4%. The
interviewing was conducted by Chilton Research Services of Radnor, PA.

Availability: Published in *The Washington Post*, January 21, 1990, p. A17.

MARION BARRY'S TRIAL

Description: Presents the results of a survey measuring the level of
satisfaction of District of Columbia residents in the results of the trial
of ex-mayor Marion Barry.

Results: Half of the respondents are satisfied with Marion Barry's conviction
on a misdemeanor drug possession charge while the jury could not reach a
verdict on 12 other charges.

Poll Extracts:

ARE YOU SATISFIED WITH THE OUTCOME OF MARION BARRY'S TRIAL?

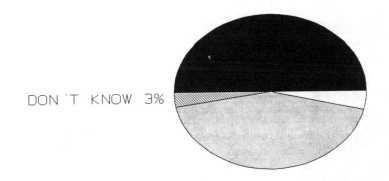

SATISFIED 50%

DON'T KNOW 3%   MIXED REACTION 4%

NOT SATISFIED 43%

Also in Source: 32% of the respondents would vote for Marion Barry to an at-
large seat on the District of Columbia Council. 33% said Barry should
serve time in jail. 74% of the respondents said that Marion Barry should
not be tried again on at least some of the charges upon which the jury
could not reach a verdict.

Poll Details: The results are based on a *Washington Post* poll of 895 self-
described registered voters in the District of Columbia conducted August
21-27, 1990. The margin of error is plus or minus 3%. The interviewing
was conducted by Chilton Research Services.

Availability: Published in *The Washington Post*, August 29, 1990, p. A1, A8.

THE ROLE OF RACE IN MARION BARRY'S INDICTMENT

Description: Presents the results of a survey concerning the motivations
leading to the indictments of Washington D.C. Mayor Marion Barry.

Results: 45% of the respondents think the indictment of Mayor Marion Barry was
racially motivated.

Poll Extracts:

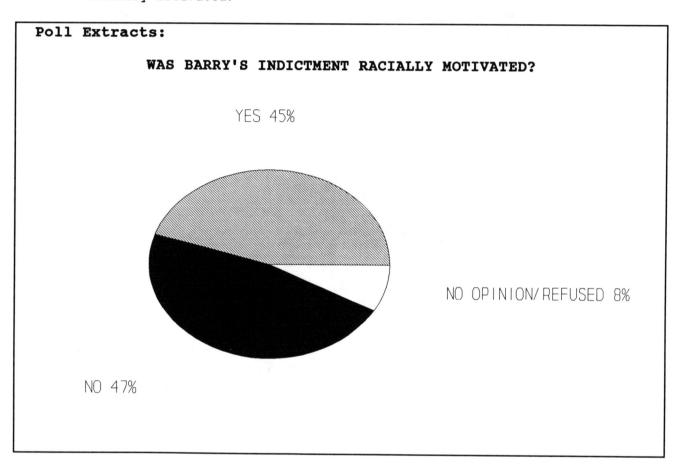

WAS BARRY'S INDICTMENT RACIALLY MOTIVATED?

YES 45%

NO OPINION/REFUSED 8%

NO 47%

Also in Source: 81% of the respondents think Marion Barry received a fair
trial. 52% are satisfied with the outcome of the trial and 62% think the
jury did a good job. 60% of the respondents think the news coverage of the
trial was generally fair. 53% think the trial increased racial tensions.

Poll Details: The results are based on telephone interviews conducted on
August 11, 1990 with 603 randomly selected District of Columbia residents
18 and older. Interviewing was conducted by Chilton Research.

Availability: Published in *The Washington Post*, August 12, 1990, p. A1, A14.

THE S&L SITUATION AND SENATOR RIEGLE

Description: Presents the results of a survey concerning the damage done to United States Senator Donald Riegle's political career due to his involvement in the savings and loan situation.

Results: 80% of the respondents said the savings and loan scandal was either very damaging or somewhat damaging to Senator Riegle.

Poll Extracts:

HOW DAMAGING HAS THE S&L CRISIS BEEN TO SENATOR RIEGLE?

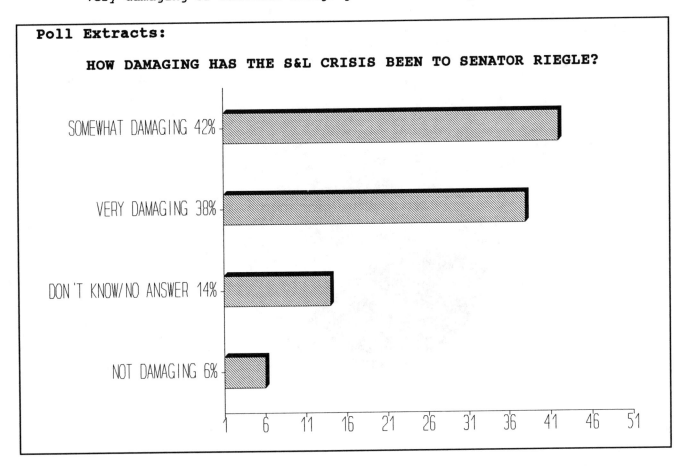

Also in Source: If Senator Riegle were up for re-election in the November 1990 general election, 23% of the respondents would vote for him, 62% would not vote for him, and 16% weren't sure or didn't know.

Poll Details: This *Detroit Free Press*-WXYZ survey was conducted by Detroit-based Market Opinion Research in a telephone poll taken October 26-28, 1990. 800 Michigan registered voters were surveyed. The margin of error is plus or minus 3.5%

Availability: Published in the *Detroit Free Press*, November 2, 1990, p. 1A, 8A.

SENATOR JOHN GLENN'S APPROVAL RATING

Description: Presents the results of a survey concerning the approval rating
        by Ohio voters of Senator John Glenn after the disclosure of his
        involvement with savings and loan executive Charles H. Keating, Jr.

Results: Almost 50% of respondents approve of the performance of United States
        Senator John Glenn.

Poll Extracts:

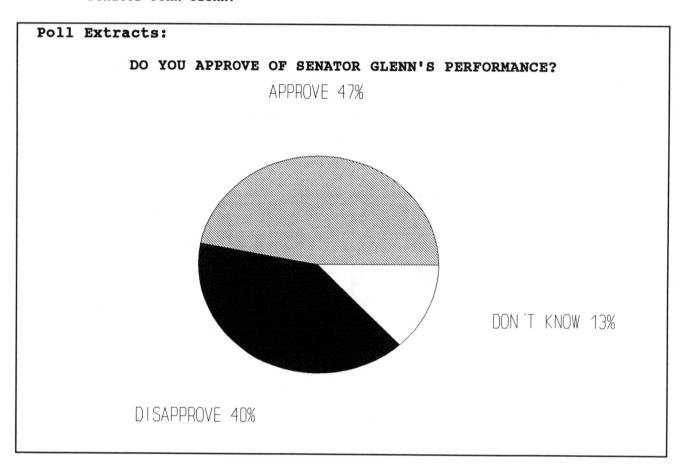

DO YOU APPROVE OF SENATOR GLENN'S PERFORMANCE?

APPROVE 47%

DON'T KNOW 13%

DISAPPROVE 40%

Also in Source: 65% of the Democrats surveyed approve of Glenn's performance,
        while 31% of Republicans and 45% of Independents share the same opinion.
        61% of the blacks and 51% of the Roman Catholics surveyed approve of
        Glenn's performance. 53% of the voters from union households also approve
        of his performance.

Poll Details: This *Columbus Dispatch* mail poll of 1,581 registered voters was
        conducted August 30 - September 6, 1990.

Availability: Published in *The Columbus Dispatch*, September 15, 1990, p. 1A.

SENATOR RIEGLE AND THE S&L SITUATION

Description: Presents the results of a survey concerning the effects of
Michigan Senator Donald Riegle's involvement in the savings and loan
situation on his re-election possibilities.

Results: Only 4% of the respondents said they would definitely vote for Donald
Riegle, while 17% said they would definitely not vote for him.

Poll Extracts:

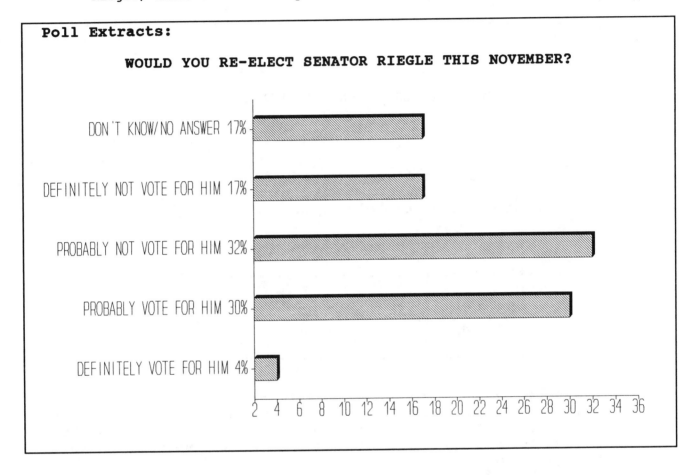

WOULD YOU RE-ELECT SENATOR RIEGLE THIS NOVEMBER?

Also in Source: 29% of the respondents said Senator Riegle's involvement in
the savings and loan situation was very damaging, 45% said somewhat
damaging, and 8% said not damaging.

Poll Details: The *Detroit Free Press*-WXYZ survey was conducted by Market
Opinion Research in two telephone polls in July/August, 1990. The results
were taken from a survey of 803 Michigan registered voters. The margin of
error is 3.5%.

Availability: Published in the *Detroit Free Press*, August 3, 1990, p. 1B, 2B.

NATIONAL RIFLE ASSOCIATION

Description: Presents the results of a survey of gun owners concerning the policies and views of the National Rifle Association.

Results: The results indicate differences between the official policies and views of the National Rifle Association and the opinions and views of gun owners.

Poll Extracts:

DO YOU FAVOR MANDATORY REGISTRATION OF:

	Yes
Semiautomatic weapons	73%
Handguns or pistols	72%
Rifles	54%
Shotguns	50%

Also in Source: 67% of the respondents said they agreed with the overall policies of the National Rifle Association. However, 87% are for a federal law requiring a 7 day waiting period and a background check for anyone who wants to buy a handgun. 31% feel that stricter gun laws would reduce violence in the United States.

Poll Details: The results were taken from a telephone poll of 605 gun owners taken for *Time*/CNN on December 15-22, 1989 by Yankelovich Clancy Shulman. Margin of error is 4%.

Availability: Published in *Time*, January 29, 1990 (volume 135, Number 5), p. 16-21.

RESTRICTIONS ON GUN OWNERSHIP

Description: Presents the results of a survey concerning the right to bear arms and the various issues surrounding gun control efforts.

Results: 37% of the respondents favor a law making it illegal to own or buy a handgun. Over 90% approve of participation in a mandatory gun-safety program for anyone buying a firearm for the first time.

Poll Extracts:

VIEWS ON VARIOUS TYPES OF GUN RESTRICTIONS:

Do you approve of mandatory participation in
a gun-safety program for anyone buying a
firearm for the first time?..........................Yes...91%

Should there be a two-week waiting period
between applying to buy a gun and taking
possession of the weapon?............................Yes...89%

Should there be a law prohibiting a convicted
felon from purchasing any type of firearm?..........Yes...88%

Should there be a law requiring that all
firearms be registered with the local police?........Yes...81%

Do you endorse outlawing semiautomatic weapons?.......Yes...75%

Also in Source: 56% of the respondents said widespread availability of handguns increased violent crime. 45% said a person is safer without a gun, while 42% said a person is safer with a gun. 65% of the respondents said gun ownership is irrelevant to our freedom in an age of nuclear weapons and supersonic fighter planes. 30% said gun ownership by private citizens helps preserve our country's freedoms.

Poll Details: This national poll was commissioned by *Parents* magazine.

Availability: Published in *Parents*, September, 1990 (volume 65, number 9), p. 28.

SUPPORT FOR GUN REGULATION

Description: This *Parade* magazine readers' poll, in the January 14, 1990 issue, asked respondents about four proposals dealing with gun regulation that were made by Warren E. Burger, Chief Justice of the United States (1969-1986).

Results: The majority of readers who responded were in favor of greater gun regulation.

Poll Extracts:

THE FOUR PROPOSALS

A 10-day waiting period should be required
before a license to purchase a gun is issued ... 67% Agreed
                                                  29% Opposed

A gun-buyer should be required to fill out
an application reciting age, residence,
employment, and criminal convictions .... 63% Agreed
                                                 20% Opposed

The transfer of a firearm should follow the
same procedure as that of a motor vehicle ...... 64% Agreed
                                                  31% Opposed

A "ballistic fingerprint" should be filed
on every weapon .... 65% Agreed
                                                  32% Opposed

---

Also in Source: Article which provides responses from leaders of the National Rifle Association and the International Association of Chiefs of Police.

Poll Details: More than 140,000 readers responded to this poll. Readers dialed a 900 number on their touch-tone telephones and answered "yes" or "no" to four questions. Some callers attempted to use a rotary phone and were unable to register their votes, although their calls were noted, resulting in percentages which do not total 100%. The poll was also disrupted on its second day as a result of the AT&T service breakdown.

Availability: Published in *Parade* magazine (*The Washington Post*), April 8, 1990, p. 10-11.

TEXANS AND GUN CONTROL

Description: Presents the results of a survey concerning Texans' views and
          attitudes toward various types of gun control.

Results: Over 80% of the respondents favor a seven-day mandatory waiting period
          to purchase a handgun.

Poll Extracts:

SHOULD THERE BE A SEVEN-DAY WAITING PERIOD TO BUY A HANDGUN?

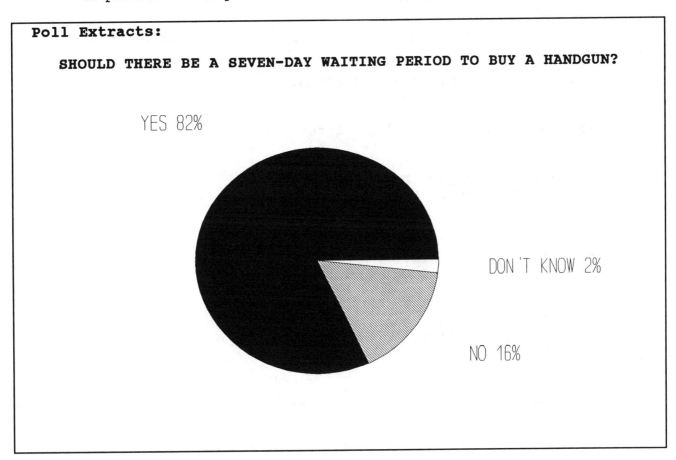

YES 82%

DON'T KNOW 2%

NO 16%

Also in Source: 69% of the respondents favor a ban on the sale of high
          caliber, fast firing assault rifles and, if their sale remains legal, 89%
          agree there should be a seven-day waiting period between sale and
          possession. 52% of the respondents own a gun.

Poll Details: The survey of 1,021 adult Texans was conducted for Harte-Hanks
          Communications by the Public Policy Resources Laborotory at Texas A&M
          University. The telephone poll taken August 4-19, 1990, has a margin of
          error of 3%.

Availability: Published in *The Dallas Morning News*, September 3, 1990, p. 1A,
          26A.

ALLERGY SUFFERERS' THOUGHTS

Description: This survey queried allergy sufferers about their problem and the medications they use to treat the symptoms.

Results: People with allergies feel misunderstood by people who don't have the same problem. They suffer from side effects of their allergy medications and feel less productive at work.

Poll Extracts:

ALLERGY SUFFERERS:

Feel allergies limit their lifestyle 34%

Say their allergies make them
less productive at work 74%

Say drowsiness is the most common side effect of
over-the-counter medicines; other effects include
nervousness, dry mouth, and insomnia 74%

Report knowing that some allergy drugs can
impair their ability to drive, although 61%
say they still drive anyway 67%

Also in Source: About one in four Americans have allergies, such as pollen and ragweed.

Poll Details: The survey was conducted by the Gallup Organization. The results are from a national sample of adults.

Availability: Published in *Health (The Washington Post)*, April 3, 1990 (volume 6, number 14), p. 5.

CHANGING THE BODY

Description: This survey queried respondents on American attitudes toward physical conditioning and self-image.

Results: "Given the opportunity to change their bodies, only 13% of the respondents to the survey said they'd stay as they were." Most adults thought that physical attractiveness was an advantage in school, career, friendship, and marriage, but tended to rate themselves as less than perfect in attractiveness, fitness, and health.

Poll Extracts:

WHEN RESPONDENTS WERE ASKED WHAT KIND OF SHAPE
THEY WERE IN, RESPONDENTS THOUGHT THAT THEIR
PHYSICAL CONDITION WAS: .... Good -- 58%
                                          Excellent -- 11%

WHEN RESPONDENTS WERE ASKED HOW PEOPLE OF THE
OPPOSITE SEX WOULD RATE THEM, 84% OF THE RESPONDENTS
THOUGHT THAT THE OPPOSITE SEX WOULD RATE THEM
AS EITHER "SOMEWHAT ATTRACTIVE" OR "VERY ATTRACTIVE."

42% OF THE MALE RESPONDENTS APPRECIATE THIN FIGURES ON
WOMEN, WHILE 44% OF THE MALE RESPONDENTS PREFER MORE
GENEROUS FIGURES.

MEN FIND THE GENERAL APPEAL OF A WOMAN'S FACE AND
FIGURE AS A WOMAN'S MOST ATTRACTIVE FEATURE; ONLY 7% OF
THE MEN FOUND THE MOST ATTRACTIVE FEATURE TO BE BREASTS.

Also in Source: The number of ads and articles about dieting in women's magazines exceeds the number of diet ads and articles in men's magazines by 10 to one. Women with eating disorders outnumber men by the same ratio.

Poll Details: This survey was sponsored by the Times Mirror Center for the People and the Press, and conducted by Princeton Survey Research Associates. 1,220 adults were surveyed by telephone.

Availability: Originally published in *The Baltimore Sun*. The information provided is based on an article printed in *The Cincinnati Enquirer*, August 21, 1990, p. B-1.

FINANCIAL PRESSURES HIT HOSPITALS

Description: Presents the results of a survey of hospital administrators concerning the effects of increasing financial pressures on hospital admissions and transfer policies.

Results: The results indicate that admissions and transfer policies have been affected by increased financial pressures.

Poll Extracts:

HAVE FINANCIAL PRESSURES CHANGED YOUR ADMISSIONS POLICIES?

YES - 37%

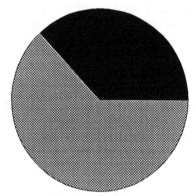

NO - 63%

Also in Source: 52% of the respondents felt that financial pressures will force a change in admissions and transfer policies in the future. A number of more specific questions and responses concerning the nature of policy changes already in effect are included in the article.

Poll Details: The poll was conducted by Professional Research Consultants of Omaha, Nebraska for *Hospitals*. 250 hospital CEOs were contacted.

Availability: Published in *Hospitals*, February 5, 1990 (volume 64, number 3), p. 64.

HEPATITIS B

Description: Respondents were queried about their knowledge of the disease "Hepatitis B," an inflammation of the liver which kills about 14 Americans every day.

Results: The majority of Americans know almost nothing about the disease.

Poll Extracts:

KNOWLEDGE OF HEPATITIS B

Respondents who acknowledged they knew little
or nothing about the disease 83%

Respondents who did not know that a vaccine
exists to prevent people from becoming infected
with Hepatitis B 69%

Also in Source: "Officials say that about 300,000 people are afflicted annually by the disease in the United States and about 5,000 people, including 300 health care workers, die of the disease or its complications. The virus, spread by blood or other body fluids, is many times more contagious than human immunodeficiency virus, the cause of AIDS, officials say."

Poll Details: As part of a patient and physician education program, SmithKline Beecham surveyed 1,000 people nationwide. The telephone survey was conducted during September 10-17, 1990. Regarding the respondents, "nearly two-thirds were married, 40% were high school graduates or had taken technical courses, and 40% had taken college courses or had college degrees."

Availability: Published in the *Dayton Daily News*, October 12, 1990, p. 2-C.

NUTRITION INFORMATION

Description: Presents the results of a survey concerning nutrition and its
impact on health. The level of nutrition information was also measured.

Results: The results indicate a mixture of solid nutritional guidelines as well
as popular misconceptions concerning American eating habits.

Poll Extracts:

NUTRITIONAL INFORMATION AND PRACTICES:

Balance, variety and moderation are
the keys to good health..................................Yes...95%

What we eat may affect our future health.................Yes...83%

Are you familiar with the basic food groups?............Yes...77%

Are there "good" foods and "bad" foods?.................Yes...67%

Are you eating more oat bran?............................Yes...52%

Are you eating more vegetables?.........................Yes....8%

Is there a difference between dietary cholesterol
and blood cholesterol?..................................Yes...85%

Also in Source: A general discussion of the implications of the study were
included in the article.

Poll Details: The survey, conducted by Gallup, was commissioned by the
American Dietetic Association and the International Food Informational
Council.

Availability: Published in the *Chicago Tribune*, February 22, 1990, p. 9B.

NUTRITIONAL CONCERNS

Description: This food labeling survey queried respondents about their
   nutritional concerns when shopping.

Results: The top nutritional concerns of the respondents were fat content,
   cholesterol, and salt content.

Poll Extracts:

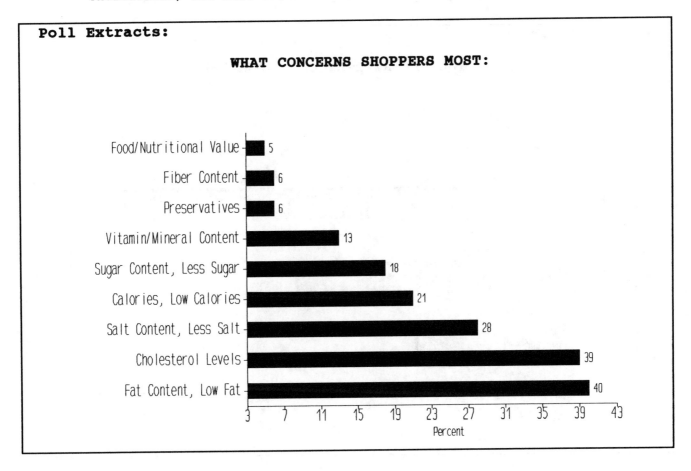

WHAT CONCERNS SHOPPERS MOST:

Also in Source: The percentage of shoppers who say they always read the
   ingredients list when making a first-time purchase. The top factors when
   food shopping.

Poll Details: The survey results are from the Food Marketing Institute.

Availability: Published in the *Chicago Tribune*, June 18, 1990, p. C1, C4.

SELF-PERCEPTION OF ONE'S HEALTH

Description: Presents the results of a survey concerning Americans' opinions
and attitudes toward their own health and physical appearance.

Results: 30% of the respondents are happy with their appearance, but 42% say
they are overwieght. 11% believe they are in excellent shape.

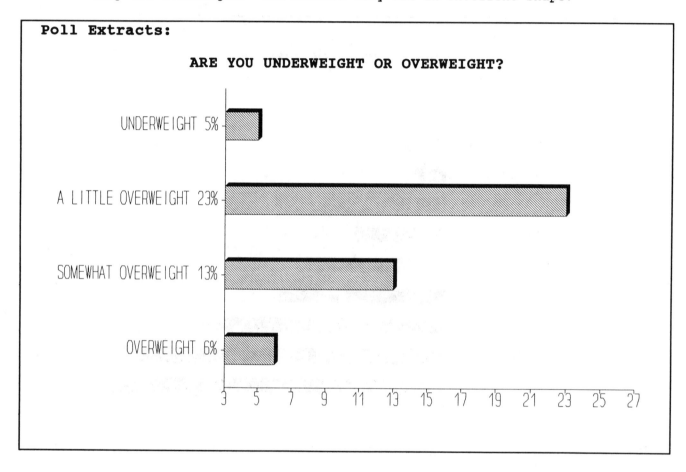

Poll Extracts:

ARE YOU UNDERWEIGHT OR OVERWEIGHT?

Also in Source: 53% of the respondents described their general health as
"good," 27% called it "excellent," and 15% said it was "fair." 5% said
their health was "poor." While 73% of the respondents believe that
exercise can improve their health and extend their lives, only 59% said
they exercise on a regular basis.

Poll Details: Princeton Survey Research Associates surveyed 1,220 adults
during the period of July 12-16, 1990, for the Times Mirror Center for
People & the Press. Margin of error is plus or minus 3%.

Availability: Published in the *Los Angeles Times*, August 19, 1990, p. A4.

WOMEN AND DIETING

Description: Presents the results of a survey concerning women's attitudes toward their own weight, body image and dieting.

Results: Many women are very critical of their own weight and body image. More than 85% of the women surveyed had gone on a weight-reducing diet at some point in their lives.

Poll Extracts:

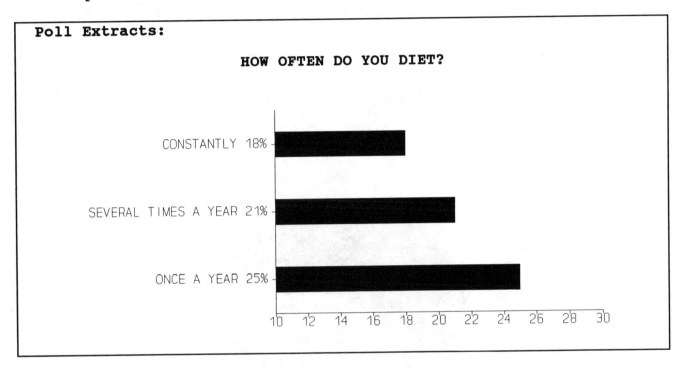

HOW OFTEN DO YOU DIET?

Also in Source: The survey includes a number of questions and responses covering the broad area of body and personal image and the effects of that image on different aspects of life.

Poll Details: *Family Circle* surveyed their Consumer Panel via a seven page questionnaire. The Consumer Panel consists of 900 women who are readers of the magazine. 739 responses were received and the author interviewed some of the women by telephone.

Availability: Published in *Family Circle*, February 1, 1990, (volume 103, number 2) p. 41, 42, 44, 46.

AFFORDABILITY OF HEALTH CARE

Description: Presents the results of a survey concerning whether people can afford a major illness. The respondents were asked the question: Suppose you became critically ill. Taking into account whatever medical insurance you have and also your current finances, do you think you would be able to afford good medical care, or not?

Results: Approximately one-third of the respondents could not afford a major illness.

Poll Extracts:

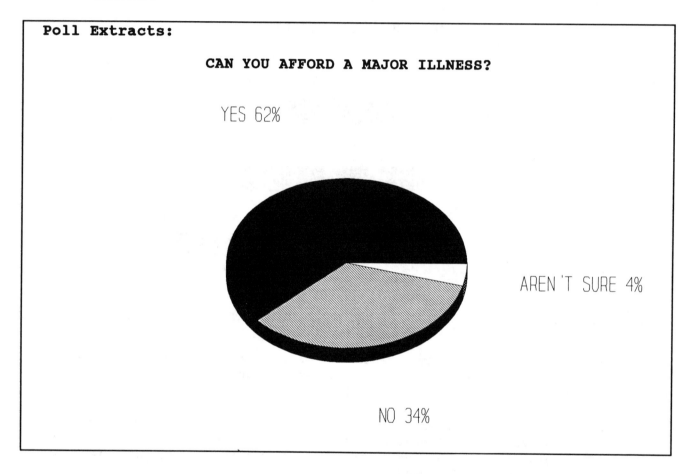

CAN YOU AFFORD A MAJOR ILLNESS?

YES 62%

AREN'T SURE 4%

NO 34%

Also in Source: 80% of the respondents agree that the uninsured should be allowed to pay less to doctors and hospitals, 8% said no, 5% said it depends, and 7% didn't know. 13% of the respondents said Georgia's health care system works well, 41% said it needs some changes, 34% said it needs a complete overhaul, and 12% weren't sure.

Poll Details: This *Atlanta Journal and Constitution* poll of 751 adults was conducted on December 1-6, 1990. The margin of error is 4%.

Availability: Published in *The Atlanta Journal and Constitution*, December 13, 1990, p. A1, A18.

CALIFORNIA HEALTH CARE SERVICES

Description: This survey is the fourth annual Gallup California Health Care Poll. The survey questioned Californians about health care issues and personal health habits.

Results: A majority of Californians would be willing to agree to higher taxes --an average of $43 per person, per month-- to provide health care for poor and uninsured persons. A majority of Californians also opposed health care rationing. (Rationing would prioritize services, and services rated least important would not be paid for.) Respondents supported taxes on traffic violations, alcohol, and firearms, but opposed sales tax increases, in order to pay for indigent health care costs.

Poll Extracts:

73% of Californians would agree to higher taxes to pay for health care for the poor and uninsured.

66% of the respondents said that poor people with no Medi-Cal coverage deserve more service.

61% of the respondents opposed health care rationing.

50% of the respondents "strongly agreed," and 34% "agreed" that employers should be required to provide basic health insurance to their employees.

Also in Source: What respondents thought was the state's greatest health threat. Responses to questions regarding personal control in right-to-die decisions. Acknowledgement of illegal drug use by whites, blacks, Latinos, and Asians.

Poll Details: 1,004 Californians were polled by telephone in an annual Gallup Poll sponsored by the California Association of Hospitals and Health Systems, and the three Hospital Councils of California.

Availability: Published in the *Los Angeles Times,* May 3, 1990, p. A3, A36.

CEOs AND MANDATED HEALTH CARE

Description: Presents the results of a survey concerning the attitudes of company CEOs toward federally mandated health care.

Results: While 68% of the respondents believe federally mandated health care would save their company money in the short run, 83% believe that such a program would cost taxpayers, including their company, more in the long run.

Poll Extracts:

ISSUES CONCERNING FEDERALLY MANDATED HEALTH CARE:

Would federally mandated health care
make your job easier?..............................Yes...78%

Would federalization save your company
money in the short run?..............................Yes...68%

Do you favor federally mandated health care?........Yes...16%

Will federalization cost taxpayers, including
your company, more in the long run?..................Yes...83%

Also in Source: When asked which areas of operation CEOs relied on for information about employee benefits planning and management, 97% named personnel and human resources with 96% naming finance and tax; corporate planning and risk management rated 21% and 17% respectively. Group insurance carriers were named by 92% as an outside resource that respondents personally relied on for advice on benefits management.

Poll Details: The survey was conducted for the Employers Council on Flexible Compensation by Swinehart Consultant Inc., an Atlanta-based survey research and political consulting firm. The survey was conducted by telephone in March 1990.

Availability: Published in *National Underwriter*, August 20, 1990, p. 37, 46.

CONSUMER HEALTH CARE ATTITUDES

Description: Presents the results of a survey concerning attitudes toward public versus private health care.

Results: While 49% of the respondents favor national health care regardless of cost, 43% called government involvement a costly mistake.

Poll Extracts:

COMPLEX ATTITUDES TOWARD A COMPLEX ISSUE:

Do you favor national health care
regardless of cost?....................................Yes...49%

Do you think governmental involvement
in health care is a costly mistake?..................Yes...43%

Should government spending on health care
increase over the next few years?....................Yes...68%

Is the amount of money currently spent on
health care too much or about the right?............Yes...52%

Would you be willing to pay more taxes to
provide health care to all?..........................Yes...53%

Also in Source: 56% of the respondents named health insurance companies as most responsible for rising health costs. 55% named hospitals as most responsible.

Poll Details: The Gallup Organization conducted a survey of 2,000 Americans for the Blue Cross and Blue Shield Association.

Availability: Published in *National Underwriters*, August 6, 1990, p. 3, 8.

CONSUMERS TRUST PHARMACISTS

Description: This poll questioned adults on their attitudes toward pharmacists.

Results: "Not only does the public trust pharmacists more than any other health professional, it regards them as an invaluable source of information and an excellent value for the money."

Poll Extracts:

RESPONDENTS THOUGHT THAT:

They are very highly or highly satisfied with the advice they receive from pharmacists 83%

It's very important that pharmacists be available as a source of information 71%

The information obtained from pharmacists contributes to their health 59%

They seek advice from pharmacists on health matters other than prescriptions and over-the-counter drugs 29%

Also in Source: "Prescription medicines are seen as least likely to contribute to the high cost of health care when compared with insurance companies, hospitals, doctors, medical technology, and overuse of medical services." The majority of Americans believe that the increased cost of prescription drugs can be traced to drug manufacturers, rather than to pharmacists.

Poll Details: This poll was conducted by the Gallup Organization for the National Association of Chain Drug Stores. 1,012 adults were interviewed by telephone.

Availability: Published in *Drug Topics*, May 7, 1990 (volume 134, number 9), p. 74.

CORPORATE LEADERS ON HEALTH CARE ISSUES

Description: Presents the results of a survey of business leaders concerning various health care issues and their impact on corporate budgets.

Results: Over 90% of the respondents are very concerned about rising health insurance premium costs. In order to trim health programs to hold down costs, over 80% of the respondents would increase the employee share of premium costs.

Poll Extracts:

HOW EXECUTIVES WILL TRIM HEALTH PROGRAMS TO HOLD DOWN COSTS

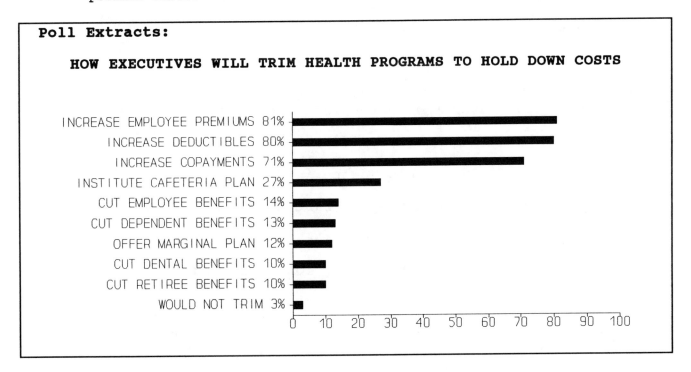

Also in Source: 45% of the respondents oppose national health insurance. 47% believe that a national health insurance program will be in place in ten years. According to the respondents, stress is the most serious workforce health problem.

Poll Details: In November 1989, a four-page questionnaire was sent to 1,500 executives who were randomly selected from the circulation list of *Business & Health*. Response rate was 28%.

Availability: Published in *Business & Health*, April, 1990 (volume 8, number 4), p. 24-26, 30-31, 34, 36-38.

THE COST OF FREE HEALTH CARE

Description: Presents the results of a survey concerning different health care
issues. Specific questions were asked concerning the popularity of free
health care if certain conditions were to be assumed.

Results: Over 70% of the respondents were in favor of having the government
provide free health care. However, significantly fewer respondents would
be in favor of the concept if certain conditions would be attached.

Poll Extracts:

FREE HEALTH CARE?

Would you favor free government provided health care?

Yes...73%

But, would you be in favor if

-it would mean traveling farther to the doctor?

Yes...43%

-it would mean waiting longer for care?

Yes...36%

-it would restrict your choice of health care providers?

Yes...29%

Also in Source: The top priorities in health care were access to quality
care, freedom to choose doctors, and cost. 68% said they were very
satisfied with the quality of health care they received, while 5% were
dissatisfied. 26% of the respondents cited AIDS as the country's greatest
health threat; 15% said rising costs; 13% said cancer; 10% drugs.

Poll Details: Gallop surveyed 2,000 adults nationwide.

Availability: Published in *USA Today*, February 19, 1990, p. 1A

HEALTH CARE QUALITY

> **Description:** Presents the results of a survey of Americans concerning the
> quality of health care.

> **Results:** Nearly 60% of the respondents felt that health care quality has
> improved in the last several years.

Poll Extracts:

HAS HEALTH CARE IMPROVED, DECLINED, OR STAYED THE SAME?

IMPROVED - 58%

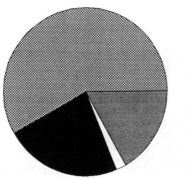

DECLINED - 17%

UNSURE - 2%

STAYED THE SAME - 23%

> **Also in Source:** The article includes two other news items concerning health
> care quality.

> **Poll Details:** The poll was conducted by the American Medical Association's
> Office of Issue and Communications Research. The organization surveyed
> 1,500 adults.

> **Availability:** Published in *Hospitals,* February 5, 1990 (volume 64, number 3),
> p. 20.

HELPING HOSPITALS STAY OPEN

Description: Presents the results of a survey concerning the willingness of
hospital CEOs to accept reduced rates at their hospitals to help ensure
that hospitals in underserved areas stay open.

Results: Approximately three-quarters of the respondents said they would not be
willing to accept lower rates to keep hospitals in underserved areas open.

Poll Extracts:

WOULD YOU ACCEPT LOWER RATES TO KEEP UNDERSERVED HOSPITALS OPEN?

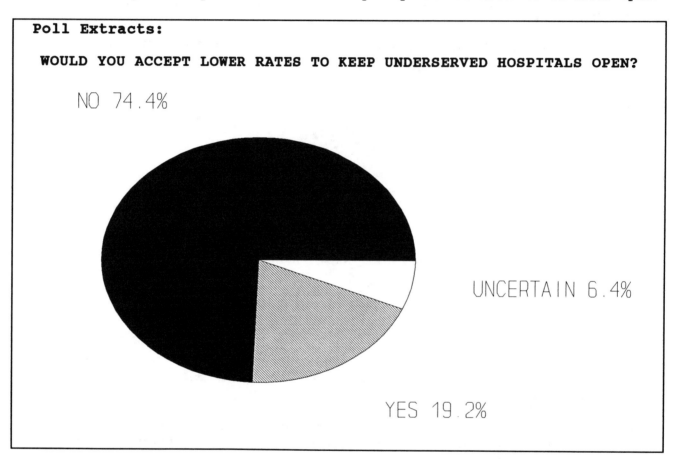

NO 74.4%

UNCERTAIN 6.4%

YES 19.2%

Also in Source: A discussion of the issue is included in the article.

Poll Details: 250 hospital CEOs were surveyed by *Hospitals* magazine.,

Availability: Published in *Hospitals*, July 5, 1990 (volume 64, number 13),
p. 66.

HOSPITAL SERVICES WHICH COULD BE CUT

Description: Presents the results of a survey identifying those hospital
services which would be curtailed if the institution were at risk of
financial failure.

Results: 22% of the respondents said they would scale back obstetrical services
if their institution were at financial risk.

Poll Extracts:

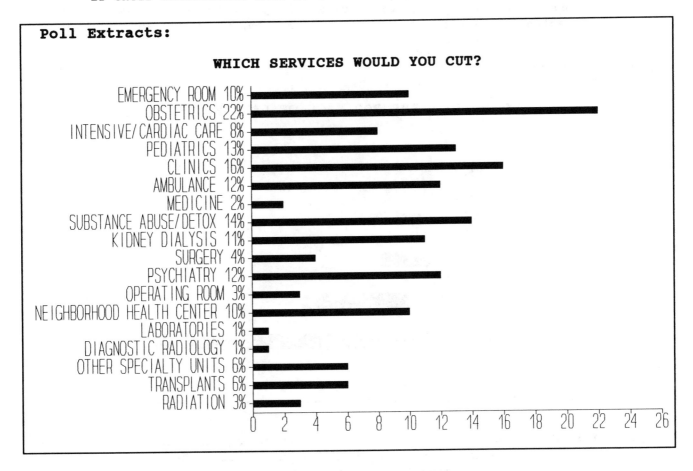

WHICH SERVICES WOULD YOU CUT?

Also in Source: 53% of the respondents said emergency room services are
unprofitable, 46% cited obstetrics, and 30% cited intensive and cardiac
care units.

Poll Details: The survey of 1,754 hospital executives was conducted by
Deloitte & Touche of Boston, MA.

Availability: Published in *The Washington Post Health Magazine*, August 7,
1990, p. 5.

LEADERSHIP VOID HURTS HEALTH POLICY

Description: Presents the results of a survey concerning the lack of
leadership in the area of health care policy. The survey asked the
respondents to identify groups that are responsible for this lack of
leadership.

Results: Over half of the respondents blamed Congress for the lack of
leadership in the area of health care policy. They also blamed, in order,
the health care field, the Bush Administration, consumers and big business.

Poll Extracts:

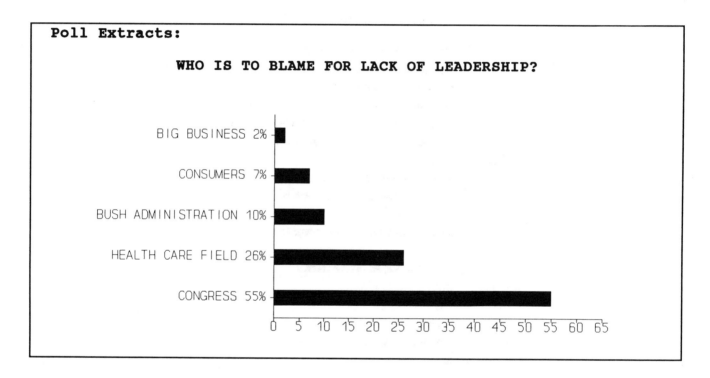

Also in Source: Almost 60% agreed with the statement that the failure of the
Bush Administration to fill key health care positions has hurt the
formation of Medicare policy and regulations. A general discussion of the
issue is also included in the article.

Poll Details: The poll was conducted for *Hospitals* by Professional Research
Consultants. 183 hospital CEOs were surveyed in November, 1989.

Availability: Published in *Hospitals*, January 5, 1990 (volume 64, number 1),
p. 66.

LONG-TERM HEALTH CARE ATTITUDES

Description: Provides the findings of a survey about attitudes toward long-term care for people with chronic problems who need help with daily living, either in their homes or in a nursing home.

Results: More than two-thirds of Americans would strongly support a government-sponsored program to provide citizens of all ages with some form of in-house and nursing home care.

Poll Extracts:

ATTITUDES TOWARD LONG-TERM CARE:

Are you concerned about the cost
of long-term care?....................................Yes...64%

Are you "not very" or "not at all confident"
that you would be able to pay for
long-term care?......................................Yes...53%

Do you believe that nursing home
costs would wipe out your savings?..................Yes...73%

Do you believe that long-term care costs
would be paid by private insurance?.................Yes...48%
(Only a small number of private policies cover long-term care.)

Also in Source: Reports the percentage of Americans who have had direct or indirect experience with the problems of providing long-term care. The source reports that the survey demonstrates consensus on three components of a federal long-term care program.

Poll Details: The survey was sponsored by the American Association of Retired Persons (AARP) and was conducted by Daniel Yankelovich Group Inc. The survey polled 1,500 adults, of whom 500 were aged 18-49, 500 were 50-64, and 500 were 65 and over.

Availability: Published in *AARP Bulletin*, February 1990 (volume 31, number 2), p. 1, 5.

MENTAL ILLNESS AND MENTAL HEALTH FACILITIES

Description: This survey studied what Americans think about mental illness.

Results: A majority of respondents thought that: mental illnesses are increasing, mental illnesses are curable, mental health facilities should not be placed in their neighborhoods. "Survey figures show that white, affluent men who were well-educated were most likely to oppose a mental health institution in their neighborhood for fear of falling property values."

Poll Extracts:

CONCERNING MENTAL HEALTH:

90% of the respondents saw mental illness as a serious problem.

74% of the respondents realized mental illnesses are curable.

70% of Americans believed that mental illness is on the rise.

More than 50% of the respondents believed that maintaining a normal life in the community is essential for recovery.

Only one out of three persons, of the 70% who believed that mental illness is on the rise, would welcome a mental health facility in their neighborhood.

Also in Source: Nearly 25 million Americans are in need of care in a community mental facility.

Poll Details: This survey was funded by the Robert Wood Johnson Foundation.

Availability: Published in the *Dayton Daily News*, April 9, 1990, p. 1-C.

NATIONAL HEALTH INSURANCE STRONGLY SUPPORTED

Description: This was an *AARP Bulletin* readers' poll. "Readers were asked if the country should expand the Medicaid program, mandate employer-provided health insurance, change the way insurance is regulated or institute government-sponsored national health insurance. Members could choose one option or a combination. They also were given space to comment and suggest solutions of their own."

Results: The majority of respondents favored a government-sponsored national health insurance program.

Poll Extracts:

FROM THE RESPONSES TALLIED, READERS FAVORED:

A government-sponsored national health insurance program 84%

Toughening insurance regulation 25%

Expanding Medicaid 16%

A plan to mandate health insurance through employers 12%

Also in Source: Several results from two 1989 surveys on national health insurance (an AARP member poll and a Gallup poll). In both of these surveys the percentage of respondents supporting a national health insurance program was much lower than the 84% level of support found in the readers' poll. The number of Americans who have no medical insurance.

Poll Details: Votes counted exceed 100% because many people chose more than one proposal. 70,000 readers responded to the poll. A sample 2,733 responses were tallied, providing a margin of error of 2%. The *AARP Bulletin* poll does not constitute a scientific sample, so the opinions expressed should not be considered as representative of AARP's (American Association of Retired Persons) entire membership.

Availability: Published in the *AARP Bulletin*, May 1990 (volume 31, number 5), p. 1, 13.

NATIONAL HEALTH PLAN

Description: Presents the results of a survey of business executives
concerning a government-run national health plan.

Results: An overwhelming majority of the respondents are opposed to a national
health plan.

Poll Extracts:

HEALTH BENEFITS PAYMENT ALTERNATIVES:

Would you reject a health care system that has
a budget controlled by the government?............Yes...94%

Do you favor improved private sector efforts
to control health care costs?....................Yes...62%

Do you favor more government regulation
to control physician and hospital costs?.........Yes...31%

Would you rather shift more of the health
costs to the employee?...........................Yes...75%

Also in Source: A brief discussion of the issue is included in the article.

Poll Details: The poll was conducted by Roper Organization Inc. for the Health
Insurance Association of America. 100 business executives were surveyed.

Availability: Published in *USA Today*, March 27, 1990, p.6B.

PATIENTS ACCESS DOCTORS

Description: Presents the results of a survey concerning patients' attitudes towards their doctors.

Results: Over 80% of the respondents are very or somewhat satisfied with a recent visit to their doctor.

```
┌─────────────────────────────────────────────────────────────────────────┐
│  Poll Extracts:                                                           │
│                                                                           │
│                   FROM THE PATIENT'S PERSPECTIVE:                         │
│                                                                           │
│    Are you very or somewhat satisfied with                                │
│    a recent visit to the doctor?........................Yes...85%         │
│                                                                           │
│    Are you satisfied with the amount of time                              │
│    you had to wait to see the doctor?...................Yes...69%         │
│                                                                           │
│    Do doctors involve patients enough in                                  │
│    deciding on treatment?...............................No....60%         │
│                                                                           │
│    Do doctors care as much about patients                                 │
│    as they used to?.....................................No....51%         │
│                                                                           │
└─────────────────────────────────────────────────────────────────────────┘
```

Also in Source: 25% of the respondents said doctors' fees are usually reasonable. 60% say doctors are usually up-to-date on the latest advances in medicine.

Poll Details: The Gallup Organization polled 1,500 adults nationwide for the American Medical Association.

Availability: Published in *USA Today*, July 9, 1990, p. 1D.

PATIENTS' THOUGHTS ABOUT DOCTORS

Description: This nationwide survey queried respondents on their perceptions about doctors, and the treatments rendered by doctors.

Results: An equal percentage of patients (43%) think that the most important qualities of a good doctor are "ability," and "concern" for patients. 27% of the respondents said that delays in seeing the doctor (patient kept waiting) are what they dislike most about physicians. 43% of the respondents thought that it takes two or more visits to their doctor before he or she finds out what's wrong with them. Seven out of 10 patients thought that their physicians get some kind of financial benefit from the tests they order.

Poll Extracts: **DO MOST DOCTORS ORDER TOO MANY TESTS OR TOO FEW?**

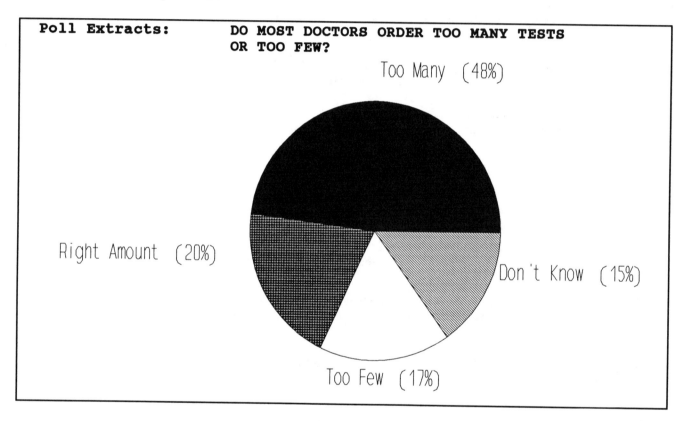

Also in Source: What respondents believed the average physician's salary amounts to in a year. The percentage of white, black, and Latino respondents who believed their doctors are good or fairly good. Respondents who said they have a personal doctor, and also the percentage of respondents who had a personal doctor by geographic region. The types of patients who were more likely to go to a female physician.

Poll Details: This nationwide survey was conducted by telephone this past winter by the *Los Angeles Times* Poll. The *Los Angeles Times* Poll, directed by I.A. Lewis, interviewed 2,046 people. The margin of error is estimated to be 3%.

Availability: Published in the *Los Angeles Times Magazine*/Part 2, April 29, 1990, p. 24, 38.

PRESIDENT BUSH'S NATIONAL HEALTH POLICY

Description: This poll queried hospital chief executive officers about
President Bush's commitment to a national health policy and whether Health
and Human Services Secretary Louis Sullivan's efforts would result in a
more coherent and comprehensive national health policy. (In his State of
the Union Address, President Bush called on Health and Human Services
Secretary Louis Sullivan to begin work on a new national health policy.)

Results: 40.4% of the respondents did not think Secretary Louis Sullivan's
efforts would result in a more coherent and comprehensive national health
policy, 33.2% thought his efforts would, and 26.4% were uncertain. The
majority of the respondents did not believe President Bush is personally
committed to developing a new health policy.

Poll Extracts:

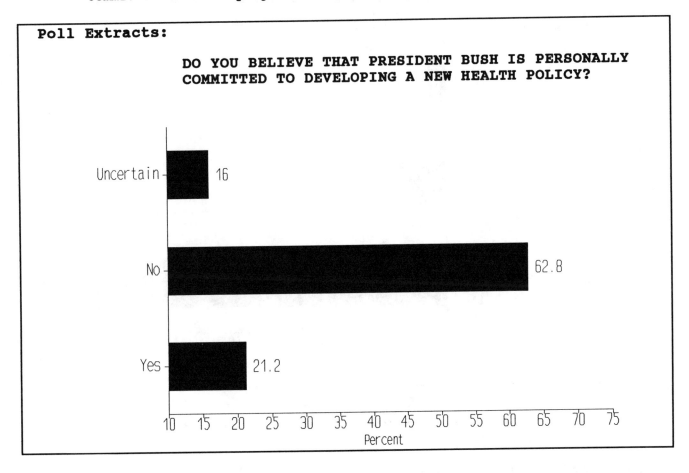

DO YOU BELIEVE THAT PRESIDENT BUSH IS PERSONALLY
COMMITTED TO DEVELOPING A NEW HEALTH POLICY?

Also in Source: Brief article containing several statements by hospital
presidents on the issue of a national health policy.

Poll Details: The results are based on responses from 250 hospital chief
executive officers surveyed by *Hospitals* magazine. The survey was
conducted by Professional Research Consultants.

Availability: Published in *Hospitals*, May 5, 1990 (volume 64, number 9),
p. 58.

THE PUBLIC'S VIEW ON RIGHT-TO-DIE

Description: Respondents were queried about their view on right-to-die, as in the case of Nancy Cruzan.

Results: If they were in a coma with no brain activity and were being kept alive by a feeding tube, the majority of respondents would want their feeding tube removed so that they could die. The majority of respondents (81%) also believed that a close family member should have the right to decide on feeding tube removal.

Poll Extracts: **"SUPPOSE YOU WERE IN A COMA WITH NO BRAIN ACTIVITY AND WERE BEING KEPT ALIVE BY A FEEDING TUBE. WOULD YOU WANT YOUR DOCTOR TO REMOVE THE FEEDING TUBE AND LET YOU DIE, OR NOT?"**

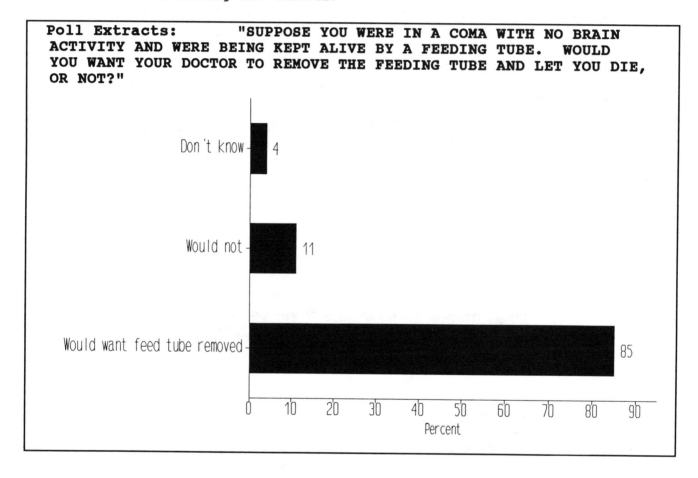

Also in Source: Excerpts from the U.S. Supreme Court Opinions on the Missouri right-to-die case.

Poll Details: This *New York Times*/CBS News Poll was based on telephone interviews with 1,515 adults conducted March 30 - April 2, 1990.

Availability: Published in *The New York Times*, June 26, 1990, p. A18.

STRIKING FOR HEALTH BENEFITS

Description: Presents the results of a study to determine the importance of the issue of health benefits in the decision to go on strike.

Results: Disputes over health coverage motivated 78% of those who went on strike in 1989.

Poll Extracts:

YES, I WENT ON STRIKE OVER HEALTH BENEFITS.

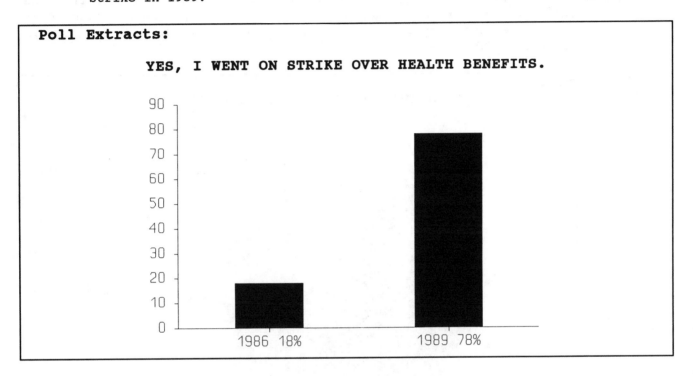

Also in Source: The article includes a general discussion of this issue.

Poll Details: The study examined strikes involving more than 1,000 workers each. The Service Employees Union used news reports and interviewed strikers.

Availability: Published in the *Los Angeles Times*, February 20, 1990, p. D5.

CELEBRATING THE HOLIDAYS

Description: Respondents were asked about the number of parties that they
would attend during the holiday season, and how many miles they would be
traveling to spend time with friends and family.

Results: About half of the respondents thought that they would attend from one
to three parties during the holidays. 70% of the respondents thought that
they would be traveling less than 100 miles, 23% from 100 to 1,000 miles,
and 5% over 1,000 miles.

Poll Extracts:

"HOW MANY PARTIES WILL YOU GO TO?"

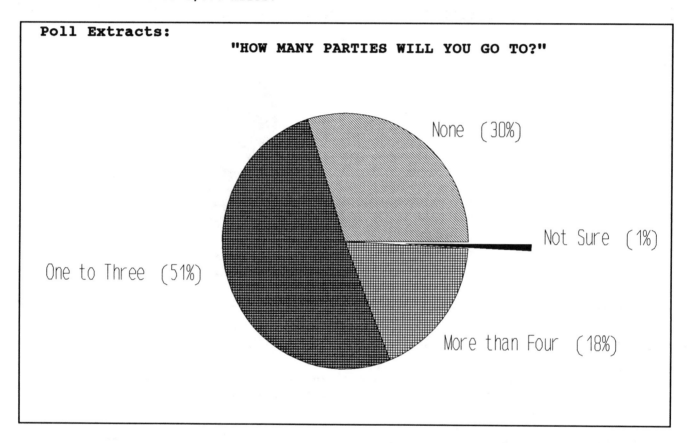

None (30%)

Not Sure (1%)

One to Three (51%)

More than Four (18%)

Also in Source: Whether respondents thought they would be spending more or
less for gifts compared to 1989, and the amount that they thought they
would spend in 1990.

Poll Details: This *Atlanta Journal and Constitution* poll was conducted from
December 6-9, 1990. 751 adults from across Georgia were interviewed by
telephone. The margin of error was 4%.

Availability: Published in *The Atlanta Journal and Constitution*, December 15,
1990, p. A-1, A-8.

HOW NEW YEAR'S EVE IS CELEBRATED

Description: Designed to find out how Americans actually celebrate New Year's
Eve, and also the types of beverages that Americans buy for that night.

Results: The poll indicated that most Americans celebrate New Year's Eve quietly
in their own home, or at a friend's or relative's home. Only 25% of Americans
partied on New Year's Eve. Young adults were most likely to go to a party.

Poll Extracts:

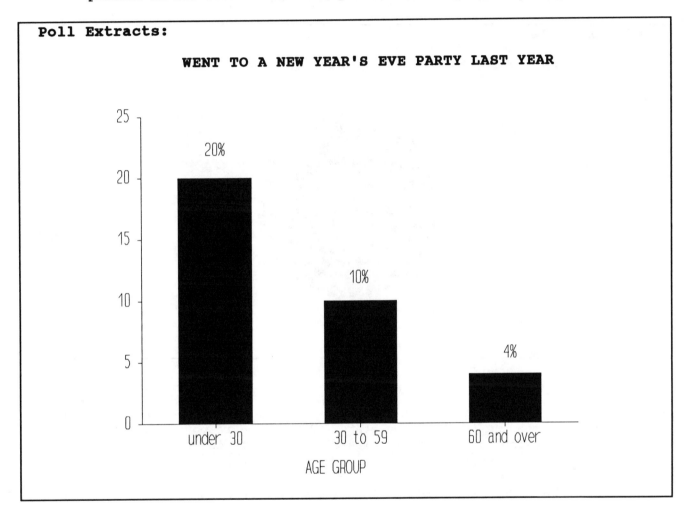

WENT TO A NEW YEAR'S EVE PARTY LAST YEAR

Also in Source: More Americans buy beer than champagne to bring in the New Year.
In general, people under age 30 are more likely than older adults to buy
alcoholic beverages for New Year's Eve. Men are twice as likely as women to
buy beer or hard liquor for New Year's Eve.

Poll Details: The poll was conducted by the Roper Organization.

Availability: Published in *American Demographics*, January 1990 (volume 12,
number 1), p. 4.

CALIFORNIA'S PROPOSITION 103

Description: Presents the results of a nationwide survey measuring the
        awareness of California's Proposition 103 and whether they would favor such
        a proposition in their own state.

Results: Approximately three-quarters of the respondents were not aware of the
        insurance-related state referendum known as Proposition 103.

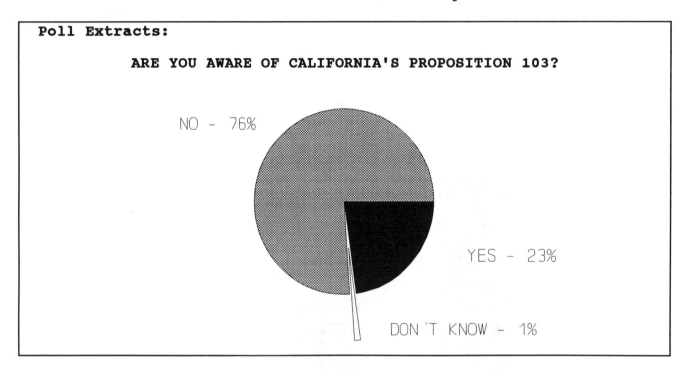

Poll Extracts:

ARE YOU AWARE OF CALIFORNIA'S PROPOSITION 103?

NO - 76%

YES - 23%

DON'T KNOW - 1%

Also in Source: Nearly 60% of those respondents who were aware of Proposition
        103 and who did not reside in California said they would like to see a
        similar measure in their own state. 20% of the respondents were aware of
        any organized consumer activities aimed at achieving better insurance
        conditions in their state.

Poll Details: The nationwide poll of 1,000 consumers was conducted by the
        Gallop Organization for *Best's Review*.

Availability: Published in *Best's Review*. *Property-Casualty Insurance Edition*,
        January 1990 (volume 89, number 9), p. 12.

INSURANCE COMPANIES OVERCHARGE

Description: Consumers were queried about their attitudes toward profits in the property/casualty insurance industry.

Results: The majority of consumers believe that the insurance industry achieves its profits by overcharging for premiums, and that property/casualty insurers earn excessive profits. 35% "strongly agreed," and 32% "agreed" that insurance companies that sell auto, homeowners, and business insurance make a killing, but pretend they are not making money.

Poll Extracts: INSURANCE INDUSTRY ACHIEVES ITS PROFITS BY: OVERCHARGING FOR PREMIUMS, CHARGING FAIR AND ADEQUATE PREMIUMS AND INVESTING AND MANAGING THIS MONEY WISELY, UNDERCHARGING, BUT MAKING UP THE DIFFERENCE THROUGH INVESTMENTS?

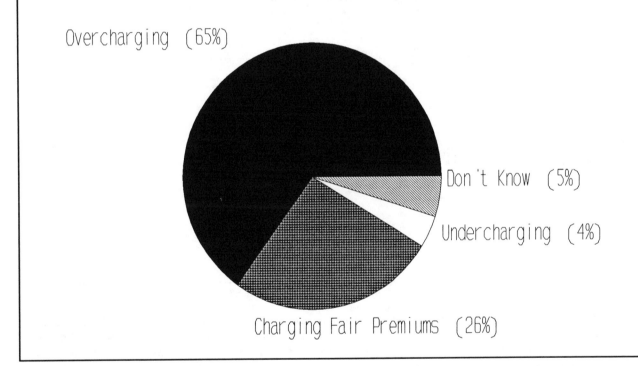

Overcharging (65%)

Don't Know (5%)

Undercharging (4%)

Charging Fair Premiums (26%)

Also in Source: Attitudes toward the profitability of companies that sell auto, homeowners, and business insurance, as compared to companies in other industries. The areas in which respondents believe insurers have the best chance of cutting costs. Whether the commissions that insurance agents receive for the policies they sell are too high or too low.

Poll Details: The Gallup Organization conducted a telephone poll of 1,000 consumers. The margin of error is plus or minus 3%.

Availability: Published in *Best's Review*, Property/Casualty Insurance Edition, May 1990 (volume 91, number 1), p. 16.

INSURER SOLVENCY

Description: Presents the results of a survey concerning consumer confidence in the financial stability of insurers.

Results: Over 50% of the respondents think, when compared to other types of insurers, health insurance companies are in the most danger of going bankrupt.

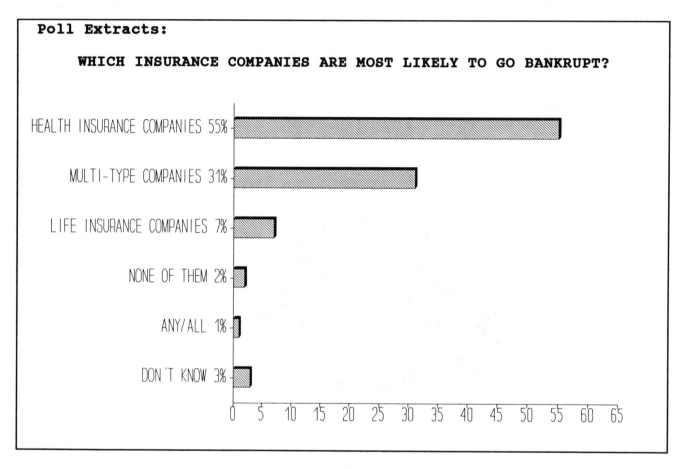

Poll Extracts:

WHICH INSURANCE COMPANIES ARE MOST LIKELY TO GO BANKRUPT?

Also in Source: 31% of the respondents said it would be extremely unusual for an insurer to go bankrupt, and 34% said a few go bankrupt each year but there is no major problem. 54% of the respondents said that if an insurer does go bankrupt people with claims are left with nothing, 20% said the claims are paid by a special state fund, and 17% said the claims are paid by the federal government.

Poll Details: The Gallup Organization surveyed 1,000 people for *Best's Review*. The margin of error is plus or minus 3%.

Availability: Published in Best's Review Property/Casualty Insurance Edition (volume 91, number 3), p. 16.

INSURERS PERFORMANCE DURING A DISASTER

Description: Presents the results of a survey of consumers concerning the behavior of insurance companies during and after disasters such as hurricanes, tornadoes and earthquakes.

Results: The results reflect a number of distinct opinions. While over half of the respondents` felt that insurers performed exceptionally well in response to disasters, an almost equal number believe insurers seem to take advantage of desperate people and try to pay less than they should.

Poll Extracts:

PERFORMANCE ON CLAIMS HANDLING:

	Agree
Insurers do just what they should................63%
Insurers seem to perform exceptionally well in disasters................51%
Insurers seem to take advantage of desperate people and try to pay less than they should................49%
Insurers requirements for evidence of losses and damages are fair and reasonable........77%
Insurers too often get inflated claims for losses................75%
Insurers ask for too much documentation.............45%

Also in Source: A general discussion of the results of the survey is included in the article.

Poll Details: The telephone poll of 1,002 consumers was conducted for *Best's Review* by the Gallop Organization. Margin of error is plus or minus 3%.

Availability: Published in *Best's Review. Property-Casualty Insurance Edition,* March 1990 (volume 90, number 11), p. 10.

ARAB AMERICANS AND THE MIDDLE EAST

Description: Presents the results of a survey of Arab Americans concerning
their views on the political and social future of the Middle East.

Results: Almost 90% of the respondents felt that a Lebanese government should
reflect the country's social and demographic makeup. Over 90% of the
respondents felt that no solution was possible if Israel maintains control
of the West Bank. Over 90% also felt that the recognition of Palestine
would help the peace process.

Poll Extracts:

THE FUTURE OF THE MIDDLE EAST:

Should Lebanon be divided into a
Christian state and a Muslim state?...................No....75%

Should the Lebanese government reflect the
country's social and demographic makeup?.............Yes...88%

Will there be a solution to Palestine-Israel conflict
if Israel maintains control of the West Bank but
grants local self rule?...............................No....96%

Would the recognition of Palestine as a state
help solve the conflict?..............................Yes...94%

Does United States policy favor Israel unfairly?.....Yes...96%

Also in Source: The poll contains a wide variety of questions concerning the
opinions of Arab Americans. Subjects include legalized abortion, the Equal
Rights Amendment, prayer in public schools, and American politics.

Poll Details: The results of the survey were compiled from a mail survey of
2,626 members of the American Arab Anti-Discrimination Committee. The
organization consists mostly of U.S. citizens of Arab descent or Arabs
living in the United States.

Availability: Published in *The Detroit News and Free Press*, March 24, 1990,
p. 1A, 20A.

CANADIANS LOOK AT THE UNITED STATES

Description: Presents the results of a survey of Canadians concerning their attitudes toward the United States.

Results: Canadians generally feel that they enjoy better health care, a higher quality of living and greater world respect than Americans. However, one in six Canadians would choose union with the United States if the province in which they live could obtain statehood and the right to elect members to Congress.

Poll Extracts:

INCLINED TO JOIN THE USA IF THEIR PROVINCE COULD BECOME A STATE:

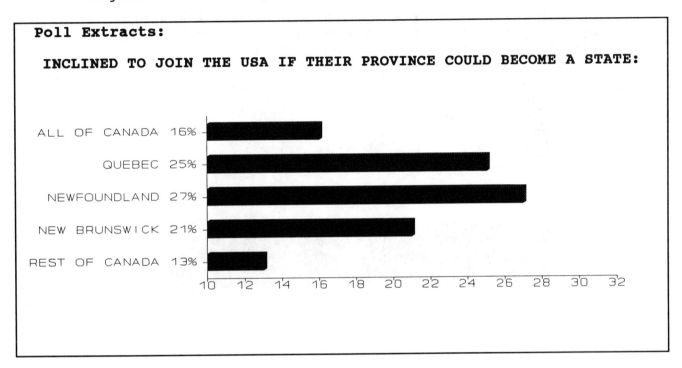

Also in Source: 89% rated Canada's health care better than health care in the United States while 66% said the quality of life was better in Canada. 63% felt that Canada was more respected world wide. However, only 36% felt Canada's economy was better and 22% thought their politicians were superior to those found in the United States.

Poll Details: This poll of 1,500 Canadians is the sixth annual year-end survey of the national mood.

Availability: Published in *MACLEAN'S*, January 1, 1990, p. 37-38.

CHANGE IN SOUTH AFRICA

Description: Americans were asked if they thought the system of racial separation in South Africa would end peacefully.

Results: The majority of respondents felt that the South African system of racial separation would not end peacefully.

Poll Extracts:

DO YOU FEEL THE RECENT ACTIONS BY THE SOUTH AFRICAN GOVERNMENT WILL LEAD TO A PEACEFUL SETTLEMENT OF THAT COUNTRY'S SYSTEM OF RACIAL SEPARATION?

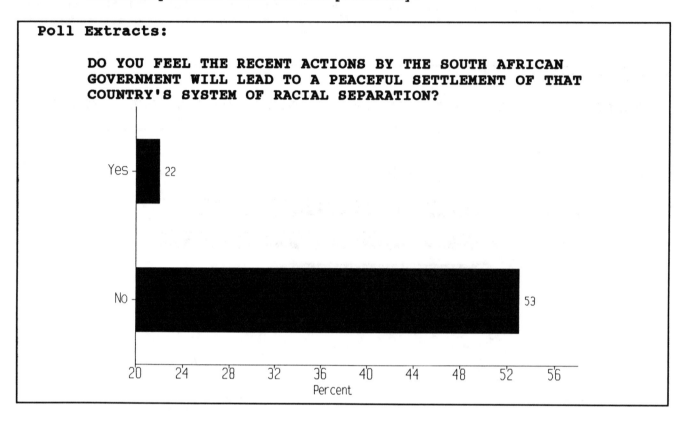

Also in Source: Attitudes toward the Congressional and the Bush Administration's handling of the savings and loan industry crisis. President Bush's favorability rating.

Poll Details: This telephone poll was conducted by KRC Communications Research on June 10-12, 1990. 1,002 registered voters were interviewed. The margin of error is 3%.

Availability: Published in *The Boston Globe*, June 14, 1990, p. 4.

CHANGES IN EASTERN EUROPE AND U.S.S.R.

Description: Presents the results of a survey concerning a wide range of
questions centering primarily on the changes in the Soviet Union and
Eastern Europe and their impact on international relations.

Results: More than three-fourths of the respondents agreed that the changes
that have occurred in the Soviet Union and the Eastern Bloc countries will
result in a more peaceful world.

Poll Extracts:

IS THE WORLD A SAFER PLACE?

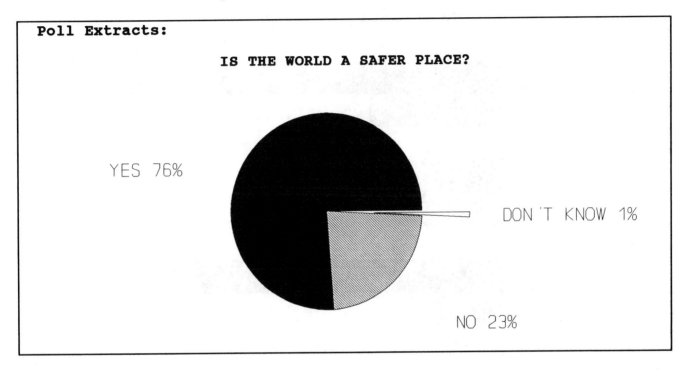

YES 76%

DON'T KNOW 1%

NO 23%

Also in Source: 56% of the respondents felt that the United States is
becoming less influential in world affairs. 73% have a favorable
impression of Mikhail Gorbachev and 80% have the same impression of George
Bush. Terrorism is seen as the greater threat to the security of the
United States by 82% of the respondents compared to 15% who see the
military power of the Soviet Union as a greater threat. 65% said that it
is very important to the United States that Gorbachev remain in power. As
a result of the changes in the Soviet Union and Eastern Europe, 49% of the
respondents agree that the U.S. can make major cuts in military spending
while the same percentage disagree. 82% said they never expected in their
lifetime to see the changes that have occurred in the Soviet Union and
Eastern Europe.

Poll Details: The results are based on a *Washington Post*-ABC News national
telephone survey of 1,526 adults conducted on May 17 through May 21, 1990.
Margin of error is 3%. Interviewing was conducted by Chilton Research.

Availability: Published in *The Washington Post*, May 27, 1990, p. 24.

THE COLD WAR

Description: Respondents were asked if they think the Cold War is over or if they think it continues.

Results: The majority of Americans believe that the Cold War is not finished.

Poll Extracts:

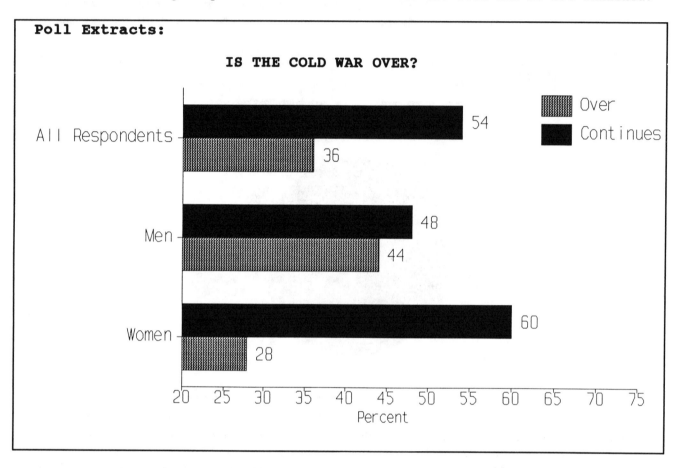

Also in Source: Respondents' attitudes toward President Bush, the June 1990 Bush-Gorbachev summit meeting, Bush's foreign policy, and Lithuanian independence.

Poll Details: KRC Communications Research interviewed 1,002 randomly chosen registered voters by telephone on June 3-5, 1990. The margin of error is 3%.

Availability: Published in *The Boston Globe*, June 7, 1990, p. 12.

DOES A REUNITED GERMANY THREATEN EUROPE?

Description: Respondents were asked if a reunited Germany posed a threat in
Europe.

Results: The majority of respondents (67%) were not concerned that a reunited
Germany would be a threat to peace in Europe. A minority of respondents
believed that if the unification of East and West Germany did take place,
Germany would try to dominate Europe economically.

Poll Extracts:
IF EAST AND WEST GERMANY ARE REUNITED, DO YOU THINK GERMANY WOULD TRY TO DOMINATE EUROPE ECONOMICALLY?

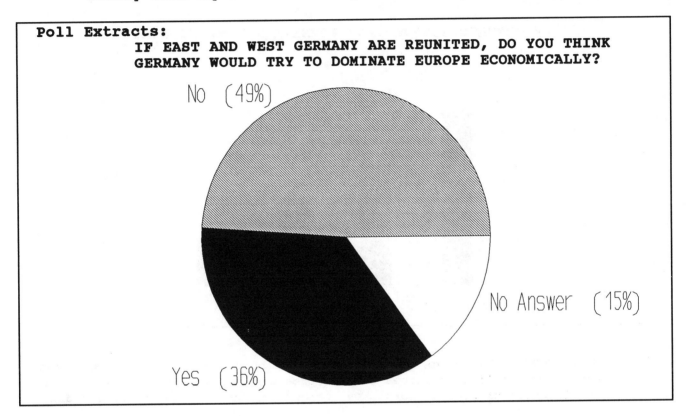

Also in Source: Poll questions regarding: the end of the Cold War, the
Lithuanian crisis, the popularity of President Bush and President
Gorbachev, world domination by the Soviets, and foreign aid.

Poll Details: This *New York Times*/CBS News Poll is based on telephone
interviews with 1,515 adults from the U.S., except Alaska and Hawaii. The
poll was conducted from March 30, 1990 - April 2, 1990. "The results have
been weighted to take into account household size and number of residential
telephone lines, and to adjust for variations in the sample relating to
region, sex, age and education. In theory, in 19 cases out of 20 the
results based on such samples will differ by no more than three percentage
points in either direction from what would have been obtained by seeking
out all American adults." The sampling error for smaller subgroups within
the poll will be larger. Further details are provided in the source as to
how the telephone numbers of the respondents were selected.

Availability: Published in *The New York Times*, April 6, 1990, p. A8.

FOREIGN AID

Description: Presents the results of a survey concerning the distribution of
U.S. foreign aid to specific countries.

Results: The order of preference for foreign aid is Panama, Poland, East
Germany, and the Soviet Union.

Poll Extracts:

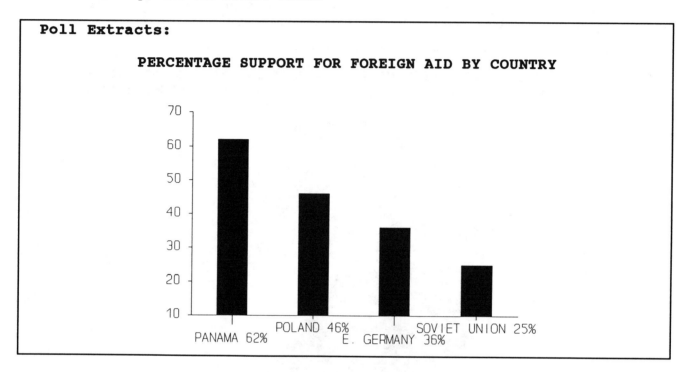

PERCENTAGE SUPPORT FOR FOREIGN AID BY COUNTRY

Also in Source: The survey included questions on a number of national issues.
Voters were polled on issues such as presidential performance, support for
the invasion of Panama, Gorbachev, Congress, the death penalty, and drugs.

Poll Details: The survey of voters was conducted by *The Wall Street
Journal*/NBC News.

Availability: Published in *The Wall Street Journal*, January 19, 1990, p. 1.

ISRAEL AND THE PALESTINIANS

Description: Respondents were questioned about their sympathy/support for
    Israel, Palestinians, and Arab nations.

Results: Americans still solidly support Israel, but support is not as deep as
    it used to be. 61% of the respondents support sustaining or increasing
    U.S. aid to Israel. 47% support giving the Palestinians a homeland in the
    occupied territories of the West Bank and the Gaza Strip (a proposal that
    is opposed by the Israeli Government). When respondents were asked if they
    were more "in sympathy" with Israel or with Arab nations, 40% were with
    Israel and 19% were with Arab nations.

Poll Extracts:

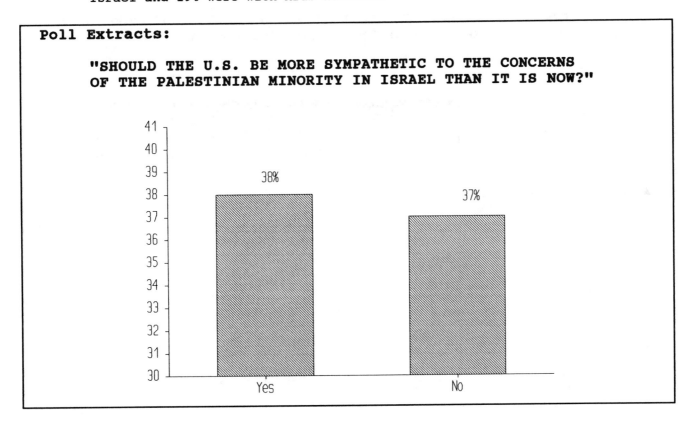

"SHOULD THE U.S. BE MORE SYMPATHETIC TO THE CONCERNS
OF THE PALESTINIAN MINORITY IN ISRAEL THAN IT IS NOW?"

Also in Source: The results from a similar *New York Times*/CBS News poll
    conducted in 1988. A chart detailing American sympathy for Israel/Arab
    nations from 1974-1990.

Poll Details: 1,084 adults around the U.S., excluding Alaska and Hawaii, were
    interviewed in this *New York Times*/CBS News poll. The poll was conducted
    by telephone during June 5-8, 1990. Further details on how the
    respondents' telephone numbers were chosen are provided in the source. The
    margin of sampling error is 3%.

Availability: Published in *The New York Times*, July 9, 1990, p. A1, A9.

ISRAEL'S ROLE IN THE MIDDLE EAST

Description: Presents the results of a survey concerning the role Israel plays
in the Middle East and the affect of the killings by Isaeli security forces
on the Temple Mount in October 1990 will have on that role.

Results: Almost 80% of the respondents think Israel's occupation of the West
Bank should be considered a separate issue and not part of an overall
diplomatic solution to Iraq's invasion of Kuwait.

Poll Extracts:

**SHOULD ISRAEL'S OCCUPATION OF THE WEST BANK BE CONSIDERED AS A
SEPARATE ISSUE OR PART OF AN OVERALL MIDDLE EAST SOLUTION?**

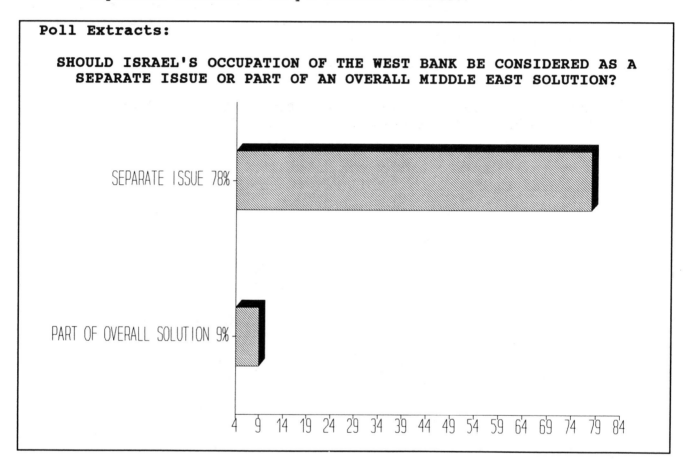

Also in Source: Since the invasion of Kuwait by Iraq, 30% of the respondents
think Israel has become a more important ally to the United States, 11%
think less important, and 52% think their importance has not changed. 56%
of the respondents think Israeli forces overreacted on the Temple Mount,
while 33% said the forces did what they had to do to protect themselves and
civilians. 60% of the respondents feel the United States should pressure
Israel to compromise its position to achieve peace, while 31% feel the U.S.
should not.

Poll Details: The results are taken from a *Newsweek* opinion poll on October
11-12, 1990.

Availability: Published in *Newsweek*, October 22, 1990 (volume CXVI, number
17). p. 34, 35, 37, 38, 40.

NORIEGA ON TRIAL

Description: Presents the results of a survey concerning the legal future of Panama's former dicator Manuel Noriega.

Results: Among the results, 70% of the respondents want Noriega to face the maximum possible sentence while over 20% think he should be allowed to plea bargain for a lighter sentence.

Poll Extracts:

ISSUES SURROUNDING THE ARREST AND TRIAL OF MANUEL NORIEGA:

Should Manuel Noriega face the maximum
possible sentence?.................................Yes....70%

Should Noriega be allowed to
plea bargain for a lighter sentence?..............Yes....21%

Can Noriega receive a fair trial
in a U.S. court?..................................Yes....72%

Would you like to be on his jury?.................Yes....39%

Does the U.S. have the right to bring foreign
leaders to trial in the U.S.?....................Yes....72%

Was the arrest of Noriega worth the loss
23 soldiers in the invasion?.....................Yes....55%

Also in Source: The article also includes a brief update on the U.S. invasion of Panama. For example, the latest estimate reports that more than 1,000 civilians died in the assault.

Poll Details: The survey of 819 adults on January 5-6, 1990 was conducted by Gordon S. Black Corporation. Sampling error is plus or minus 3.5%.

Availability: Published in *USA Today*, January 8, 1990, p. 1A.

SUPERPOWER SUMMITS

Description: Presents the results of a survey concerning the role and purpose of superpower summits between the Soviet Union and the United States.

Results: Almost half of the respondents said the purpose of superpower summits between the United States and the Soviet Union should be to set groundwork for further agreements. Less than 20% thought the purpose of these summits is to make agreements.

Poll Extracts:

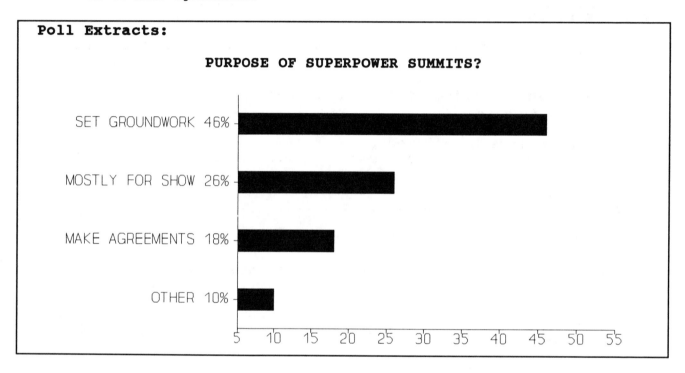

PURPOSE OF SUPERPOWER SUMMITS?

SET GROUNDWORK 46%

MOSTLY FOR SHOW 26%

MAKE AGREEMENTS 18%

OTHER 10%

5 10 15 20 25 30 35 40 45 50 55

Also in Source: 35% of the respondents predicted President Bush would get a better deal at the upcoming summit with Mikhail Gorbachev in Washington, D.C., 31% thought Gorbachev would do better, and 13% felt they would do the same.

Poll Details: The poll is based on telephone interviews with 800 Michigan adults conducted May 20 through 22, 1990. The survey was designed and analyzed with the Gannett Company Inc. research department. The margin of error is 3.5%.

Availability: Published in *The Detroit News and Free Press,* May 27, 1990, p. 1A, 6A.

SUPPORT FOR PANAMA POLICIES

Description: Presents the results of a survey concerning the level of support for the December 1989 invasion of Panama by the United States.

Results: Over 70% of the respondents supported the invasion of Panama.

Poll Extracts:

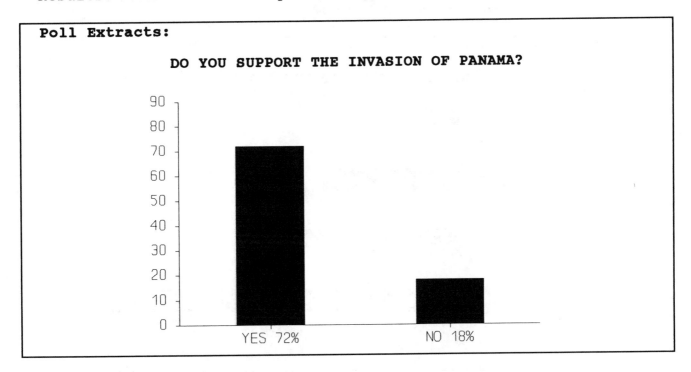

Also in Source: 67% of American voters felt that Manuel Noriega can get a fair trial in the United States. 10% felt that his capture will make a significant difference in reducing the flow of drugs into the United States. 42% felt that Noriega's removal will make a little difference and 45% felt that there will be almost no impact.

Poll Details: The survey of voters was conducted by *The Wall Street Journal*/NBC News.

Availability: Published in *The Wall Street Journal*, January 19, 1990, p. A1.

TRUSTWORTHINESS OF NATIONAL ALLIES

Description: Presents the results of a survey measuring the level of trust towards the allies of the United States.

Results: The allies which are trusted the least are, in order, Japan, West Germany, France, and Great Britain.

Poll Extracts:

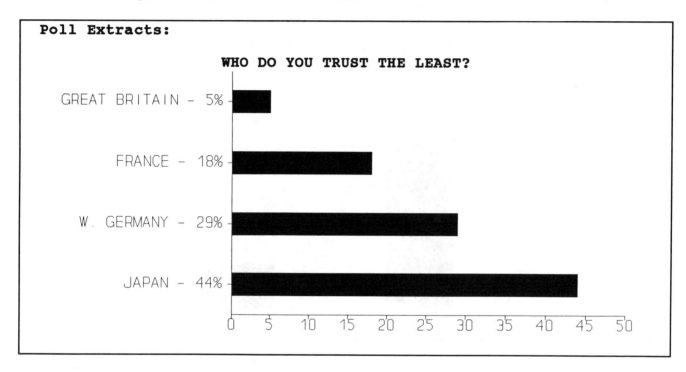

WHO DO YOU TRUST THE LEAST?

Also in Source: The article includes a number of other questions covering a wide range of topics.

Poll Details: The poll was conducted by Audits & Surveys Inc. for *People Weekly*. They contacted 1,000 *People Weekly* readers. This is the magazine's 11th annual poll.

Availability: Published in *People Weekly*, January 8, 1990 (volume 33, number 1), p. 58-68.

THE VIETNAM WAR REVISITED

Description: Presents the results of a survey measuring the attitudes of Americans toward the Vietnam War 15 years later.

Results: Over 60% of Vietnam War veterans are proud of America's role in the war while less than 40% of the general U.S. population share the same opinion. On the other hand, 28% of Vietnam War veterans are not proud of America's involvement compared to 48% of the general public.

Poll Extracts:

ARE YOU PROUD OF THE ROLE THE U.S. PLAYED IN VIETNAM?

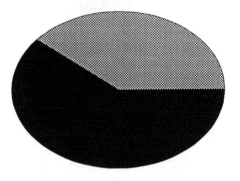

YES, U.S. PUBLIC 39%

YES, VIETNAM VETS 61%

Also in Source: Almost half of the respondents, the general public and Vietnam War veterans, feel that the U.S. should re-establish diplomatic ties with Vietnam. 51% of Vietnam War veterans believe the U.S. should admit more Vietnamese boat people compared to only 35% of the general public. 84% of Vietnam War veterans believe American MIA's are still alive in Vietnam. 62% of the general population share the same opinion.

Poll Details: The telephone poll of 1,000 adult Americans was conducted by Yankelovich Clancy Shulman on April 9, 10, 1990 for *Time*/CNN. Sampling error was plus or minus 3%. The poll also questioned 208 veterans at the Vietnam War Memorial in Washington, D.C. on April 7, and April 12-14, 1990.

Availability: Published in *Time*, April 30, 1990 (volume 135, number 18), p. 18-21.

VIEWS ON A UNITED GERMANY

Description: Presents the results of a survey concerning the prospect of a
    united Germany.

Results: Over 40% of the U.S. general public has some concern about East and
    West Germany becoming one country again.

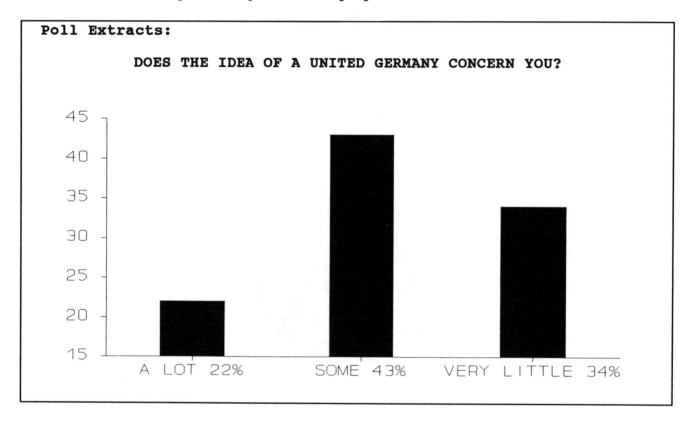

Poll Extracts:

DOES THE IDEA OF A UNITED GERMANY CONCERN YOU?

A LOT 22%   SOME 43%   VERY LITTLE 34%

Also in Source: 42% of the U.S. Jewish population have a lot of concern about
    a united Germany, 32% have some concern and 24% have very little concern.
    51% of the respondents believe the Cold War is mostly over while 41% feel
    the Cold War is still going on.

Poll Details: *The Wall Street Journal*/NBC News poll was conducted by the
    polling firms of Peter Hart, a Democrat, and Robert Teeter, a Republican.
    The telephone survey of 1,003 Americans was taken on March 10-13, 1990.

Availability: Published in *The Wall Street Journal*, March 16, 1990, p. A14.

AFTER THE HOSTAGES ARE FREE

Description: Respondents were queried about what actions should be taken with
the U.S. troops after Saddam Hussein releases the hostages.

Results: After the hostages are released, respondents thought we should:
remove the military troops -- 13%, leave the troops and enforce the
embargo, but don't invade -- 43%, invade Iraq if it doesn't leave Kuwait by
January 15, 1990 -- 37%, didn't know -- 7%.

Poll Extracts: **"IF HUSSEIN RELEASES THE HOSTAGES AND PULLS HIS
TROOPS OUT OF MOST OF KUWAIT, BUT HOLDS ON TO AN OILFIELD AND
SOME OTHER LAND IN KUWAIT, DO YOU THINK WE SHOULD:"**

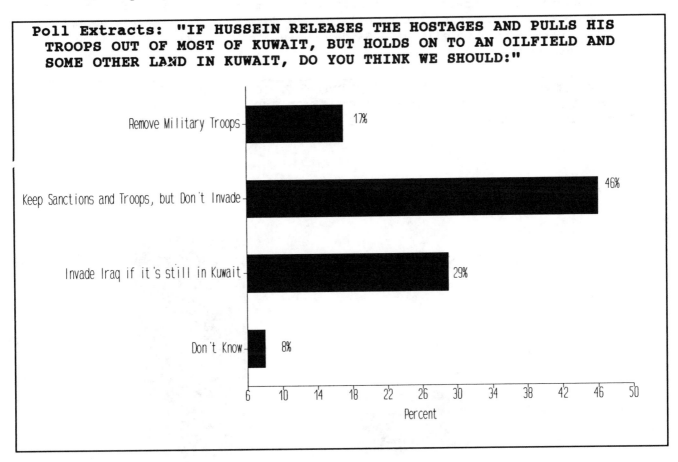

Also in Source: Approval for President Bush's handling of the Iraqi crisis.
Approval for President Bush's overall performance as president. Support
for a long-term American military presence in the Persian Gulf even if
Saddam Hussein pulls his troops out of Kuwait.

Poll Details: This *Los Angeles Times* poll surveyed 2,205 adult men and women.
The telephone survey was conducted December 8-12, 1990. The margin of
error is 3%.

Availability: Published in the *Los Angeles Times*, December 14, 1990,
p. A1, A30.

ASSASSINATION AS A SOLUTION

Description: Respondents were asked if they would support the assassination of
   Iraqi leader Saddam Hussein as a way to end the current crisis. If Iraq
   were to withdraw from Kuwait, respondents were asked if military action
   should be taken to eliminate Saddam Hussein's war-making capability, Saddam
   Hussein himself, both, or neither.

Results: Just over half of the respondents opposed the assassination of Saddam
   Hussein. Even if Iraq were to withdraw from Kuwait, 11% of the respondents
   supported military action to eliminate Saddam Hussein, and 23% supported
   military action to eliminate Saddam Hussein's war-making capability and
   Saddam Hussein.

Poll Extracts: **WOULD YOU SUPPORT A COVERT ASSASSINATION
OF SADDAM HUSSEIN AS A WAY TO QUICKLY END THE CRISIS, OR
WOULD YOU OPPOSE SUCH A PLAN AS WRONG EVEN IF IT WORKED?**

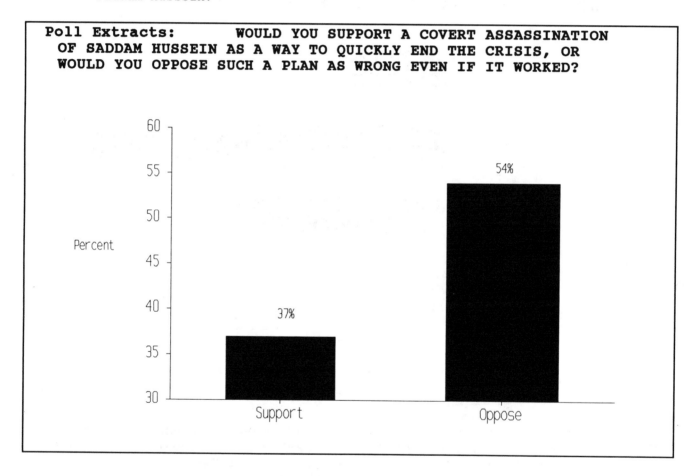

Also in Source: Support for quick military action against Iraq or a more
   diplomatic solution to the crisis. The percentage of respondents who
   approved of the way President Bush was handling the Iraqi crisis. If
   fighting were to begin and U.S. hostages were held at Iraqi positions, the
   percentage of respondents who thought President Bush should still order
   attacks on those positions.

Poll Details: This *Newsweek* poll was conducted by the Gallup Organization.
   755 adults across the nation were interviewed by telephone on October 18
   and October 19, 1990. The margin of error is 4%.

Availability: Published in *Newsweek*, October 29, 1990 (volume CXVI, number
   18), p. 25, 29, 33.

AUTHORIZING FORCE AGAINST IRAQ

Description: Respondents were queried about the United Nations Security
Council resolution authorizing the use of force against Iraq if Iraq fails
to withdraw from Kuwait by January 15, 1991.

Results: A majority of the respondents approved of the United Nations
resolution but did not believe that the U.N. resolution would convince Iraq
to withdraw from Kuwait.

Poll Extracts:
**RESPONDENTS WHO APPROVE OF THE U.N. SECURITY COUNCIL
RESOLUTION AUTHORIZING THE USE OF FORCE AGAINST IRAQ.**

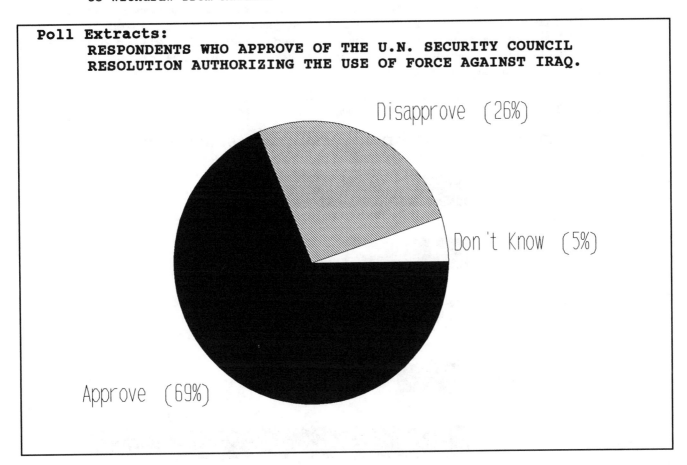

Also in Source: The percentage of respondents who approved of the way George
Bush was handling the Iraqi crisis. Support for the use of military force
against Iraq. Respondents who approved of Secretary of State James Baker
being sent to Iraq, and respondents who thought that a diplomatic solution
would arise out of his visit.

Poll Details: This *Washington Post*-ABC News poll interviewed 758 randomly
selected adults on November 30 and December 1, 1990. The margin of error
is 4%.

Availability: Published in *The Washington Post*, December 4, 1990, p. A27, A29.

AVOID WAR WITH IRAQ

Description: Respondents were queried about President George Bush's handling of the crisis with Iraq and their willingness to see the U.S. enter into war.

Results: 71% of the respondents agreed with the way President Bush is handling the crisis. Characteristics of the respondents who were more willing to have the nation go to war than other respondents were: men more than women, young more than old, richer more than poorer, conservatives more than liberals, and Republicans more than Democrats. When asked if they would support a war to defend Kuwait, Saudi Arabia, Israel, or oil: 53% of the Democrats would not support such a war, but only 27% of the Republicans would not support such a war.

Poll Extracts:

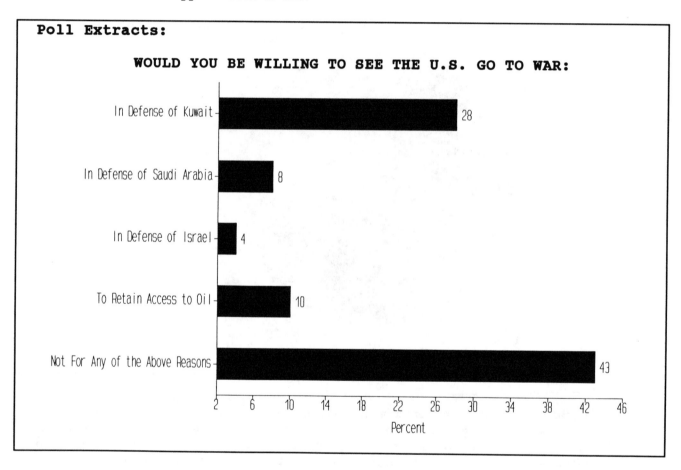

WOULD YOU BE WILLING TO SEE THE U.S. GO TO WAR:

Poll Details: This *Boston Globe*/WBZ-TV poll has a margin of error of 5%. 436 persons were interviewed by KRC Communications Research for the poll.

Availability: Published in *The Boston Globe*, September 1, 1990, p. 2.

CONGRESS AND PRESIDENT BUSH

Description: Respondents were asked if President Bush, in case he decides to go to war with Iraq, should first ask for Congressional permission before attacking Iraq and if there should be a special session of Congress to debate Persian Gulf policy and clarify the U.S. role in the region.

Results: The majority of respondents believe that President Bush should obtain Congressional approval before he orders an attack against Iraq. 71% of the respondents thought that a special session of Congress should be called, so that U.S. policy in the Persian Gulf could be debated.

Poll Extracts:

**"IF BUSH DECIDED TO GO TO WAR WITH IRAQ,
DO YOU THINK HE SHOULD ASK PERMISSION FROM CONGRESS
BEFORE LAUNCHING AN ATTACK, OR NOT?"**

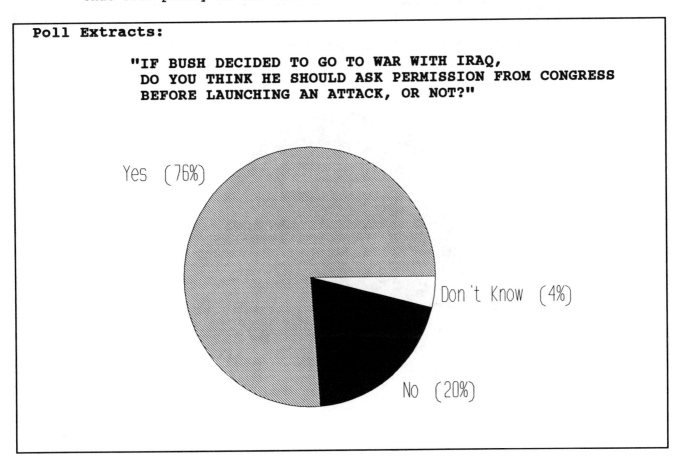

Also in Source: Approval for the way President Bush is handling the Iraqi crisis. Respondents who believe President Bush is moving "too quickly" or "too slowly" against Iraq. Respondents who approved of President Bush's announcement to send additional troops to the Persian Gulf. Results from similar polls conducted prior to this poll.

Poll Details: This *Washington Post*-ABC News poll was conducted by the ICR Survey Research Group and Chilton Research. 515 adults across the nation were interviewed November 14-15, 1990. The margin of error is 5%.

Availability: Published in *The Washington Post*, November 17, 1990, p. A1, A18.

DESERT VIETNAM?

Description: Respondents were asked if they approved of sending American troops to the Persian Gulf to defend Saudi Arabia against a possible Iraqi attack and if they thought the U.S. might be getting involved in another Vietnam.

Results: 74% of the respondents approved of President Bush's decision to send American troops to Saudi Arabia. Just over half of the respondents thought it was likely that the U.S. could become "bogged down" in another Vietnam.

Poll Extracts:

IS THE IRAQI CRISIS LIKELY TO BECOME ANOTHER VIETNAM?

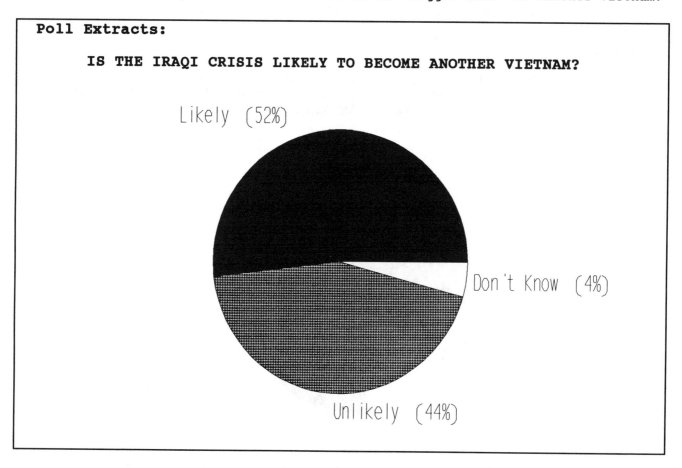

Likely (52%)

Don't Know (4%)

Unlikely (44%)

Also in Source: Respondents who were worried that the economic impact of the Middle East crisis could help start a recession in California. The percentage of Californians who oppose offshore drilling for oil.

Poll Details: This *Los Angeles Times* poll surveyed 1,586 registered voters throughout California. The poll was conducted August 17-22, 1990. The margin of error is 3%.

Availability: Published in the *Los Angeles Times*, August 26, 1990, p. A7, A13.

FIGHTING FOR OIL

Description: Respondents were asked what the U.S. was hoping to achieve in the Middle East and if it was worth fighting for the liberation of Kuwait.

Results: 42% of the respondents did not think it was worth fighting for the liberation of Kuwait. Half of the respondents thought that the U.S. main goal was to protect the oil supply.

Poll Extracts:

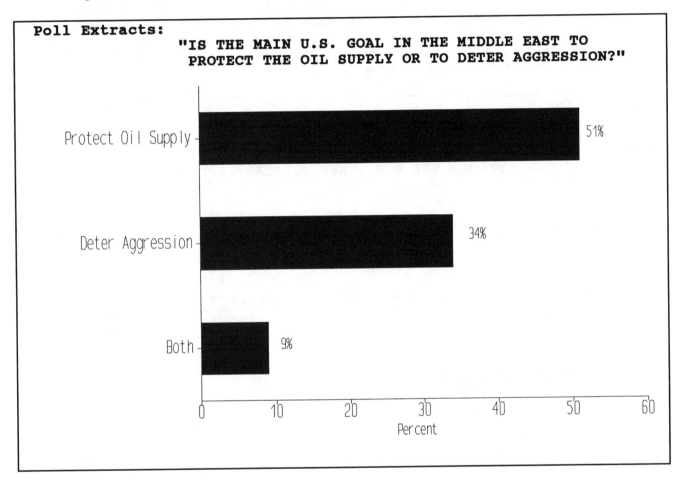

"IS THE MAIN U.S. GOAL IN THE MIDDLE EAST TO PROTECT THE OIL SUPPLY OR TO DETER AGGRESSION?"

Also in Source: Whether the likelihood of war has increased in the past several weeks. How long the U.S. and its allies should wait before giving up on the economic sanctions as a solution.

Poll Details: Yankelovich Clancy Shulman conducted this poll for *Time*/CNN. 500 adult Americans were interviewed by telephone on November 14, 1990. The margin of error is 4.5%.

Availability: Published in *Time*, November 26, 1990 (volume 136, number 23), p. 31, 33.

FIGHTING IN THE PERSIAN GULF

Description: Respondents were given several situations that might develop in the Persian Gulf crisis, and then asked if the U.S. should take military action in such a situation.

Results: U.S. military action against acts of outright aggression by Iraq would be supported by a majority of the respondents. 39% of the respondents believe military action should be taken "if the U.S. develops a major shortage of oil that threatens an economic recession and closes some of our factories." 27% of the respondents thought that military action should be taken "if the U.S. develops a major shortage of oil that increases the price of gasoline to over $2 a gallon."

Poll Extracts:

SHOULD THE U.S. TAKE MILITARY ACTION:

If Iraq refuses to withdraw from Kuwait? ...... 43% -- Yes
                                                42% -- No

If terrorists loyal to Iraq kill Americans
anywhere? .... 67% -- Yes
                                             21% -- No

If Iraq imprisons or mistreats Americans
left in Kuwait? .... 70% -- Yes
                                            18% -- No

If Iraq invades Saudi Arabia? .... 74% -- Yes
                                              18% -- No

Also in Source: Accompanying article on the need for the U.S. to define its long-term objectives in the Persian Gulf.

Poll Details: This *Wall Street Journal*/NBC News poll questioned 805 registered voters from August 18-19, 1990.

Availability: Published in *The Wall Street Journal*, August 30, 1990, p. A12.

HOSTAGES IN IRAQ: SHOULD THE U.S. ATTACK?

Description: Presents the results of a survey concerning the treatment of hostages in Iraq as grounds for a United States attack.

Results: Over 60% of the respondents say the United States should attack Iraq if Saddam Hussein mistreats hostages.

Poll Extracts:

THE HOSTAGES IN IRAQ:

Should the United States attack Iraq if Saddam
Hussein mistreats hostages?.........................Yes...56%

Given this mistreatment, should the United
States attack Iraq even if hostages would
die as a result?....................................Yes...41%

Also in Source: President Bush's approval rating was 59%.

Poll Details: The telephone poll, conducted by ABC News, was conducted on November 2-4, 1990. The random sampling of 1,093 voters has an error rate of plus or minus 3.5%.

Availability: Published in *USA Today*, November 6, 1990, p. 4A.

THE IRAQI CRISIS AND HISTORICAL COMPARISONS

Description: Presents the results of a poll which asked respondents if Saddam
Hussein is comparable to Adolf Hitler, and if the whole situation in the
Middle East is a lot like Vietnam.

Results: The majority of respondents thought that Saddam Hussein is comparable
to Adolf Hitler. 42% of the respondents thought that the current situation
in the Middle East is a lot like Vietnam in the 1960s. More women (47%)
than men (35%) thought that the situation in the Middle East is a lot like
Vietnam.

Poll Extracts:

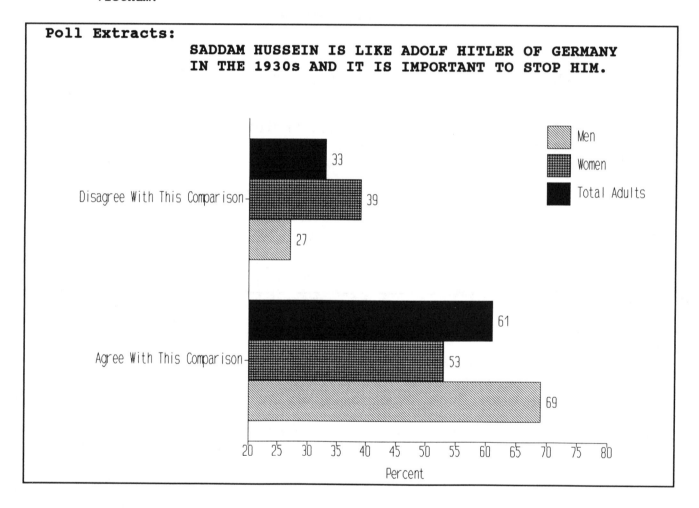

Also in Source: Support for the actions taken against Iraq. Respondents who
believe that the administration was too quick to send military forces.
President Bush's approval rating. Approval for President Bush's handling
of the crisis. Expectations for war with Iraq.

Poll Details: This *New York Times* poll was conducted by telephone interviews
with 670 adults nationwide, excluding Alaska and Hawaii. The poll was
conducted on August 9-10, 1990. Further details as to how the respondents
were selected is provided in the source. The margin of sampling error is
4%.

Availability: Published in *The New York Times*, August 12, 1990, p. 1, 13.

KEEP THE HOSTAGES SAFE

Description: Presents the results of a poll which questioned respondents about
the crisis with Iraq.

Results: 49% of the respondents thought that it was "very likely" that the U.S.
would be involved in a war with Iraq. 73% of the respondents believe that
getting involved in the conflict with Iraq was the right thing to do. 57%
of the respondents do not believe that our involvement will lead to a
situation like Vietnam. 70% of the respondents approve of President Bush's
decision to call up the military reserves.

Poll Extracts:

**"IS IT MORE IMPORTANT TO PROTECT THE LIVES OF HOSTAGES
OR TO DEFEND U.S. INTERESTS IN THE MIDDLE EAST?"**

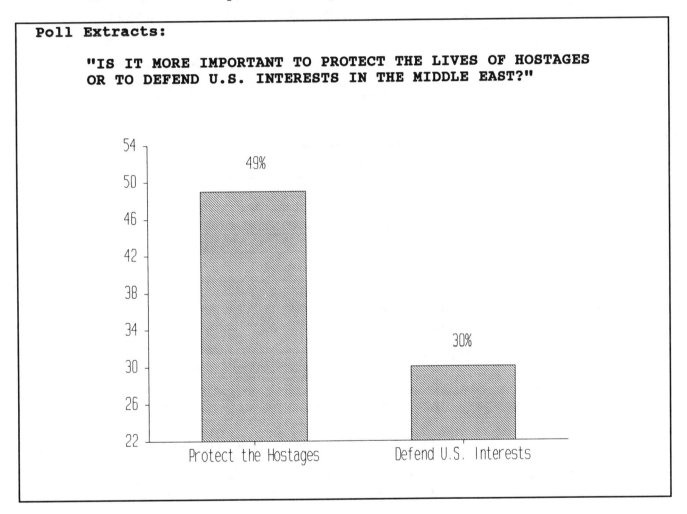

Also in Source: Whether respondents favor or oppose strong actions against
Iraq, when presented with several possible consequences.

Poll Details: This *Time* poll was conducted by Yankelovich Clancy Shulman on
August 23, 1990. 500 adults were interviewed by telephone. The sampling
error is 4.5%.

Availability: Published in *Time*, September 3, 1990 (volume 136, number 10),
p. 29-32.

NUCLEAR WEAPONS IN THE PERSIAN GULF

Description: Presents the results of a survey concerning a variety of issues involving the crisis in the Persian Gulf, including the use of nuclear weapons in a potential conflict.

Results: 60% of the respondents said the United States should use nuclear weapons if Iraq uses nuclear weapons against American troops.

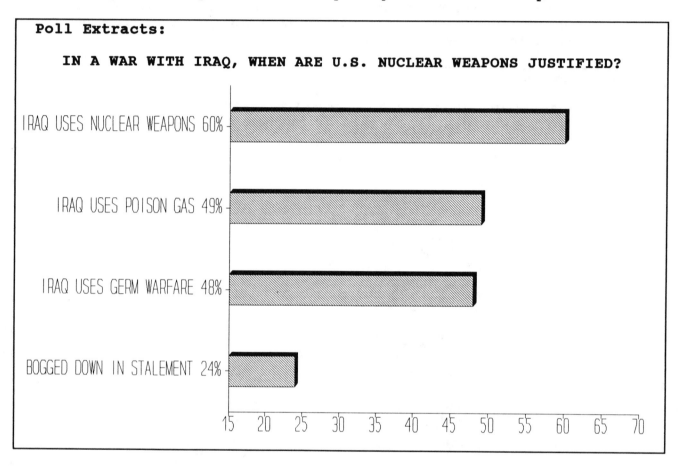

Poll Extracts:

IN A WAR WITH IRAQ, WHEN ARE U.S. NUCLEAR WEAPONS JUSTIFIED?

IRAQ USES NUCLEAR WEAPONS 60%

IRAQ USES POISON GAS 49%

IRAQ USES GERM WARFARE 48%

BOGGED DOWN IN STALEMENT 24%

15 20 25 30 35 40 45 50 55 60 65 70

Also in Source: 36% of the respondents feel President George Bush is moving too quickly toward a war with Iraq, while 59% feel he is not. 68% approve of the United Nations resolution setting a January 15, 1991, deadline for Iraq to pull out of Kuwait and allowing the use of force against Iraq. 25% of the respondents disapprove of such a resolution.

Poll Details: The results of the poll were taken from a telephone survey of 1,000 adult Americans for *Time*/CNN on November 27-28, 1990 by Yankelovich Clancy Shulman. The sampling error is plus or minus 3%.

Availability: Published in *Time*, December 10, 1990 (voulme 136, number 25), p. 42.

PEACEFUL OUTCOME PREDICTED FOR THE IRAQI CRISIS

Description: Presents the results of a survey which asked respondents if they
thought the crisis in the Persian Gulf would be settled peacefully.

Results: 53% of the respondents thought that the Iraqi crisis can be resolved
without military action. 19% of the respondents thought that it was "very
unlikely" and 24% thought that it was "somewhat unlikely" that the Iraqi
crisis would be resolved peacefully.

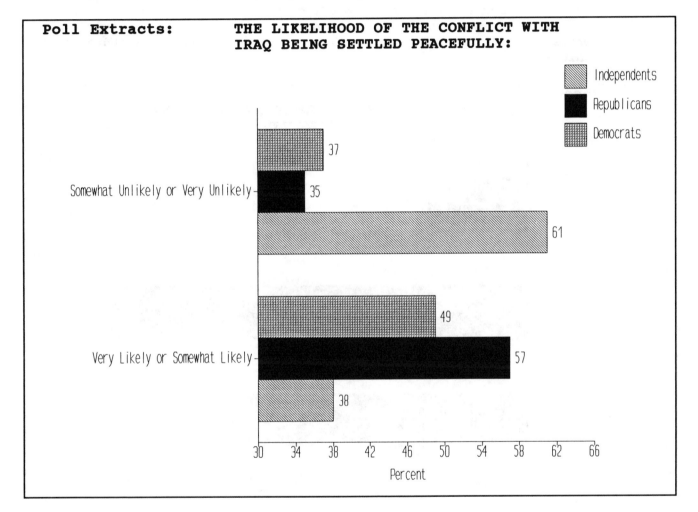

Poll Extracts: **THE LIKELIHOOD OF THE CONFLICT WITH
                            IRAQ BEING SETTLED PEACEFULLY:**

Also in Source: The percentage of respondents in two previous polls who
thought that the Iraqi crisis could be resolved without military action.
The percentage of respondents who believe that U.S. allies should pay
between one-half and three-fourths of the cost of the Middle East
operation. President Bush's favorability rating. Respondents rating of
President Bush's job performance; and his handling of the economy and
federal deficit. The percentage of respondents who said they would re-
elect President Bush for a second term in office.

Poll Details: KRC Communications Research interviewed 1,003 registered voters
nationwide by telephone on September 2-4, 1990. The margin of sampling
error is 3%.

Availability: Published in *The Boston Globe*, September 6, 1990, p. 10.

PREPARING FOR WAR WITH IRAQ

Description: Presents the results of a poll which questioned respondents about the likelihood of the U.S. entering into a war with Iraq. Respondents were also questioned about their support for U.S. troops in Saudi Arabia, and their perception of what was important in the crisis.

Results: The majority of respondents think that the U.S. will be engaged in a war with Iraq. 75% of the respondents favor President Bush's decision to send U.S. troops and aircraft to Saudi Arabia. Dealing with the Iraqi crisis, respondents thought it was important to: protect the lives of Americans -- 84%; defend Saudi Arabia -- 70%; force Iraq to withdraw from Kuwait -- 67%.

Poll Extracts:

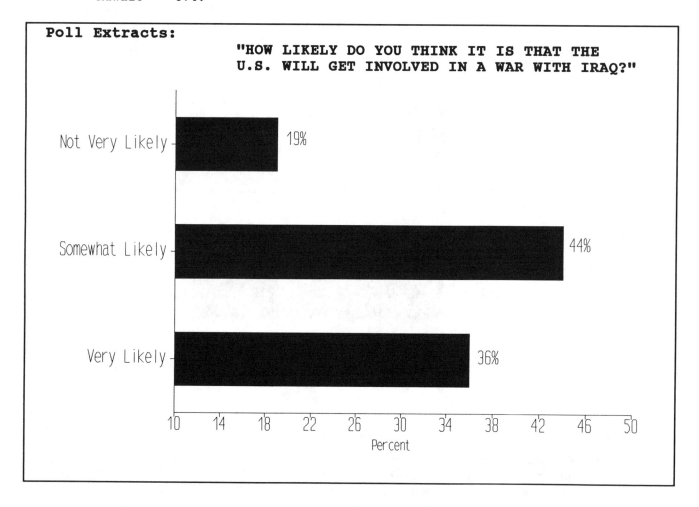

"HOW LIKELY DO YOU THINK IT IS THAT THE U.S. WILL GET INVOLVED IN A WAR WITH IRAQ?"

Also in Source: Whether respondents favor or oppose strong actions against Iraq, when presented with several possible consequences.

Poll Details: This *Time*/CNN poll was conducted by Yankelovich Clancy Shulman on August 9, 1990. 500 adults were interviewed by telephone. The sampling error is 4.5%.

Availability: Published in *Time*, August 20, 1990 (volume 136, number 8), p. 20-22.

REASONS FOR FIGHTING IRAQ

Description: Respondents were asked if the U.S. should soon start military operations against Iraq or wait to see what Iraq does. Respondents were also asked what was a good justification for using military action against Iraq.

Results: 71% of the respondents thought that the U.S. should wait and see what Iraq does before U.S. troops begin military action against Iraq. Over half of the respondents felt that stopping Saddam Hussein from developing nuclear weapons was enough justification for starting military action against Iraq.

Poll Extracts:

WHICH OF THE FOLLOWING IS GOOD ENOUGH OR NOT GOOD ENOUGH A REASON FOR THE UNITED STATES TO TAKE MILITARY ACTION AGAINST IRAQ?

To restore the government of
Kuwait and defend Saudi Arabia
against aggression .... 35% -- Good Enough
                                 56% -- Not Good Enough

To stop Saddam Hussein from
developing nuclear weapons ...... 54% -- Good Enough
                                  39% -- Not Good Enough

To protect the source of much
of the world's oil .... 31% -- Good Enough
                                 62% -- Not Good Enough

Also in Source: Respondents' attitudes toward President Bush's use of American military forces in the Persian Gulf.

Poll Details: This *New York Times*/CBS News poll involved 1,370 adults across the nation, excluding Alaska and Hawaii. The telephone poll was conducted during November 13-15, 1990. The margin of error is 3%.

Availability: Published in *The New York Times*, November 20, 1990, p. A12.

RELEASING THE HOSTAGES

Description: Respondents were queried on several possible scenarios in the
Persian Gulf.

Results: 66% of the respondents would see the following as a success for U.S.
policy: Iraq withdraws from Kuwait, the former government is restored --
later the Arab countries work out an agreement that will meet some of
Iraq's demands for territory.

Poll Extracts:

**IF SADDAM HUSSEIN RELEASES ALL THE U.S. HOSTAGES SOON,
HOW WOULD THAT AFFECT YOUR SUPPORT FOR U.S. MILITARY
ACTION AGAINST IRAQ?**

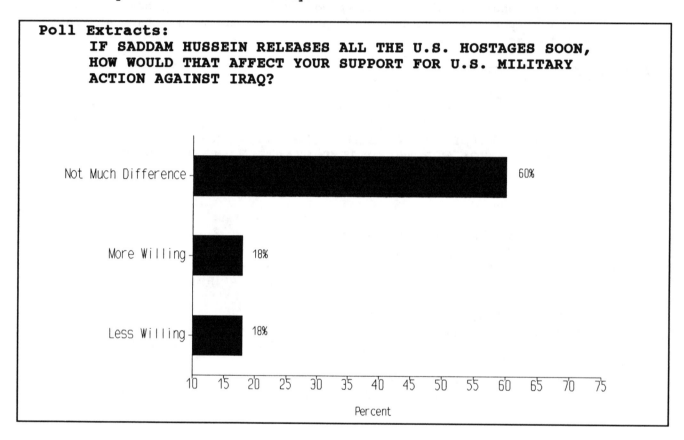

Also in Source: Support for U.S. military action to remove Iraq from Kuwait,
if Iraq refuses to leave. Respondents who saw President Bush's decision to
receive the Iraqi foreign minister and send Secretary of State James Baker
to Iraq, as more of an attempt to justify starting a war than as a real
negotiation to avoid war.

Poll Details: This *Newsweek* poll was conducted by the Gallup Organization.
769 adults across the nation were interviewed by telephone December 6 and
December 7, 1990.

Availability: Published in *Newsweek*, December 17, 1990 (volume CXVI, number
25), p. 22.

SADDAM HUSSEIN AND ADOLF HITLER

Description: Respondents were asked about the comparison of Saddam Hussein and Adolf Hitler and whether military action against Iraq should begin quickly.

Results: Over half of the respondents agreed with the comparison of Saddam Hussein to Adolf Hitler. 70% of the respondents thought that before beginning military action against Iraq, President Bush should wait to see if economic sanctions are effective.

Poll Extracts:

"SOME PEOPLE HAVE COMPARED SADDAM HUSSEIN TO ADOLF HITLER. DO YOU AGREE OR DISAGREE WITH THIS COMPARISON?"

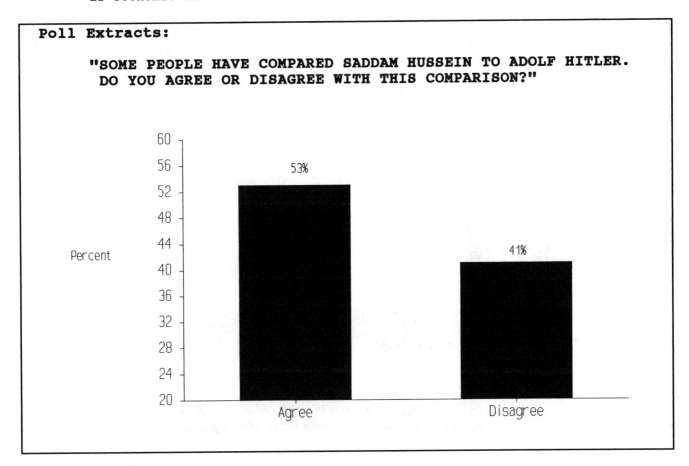

Also in Source: The percentage of respondents who thought that U.S. forces would end up in combat.

Poll Details: This *Newsweek* poll was conducted by the Gallup Organization. 754 adults across the nation were interviewed by telephone on November 15 and November 16, 1990. Don't know and other responses were not shown. The margin of error is 4%.

Availability: Published in *Newsweek*, November 26, 1990 (volume CXVI, number 22), p. 26.

SANCTIONS OR FORCE

Description: Respondents were asked whether Congress should be able to openly debate whether the U.S. should fight Iraq or whether the public debate would damage the effort to persuade Iraq to leave Kuwait. Respondents were also asked what the U.S. should do if Iraq had not withdrawn its troops from Kuwait by January 15, 1991.

Results: 69% of the respondents thought that Congress should be able to debate openly whether the U.S. should fight Iraq. Respondents were about evenly divided on starting military actions against Iraq or waiting to see if the trade embargo and other economic sanctions will work after the arrival of the January 15, 1991 deadline.

Poll Extracts:

IF IRAQ HAS NOT WITHDRAWN FROM KUWAIT BY JANUARY 15, 1991

SHOULD THE U.S. START MILITARY ACTIONS AGAINST IRAQ, OR SHOULD THE U.S.
WAIT LONGER TO SEE IF THE TRADE EMBARGO AND OTHER ECONOMIC SANCTIONS WORK?

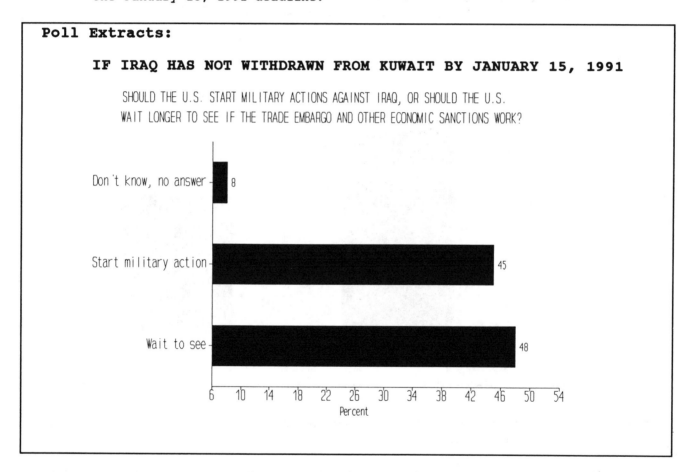

Also in Source: Views of the respondents on sending troops to Saudi Arabia, and on what action to take if Iraq does not withdraw by January 15, 1991; results broken down by sex, race, education, political affiliation, political outlook, and age group.

Poll Details: This *New York Times*/CBS News poll was conducted December 9-11, 1990. 1,044 adults across the nation, excluding Alaska and Hawaii, were interviewed by telephone. The results have been weighted to take into account variations in the sample relating to region, race, sex, age, and education. The margin of error is 3%. Further details on how the survey was conducted are provided in the source.

Availability: Published in *The New York Times*, December 14, 1990, p. A1, A14.

STARTING A WAR

Description: This survey asked 62 questions about attitudes on the Persian Gulf.

Results: Americans strongly support President Bush's goals in the Persian Gulf, but 90% of the respondents are not ready for the United States to begin a war. If Iraq were to attack American forces in the Persian Gulf: 49% of the respondents favored a response limited to the force required for defense, while 47% favored a massive counterattack and all-out war.

Poll Extracts: **DO YOU BELIEVE THAT THE UNITED STATES GOVERNMENT WOULD TELL THE AMERICAN PEOPLE THAT IRAQ HAD STARTED THE WAR WHEN THE UNITED STATES ACTUALLY HAD STARTED IT?**

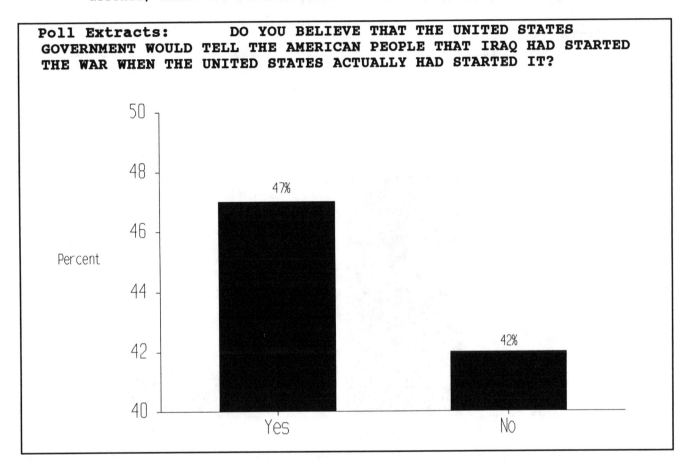

Also in Source: The percentage of respondents who thought it was very important or extremely important that the Kuwaiti royal family be returned to power. The percentage of respondents who thought: the main goal in the Persian Gulf was maintaining the flow of oil, President Bush's main goal in the Persian Gulf was to maintain the flow of oil.

Poll Details: 1,000 adults were interviewed in this survey for Americans Talk Security, a bipartisan group of polling and consulting firms. The survey was conducted September 21-26, 1990. The margin of error is 3.2%.

Availability: Published in *The New York Times*, October 1, 1990, p. A9.

SUPPORT FOR ACTIONS AGAINST IRAQ

Description: Respondents were asked if they supported an economic blockade of Iraq to keep all goods including food and medicine from entering Iraq. Respondents were also asked if the U.S. did the right thing in sending troops to Saudi Arabia.

Results: The majority of respondents favor the U.S. Navy enforcing an economic blockade of Iraq. The majority of respondents also feel that the U.S. did the right thing in sending troops to Saudi Arabia.

Poll Extracts:

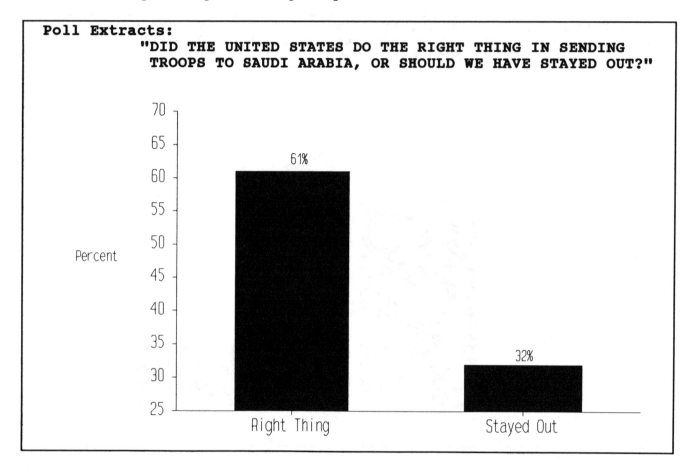

"DID THE UNITED STATES DO THE RIGHT THING IN SENDING TROOPS TO SAUDI ARABIA, OR SHOULD WE HAVE STAYED OUT?"

Also in Source: Approval ratings for how President Bush has handled his responsibilities. The percentage of respondents who believe the Iraqi crisis will be resolved without fighting. The percentage of respondents who believe the U.S. is involved mainly to protect oil supplies.

Poll Details: This *New York Times*/CBS News poll involved 960 adults across the nation, excluding Alaska and Hawaii. Telephone interviews were conducted October 8-10, 1990. "The results have been weighted to take account of household size and number of residential phone lines and to adjust for variations in the sample relating to region, race, sex, age and education." The margin of error is 3%. Further details are provided in the source.

Availability: Published in *The New York Times*, October 14, 1990, p. 1, 25.

TROOPS IN SAUDI ARABIA

Description: Respondents were queried about U.S. troops in Saudi Arabia and U.S. military options against Iraq.

Results: 81% of the respondents approved of the decision to send U.S. troops to Saudi Arabia. The respondents thought that: U.S. troops should stay until the crisis is over -- 52%; U.S. troops are likely to end up in combat against Iraqi forces -- 73%. Men were more supportive than women about sending troops to Saudi Arabia and having them stay there until the crisis is resolved. The most favored military action is a naval blockade of Iraq.

Poll Extracts:

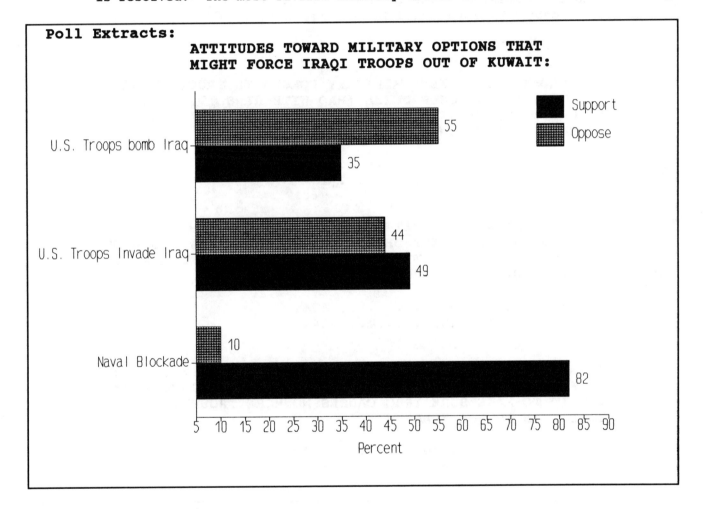

ATTITUDES TOWARD MILITARY OPTIONS THAT MIGHT FORCE IRAQI TROOPS OUT OF KUWAIT:

Also in Source: The percentage of respondents willing to pay 50 cents or more per gallon of gasoline in order to make the ban on Iraqi oil effective.

Poll Details: This *USA Today* poll interviewed 610 people by telephone. The nationwide poll was conducted by Gordon S. Black Corp. on August 8, 1990. The margin of sampling error is 4%.

Availability: Published in *USA Today*, August 9, 1990, p. 1A.

U.S. POLICY IN THE CRISIS WITH IRAQ

Description: Presents the results of a poll which asked respondents about
their perspectives on U.S. policy in the Middle East crisis.

Results: 48% favored and 46% opposed invading Kuwait to force Iraq out (after
considering the risk of starting a war with Iraq). 75% of the respondents
thought that the U.S. should not fire the first shot and should instead
wait until Iraq attacks American forces first. 79% of the respondents
would continue to support the economic embargo against Iraq "even if it
results in massive famine in Iraq." 51% of the respondents thought that
the economic blockade would force Iraq out of Kuwait.

Poll Extracts:

"SHOULD THE U.S. KEEP MILITARY FORCES IN SAUDI ARABIA
AND THE PERSIAN GULF UNTIL IRAQ WITHDRAWS ITS TROOPS
FROM KUWAIT, EVEN IF IT MEANS KEEPING AMERICAN FORCES
THERE FOR MANY MONTHS OR EVEN YEARS?"

Yes 75%
No 23%

"DO YOU THINK A WAR BETWEEN THE UNITED STATES AND IRAQ
WOULD BE A RELATIVELY SHORT WAR LASTING A FEW WEEKS OR
MONTHS OR DO YOU THINK SUCH A WAR WOULD LAST FOR A LONG
TIME, A YEAR OR MORE?"

Short War 63%
Long War 34%

"THE U.S. SHOULD KEEP ITS MILITARY FORCES IN THE MIDDLE
EAST ON A PERMANENT BASIS EVEN IF IRAQ WITHDRAWS FROM
KUWAIT TO MAKE SURE IRAQ CAUSES NO MORE TROUBLE IN THE
REGION IN FUTURE YEARS."

Agree 46%
Disagree 52%

Also in Source: Approval of President Bush's handling of the Iraqi crisis.
Whether our allies should help pay the cost of this operation. Will the
U.S. become involved in a war with Iraq. Whether the Soviet Union is
helping or hurting the chances of a settlement in the crisis. For several
of the questions asked, responses from two similar polls that were
conducted in August, 1990.

Poll Details: This *Washington Post*/ABC News telephone poll was conducted
September 6-9, 1990. 1,011 randomly selected adults across the nation were
interviewed by Chilton Research Services. The margin of error is 3%.

Availability: Published in *The Washington Post*, September 11, 1990, p. A1, A9.

U.S. TROOPS SHOULD STAY UNTIL THE END

Description: This poll queried Texans about the direction U.S. policy should take in forcing Iraqi troops out of Kuwait.

Results: The majority of respondents supported U.S. troops in the Persian Gulf until Iraqi troops withdraw from Kuwait. 45% of the respondents favored an invasion of Kuwait to force out Iraq, even if it meant risking war with Iraq (39% opposed).

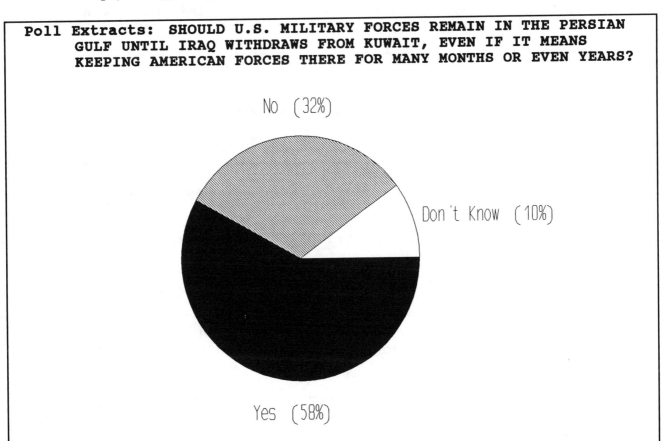

Poll Extracts: SHOULD U.S. MILITARY FORCES REMAIN IN THE PERSIAN GULF UNTIL IRAQ WITHDRAWS FROM KUWAIT, EVEN IF IT MEANS KEEPING AMERICAN FORCES THERE FOR MANY MONTHS OR EVEN YEARS?

No (32%)

Don't Know (10%)

Yes (58%)

Also in Source: "The Texas Poll found that native Texans' enthusiasm for a prolonged U.S. presence in Saudi Arabia lagged behind support expressed by newcomers."

Poll Details: 1,008 Texans were interviewed by telephone for Harte-Hanks Communications Inc. by the Public Policy Resources Laboratory of Texas A&M University. The margin of error is 3%.

Availability: Published in *The Dallas Morning News*, November 13, 1990, p. 1A, 6A.

VIEWS ON THE IRAQI CRISIS

Description: Respondents were queried about their support for U.S. involvement in the Iraqi crisis.

Results: 81% of the respondents anticipated war with Iraq. 54% approved of the U.S. keeping troops in Saudi Arabia until Iraq leaves Kuwait, even if it takes months or even years. Respondents thought that there was reason enough to begin a military action against Iraq in order to: drive Iraq out of Kuwait -- 59%, stop Saddam Hussein from obtaining nuclear weapons -- 78%, and protect a major source of the world's oil -- 58%.

Poll Extracts:

VIEWS ON THE IRAQI CRISIS

	Blacks	Whites
Have a family member in the armed forces or reserves --	54%	27%
U.S. has tried enough diplomacy --	30%	55%
U.S. was too quick to send troops --	59%	39%
President Bush adequately explained the reasons for sending the troops --	33%	60%
U.S. should fight to free Kuwait --	39%	64%

Also in Source: Approval for the way President George Bush is handling his job. The percentage of respondents who thought that the Bush Administration had been too quick to get the U.S. military involved, and the percentage who thought that the Bush Administration had tried hard enough to find a diplomatic solution.

Poll Details: This poll was conducted during December 6-9, 1990 by Voice Information Services Inc., an operating unit of *The Atlanta Journal and Constitution*. 751 adult Georgians were randomly interviewed by telephone. The margin of error is 4%, with the potential sampling error larger for subgroups.

Availability: Published in *The Atlanta Journal and Constitution*, December 14, 1990, p. A-1, A-10.

WAR WITH IRAQ

Description: Respondents were queried about the possibility of war with Iraq, and about U.S. military options.

Results: 60% of the respondents believed that the U.S. would be involved in a war with Iraq. 68% of the respondents thought that the U.S. should not invade Iraq in order to force Iraq to withdraw from Kuwait. 63% of the respondents supported keeping U.S. military forces in Saudi Arabia and the Persian Gulf until Iraq withdraws from Kuwait, even if it takes many months or even years. Even with respondents aware of the fact that U.S. ships would be within the range of Iraq's missiles during a blockade of Iraq's ports, 69% of the respondents favored a blockade.

Poll Extracts:

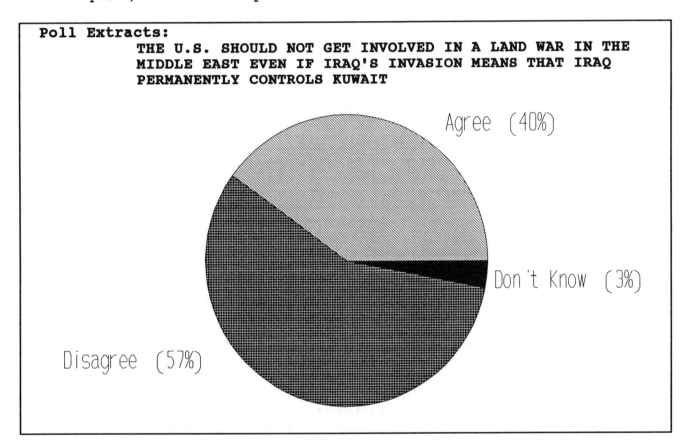

THE U.S. SHOULD NOT GET INVOLVED IN A LAND WAR IN THE MIDDLE EAST EVEN IF IRAQ'S INVASION MEANS THAT IRAQ PERMANENTLY CONTROLS KUWAIT

Agree (40%)

Don't Know (3%)

Disagree (57%)

Also in Source: Approval/disapproval of President Bush's decision to send U.S. troops to Saudi Arabia and the Persian Gulf. The percentage of respondents who thought that the oil and gas price increases which took place after Iraq invaded Kuwait were: "oil suppliers just using the situation to make more money." Respondents who thought that President Bush had been too tough, not tough enough, or as tough as needed with Iraq.

Poll Details: This *Washington Post*/ABC News telephone survey was conducted on August 8, 1990 by Chilton Research Services of Radnor, PA. 769 adults were interviewed, with the margin of error for the overall poll results being 4%.

Availability: Published in *The Washington Post*, August 10, 1990, p. A1, A26.

WHEN DIPLOMACY FAILS TO WORK

Description: Respondents were asked what action the U.S. should take if diplomacy failed to convince Iraq to withdraw from Kuwait.

Results: The largest group of respondents thought that the U.S. should maintain its troops in the Persian Gulf and only attack if Iraq were to attack first. "Women, political independents, Hispanics, the elderly, and those who earn less than $30,000 a year were the most reluctant to attack."

Poll Extracts:

"IF DIPLOMATIC EFFORTS TO END THE PERSIAN GULF CRISIS CONTINUE TO PROVIDE NO SOLUTION, DO YOU THINK THE UNITED STATES SHOULD ..."

Maintain its current presence and only attack
if Iraq attacks first .... 47% -- Agree

Attack Iraqi targets .... 27% -- Agree

Withdraw from the region while continuing to
negotiate the removal of Iraq from Kuwait .... 17% -- Agree

Don't know/refused .... 9% -- Agree

Also in Source: The popularity rating of President Bush. Three of every five Americans have never heard of John Sununu, President Bush's chief of staff.

Poll Details: This *Boston Globe*-WBZ TV poll was conducted by KRC Communications Research. 1,000 registered voters were interviewed by telephone October 21-23, 1990. The margin of error is 3%.

Availability: Published in *The Boston Globe*, October 26, 1990, p. 3.

WHY AMERICAN TROOPS ARE IN THE PERSIAN GULF

Description: Respondents were questioned about their perceptions of: what are the U.S. objectives for the American troops; what would constitute a victory for the U.S.; other areas of interest relating to the crisis.

Results: Respondents believe that U.S. troops were sent to Saudi Arabia mainly to protect U.S. oil supplies. Respondents thought that a U.S. victory in the crisis with Iraq could be claimed if: the Iraqis were forced out of Kuwait -- 24%; the government of Saddam Hussein was overthrown -- 24%; American hostages were released unharmed -- 23%; an attack against Saudi Arabia was prevented -- 5%. "The public's support for U.S. military involvement in the Persian Gulf increases sharply with education, according to the survey. For example, the commitment of troops was supported by only 45% of high school dropouts but by 61% of those who received a diploma. And among people who went to college, backing for the troop deployment rose to 72%." To show that countries cannot just "get away" with aggression, 53% of the respondents thought it would be worth risking the lives of U.S. troops.

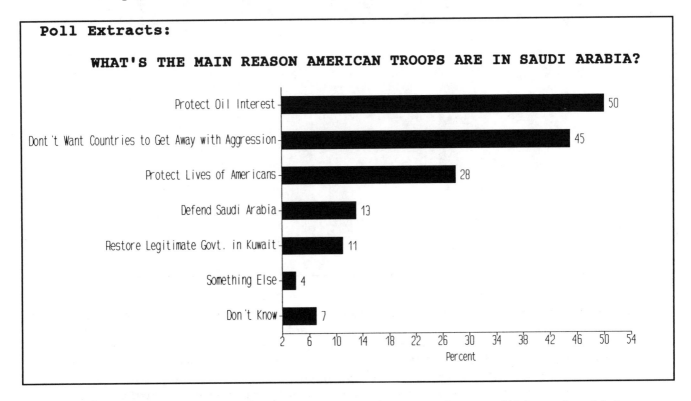

Poll Extracts:

WHAT'S THE MAIN REASON AMERICAN TROOPS ARE IN SAUDI ARABIA?

Protect Oil Interest — 50
Dont't Want Countries to Get Away with Aggression — 45
Protect Lives of Americans — 28
Defend Saudi Arabia — 13
Restore Legitimate Govt. in Kuwait — 11
Something Else — 4
Don't Know — 7

Percent

Also in Source: Approval rating of President Bush. Conditions in which respondents would support going to war with Iraq. The percentage of respondents who support offshore oil drilling in light of the current Middle East situation. The percentage of respondents who think the federal government should spend less for national defense.

Poll Details: This *Los Angeles Times* poll interviewed 1,206 adults by telephone on August 29, 1990. The random sample had a margin of error of 4%.

Availability: Published in the *Los Angeles Times*, August 31, 1990, p. A1, A16.

WILL IRAQ BECOME ANOTHER VIETNAM?

Description: Presents the results of a survey concerning the Persian Gulf crisis.

Results: Over 40% of the respondents believe that if fighting begins with Iraq it is very likely or somewhat likely to become another prolonged situation like the Vietnam War.

Poll Extracts:

IF FIGHTING BEGINS, WILL IRAQ BECOME A PROLONGED VIETNAM-STYLE WAR?

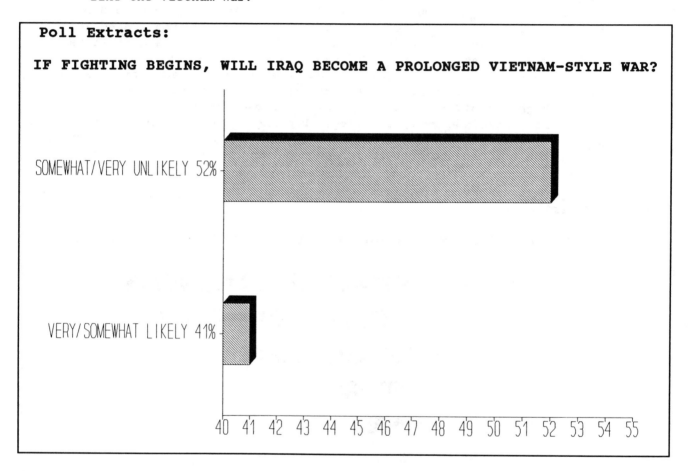

Also in Source: After January 15, 1991, 49% of the respondents feel sanctions should be allowed to work, 42% said attack, and 9% didn't know. 60% feel President George Bush is focusing on the correct balance of military and diplomatic solutions. 11% feel Bush is focusing too much on diplomatic solutions and 22% said he is focusing too much on military solutions. 56% of the respondents are becoming increasingly concerned regarding United States actions against Iraq. 31% said their feelings have not changed and 10% claim they have become more comfortable.

Poll Details: Gordon S. Black conducted a telephone survey of 704 adults on December 9 and 10, 1990 for *USA Today*. The poll has a 4% margin of error.

Availability: Published in *USA Today*, December 13, 1990, p. 1A, 4A.

WILL THE U.S. GO TO WAR?

Description: Presents the results of a survey concerning various issues
surrounding the Persian Gulf crisis.

Results: Over 40% of the respondents believe United States forces will fight
Iraq. Approximately half of the respondents approve of how President
George Bush is handling the crisis.

Poll Extracts:

WILL THE U.S. FIGHT IN THE PERSIAN GULF?

Is it very likely United States forces
will fight Iraq?..Yes...44%

Do you approve of how President Bush
is handling the crisis?...Yes...51%

Is United States combat in Iraq "somewhat likely"
of "very likely?"...Yes...81%

Also in Source: 10% of the respondents are "more comfortable" with United
States actions while 57% are "increasingly concerned." 50% say saving the
1,000 U.S. hostages in Iraq and Kuwait is the top priority.

Poll Details: The Gordon S. Black telephone poll of 615 adults was conducted
November 12, 1990 for *USA Today*. The margin of error is plus or minus 4%.

Availability: Published in *USA Today*, November 13, 1990, p. 1A.

ATTITUDES TOWARD JAPAN

Description: Presents the results of a survey concerning general attitudes of Americans toward Japan.

Results: Compared to 1985 and 1989, the percent of Americans expressing positive attitudes toward Japan in 1990 has eroded, while negative attitudes toward Japan have increased.

Poll Extracts:

YES, I HAVE GENERALLY FRIENDLY FEELINGS TOWARD JAPAN

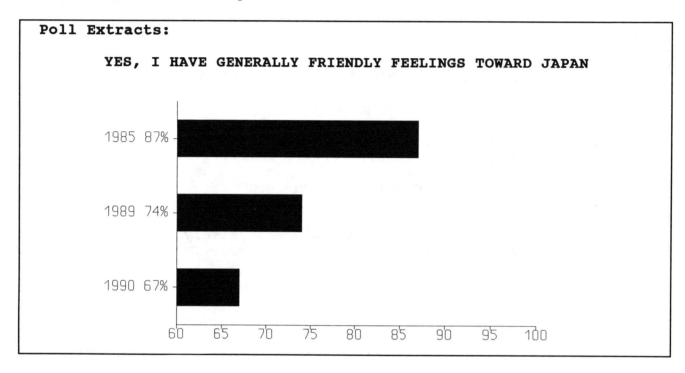

Also in Source: In January 1990, 25% of Americans said their feelings toward Japan were generally unfriendly. This compares to 19% in June 1989 and 8% in 1985.

Poll Details: The survey was conducted by *The New York Times*/CBS News. 1,557 Americans were contacted by telephone on January 13-15, 1990.

Availability: Published in *The New York Times*, February 6, 1990, p. B7.

ATTITUDES TOWARD JAPAN

Description: Presents the results of polls on six questions regarding Japan.

Results: A majority of Americans feel that Japan unfairly restricts the sales of U.S. goods in Japan, and a majority also feel that the U.S. should restrict Japanese imports.

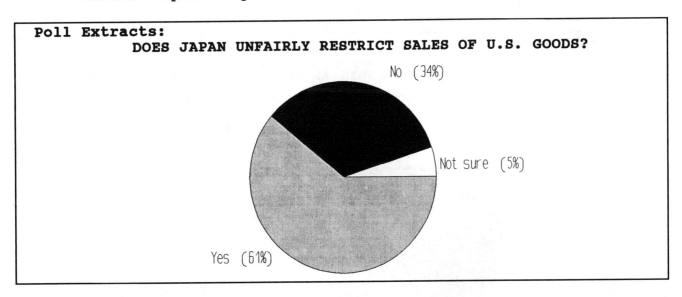

Poll Extracts:
DOES JAPAN UNFAIRLY RESTRICT SALES OF U.S. GOODS?

No (34%)

Not sure (5%)

Yes (61%)

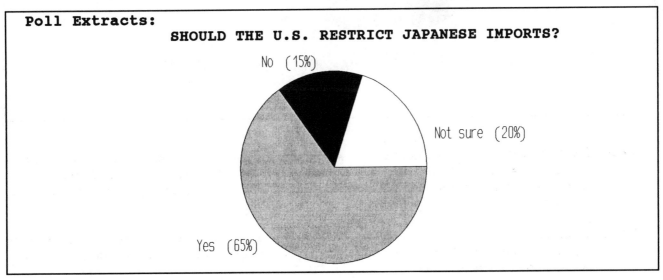

Poll Extracts:
SHOULD THE U.S. RESTRICT JAPANESE IMPORTS?

No (15%)

Not sure (20%)

Yes (65%)

Also in Source: A majority of Americans felt: the trade deficit with Japan was "very serious," Japanese investment in the U.S. should be discouraged, Japan was the least trustworthy ally out of four choices, and they would disapprove of the Japanese buying a major U.S. bank.

Poll Details: The polls were conducted by Louis Harris & Associates, Inc., People, Yankelovich/Time, and Yankelovich/Time-CNN. The poll extracts represent Yankelovich/Time-CNN polls.

Availability: Published in *Fortune*, February 26, 1990 (volume 121, number 5), p. 50-60.

ATTITUDES TOWARD JAPANESE INVESTMENTS

Description: Presents the results of a poll commissioned by the Japanese
government concerning attitudes of Americans toward Japanese-owned firms
and Japanese investments in the United States.

Results: Almost half of the respondents felt that Japanese investments were bad
for the United States.

Poll Extracts:

JAPANESE INVESTMENTS IN THE U.S.A. ARE –

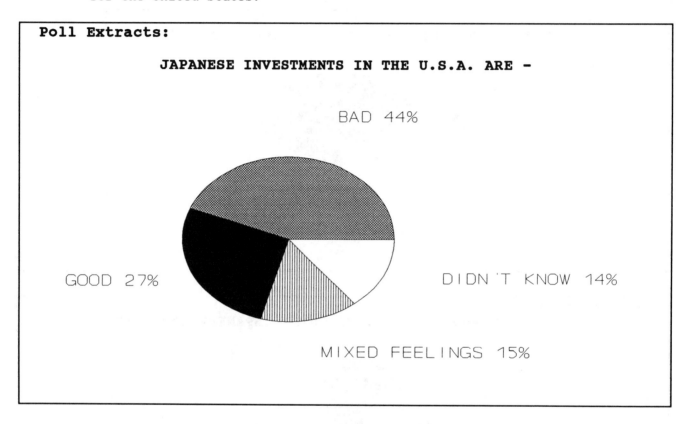

BAD 44%

GOOD 27%   DIDN'T KNOW 14%

MIXED FEELINGS 15%

Also in Source: To the question, "Which foreign-owned company would you most
want to see buying an office on your street," 31% said they preferred a
Canadian-owned firm, 9% a Japanese firm, 7% said a British firm, 6% a West
German firm and 2% a French firm.

Poll Details: The poll, conducted in January 1990 throughout the United States
by the Roper Organization Inc., involved interviews of 1,994 adults. The
margin of error was 3%.

Availability: Published in *The Wall Street Journal*, February 20, 1990, p. A16.

DISTRUST OF JAPAN

Description: This poll measured U.S. opinion on the trustworthiness of Japan as an American ally.

Results: U.S. distrust of the Japanese is at its highest level in 30 years.

Poll Extracts:

RESPONDENTS WHO BELIEVE THAT JAPAN IS NOT A DEPENDABLE ALLY:

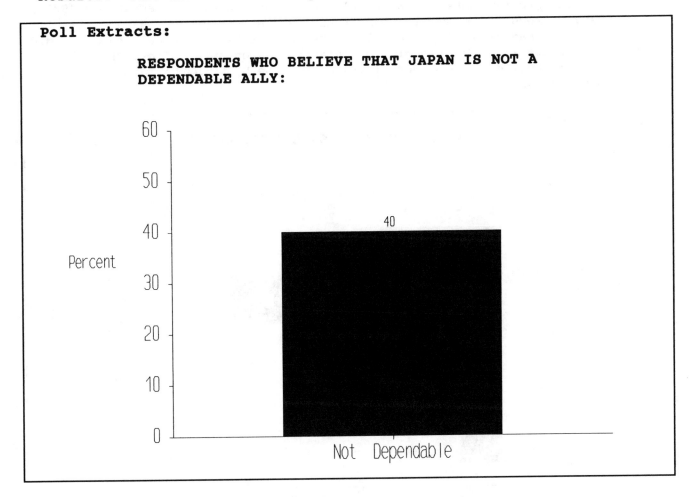

Also in Source: The results from a separate poll of U.S. scholars, business officials, politicians, and other opinion leaders who were asked if they considered a resurgence of Japanese militarism very likely or fairly likely. The percentage of Japanese respondents who had friendly feelings toward Americans in an October 1989 public opinion poll.

Poll Details: The first poll in this series was conducted in 1960. The Japanese Foreign Ministry commissioned the poll which was conducted by the U.S.-based Gallup Organization Inc. The company polled 1,502 U.S. citizens in February 1990.

Availability: Published in *The Atlanta Journal and Constitution*, April 8, 1990, p. C-4.

JAPANESE OPINION OF AMERICANS

Description: This poll queried Japanese respondents on their opinions about
Americans, trade with the U.S., and general relations with the U.S.

Results: The Japanese thought that the following were serious or somewhat
serious problems in the U.S. workplace: drug and alcohol addiction (93%),
lazy workers (66%), and too many racial and ethnic groups (57%). 33% of
the Japanese respondents have less respect for America today than they did
five years ago. The majority of Japanese respondents believe that the
reason there's an imbalance of trade with the U.S. is that Japanese
products are better.

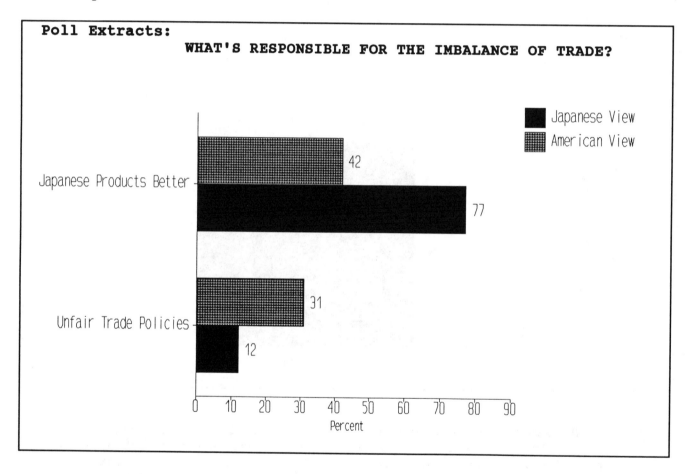

Poll Extracts:

WHAT'S RESPONSIBLE FOR THE IMBALANCE OF TRADE?

Also in Source: Article detailing what Japanese think about Americans,
including several quotes from Japanese personalities. Excerpts from Lee
Iacocca's analysis of the results of the *Newsweek* Poll.

Poll Details: "For this special *Newsweek* Poll, a Japanese affiliate of the
Gallup Organization interviewed a national sample of 785 Japanese adults by
phone January 19-24, 1990. The margin of error is plus or minus 4
percentage points. "Don't Know" and other answers were omitted. U.S. views
from *Newsweek* Polls by Gallup in May and September 1989 and in February
1988."

Availability: Published in *Newsweek*, April 2, 1990 (volume 115, number 14),
p. 18-24.

JAPANESE RESPECT FOR THE UNITED STATES

Description: Presents the results of a survey measuring the level of respect the Japanese have for the United States today compared to five years ago.

Results: One-third of the respondents said their respect for the United States has decreased over the past five years.

Poll Extracts:

HOW HAS YOUR RESPECT FOR THE U.S. CHANGED OVER THE PAST FIVE YEARS?

DECREASED 33%

INCREASED 11%

NO OPINION 56%

Also in Source: 71% of the respondents said Japanese products are superior to American products, 11% said they weren't, and 18% had no opinion. 14% of the respondents think their standard of living is better than that of Americans and Europeans, 32% think it's about the same, 32% think it's worse, and 22% are undecided.

Poll Details: The survey of Japanese citizens was conducted for *Fortune* by Chuo Chosa Sha, a Tokyo research organization.

Availability: Published in *Fortune*, *Pacific Rim Special Issue*, Fall 1990 (volume 122, number 8), p. 17.

PERSPECTIVES ON JAPAN

Description: Presents the results of a survey concerning Americans' attitudes toward Japan.

Results: When asked whether Americans had positive or negative attitudes toward specific Pacific Rim countries, Australia ranked as the most positive with, Japan coming in second.

Poll Extracts:

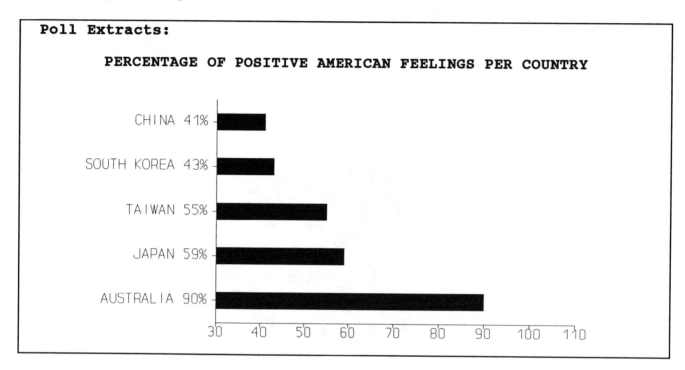

PERCENTAGE OF POSITIVE AMERICAN FEELINGS PER COUNTRY

Also in Source: 91% of the respondents perceive Japanese products as being average or above average in quality. 13% prefer buying Japanese products over American products. 58% said they would be willing to work for a Japanese company, compared with 66% for a German company, 81% for a British company, and 88% for a Canadian company.

Poll Details: The poll was conducted in two separate telephone surveys in January and October 1989, and involved a random sample of 1,614 respondents. The first survey of 1,008 people had a margin of error of plus or minus 3%. The second poll of 606 samples had a margin of error of 4%.

Availability: Published in *The Cincinnati Enquirer*, February 25, 1990, p. H-2.

TRADING WITH JAPAN

Description: Presents the results of a survey concerning the trade situation
between the United States and Japan.

Results: A majority of Americans felt that Japan unfairly restricts the sales
of U.S. goods in Japan.

Poll Extracts:

DOES JAPAN UNFAIRLY RESTRICT SALES OF U.S. GOODS?

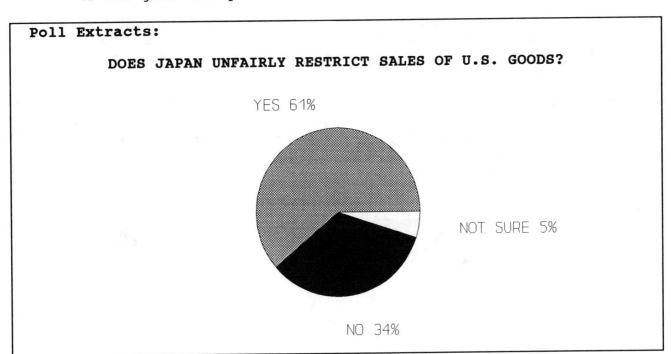

YES 61%

NOT SURE 5%

NO 34%

Also in Source: 65% of Americans felt that the U.S. should restrict Japanese
imports. A majority of Americans felt: that the trade deficit with Japan
was "very serious", that Japanese investment in the U.S. should be
discouraged, that Japan was the least trustworthy ally out of four choices,
and that they would disapprove of the Japanese buying a major U.S. bank.

Poll Details: The survey was conducted by Louis Harris & Associates, Inc.,
People, Yankelovich/*Time*, and Yankelovich/*Time*/CNN.

Availability: Published in *Fortune*, February 26, 1990 (volume 121, number 5),
p. 50-60.

U.S. ON THE DEFENSIVE

Description: U.S. respondents were queried about American security, and both
American and Japanese respondents were asked who they thought would be the
number one economic power in the next century.

Results: 58% of the U.S. respondents picked Japan as the United States
strongest competitor. 58% of the respondents saw the economic power of
Japan as a greater threat to U.S. security than the military power of the
Soviet Union. Fewer than one-third of the U.S. respondents thought that
the U.S. would be the number one economic power in the world during the
next century.

Poll Extracts:

**RESPONDENTS IN THE U.S. AND JAPAN WERE ASKED WHO THEY
THOUGHT WOULD BE THE NUMBER ONE ECONOMIC POWER IN THE
WORLD IN THE NEXT CENTURY:**

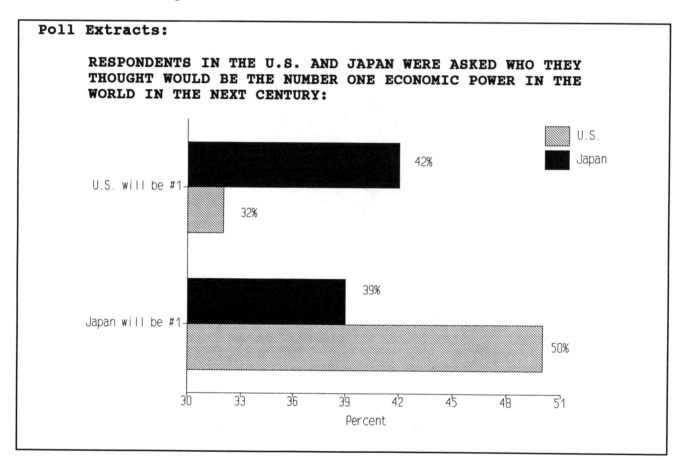

Also in Source: Japanese and American attitudes toward economic competition,
trade restrictions, and overall feelings toward the other country. U.S.
attitudes toward foreign investment.

Poll Details: This *New York Times*/CBS News/Tokyo Broadcasting System poll is
based on telephone interviews in the U.S., and on personal interviews in
Japan. 1,084 adults were interviewed in the U.S. from June 5-8, 1990,
excluding Alaska and Hawaii. 1,468 adults were interviewed in Japan from
May 31 - June 7, 1990. Further details as to how the poll was conducted is
provided in the source. The margin of sampling error is 3%.

Availability: Published in *The New York Times*, July 10, 1990, p. A11.

AMERICAN AND SOVIET LIFE

Description: This poll queried people in the Soviet Union and the United States about different parts of their lives.

Results: Regarding their overall satisfaction with life, 92% of U.S. citizens are satisfied, while 62% of Soviet citizens are dissatisfied. Regarding the availability of consumer goods, 90% of U.S. citizens are satisfied, and 90% of the Soviet citizens are dissatisfied. Regarding the quality of service to the consumer, 80% of U.S. citizens are satisfied, and 85% of Soviet citizens are dissatisfied. Regarding the quality of health care, 65% of U.S. citizens are satisfied, and 76% of Soviet citizens are dissatisfied. Regarding the economy, 66% of U.S. citizens described the U.S. economy as somewhere in between good and bad, while 72% of the Soviet citizens described their economy as bad.

Poll Extracts:

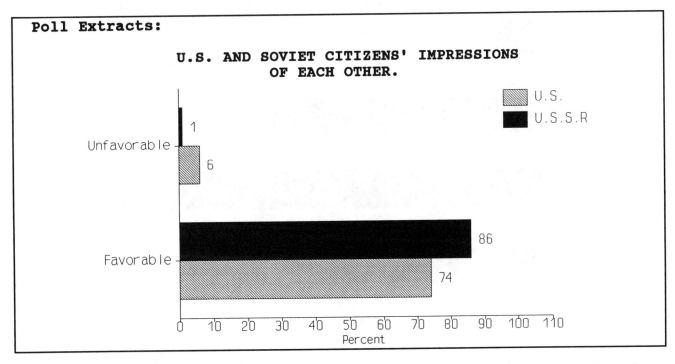

Also in Source: The number of Soviet respondents who estimate that there is a fairly high chance of a public revolt against the government of the Soviet Union. Soviet opinion as to when their economy will improve. The number of Soviets who think Gorbachev and his reforms will survive. Soviet and American opinion on the condition of their family finances as compared to last year.

Poll Details: This survey was conducted as part of *The Los Angeles Times Poll*, directed by I.A. Lewis. The Soviet interviews were conducted by the Soviet Academy of Sciences, with 1,485 citizens on May 9-24, 1990, Soviet respondents were randomly selected from a complete list of people holding internal "passports" in the area west of the Urals. The U.S. part of the survey was conducted by *The Times Poll* on May 10-14, 1990, with 2,144 adults. The margin of error in each country was plus or minus 3%. The University of Houston cooperated in the project.

Availability: Published in the *Los Angeles Times*, June 1, 1990, p. A1, A15.

DEALING WITH THE SOVIETS

Description: This poll asked respondents about their views on arms control with the Soviets, and if they expected a nuclear war to occur within the next 10 years.

Results: 10% of the respondents thought that one superpower would gain more than the other by reaching an arms control agreement. 18% of the respondents thought that the world was likely to get into a nuclear war in the next 10 years.

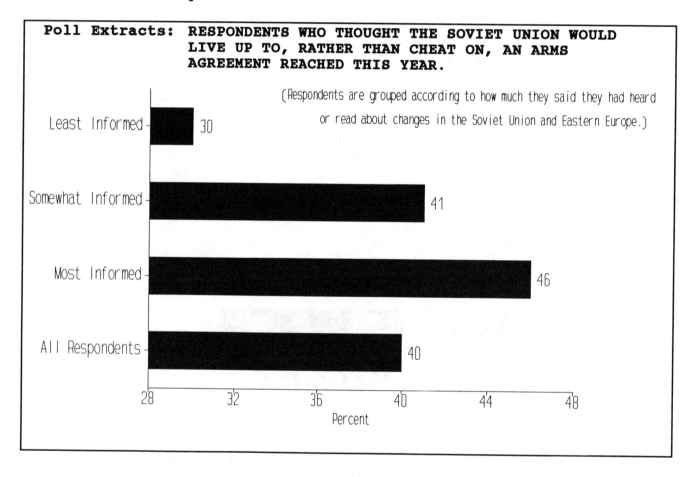

Poll Extracts: **RESPONDENTS WHO THOUGHT THE SOVIET UNION WOULD LIVE UP TO, RATHER THAN CHEAT ON, AN ARMS AGREEMENT REACHED THIS YEAR.**

(Respondents are grouped according to how much they said they had heard or read about changes in the Soviet Union and Eastern Europe.)

Least Informed — 30

Somewhat Informed — 41

Most Informed — 46

All Respondents — 40

Percent

Also in Source: The expectations of respondents in previous polls, as to whether the world would enter into nuclear war within the following 10 years. Views toward equality or superiority in U.S. versus Soviet military strength. The popularity of President Bush and Soviet President Gorbachev. Views on the June 1990 summit meeting.

Poll Details: This *New York Times*/CBS News Poll is based on telephone interviews with 1,140 adults from across the U.S., excluding Alaska and Hawaii. The margin of error is plus or minus 3%. Further details as to how the telephone numbers of the respondents were selected, and how the results have been weighted, are provided in the source.

Availability: Published in *The New York Times*, May 30, 1990, p. A12.

GOOD RELATIONS WITH GORBACHEV OR LITHUANIA?

Description: Respondents were asked about the U.S. response to the Lithuanian declaration of independence from the Soviet Union.

Results: The largest percentage of respondents thought that maintaining good relations with President Gorbachev was more important than supporting Lithuania's independence movement. More respondents approved (39%) than disapproved (19%) of President Bush's handling of the Lithuanian crisis.

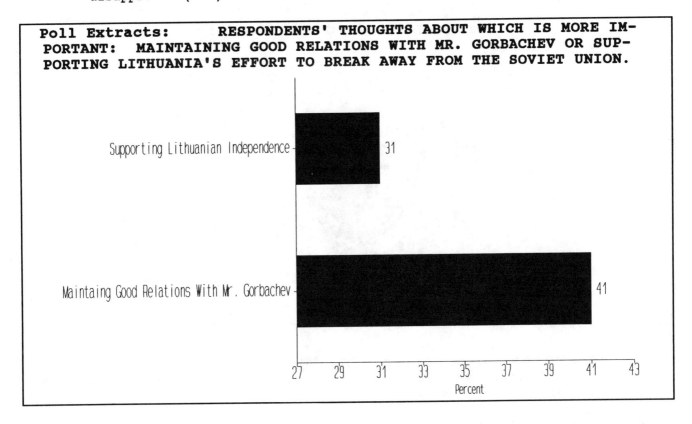

Poll Extracts: RESPONDENTS' THOUGHTS ABOUT WHICH IS MORE IMPORTANT: MAINTAINING GOOD RELATIONS WITH MR. GORBACHEV OR SUPPORTING LITHUANIA'S EFFORT TO BREAK AWAY FROM THE SOVIET UNION.

Supporting Lithuanian Independence — 31

Maintaing Good Relations With Mr. Gorbachev — 41

Percent

Also in Source: Poll questions regarding: the end of the Cold War, German reunification, the popularity of President Bush and President Gorbachev, world domination by the Soviets, and foreign aid.

Poll Details: This *New York Times*/CBS News Poll is based on telephone interviews with 1,515 adults from the U.S., except Alaska and Hawaii. The poll was conducted from March 30, 1990 - April 2, 1990. "The results have been weighted to take account of household size and number of residential telephone lines and to adjust for variations in the sample relating to region, sex, age and education. In theory, in 19 cases out of 20 the results based on such samples will differ by no more than three percentage points in either direction from what would have been obtained by seeking out all American adults." The sampling error for smaller subgroups within the poll will be larger. Further details are provided in the source as to how the telephone numbers of respondents were selected.

Availability: Published in *The New York Times*, April 6, 1990, p. A8.

GORBACHEV AS MAN OF THE DECADE

Description: Presents the results of a poll assessing Mikhail Gorbachev in
response to being chosen *Time's* Man of the Decade.

Results: Nearly 85% of those who responded felt that Gorbachev has made the
world safer.

Poll Extracts:

GORBACHEV HAS MADE THE WORLD:

SAFER 84.2%

OTHER 1.4%

NOT MUCH DIFFERENT 9.2%

MORE DANGEROUS 5.2%

Also in Source: 73% felt that the U.S. defense budget should be cut a lot,
15% said cut a little, 8.4% said it should be kept the same, and 3.2% said
that it should be increased.

Poll Details: After *Time* named Gorbachev their Man of the Decade they asked
their readers to assess Gorbachev's performance. They also asked for their
readers views on U.S. defense expenditures. A total of 3,297 readers
responded.

Availability: Published in *Time,* February 12, 1990 (volume 135, number 7),
p. 10.

LITHUANIAN RECOGNITION

Description: Respondents were asked if the U.S. should recognize Lithuanian independence from the Soviet Union.

Results: The majority of respondents felt that the U.S. should recognize Lithuanian independence.

Poll Extracts:

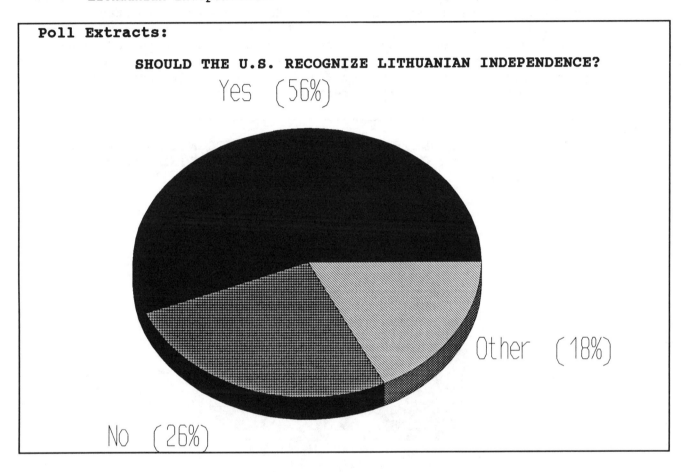

SHOULD THE U.S. RECOGNIZE LITHUANIAN INDEPENDENCE?

Yes (56%)

Other (18%)

No (26%)

Also in Source: Attitudes on summit meetings between the superpowers, arms control negotiations, and troop reductions in Europe.

Poll Details: *The Detroit News* poll was designed and analyzed with the Gannett Co. Inc. research department. The telephone poll of 800 Michigan adults was conducted May 20-22, 1990. The margin of error is plus or minus 3.5%.

Availability: Published in *The Detroit News and Free Press*, May 27, 1990, p. 1A, 6A.

LITHUANIAN SUPPORT IN THE U.S.

Description: Respondents were queried about U.S. support for the Lithuanian
declaration of independence from the Soviet Union.

Results: 61% of the respondents thought it was more important to maintain
friendly ties with President Gorbachev rather than support the Lithuanians'
efforts for independence. Only 23% thought it was more important to
support Lithuania, with 16% not sure. If the Soviet Union were to use
military force to prevent the Lithuanians from establishing an independent
nation, 61% of the respondents thought the U.S. should not cancel the
upcoming June 1990 summit between President Bush and President Gorbachev
(31% thought the U.S. should cancel).

Poll Extracts:
**DO YOU THINK THE UNITED STATES SHOULD RECOGNIZE LITHUANIA
AS AN INDEPENDENT COUNTRY, OR SHOULD THE UNITED STATES NOT
GET INVOLVED?**

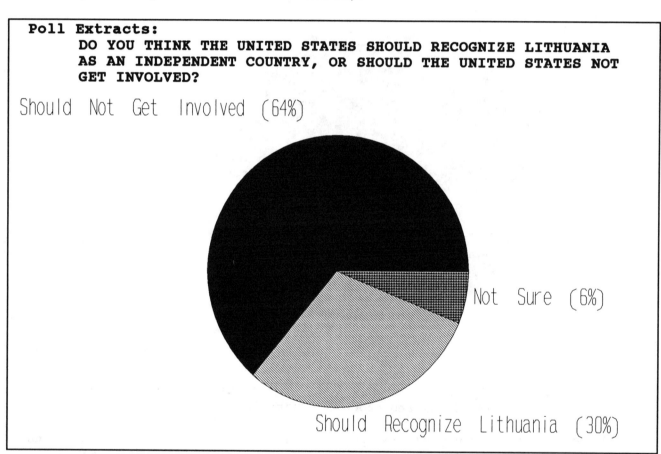

Should Not Get Involved (64%)

Not Sure (6%)

Should Recognize Lithuania (30%)

Also in Source: Article discussing U.S.-Soviet tensions in relation to the
developing Lithuanian situation.

Poll Details: The above information is from *The Wall Street Journal*/NBC News
Poll.

Availability: Published in *The Wall Street Journal*, April 19, 1990,
p. A1, A10.

SOVIET POPULARITY INCREASES

Description: Respondents were questioned about the Soviet Union and Soviet President Gorbachev.

Results: President Bush's and Soviet President Gorbachev's popularity continues to remain high. 33% of the respondents thought that President Gorbachev is doing more to reduce East-West tensions than George Bush. A small minority of respondents had unfavorable feelings toward the Soviet Union generally. 29% of the respondents believed that the Soviets seek to dominate the world. 50% of the respondents thought that the Soviet Union cannot be trusted to live up to arms control agreements.

Poll Extracts:

ARE YOUR FEELINGS TOWARD THE SOVIET UNION GENERALLY ...

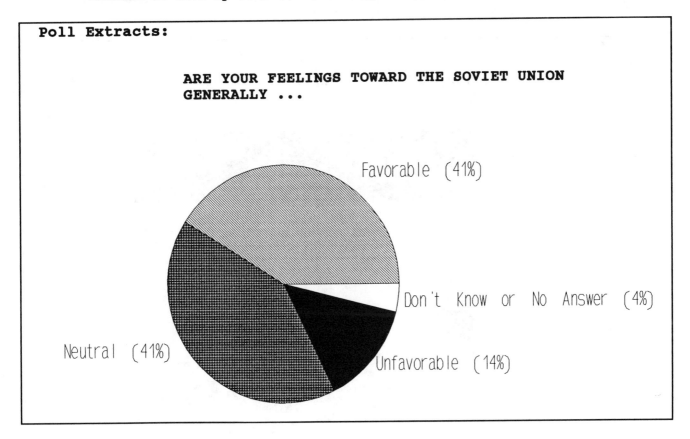

Also in Source: Responses from a similar poll conducted in November 1989. Reaction to the Baltic states' independence movement. The percentage of respondents who thought that the U.S. should significantly reduce its military spending because of reduced tensions between the U.S. and the Soviet Union. The percentage of respondents who thought that the U.S. should immediately begin reductions in its military forces in Western Europe.

Poll Details: This national Media General-Associated Press telephone poll was conducted May 11-20, 1990 with 1,143 adults. The margin of error is plus or minus 3%.

Availability: Published in *The Atlanta Journal and Constitution*, May 28, 1990, p. A-16.

THE SOVIET THREAT TO U.S. SECURITY

Description: This poll queried Americans about their opinion of the Soviet threat to U.S. national security, trustworthiness of the Soviets in arms agreements, the Soviet goal of world domination, and Soviet President Gorbachev.

Results: 77% of the respondents believe that the Soviet Union is more interested in national security than world domination. 47% of the respondents believe that the Soviet Union cannot be trusted to keep arms agreements. President Gorbachev received an 81% favorability rating among Americans. 57% of Americans believe it is unlikely that Gorbachev will fall from power.

Poll Extracts:

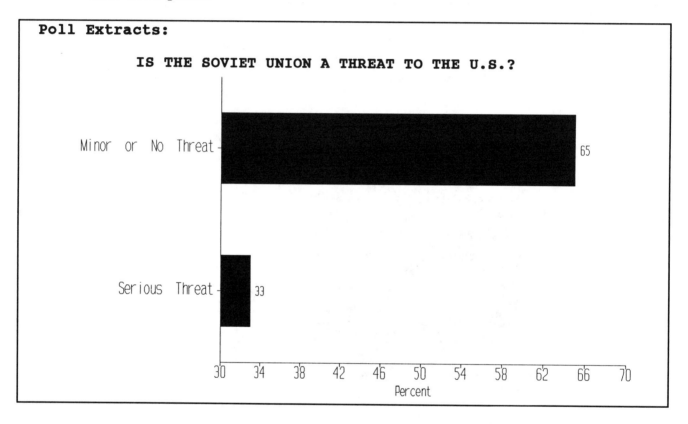

IS THE SOVIET UNION A THREAT TO THE U.S.?

Also in Source: The results from several polls that asked similar questions, and that were conducted in previous years.

Poll Details: Michigan pollster Fred Steeper conducted the survey for Americans Talk Security, a bipartisan group that examines American attitudes toward defense and security. The national telephone survey of 1,000 adults was conducted during February and March 1990. The margin of error was plus or minus 3%.

Availability: Published in the *Chicago Tribune*, May 27, 1990, section 1, p. 19.

SOVIET UNION/UNITED STATES RELATIONS

Description: Presents the results of a survey concerning the relationship between the United States and the Soviet Union.

Results: Almost 70% of the American respondents describe the relationship between the United States and the Soviet Union as friendly.

Poll Extracts:

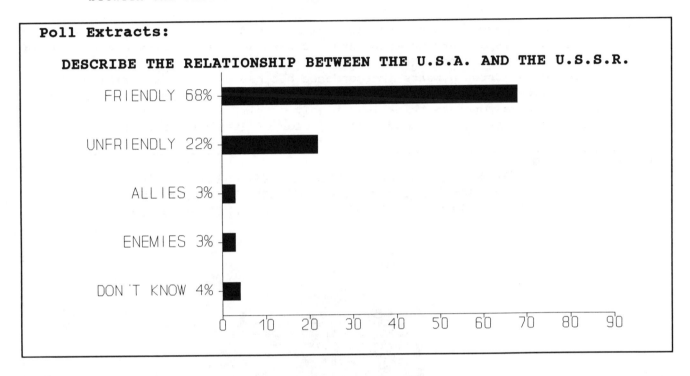

DESCRIBE THE RELATIONSHIP BETWEEN THE U.S.A. AND THE U.S.S.R.

Also in Source: 53% of the Soviet respondents described the relationship between the United States as friendly, 36% said unfriendly, 1% said enemies, 4% as allies, and 6% didn't know. 52% of the Americans polled would like to see a unified Germany as part of NATO while 73% of the Soviets polled would like to see a neutral unified Germany.

Poll Details: In the United States, the *Los Angeles Times* poll interviewed 2,144 Americans by telephone from May 10 through May 14, 1990. The phone numbers were selected randomly by computer. In the Soviet Union, door-to-door interviews of 1,485 people were conducted from May 9 through May 24, 1990 by the Soviet Academy of Sciences in Moscow. Those interviewed were selected randomly from the complete list of internal "passport" holders. All Soviet citizens age 16 and older are required to carry these passports as identification papers.

Availability: Published in the *Los Angeles Times*, May 31, 1990, p. A14.

U.S. ADVICE FOR LITHUANIA

Description: This poll asked Americans about the Baltic states' (Lithuania, Latvia, and Estonia) move toward independence from the Soviet Union. Respondents were also asked if Soviet President Gorbachev's embargo of oil and other supplies to Lithuania had affected their opinion of President Gorbachev.

Results: The respondents supported gradual independence for the Baltic states. 57% of the respondents were in favor of Lithuania's and Latvia's actions of claiming independence. Estonia's actions are favored by only 8% of the respondents (Estonia wants independence but has not laid a formal claim to it). Since President Gorbachev began his embargo of supplies to Lithuania, 34% of the respondents think less highly of him, while 48% of the respondents have not changed their opinion of President Gorbachev.

Poll Extracts:

SHOULD LITHUANIA BACK OFF FROM ITS CLAIM OF INDEPENDENCE FROM THE SOVIET UNION OR GO FORWARD WITH ITS CLAIM OF INDEPENDENCE?

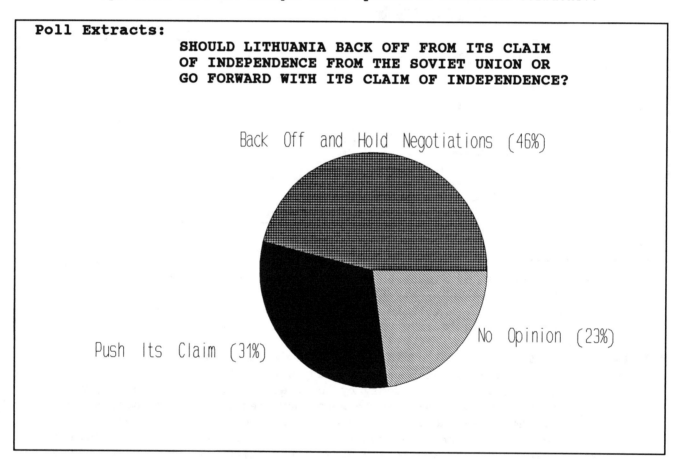

Back Off and Hold Negotiations (46%)

No Opinion (23%)

Push Its Claim (31%)

Also in Source: Attitudes toward the Soviet Union. The number of respondents who support budget and force reductions for the U.S. military, in response to improved relations between the U.S. and the Soviet Union.

Poll Details: This national Media General-Associated Press telephone poll was conducted during May 11-20, 1990 with 1,143 adults. The margin of error is plus or minus 3%.

Availability: Published in *The Atlanta Journal and Constitution*, May 28, 1990, p. A-16.

ARAB AMERICANS AND THE MEDIA

Description: Presents the results of a survey of Arab Americans concerning their views of the American news media.

Results: There is a strong distrust of the American news media among Arab Americans.

Poll Extracts:

IS THE MEDIA FAIR?

Do you believe most American news organizations
are biased in favor of Israel?......................Yes....91%

Do you believe the film and television
industry is guilty of perpetuating negative
stereotypes concerning Arabs?......................Yes....85%

Also in Source: The poll contains a wide variety of questions concerning the opinions of Arab Americans. Subjects include legalized abortion, the Equal Rights Amendment, prayer in public schools, and American politics.

Poll Details: The results were compiled from a mail survey of 2,626 members of the American Arab Anti-Discrimination Committee. The Committee is made up of mostly U.S. citizens of Arab descent or Arabs living in the United States.

Availability: Published in *The Detroit News and Free Press*, March 24, 1990, p. 1A, 20A.

AWARENESS OF THE NEWS

Description: Presents the results of a survey concerning the attention given to certain news stories.

Results: The United States deployment of troops into the Middle East received the most attention.

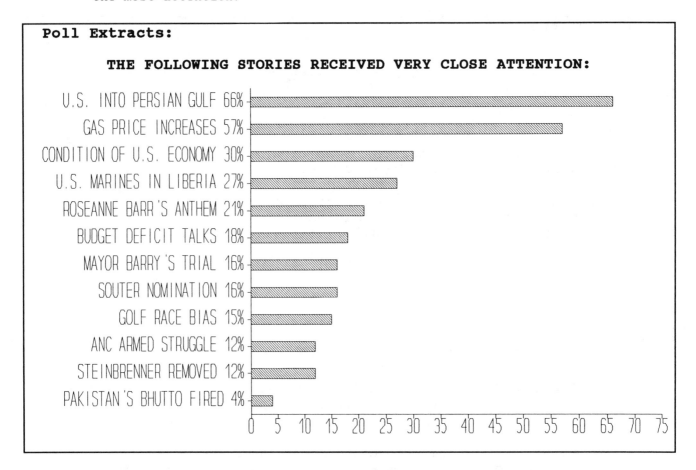

Poll Extracts:

THE FOLLOWING STORIES RECEIVED VERY CLOSE ATTENTION:

- U.S. INTO PERSIAN GULF 66%
- GAS PRICE INCREASES 57%
- CONDITION OF U.S. ECONOMY 30%
- U.S. MARINES IN LIBERIA 27%
- ROSEANNE BARR'S ANTHEM 21%
- BUDGET DEFICIT TALKS 18%
- MAYOR BARRY'S TRIAL 16%
- SOUTER NOMINATION 16%
- GOLF RACE BIAS 15%
- ANC ARMED STRUGGLE 12%
- STEINBRENNER REMOVED 12%
- PAKISTAN'S BHUTTO FIRED 4%

Also in Source: 66% of the respondents knew that the Soviet Union is supporting American efforts to have Iraq withdraw from Kuwait and 64% knew that other countries would be sending forces to Saudi Arabia along with the United States.

Poll Details: This Times Mirror News Interest Index interviewed 1,213 adults on August 9-12, 1990, and has a margin of error of 3%.

Availability: Published in the *Los Angeles Times*, August 15, 1990, p. A7.

CLOSELY WATCHED NEWS STORIES

Description: Presents the results of a survey measuring the amount of relative attention given certain news stories.

Results: President Bush's call for higher taxes was cited as the most closely watched news story.

Poll Extracts:

WHICH STORIES HAVE YOU WATCHED CLOSELY?

1. President Bush's call
   for higher taxes.......................................64%

2. Reports about the fires
   in Southern California..............................64%

3. Supreme Court decision finding laws
   against flag burning unconstitutional...............63%

4. Nelson Mandela's visit to the U.S....................57%

5. Earthquake in Iran....................................56%

6. Supreme Court decision on
   the right to die.....................................56%

7. Alzheimer's victim from Oregon
   who died using suicide machine.......................55%

8. Trial of Washington Mayor Marion Barry...............53%

9. Financial troubles of Donald Trump...................42%

10. AIDS conference in San Francisco.....................32%

Also in Source: 63% of the respondents said they saw on television the FBI's hidden camera videotape of Marion Barry in a hotel room. After seeing the videotape, 52% said it didn't change their opinion of Marion Barry, 13% were more sympathetic, and 33% were less sympathetic.

Poll Details: The Times Mirror Interest Index results are based on telephone interviews conducted under the direction of Princeton Survey Research Associates among 1,231 adults during July 5-8, 1990. Interviewing services were provided by the Gallup Organization. Sampling error is plus or minus 3%.

Availability: Published in *The Washington Post*, July 30, 1990, p. A6.

DEBORAH NORVILLE OR JANE PAULEY?

Description: Presents the results of a survey comparing the popularity of
Deborah Norville and Jane Pauley as host of the *Today Show* on NBC.

Results: Nearly 70% of the respondents favored Jane Pauley as host of the *Today
Show.*

Poll Extracts:

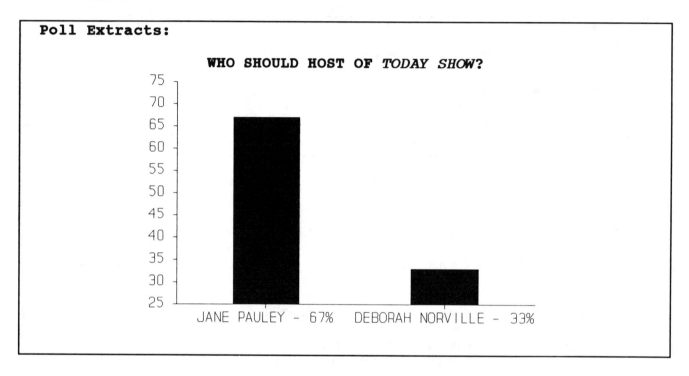

WHO SHOULD HOST OF *TODAY SHOW*?

JANE PAULEY - 67%   DEBORAH NORVILLE - 33%

Also in Source: Deborah Norville achieved her highest ratings from the 18-24
age group. The article also includes a number of other questions
concerning a wide variety of celebrities.

Poll Details: The poll was conducted by Audits & Surveys Inc. for *People
Weekly*. They contacted 1,000 *People Weekly* readers. This is the
magazine's 11th annual poll.

Availability: Published in *People Weekly*, January 8, 1990 (volume 33, number
1), p.58-68.

DOES EXPOSURE TO VIOLENCE AFFECT BEHAVIOR?

Description: Presents the results of a survey concerning whether the sexual
violence portrayed in the media, movies, and music might lead children to
feel that rape is acceptable behavior.

Results: Almost 90% of the respondents agree that sexual violence seen on
television, in the movies, or heard in song lyrics leads children to feel
that rape is acceptable behavior.

Poll Extracts:

DOES SEXUAL VIOLENCE IN THE MEDIA LEAD TO RAPE?

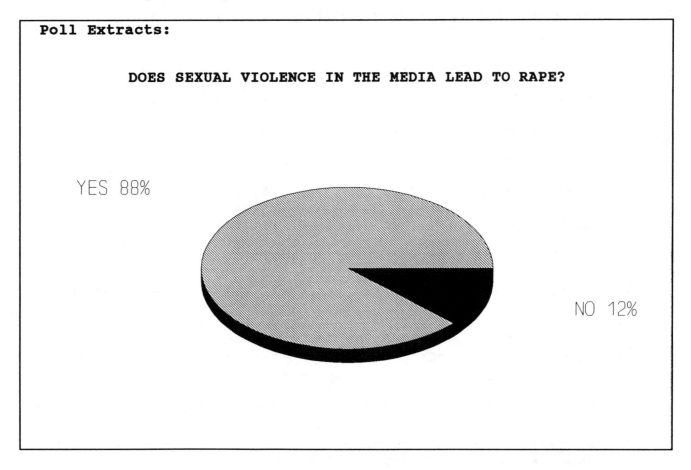

YES 88%

NO 12%

Also in Source: 56% of the respondents feel that prison is the appropriate
fate for juvenile rapists, while 44% say they should be sent to a treatment
center. 99% said we should be tougher on juvenile offenders compared to 1%
who said we shouldn't. 94% of the respondents said juvenile rapists who
were themselves victims of abuse should not be given a lighter sentence,
while 6% said they should.

Poll Details: Nearly 3,000 readers of *Redbook* magazine responded to a
questionnaire in the April 1990 issue.

Availability: Published in *Redbook*, October 1990 (volume CLXXV, number 6),
p. 160.

FAVORITE CARTOONS

Description: Presents the results of a survey identifying favorite cartoons or animated characters.

Results: Bugs Bunny was the favorite cartoon or animated character.

Poll Extracts:

WHAT IS YOUR FAVORITE CARTOON OR ANIMATED CHARACTER?

1. Bugs Bunny...20.5%

2. Mickey Mouse.......................................10.3%

3. Road Runner..5.9%

4. Donald Duck..3.8%

5. Garfield the Cat...................................3.6%

6. Bart Simpson.......................................1.7%

7. The Flintstones....................................1.7%

8. Popeye...1.6%

9. Daffy Duck...1.4%

10. Winnie the Pooh....................................1.4%

Also in Source: The most hated cartoon or animated character by both adult men and women are the Teenage Mutant Ninja Turtles.

Poll Details: This random telephone survey of 1,000 people was conducted in July, 1990 by the Gallup Organization for *Advertising Age*. The margin of error was plus or minus 3.1%.

Availability: Published in *Advertising Age*, September 17, 1990 (volume 61, number 38), p. 3, 73.

POLICE ATTITUDES TOWARD NEWSPAPERS

Description: Presents the results of a survey concerning the similarities or differences among police attitudes towards newspapers.

Results: Measuring attitudes toward newspapers on a scale of one to five with five being most critical, most police officers rate newspapers approximately 4.5.

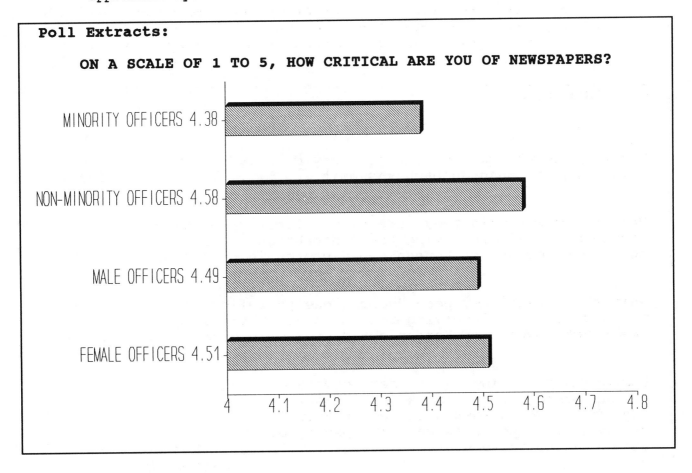

Poll Extracts:

ON A SCALE OF 1 TO 5, HOW CRITICAL ARE YOU OF NEWSPAPERS?

MINORITY OFFICERS 4.38

NON-MINORITY OFFICERS 4.58

MALE OFFICERS 4.49

FEMALE OFFICERS 4.51

4   4.1   4.2   4.3   4.4   4.5   4.6   4.7   4.8

Also in Source: Measuring cooperation from the public on a scale of one to five with one meaning citizens are eager to help police and five meaning they are apt to obstruct, minority officers rank 2.43, non-minority officers rank 2.18, male officers rank 2.22, and female officers rank 2.48.

Poll Details: The results are based on a study by the Claremont Graduate School. 1,000 police officers were surveyed.

Availability: Published in the *Los Angeles Times*, September 2, 1990, p. B1, B6.

RACIAL TENSIONS ARISE MINORITY INTEREST

Description: This monthly survey queries respondents about which news stories they have paid close attention to in the last month.

Results: More respondents were paying attention to the Bush-Gorbachev summit meeting than to any other news story in the last month. However, among non-whites, the news stories that captured the most interest were the racial tensions that occurred in New York City -- the "Bensonhurst" trial of two white men convicted of charges related to the killing of a black teen-ager in Brooklyn, and the boycott of Korean-owned stores by blacks in Brooklyn.

Poll Extracts:

Respondents who said they were "very closely"
following the Bush-Gorbachev summit 38%

Non-whites who said they were "very closely" following
the news stories involving the Bensonhurst trial, and
the black boycott of Korean-owned stores in Brooklyn 38%

Whites who said they were "very closely" following
the news stories involving the Bensonhurst trial, and
the black boycott of Korean-owned stores in Brooklyn 13%

Respondents' rating of the news coverage
of the Bensonhurst trial and the black
boycott of Korean-owned stores in Brooklyn,
by the the respondents who were paying close
attention to those stories .... Excellent - 7%
                                                Fair or Poor - 58%

Also in Source: The attention given to news stories that people followed was usually according to income and age, rather than race. The majority of those people who were following the racial tensions in New York City closely thought that the coverage given to the story by the press was only "fair" or "poor."

Poll Details: The Times Mirror News Interest Index is a monthly survey conducted by the Times Mirror Co.

Availability: Published in the *Los Angeles Times*, June 8, 1990, p. A22.

TOP COMICS

Description: Presents the results of a survey identifying readers' favorite
                 and least favorite comic strips.

Results: Calvin & Hobbes was ranked as the favorite comic strip and Alex's was
             the least favorite.

Poll Extracts:

MOST LIKED COMICS

1. Calvin & Hobbes
2. For Better or Worse
3. Sally Forth
4. Cathy
5. Modesty Blaise

MOST DISLIKED COMICS

1. Alex's
2. Doonesbury
3. Brenda Starr
4. Modesty Blaise
5. Mister Boffo

Also in Source: Calvin & Hobbes, For Better or Worse, Peanuts, The Lockhorns,
                    and Sally Forth were the most read comic strips by those readers who
                    responded to the survey.

Poll Details: 17,595 readers of the *Detroit Free Press* returned ballots which
                  were published in the June 10, 1990 issue of the paper.

Availability: Published in the *Detroit Free Press*, August 19, 1990, p. 1H, 6H

TOP NEWS STORIES OF 1990

Description: Presents the results of a vote among broadcast and newspaper
members of the Associated Press concerning the top news stories of 1990.

Results: The invasion of Kuwait by Iraq was voted the top news story of 1990.
The second most important news story was the reunification of East and West
Germany.

Poll Extracts:

THE MOST IMPORTANT NEWS STORIES OF 1990

1. Iraq invades Kuwait

2. East and West Germany reunite

3. Soviet turmoil over political and economic reform

4. The savings and loan bailout and scandals

5. Warming U.S.-Soviet relations

6. Federal budget debate ends with tax increases

7. U.S. economic slump

8. Fledgling democracies in Eastern Europe

9. Panamanian President Manuel Noriega faces trial on drug charges

10. British Prime Minister Margaret Thatcher steps down

Also in Source: Also included in the article is a list of the top news
stories involving the State of Michigan. The top news story in the State
of Michigan was the defeat of Governor James Blanchard by State Senator
John Engler.

Poll Details: The broadcast and newspaper members of the Associated Press
voted for the top news story of 1990.

Availability: Published in *The Detroit News and Free Press*, December 29, 1990,
p. 9A.

BEST ALBUMS OF THE YEAR

Description: Presents the results of an annual survey identifying the best
album of the year by a critics poll of *Down Beat* magazine.

Results: Cecil Taylor's *In Berlin* (FMP) was selected as the best jazz album of
the year in Down Beat's 38th annual critics poll.

Poll Extracts:

BEST ALBUMS OF THE YEAR:

Jazz Album..............Cecil Taylor, *In Berlin* (FMP)

Blues Album............John Lee Hooker, *The Healer* (Chameleon)

R&B/Soul..............Neville Brothers, *Yellow Moon* (A&M)

Rock Album............Pixies, *Doolittle* (Elektra)

World Beat.............Peter Gabriel, *Passion* (Geffen)

Rap...................Public Enemy, *Fear of a Black Planet*
(Def Jam)

Reissue...............Clifford Brown, Brownie: *The Complete
Emarcy Recordings* (Emarcy)

Record Label..........Blue Note

Also in Source: The article also includes the critics' selections for best
artists of the year in specific areas.

Poll Details: 64 critics voted for this year's selections distributing ten
points among up to three choices in each of two categories.

Availability: Published in *Down Beat*, August 1990 (volume 57, number 8),
p. 18-20, 22.

BEST GUITAR PLAYER

Description: Presents the results of a poll to determine the best guitar
player of 1989. An overall winner was selected as well as the best players
in specific areas including rock, blues, metal, country, acoustic,
fingerstyle & pickstyle, jazz, bass, pedal & lap steel, guitar synthesist,
experimental and guitar album.

Results: The overall winner and best rock guitar player in 1989 was Joe
Satriani.

```
Poll Extracts:

                         BEST GUITAR PLAYERS:

    Overall.....................................Joe Satriani
    Rock........................................Joe Satriani
    New Talent & Blues..........................Jeff Healey
    Metal.......................................Kirk Hammett
    Country.....................................Ricky Skaggs
    Acoustic Fingerstyle........................Michael Hedges
    Pedal & Lap Steel...........................Jay Dee Maness
    Experimental................................Adrian Belew
    Guitar Synthesist...........................Allan Holdsworth
    Guitar Album................................High Tension Wires
    Jazz........................................Larry Carlton
    Fusion......................................Frank Gambale
    Classical...................................Christopher Parken
    Flamenco....................................Paco Pena
    Studio......................................Steve Lukather
    Slide.......................................Ry Cooder
    Rock Bass...................................Billy Sheehan
    Jazz Bass...................................Stuart Hamm
```

Also in Source: The article also lists the top three vote receivers in each
specific area. A list of those guitarists who have been voted the best in
any category at least five times over the past 20 years is provided. The
article also includes a summary listing of each winner from the past 20
years.

Poll Details: The poll's target audience is the readers of *Guitar Player.*

Availability: Published in *Guitar Player,* January 1990 (volume 24, number 1),
p. 22-29.

GOSPEL MUSIC ENRICHES SOULS

Description: This poll asked readers at *Ebony* magazine to pick their favorite type of music, their favorite singers, and a wide variety of questions.

Results: Gospel music was chosen as the favorite form of music by more respondents than any other type of music. Luther Vandross was chosen as the favorite male singer, and Anita Baker was chosen as the favorite female singer.

Poll Extracts:

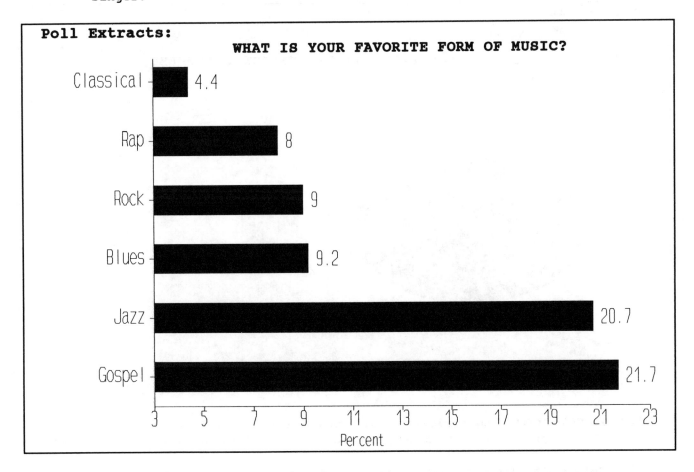

WHAT IS YOUR FAVORITE FORM OF MUSIC?

Also in Source: Readers chose their favorite: new singing group or band, established singing group or band, rap artist, sport, alcoholic spirit, beverage, food, male and female movie star, movie in the last 12 months, and TV show. Answers to poll questions covering a number of other areas not related to music.

Poll Details: Thousands of readers responded to the poll, and the replies were tabulated by Market Facts, Inc.

Availability: Published in *Ebony*, April 1990 (volume 45, number 6), p. 122-124, 126-128.

NATIONAL ANTHEM

Description: Presents the results of a survey concerning attitudes towards *The Star Spangled Banner*. The poll specifically asked whether *The Star Spangled Banner* should be replaced by *America, the Beautiful* as the national anthem.

Results: Almost 30% of the respondents favored replacing *The Star Spangled Banner* with *America, the Beautiful* as the national anthem.

Poll Extracts:

WHICH DO YOU FAVOR AS THE NATIONAL ANTHEM?

THE STAR SPANGLED BANNER 67%

NO OPINION 5%

AMERICA, THE BEAUTIFUL 28%

Also in Source: The survey also indicated that 53% of those polled felt *The Star Spangled Banner* is easy to sing and 64% claimed to know all the words.

Poll Details: The national telephone poll of 1,000 adult Americans was conducted by Yankelovich Clancy Shulman on January 31 and February 1, 1990 for *Time*/CNN. Sampling error was 3%.

Availability: Published in *Time*, February 12, 1990 (volume 135, number 7), p. 27.

RAP MUSIC

Description: Presents the results of a survey concerning possible restrictions
to be placed on the sale and playing of rap music.

Results: Almost half of the respondents would restrict rap music to adults.

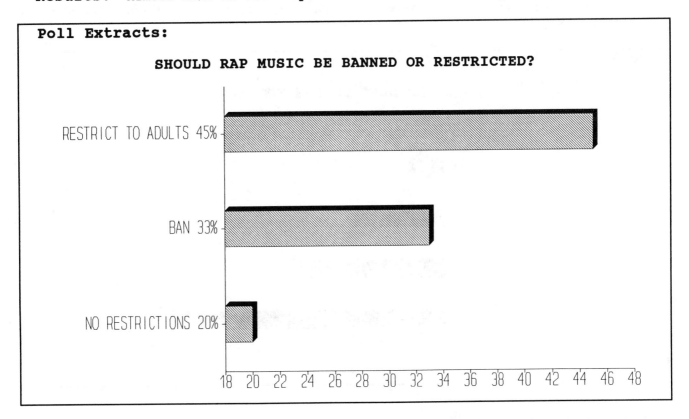

Poll Extracts:

SHOULD RAP MUSIC BE BANNED OR RESTRICTED?

Also in Source: 86% of the respondents over the age of 55 would like to see
rap music either banned or restricted to adults. 77% of the respondents
aged 35 to 54 and 73% between the ages of 18 to 34 would like to see a
similar ban or restriction.

Poll Details: This nationwide telephone poll of 811 adults was conducted on
June 25-26, 1990, by Gordon S. Black Corporation for *USA Today*.

Availability: Published in *USA Today*, July 3-4, 1990, p. 1A, 11A

TOO OLD TO ROCK AND ROLL

Description: This poll asked which musical groups are too old to rock and roll.

Results: 15% of the respondents felt that the Beach Boys were too old to continue playing rock and roll. Less than 10% of those asked said that the Rolling Stones, Paul McCartney, and The Who were also too old.

Poll Extracts:

A TAD LONG IN THE TOOTH:

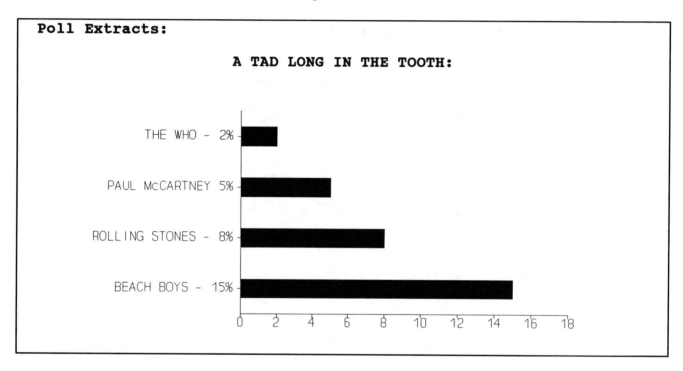

Also in Source: 68% of the respondents agreed with the statement that "there's no such thing as too old to rock and roll." The article also includes a number of other questions concerning a wide variety of celebrities.

Poll Details: The choices of musical groups were provided. The poll was conducted by Audits & Surveys Inc. for *People Weekly*. They contacted 1,000 *People Weekly* readers. This is the magazine's 11th annual poll.

Availability: Published in *People Weekly*, January 8, 1990 (volume 33, number 1), p. 58-68.

TOP PERFORMERS OF 1990

Description: This *Playboy* magazine poll asked readers to choose the top performers of 1990.

Results: The readers chose winners in 14 different categories.

Poll Extracts:

1990 TOP PERFORMERS

Group / Rock .... Rolling Stones

Group / Country .... Alabama

Group / R & B .... Fine Young Cannibals

Group / Jazz .... Spyro Gyra

Male Vocalist / Jazz .... Al Jarreau

Male Vocalist / Country .... Randy Travis

Male Vocalist / Rock .... John Cougar Mellencamp

Male Vocalist / R & B .... Bobby Brown

Female Vocalist / Jazz .... Sade

Female Vocalist / Country .... Reba McEntire

Female Vocalist / Rock .... Paula Abdul

Female Vocalist / R & B .... Anita Baker

Instrumentalist / Rock .... Jeff Healy

Instrumentalist / Jazz .... Kenny G

Also in Source: The readers' favorite: movie sound track, albums of the year, music video, concert of the year, and veejay.

Poll Details: More than 15,000 ballots were returned in this readers poll.

Availability: Published in *Playboy*, May 1990 (volume 37, number 5), p. 98-100.

BUDGET MADNESS

> **Description:** Presents the results of a survey concerning the federal budget
> process involving the White House and Congress.

> **Results:** 70% of the respondents feel that if the Bush Administration and
> Congress reach agreement on a budget deficit plan, it will be one that
> avoids the real issue.

Poll Extracts:

WILL THE BUDGET AGREEMENT BE A MEANINGFUL AGREEMENT OR?

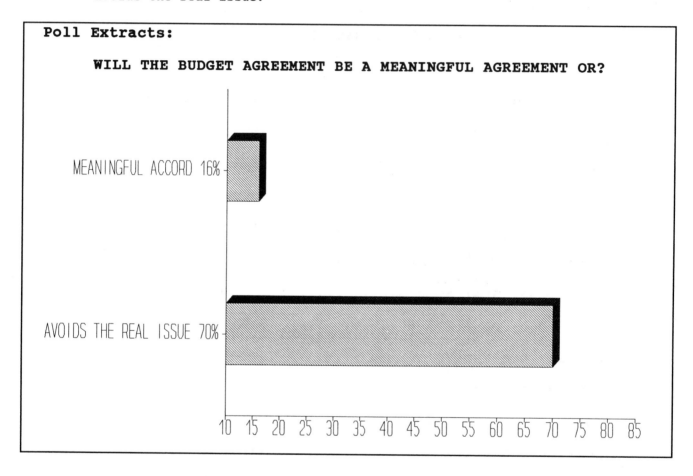

MEANINGFUL ACCORD 16%

AVOIDS THE REAL ISSUE 70%

10 15 20 25 30 35 40 45 50 55 60 65 70 75 80 85

> **Also in Source:** 75% of the respondents said that their Congress member's
> budget vote will affect their choice in the November election. 66% said
> the budget deficit really does matter. 42% of the respondents blame the
> Democrats in Congress for the difficulty in reaching a budget agreement,
> while 29% blame the Bush Administration.

> **Poll Details:** The results are taken from a telephone poll of 500 adult
> Americans for *Time*/CNN on September 13, 1990, by Yankelovich Clancy
> Shulman. Sampling error is plus or minus 4.5%

> **Availability:** Published in *Time*, September 24, 1990 (volume 136, nmuber 13),
> p. 50.

CAMPAIGN FINANCING

Description: Presents the results of a survey about the issues surrounding the financing methods used for funding campaigns for public office.

Results: 30% of the respondents said the $5,000 per election PAC limit should be maintained while approximately one-quarter of the respondents would like to abolish PACs.

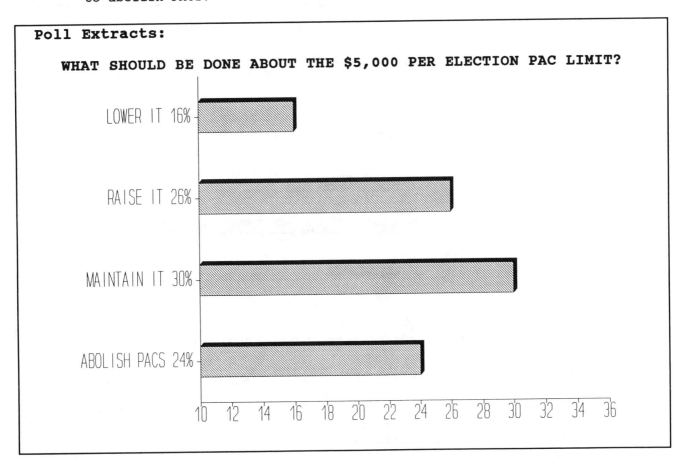

Poll Extracts:

WHAT SHOULD BE DONE ABOUT THE $5,000 PER ELECTION PAC LIMIT?

LOWER IT 16%

RAISE IT 26%

MAINTAIN IT 30%

ABOLISH PACS 24%

10 12 14 16 18 20 22 24 26 28 30 32 34 36

Also in Source: 19% of the respondents favor comprehensive public financing of congressional campaigns with set spending limits, 38% favor partial public financing of campaigns with a system of spending limits with matching funds, and 20% favor voluntary spending limits that penalize non-compliants. 53% of the respondents favor making free television broadcasting time available to candidates. 71% favor requiring TV stations to sell candidates fixed time at the lower, pre-emtive rate. 7% favor legislation to make political ads less negative.

Poll Details: The results are based on *Campaigns & Elections* survey of a randomly selected sample of 79 political professionals conducted by fax between April 26 and May 2, 1990.

Availability: Published in *Campaigns & Elections*, June/July 1990 (volume 11, number 2), p. 7, 8.

CAMPAIGN REFORM

Description: Presents the results of a survey concerning the need for campaign reform.

Results: The majority of Americans feel that the congressional campaign finance system needs reform.

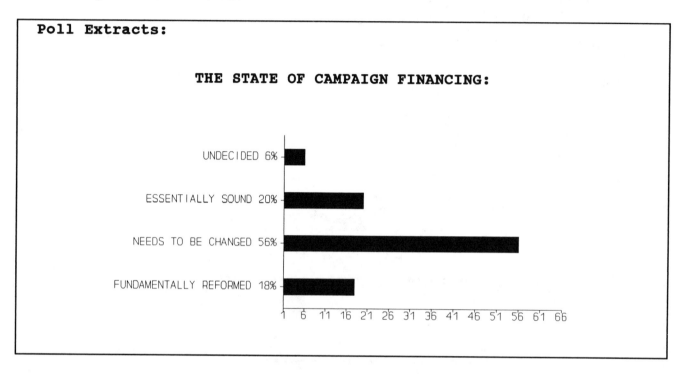

Poll Extracts:

THE STATE OF CAMPAIGN FINANCING:

UNDECIDED 6%

ESSENTIALLY SOUND 20%

NEEDS TO BE CHANGED 56%

FUNDAMENTALLY REFORMED 18%

1 6 11 16 21 26 31 36 41 46 51 56 61 66

Also in Source: Campaign reform ranks low as a major concern below drugs and crime (38%); education (16%); the economy (16%); taxes (13%); and the environment (9%). Campaign finance was rated highest by 5%, barely above "don't know" (2%). A number of other questions concerning campaign financing are included in the article.

Poll Details: The poll was sponsored by People for the American Way, Ralph Nader's Public Citizen, the Advocacy Institute and the ARCA. The poll has a margin of error of plus or minus 3.3%.

Availability: Published in *The Cincinnati Enquirer*, March 4, 1990, p. A-12.

CONGRESSIONAL CORRUPTION

Description: Presents the results of a survey concerning financial corruption among Congress.

Results: Over 40% of the respondents think at least half the members of Congress is financially corrupt. Over 50% think some or hardly any members of Congress are financially corrupt.

Poll Extracts:

JUDGING CONGRESS:

How many members of Congress are financially corrupt?

Some or hardly any...................................51%
About half or more..................................42%

Is your own U.S. Representative financially corrupt?

No..62%
Yes...16%

Is either Senator from your state financially corrupt?

No..62%
Yes...19%

Also in Source: 40% of the respondents approve of the way Congress is handling its job. 60% of the respondents approve of the way their U.S. Representative is doing his or her job, but only 43% think their U.S. Representative deserves re-election. 59% of the respondents said George Bush and the Congress are not making a serious effort to reduce the federal deficit.

Poll Details: This *New York Times*/CBS News Poll is based on telephone interviews with 1,422 adults nationwide conducted August 16-19, 1990.

Availability: Published in *The New York Times*, September 4, 1990, p. A1, A13.

CONGRESSIONAL PRIORITIES

Description: Presents the results of a survey concerning whether members of Congress are more interested in solving the nation's problems or in getting re-elected.

Results: Over 40% of the respondents said the members of Congress are more interested in re-election than in solving the problems of the nation.

Poll Extracts:

ARE CONGRESS MEMBERS WORKING AT SOLVING PROBLEMS OR RE-ELECTION?

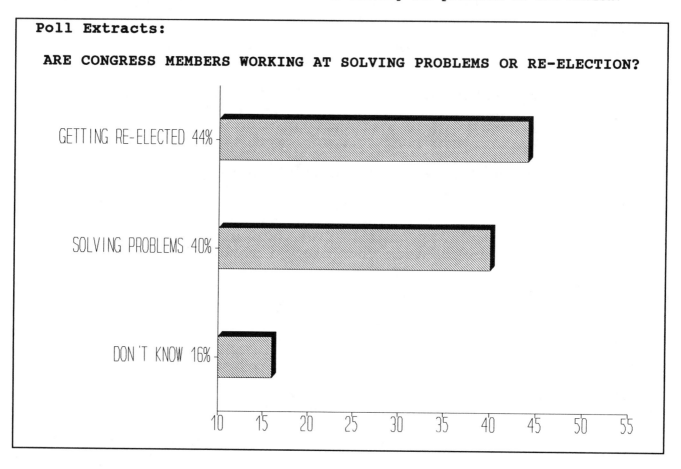

GETTING RE-ELECTED 44%

SOLVING PROBLEMS 40%

DON'T KNOW 16%

10 15 20 25 30 35 40 45 50 55

Also in Source: Polls indicate that support for incumbents, both Democrats and Republicans, is down by an average of 8%.

Poll Details: Market Opinion Research conducted the poll of 1,000 registered voters. The sampling error is 3.2%.

Availability: Published in *USA Today*, September 9, 1990, p. 11A.

THE DEFICIT REDUCTION AGREEMENT

Description: Respondents were queried on their attitudes toward the 1991
deficit reduction package.

Results: 52% of the respondents disapproved of the package. 69% of the
respondents did not believe that the agreement would achieve major deficit
reduction. 56% of the respondents thought the agreement favored the
wealthy.

Poll Extracts:

**RESPONDENTS WHO EXPECTED THE DEFICIT REDUCTION AGREEMENT
TO HAVE A MAJOR IMPACT ON THEIR LIVES, GROUPED BY INCOME:**

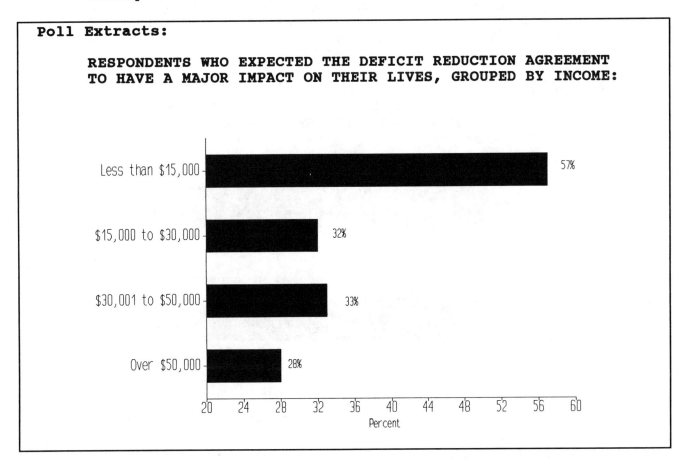

Also in Source: The percentage of respondents who disapprove of the planned
luxury tax. The most unpopular and second most unpopular change included
in the plan.

Poll Details: The Gordon S. Black Corp. conducted this nationwide telephone
poll for *USA Today*. 852 adults were interviewed on October 1, 1990. The
margin of error is 3.5%.

Availability: Published in *USA Today*, October 2, 1990, p. 1A, 3A.

THE DEMOCRATS IN CONGRESS

Description: The poll asked voters what the Democratic-controlled Congress is
doing.

Results: A majority of respondents could not answer as to what the Democrats in
Congress are doing. President Bush was popular with respondents, with much
of his support being "soft." 41% of the respondents thought the
Republicans would do a better job in leading the country. 46% percent of
the respondents thought the country was headed in the right direction, when
asked about the country generally. 49% percent thought the country was
headed in the wrong direction, when asked about the nation's economic
situation.

Poll Extracts:

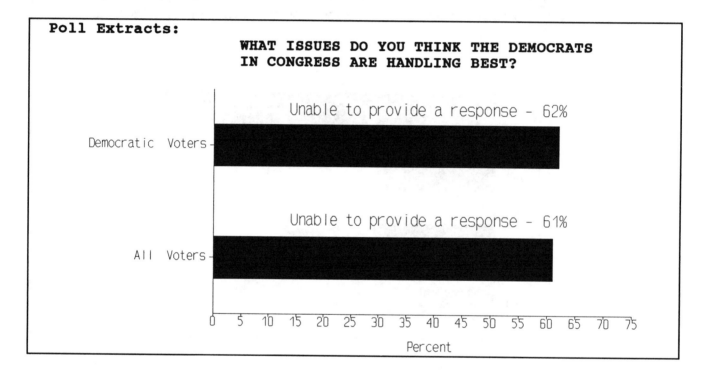

Also in Source: The percentage of respondents who thought the Democrats would
do a better job of leading the country.

Poll Details: This was a telephone poll of 1,494 people who described
themselves as registered voters. The poll was conducted by Greenberg-
Lake: the Analysis Group, and the Garin-Hart Strategic Research Group,
during February 26-March 1, 1990. The margin of sampling error was plus or
minus 3%. The poll was produced for Democrats for the 90's, a Washington
advocacy group for the Democratic Party.

Availability: Published in *The New York Times*, March 16, 1990, p. A12.

EVALUATING THE POLITICAL PARTIES

Description: Presents the results of a survey concerning the level of trust in the abilities of the Democratic and Republican parties to deal effectively with a number of national issues.

Results: Among the results, over half of the respondents feel the Republicans can do a better job handling the nation's economy. On the other hand, 53% feel that the Democrats will do a better job helping the middle class.

Poll Extracts:

WHICH POLITICAL PARTY DO YOU TRUST TO DO A BETTER JOB?

	DEMOCRATS	REPUBLICANS
Handling the nation's economy	33%	52%
Handling the crime problem	31%	43%
Handling foreign affairs	29%	55%
Handling the homeless problem	56%	25%
Improving education	45%	36%
Reducing the drug problem	28%	47%
Maintaining a strong national defense	25%	62%
Helping the middle class	53%	32%
Holding taxes down	37%	47%
Protecting the environment	46%	31%

Also in Source: Overall, 50% of the respondents felt that the Republicans can do a better job in coping with the main problems the nation faces over the next few years. 38% felt that the Democrats could be trusted with the same task.

Poll Details: The results are based on a *Washington Post*-ABC News telephone survey of 1,518 randomly selected adults conducted January 11-15, 1990. Margin of error is plus or minus 3%. Interviewing was done by Chilton Research of Radnor, PA.

Availability: Published in *The Washington Post*, January 29, 1990, p. A1, A8.

THE FEDERAL BUDGET DEFICIT

Description: Respondents were asked to rate the performance of the Bush
administration in reducing the federal budget deficit.

Results: Almost two of three respondents thought that the Bush administration
was performing a below average or poor job of reducing the federal budget
deficit.

Poll Extracts:

"HOW WOULD YOU RATE THE JOB THE BUSH ADMINISTRATION IS DOING ON REDUCING THE FEDERAL BUDGET DEFICIT?"

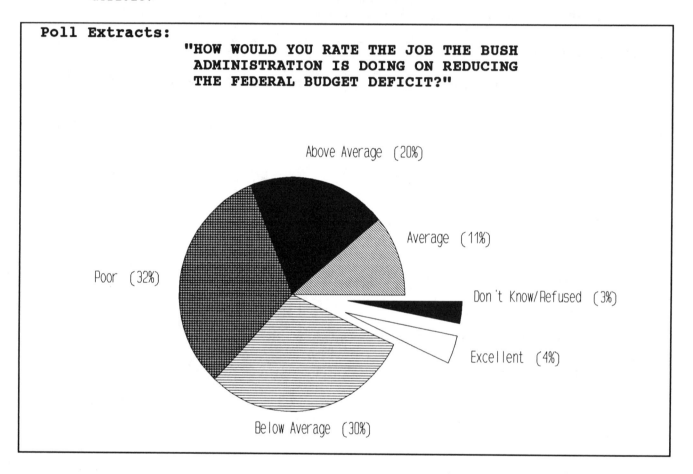

Also in Source: The approval rating of President Bush overall, and on matters
of foreign policy. Respondents who thought the economy was heading for a
recession.

Poll Details: This *Boston Globe*-WBZ-TV poll was conducted by KRC
Communications Research. A nationwide telephone poll of 1,004 registered
voters took place during October 7-9, 1990.

Availability: Published in *The Boston Globe*, October 11, 1990, p. 26.

FLAG BURNING AND CONGRESSIONAL VOTING

Description: Respondents were asked if their Congressional representative were to vote against the proposed constitutional amendment prohibiting flag burning, would that action would influence their vote for that representative in future elections.

Results: One out of four voters would be more likely to vote for his or her Congressional representative if that representative voted against the proposed constitutional amendment.

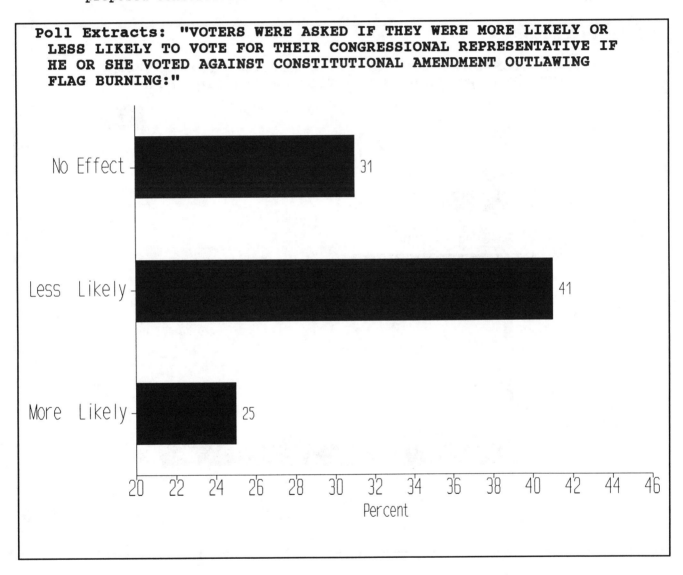

Poll Extracts: **"VOTERS WERE ASKED IF THEY WERE MORE LIKELY OR LESS LIKELY TO VOTE FOR THEIR CONGRESSIONAL REPRESENTATIVE IF HE OR SHE VOTED AGAINST CONSTITUTIONAL AMENDMENT OUTLAWING FLAG BURNING:"**

Poll Details: This information is from a KRC Communications Research telephone poll of 1,004 registered voters conducted June 17, 1990. The sampling error is 3%.

Availability: Published in *USA Today*, June 25, 1990, p. 11A.

FLAG DESECRATION AND CONGRESS

Description: Representatives and senators in Congress were asked about their support for the proposed constitutional amendment on flag burning.

Results: The proposed amendment, "The Congress and the United States shall have power to prohibit the physical desecration of the flag of the United States," does not seem to have enough support to be passed in either the House or the Senate (289 votes are needed to pass the House, and 67 votes are needed to pass the Senate).

Poll Extracts:

CONGRESSIONAL SUPPORT FOR THE CONSTITUTIONAL AMENDMENT PROHIBITING PHYSICAL DESECRATION OF THE U.S. FLAG:

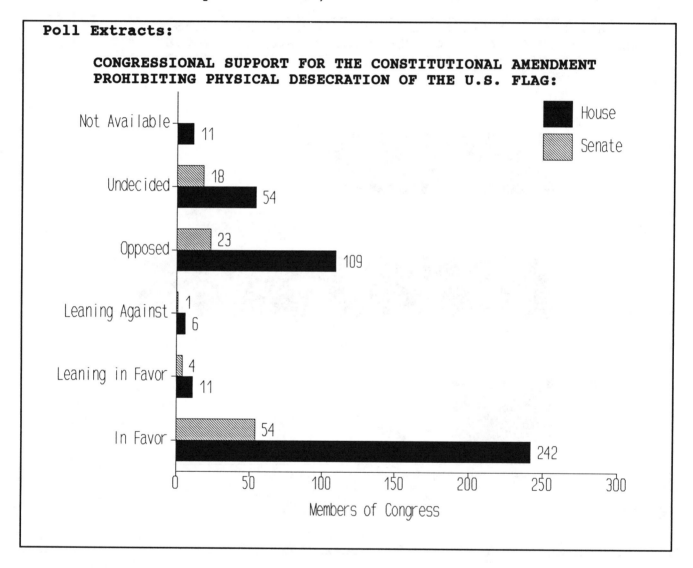

Poll Details: The Associated Press conducted this poll of Congress.

Availability: Published in the *Dayton Daily News*, June 20, 1990, p. 7-A.

GENDER ISSUES IN CALIFORNIA

Description: Respondents were queried about their preferences in the California governors race and related gender issues which had arisen in the campaign.

Results: Diane Feinstein, campaigning for the Democratic gubernatorial nomination, leads her opponent, John K. Van de Kamp, by 13 percentage points (42% to 29%), while 27% of registered Democrats are still undecided. Respondents were queried in relation to Feinstein's plan to reserve half the jobs in her administration for women. When respondents were asked about the statement, "The government ought to see to it that there is an even balance between the number of men and women in public office," only 33% agreed, while 58% disagreed. The majority of voters believe it is unimportant whether a woman becomes governor, but more of Feinstein's supporters are women, when compared to her opponent's supporters.

Poll Extracts:

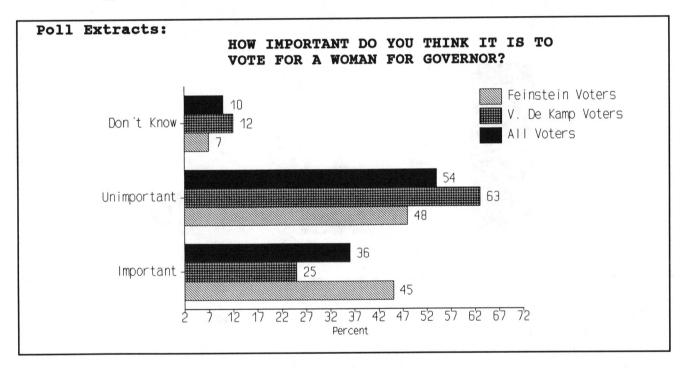

HOW IMPORTANT DO YOU THINK IT IS TO VOTE FOR A WOMAN FOR GOVERNOR?

Also in Source: The percentage of Democratic voters who "think that the decision to have an abortion is a choice that must be made only by the woman herself." Women interviewers tended to elicit responses that were more supportive of the woman candidate, more supportive of seeing a quota for women in public office, and tended to see electing a woman as more important.

Poll Details: This *Los Angeles Times* Poll was conducted during May 31–June 2, 1990, among 920 registered Democrats. In this telephone poll, a computer was used to randomly select the telephone numbers that were called. The households that were contacted represent a cross-section of Democratic households in California. The margin of error is plus or minus five percentage points.

Availability: Published in the *Los Angeles Times*, June 4, 1990, p. A1, A28.

JESSE JACKSON FOR PRESIDENT

Description: Presents the results of a survey of *Ebony* readers concerning a
   wide range of topics and personalities. This question deals with the
   possibility of Jesse Jackson running again for president.

Results: Approximately 60% of the respondents agreed that Jesse Jackson should
   again seek the presidency.

Poll Extracts:

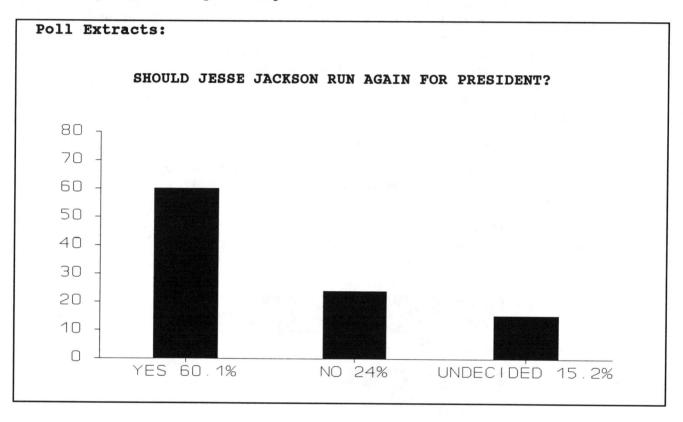

SHOULD JESSE JACKSON RUN AGAIN FOR PRESIDENT?

Also in Source: The poll includes a number of questions covering a wide
   variety of topics and personalities.

Poll Details: The survey of *Ebony* readers was conducted by Market Facts, Inc.

Availability: Published in *Ebony*, April, 1990 (volume XLV, number 6),
   p. 122-124, 126-128.

LEADING THE NATION

Description: Respondents were asked who would provide the best leadership on a variety of issues, the Democrats in Congress or the Republicans in the White House.

Results: The Republicans were thought to provide better leadership for strengthening the economy and combatting drugs, while the Democrats were seen to surpass the Republican leadership on all other issues.

Poll Extracts: **"IN THE DAYS AHEAD DO YOU THINK THE DEMOCRATS IN CONGRESS OR THE REPUBLICANS IN THE WHITE HOUSE WILL DO A BETTER JOB OF PROVIDING LEADERSHIP ON ..."**

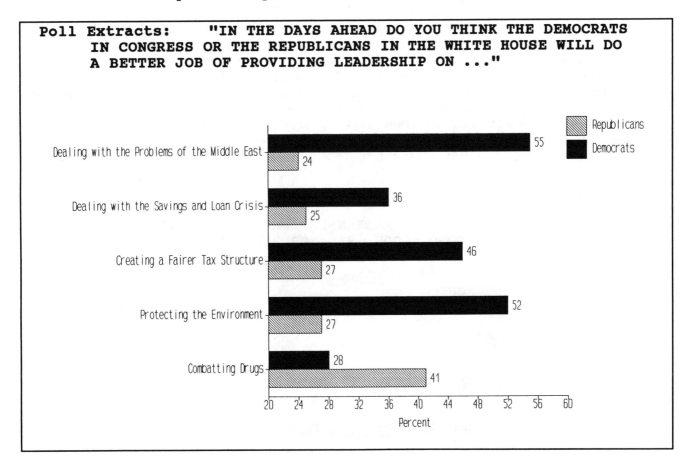

Also in Source: The approval rating for President Bush, his handling of the economy, his overall job rating, and the Bush administration's handling of foreign policy,

Poll Details: This *Boston Globe*-WBZ-TV poll was conducted by KRC Communications Research. 1,004 registered voters across the nation were interviewed by telephone during October 28-30, 1990. The margin of error is 3%.

Availability: Published in *The Boston Globe*, November 1, 1990, p. 1, 26.

LESTER MADDOX AND RACE RELATIONS

Description: This poll asked respondents about the Democratic and Republican
primary candidates for governor in Georgia: who they would vote for, and
whether their opinion of the candidates was favorable, not favorable, or if
they had no opinion on the candidate (one of the Democratic candidates for
governor being Lester Maddox - former governor of Georgia in the late
1960s). Respondents were also asked about their view on race relations in
Georgia, and on segregation.

Results: When asked who they would vote for if the Democratic primary for
governor was held that same day, Lester Maddox received 3.3% of the votes.
Georgians' views of Lester Maddox were 23% - favorable, 49% - not
favorable, and 29% - no opinion. "50% of the whites polled rated him
unfavorably, 24% gave him a favorable rating, and 26% had no opinion. 44%
of blacks polled expressed disfavor for Mr. Maddox, and 16% rated him
favorably - although no black voter polled said he would vote for Mr.
Maddox." Strict segregation of the races was supported by 3.3% of the
respondents, with 62% supporting integration, and 30% favoring something in
between.

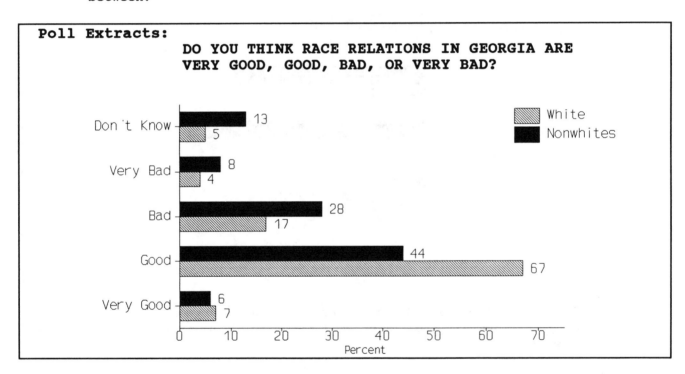

Poll Extracts:

**DO YOU THINK RACE RELATIONS IN GEORGIA ARE
VERY GOOD, GOOD, BAD, OR VERY BAD?**

Poll Details: The telephone poll is based on interviews with 652 adults in
Georgia, who were identified as likely voters in the Democratic and
Republican primaries. The poll was conducted April 13-24, 1990, except for
Easter Sunday. "In theory, one can say with 95% certainty that the survey
results represent the views of all likely primary voters in Georgia with a
margin of error of plus or minus four percentage points." Results based on
subgroups have a larger margin of error. The questionnaire for the survey
was prepared with the paid assistance of Merle Black, of Emory University,
who also analyzed the results. Further details are provided in the source.

Availability: Published in *The Atlanta Journal and Constitution*, April 29,
1990, p. A-14.

MASSACHUSETTS PRIORITIES

Description: Presents the results of a survey concerning the important issues in the governor's race in the State of Massachusetts.

Results: The candidates' stand on taxes is the most important issue to most of the respondents in the race for governor of Massachusetts.

Poll Extracts:

IN YOUR VOTE FOR GOVERNOR, WHICH ISSUE IS MOST IMPORTANT?

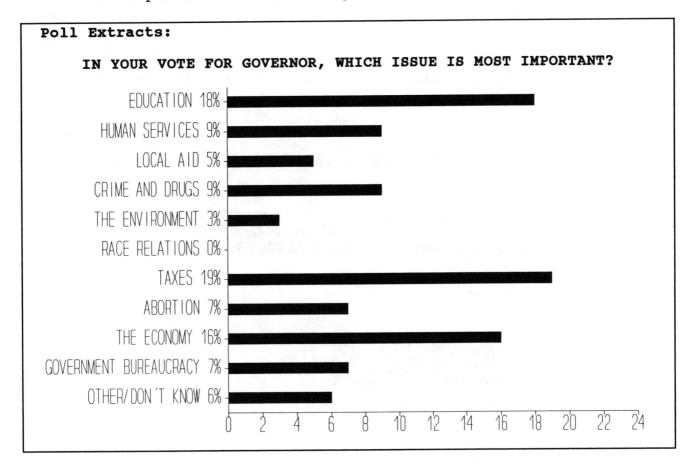

Also in Source: 43% of the respondents have more confidence in their local government than in the state or federal level. 81% think the state government is out of touch with the state's residents. 48% think state government serves politicians, while 13% think the government serves all the people.

Poll Details: This *Boston Globe*/WBZ-TV poll was conducted by KRC Communications Research. 173 Democrats, 183 Independents, and 71 Republicans were surveyed by telephone August 26-30, 1990.

Availability: Published in *The Boston Globe*, September 3, 1990, p. 1, 8, 9.

MOVEMENT TOWARD THE DEMOCRATS

Description: Respondents were queried on several issues as to which political
party, the Democrats or the Republicans, would do a better job of handling
that issue.

Results: Voters are moving toward the Democrats. Voters sense that the
Democrats are working for the average person, while the Republicans are
working for the wealthy. "Voters believe, 47% to 18%, that the Democratic
Party would do a better job helping the middle class. The voters also
believe the Democrats would do a better job looking out for the poor, 60%
to 10%." The Republicans are seen as most likely to look out for the
wealthy, 64% to 13%.

Poll Extracts:

"WHICH PARTY DO YOU THINK WOULD DO A BETTER JOB AT ...?"

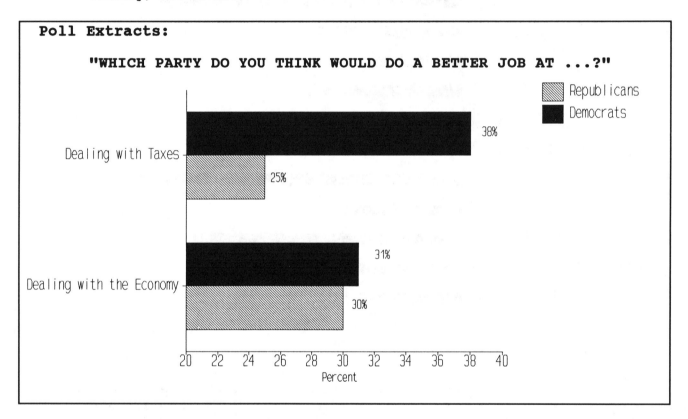

Also in Source: Responses to a similar poll conducted during November 1989.
The percentage of respondents who blamed the Republicans or Democrats as
being responsible for the savings-and-loan crisis. The percentage of
respondents who trust the Democrats more than the Republicans to handle the
savings-and-loan crisis. Respondents who planned to vote for the
Republican or Democratic candidate in the next congressional election.

Poll Details: The Peter Hart and Robert Teeter organization interviewed 1,019
registered voters nationwide. The poll was conducted from October 19-25,
1990. "The results of the survey were minimally weighted by age, region,
and party identification to ensure that the poll accurately reflects
registered voters nationwide." The margin of error is 3.2%. Additional
details can be found in the source.

Availability: Published in *The Wall Street Journal*, October 25, 1990, p. A24.

POLITICAL PARTY AFFILIATIONS

Description: Presents the results of a survey concerning the relative
popularity and loyality of the two major national political parties.

Results: 44% of respondents identified themselves as Republicans or said they
leaned in that direction in 1989. 46% of the respondents identified
themselves as Democrats or leaned in that direction.

Poll Extracts:

PARTY AFFILIATION BY INCOME:

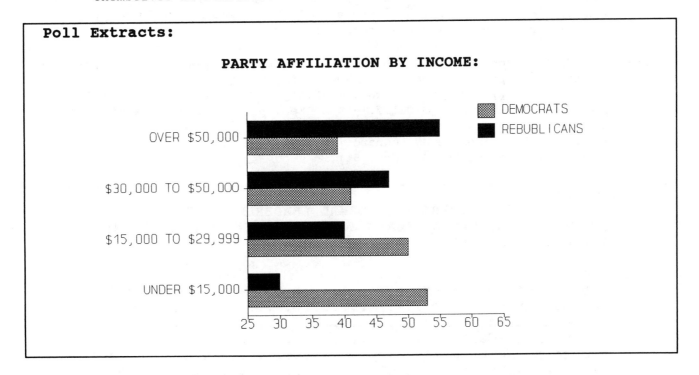

Also in Source: The article also provides party affiliation percentages by
sex, race and age. A general discussion of the survey's implications is
also included in the source.

Poll Details: The results of the survey, conducted by *The New York Times*/CBS
News, are based on telephone interviews with 1,557 adults nationwide on
January 13-15, 1990.

Availability: Published in *The New York Times*, January 21, 1990, p.A15.

POWER IN CONGRESS

Description: This poll asked Congressional aides to name the two or three most effective and influential members of Congress, excluding the formal leadership. It also asked the respondents to name two or three members of Congress in a position to have a major influence on legislation who have been the most ineffective, and especially those members of Congress who have failed to live up to their potential. In addition, respondents were asked to name two or three congressional staff members who have played the greatest role in shaping the course of major legislation.

Results: Respondents thought that the most ineffective members of Congress are: Richard A. Gephardt (D-Mo.)-12%, Newt Gringrich (R-Ga.)-10%, Robert H. Michel (R-Ill.), Dan Rostenkowski (D-Ill)-6%, Claiborne Pell (D-R.I.)-5%, and Glenn M. Anderson (D-Calif.)-5%. The top congressional staff members in influencing major legislation are Heather S. Foley (16%), George Kundanis (13%), Robert J. Leonard (9%), William R. Pitts (7%), Sheila P. Burke (6%), and Martha S. Pope (6%).

Poll Extracts:

"EXCLUDING THE FORMAL LEADERSHIP, WHO DO YOU THINK ARE THE TWO OR THREE MOST EFFECTIVE AND INFLUENTIAL MEMBERS OF CONGRESS?"

John D. Dingell (D-Mich.)	36%
Dan Rostenkowski (D-Ill.)	28%
Lloyd Bentsen (D-Tex.)	17%
Sam Nunn (D-Ga.)	13%
Edward M. Kennedy (D-Mass.)	9%
Jamie L. Whitten (D-Miss.)	7%
Henry A. Waxman (D-Calif.)	7%
Robert C. Byrd (D-W. Va.)	7%
Leon E. Panetta (D-Calif.)	6%
Vic Fazio (D-Calif.)	6%
Bill Bradley (D-N.J.)	5%
All other mentions	71%
Don't know	1%
Refused	0%

Also in Source: The industries that are most effective and ineffective in lobbying Congress. The business executives that are the most effective in representing their interests to Congress.

Poll Details: This *Business Week*/Harris Poll surveyed 304 of the most senior Congressional staffers (177 Democrats and 127 Republicans) from the House and the Senate. Approximately two-thirds of the Congressional aides work in members' offices, with the rest of the aides on committees.

Availability: Published in *Business Week*, April 16, 1990 (number 3155), p. 58-59.

PRESIDENT BUSH'S POLITICAL INFLUENCE

Description: Presents the results of a survey concerning President George Bush's current level of political influence.

Results: Over 60% of the respondents believe President Bush is losing political influence.

Poll Extracts:

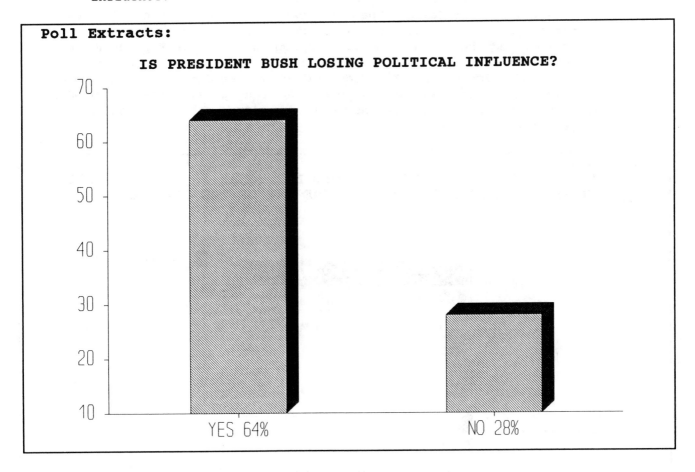

IS PRESIDENT BUSH LOSING POLITICAL INFLUENCE?

Also in Source: 48% of the respondents approve of the way George Bush is handling his job as president, while 36% disapprove.

Poll Details: For this *Newsweek* poll, the Gallup Organization interviewed a national sample of 753 adults by telephone on October 25-26, 1990. The margin of error is plus or minus 4%.

Availability: Published in *Newsweek*, November 5, 1990 (volume CXVI, number 19), p. 20-22.

THE TEXAS GUBERNATORIAL CAMPAIGN

Description: Voters in Texas were asked which candidate (Ann Richards or Clayton Williams) they voted for in the 1990 Texas gubernatorial election and why they voted for that candidate.

Results: More of the respondents chose Ann Richards than Clayton Williams to be the new governor of Texas. The top three issues for Clayton Williams supporters in deciding how they voted for governor were: crime/drugs, education, and the Texas economy. The top three issues for Ann Richards supporters in deciding how they voted for governor were: education, ethics, and crime/drugs. The factor which mattered the most in deciding how Clayton Williams supporters voted was "toughness." The factor which mattered the most in deciding how Ann Richards supporters voted was "experience."

Poll Extracts:
"IN DECIDING WHO YOU WOULD VOTE FOR TODAY IN THE RACE FOR GOVERNOR, HOW IMPORTANT WAS THE SEX OF THE CANDIDATE?"

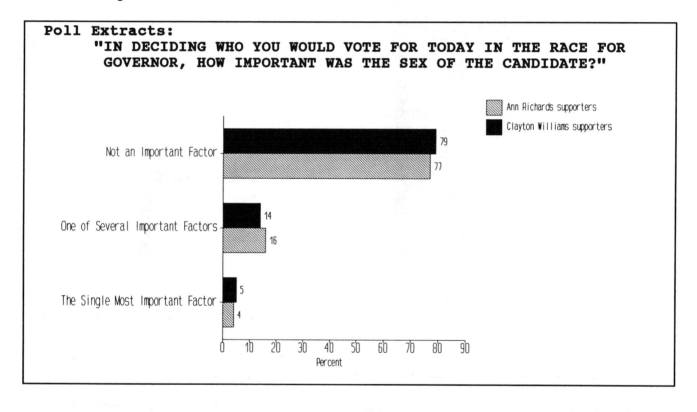

Also in Source: Which gubernatorial candidate's campaign the respondents believed to be more negative. When the respondents made their decision as to which gubernatorial candidate they would vote for. How the respondents viewed themselves politically (moderate, conservative, liberal) and which political party they usually associated themselves with (Democrat, Republican, Independent).

Poll Details: This exit survey was designed and conducted by the New York based Voter Research and Surveys (an association of ABC News, CNN, CBS News, and NBC News) with the support of Chilton Research Services, for *The Dallas Morning News*. 2,333 voters were interviewed as they left polling places around Texas on November 6, 1990. The margin of error is 2.5%.

Availability: Published in *The Dallas Morning News*, November 7, 1990, p. 16A.

TEXAS POLITICS

Description: Presents the results of a survey of Dallas Democrats concerning the importance of possible drug use by candidates running for public office.

Results: Over 40% of the respondents said that it was not important to know if a candidate ever used illegal drugs.

Poll Extracts:

HOW IMPORTANT IS IT TO KNOW IF A CANDIDATE HAS USED ILLEGAL DRUGS?

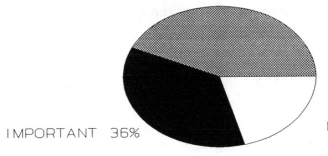

NOT IMPORTANT 43%

IMPORTANT 36%

NO ANSWER/NO OPINION 21%

Also in Source: The poll was commissioned in response to allegations that Texas gubernatorial candidate Ann Richards had used illegal drugs. She declined to respond to the allegations.

Poll Details: The *Dallas Morning News* polled 206 voters. Sampling error was 7%.

Availability: Published in *USA Today*, March 5, 1990, p. 5A.

THROW THE BUMS OUT?

Description: Presents the results of a survey concerning whether the present members of Congress should be returned to office based on the difficulty they have had in passing a deficit-reduction plan.

Results: Over 50% of the respondents would fire Congress for the difficulty it has had in passing the budget-reduction plan, but approximately 60% would not vote his or her Representative out of office.

Poll Extracts:

ARE THE INCUMBENTS IN DANGER?

If you could, would you fire Congress for the difficulty it has had in passing a budget-reduction plan?.............................Yes...52%

Do you think your Representative should be voted out of office?............................No....57%

Also in Source: A general discussion of the budget-reduction issue is included in the article.

Poll Details: The results were taken from a telephone survey of 500 adult Americans for *Time*/CNN by Yankelovich Clancy Shulman. Sampling error is plus or minus 4.5%.

Availability: Published in *Time*, October 22, 1990 (volume 136, number 17), p. 29.

WASHINGTON, D.C. MAYOR'S RACE

Description: Presents the results of a survey concerning the next election for mayor of Washington, D.C.

Results: If Marion Barry were to run for re-election, he would receive 23% of the vote. John Ray would also receive 23% of the vote.

Poll Extracts:

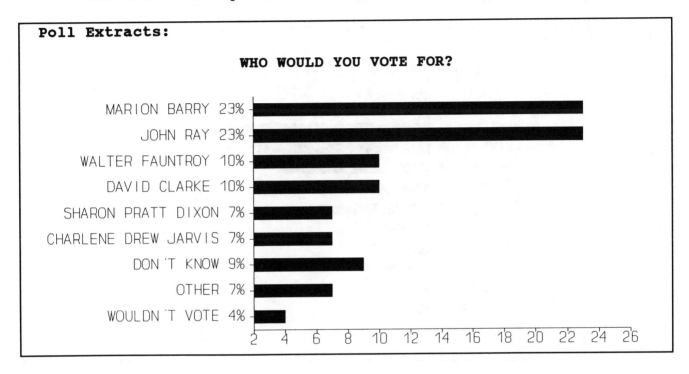

WHO WOULD YOU VOTE FOR?

- MARION BARRY 23%
- JOHN RAY 23%
- WALTER FAUNTROY 10%
- DAVID CLARKE 10%
- SHARON PRATT DIXON 7%
- CHARLENE DREW JARVIS 7%
- DON'T KNOW 9%
- OTHER 7%
- WOULDN'T VOTE 4%

Also in Source: If Marion Barry were not to run for another term, John Ray would be favored by 29% of the voters followed by Walter Fauntroy with 16%, and David Clarke with 12%.

Poll Details: The results are based on a *Wasington Post* telephone survey of 760 self-described registered Democrats in the District of Columbia conducted on May 17 through 22, 1990. Margin of error is plus or minus 4%. Interviewing was conducted by Chilton Research Services.

Availability: Published in *The Washington Post*, May 25, 1990, p. A1, A8.

WASHINGTON D.C. POLITICS

Description: Presents the results of a poll of Washington D.C. registered
Democrats concerning their choice for mayor.

Results: A quarter of the respondents would vote for Marion Barry, 19% for
Jesse Jackson and 14% for John Ray.

Poll Extracts:

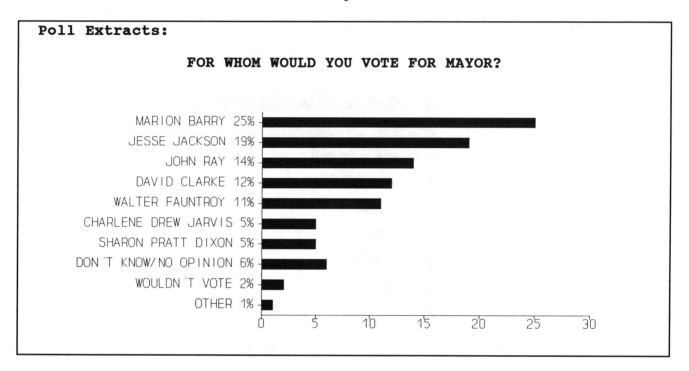

FOR WHOM WOULD YOU VOTE FOR MAYOR?

Also in Source: Voters were also asked how they would vote if Marion Barry
and Jesse Jackson decided not to run for the position. 52% of those
interviewed said Barry should resign and 71% said he should not run for
mayor. Also, 71% said that Barry needs to apologize to the voters for his
behavior.

Poll Details: The results are based on a *Washington Post* telephone survey of
800 self-described registered voters in the District of Columbia conducted
on February 16-19, 1990. Margin of error is plus or minus 4%.
Interviewing was conducted by Chilton Research Services of Radnor, PA.

Availability: Published in *The Washington Post*, February 22, 1990, p. A9.

WHO WANTS TO BE PRESIDENT?

Description: College women were asked if they would like to be president.
They were also asked if a woman or African American should be president.

Results: 67% of the respondents would not like to be president, only 8% thought
they would like to be president. The majority of respondents thought that
an African American or a woman should be president.

Poll Extracts:

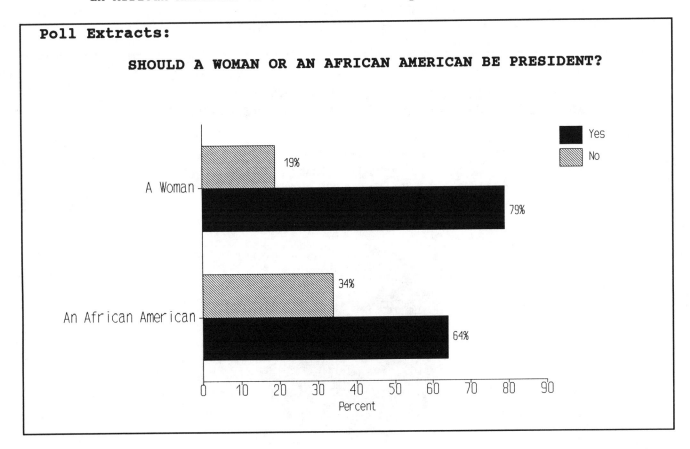

SHOULD A WOMAN OR AN AFRICAN AMERICAN BE PRESIDENT?

Also in Source: Liberal and conservative respondents who agreed or disagreed
that the American political system is the best in the world. Respondents
who were registered to vote and who thought they could effect change by
voting. Views on the Republican and Democratic Parties.

Poll Details: "Data compiled by R.H. Bruskin Associates, from a survey of 504
female college students on 16 campuses across the country."

Availability: Published in *In View*, November/December 1990 (volume 2,
issue 5), p. 16.

WILL THE DEMOCRATS OR REPUBLICANS GO TOO FAR?

Description: Respondents were asked if they thought Congress could deal with the major issues facing the nation, and whether they thought the Democrats or Republicans in Congress could do more damage to the nation.

Results: 42% of the respondents did not think Congress was capable of dealing with the "big issues" facing the United States. The Republicans, by their assistance to the rich, while cutting services to the average American and the poor, were seen as posing the greatest danger to the country.

Poll Extracts:

"WHICH OF THESE TWO STATEMENTS WOULD YOU SAY REPRESENTS THE GREATEST DANGER FOR THE COUNTRY:

The Democrats in Congress will go too far in keeping costly government services that are wasteful and out-of-date; or
The Republicans will go too far in helping the rich and cutting needed government services that benefit average Americans as well as the poor."

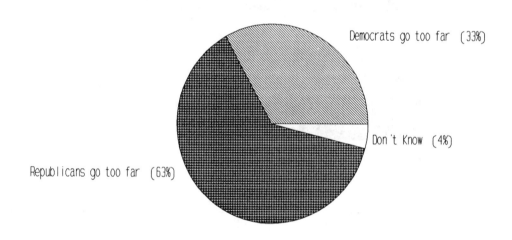

Democrats go too far (33%)

Don't Know (4%)

Republicans go too far (63%)

Also in Source: Respondents who blamed President Bush, the Democrats in Congress, or the Republicans in Congress for the federal budget situation. Approval or disapproval of the way President Bush is handling his job.

Poll Details: Chilton Research interviewed 756 randomly selected adults across the nation by telephone. The interviews were conducted during October 5-7, 1990. The margin of error is 4%.

Availability: Published in *The Washington Post*, October 9, 1990, p. A8.

BIRTH CONTROL AND MORALS

Description: This poll looked at the public's attitude toward each side's position in the abortion debate. Examined respondents' attitudes toward various methods of family planning, as to what they considered as morally acceptable.

Results: The majority of Americans support a woman's right to abortion. Americans don't approve of abortion as a method of birth control. Slightly more men than women support the right of choice. Significant numbers on both sides of the abortion debate recognize the validity of the opposing side's point of view.

Poll Extracts:

**WHEN QUESTIONED ABOUT FAMILY PLANNING AND
WHAT IS CONSIDERED AS MORALLY ACCEPTABLE METHODS:**

Birth control pills are morally acceptable 89%

Diaphragms are morally acceptable 80%

A "morning after" pill, which would prevent
a fertilized egg from developing 57%

Abortion 33%

Also in Source: The most convincing arguments for and against abortion, as seen by the people for and against abortion. The percentage of those surveyed who favor or are opposed to abortion. Arguments on both sides of the issue which are recognized as being valid by their opponents. Catholic versus Protestant opinion.

Poll Details: The survey was commissioned by *Parents* Magazine.

Availability: Published in *Parents*, March 1990 (volume 65, number 3), p. 30.

BIRTH CONTROL PILLS

Description: This study looked at mistakes made by users of birth control
pills.

Results: Only about 11% of women who use birth control pills use them properly
all the time.

Poll Extracts:

MISTAKES MADE BY WOMEN USING THE PILL

Took pills at different times of the day............ 83%

Didn't take a pill every day....................... 58%

Didn't make up missed pills or stopped
taking pills before the end of a month............. 16%

Didn't use back-up methods when needed............. 40%

Didn't take pills in the right order............... 2%

Borrowed pills from other women.................... 2%

Also in Source: The approximate percentage of all couples using birth control
that rely on the pill as their birth control method. The percentage of new
users who get pregnant within a year as found by a national study.

Poll Details: The study was conducted with 612 women, ages 14-36, who got
prescriptions at three Detroit-area clinics. Researchers, including
Deborah Oakley, at the University of Michigan, Ann Arbor, conducted the
study.

Availability: Published in *USA Today,* February 21, 1990, p. 1D.

DISCRIMINATION AGAINST PREGNANT WOMEN

Description: Presents the results of a survey concerning the presence of discrimination toward pregnant women in the workplace.

Results: Over 40% of the respondents said pregnancy adversely affects job performance and would consider not hiring or promoting a pregnant worker.

Poll Extracts:

PREGNANCY IN THE WORKPLACE:

Does pregnancy adversely effect
job performance?...Yes...41%

Would you consider not hiring or promoting
a pregnant worker?...Yes...42%

Do you know of someone who has delayed or
avoided pregnancy because of concern about
their employer's reaction?..................................Yes...30%

Would you support legislation to help pregnant
employees?...Yes...68%

Also in Source: Men were more likely than women to view pregnant employees as reducing work-group productivity and to rate pregnant employees' performance lower.

Poll Details: Researchers Hal Gueutal and Elisabeth Taylor of the State University of New York at Albany surveyed 133 women and 122 men who work at eight businesses in the Northeast.

Availability: Published in *The Cincinnati Enquirer*, July 30, 1990, p. A-6.

UNMARRIED PREGNANT TEENAGERS

Description: This survey of *Ladies Home Journal* readers asked mothers to respond to questions about their children and sex, and a variety of other subjects.

Results: 42% of the respondents said that sex was the hardest subject to talk about with their children. "53% of the respondents would give contraceptives to sexually active teenagers who asked for them."

Poll Extracts:

IF THEIR UNMARRIED TEENAGE DAUGHTER BECAME PREGNANT, RESPONDENTS WOULD:

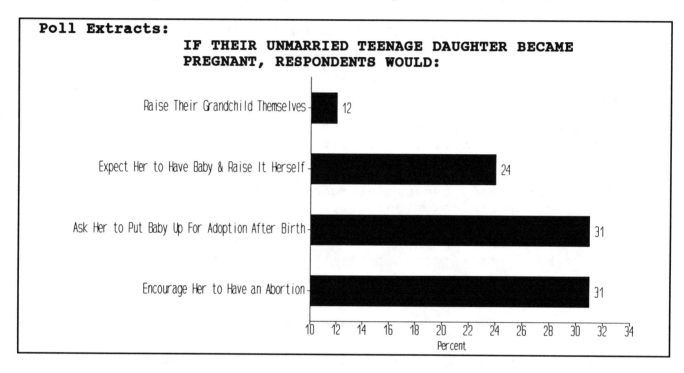

Raise Their Grandchild Themselves	12
Expect Her to Have Baby & Raise It Herself	24
Ask Her to Put Baby Up For Adoption After Birth	31
Encourage Her to Have an Abortion	31

Percent

Also in Source: The number of respondents who were pregnant when they got married. The number of respondents who have had an abortion. What mothers feel are the joys and frustrations of being a mother. Attitudes of mothers toward working outside of the home.

Poll Details: 22,000 readers responded to the survey. Characteristics of the respondents are as follows: 41% live in the suburbs, 29% cities, 30% rural areas; 80% are married; 59% are 25-39 years old, 25% are 40-49 years old, 13% are 50 or older, 4% are under 20 years old; 23% have one child, 42% have two children, 35% have three or more; 65% are currently employed, 30% not employed, 5% retired; 46% have school-age kids, 34% have toddlers/preschoolers or teenagers, 27% have adult children; 72% had their first child in their twenties, 17% were teenagers, 11% were in their thirties, and 0.4% were in their fourties; 25% have a high school education, 46% have some business or college education, 24% are college graduates; 20% have family incomes under $25,000, 33% have incomes between $25,000 and $39,000, 40% have incomes of $40,000 or more.

Availability: Published in *Ladies Home Journal*, May 1990 (volume 107, number 5), p. 132, 134, 136.

APPROVAL OF THE PRESIDENT - AFTER ONE YEAR

Description: The poll measured the public's approval of President George Bush after his first year in office. The poll also assessed perceptions as to the progress made by President Bush on various domestic issues.

Results: The President's approval rating is the highest since John F. Kennedy's, when compared to previous administrations following their first year in office.

Poll Extracts: **PUBLIC APPROVAL OF THE PRESIDENT AFTER ONE YEAR IN OFFICE**

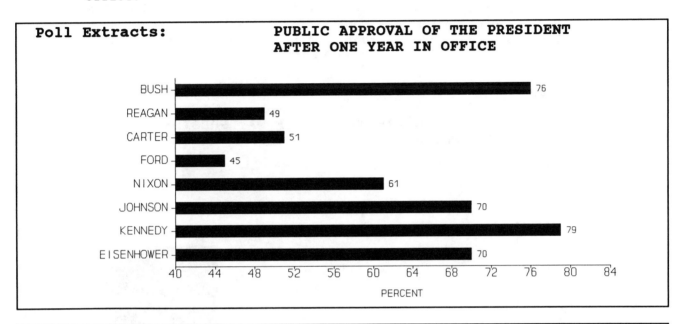

Poll Extracts:

% of all adults seeing progress

So far has George Bush really made progress in:

dealing with the drug problem, or has he mainly just talked about it?   54%

Also in Source: Information on attitudes toward the President and foreign relations, the President and the invasion of Panama, the President and taxes, the President and domestic issues. In addition to the group surveyed as a whole, there was a breakdown of the questions on domestic issues by Democratic and Republican response.

Poll Details: This New York Times/CBS News poll is based on telephone interviews with 1,557 adults around the U.S., excluding Alaska and Hawaii, conducted January 13-15, 1990. The results have been weighted to adjust for variations in the sample.

Availability: Published in *The New York Times*, January 19, 1990, p. A1, A20.

BLACK APPROVAL OF PRESIDENT BUSH

Description: This poll questioned black adults as to whether they approved of
the way President Bush is handling foreign policy, the drug problem, and
his job in general.

Results: 56% of black Americans approve of the way President Bush is doing his
job. 26% of the blacks surveyed disapproved of the job he was doing. One-
third of the black respondents said their opinion of President Bush had
improved since he became president. 45% of the black respondents thought
that President Bush cares a great deal or cares some about people like
themselves.

Poll Extracts:

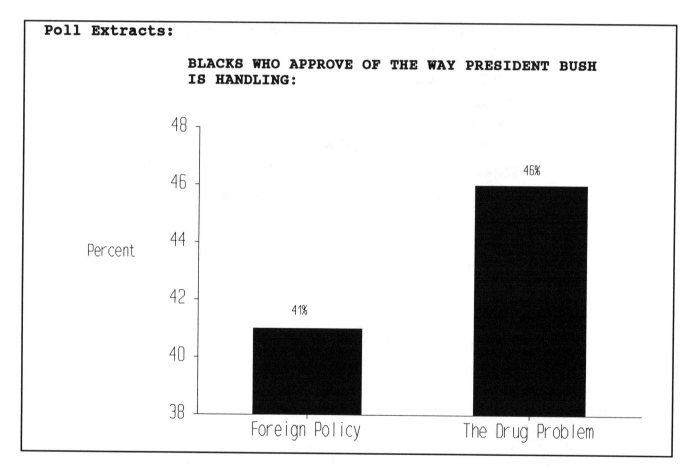

**BLACKS WHO APPROVE OF THE WAY PRESIDENT BUSH
IS HANDLING:**

Also in Source: President Bush has received the highest level of sustained
approval for a Republican president, by black Americans, since President
Dwight D. Eisenhower. Responses to the questions concerning foreign
policy, the drug problem, and whether President Bush cares about people
like the respondents, were broken down by the age, education, sex, and
income characteristics of the respondents.

Poll Details: A telephone survey of 1,515 adults, including 403 blacks, was
conducted from March 30, 1990 through April 2, 1990. The margin of error
is 5% for blacks, and 3% for the entire sample. Further details as to how
the survey was conducted are provided in the source.

Availability: Published in *The New York Times*, April 13, 1990, p. A12.

BUSH'S APPROVAL RATING

Description: Presents the results of a survey concerning the performance of
George Bush as President of the United States.

Results: President Bush's overall approval rating in July 1990 was 50%. Most
of his high marks come in foreign policy areas with lesser grades in
domestic concerns.

Poll Extracts:

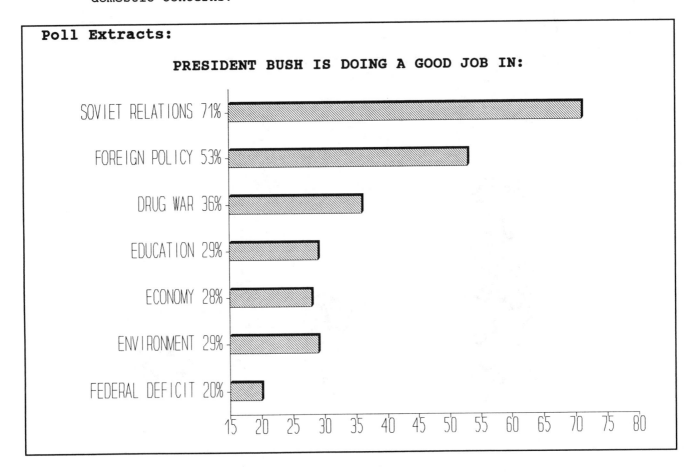

PRESIDENT BUSH IS DOING A GOOD JOB IN:

SOVIET RELATIONS 71%
FOREIGN POLICY 53%
DRUG WAR 36%
EDUCATION 29%
ECONOMY 28%
ENVIRONMENT 29%
FEDERAL DEFICIT 20%

15 20 25 30 35 40 45 50 55 60 65 70 75 80

Also in Source: 59% of the respondents think Bush will be re-elected to a
second term. Barbara Bush's approval rating is 77% while Dan Quayle's is
24%.

Poll Details: This Gordon S. Black telephone survey of 813 adults nationwide
was conducted for *USA Today* on July 16-17, 1990 about two weeks before Iraq
invaded Kuwait. The margin of error is 3.5%.

Availability: Published in *USA Today*, July 20-22, 1990, p. 1A, 6A.

BUSH'S SAUDI ARABIA DECISION

Description: Presents the results of a survey concerning the approval of
President George Bush's decision to send troops to Saudi Arabia to defend
against a possible invasion by Iraq.

Results: Over 60% of the respondents approve of Mr. Bush's decision to send
U.S. troops to Saudi Arabia.

Poll Extracts:

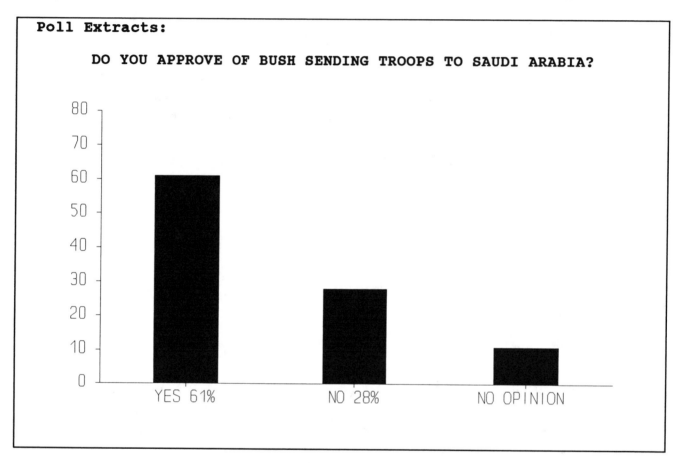

DO YOU APPROVE OF BUSH SENDING TROOPS TO SAUDI ARABIA?

Also in Source: A general discussion of the issue is included in the article.

Poll Details: Based on a CBS News Poll of 376 adults nationwide contacted by
telephone on August 7, 1990 five days after Iraq invaded Kuwait.

Availability: Published in *The New York Times*, August 9, 1990, p. A1, A20.

CHINESE AND SOVIET RELATIONS

Description: Respondents were asked to rate the Bush Administration's handling of relations with the Soviets and the Chinese.

Results: The Bush Administration's handling of relations with the Soviets are viewed favorably by 80% of the respondents. Relations with China were seen as below average or poor by 38% of the respondents.

Poll Extracts:

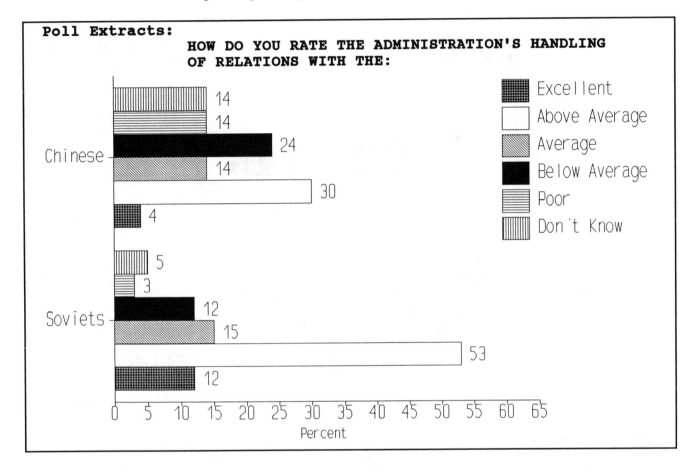

Also in Source: Respondents rated Bush's handling of the economy. They also answered whether or not they thought public education and the quality of the environment would improve during the next two years.

Poll Details: KRC Communications Research interviewed 1,002 registered voters by telephone on May 28-30, 1990. The margin of error is 3%.

Availability: Published in *The Boston Globe*, May 31, 1990, p. 7.

THE CIVIL RIGHTS BILL

Description: Supporters of Republican and Democratic candidates were asked what action President Bush should have taken with the civil rights bill.

Results: A majority of the Republican supporters felt that President Bush should have vetoed the civil rights bill while a majority of Democratic supporters felt that he should have signed it.

Poll Extracts:

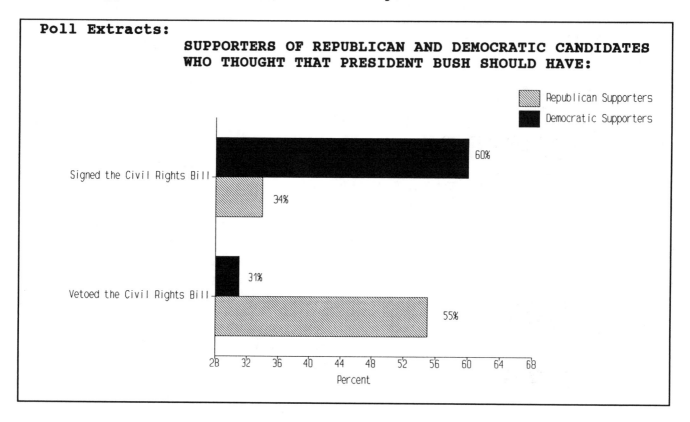

SUPPORTERS OF REPUBLICAN AND DEMOCRATIC CANDIDATES WHO THOUGHT THAT PRESIDENT BUSH SHOULD HAVE:

Also in Source: The mood of the nation measured on a scale using the worst and best possible situation as a means of reflecting how things are going in the United States. Views on economics, policy issues, and the way President Bush and Congress are handling their jobs.

Poll Details: This *New York Times*/CBS News poll interviewed 1,445 adults across the United States, excluding Alaska and Hawaii. Telephone interviews were conducted from October 28 to October 31, 1990. The results have been weighted to adjust for variations in the sample such as region, race, sex, age, and education. The margin of error is 3%. Further information as to how the poll was conducted is provided in the source.

Availability: Published in *The New York Times*, November 4, 1990, p. 1, 34.

CONGRESSIONAL APPROVAL OF MILITARY ACTIONS

Description: Respondents were asked about President Bush's explanation as to why U.S. troops are in the Middle East and his ability to engage those troops in action.

Results: Respondents were about evenly divided as to whether President Bush had done a good job (49%) or a poor job (45%) of informing the American people why U.S. troops are in the Middle East. The majority of respondents also felt that utilizing military force against Iraq should not occur without congressional approval.

Poll Extracts:
"SHOULD PRESIDENT BUSH HAVE THE OPTION OF USING MILITARY FORCE AGAINST IRAQ WITHOUT CONGRESS'S AUTHORIZATION?"

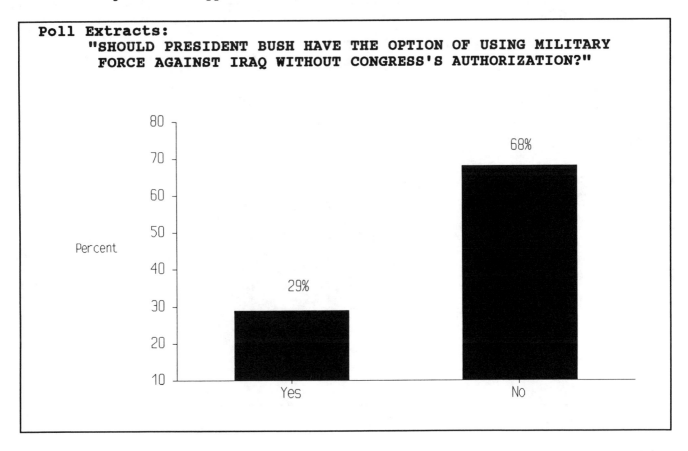

Also in Source: Opinions on the Persian Gulf crisis.

Poll Details: Yankelovich Clancy Shulman conducted this poll for *Time*/CNN. 500 adult Americans were interviewed by telephone on November 14, 1990. The margin of error is 4.5%.

Availability: Published in *Time*, November 26, 1990 (volume 136, number 23), p. 31, 33.

DIPLOMACY OR FORCE

Description: Respondents were asked about President Bush's use of American military forces in the Persian Gulf.

Results: Respondents feel that the U.S. military involvement and build-up in Saudi Arabia has not been clearly justified by President Bush. 47% of the respondents believe that the President has sent American military forces to the Persian Gulf too fast and has not worked hard enough to find diplomatic solutions.

Poll Extracts:

HAS PRESIDENT BUSH FAILED TO EXPLAIN CLEARLY ENOUGH WHY THE UNITED STATES IS SENDING TROOPS TO SAUDI ARABIA?

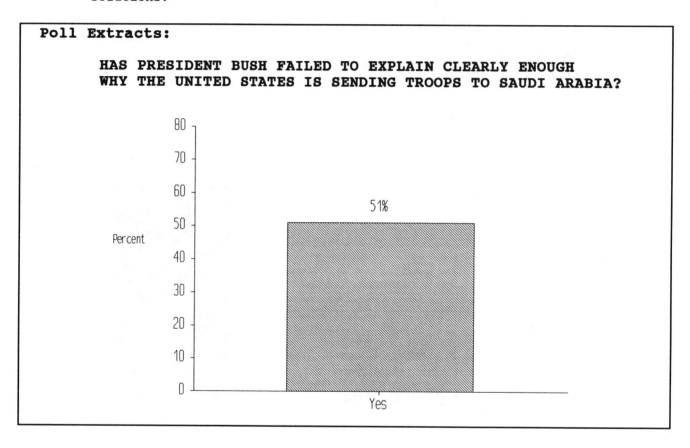

Also in Source: The percentage of respondents who: expected the U.S. and Iraqi troops to end up fighting each other, believed the U.S. should attack soon, and accepted or rejected several ideas as good enough reasons for fighting Iraq.

Poll Details: This *New York Times*/CBS News poll involved 1,370 adults across the nation, excluding Alaska and Hawaii. The telephone poll was conducted during November 13-15, 1990. The margin of error is 3%.

Availability: Published in *The New York Times*, November 20, 1990, p. A12.

ENVIRONMENTAL POLICY

Description: This survey queried respondents about President Bush and his
environmental record.

Results: The majority of respondents think President Bush has not made much
progress in protecting the environment. But, 57% do trust him to make the
right decisions concerning the environment.

Poll Extracts:

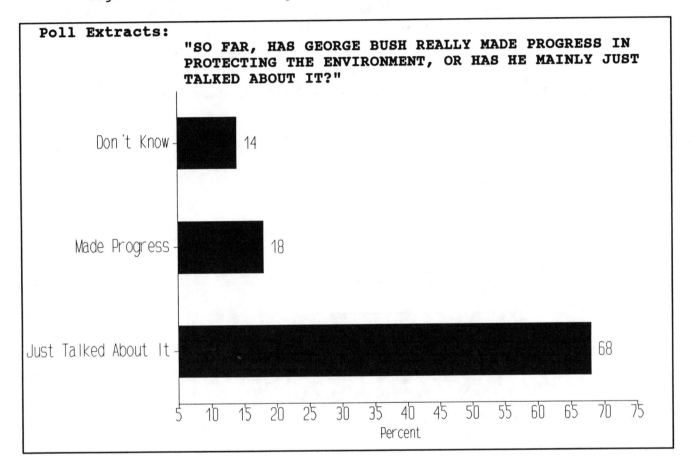

**"SO FAR, HAS GEORGE BUSH REALLY MADE PROGRESS IN
PROTECTING THE ENVIRONMENT, OR HAS HE MAINLY JUST
TALKED ABOUT IT?"**

Also in Source: The percentage of respondents who think that we must protect
the environment even if it means increased government spending and higher
taxes, or even losing jobs in the local community. The percentage of
respondents who believe that pollution is a serious problem and getting
worse.

Poll Details: This *New York Times*/CBS News Poll surveyed 1,515 people by
telephone during March 30 - April 2, 1990.

Availability: Published in *The New York Times*, April 17, 1990, p. A1, B10.

IRAQI CRISIS BOOSTS POPULARITY

Description: This poll asked respondents to rate President Bush's performance in a number of areas.

Results: 76% of the respondents approve of the way George Bush is handling his job as President. (This level of support was last reached after President Bush ordered the invasion of Panama last December.) Approval for the President's performance is highest for his conduct of foreign affairs, and much lower for his handling of domestic affairs.

Poll Extracts:

RESPONDENTS WHO APPROVE OF THE WAY PRESIDENT BUSH IS HANDLING:

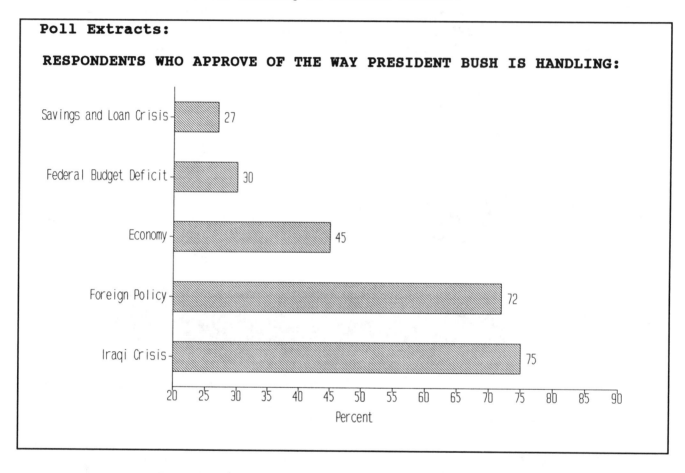

Also in Source: The percentage of respondents who support the decision to send troops to the Persian Gulf. The percentage of respondents who would be willing to pay higher taxes in order to protect Saudi Arabia. A chart breaking down the respondents approval ratings into the Republican, Democratic, and Independent response.

Poll Details: This *New York Times*/CBS News poll is based on telephone interviews with 1,422 adults. The poll was conducted on August 16-19, 1990.

Availability: Published in *The New York Times*, August 22, 1990, p. A1, A13.

LITHUANIAN INDEPENDENCE

Description: Respondents were queried about President Bush's reaction to the
events in Lithuania.

Results: Most of the respondents thought President Bush's reaction to the
Lithuanian situation was "about right." But, 29% thought that President
Bush was doing an excellent, or above average job, in dealing with the
Soviets on the issue of Lithuanian independence.

Poll Extracts:

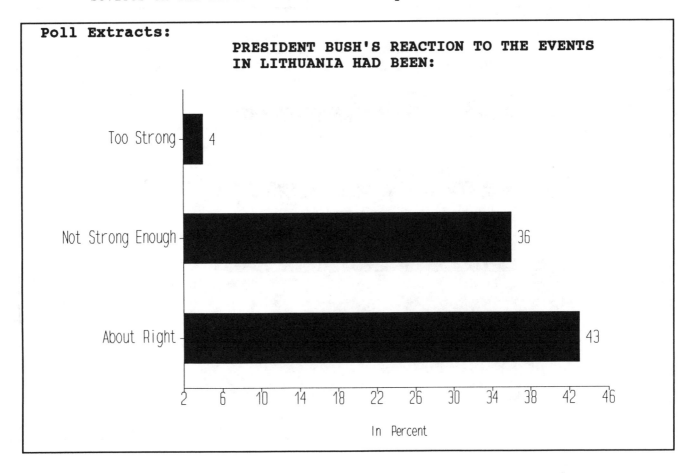

PRESIDENT BUSH'S REACTION TO THE EVENTS
IN LITHUANIA HAD BEEN:

Too Strong — 4
Not Strong Enough — 36
About Right — 43

In Percent

Also in Source: Respondents' attitudes toward President Bush, the June 1990
Bush-Gorbachev summit meeting, Bush's foreign policy, and the Cold War.

Poll Details: KRC Communications Research interviewed 1,002 registered voters,
chosen at random, by telephone on June 3-5, 1990. The margin of error is
3%.

Availability: Published in *The Boston Globe*, June 7, 1990, p. 12.

LONG-TERM PROBLEMS

Description: Respondents were asked to rate the job that President Bush is
        doing in dealing with the long-term problems of the economy, health care,
        education, and the environment.

Results: President Bush is rated as doing an excellent job in handling several
        long-term problems by 5% or fewer of the respondents.

Poll Extracts:

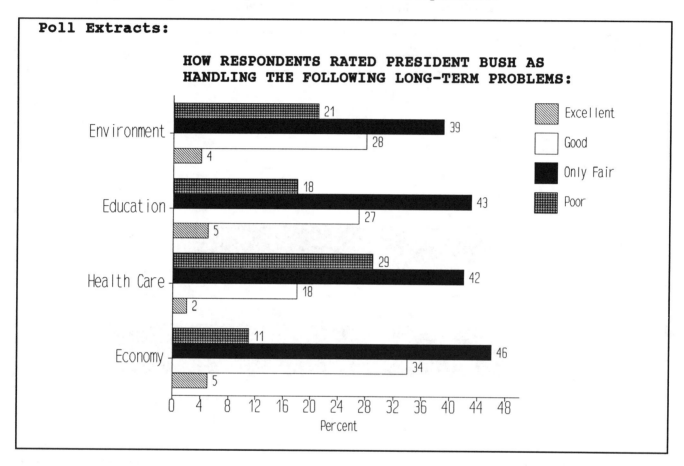

**HOW RESPONDENTS RATED PRESIDENT BUSH AS
HANDLING THE FOLLOWING LONG-TERM PROBLEMS:**

Also in Source: Accompanying article on the nation's loss of leadership.

Poll Details: The Poll Extracts information is from a Times Mirror poll.

Availability: Published in the *Los Angeles Times,* April 13, 1990, p. A19.

POPULARITY OF GEORGE BUSH AND MIKHAIL GORBACHEV

Description: Respondents were polled for their approval ratings of President George Bush and Soviet leader Mikhail Gorbachev. They were also questioned about Gorbachev as a reformer, and his chances of changing his society.

Results: President Bush received the same job approval rating as Mikhail Gorbachev. 62% of the respondents thought that Gorbachev is a sincere reformer who is trying to turn the Soviet Union into a more democratic country that will cooperate with the United States in the years ahead. 23% of the respondents see Gorbachev as a committed communist and adversary. 56% think Gorbachev will remain in power, 38% think he could be out of power within a year, and 71% believe that even if Gorbachev is removed from power, the movement toward democracy will continue within the Soviet Union.

Poll Extracts:

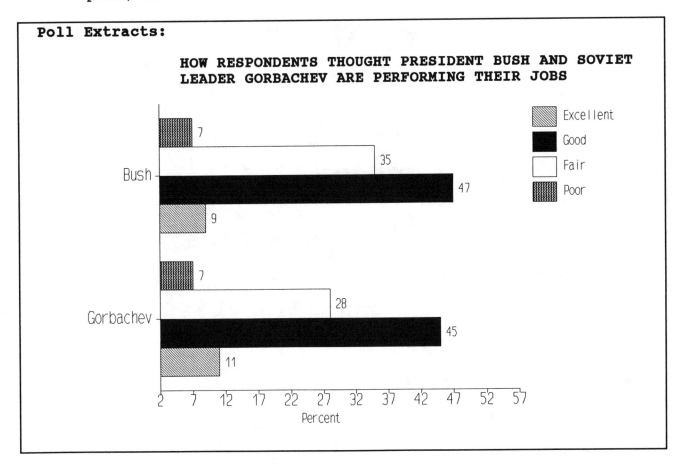

Poll Details: This telephone poll of 800 adults in the State of Michigan was conducted in the week prior to May 28, 1990.

Availability: Published in *The Detroit News and Free Press*, May 28, 1990, p. 1A, 4A.

PRESIDENT BUSH AND NATIONAL ISSUES

Description: This poll attempted to query respondents about whether President
George Bush is doing a "good" or "poor" job in several areas.

Results: Approval of the President is highest in his handling of foreign
relations, and falls in his handling of domestic affairs.

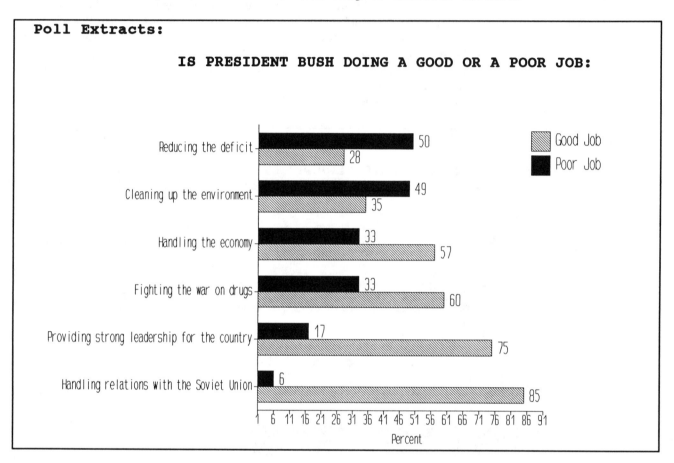

Poll Extracts:

IS PRESIDENT BUSH DOING A GOOD OR A POOR JOB:

Also in Source: The percentage of respondents who approve of George Bush's
overall job performance. A discussion of why President Bush is so popular.

Poll Details: Results are from a *Time*/CNN telephone poll of 500 adult
Americans on February 14, 1990. The poll was conducted by Yankelovich
Clancy Shulman. The sampling error is 4.5%.

Availability: Published in *Time*, February 26, 1990 (volume 135, number 9),
p. 36.

PRESIDENT BUSH AND THE ECONOMY

Description: Presents the results of a survey concerning President George
Bush's performance in handling a number of issues, including the economy.

Results: Almost 60% of the respondents disapprove of President Bush's handling
of the savings and loan crisis, over 60% disapprove of his handling of the
federal deficit, and 54% disapprove of possible increased taxes.

Poll Extracts:

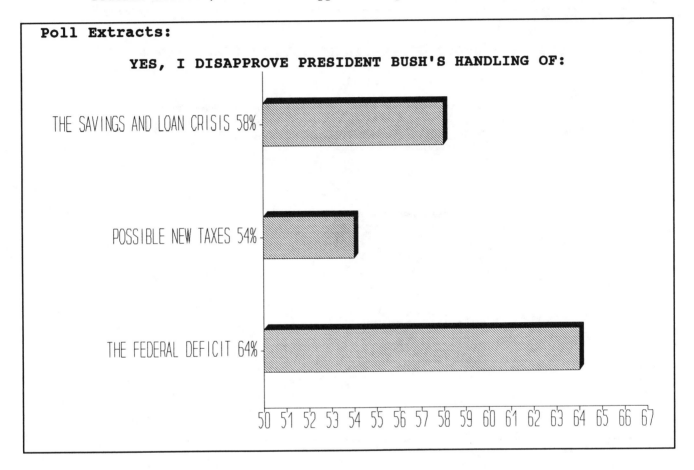

YES, I DISAPPROVE PRESIDENT BUSH'S HANDLING OF:

THE SAVINGS AND LOAN CRISIS 58%

POSSIBLE NEW TAXES 54%

THE FEDERAL DEFICIT 64%

50 51 52 53 54 55 56 57 58 59 60 61 62 63 64 65 66 67

Also in Source: 63% of the respondents approve of the overall job Bush is
doing. 82% approved of his handling of relations with the Soviet Union.
Asked to cite President Bush's greatest achievement, 37% mentioned foreign
policy particularly the changes in the Soviet Union and Eastern Europe.

Poll Details: The results are based on a nationwide telephone poll of 1,240
adults on July 6-8, 1990. The survey was conducted by the Gallup
Organization.

Availability: Published in *The New York Times*, July 11, 1990, p. A10.

PRESIDENT'S APPROVAL RATING DROPS

Description: Presents the results of a survey concerning President George
Bush's continuing slide in the approval rating polls.

Results: President Bush's approval rating has dropped 15% from August 23, 1990
to October 10, 1990.

Poll Extracts:

YES, I APPROVE OF PRESIDENT BUSH'S PERFORMANCE:

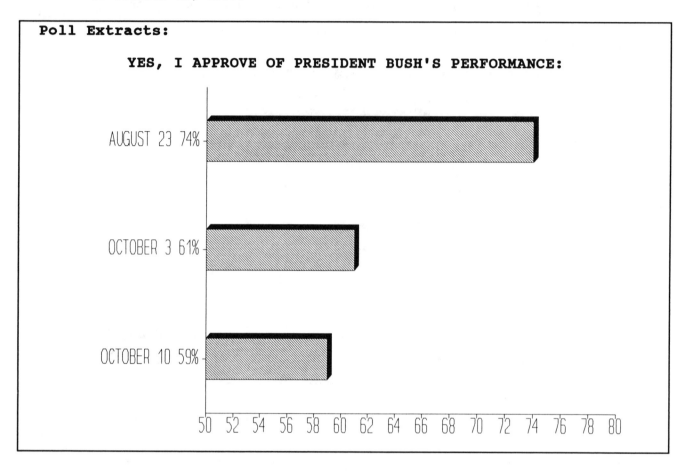

Also in Source: 67% of the respondents feel Bush is doing a good job handling
foreign policy, while 26% feel he is doing a poor job. 34% feel he doing a
good job handling the economy, while 56% think he is doing a poor job. 35%
feel he is doing a good job working with Congress on the budget deficit and
56% think he is doing a poor job. 58% of the respondents think the United
States is in a recession.

Poll Details: The results were taken from a telephone poll of 500 adult
Americans for *Time*/CNN by Yankelovich Clancy Shulman. Sampling error is
plus or minus 4.5%.

Availability: Published in *Time*, October 22, 1990 (volume 136, number 17),
p. 26-28.

PRESIDENTIAL POPULARITY AFTER THE PANAMA INVASION

Description: The poll measured public support for President George Bush, the Republican Party, and the invasion of Panama.

Results: After almost one year in office, President Bush is one of the most popular presidents in recent years. More Americans now believe the Republican Party is best suited to solve this nation's problems. Over 80% believe the military invasion in Panama was a success. Nine in ten respondents thought Gen. Manuel Antonio Noriega was guilty in relation to the drug charges against him, but seven in ten thought that he could still receive a fair trial.

Poll Extracts:

RESPONDENTS WHO:

Approve of the job George Bush
has done as president................... 79%

Trust the Republican Party to do
a better job of coping with the
country's biggest problems.............. 50%

Trust the Democratic Party to do
a better job of coping with the
country's biggest problems.............. 38%

Also in Source: The percentage of respondents who approve of the use of U.S. Navy ships to block shipments of cocaine, off of Columbia. The percentage of respondents who do not approve of President Bush's plan to attend a drug summit in Cartagena, Columbia. The percentage of respondents -- blacks, self-described liberals, Democrats, and Democrats who voted for Michael S. Dukakis for president in 1988 -- who approve of President Bush's job performance.

Poll Details: This *Washingtion Post*-ABC News Poll was conducted January 11-15, 1990, and interviewed 1,518 randomly selected adults by telephone. The sampling error is 3%.

Availability: Published in *The Washington Post*, January 18, 1990, p. A9.

PRESIDENTIAL POPULARITY FALLS

Description: Respondents were asked if they approved of the way President Bush
was handling his job.

Results: Just over half of the respondents approved of the way President Bush
was handling his job, down from similar polls conducted in August and
September 1990.

Poll Extracts:

"DO YOU APPROVE OF THE WAY GEORGE BUSH IS HANDLING HIS JOB?"

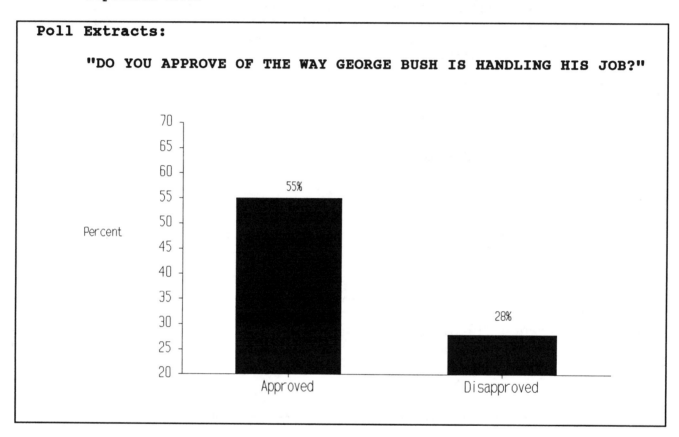

Also in Source: Respondents who were aware of the impact that the proposed
budget compromise (which was later discarded) would have had on: Medicare
fees, gasoline taxes, alcohol taxes, and cigarette taxes. Dissatisfaction
had increased in all demographic and political groups for the way President
Bush was handling his job. President Bush's approval rating had fallen by
15% or more among older people, blacks, and Democrats.

Poll Details: This nationwide survey of 1,213 adults was done for The Times
Mirror Center for The People & The Press by Princeton Survey Research
Associates. The survey was conducted October 4-7, 1990.

Availability: Published in the *Los Angeles Times*, October 9, 1990, p. A1, A13.

PRESIDENTIAL RESPONSIBILITIES

Description: Respondents were asked if they approved or disapproved of how President Bush has handled several of his responsibilities.

Results: President Bush's overall job rating was the worst of his Presidency (60% approval). Compared to the results of a similar poll conducted in August 1990, approval has fallen for the way President Bush has handled his responsibilities in a number of areas. "Those 65 and over, an age group which votes more heavily than any other, are now evenly divided between the 41% who express approval of Mr. Bush's handling of his job and the 41% who express disapproval. That is a sharp shift from the 70% of older Americans who expressed approval and the 17% who expressed disapproval in August."

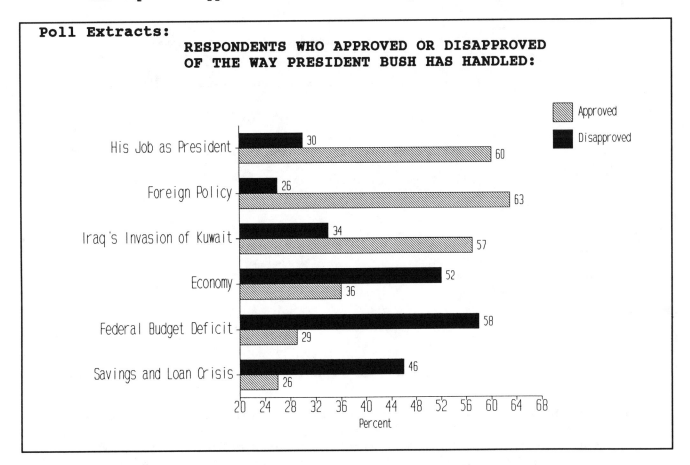

Poll Extracts:

RESPONDENTS WHO APPROVED OR DISAPPROVED OF THE WAY PRESIDENT BUSH HAS HANDLED:

Also in Source: Responses to polls on President Bush's handling of Iraq's invasion of Kuwait from August and September 1990. Questions dealing with the Persian Gulf conflict.

Poll Details: This *New York Times*/CBS News poll involved 960 adults across the nation, excluding Alaska and Hawaii. Telephone interviews were conducted October 8-10, 1990. "The results have been weighted to take account of household size and number of residential phone lines and to adjust for variations in the sample relating to region, race, sex, age, and education." The margin of error is 3%. The margin of error for people 65 years of age or older is 8%. Further details are provided in the source.

Availability: Published in *The New York Times*, October 14, 1990, p. 1, 25.

PRESIDENTIAL VACATIONS

Description: Presents the results of a survey concerning President George Bush working at his summer home in Maine after ordering American troops to the Middle East.

Results: Over half of the respondents said it was appropriate for President Bush to be in Maine during the Middle East crisis.

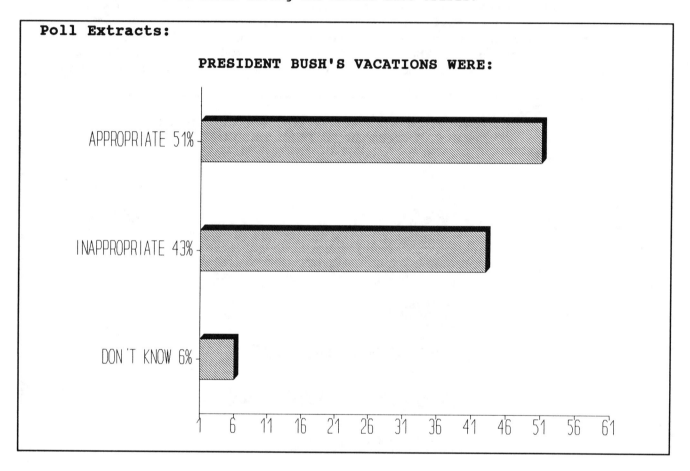

Poll Extracts:

PRESIDENT BUSH'S VACATIONS WERE:

APPROPRIATE 51%

INAPPROPRIATE 43%

DON'T KNOW 6%

1   6   11   16   21   26   31   36   41   46   51   56   61

Also in Source: President Bush's favorability rating was 81%. By a 57% to 25% margin, voters said Bush will force Iraq out of Kuwait. 46% of the respondents said a diplomatic success in the Middle East is somewhat or very unlikely. Bush's handling of energy policy matters was rated as below average or poor by 39% of the respondents. The poll found less than 15% of voters believe oil prices will drop by next year. An increase in oil prices was predicted by 66% with 17% predicting price levels will be about the same.

Poll Details: KRC Communications Research contacted 1,004 registered voters nationwide by telephone August 26-28, 1990. The poll's margin of error was 3%.

Availability: Published in *The Boston Globe*, August 30, 1990, p. 2.

THE PRESIDENT'S REPORT CARD

Description: One week before President George Bush's first anniversary in office, respondents were asked to grade the President.

Results: A majority of respondents think that President Bush merits a grade above a "C" grade. 74% of the respondents gave President Bush high marks on Soviet relations. 25% of the respondents gave President Bush high marks for his handling of the deficit.

Poll Extracts:

RESPONDENTS WHO THINK:

President Bush merits an "A" or "B" grade........ 63%

They feel better about President Bush because of the way he handled the Panama crisis............. 62%

President Bush has "taken charge" in Washington instead of reacting to events.................... 45%

President Bush merits an "A" or "B" grade on cleaning the environment......................... 28%

President Bush merits an "A" or "B" grade on education...................................... 34%

Also in Source: More respondents rated Barbara Bush with an "A" or "B" grade than President Bush received. Vice President Dan Quayle was graded with low marks. The percentage of respondents who felt President Bush deserved an "A" or "B" grade in the following areas: foreign policy, terrorism, drug problems, and the economy.

Poll Details: The poll of 810 adults was conducted by Gordon S. Black Corp., on January 10-11, 1990. The margin of error is 3.5%.

Availability: Published in *USA Today*, January 15, 1990. p. 1A, 4A.

SHOULD THE U.S. GO TO WAR

Description: Presents the results of a survey concerning the support for U.S. troops going into battle in the Middle East.

Results: Half of the respondents would approve of U.S. troops engaging in war to force Iraqi President Saddam Hussein from Kuwait.

Poll Extracts:

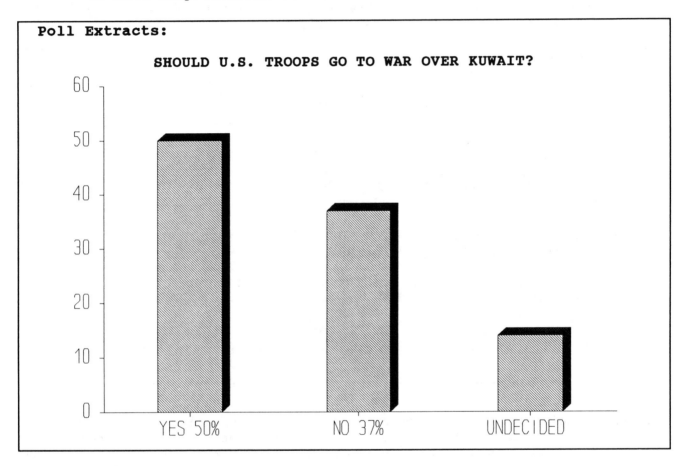

SHOULD U.S. TROOPS GO TO WAR OVER KUWAIT?

Also in Source: 80% of the respondents approve of the overall job George Bush is doing as President of the United States. 73% approve of the way Bush is handling the Middle East situation. 40% said the fact that Americans are being held hostage made them "more favorable" toward a war with Iraq.

Poll Details: The *Chicago Tribune* poll of 1,000 people was conducted throughout Illinois by telephone on August 28 - September 1, 1990. There was a 3% margin of error.

Availability: Published in the *Chicago Tribune*, September 9, 1990, Section 1, p. 18.

SUPPORT FOR THE RE-ELECTION OF PRESIDENT BUSH

Description: Respondents were asked about their support for President Bush and whether they would re-elect George Bush.

Results: 53% of the respondents gave President Bush an "excellent" or "above average" rating for foreign policy. 55% of the respondents were critical of President Bush's leadership on the national economy.

Poll Extracts:
"IF ELECTION DAY WAS TOMORROW, AND YOU WERE VOTING FOR PRESIDENT, WOULD YOU VOTE TO RE-ELECT GEORGE BUSH OR WOULD YOU VOTE FOR SOMEONE ELSE?"

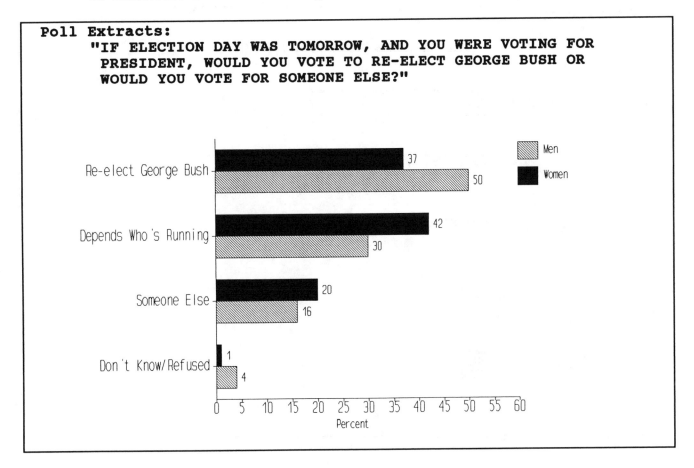

Also in Source: The political party that respondents thought was looking out for the interests of the wealthy and the interests of the middle class. The percentage of respondents who would vote to re-elect their congressman.

Poll Details: This nationwide *Boston Globe*/WBZ-TV poll was conducted by KRC Communications Research. 1,002 registered voters were interviewed by telephone October 14-16, 1990. The margin of error is 3%.

Availability: Published in *The Boston Globe*, October 18, 1990, p. 1, 107.

TEXANS RATE BUSH

>   **Description:** Presents the results of a survey measuring President George
>   Bush's approval rating in the state of Texas.

>   **Results:** Over 71% of the respondents think President Bush is doing a good or
>   excellent job.

Poll Extracts:

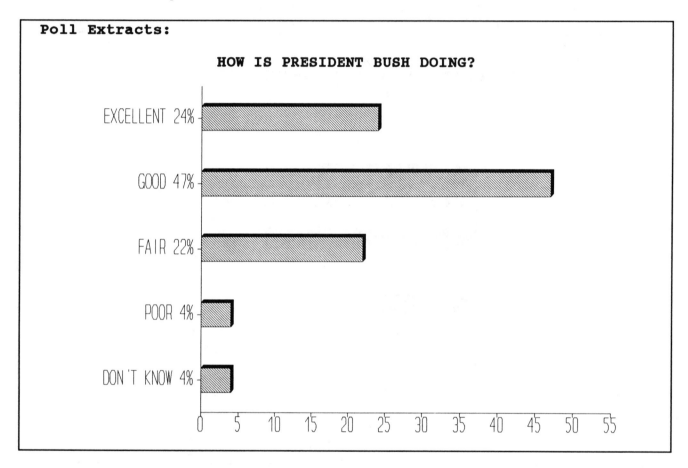

HOW IS PRESIDENT BUSH DOING?

>   **Also in Source:** 32% of the respondents said their opinion of President Bush
>   would lessen if he broke his promise not to raise taxes, 64% said it
>   wouldn't, and 4% didn't know.

>   **Poll Details:** The survey of 1,021 adults was conducted August 4-19, 1990, by
>   the Public Policy Resources Laboratory at Texas A&M University for Harte-
>   Hanks Communications Inc. The margin of error is plus or minus 3%.

>   **Availability:** Published in *The Dallas Morning News,* September 4, 1990,
>   p. 1A, 7A.

WORRIED ABOUT THE WEALTHY

Description: This poll asked respondents about the way President Bush is handling his job and about economic conditions in the United States. Respondents were also asked about President Bush's relations with wealthy Americans.

Results: 54% of the respondents approved and 34% disapproved of the way George Bush was handling his job as President. Only 29% of the respondents approved of the way President Bush was handling economic conditions in the United States. The majority of respondents thought that President Bush was overly concerned about the wealthy.

Poll Extracts:

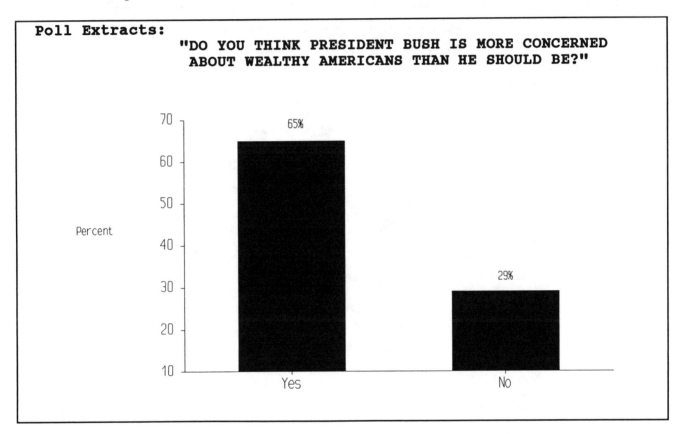

"DO YOU THINK PRESIDENT BUSH IS MORE CONCERNED ABOUT WEALTHY AMERICANS THAN HE SHOULD BE?"

Also in Source: Respondents thought that wealthy Americans do not have to pay their fair share of taxes. Where the respondents placed the blame for the inability to reach an agreement on a federal budget to reduce the deficit: President Bush, Republicans in Congress, Democrats in Congress, special interest/lobbying groups, or American voters who oppose higher taxes or spending cuts. Respondents who favored a limit on the number of terms a person can serve as a member of the House or Senate.

Poll Details: This *Newsweek* poll was conducted by the Gallup Organization. 757 adults across the nation were interviewed by telephone October 11 and October 12, 1990. The margin of error is 4%.

Availability: Published in *Newsweek*, October 22, 1990 (volume CXVI, no. 17), p. 23.

ABORTION AND CATHOLIC BISHOPS

Description: Respondents were queried about the involvement of Catholic
          bishops in abortion politics and the use of church penalties against
          supporters of abortion.

Results: The majority of Catholic respondents and non-Catholic respondents
          object to the Catholic bishops' high-profile involvement in abortion
          politics. "Voters also strongly oppose excommunication or other church
          penalties against women who have abortions, doctors who perform abortions,
          and politicians who support abortion rights, the poll found."

Poll Extracts:

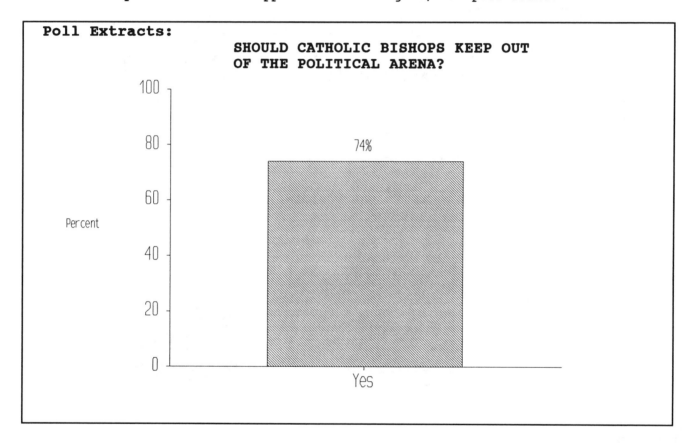

**SHOULD CATHOLIC BISHOPS KEEP OUT
OF THE POLITICAL ARENA?**

Also in Source: "The Conference of Catholic Bishops criticized the poll for
          failing to distinguish between churchgoing Catholics and those who do not
          attend church."

Poll Details: KRC Research and Consulting, a New York City-based public
          opinion research group, conducted the nationwide telephone poll in October
          1990. 2,002 voters participated in the poll which was paid for by
          Catholics for a Free Choice. The margin of error was 2%.

Availability: Published in the *Detroit Free Press*, October 26, 1990, p. 2A.

BABY BOOMERS' BELIEFS

Description: The preliminary findings in a regional analysis of religious characteristics of the baby boom generation are presented.

Results: Younger baby boomers may be carrying deeper personal beliefs, and affirming traditional Christian-Judeo beliefs more than older boomers.

Poll Extracts:

PERSONAL BELIEFS OF OLDER AND YOUNGER BABY BOOMERS:

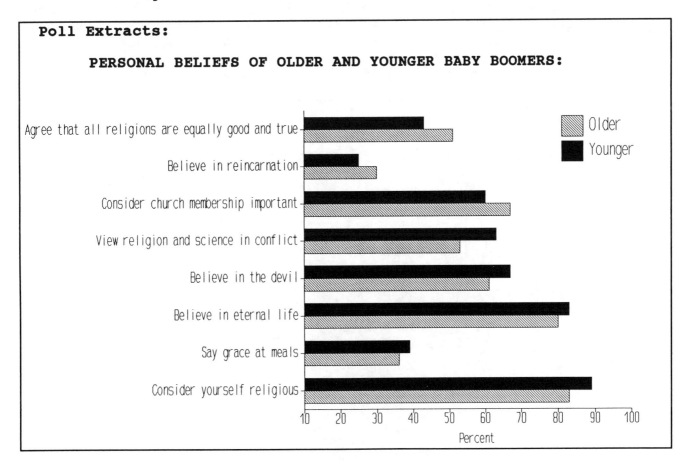

Also in Source: The percentages of older and younger baby boomers who would call upon an institution for a baptism, a wedding, or a funeral.

Poll Details: The responses are based on telephone interviews with 536 adults in California, Massachusetts, Ohio, and North Carolina. The older group of adults was born between 1946 and 1955. The younger group of adults was born between 1956 and 1965. The data in this poll was obtained from Dr. Wade Clark Roof of the University of California at Santa Barbara.

Availability: Published in *The Atlanta Journal and Constitution*, March 3, 1990, p. B9.

BELIEFS AND CHURCH ATTENDANCE IN TEXAS

Description: This telephone poll queried respondents about various aspects of
religion in Texas.

Results: The majority of Texans believe religion is very important in their
daily lives. "53% of the respondents described their religious convictions
as predominantly traditional." 2% of the respondents described themselves
as agnostic or atheist, but 9% of this group also said they attend church
every week. 52% of the respondents attend church or religious activities
every week, or several times a week. 23% attend church or religious
activities from nearly every week to two-to-three times a month.

Poll Extracts:

TEXANS SAY RELIGION IN THEIR DAILY LIFE IS:

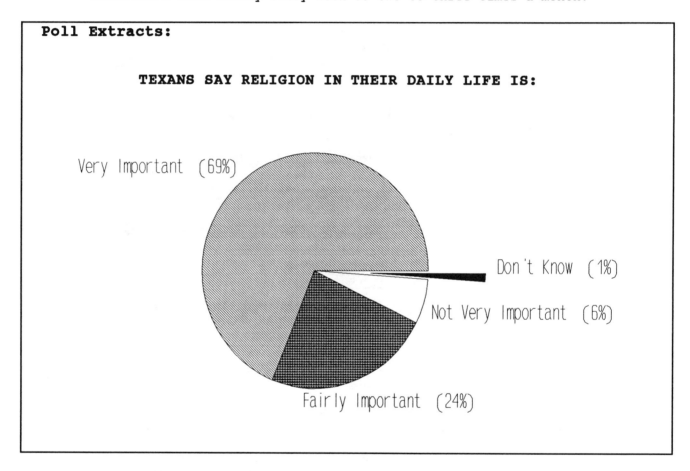

Very Important (69%)

Don't Know (1%)

Not Very Important (6%)

Fairly Important (24%)

Also in Source: The percentage of respondents is stated according to their
current religious preference. Texans who were familiar with the term "new
age" when associated with religion, and the percentage of this group who
had a positive or negative view of it.

Poll Details: "The Public Policy Resources Laboratory at Texas A&M University
conducted the telephone poll April 28–May 12 for Harte-Hanks Communications
Inc. The survey of 1,007 adults statewide has a margin of error of 3
percentage points."

Availability: Published in *The Dallas Morning News*, June 9, 1990, p. 1A, 14A.

BLACK CATHOLICS

Description: This survey of black Catholics asked a variety of questions
    dealing with church membership.

Results: 40% of the respondents have encountered racism in the church. 18% of
    the respondents picture Jesus to be black. 92% of the respondents felt
    that black Catholics would not be better served by a separate Catholic
    sect. 51% of the respondents said that the Mass they usually attend is
    celebrated in a style strongly influenced by black culture.

Poll Extracts:

**"IF GIVEN THE CHOICE, I'D RATHER WORSHIP WITH AN
ALL-BLACK CONGREGATION THAN WITH AN INTEGRATED
CONGREGATION."**

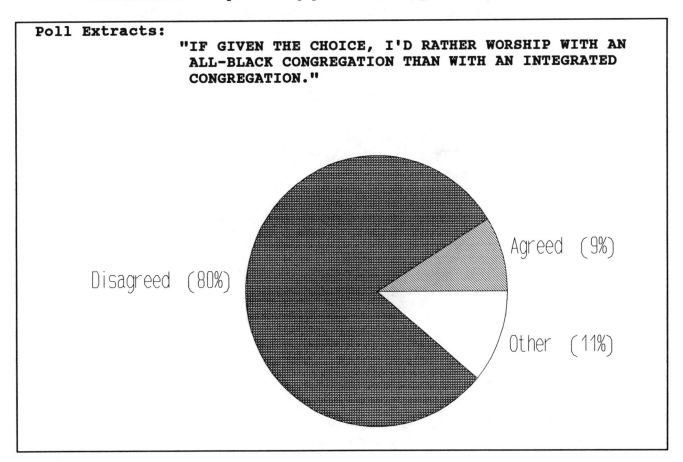

Also in Source: The percentage of respondents who: find more racism in the
    church than in society at large, read the bible, believe preaching is the
    best part about the black liturgy, would encourage their child to be a
    Catholic priest or nun, often ask saints to intercede for them with God,
    and believe that God answers their prayers.

Poll Details: This *U.S. Catholic* survey of black Catholics was stated to be
    "small and informal."

Availability: Published in the *U.S. Catholic*, October 1990 (volume 55,
    number 10), p. 6-15.

BLACK CHURCH EFFECTIVENESS

Description: This poll asked respondents if black churches are more effective
in supporting black causes than 10 years ago.

Results: The majority of respondents thought that black churches are more
effective now.

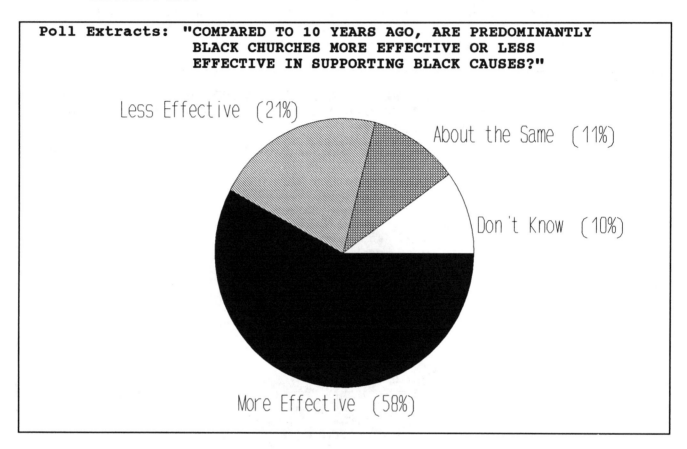

**Poll Extracts: "COMPARED TO 10 YEARS AGO, ARE PREDOMINANTLY
BLACK CHURCHES MORE EFFECTIVE OR LESS
EFFECTIVE IN SUPPORTING BLACK CAUSES?"**

Less Effective (21%)

About the Same (11%)

Don't Know (10%)

More Effective (58%)

Also in Source: Perspectives on the provision of various city services from
the City of Detroit, by all respondents and also by black and white
subgroups. Residents of Detroit who would move out of Detroit if they
could.

Poll Details: This Market Opinion Research/*Detroit Free Press* poll interviewed
700 Detroit area residents during November 28-30, 1990. The margin of
error was 3.8%.

Availability: Published in the *Detroit Free Press*, December 18, 1990,
p. 1A, 8A.

CONFESSION

Description: A study of why the majority of active Catholics seldom, if ever, confess their sins to a priest.

Results: The decline in Catholics participating in confession was attributed to "a less pervasive sense of sin" by U.S. bishops. Parishioners ranked "a less pervasive sense of sin" in seventh place for why confession has declined, along with "general confusion over what is right or wrong." Reconciliation with God through other means -- receiving Communion, personal prayer, an act or contrition, talking with a friend -- was the biggest reason given by lay Catholics for not confessing their sins. Each example was cited by more than 50% of the lay people surveyed.

Poll Extracts:

HOW OFTEN 2,500 PRIESTS CONFESSED SINS:

Weekly 8%
Monthly 27%

HOW OFTEN LAY CATHOLICS IN 3 UNNAMED DIOCESES WENT TO CONFESSION:

Weekly 4%
Monthly 5%

Also in Source: Two older polls on confession were briefly mentioned.

Poll Details: The results of this 1988 survey were released by the Bishops Committee for Pastoral Research and Practices.

Availability: Published in the *Los Angeles Times*, February 24, 1990, p. F16.

FAVORITE HYMNS

Description: Respondents were asked to identify their favorite hymns.

Results: "Amazing Grace" was the favorite hymn of respondents. It was followed
   by "How Great Thou Art," "In the Garden," "The Old Rugged Cross," and "What
   a Friend We Have in Jesus."

Poll Extracts:

PRESIDENT GEORGE BUSH'S FAVORITE HYMN:

"Eternal Father, Strong to Save"

MRS. BUSH'S FAVORITE HYMNS:

"Nearer My God to Thee"
"The Church's One Foundation"
"Amazing Grace"

Poll Details: Responses are from a survey of 10,000 newspaper readers by
   syndicated religion columnist George R. Plagenz.

Availability: Published in *The Atlanta Journal and Constitution*, March 3,
   1990, p. B9.

REGULAR CHURCH ATTENDANCE

Description: Presents the results of a survey of *Ebony* readers concerning a
wide range of topics and personalities. This particular question deals
with regular church attendance.

Results: Almost half of the respondents said they attend church regularly while
almost 30% said they attend occasionally.

Poll Extracts:

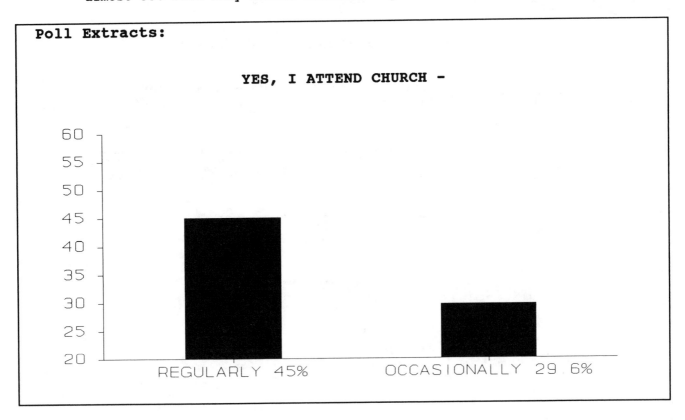

Also in Source: The poll includes a number of questions covering a wide
variety of topics and personalities.

Poll Details: The survey of *Ebony* readers was conducted by Market Facts, Inc.

Availability: Published in *Ebony*, April, 1990 (volume XLV, number 6),
p. 122-124, 126, 127, 128.

RELIGIOUS ACTIVITIES AND ATTITUDES

Description: Presents the results of a survey concerning religious attitudes and activities of Los Angeles County residents.

Results: Over one-third of the respondents said they attend church in a given week and the same figure read the Bible at least once a week.

Poll Extracts:

L.A. COUNTY RELIGIOUS ATTITUDES AND ACTIVITIES

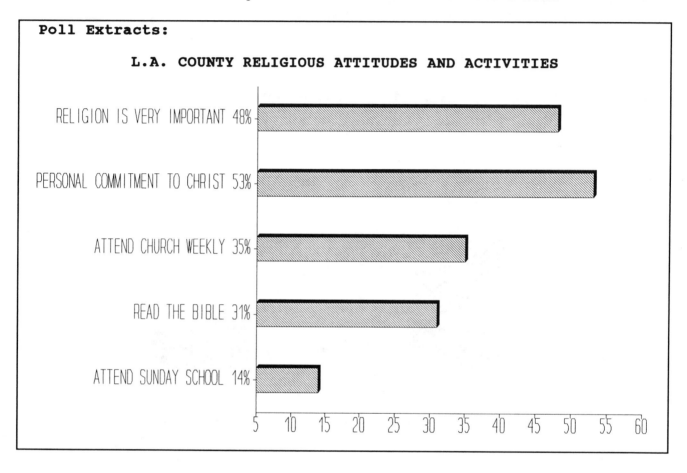

Also in Source: Nationwide, 44% attend church in a given week, 41% read the Bible once a week, 53% say religion is very important to life, and 64% made a "personal commitment" to Christ.

Poll Details: Barna Research Group conducted a telephone survey of 600 Los Angeles residents during the Summer of 1990.

Availability: Published in the *Los Angeles Times*, September 15, 1990, p. F16.

RELIGIOUS BELIEFS AND PRACTICES

Description: The preliminary findings concerning the State of Ohio, in a
regional analysis of religion, are presented in this poll. The Midwest,
the West Coast, the East, and the South, are represented by Ohio,
California, Massachusetts, and North Carolina.

Results: In comparing Ohioans' religious beliefs and practices with other
states, "Ohioans' always come out in or near the middle." Respondents from
California and Massachusetts were more liberal in their beliefs, and less
likely to attend church regularly. Respondents from North Carolina were
more conservative than the other respondents.

Poll Extracts:

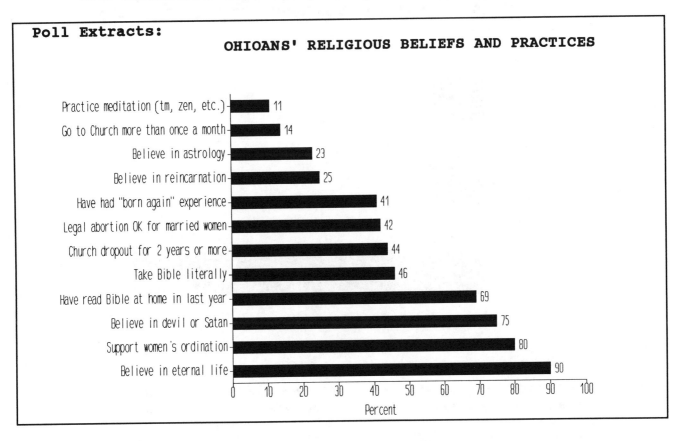

OHIOANS' RELIGIOUS BELIEFS AND PRACTICES

Belief/Practice	Percent
Practice meditation (tm, zen, etc.)	11
Go to Church more than once a month	14
Believe in astrology	23
Believe in reincarnation	25
Have had "born again" experience	41
Legal abortion OK for married women	42
Church dropout for 2 years or more	44
Take Bible literally	46
Have read Bible at home in last year	69
Believe in devil or Satan	75
Support women's ordination	80
Believe in eternal life	90

Also in Source: The percentage of respondents who have had born-again
experiences. A brief discussion detailing how the study was designed to
discover what is currently going on among conservative, moderate, and
liberal Protestants.

Poll Details: Adults between the ages of 24 and 60 were interviewed by
telephone during the fall of 1988. The research was conducted by Dr.
Phillip E. Hammond, chairman of the Department of Religious Studies at the
University of California at Santa Barbara. The results of the survey are
detailed in *Progressions*, a report by the Lilly Endowment. The data
presented in the "Poll Extracts" represents data collected by telephone
interviews with 650 adults ages 24-60, during September through November
1988.

Availability: Published in the *Dayton Daily News*, March 17, 1990, p. 6-C.

RELIGIOUS INFLUENCE IN AMERICA

Description: This poll asked respondents various questions dealing with religion in public life.

Results: 75% of the respondents thought that it was all right for religious leaders such as priests, ministers, and rabbis to speak out on social issues. 54% of the respondents did not think it was right for religious leaders to endorse political candidates.

Poll Extracts: **"DO YOU BELIEVE THAT RELIGION CAN ANSWER ALL OR MOST OF TODAY'S PROBLEMS, OR THAT RELIGION IS LARGELY OLD-FASHIONED AND OUT OF DATE?"**

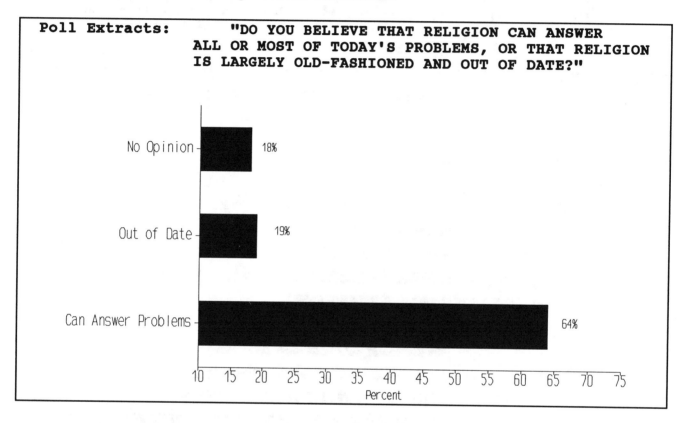

Also in Source: How important the respondents say religion is in their lives, listed by religious affiliation. Responses to poll questions by the following religious subgroups: mainline Protestant, evangelical Protestant, and Catholic. Churches that gained or lost members when membership for 1965 and 1988 is compared. Groups that respondents in 1989 said they would welcome or not welcome as potential neighbors. The percentage of respondents who thought that the Boy Scouts should drop the reference to God from the Boy Scout oath. Whether religion is increasing or decreasing its influence as a whole in American life.

Poll Details: The sources of the poll results were the Associated Press and the Gallup Organization. Results are based on a telephone poll by ICR Survey Research Group. 1,006 adults were interviewed November 16-20, 1990. The margin of error is 3% for the entire sample and larger for subgroups.

Availability: Published in *The Columbus Dispatch,* December 23, 1990, p. 1C, 4C.

SUPERSTITION AND ASTROLOGY

Description: Presents the results of a poll on superstition and astrology.

Results: It was found that Catholics were more superstitious than Protestants, with both groups having about the same faith in astrology. 18% of all the respondents were "very" or "somewhat" superstitious.

Poll Extracts:

RESPONDENTS WHO WERE "VERY" OR "SOMEWHAT" SUPERSTITIOUS

Catholic 23%
Protestant 15%

RESPONDENTS WHO BELIEVED IN ASTROLOGY

Catholic 27%
Protestant 25%

Also in Source: The percentage of church members and non-members who believe in extrasensory perception (ESP).

Poll Details: This nationwide Gallup Organization poll of 1,236 people was conducted in June 1990. The margin of error is 4%.

Availability: Published in *The Dallas Morning News*, October 27, 1990, p. 41A.

FAVORITE RESTAURANT CHAINS

Description: Restaurant chains were rated in a customer survey.

Results: Burgers from Wendy's, and pizza from Pizza Hut, were preferred by people who eat at fast-food restaurants.

Poll Extracts:

WINNERS IN THE VARIOUS CATEGORIES:

Sandwiches....................... Subway

Mexican.......................... Chi-Chi's

Dinner Houses.................... The Olive Garden

Seafood.......................... Red Lobster

Family Dining.................... Bob Evans

Cafeterias....................... Luby's

Chicken.......................... Chick-Fil-A

Steak............................ Stuart Anderson's

Sweets........................... Mrs. Fields

Poll Details: 6,694 households rated more than 100 fast-food chains in *Restaurant & Institutions'* 10th annual customer survey. The chains were rated according to: food quality, value, service, atmosphere, cleanliness, and overall satisfaction.

Availability: Published in *USA Today*, March 14, 1990, p. 4D.

RESTAURANT RESERVATIONS

Description: This poll queried respondents about restaurant reservations.

Results: The majority of customers don't make reservations. "50% of the restaurants where the check for a couple averages $50 and up reported no-shows, as did 30% of the restaurants with checks averaging $30 to $49.99 and 25% of the restaurants with checks of $16 to $29.99."

Poll Extracts:

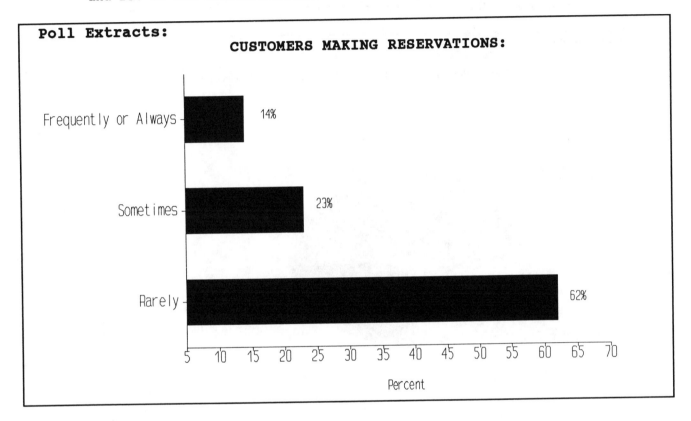

CUSTOMERS MAKING RESERVATIONS:

Poll Details: A Gallup survey for the National Restaurant Association.

Availability: Published in *The Cincinnati Enquirer*, March 8, 1990, p. B-1.

IRA POPULARITY

Description: Presents the results of a survey concerning the level of interest in individual retirement accounts as long-term savings plans.

Results: One-third of the respondents said they have an IRA and approximately half of those respondents made a contribution to the account in 1989. Also, almost 20% of the respondents believe that all of the incentives removed by the Tax Reform Act of 1987 will be restored in 1990.

Poll Extracts:

IRA TAX DEDUCTIONS WILL BE RESTORED:

PARTIAL DEDUCTION 32%

FULL DEDUCTION 19%

NO CHANGE 23%

NO ANSWER 26%

Also in Source: The survey also found that IRAs are most popular among the educated and affluent. Half of the college graduates polled said they have an IRA, double the proportion of those with no more than a high school diploma. Two out of three respondents with an annual income of more than $60,000 said they had an IRA compared with one in eight among those that earn less than $20,000 a year.

Poll Details: The survey was conducted by the Gallup Organization for *Bank Advertising News*. 1,000 adults were contacted in February, 1990.

Availability: Published in *American Banker*, April 2, 1990 (volume CLV, number 63), p. 6.

PLANNING FOR RETIREMENT HOUSING

Description: This survey of Americans age 55 and older asked respondents about their retirement housing plans and needs.

Results: 88% of the respondents never discuss housing needs with anyone. 35% spend no time planning their future housing needs. "86% of the respondents want to live in their present homes and never move." 16% are considering, or would seriously consider, house sharing (15% had tried it).

Poll Extracts:

HOW MUCH TIME AMERICANS (AGE 55 AND OLDER) SPEND PLANNING THEIR FUTURE HOUSING NEEDS.

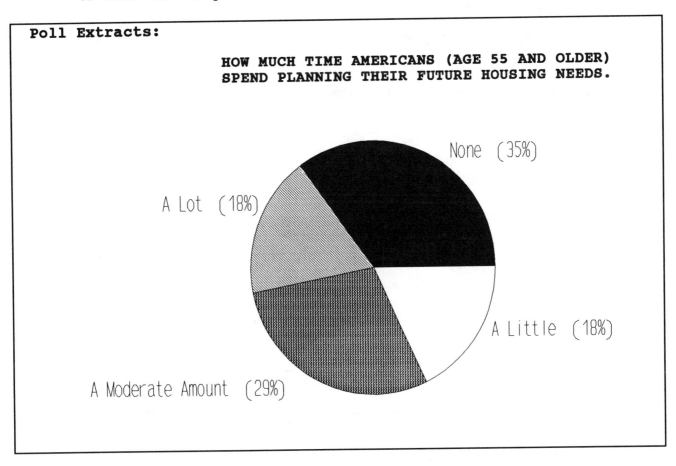

None (35%)

A Lot (18%)

A Little (18%)

A Moderate Amount (29%)

Also in Source: The percentage of respondents who live in single-family detached houses, and the percentage of those houses that have been paid for in full.

Poll Details: The survey involved 1,514 Americans, and was conducted for the American Association of Retired Persons (AARP) by Market Facts Inc.

Availability: Published in *AARP Bulletin*, June 1990 (volume 31, number 6), p. 6.

WORKING AFTER RETIREMENT

Description: A national survey of men and women retirees, at the ages they traditionally drop out of the workforce, to determine if they would consider returning to the workforce.

Results: Almost one-fourth of the retirees are able and willing to go back to work. "There is an available labor pool of older people that is far larger, more qualified, more flexible, and more committed than previously believed."

```
Poll Extracts:


   NON-WORKING RETIREES WHO ARE ABLE AND WILLING TO:


   Go back to work................................... 24%

   Take seasonal jobs................................ 83%

   Work standing up.................................. 60%

   Work alone........................................ 73%

   Commute more than 30 minutes..................... 60%

   Work evenings and weekends....................... 54%
```

Also in Source: The percentage of retirees who were high school or college graduates, compared to their counterparts still in the workforce.

Poll Details: The results are from a 1989 national survey of 1,751 men (aged 55-64) and 1,758 women (aged 50-59), by Louis Harris and Associates, Inc. The results were analyzed for The Commonwealth Fund by ICF Inc., a Washington consulting firm.

Availability: Published in *Washington Post Health*, February 13, 1990 (volume 6, number 7), p. 18.

BANKING BY PHONE

Description: This poll asked consumers if banking by phone would make banking more convenient.

Results: The majority of respondents thought that banking by phone would make banking more convenient.

Poll Extracts:

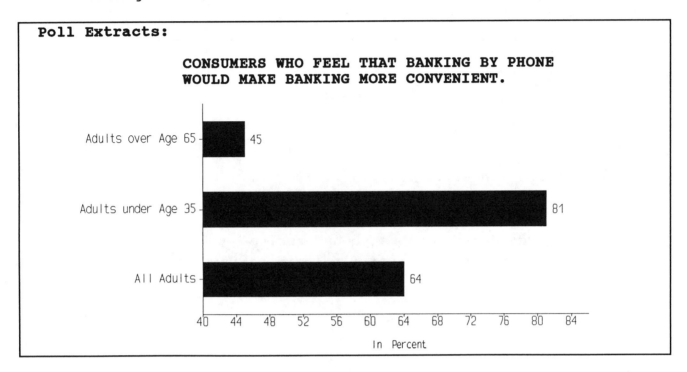

CONSUMERS WHO FEEL THAT BANKING BY PHONE WOULD MAKE BANKING MORE CONVENIENT.

In Percent

Also in Source: A poll of retail banking institutions indicates that 37% offer banking by phone, and 8% plan to introduce it within the next two years. "More and more financial institutions are looking at banking by phone, not only as a customer convenience, but also as a way to cut costs, the study found."

Poll Details: The poll was conducted by ICR Survey Research in April and May, 1990, and commissioned by International Business Machines Corp. 1,001 adults participated in the poll.

Availability: Published in the *Chicago Tribune*, May 25, 1990, section 3, p. 4.

CONSUMER ATTITUDES TOWARD BANKS

Description: Presents the results of a survey concerning consumer attitudes toward bank policies and activities.

Results: More than 60% of the respondents said banks should not get involved in new lines of business. One in three of the respondents said it was a good idea for banks to underwrite life insurance.

Poll Extracts:

TOMORROW'S BANKS

Should banks get involved in new lines of business,
including mutual funds, travel services,
and life insurance?.....................................No...66%

Is it a good idea for banks to underwrite
life insurance?..Yes..33%

Also in Source: Of the two-thirds who think banks should not underwrite life insurance, half said underwriting activities would put both a bank and its depositors at risk. Of those consumers who think banks should underwrite insurance, four out of ten perceive banks as safer institutions than insurance companies due to stricter regulation.

Poll Details: 802 consumers were surveyed by telephone in July 1990, by Synergistics Research Corporation.

Availability: Published in *American Banker*, August 10, 1990 (volume CLV, number 156), p. 8.

GEORGIANS VIEWS ON THE SAVINGS AND LOAN CRISIS

Description: Presents the results of a survey of the residents of the state of Georgia concerning their views of the savings and loan situation.

Results: Over 70% of the respondents feel the savings and loan problem is very serious. Almost 80% feel the bailout will cause higher taxes.

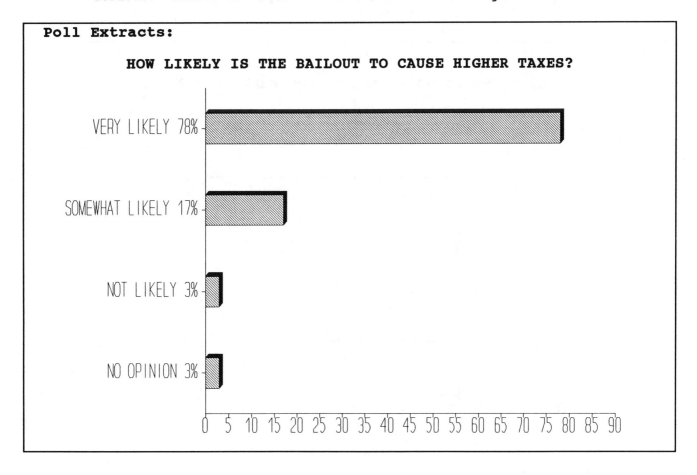

Also in Source: 45% of the respondents blame the savings and loan executives and 24% blame the Reagan Administration for the S&L crisis. 16% blame Congress and 13% said they didn't know who to blame. 46% said they believe defense should be cut.

Poll Details: The results of *The Atlanta Journal and Constitution* poll are based on telephone interviews with 708 adults in Clayton, DeKalb, Fulton, and Gwinett counties. It was conducted August 12-14, 1990. The margin of error is 4%.

Availability: Published in *The Atlanta Journal and Constitution*, August 26, 1990, p. A1, A12.

HOW SAFE IS YOUR BANK?

Description: Presents the results of a survey concerning the stability of the banking system in the United States.

Results: Almost 90% of the respondents ranked their regular commercial banks as somewhat or very safe, with the percent saying their money is safe in a savings and loan nearly 30% lower.

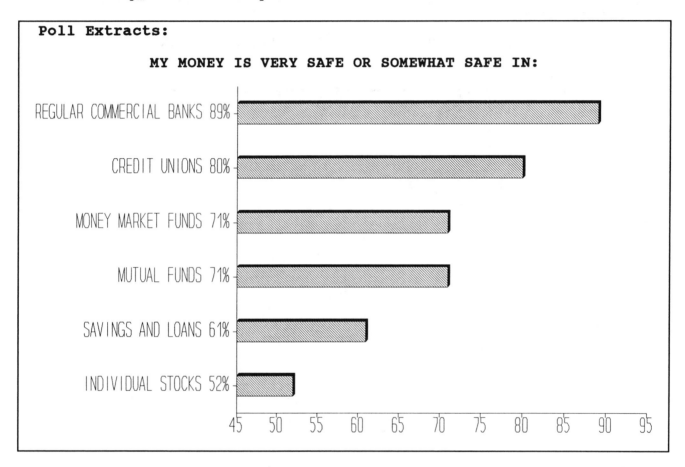

Poll Extracts:

MY MONEY IS VERY SAFE OR SOMEWHAT SAFE IN:

REGULAR COMMERCIAL BANKS 89%
CREDIT UNIONS 80%
MONEY MARKET FUNDS 71%
MUTUAL FUNDS 71%
SAVINGS AND LOANS 61%
INDIVIDUAL STOCKS 52%

45 50 55 60 65 70 75 80 85 90 95

Also in Source: 27% of the respondents expect more regular commercial banks to fail, 23% expect fewer to fail, and 47% said about the same number will fail. 57% think the federal government will have to bail out some regular commercial banks. 57% said FDIC's deposit guarentee should be kept at $100,000.

Poll Details: Louis Harris & Associates surveyed 1,254 adults on June 21-26, 1990 for *Business Week*. Margin of error is 3%.

Availability: Published in *Business Week*, July 16, 1990, number 3169, p. 146-152.

IS BANK COERCION A CONCERN?

Description: Presents the results of a survey concerning consumers' views on the issue of bank coercion. The insurance industry frequently cites the issue of possible coercion as a major reason why banks should not be permitted to invest further in the insurance business.

Results: Over half of the respondents felt that banks should not be allowed to sell all types of insurance such as automobile, health, homeowners, life, etc.

Poll Extracts:

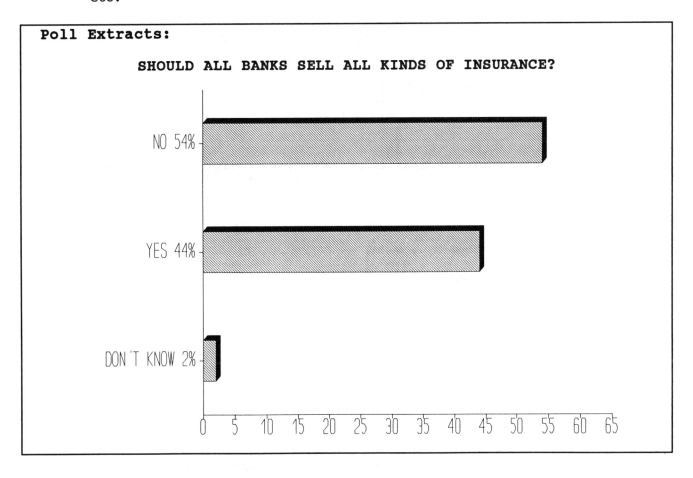

SHOULD ALL BANKS SELL ALL KINDS OF INSURANCE?

Also in Source: 65% of the respondents said they would feel free to shop around if the bank to which they applied for a mortgage or car loan offered to sell them insurance for these purchases. 13% would welcome it as a convenience, 11% would worry that the bank would charge higher rates for the insurance, and 9% would feel obligated to buy from them because if they didn't, the loan might be rejected.

Poll Details: 1,000 consumers were contacted by the Gallup Organization for *Best's Review*. The margin of error is plus or minus 3%.

Availability: Published in *Best's Review Property/Casualty/Insurance Edition*, September, 1990 (volume 91, number 5), p. 12.

PARTY POLITICS AND THE S&L CRISIS

Description: Presents the results of a survey concerning the relationship
between the two political parties and the savings and loan situation.

Results: Almost 40% of the respondents feel the Republicans are more
responsible for the savings and loan problems compared to less than 20% who
blame the Democrats.

Poll Extracts:

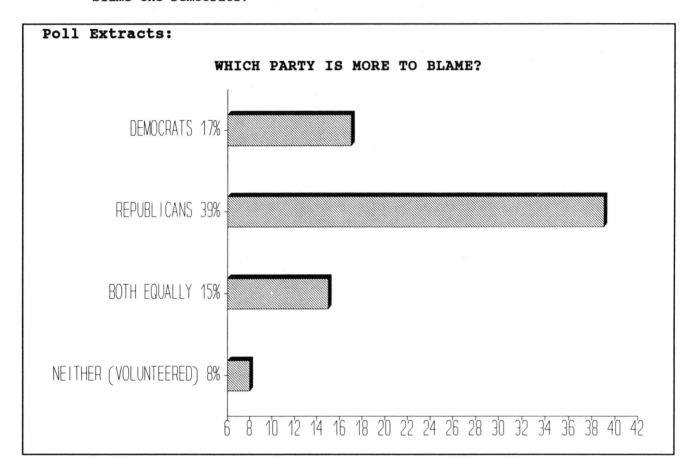

WHICH PARTY IS MORE TO BLAME?

Also in Source: 79% of the respondents favor appointing a special prosecutor
to investigate the industry; 60% favor doubling the number of auditors
examining the thrifts' books. 43% favor getting rid of the S&Ls entirely
by forcing them to become commercial banks. 30% trust the Democrats more
and 31% trust the Republicans more to handle the problem. 38% of the
respondents approve of President Bush's handling of the situation, while
37% disapprove.

Poll Details: *The Wall Street Journal*/NBC News poll was based on a nationwide
telephone survey of 1,555 registered voters conducted July 6-11, 1990, by
Peter Hart and Robert Teeter.

Availability: Published in *The Wall Street Journal*, July 13, 1990, p. A1, A4.

POSTAL RATES AND SERVICE

Description: This poll queried respondents about the U.S. postal service and the proposed price increase of a first class stamp, from 25 to 30 cents, by early 1991.

Results: 82% of respondents are satisfied with the service provided by the U.S. Postal Service. 62% of respondents feel that the proposed 5 cent increase is unjustified. 86% would prefer the cost for junk mail to increase, instead of first class stamps.

Poll Extracts:

RESPONDENTS SAID THAT IF THE PRICE OF A STAMP INCREASED TO 30 CENTS:

Service would not change 53%

Service would get worse anyway 35%

Also in Source: The percentage of respondents who would, and wouldn't, pay more than 30 cents to improve service. The percentage of respondents who would send fewer letters if the price of stamps increased to 40 cents, and 50 cents. The percentage of respondents who felt that they had been inconvenienced in the last year because their mail was delivered late.

Poll Details: This *USA Today* telephone poll of 823 respondents was conducted on March 7-8, 1990, by the Gordon S. Black Corporation. The poll has a 3.5% sampling error.

Availability: Published in *USA Today*, March 9-11, 1990, p. 1A.

SAVINGS AND LOAN WORRIES

Description: Presents the results of a survey concerning the savings and loan crisis.

Results: Two-thirds of the respondents call the S&L crisis very serious. More than 70% don't expect the government to recover the lost money.

Poll Extracts:

AN APPARENT LACK OF CONFIDENCE:

Is the S&L situation very serious?....................Yes...66%

Will the government recover the lost money?..........No....73%

Will the government do a good job
solving the crisis?..................................No....71%

Will the criminals be prosecuted?....................No....62%

Will the way the crisis is handled affect
the way you vote in congressional and
national elections?..................................Yes...53%

Also in Source: A general discussion of the savings and loan situation in included in the article.

Poll Details: The Gordon S. Black Corporation polled 631 adults by telephone for *USA Today*. The poll's margin of error is 4%.

Availability: Published in *USA Today*, July 13-15, 1990, p. 1A.

SERVICES FOR BUSINESS TRAVELERS

Description: Respondents were asked about their expectations from airline
companies. Respondents were also asked which companies provide what they
expect.

Results: The most important services airline companies provide business
travelers are: on-time arrival, prompt baggage delivery, and efficient
check-in. Delta Airlines received the highest on-time satisfaction rating,
and the highest overall satisfaction rating.

Poll Extracts:

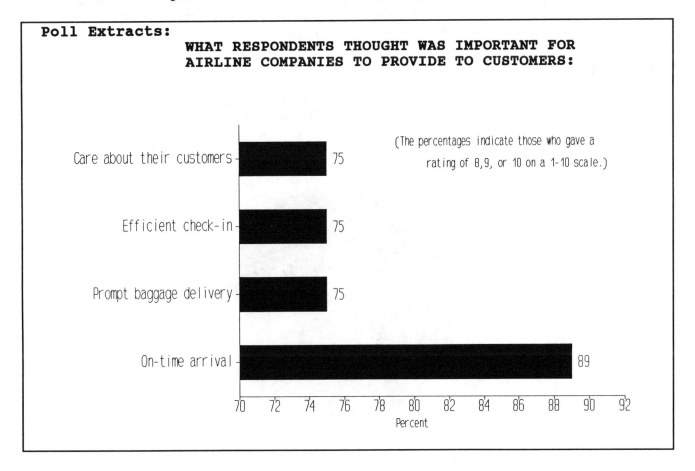

Also in Source: Respondents' expectations from hotel and car rental
companies. Hotel and car rental companies ranking first in overall
customer satisfaction. Respondents' perception of airline, hotel, and car
rental company personnel in demonstrating their personal care about
customers.

Poll Details: This quarterly Executive Travel Index study is from Opinion
Research Corp., Princeton, New Jersey. The study was conducted with 400
executives from companies listed in the Fortune 500 and Fortune Service 500
editions, and in Dun & Bradstreet's *Million Dollar Directory*. The
respondents traveled on business an estimated 45 days in the past year,
averaging 34 nights in hotels, 34 trips on commercial airlines, and 20 days
with a rented car.

Availability: Published in *Travel Weekly*, May 28, 1990, p. 29-30.

SHOPPERS' THOUGHTS ABOUT MANUFACTURERS

Description: Consumers were surveyed on their attitudes towards pricing and
their knowledge of prices. "Shoppers were asked where they shopped, how
they felt about various issues concerning price, and then were given a list
of 25 common grocery items and were asked to give the prices for any items
they regularly purchased."

Results: The majority of the shoppers surveyed agreed that manufacturers are
bringing too many new products into the marketplace that aren't really new
or necessary. Shoppers also thought that retailers and manufacturers are
making too much money on the grocery bill.

Poll Extracts:

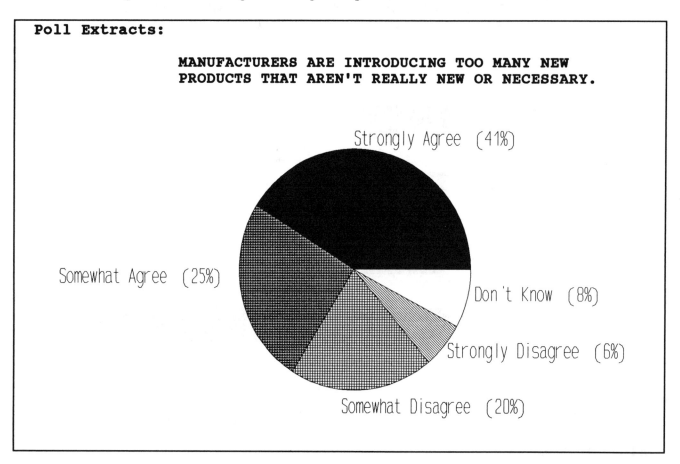

**MANUFACTURERS ARE INTRODUCING TOO MANY NEW
PRODUCTS THAT AREN'T REALLY NEW OR NECESSARY.**

Strongly Agree (41%)

Somewhat Agree (25%)

Don't Know (8%)

Strongly Disagree (6%)

Somewhat Disagree (20%)

Also in Source: Questions relating to what shoppers knew about the prices
they paid, and the importance of price to shopping behavior.

Poll Details: *Supermarket Business* sponsored this market study of Birmingham,
Alabama and Phoenix, Arizona. These two cities were chosen because one is
a fairly stable market, where the "Everyday Low Prices" concept is well
established, and the other is rather unstable with only a few stores
offering "Everyday Low Prices." The survey was conducted by two local
independent market research firms, who contacted the primary shopper in a
total of 480 households by telephone.

Availability: Published in *Supermarket Business*, June 1990 (volume 45,
number 6), p. 15, 19, 21.

WHO'S TO BLAME FOR THE THRIFTS CRISIS?

Description: Presents the results of a survey concerning the handling of the savings and loan crisis.

Results: Over 40% of the respondents blame the Reagan Administration for the S&L crisis, while less than 10% blame the Bush Administration.

Poll Extracts:

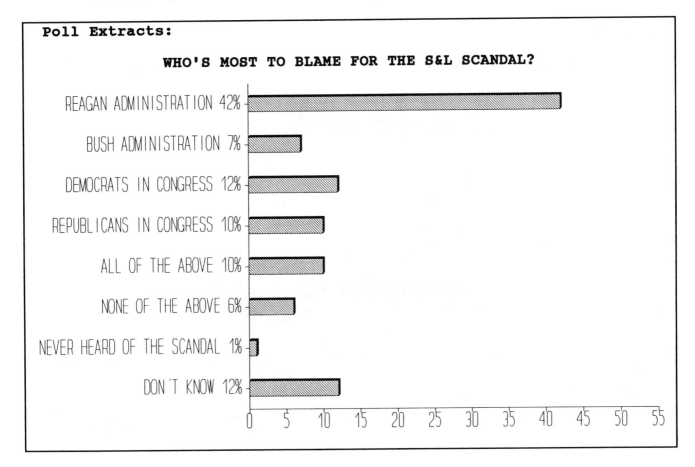

WHO'S MOST TO BLAME FOR THE S&L SCANDAL?

Also in Source: 72% of the respondents have a fair amount or not much confidence at all in this country's savings and loan institutions. 52% are fairly or very unsure that the federal insurance system will be able to pay people their money if their savings and loan institution goes out of business. 29% identify bad management as the most important cause of the scandal. 74% said Neil Bush's business affairs have nothing to do with his father's policies.

Poll Details: Results are based on a *Washington Post*-ABC News telephone survey of 1,509 randomly selected adults nationwide conducted on July 19-24, 1990. Margin of sampling error for the overall results is plus or minus 3%.

Availability: Published in *The Washington Post*, July 27, 1990, p. F1, F4.

SEXUAL HONESTY

Description: Presents the results of a survey concerning the willingness of individuals to disclose a single episode of sexual infidelity.

Results: 22% of male respondents and 35% of female respondents said they would disclose a single episode of sexual infidelity.

Poll Extracts:

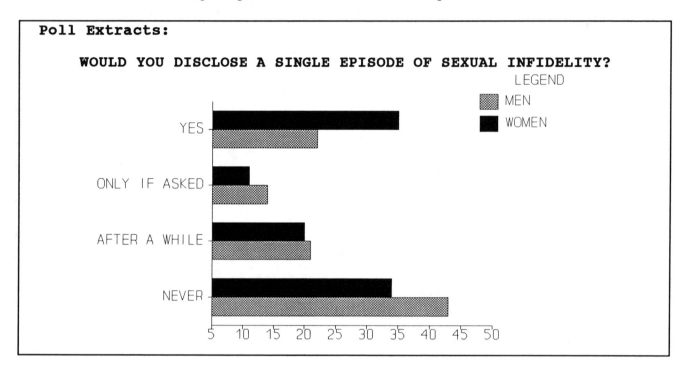

WOULD YOU DISCLOSE A SINGLE EPISODE OF SEXUAL INFIDELITY?

LEGEND
MEN
WOMEN

Also in Source: The article also includes other questions concerning the level of honesty involving past sexual experience. For example, 34% of the male respondents had lied in order to have sex. 10% of the female respondents had lied in order to have sex.

Poll Details: The results are based on a survey of 665 18-to-25-year-old students attending colleges in southern California. They completed 18-page questionnaires assessing sexual behavior.

Availability: Published in *The New England Journal of Medicine*, March 15, 1990, (volume 322, number 11) p. 774.

AMERICA'S RACE RELATIONS

Description: Presents the results of a survey of the state of race relations
in the United States.

Results: Approximately one-third of both black and white respondents feel that
whites would have a better chance at being hired when a black person and
white person of equal intelligence and skill apply for the same kind of
job.

Poll Extracts:

GIVEN EQUAL CANDIDATES, WHITES HAVE A BETTER CHANCE OF BEING HIRED:

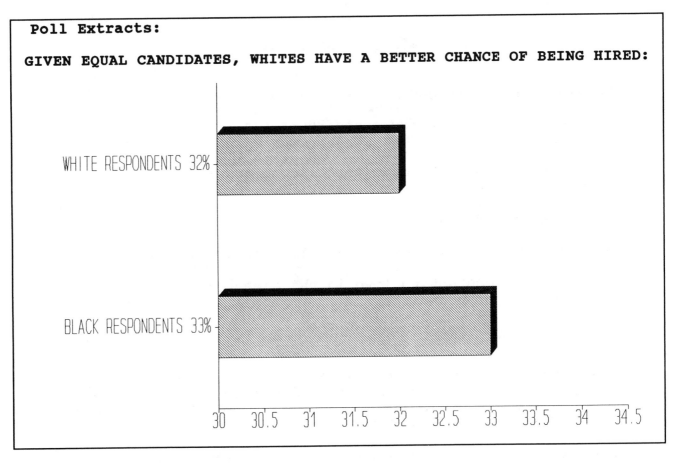

WHITE RESPONDENTS 32%

BLACK RESPONDENTS 33%

30   30.5   31   31.5   32   32.5   33   33.5   34   34.5

Also in Source: 50% of black respondents and 68% of white respondents think
the conditions for black people in this country with regard to housing,
education, job opportunities, social acceptence by whites, etc. are
excellent or good. 29% of the respondents say Hispanics have taken away
jobs from Americans and 50% say they have added to the welfare rolls.

Poll Details: The poll was conducted by the Roper Organization.

Availability: Published in *The Christian Science Monitor*, July 13, 1990
(volume 82, number 159), p. 18.

AMERICA'S THOUGHTS AND FEELINGS

Description: Presents the results of a wide-ranging survey concerning a number of topics and issues.

Results: Among the survey results, 40% of the respondents think people shouldn't chew gum in public and almost 70% support pollution standards "even if it means shutting down some factories."

Poll Extracts:

VIEWS OF AMERICANS

Should people chew gum in public?..................No....40%

Do you support pollution standards "even
if it means shutting down some factories?".........Yes...69%

Should police use whatever force is necessary
to maintain law and order?.........................Yes...60%

Do men prefer the clean-shaven look on men?........Yes...50%

Do women prefer the clean-shaven look on men?......Yes...55%

Would you be content to live in the same town
for the rest of your life?.........................Yes.73.5%

Also in Source: The percentage of people who say that "religion is an important part of my life" has declined steadily since 1981. The percentage of people who say couples should live together before marriage has risen steadily since 1981.

Poll Details: This annual *Life Style Study* is conducted by DDB Needham. Once a year 4,000 adults are asked up to 1,000 questions via the mail. The sample is constructed to eliminate the very poor and the very rich. The survey has a maximum margin of error of 1.5%.

Availability: Published in *Advertising Age*, September 24, 1990 (volume 61, number 39), p. 24, 25.

ATTITUDES TOWARD LAWYERS

Description: This survey of Washington, D.C. area residents asked them about
their attitudes toward lawyers.

Results: 58% of the respondents believed that lawyers are overpaid for what
they do. 48% of the respondents thought that lawyers are usually most
interested in making money for themselves rather than upholding our legal
system or helping their clients. 30% of the respondents thought that they
tended to deal more cautiously with lawyers in their business and personal
life than they deal with others. After forming a trust index for people in
various occupations, lawyers were rated above cab drivers, politicians, and
car salesmen, but below teachers, dentists, police, physicians, government
workers, plumbers, and journalists.

Poll Extracts:

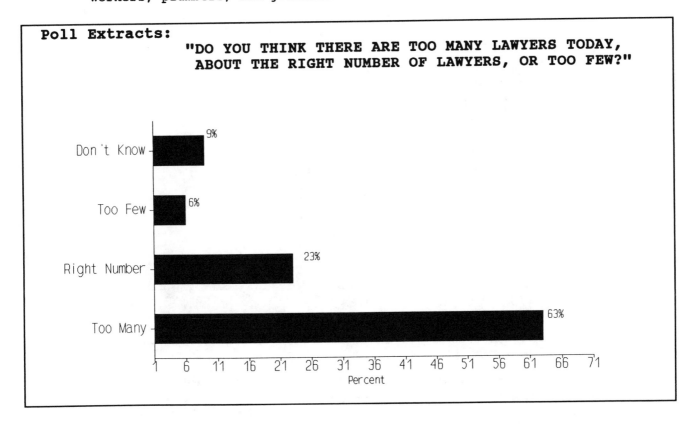

"DO YOU THINK THERE ARE TOO MANY LAWYERS TODAY,
ABOUT THE RIGHT NUMBER OF LAWYERS, OR TOO FEW?"

Also in Source: The percentage of respondents who thought: there are too
many lawsuits, lawyers encourage people to sue so they can make more money,
juries award too much money in lawsuits, and there would be fewer lawsuits
if there were fewer lawyers.

Poll Details: 400 Washington, D.C. area residents were randomly selected and
interviewed by telephone during September 1990. The survey was conducted
by Mellman & Lazarus for *The Washingtonian*. The margin of error is 5%.
Due to rounding, the percentages may not total 100.

Availability: Published in *The Washingtonian*, November 1990 (volume 26,
number 2), p. 136-137.

THE COST OF A CHILD'S HEALTH

Description: Presents the results of a survey concerning the willingness of adults to pay more taxes to improve health care for poor children.

Results: Almost 60% of the respondents would agree to a $100 annual tax increase to fund health care for poor children.

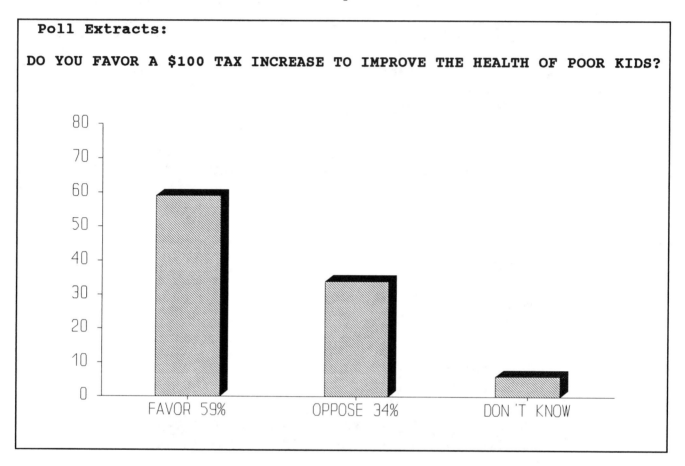

Poll Extracts:

DO YOU FAVOR A $100 TAX INCREASE TO IMPROVE THE HEALTH OF POOR KIDS?

Also in Source: 60% of the respondents said "the situation for children in America" has grown worse over the past five years. 65% of the Democrats and 51% of the Republicans polled approve of the tax increase to aid poor children. 62% of the respondents from the south approve of the tax.

Poll Details: The nationwide poll of 1,000 adults in June, 1990 was conducted by Penn & Schoen Associates Inc. for the National Association of Children's Hospitals.

Availability: Published in *The Atlanta Journal and Constitution*, July 20, 1990, p. A-3.

FEAR OF HOMELESSNESS

Description: This poll queried heads of households about homelessness and its solutions.

Results: The majority of respondents are sympathetic toward the homeless and fear that the loss of their jobs, a serious illness, or injury could easily turn them into homeless persons.

Poll Extracts:

RESPONDENTS WHO FEEL:

Housing is a basic human right 86%

They could easily become homeless 57%

The lack of affordable housing is to blame
for much of the homeless problem 79%

They would be willing to pay an additional
$100 in taxes to help find permanent
solutions to homelessness 58%

Also in Source: The Massachusetts' rent subsidy program, central to that state's homelessness prevention policy, was proposed for elimination in the next fiscal year's budget.

Poll Details: This survey was commissioned by the Boston Foundation on behalf of the Coalition for the Homeless and other advocacy groups. The survey was conducted in late April 1990, and 259 randomly selected heads of households were interviewed.

Availability: Published in *The Boston Globe*, June 20, 1990, p. 26.

A FEMALE PRESIDENT

Description: Presents the results of a survey concerning womens' views on the issue of a female seeking and being elected president of the United States.

Results: Elizabeth Dole is the favorite among possible female presidential candidates.

Poll Extracts:

WHO WOULD YOU LIKE TO SEE AS THE FIRST WOMAN PRESIDENT?

1. Elizabeth Dole

2. Patricia Shroeder

3. Nancy Kassebaum

4. Ann Richards

5. Dianne Feinstein

6. Kay Orr

Also in Source: 35% of the respondents would prefer voting for a woman for president of the United States; 25% would prefer voting for a man. 78% believe that an election should be decided on an individual basis and not because it is an important social goal to have women and minorities in office. 52% of the respondents would prefer having a woman deciding economic and tax policy. Fewer than 10% wanted a man making the final decision on abortion.

Poll Details: 6,988 women took part in the *McCall's* survey. This detailed analysis is based on 5,284 early returns received during the first three weeks after publication of the June issue.

Availability: Published in *McCall's*, September 1990 (volume CXII, number 12), p. 89, 91, 92.

GIVING TO CHARITY

Description: Respondents were queried about contributing time and money to charities.

Results: "Nearly 90% of respondents say they donate time or money or both to causes ranging from local homeless shelters, churches and schools to the environment." "Westerners are the least likely to feel an obligation to help those less fortunate than themselves, the most likely to turn down a panhandler, and the most likely to refuse to give to a charitable organization (they were tied with Southerners on that score)." More men than women have turned down a panhandler because the panhandler "didn't deserve it." People aged 35-54 felt more obligated to give time or money than did younger or older aged respondents.

Poll Extracts:

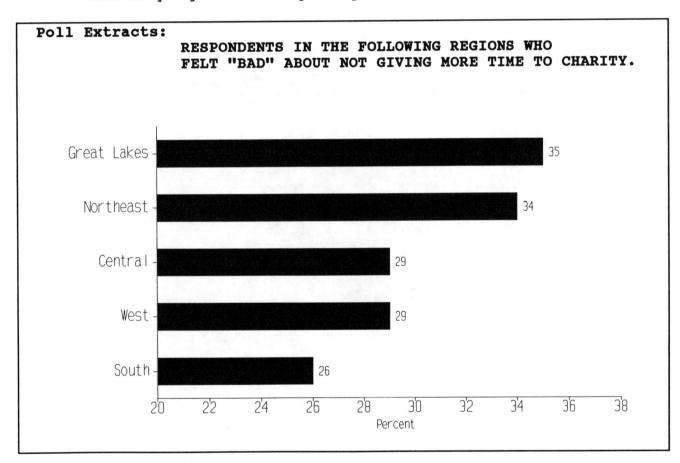

RESPONDENTS IN THE FOLLOWING REGIONS WHO
FELT "BAD" ABOUT NOT GIVING MORE TIME TO CHARITY.

Also in Source: The percentage of women and men who do something special for charity at the holidays. "Individuals with incomes under $10,000 give more than 5% to charity. Those who make more than $100,000 give about 2%."

Poll Details: This *USA WEEKEND* poll was conducted by Gordon S. Black Corp. 801 adults were interviewed by telephone across the United States. The margin of error is 3.5%.

Availability: Published in *USA WEEKEND*, December 21-23, 1990, p. 4-5.

GOALS OF YOUNG MEN AND YOUNG WOMEN

Description: This poll queried male and female respondents about their most important goals and whether they thought it was easier to be a man or woman.

Results: More of the male respondents thought that their most important goal was a successful career. More of the female respondents thought that their most important goal was a happy marriage. The majority of both male and female respondents thought that it was easier to be a man than a woman.

Poll Extracts:

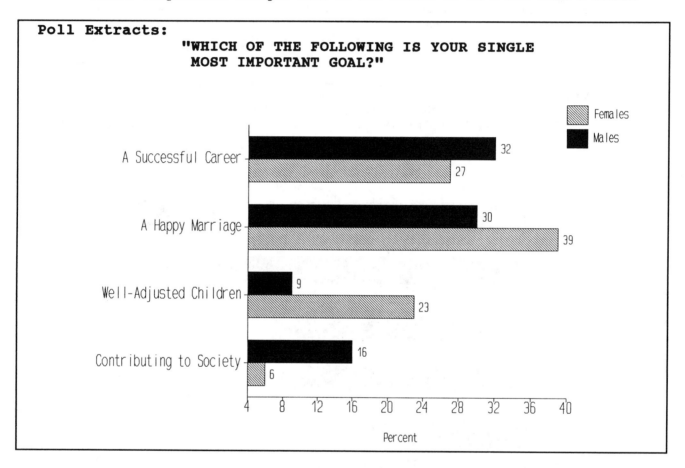

"WHICH OF THE FOLLOWING IS YOUR SINGLE MOST IMPORTANT GOAL?"

Also in Source: Attitudes toward marriage and raising a child.

Poll Details: This poll was conducted by Yankelovich Clancy Shulman for *Time* magazine. 505 Americans aged 18-24 were polled during September 5-11, 1990. The margin of error is 4.5%.

Availability: Published in *Time*, Fall 1990 (volume 136, number 19), p. 14.

HAVE RACE RELATIONS IMPROVED?

Description: Presents the results of a survey concerning the present state of
race relations in the state of Michigan.

Results: Almost 50% of the respondents feel race relations have stayed the same
over the past five years. Almost 30% said relations between the races have
improved over that time period.

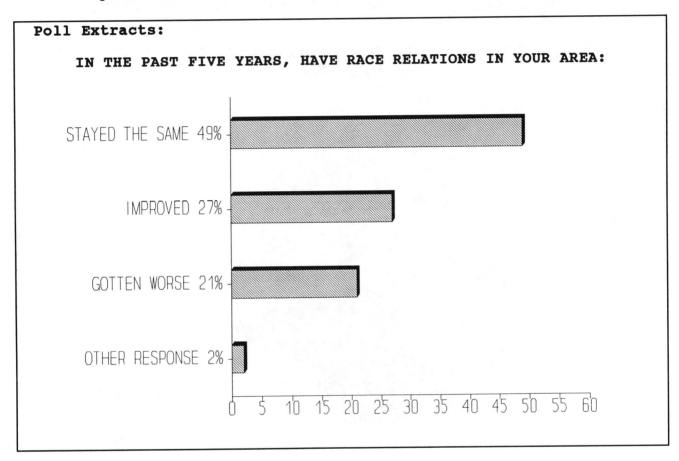

Poll Extracts:

IN THE PAST FIVE YEARS, HAVE RACE RELATIONS IN YOUR AREA:

STAYED THE SAME 49%

IMPROVED 27%

GOTTEN WORSE 21%

OTHER RESPONSE 2%

0 5 10 15 20 25 30 35 40 45 50 55 60

Also in Source: 51% of white respondents and 38% of black respondents feel
race relations have stayed the same over the past five years. 18% of white
respondents and 39% of black respondents think race relations have
worsened. 27% of white respondents and 22% of black respondents say
relations between the races have improved over the past years.

Poll Details: The *Detroit Free Press*-WXYZ-TV survey was conducted by Market
Opinion Research in a telephone survey taken September 21-23, 1990. The
margin of error is plus or minus 3.5%. 800 registered Michigan voters were
polled.

Availability: Published in *The Detroit News and Fress Press*, September 29,
1990, p. 1A, 5A.

THE HOMELESS

Description: This survey asked questions about daily life that the U.S. Census
did not ask.

Results: When telephoning someone, 54% of the respondents were more aggravated
by hearing the phone ring endlessly, while the remainder of the respondents
were more aggravated by getting the answering machine. The results did not
seem to establish any trends, as each question seemed to be independent of
each of the other questions.

Poll Extracts: **HOW MANY DIFFERENT HOMELESS PEOPLE DO
YOU PASS IN A WEEK?**

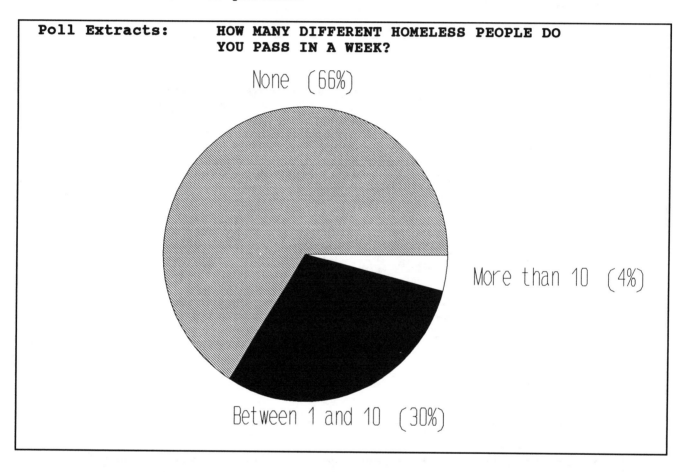

Also in Source: The number of shoes that people own/need, how many times
respondents had called their mothers that week, respondents who own a
microwave, how many frozen dinners are in the respondent's freezer, the
amount of the work-week that is fun, methods of getting out of bed, what do
respondents expect to earn in the year 2000, how many rolls of toilet paper
have been stashed away by the respondent, and how many plants live with the
respondents.

Poll Details: The answers were from 38,465 readers of *USA WEEKEND.*

Availability: Published in *USA WEEKEND,* March 16-18, 1990, p. 4, 5.

THE HOMELESS AND THE BUSH ADMINISTRATION

Description: The poll measured feelings toward the Bush Administration's programs to help the homeless.

Results: The majority of respondents felt that President Bush's Administration had not done enough for the homeless.

Poll Extracts:
DO YOU THINK THE BUSH ADMINISTRATION HAS DONE ALL IT SHOULD TO HELP THE HOMELESS, OR DO YOU THINK IT HAS NOT SHOWN ENOUGH CONCERN?

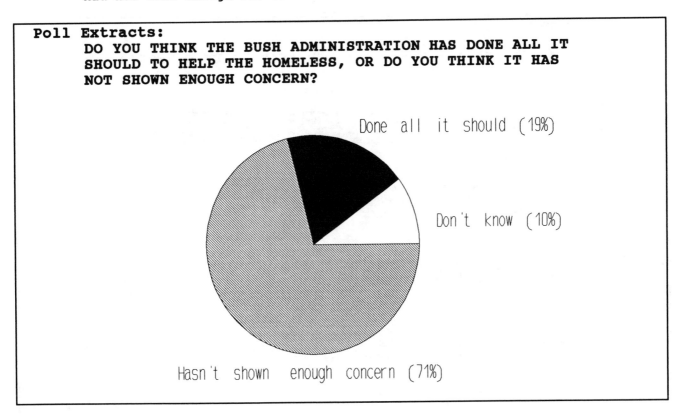

Done all it should (19%)

Don't know (10%)

Hasn't shown enough concern (71%)

Also in Source: A timeline chart based on 14 *New York Times*/CBS News Polls and one *New York Times* poll, which shows the percentage of adults who believe homelessness is the most important problem facing the country, from April 1986 through January 1990.

Poll Details: This *New York Times*/CBS News Poll was conducted January 13-15, 1990, with 1,557 adults.

Availability: Published in *The New York Times*, January 28, 1990, p. 1, 22.

HOW MUCH IS ENOUGH?

Description: Presents the results of a survey measuring the desired income
levels of different age groups of Americans.

Results: Over 60% of the respondents age 18 through 49 require a household
income of at least $40,000.

Poll Extracts:

YES, I NEED AT LEAST $40,000 PER YEAR TO BE COMFORTABLE:

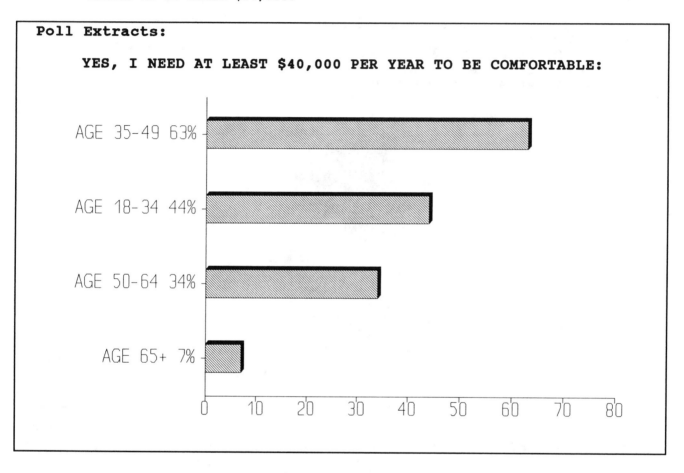

Also in Source: On the average, each age group says an additional $10,000 per
year would satisfy their needs.

Poll Details: This *Detroit Free Press*-WXYZ poll of 803 registered Michigan
voters was conducted by Market Opinion Research during August, 1990.

Availability: Published in the *Detroit Free Press*, August 9, 1990, p. 1H, 4H.

I WANNA BE RICH

Description: Presents the results of a survey concerning attitudes toward accumulated personal wealth.

Results: Almost 60% of the respondents said if they had a choice they would like to be rich.

Poll Extracts:

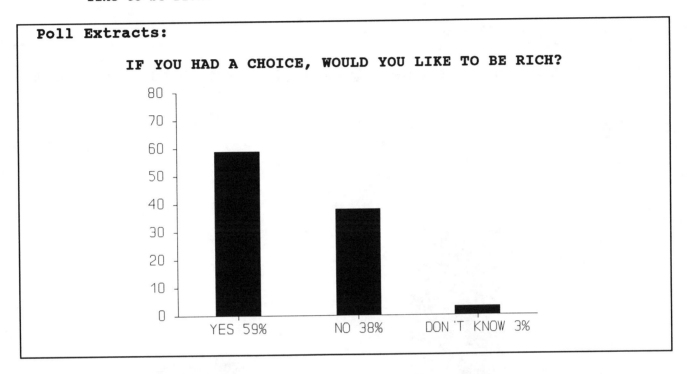

IF YOU HAD A CHOICE, WOULD YOU LIKE TO BE RICH?

YES 59%   NO 38%   DON'T KNOW 3%

Also in Source: Half of all Americans believe one can be rich with an income lower than $95,000 a year while the other half thinks an income greater than $95,000 is needed to be rich. 67% of the respondents feel that it is not very likely or not at all likely that they will ever be rich. 9% said it is very likely and 23% said somewhat likely. 42% said the rich did a fair job in terms of contributing back to society. 25% of the respondents said they would be very willing to work between 12 and 14 hours a day to be rich. 8% said they would be very willing to work at a job they hated, 1% would be very willing to do something illegal, 2% said they would be very willing to marry a rich person they did not love, and 4% would be very willing to not see much of the family to become rich.

Poll Details: The results are based on telephone interviews of a randomly selected sample of 1,255 adults, 18 or older, conducted May 17-20, 1990. The margin of error is plus or minus 4%.

Availability: Published in the *Dayton Daily News*, July 1, 1990, p. 1-E, 2-E.

THE IDEAL MATE

Description: Presents the results of a survey concerning desired traits and characteristics to be found in respondents' mates.

Results: 80% of the male respondents would prefer their mate have great sexual skill than great wealth, while 58% of the female respondents share that same opinion.

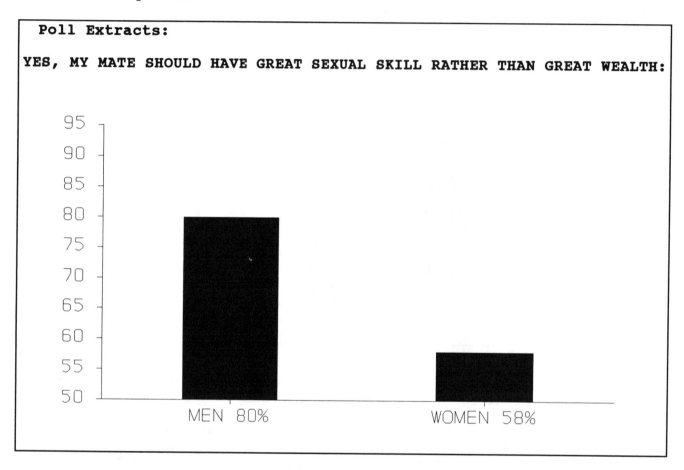

Poll Extracts:

YES, MY MATE SHOULD HAVE GREAT SEXUAL SKILL RATHER THAN GREAT WEALTH:

Also in Source: 66% said they would rather see their ideal mate in an exercise bike than an easy chair. 52% said their ideal mate would want to attend plays and concerts. 75% would dress their mate in classic clothes. 78% of women and 69% of men want a mate who loves to shop. 86% of women want someone who says "I love you" daily; 73% of men agree. 63% say an ideal mate should have many friends of both sexes.

Poll Details: 10,935 people completed a mail-in survey printed in *USA Weekend*. 79% of the respondents were women.

Availability: Published in *USA Weekend*, July 13-15, 1990, p. 4, 5.

IMPRESSIONS OF AMERICAN AND JAPANESE SOCIETY

Description: This poll examined American impressions of American society and
Japanese society.

Results: 46% of the U.S. registered voters surveyed believe that the U.S. is
more intolerant of other races than is Japan. 51% of Americans think that
Japanese society has more of a long-term perspective than does the U.S.
Americans think that the U.S. is more devoted to democracy (89%), and free
speech (93%). 70% of Americans think that the U.S. is more honest in
dealing with others and others' countries.

Poll Extracts:

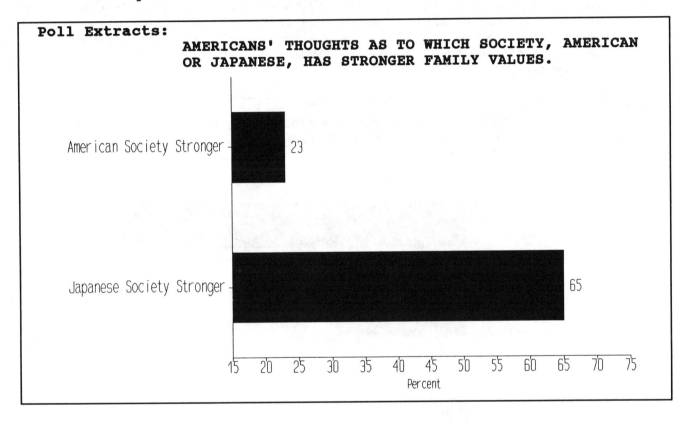

AMERICANS' THOUGHTS AS TO WHICH SOCIETY, AMERICAN
OR JAPANESE, HAS STRONGER FAMILY VALUES.

Also in Source: A second related poll which was conducted in Japan for *The
Wall Street Journal* by Nippon Research. This second poll examined Japanese
impressions of Japanese society and American society.

Poll Details: This poll was conducted for *The Wall Street Journal* and NBC by
political pollsters Peter Hart and Robert Teeter.

Availability: Published in *The Wall Street Journal*, June 15, 1990, p. A6.

IS AMERICA THE BEST?

Description: Americans were polled on the United States position as world
leader.

Results: 54% of the respondents thought that it was important for the U.S. to
be the best country in the world, even if it requires a personal sacrifice.
Almost half of the respondents thought that the U.S. would maintain its
position as world leader over the next few decades. Respondents currently
felt that when comparing the U.S., Japan, and Western Europe, the U.S. was
the best country in the following areas: quality of life -- 87%, popular
culture -- 84%, individual opportunity to succeed -- 83%, political systems
and institutions -- 82%, and assuming a leadership position in the
international arena --80%. 52% of Americans said that Japan was the leader
in scientific and technological achievements, and also in educating its
citizens.

Poll Extracts:

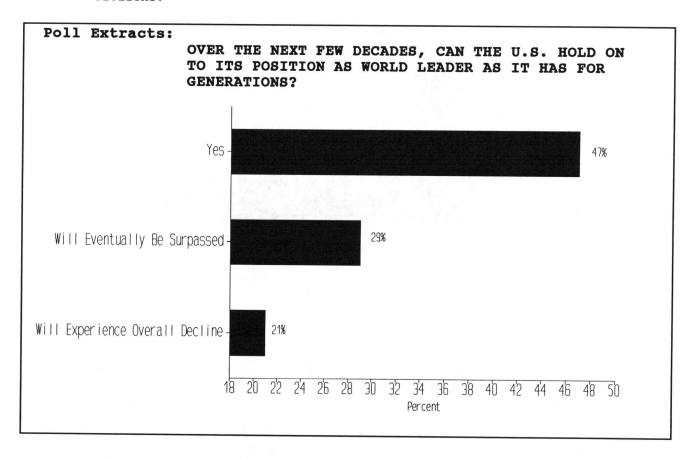

OVER THE NEXT FEW DECADES, CAN THE U.S. HOLD ON
TO ITS POSITION AS WORLD LEADER AS IT HAS FOR
GENERATIONS?

Also in Source: Other areas in which respondents rated the U.S. highest, when
compared to Japan and Western Europe. Areas in which by 2010 the U.S. is
expected to be the leader, when compared to Japan and Western Europe.

Poll Details: This national public opinion poll was commissioned by *Parents*
magazine.

Availability: Published in *Parents,* November 1990 (volume 65, number 11),
p. 30.

LOS ANGELES QUALITY OF LIFE

Description: Presents the results of a survey concerning the quality of life in Los Angeles, California.

Results: Only one-third of the respondents strongly felt it is easy to meet people and make friends in Los Angeles County.

Poll Extracts:

LOS ANGELES RESIDENTS SPEAK:

Is it easy to meet people and make friends?...........Yes...33%

Do you feel a part of your community?................Yes...40%

Will you move in the next three years?...............Yes...42%

Are there enough services for the elderly?...........Yes...19%

Is Los Angeles a good place to raise children?.......Yes...14%

Also in Source: A discussion of the county's religious attitudes and activities is also included in the article.

Poll Details: Barna Research Group surveyed 600 adults during the Summer of 1990.

Availability: Published in the *Los Angeles Times*, September 15, 1990.

MAKING RACIAL REMARKS

Description: This survey asked respondents about racial remarks and race
relations in Michigan.

Results: 60% of the respondents knew someone personally who had made "racial
remarks" that they wouldn't repeat if members of that race were present.
When respondents were asked if they had ever made such "racial remarks,"
only 30% said that they had made such remarks. 39% of the blacks and 18%
of the whites thought that race relations have gotten worse in the past
five years in their area.

Poll Extracts:

DURING THE PAST FIVE YEARS, RACE RELATIONS IN YOUR AREA HAVE:

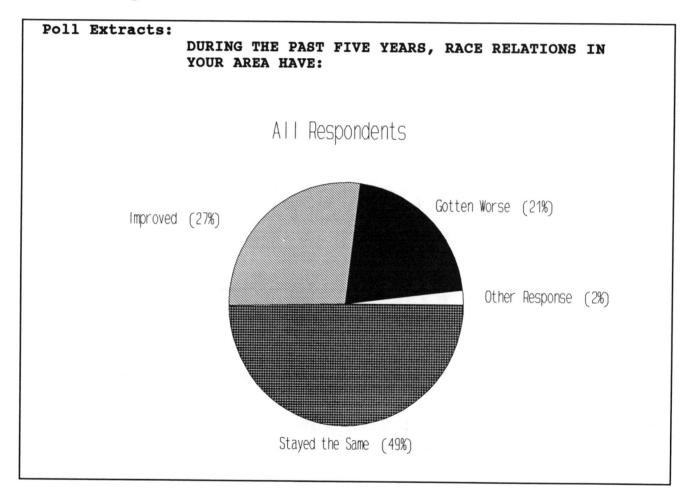

All Respondents

Improved (27%)

Gotten Worse (21%)

Other Response (2%)

Stayed the Same (49%)

Also in Source: The percentage of black and white respondents who have
personally experienced discrimination in the past five years.

Poll Details: This *Detroit Free Press*/WXYZ-TV survey was conducted by Market
Opinion Research of Detroit. 800 Michigan registered voters were
interviewed on September 21-23, 1990. The margin of error is 3.5%.

Availability: Published in the *Detroit Free Press*, September 29, 1990,
p. 1A, 5A.

MEN WORK - WOMEN STAY HOME

Description: This poll asked, "If the clock could be turned back to the idealized world of the 1950's, when women stayed home and men went to work, would you do so?"

Results: The majority of women would not turn back the clock.

Poll Extracts:
"IF YOU COULD TURN BACK THE CLOCK TO THE IDEALIZED WORLD OF THE 1950'S, WHEN WOMEN STAYED HOME AND MEN WENT TO WORK, WOULD YOU DO SO?"

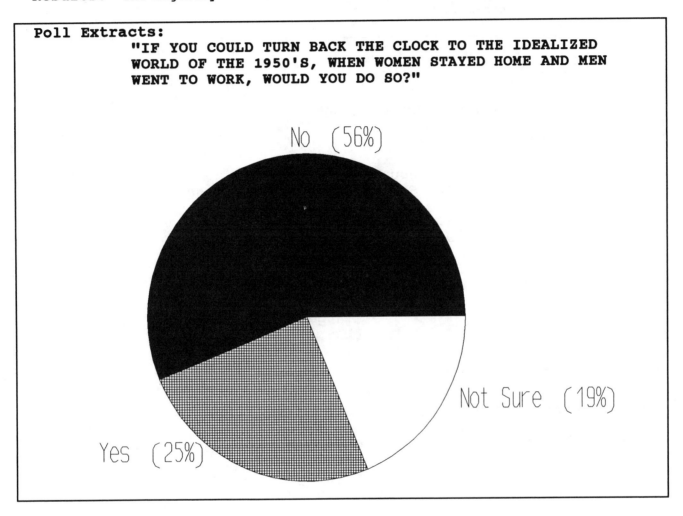

Also in Source: Other questions in the poll deal with the issues, problems, and concerns relating to women and work.

Poll Details: This *Parents* magazine readers' poll had 30,000 readers return the magazine's questionnaire.

Availability: Published in *Parents*, June 1990 (volume 65, number 6), p. 107-108, 110, 112, 114.

MOST POPULAR PET NAMES

Description: This survey asked respondents about their preferred pet names.

Results: 26% of the respondents preferred "honey" as a term of endearment. "Honey" was favored among spouses by 32%, among women by 31%, and among Midwesterners by 31%. Sterotypes of men and women as reflected by pet names are increasingly less accepted.

Poll Extracts:

THE TOP TEN LOVE NAMES.

1. Honey
2. Special Someone's Real Name
3. Baby
4. Sweetheart
5. Dear
6. Lover
7. Darling
8. Sugar
9. Tied -- Pumpkin
            Angel

Poll Details: Korbel Champagne Cellars surveyed 1,000 adults nationwide.

Availability: Published in the *Detroit Free Press*, May 29, 1990, p. 1F.

MOTHERS AND RACE RELATIONS

Description: This readers' survey of mothers asked respondents about their hopes and fears for their children.

Results: 89% of all mothers would encourage their children to have friends of a different religion or race. About 25% of the mothers would be upset if their child married someone of a different religious faith, but would still accept the decision.

Poll Extracts:

REACTION OF MOTHERS TO INTERRACIAL MARRIAGE:

50% of the mothers would accept their child's decision to marry outside of their race.

25% of the mothers would find their child's interracial marriage intolerable.

Also in Source: What mothers feel are the joys and frustrations of being a mother; attitudes toward working and being a mother; attitudes toward sex and abortion in relation to their children.

Poll Details: 22,000 readers responded to the survey. Characteristics of the respondents are as follows: 41% live in the suburbs, 29% cities, 30% rural areas; 80% are married; 59% are 25-39 years old, 25% are 40-49 years old, 13% are 50 or older, 4% are under 20 years old; 23% have one child, 42% have two children, 35% have 3 or more; 65% are currently employed, 30% not employed, 5% retired; 46% have school age kids, 34% have toddlers/preschoolers or teenagers, 27% have adult children; 72% had their first child in their twenties, 17% were teenagers, 11% were in their thirties, and 0.4% were in their forties; 25% were high school graduates, 46% had some business or college education, 24% were college graduates; 20% have family incomes under $25,000, 33% have family incomes between $25,000 and $39,999, and 40% have incomes of $40,000 or more.

Availability: Published in *Ladies Home Journal*, May 1990 (volume 107, number 5), p. 132, 134, 136.

PRIVACY

Description: Respondents were asked about their attitudes on personal privacy, and the access and use of consumer information for credit, insurance, employment, and direct marketing purposes.

Results: 57% of the respondents think that consumers being asked to provide excessively personal information is a major problem with organizations that collect information. 54% think that inaccuracy and mistakes are also a major problem. 71% of the respondents agreed with the statement, "Consumers have lost control over how personal information about them is circulated and used by companies." 30% of the respondents decided that rather than provide some requested information, they would forgo applying for a job, credit insurance, or something similar. 80% of the respondents thought that the right to privacy should have been written into the Declaration of Independence.

Poll Extracts:

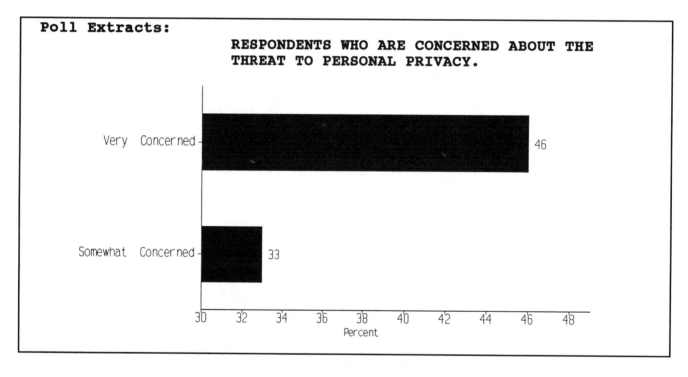

RESPONDENTS WHO ARE CONCERNED ABOUT THE THREAT TO PERSONAL PRIVACY.

Also in Source: Opinions on private social practices such as marijuana smoking, prostitution, homosexual relations, and abortion. Support for random drug testing in the workplace, spot checks for drunk drivers, and the testing of new employees for AIDS. Responses from a similar poll conducted in 1978.

Poll Details: This poll was conducted by Louis Harris & Associates, and was paid for by Equifax Inc., an Atlanta-based credit reporting company.

Availability: Published in *The Atlanta Journal and Constitution*, June 12, 1990, p. A-1, A-4.

PROBLEMS IN OHIO

Description: This poll queried Ohioans about the most important problem facing Ohioans.

Results: Environmental problems have become a primary concern of Ohioans. Combining the two issues of pollution and solid waste disposal, the environment becomes the second most important problem in Ohio, with the first being drug and alcohol abuse. Whites and blacks had very different views as to Ohio's most important problem. Whites viewed pollution (a little over 15%) and solid waste (5.9%) as the top problem in Ohio. 47% of blacks thought that drug and alcohol abuse was the top problem in Ohio, and none of the blacks thought the environment was the most important problem. The environment was seen as the top problem more frequently by younger respondents than older respondents.

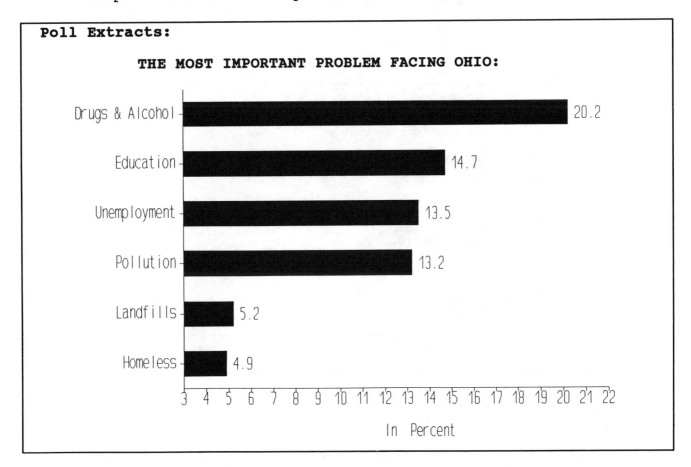

Poll Extracts:

THE MOST IMPORTANT PROBLEM FACING OHIO:

In Percent

Poll Details: The Ohio Poll surveyed 628 randomly selected adults throughout Ohio. The poll was conducted five days after the 20th anniversary of the first Earth Day.

Availability: Published in the *Dayton Daily News*, June 4, 1990, p. 3-A.

RACIAL CONSPIRACIES

Description: Respondents were asked about several supposed racial plots or conspiracies and whether or not these plots might be true.

Results: For black respondents, 10% thought it was true and 19% thought it might be true that the AIDS virus was deliberately created in a laboratory in order to infect black people. For black respondents, 25% thought it was true and 33% thought it might be true that the government deliberately makes drugs easily available in poor black neighborhoods.

Poll Extracts:

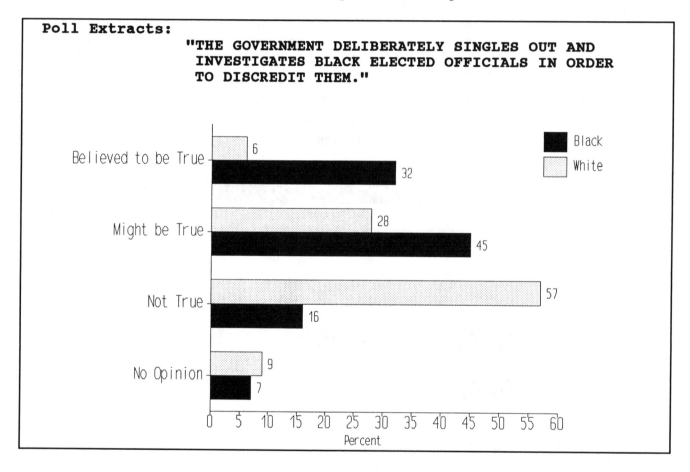

"THE GOVERNMENT DELIBERATELY SINGLES OUT AND INVESTIGATES BLACK ELECTED OFFICIALS IN ORDER TO DISCREDIT THEM."

Also in Source: Responses to poll questions according to black and white respondents.

Poll Details: This *New York Times*/WCBS-TV News telephone poll of 1,047 adults was conducted during June 17-20, 1990. The poll included 408 black respondents and 484 white respondents. The margin of error was 5% for blacks and 4% for whites.

Availability: Published in the *Dayton Daily News*, November 2, 1990, p. 1-C, 4-C.

REAL TEXANS

Description: This poll of native and non-native Texans asked respondents what it takes to be a true Texan.

Results: 56% of native Texans thought that a person born elsewhere is not a Texan -- no matter how long that person has lived in Texas. 45% of the respondents thought that a person who moves to Texas is a Texan. 40% of the respondents thought that a person who lived in Texas 10 years ago and left is still a Texan.

Poll Extracts:

"A PERSON BORN IN TEXAS IS A TEXAN, NO MATTER WHERE HE OR SHE MAY MOVE TO."

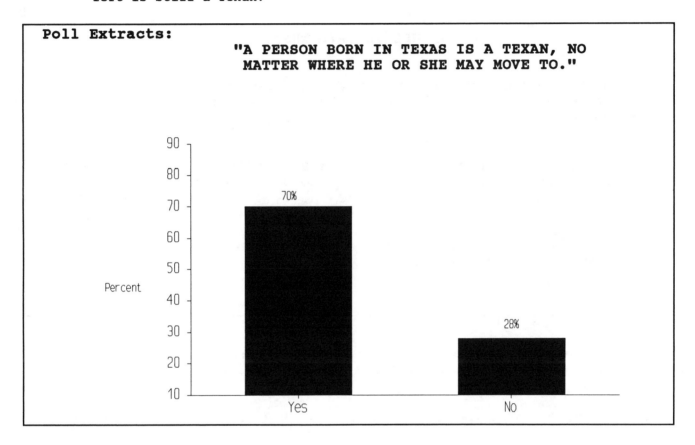

Also in Source: Respondents who thought President George Bush is a Texan. Respondents who thought that thinking like a Texan does not make a person a Texan.

Poll Details: The Texas Poll was conducted by the Public Policy Resources Laboratory of Texas A&M University. This telephone poll was conducted during October 19-29, 1990. Harte-Hanks Communications Inc. sponsored the poll of 1,008 adults across Texas. The margin of error is 3%.

Availability: Published in *The Dallas Morning News*, November 19, 1990, p. 1A, 8A.

SEXUAL COERCION

Description: This survey of males queried respondents about the use of deception or coercion to obtain sex.

Results: Almost half of the respondents said they would use deception or coercion to obtain sex.

Poll Extracts:

RESPONDENTS SAID THAT:

They had tried to coerce a woman to have sex by saying things they didn't mean or threatening to end the relationship .... Yes -- 60%

There was a likelihood of "forcing a female to do something sexual she didn't want to do" if they wouldn't be punished or found out .... Yes -- 44%

There was a likelihood of their raping a woman if they could get away with it .... Yes -- 11%

Also in Source: Respondents who had provided alcohol or drugs to obtain sex. Respondents who had reported behavior that legally is rape or attempted rape.

Poll Details: 262 male students were surveyed at the University of Florida.

Availability: Published in *The Atlanta Journal and Constitution,* November 6, 1990, p. E-3.

THE SIXTIES GENERATION

Description: This poll queried respondents about the lasting effects of the
1960s.

Results: Respondents believed that the sixties brought about 3 changes that
were for the most part good for society, while 2 changes had caused more
harm than good.

```
┌─────────────────────────────────────────────────────────────────────────┐
│  Poll Extracts:                                                           │
│                                                                           │
│                                                                           │
│   30-TO-49-YEAR-OLDS WERE ASKED IF THESE WERE POSITIVE                     │
│   CHANGES IN SOCIETY?                                                      │
│                                                                           │
│                                                                           │
│   Feminism ............................. More than 75% --Yes              │
│                                                                           │
│   Willingness to question authority .... More than 75% --Yes              │
│                                                                           │
│   Increased openness about sexuality ... More than 75% --Yes              │
│                                                                           │
│   Liberal attitudes about drugs ................. 81% --No                │
│                                                                           │
│   Greater tolerance of homosexuality                                      │
│   as an alternative lifestyle ................... 59% --No                │
│                                                                           │
└─────────────────────────────────────────────────────────────────────────┘
```

Also in Source: What 30-to-49-year-olds say about the youth of today, in
comparison to themselves as youths.

Poll Details: The poll queried 30-to-49-year-olds.

Availability: Published in *American Demographics*, March 1990 (volume 12,
number 3), p. 14-15.

SOCIAL PROBLEMS

Description: This poll looked at American feelings toward national problems now and in the future.

Results: Americans are worried that their children's lives will be worse than their own and are skeptical about any government solutions to current national problems. 49% of respondents believe that the country is headed on the wrong track. Drugs are seen as the most important problem facing the country today by 40% of the respondents. 55% disapprove of the way Congress is doing its job. 42% believe that things will get better for the country overall, during the next 10 years. A majority of respondents think that it will be more difficult for young people in the year 2000 to find a good job, afford college, buy a house, afford children, or save money.

Poll Extracts:

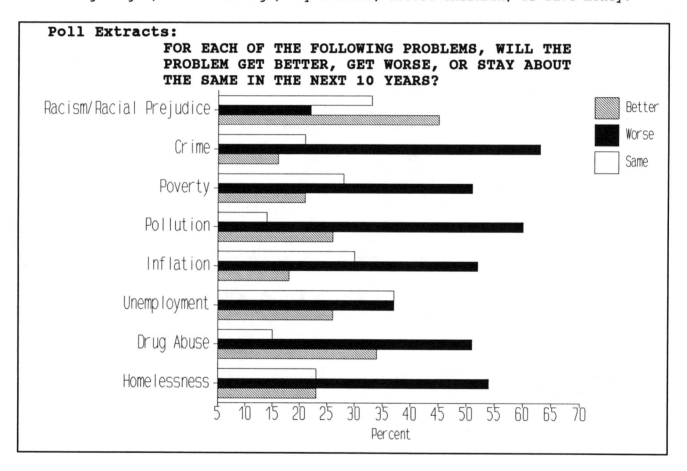

FOR EACH OF THE FOLLOWING PROBLEMS, WILL THE PROBLEM GET BETTER, GET WORSE, OR STAY ABOUT THE SAME IN THE NEXT 10 YEARS?

Also in Source: Countries which respondents believe to be the strongest economic powers in the world today, and also in the year 2000. The results from a separate poll on power in government, and defense funds.

Poll Details: A Washington Post-ABC News telephone survey of 1,518 randomly selected adults. The survey was conducted by Chilton Research of Radnor, Pennsylvania on January 11-15, 1990. The margin of sampling error is 3%.

Availability: Published in the *Washington Post*, January 21, 1990, p. A1, A24.

TEEN-AGE RACISM

Description: 10th, 11th, and 12th grade students were surveyed about their attitudes regarding race relations.

Results: It was concluded that racial intolerance exists all over the nation and among every racial and ethnic group.

Poll Extracts:

RESPONDENTS SAID THAT:

If they were to come upon a racial attack in progress, they would join in or they would feel that the group being attacked deserved what it was getting .... 47% Yes

They would tell a teacher or other school official about a racial episode they had witnessed .... 25% Yes

---

Also in Source: Increases in racially motivated crimes since 1987. The percentage of respondents who said they had seen a bias-motivated attack. The percentage of black, white, and Hispanic respondents who said they had been the target of racial or religious bias.

Poll Details: Louis Harris and Associates surveyed 1,865 10th, 11th, and 12th grade students. The survey was conducted for Northeastern University and Reebok International. The margin of error is 3%.

Availability: Published in *The Boston Globe*, October 18, 1990, p. 35, 41.

THE TWENTYSOMETHING GENERATION

Description: Presents the results of a survey of 18- to 29-year-old Americans
concerning the views and priorities of their generation.

Results: 77% of the respondents find the easygoing life style of the 1960s
attractive, 70% enjoy the music of the '60s, and 79% think the
experimentation with drugs during that period unattractive.

Poll Extracts:

WHICH ASPECTS OF THE '60S DO YOU FIND ATTRACTIVE OR UNATTRACTIVE?

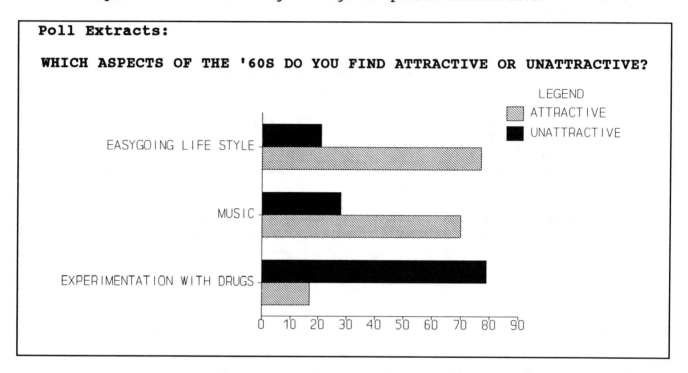

Also in Source: 58% of the respondents agree that there is no point to
staying in a job unless you are completely satisfied. 65% say it will be
much harder for their generation to live as comfortably as previous
generations. 64% of the respondents said they would spend more time with
their children than their parents did with them.

Poll Details: This Yankelovich Clancy Shulman telephone survey of 602 18- to
29-year-old Americans was taken for *Time*/CNN on June 13 through 17, 1990.
Sampling error is plus or minus 4%.

Availability: Published in *Time*, July 16, 1990 (volume 136, number 3),
p. 56-62.

U.S. ENERGY POLICY

Description: The results of several polls on energy conservation and U.S. energy policy are presented.

Results: 90% of the respondents in a Penn and Schoen Associates poll thought that the government needs to adopt a new national energy policy to encourage conservation and reduce U.S. dependence on foreign oil. 68% of the respondents from a Yankelovich Clancy Shulman poll thought that the U.S. has done a poor job of conserving energy.

Poll Extracts:

"DO YOU THINK THE ENERGY PROBLEM IN THIS COUNTRY CAN BE SOLVED BY CUTTING BACK ON THE USE OF ENERGY OR SHOULD THE MAIN EMPHASIS BE ON INCREASING ENERGY PRODUCTION?"

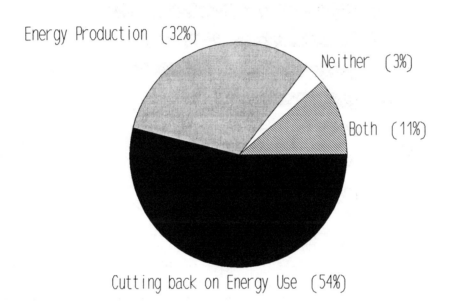

Energy Production (32%)

Neither (3%)

Both (11%)

Cutting back on Energy Use (54%)

Also in Source: Support for a tax increase on gasoline and lowering the speed limit. The percentage of respondents who thought they had been doing a good job of conserving energy. Actions that respondents had taken in order to reduce their use of energy.

Poll Details: For the polls presented, the source of each poll was provided along with the date the poll was conducted. The source of the poll extracts information was: Cambridge Reports/Research International, September 1990.

Availability: Published in *The Christian Science Monitor*, November 30, 1990, p. 19.

WAKING UP TO $1,000,000

Description: Respondents were asked what they would do if they one day woke up
as a millionaire.

Results: 50% of the respondents who are currently in the workforce would
continue to work full-time. 68% of those respondents who would continue to
work full or part-time, would do the same type of work they do now.

Poll Extracts:

**WHAT RESPONDENTS WOULD DO WITH $1 MILLION IF IT
WERE TO UNEXPECTEDLY COME THEIR WAY:**

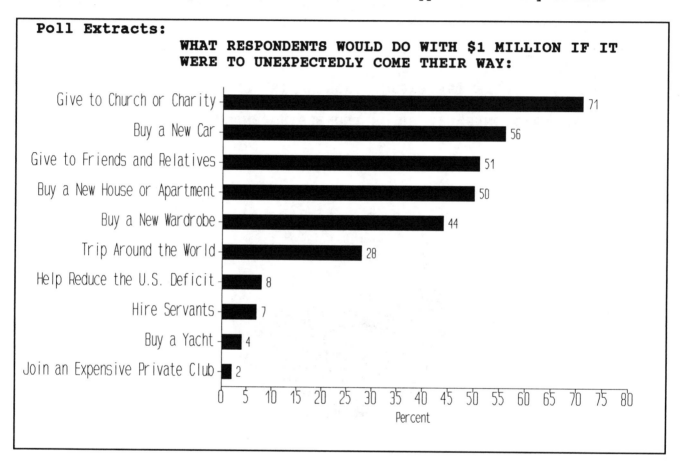

Also in Source: Most of the respondents agreed that $1 million is not enough
money to be "really rich." The percentage of respondents with children,
who would have educated their children differently if they had $1 million.
The percentage of respondents who thought they would be happier if they
suddenly came into $1 million.

Poll Details: This nationwide public opinion poll was commissioned by *Parents*
magazine.

Availability: Published in *Parents*, October 1990 (volume 65, number 10),
p. 34.

WASHINGTON, D.C. LIFESTYLES

Description: Presents the results of a survey concerning favorite lifestyles or pastimes of adults in the Washington, D.C. area.

Results: The favorite activity of Washington, D.C. area residents is foreign travel followed by participation in cultural or arts events. The least favorite pastime is recreational vehicle/four wheel drive based activites.

Poll Extracts:

Top ten "lifestyles" in Washington

1. Foreign travel
2. Cultural/arts events
3. Personal/home computer
4. Tennis frequently
5. Current affairs/politics
6. Real estate investments
7. Running/jogging
8. Wines
9. Career-oriented activities
10. Gourmet cooking/fine foods

Bottom ten "lifestyles" in Washington

1. Recreational vehicle/4 wheel drive
2. Fishing frequently
3. Hunting frequently
4. Motorcycles
5. Grandchildren
6. Camping/hiking
7. Bible/devotional reading
8. Sewing
9. Bowling
10. Crafts

Also in Source: In a survey that divided the country into 212 marketing regions, the Washington, D.C. area ranked first in the percentage of residents between the ages of 18 and 34 who earned more than $50,000 in 1989 (8%) and first in the percentage of people between 35 and 44 making that much (11.9%). Boston was second and Hartford-New Haven was third.

Poll Details: The survey was conducted by National Demographics and Lifestyles, a Denver-based market-research firm.

Availability: Published in *The Washington Post*, May 25, 1990, p. F1, F10.

WHAT'S IN A NAME?

Description: Presents the results of a survey concerning the debate surrounding the issue of changing names at marriage.

Results: 75% of the respondents said they wouldn't give up their birth name at marriage.

Poll Extracts:

AT MARRIAGE, WHAT WOULD YOU DO?

TAKE HUSBAND'S NAME 25%

KEEP BIRTH NAME 75%

Also in Source: The options preferred by the 75% who would not give up their birth name include: 34% would use their own name only; 24% would use a husband's last name with their own name as a middle name; 14% would use names according to the situation - such as their name professionally and their husband's name socially; 13% would hyphenate their husband's and their own name; 9% would make up a new name; and 6% didn't change names for the second marriage although they did so for the first.

Poll Details: *USA Today* received 189 responses to their request for letters on changing names at marriage.

Availability: Published in *USA Today,* August 28, 1990, p. 5D.

WOMEN AT WORK

Description: Presents the results of a survey concerning comparisons between at-home mothers and mothers who work outside the home.

Results: Almost 60% of the mothers who work outside the home admire at-home mothers.

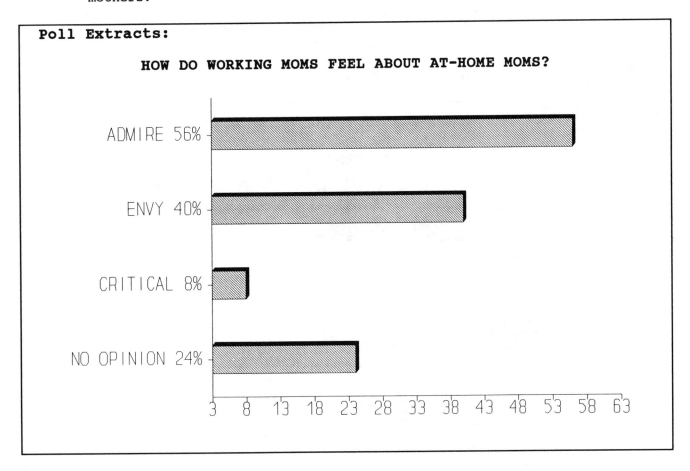

Poll Extracts:

HOW DO WORKING MOMS FEEL ABOUT AT-HOME MOMS?

Also in Source: 49% of the at-home mothers are critical of mothers who work outside the home. 94% of the mothers who work outside the home said they need the money, 82% said they need the stimulation, and 80% said they like the company of other adults. 88% of working moms said there is not enough time for themselves, 74% said they are tired all the time, 67% said there is not enough time for the family, and 59% said they were tense and short-tempered. 76% of at-home moms said there is not enough time for themselves, 71% said there is not enough time with other adults, 48% said there is not enough diversity, and 44% said there is too much boredom.

Poll Details: The results are taken from a readers survey of *Parents* magazine.

Availability: Published in *Parents*, July, 1990 (volume 65, number 7), p. 64-67, 70, 116.

THE WOMEN'S MOVEMENT

Description: This poll asked males about the impact of the women's movement on men, women, and children. Men were also asked about their wives' careers.

Results: Men thought that the women's movement had made things better for women, but worse for children and men. 58% of the married men thought that their careers were more important than their wives' careers, and less than 50% were happy about their wives' jobs. More than 80% of the married men said that if their wives made more money than they did, it wouldn't bother them. 45% of the men were willing to rearrange their careers and relocate if their wives were offered jobs that required moving.

Poll Extracts:

SINCE THE WOMEN'S MOVEMENT BEGAN IN THE 1960s, HAS IT MADE THINGS BETTER OR WORSE FOR MEN, WOMEN, AND CHILDREN?

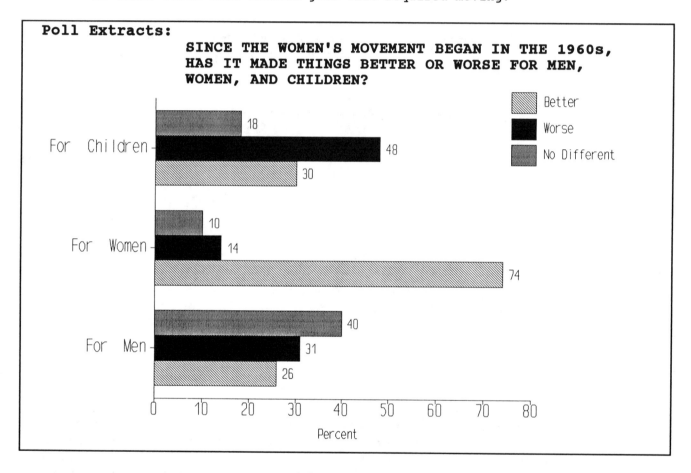

Also in Source: Responses to questions dealing with families, work, sex, and values.

Poll Details: Peter D. Hart Associates of Washington, D.C., interviewed 815 American men from age 18 through retirement. The margin of error was 4%.

Availability: Published in *Men's Life*, Fall Issue 1990 (volume 1, number 1), p. 64-70.

WOMEN'S VIEWS OF MEN

Description: Women were queried about their attitudes toward men.

Results: "American women increasingly believe most men are mean, manipulative, oversexed, self-centered, and lazy." But, more than 90% of the women said marriage is better than living alone.

Poll Extracts:

WOMEN SAY:

Most men are basically selfish and self-centered ... 42% Agree

Most men are basically kind, gentle, and thoughtful .... 51% Agree

Most men look at a woman and immediately think how it would be to go to bed with her .... 54% Agree

Most men think only their own opinions about the world are important .... 58% Agree

Most men find it necessary for their egos to keep women down .... 55% Agree

Most men are interested in their work and life outside the home and don't pay much attention to things going on at home .... 53% Agree

---

Also in Source: Today's women tended to rate men more negatively in a number of areas when their responses are compared to identical questions asked 20 years ago.

Poll Details: The survey was conducted July 22 - August 12, 1989, and was financed by Philip Morris USA in the name of its Virginia Slims cigarettes. A random sample of 3,000 women were interviewed in person across the country. The margin of error is plus or minus 2%.

Availability: Published in *The Columbus Dispatch*, April 26, 1990, p. 1A.

BASEBALL LABOR DISPUTE

Description: Presents the results of a survey concerning various issues surrounding the difference between players' and owners' contract proposals.

Results: 60% of the respondents said they would pay at least 31 cents more per ticket to end the lockout. Players want salary concessions that owners say could cost $18 million, or 31 cents for each of the 55 million tickets sold during the 1989 season.

Poll Extracts:

THE FANS TALK:

Would you pay 31 cents per ticket more
to end the players lockout?......................Yes....60%

Will you boycott games because
of the dispute?..................................Yes....10%

If the dispute is settled on time,
would you attend the same number of games?.......Yes....63%

Do players care more about the fans
than owners do?..................................Yes....43%

Do you support the owners?.......................Yes....37%

Do you support the players?......................Yes....33%

Also in Source: A brief discussion of the issue is included in the article.

Poll Details: The *USA Today* poll contacted 604 fans. The poll was conducted by Gordon S. Black and has a 4% margin of error.

Availability: Published in *USA Today*, March 15, 1990, p. 1A.

BASEBALL SETTLEMENT

Description: Presents the results of a survey concerning the labor dispute
involving professional baseball.

Results: The respondents are split over the best way to settle the labor
dispute. Almost 30% feel that a federal mediator should be appointed.

Poll Extracts:

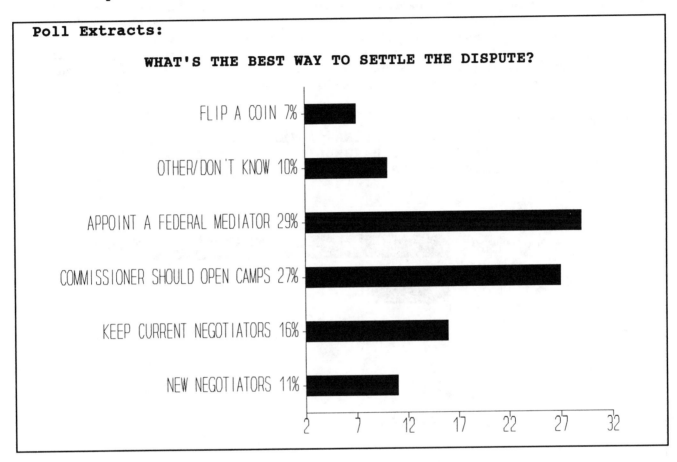

WHAT'S THE BEST WAY TO SETTLE THE DISPUTE?

FLIP A COIN 7%

OTHER/DON'T KNOW 10%

APPOINT A FEDERAL MEDIATOR 29%

COMMISSIONER SHOULD OPEN CAMPS 27%

KEEP CURRENT NEGOTIATORS 16%

NEW NEGOTIATORS 11%

2 7 12 17 22 27 32

Also in Source: The respondents replied to a number of other questions
concerning baseball's labor problems.

Poll Details: The poll was conducted by Gordon S. Black for *USA Today*. 432
baseball fans were interviewed by telephone on March 13-14, 1990. The poll
has a margin of error of plus or minus 5%.

Availability: Published in *USA Today*, March 15, 1990, p. 10C.

BO DON'T KNOW ERNIE

Description: Michigan respondents were queried about Bo Schembechler's
decision not to renew Ernie Harwell's contract after the 1991 baseball
season (Ernie Harwell having been the broadcaster for the Detroit Tigers
baseball team for 31 years), hours after the announcement of the decision.

Results: The majority of the respondents disapproved of the decision to let
Ernie Harwell go. Of the respondents who disapproved, 25.9% thought that
the Detroit Tigers owner (Thomas Monaghan) should overrule Bo
Schembechler's decision, and 14.1% thought that Bo Schembechler should be
fired. 28% of the respondents would not listen to Detroit Tigers radio
games as frequently after Ernie Harwell leaves the Detroit Tigers.

Poll Extracts:

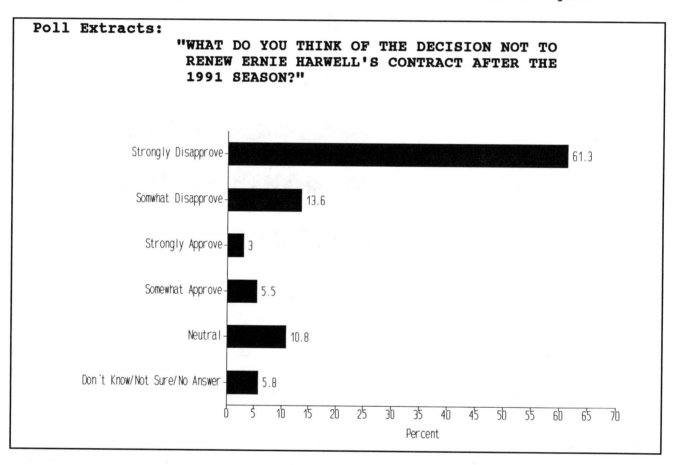

**"WHAT DO YOU THINK OF THE DECISION NOT TO
RENEW ERNIE HARWELL'S CONTRACT AFTER THE
1991 SEASON?"**

Also in Source: Respondents whose opinion of Bo Schembechler had changed
based on his conduct as Detroit Tigers president. The location respondents
would like to see the Detroit Tigers move to, if they move from their
current location in Detroit.

Poll Details: 500 Michigan residents were surveyed by Market Opinion Research
of Detroit on December 19, 1990. The margin of error is 4.5%.

Availability: Published in the *Detroit Free Press*, December 21, 1990, p. 14A.

COLLEGE FOOTBALL NATIONAL CHAMPION

Description: Presents the results of a survey to determine the best college
football team of the 1989 season.

Results: 70% of the respondents picked Notre Dame as the best football team in
the nation.

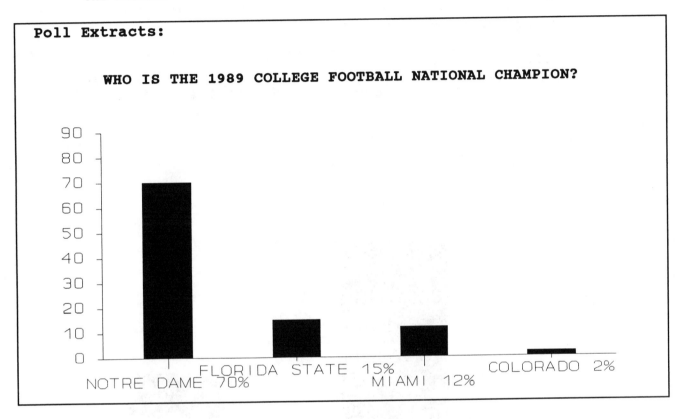

Poll Extracts:

WHO IS THE 1989 COLLEGE FOOTBALL NATIONAL CHAMPION?

NOTRE DAME 70%   FLORIDA STATE 15%   MIAMI 12%   COLORADO 2%

Also in Source: 70% of the respondents felt a playoff game would be a better
way of selecting a national champion in college football.

Poll Details: 4,329 readers of *USA Today* telephoned the newspaper with their
selection.

Availability: Published in *USA Today*, January 3, 1990, p. 1A.

THE DESIGNATED HITTER

Description: This poll asked males about what topics they talk about with other men, and their opinion on the American League's designated hitter rule.

Results: Men frequently talked to other men about: women -- 23%, sports -- 20%, work -- 19%, hobbies and leisure activities -- 17%, children -- 10%, politics -- 6%, and religion -- 4%.

Poll Extracts:

"DO YOU FEEL THE AMERICAN LEAGUE'S DESIGNATED HITTER RULE SHOULD BE KEPT OR REPEALED?"

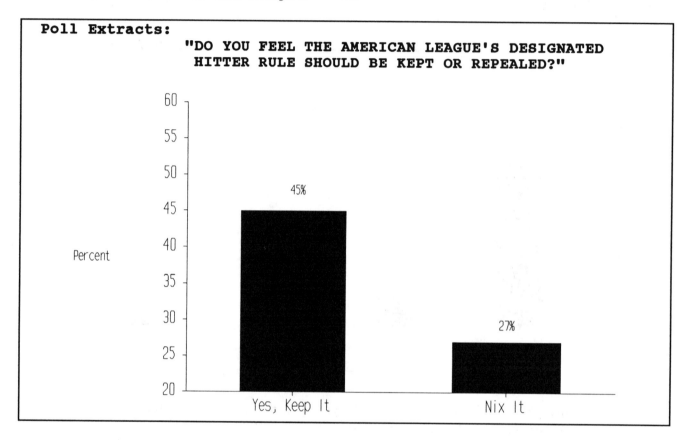

Also in Source: Responses to questions dealing with families, work, sex, and values.

Poll Details: Peter D. Hart Associates of Washington, D.C., interviewed 815 American men from age 18 through retirement. The margin of error was 4%.

Availability: Published in *Men's Life*, Fall Issue 1990 (volume 1, number 1), p. 64-70.

FAVORITE SUNSCREENS

Description: Presents the results of an informal poll of Nudist Society members concerning their opinions toward the effectiveness of different brands of sunscreens.

Results: Coppertone products ranked as the favorite sunscreen of members of the Nudist Society.

Poll Extracts:

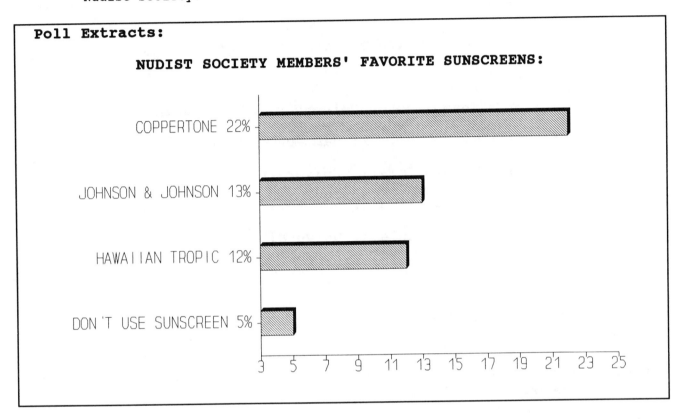

NUDIST SOCIETY MEMBERS' FAVORITE SUNSCREENS:

Also in Source: The article includes a number of informal surveys across a broad range of topics.

Poll Details: At least 100 members of the Nudist Society were polled. Only the top recommendations are listed.

Availability: Published in *USA Today*, June 29-July 1, 1990, p. 2E.

HEISMAN TROPHY FAVORITES

Description: Presents the results of a survey identifying the leading candidates for the 1990 Heisman Trophy.

Results: University of Virginia quarterback Shawn Moore is favored to win the Heisman Trophy but Ty Detmer was the actual winner.

Poll Extracts:

WHO WILL WIN THE HEISMAN TROPHY?

1. Shawn Moore, University of Virginia

2. Ty Detmer, Brigham Young University

3. Raghib Ismail, University of Notre Dame

4. David Klingier, University of Houston

5. Eric Bieniemy, University of Colorado

Also in Source: A general discussion of the Heisman Trophy race is included in the article.

Poll Details: This *USA Today*-Gannett News Service nationwide poll of 106 voters was taken in late October 1990.

Availability: Published in *USA Today*, October 30, 1990, p. 1C.

THE METS OR THE YANKEES?

Description: Presents the results of a survey measuring the comparative fan
interest of New Yorkers in either the New York Yankees or the New York
Mets.

Results: The New York Mets have almost three times as many fans as do the New
York Yankees.

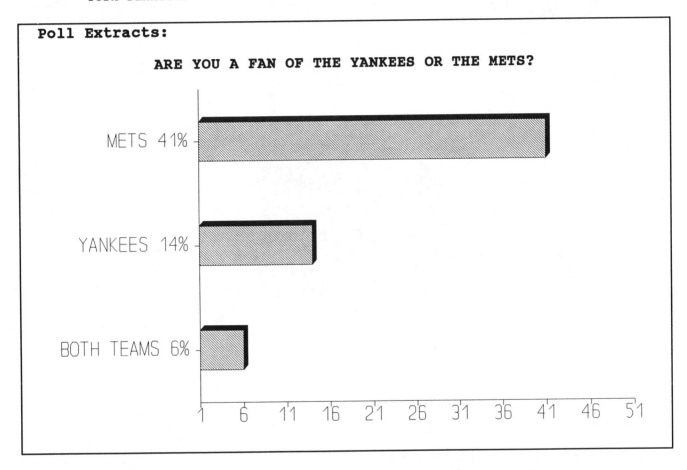

ARE YOU A FAN OF THE YANKEES OR THE METS?

Poll Extracts:

Also in Source: One out of ten Yankee fans had a favorable impression of
George Steinbrenner. 53% of those who described themselves as Yankee fans
said their opinion of Steinbrenner was "not favorable," 14% said they were
undecided, 22% said they hadn't heard enough about him, and 1% refused
comment.

Poll Details: The *New York Times*/WCBS-TV Poll was conducted by telephone with
1,047 New Yorkers 18 years old or older. It was designed to sample a cross
section of New Yorkers. The poll had a margin of error of plus or minus
3%.

Availability: Published in *The New York Times*, July 1, 1990, p. 1S.

PETE ROSE

Description: Presents the results of a survey concerning support for Pete
Roses's admission to Baseball's Hall of Fame.

Results: Almost 90% of the respondents said Pete Rose should be admitted to
the Hall of Fame.

Poll Extracts:

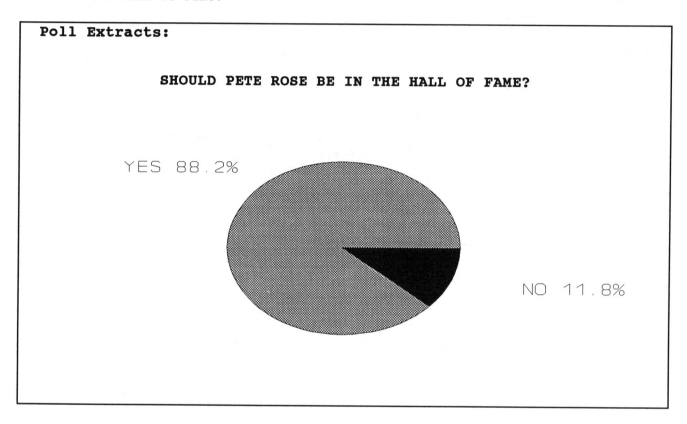

SHOULD PETE ROSE BE IN THE HALL OF FAME?

YES 88.2%

NO 11.8%

Also in Source: A brief discussion of the issue is included in the article.

Poll Details: The results are based on 23,685 telephone responses to a *USA
TODAY/INSPORT* Hot Line over the weekend of February 24-25, 1990.

Availability: Publised in *USA Today,* February 27, 1990, p. 2C.

PETE ROSE'S PUNISHMENT

Description: Presents the results of a survey concerning the appropriate punishment for ex-baseball player and manager Pete Rose.

Results: Americans overwhelmingly believe Pete Rose deserves jail time for not paying taxes, but most say he should be allowed to work in baseball and have a chance to be elected to the Hall of Fame.

Poll Extracts:

WHAT SHOULD HAPPEN TO PETE ROSE?

Is Pete Rose's five-month prison
sentence proper?..Yes...81%

Has Pete Rose harmed baseball's image?..............No....56%

Should Pete Rose be allowed to work
in baseball again?.....................................Yes...63%

Should Pete Rose be elected to the
Hall of Fame?..Yes...67%

Also in Source: A general discussion of the issue is included in the article.

Poll Details: The poll was conducted for the Associated Press by ICR Survey Research Group of Media, Pennsylvania. 1,004 adults were contacted in July, 1990, and the margin of error is plus or minus 3%.

Availability: Published in *The Cincinnati Enquirer*, July 26, 1990, p. A-1.

PROFESSIONAL BASEBALL SALARIES

Description: This poll queried Ohioans about their favorite Major League
baseball teams, and their attitudes toward players' salaries.

Results: Over half of Ohioans are Major League baseball fans, and they tend to
follow the team that is closest to where they live. The fans in Ohio are
fairly evenly divided between the Cleveland Indians (38%) and the
Cincinnati Reds (37%), with other teams being supported by 25% of the
people. The majority of respondents believe that Major League baseball
players are overpaid, and should have their salaries reduced.

Poll Extracts:

WHICH BEST DESCRIBES YOUR POINT OF VIEW ABOUT THE SALARIES OF PROFESSIONAL BASEBALL PLAYERS?

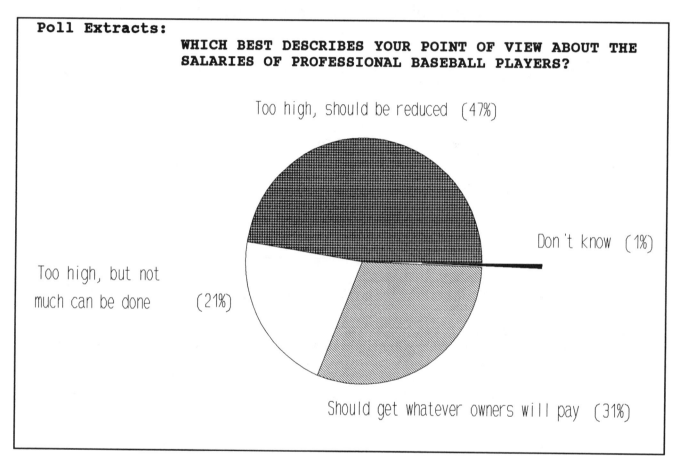

Too high, should be reduced (47%)

Don't know (1%)

Too high, but not
much can be done   (21%)

Should get whatever owners will pay (31%)

Also in Source: The percentage of northwest Ohio respondents who root for the
Cleveland Indians, the Cincinnati Reds, and the Detroit Tigers. The
results from four regions of Ohio, as to the respondents' favorite baseball
team, given the choice of the Cincinnati Reds, the Cleveland Indians, or
other.

Poll Details: The Ohio Poll was conducted for the *Dayton Daily News* and *The
Cincinnati Post* by the Institute for Policy Research at the University of
Cincinnati. The results are from a random sampling of 802 adults
statewide. The margin of error is 5%.

Availability: Published in the *Dayton Daily News*, April 9, 1990, p. 1-A, 5-A.

SAVE TIGER STADIUM

Description: This poll questioned respondents about the future of Tiger
Stadium in Detroit. Should the 78-year old stadium be renovated, or
replaced with a new stadium, and if so, where should the new stadium be
located?

Results: The majority of respondents believe Tiger Stadium should be renovated.
If a new stadium was built, respondents would like to see it located at:
the current location (33%), near the Pontiac Silverdome (13%), Ann Arbor
(3%), Dearborn (9%), and elsewhere in Detroit (19%). 42% of the people
feel that the area around the stadium is unsafe. 31% of those polled say
that the area around the stadium keeps them from attending games.

Poll Extracts:

**DO YOU BELIEVE TIGER STADIUM SHOULD BE RENOVATED,
REPLACED WITH A NEW STADIUM, OR DOESN'T IT MAKE A
DIFFERENCE?**

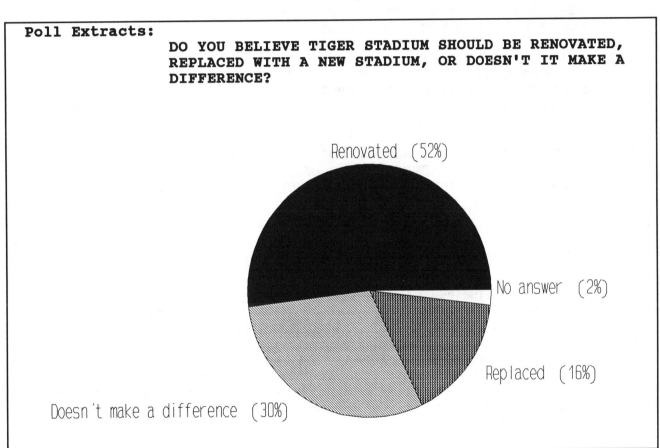

Also in Source: Polls have been conducted during the last two years which
show the majority of fans support renovation. The percentage of
respondents in favor of renovation has decreased significantly from a
similar poll conducted in February 1988.

Poll Details: The *Detroit Free Press* poll was conducted by Market Opinion
Research, a Detroit-based firm that surveyed 400 residents of Wayne,
Oakland, and Macomb counties who said they have attended a Tigers, Lions,
Pistons, or Red Wings game in the past year.

Availability: Published in the *Detroit Free Press*, May 11, 1990, p. 1A, 14A.

TOP SPORTS COLLEGES' INTEGRITY

Description: This poll queried respondents about the integrity of the nation's top sports colleges.

Results: A majority of respondents agreed that sports are overemphasized, academics neglected, and improper payments are common.

```
┌─────────────────────────────────────────────────────────────────────┐
│                                                                       │
│  Poll Extracts:                                                       │
│                                                                       │
│                                                                       │
│                                                                       │
│       COLLEGES OVEREMPHASIZE SPORTS AND NEGLECT                       │
│       ACADEMIC STANDARDS FOR ATHLETES ............... 66%            │
│                                                                       │
│                                                                       │
│       BELIEVE SCHOOLS AND BOOSTER CLUBS COMMONLY                      │
│       MAKE PAYMENTS UNDER THE TABLE TO                                │
│       STUDENT ATHLETES ............................... More than 55% │
│                                                                       │
│                                                                       │
│       CALLED IT COMMON PRACTICE FOR PROFESSORS TO                     │
│       GIVE STUDENT ATHLETES HIGHER GRADES THAN                        │
│       THEY DESERVE SO THEY CAN CONTINUE TO PLAY ..... 50%            │
│                                                                       │
│                                                                       │
│                                                                       │
└─────────────────────────────────────────────────────────────────────┘
```

Also in Source: The number or percentage of respondents who: favor athletic scholarships, favor the provisions of NCAA's Proposal No. 42 (which would prohibit schools from giving athletic scholarships to freshmen unable to meet the NCAA's academic requirements) -- black and white responses provided. The number or percentage of respondents who: would favor NCAA's Proposal No. 42 -- even if it would disqualify many blacks and other minority athletes from scholarships, believe a "C" grade average should be required for students to play sports, believe a grade average higher than "C" should be required.

Poll Details: This Media General - Associated Press national survey was conducted by telephone among a random sample of 1,108 adults, March 6-15, 1990. The margin of sampling error is 3%.

Availability: Published in *The NCAA News,* April 5, 1989 (volume 26, number 14), p. 1, 19.

WHO SHOULD BE BASEBALL'S MOST VALUABLE PLAYERS

Description: Presents the results of a survey of major league baseball players concerning their choice for Most Valuable Players in the American and National leagues.

Results: Detroit Tiger Cecil Fielder is the favorite for the American League MVP Award and Barry Bonds of the Pittsburgh Pirates is the favorite to receive the National League honor.

Poll Extracts:

WHO SHOULD BE 1990's MOST VALUABLE PLAYERS

American League

1. Cecil Fielder, Detroit Tigers
2. Rickey Henderson, Oakland A's

National League

1. Barry Bonds, Pittsburgh Pirates
2. Doug Drabek, Pittsburgh Pirates

Also in Source: Oakland's Bob Welch was the runaway choice for the American league Cy Young Award. Cleveland's Sandy Alomar easily beat out Kevin Mass of the New York Yankees for American League Rookie of the Year. Jeff Torborg of the Chicago White Sox is favored to win American League Manager of the Year. In the National League, Atlanta's Dave Justice was the big favorite for Rookie of the Year and Jim Leyland of the Pittsburgh Pirates should win the Manager of the Year Award.

Poll Details: The results of the survey were taken from a *USA Today* of major league baseball players.

Availability: Published in *USA Today*, October 16, 1990, p. 1C.

AUTOWORKERS PREPARED TO STRIKE

Description: This telephone poll gives the perspectives of 150 Detroit-area rank-and-file members, as to what is important to United Auto Workers' (UAW) members.

Results: "Two-thirds of the workers surveyed said they'll be willing to strike when UAW contracts covering 500,000 active and displaced Big Three workers expire September 14. More than half said they have made financial preparations for a walkout." In the upcoming contract talks 49% of the respondents thought job security (stronger guarantees) and tighter controls on shipping work to outside companies was the top priority. About one worker in five thought that cost-of-living allowances (COLA) on pensions was the top priority.

Poll Extracts:

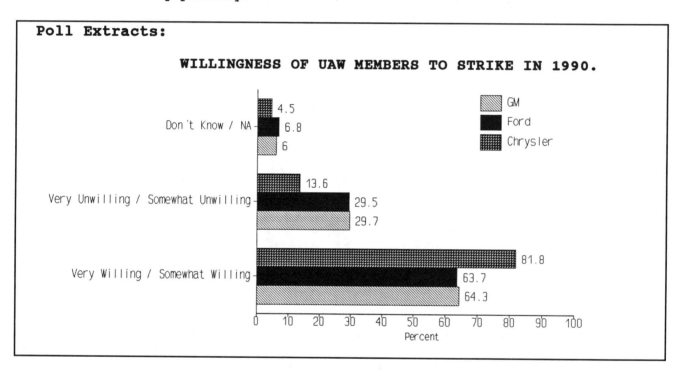

WILLINGNESS OF UAW MEMBERS TO STRIKE IN 1990.

GM
Ford
Chrysler

Don't Know / NA — 4.5 / 6.8 / 6

Very Unwilling / Somewhat Unwilling — 13.6 / 29.5 / 29.7

Very Willing / Somewhat Willing — 81.8 / 63.7 / 64.3

Percent

Also in Source: Opinions on joint programs between the UAW and the Big Three, opinions on UAW and corporate leadership, and living standards. The percentage of respondents who are willing to work less to create jobs for others. Responses are broken down according to General Motors, Ford, and Chrysler employees. The percentage of autoworkers who want more restrictive trade policies.

Poll Details: The *Detroit Free Press* poll is based on telephone interviews conducted by Nordhaus Research Inc. of Southfield, Michigan. The survey does not give a scientifically accurate picture of the UAW membership, but rather the perspectives of 150 UAW members. The 150 Big Three workers that participated were contacted through telephone calls targeting Detroit Area counties with large concentrations of blue-collar workers. The interviews were conducted between April 30 and May 14. Demographic characteristics of the sample are included in the source. The margin of error for the total sample is 7.84 percentage points at the 95% confidence level.

Availability: Published in the *Detroit Free Press*, May 18, 1990, p. 1A, 6A.

GREYHOUND STRIKE

Description: Attitudes toward labor unions, strikes in general, and the
         Greyhound strike were examined by this poll.

Results: 22% of the respondents were sympathetic toward management's position
         in the Greyhound strike, but 25% refused to take a side. 40% of the
         respondents think labor unions have too much power. 73% of those polled
         think labor unions are still needed by American workers. When asked if
         private sector workers have the right to strike without losing their jobs,
         50% of the respondents thought that "it's the chance they take." 59% of
         the respondents said they would not take the job of a striking worker.

Poll Extracts:

**AFTER THE STRIKE, SHOULD GREYHOUND BE REQUIRED TO
REHIRE THE STRIKING WORKERS?**

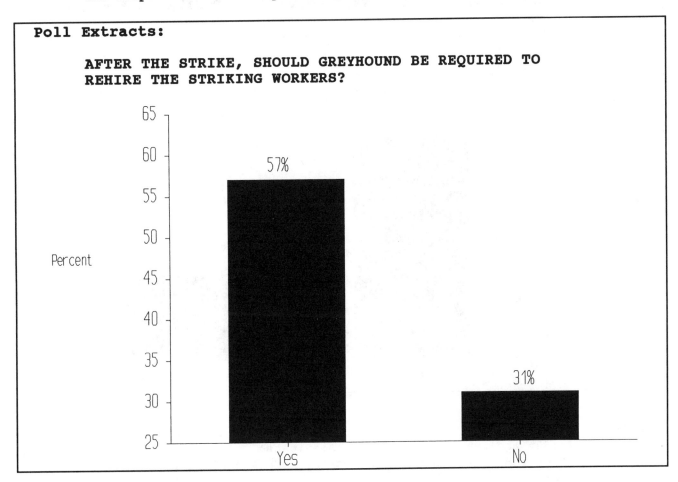

Also in Source: Discussion of the Greyhound strike.

Poll Details: This telephone poll by Yankelovich Clancy Shulman surveyed 500
         adult Americans for *Time*/CNN on March 14, 1990. The sampling error is
         4.5%.

Availability: Published in *Time*, March 26, 1990 (volume 135, number 13),
         p. 56-57, 59.

STRIKE SUPPORT

Description: This survey questioned Americans' attitudes regarding strikes.

Results: A "dramatic change" in attitudes toward strikes was recorded. The level of support for unions was at its highest level since the survey began 16 years ago. The level of support for companies was at its lowest level since the survey began.

Poll Extracts:

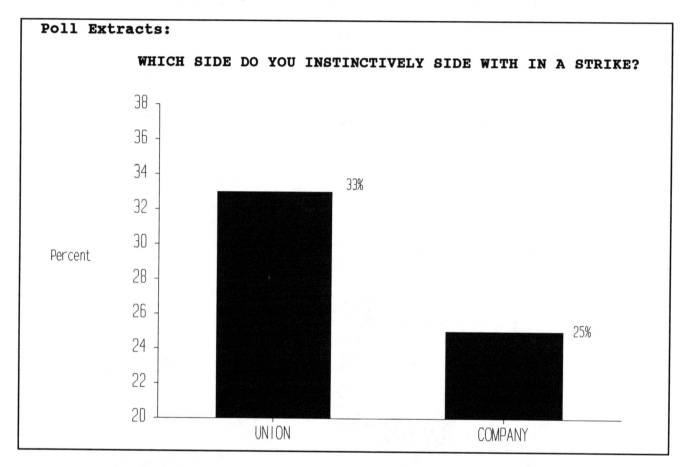

WHICH SIDE DO YOU INSTINCTIVELY SIDE WITH IN A STRIKE?

Also in Source: The level of support for companies and unions in strikes, in 1977 (32% and 28% respectively). Americans' opinions of labor leaders, and how they rank when compared to doctors, educators, businessmen, stockbrokers, and politicians.

Poll Details: The poll was conducted by the Roper Organization.

Availability: Published in the *Chicago Tribune*, February 22, 1990, section 3, p. 5.

TEACHER STRIKES

Description: Presents the results of a survey concerning the level of support
for teacher strikes.

Results: Over 70% of the respondents agreed that when teachers strike, they
usually have good reasons.

Poll Extracts:

TEACHERS ON STRIKES:

When teachers strike, do they usually
have a good reason?................................Yes...72%

Are unions very useful in improving the
pay, benefits, and working conditions of teachers?...Yes...71%

Are teacher strikes often caused by unrealistic
contract offers by school officials?.................Yes...68%

Do you agree with the statement that
"strikes against a school system don't hurt the
students because the strikes usually don't
last very long?".....................................No....75%

Are you willing to spend more money on education?....Yes...58%

Also in Source: Half of the respondents were critical of teacher unions for
holding back necessary changes to improve the quality of public education.

Poll Details: 1,003 adults took part in a telephone survey conducted by the
Roper Organization. The survey was sponsored by the U.S. Chamber of
Commerce.

Availability: Published in the *Chicago Tribune*, September 1, 1990, section 1,
p. 3.

ALCOHOL TAX INCREASE

Description: Presents the results of a survey concerning two California ballot propositions which would increase the taxes on alcoholic beverages. Proposition 126 would boost the per gallon tax on table wine and beer to 20 cents and liquor to $3.30. Proposition 134 would hike per gallon taxes on table wine from a penny to $1.29, on beer from four cents to 57.3 cents, and on liquor from $2.00 to $8.40.

Results: Almost half of the respondents said they would support both propositions which would increase the tax on alcohol.

Poll Extracts:

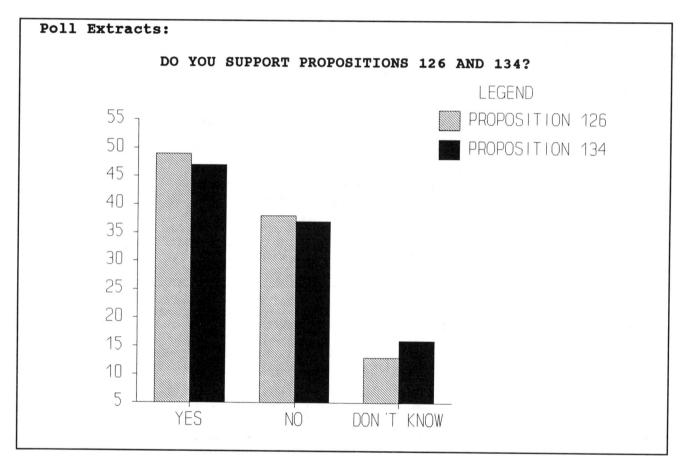

DO YOU SUPPORT PROPOSITIONS 126 AND 134?

LEGEND
PROPOSITION 126
PROPOSITION 134

Also in Source: The article also includes a survey measuring support for a proposition that addresses a long list of environmental issues. 44% of the respondents support the measure.

Poll Details: The *Los Angeles Times* poll interviewed 1,586 registered voters by telephone over a six day period in mid-August, 1990. The poll was supervised by Susan Pinkus.

Availability: Published in the *Los Angeles Times*, August 26, 1990, p. A1, A47.

CANDIDATES' CREDIBILITY

Description: Presents the results of a survey concerning the no-new-taxes
pledges forwarded by political candidates.

Results: Over 70% of the respondents do not believe a candidate for public
office when the candidate vows not to raise taxes.

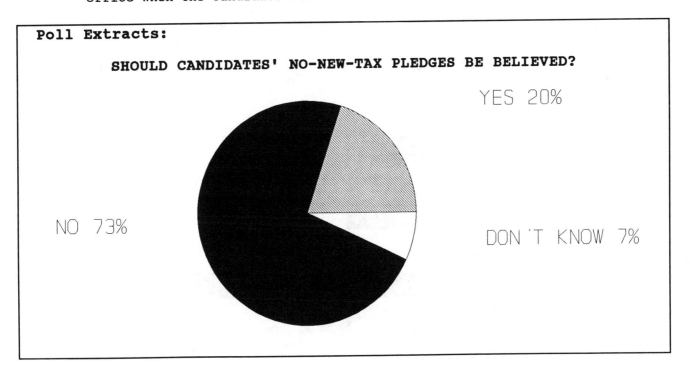

Poll Extracts:

SHOULD CANDIDATES' NO-NEW-TAX PLEDGES BE BELIEVED?

YES 20%

NO 73%

DON'T KNOW 7%

Also in Source: 32% of the respondents said it would lessen their opinion of
President Bush if he broke his promise not to raise taxes. 64% said it
would make no difference and 4% didn't know or refused to answer.

Poll Details: The survey of 1,021 Texas adults was conducted on August 4-19,
1990 by the Public Policy Resources Laboratory at Texas A&M University for
Harte-Hanks Communications. The margin of error is plus or minus 3%.

Availability: Published in *The Dallas Morning News*, September 4, 1990,
p. 1A, 7A.

ELECTRONIC TAX FILING

Description: Presents the results of a survey concerning the level of interest in filing tax returns electronically.

Results: Over two-thirds of the respondents said they are not interested in electronic filing.

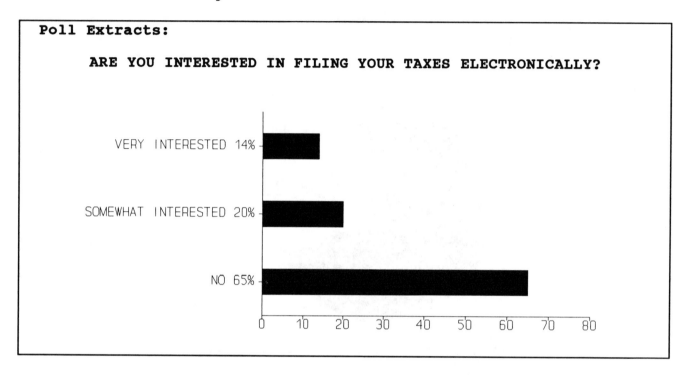

Poll Extracts:

ARE YOU INTERESTED IN FILING YOUR TAXES ELECTRONICALLY?

Also in Source: The article also presents the results of a survey concerning the popularity of individual retirement accounts.

Poll Details: The survey was conducted by the Gallup Organization for *Bank Advertising News*. 1,000 adults were contacted in February, 1990.

Availability: Published in *American Banker*, April 2, 1990 (volume CLV, number 63), p. 6.

MORTGAGE INTEREST DEDUCTIONS AND SECOND HOMES

Description: Presents the results of a survey concerning the attractiveness of second or vacation home ownership if the mortgage interest deduction is eliminated.

Results: More than half of the potential second home purchasers said the loss of the mortgage interest deduction would cause them to reconsider a vacation home purchase.

Poll Extracts:

HOW WOULD THE LOSS OF INTEREST DEDUCTION AFFECT YOUR DECISION TO PURCHASE A SECOND HOME?

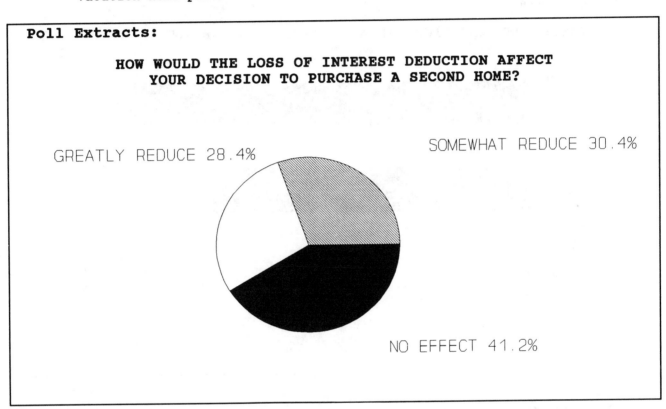

GREATLY REDUCE 28.4%   SOMEWHAT REDUCE 30.4%

NO EFFECT 41.2%

Also in Source: 20% of the respondents under 39 years of age expressed interest in purchasing a second home. 12.5% of those over 50 years old expressed the same sentiment.

Poll Details: The National Association of Realators, the International Foundation for Timesharing, and the American Resort and Residential Development Association Political Education Fund paid for the study. 5,636 people were interviewed by telephone during Spring, 1990.

Availability: Published in *The Washington Post*, August 18, 1990, p. E1, E12.

PRESIDENT BUSH'S PLEDGE

Description: Respondents were asked if they agreed that President Bush was right to abandon his pledge not to raise taxes.

Results: Just over half of the respondents thought that President Bush should not have abandoned his pledge to not raise taxes.

Poll Extracts:

"PRESIDENT BUSH WAS RIGHT TO ABANDON HIS PLEDGE NOT TO RAISE TAXES."

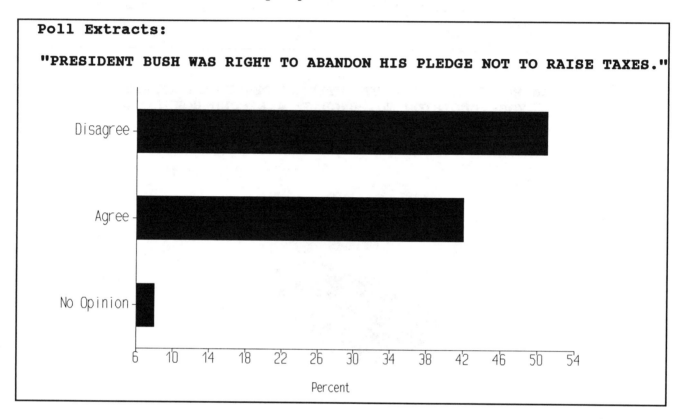

Also in Source: The percentage of respondents who blamed President Bush for the "budgetary brouhaha" that had existed (some government services were stopped in order to pressure Congress to come up with a revised budget plan). President Bush's popularity in Georgia. President Bush's popularity among black Georgians, following his veto of the 1990 Civil Rights Act.

Poll Details: This poll was conducted by Voice Information Services Inc., an operating unit of *The Atlanta Journal and Constitution*, from October 24 to October 28, 1990. 691 adults in Georgia who were identified as "likely" voters in the November 6, 1990 general election were interviewed by telephone. The margin of error is 4%. Further details are available in the source.

Availability: Published in *The Atlanta Journal and Constitution*, October 31, 1990, p. A-6.

READ MY LIPS - NO NEW TAXES

Description: This poll asked adults their thoughts about a possible tax increase.

Results: 62% are opposed to a tax increase in order to cut the deficit. 48% think it's "very likely," 38% think it's "somewhat likely" that President Bush will ask Congress to increase taxes. Should President Bush break his campaign pledge of "Read my lips, no new taxes," 12% of the respondents would feel angry, 26% would be sympathetic, and 60% think he never should have made the promise.

Poll Extracts:

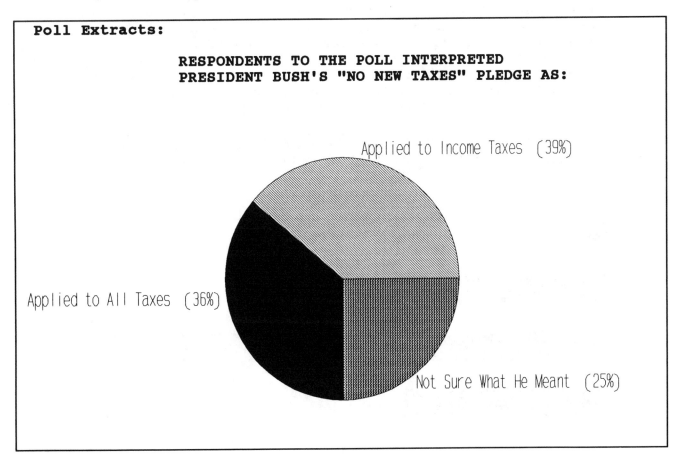

**RESPONDENTS TO THE POLL INTERPRETED
PRESIDENT BUSH'S "NO NEW TAXES" PLEDGE AS:**

Applied to Income Taxes (39%)

Applied to All Taxes (36%)

Not Sure What He Meant (25%)

Also in Source: The number of respondents, who voted for President Bush in 1988, who say they'd be less likely to vote for him if he supported new taxes.

Poll Details: This *USA Today* poll of 610 adults was conducted on May 10, 1990 by Gordon S. Black. This telephone poll has a margin of error of 4%.

Availability: Published in *USA Today*, May 11-13, 1990, p. 1A.

READ MY LIPS - WHAT DID PRESIDENT BUSH MEAN

Description: This poll queried respondents about their thoughts on President
Bush's campaign pledge of "no new taxes," the possibility of a tax increase
to reduce the federal budget deficit, and the possibility of decreased
spending in several areas.

Results: 68% of the respondents expect President Bush to ask Congress to
increase taxes. 55% believe that in order to substantially reduce the
deficit, taxes will have to be raised. If taxes had to be increased, then
respondents would find it acceptable if taxes were raised on: beer and
liquor (80%), income over $200,000 (78%), and gasoline (40%). 63% of the
respondents would find it unacceptable to create a federal sales tax. If
spending had to be cut, the respondents thought it would be acceptable to
reduce: foreign aid (83%), military spending (64%), all federal programs
(41%), spending on the environment (20%), and spending on education (12%).
82% of the respondents thought it would be unacceptable to delay Social
Security increases in order to reduce spending.

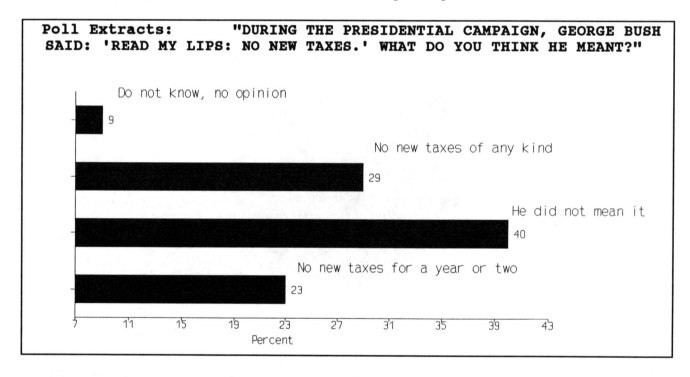

Poll Extracts: "DURING THE PRESIDENTIAL CAMPAIGN, GEORGE BUSH
SAID: 'READ MY LIPS: NO NEW TAXES.' WHAT DO YOU THINK HE MEANT?"

Also in Source: Which political party respondents view as more likely to
raise taxes. Public concern about the deficit. Differences between the
responses of younger and older respondents on the questions of taxes and
spending. The estimated effects on revenues if the government were to:
raise the federal excise tax on beer, wine, and liquor to 25 cents an ounce
of alcohol; raise the cigarette tax to 32 cents per package.

Poll Details: This *New York Times* / CBS News poll was conducted by telephone
with 1,140 adults on May 22-24, 1990. The respondents were from across the
nation, excluding Alaska and Hawaii. The sampling error is 3%, with a
larger error for subgroups. Further details are provided in the source.

Availability: Published in *The New York Times*, May 27, 1990. p. 1, 24.

REDUCING THE FEDERAL BUDGET DEFICIT

Description: Respondents were asked if they would be willing to raise taxes in order to reduce the Federal budget deficit.

Results: "Americans were most supportive of tax increases on people with incomes over $100,000 and higher taxes on beer, wine, and liquor." "The public was least supportive of raising the charges paid by people who get Medicare."

Poll Extracts:

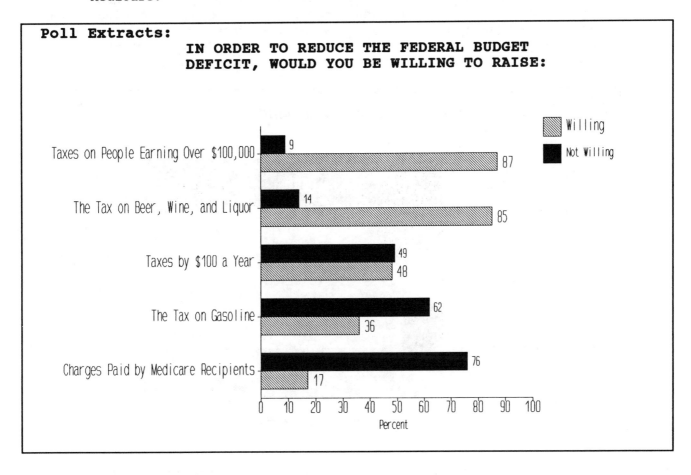

IN ORDER TO REDUCE THE FEDERAL BUDGET DEFICIT, WOULD YOU BE WILLING TO RAISE:

Also in Source: The percentage of respondents who would support reduced defense spending or fewer government services, in order to reduce the Federal budget deficit. Approval for the way President Bush is handling his job as president. Poll results which were critical of Congress.

Poll Details: This nationwide CBS News poll involved 775 adults. The respondents were interviewed by telephone on October 7, 1990.

Availability: Published in *The New York Times*, October 9, 1990, p. A21.

ROSTENKOWSKI'S TAX PLAN

Description: This poll asked respondents if they supported or opposed various features of House Ways and Means Committee Chairman Dan Rostenkowski's tax plan. It also queried respondents about President Bush's "no new taxes" pledge.

Results: 74% of the respondents support raising the income tax on the wealthy to 33%, and also support raising the taxes on alcoholic beverages and cigarettes. 52% favor a one-year freeze on all domestic spending, except programs for the poor. 71% oppose a one-year freeze on cost-of-living adjustments to Social Security. 48% of the respondents think that President Bush should not drop his pledge of "no new taxes."

Poll Extracts:

DO YOU FAVOR OR OPPOSE:

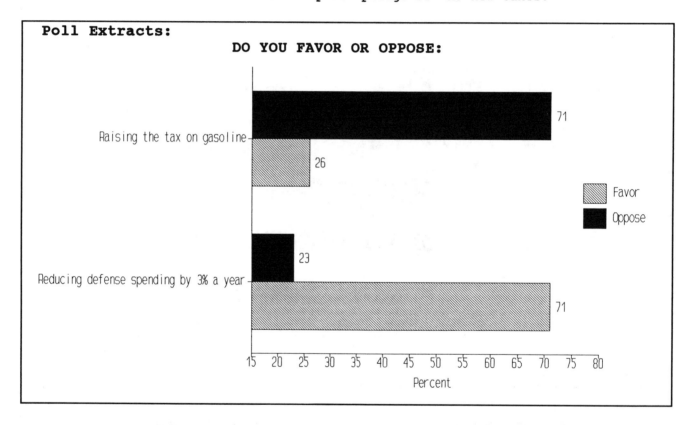

Also in Source: The percentage of respondents who felt that President Bush should not drop his pledge of "no new taxes," because: "taxes are already too high," "deficit can be reduced by other means," "the Government would use the money for other purposes than reducing the deficit." The percentage of the respondents who agree, "Democrats are too quick to suggest tax increases to reduce the federal deficit."

Poll Details: The results are from a March 14, 1990 *Time*/CNN telephone poll of 500 adult Americans. The poll was conducted by Yankelovich Clancy Shulman. The sampling error is 4.5%.

Availability: Published in *Time*, March 26, 1990 (volume 135, number 13), p. 16-17.

TAX INCREASES

> **Description:** Given the size of the national deficit, 1,000 adult Americans
> were asked if they thought their taxes will increase, decrease, or remain
> the the same.

> **Results:** 82% of the respondents felt their taxes will increase while only 1%
> felt their taxes will decrease. 16% of the respondents felt their taxes
> will remain about the same and 1% were not sure.

Poll Extracts:

**WILL TAXES INCREASE, DECREASE, OR
REMAIN THE SAME?**

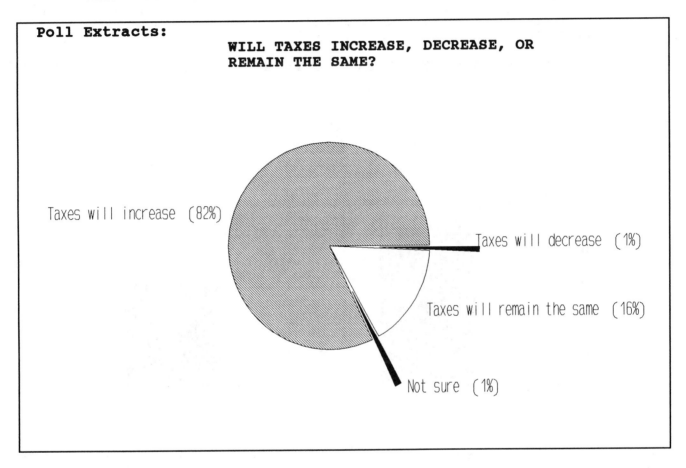

> **Also in Source:** Other questions concerning several tax issues were included
> in this survey. Areas covered include social security, new taxes, the
> deficit, capital-gains, and individual retirement accounts.

> **Poll Details:** The survey was conducted on January 22-23, 1990 for *Business
> Week* by Louis Harris & Associates. Results should be accurate to within
> 3%.

> **Availability:** Published in *Business Week*, February 5, 1990 (number 3144),
> p. 27.

TAXES AND PRESIDENT BUSH

Description: Presents the results of a survey concerning the need for
   increased taxes and President Bush's accountability in relation to his
   no-new-taxes pledge.

Results: Half of the respondents said President Bush should support a tax
   increase while slightly less than half oppose his support for a raise in
   taxes.

Poll Extracts:

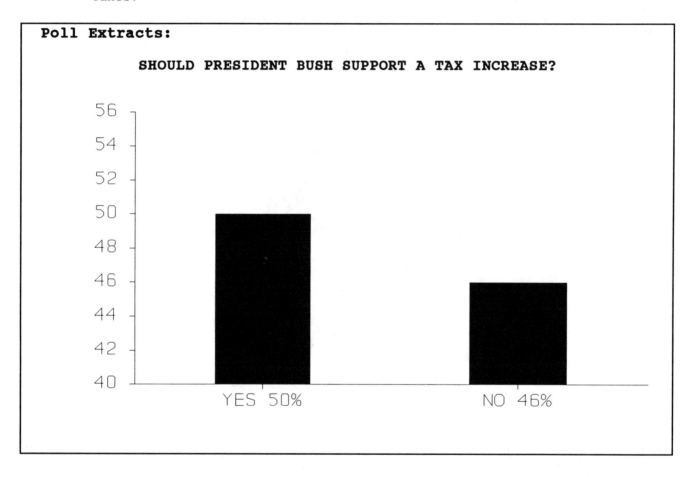

SHOULD PRESIDENT BUSH SUPPORT A TAX INCREASE?

Also in Source: 88% of the respondents think taxes are likely to rise and 49%
   said they would prefer higher taxes to living with the current budget
   deficit. Nearly two-thirds said they would not feel any differently
   towards Bush if he supported a tax-increase bill, while 18% would think
   less of him, and 14% would think more of him. 49% favored a proposal
   considered by the Bush Administration to assess a new levy on all stock and
   bond sales. The poll also found that 76% of those surveyed favored
   increasing the income tax rate for upper income individuals.

Poll Details: The survey was conducted for *The Wall Street Journal* and NBC
   News by the polling organizations of Peter Hart, a Democrat, and Robert
   Teeter, a Republican, between July 6 and 10, 1990. The margin of error for
   the nationwide survey of 1,555 registered voters is 2.6%.

Availability: Published in *The Wall Street Journal*, July 12, 1990, p. A12.

WHERE TO INCREASE TAXES

Description: Respondents were asked if they would prefer to see a tax increase
fall upon the wealthy, or upon gasoline purchases.

Results: The majority of respondents would prefer to see the tax-rate for
upper-income earners increase rather than place new taxes on gasoline.

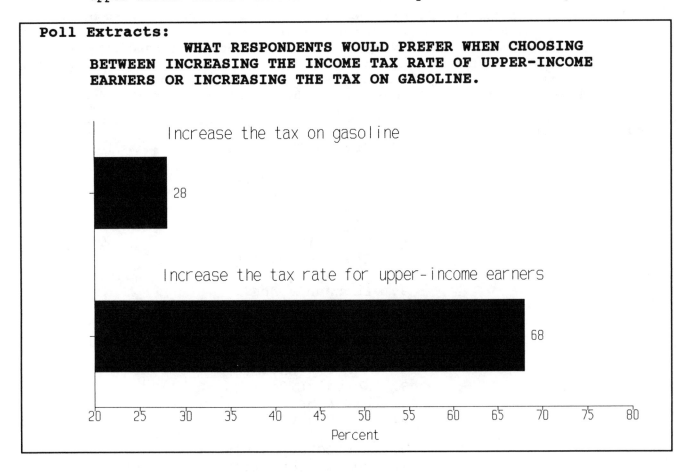

Poll Extracts:
**WHAT RESPONDENTS WOULD PREFER WHEN CHOOSING
BETWEEN INCREASING THE INCOME TAX RATE OF UPPER-INCOME
EARNERS OR INCREASING THE TAX ON GASOLINE.**

Also in Source: Discussion of various options for where taxes might be
increased: sin taxes (alcohol and tobacco), income tax rates, professional
services, and insurance companies.

Poll Details: This *Wall Street Journal*/NBC News Poll was conducted May 18-22,
1990.

Availability: Published in *The Wall Street Journal*, June 27, 1990, p. A1, A4.

BEST AND WORST TV SERIES

Description: This poll of 30 TV critics at the end of the 1989-1990 season
asked critics to list their 10 favorite shows, five least-favorite shows,
three favorite specials, movies or miniseries, and three least-favorite
special movies or miniseries.

Results: The CBS series "Murphy Brown" is ranked as the No. 1 series by the
nation's TV critics, and is seen by the critics as a modern-day "Mary Tyler
Moore Show." The critics thought the worst series was "Grand Slam" or
"Baywatch." "America's Funniest Home Videos" which is popular with viewers,
was ranked as number eight on the critic's list of the worst series, and
did not get a single vote from any of the critics as a top 10 favorite.

Poll Extracts:

THE BEST TELEVISION SERIES
1. Murphy Brown
2. Tied -- Twin Peaks
   L.A. Law
4. Wonder Years
5. Cheers
6. The Simpsons
7. Thirtysomething
8. Designing Women
9. Shannon's Deal
10. China Beach

THE WORST TELEVISION SERIES
1. Tied -- Grand Slam
   Baywatch
3. Normal Life
4. His & Hers
5. The Bradys

BEST MOVIE, SPECIAL, MINISERIES
1. Small Sacrifices
2. Traffik
3. Family of Spies

WORST MOVIE, SPECIAL, MINISERIES
1. People Like Us
2. Tied -- Challenger
   Love Boat

Also in Source: The number of first place votes each series received, and the
total point value each series obtained. The names and affiliations of the
30 critics who were polled.

Poll Details: *Electronic Media* polls the critics twice a year, once at
midseason, and again at the end of the season.

Availability: Published in *Electronic Media*, June 25, 1990 (volume 9,
number 26), p. 1, 16.

FAVORITE TELEVISION FAMILIES

Description: This survey asked questions regarding opinions about families on
television. Which is the funniest? What character is the biggest brat?
Who's most like you?

Results: The Bundys of Fox's *Married With Children* would be the family 40% of
the respondents would hate to have living next door.

Poll Extracts:

The top all-time favorite families on TV.

1. The Cosby Show

2. Family Ties

3. Roseanne

4. The Waltons

5. Little House on the Prairie

Also in Source: The television family that would be the preferred dinner
guests, son/brother most like my own, daughter/sister most like my own, the
squarest dad, the best mom, and TV remarks heard in my house.

Poll Details: The answers were from 4,700 readers of *USA WEEKEND.*

Availability: Published in *USA WEEKEND,* February 16-18, 1990, p. 10, 11.

FEELINGS ABOUT CABLE TV

Description: Respondents were asked for their opinions about cable TV.

Results: The majority of respondents favor government regulation of cable
companies. 39% of the respondents channel flip: most of the time - 39%,
some of the time - 47%, hardly ever - 14%.

Poll Extracts:

**THE CABLE INDUSTRY IS CURRENTLY NOT REGULATED. WHEN
RESPONDENTS WERE ASKED, "DO YOU FAVOR GOVERNMENT REGULATION
OF CABLE COMPANIES?" THEY REPLIED:**

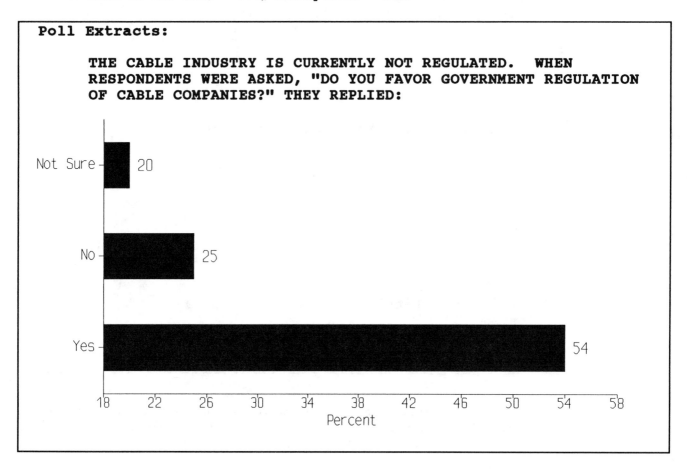

Poll Details: More than 2,800 respondents provided their opinions on cable TV
and what they would like to tell the cable industry's executives at their
Atlanta meeting.

Availability: Published in *The Atlanta Journal and Constitution*, May 21, 1990,
p. A-4.

PEOPLE'S CHOICE AWARDS

Description: This poll asked for the public's favorite television entertainers and programs in 22 categories.

Results: Bill Cosby and "The Cosby Show" won 3 awards, while Roseanne Barr won 2 awards.

```
Poll Extracts:


    WINNERS OF THE AWARDS:


    Roseanne Barr ...............  All-around female entertainer
      Bill Cosby ................  All-around male entertainer
    Roseanne Barr ...............  Female TV performer
      Bill Cosby ................  Male TV performer
    Fred Savage .................  Young TV performer
      The Cosby Show ...........   TV comedy series
    L.A. Law ...................   TV dramatic series
      Neil Patrick Harris .......  Male performer in a new TV
                                   series
    Jamie Lee Curtis ............  Female performer in a new TV
                                   series
      Doogie Howser, M.D. .......  New TV comedy series
    Rescue:  911 ................  New TV dramatic series
      Arsenio Hall ..............  Late-night talk show host
    Batman .....................   Motion picture
      Batman and
      Steel Magnolias ...........  Dramatic motion picture
    Tom Cruise ..................  Motion picture actor
      Meryl Streep ..............  Motion picture actress
    Bobby Brown .................  Male musical performer
      Paula Abdul ...............  Female musical performer
    Randy Travis and
    Kenny Rogers ................  Country music performer
      Meryl Streep ..............  World motion picture actress
    Dustin Hoffman ..............  World motion picture actor
      Look Who's Talking ........  World comedy motion picture
```

Poll Details: The poll was conducted nationwide by Gallup.

Availability: Published in *The Atlanta Journal and Constitution*, March 12, 1990, p. B-4.

STANDARDS AND CENSORSHIP

Description: This poll asked respondents if there should be standards that prohibit some types of material from being shown on television, regardless of its popularity; or whether the decision about programming should be left to the viewer. Respondents were also asked about the types of things that should or should not be allowed on television.

Results: 66% of the respondents believe that there should be standards to prohibit some material from being shown on television. If shown only late at night, 55% of the respondents thought that scenes that suggest sexual activity between adults but do not actually show it, are acceptable. Words such as "hell" or "damn" would be allowed on television at any time by 52% of the respondents. Words such as "breast" or "condom" would be allowed on television at any time by 51%.

Poll Extracts:

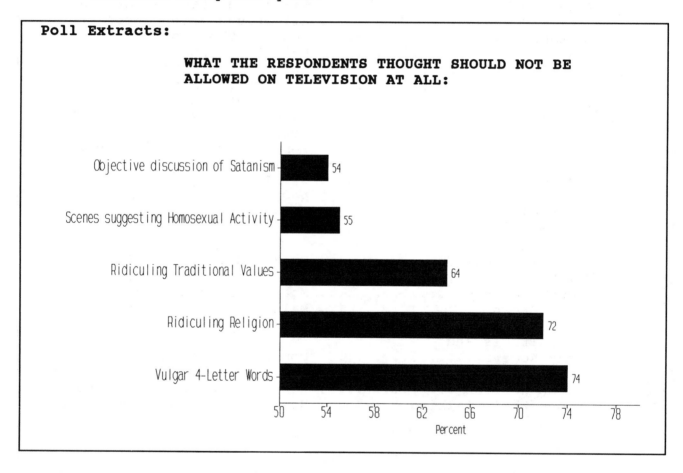

WHAT THE RESPONDENTS THOUGHT SHOULD NOT BE ALLOWED ON TELEVISION AT ALL:

Category	Percent
Objective discussion of Satanism	54
Scenes suggesting Homosexual Activity	55
Ridiculing Traditional Values	64
Ridiculing Religion	72
Vulgar 4-Letter Words	74

Also in Source: The percentage of respondents who watch TV every day; who watch one to three hours a day; and who rate TV programming as excellent, good, fair, poor, or terrible.

Poll Details: The poll was a national opinion poll commissioned by *Parents* Magazine.

Availability: Published in *Parents*, April 1990 (volume 65, number 4), p. 34.

TURNED OFF TELEVISIONS

Description: Presents the results of a survey concerning the level of
television viewing compared with a year ago. Survey also includes
questions concerning cable television and the presence of violence on TV.

Results: 70% of the respondents are watching less television today compared to
a year ago.

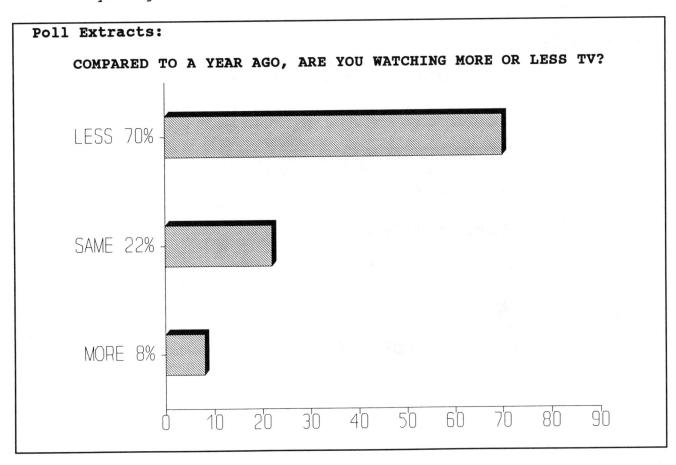

Poll Extracts:

COMPARED TO A YEAR AGO, ARE YOU WATCHING MORE OR LESS TV?

LESS 70%

SAME 22%

MORE 8%

0 10 20 30 40 50 60 70 80 90

Also in Source: 78% of the respondents have cable television. 56% are
watching more cable, 22% are watching the same, and the same are watching
less. 58% of the respondents said television is too predictable, 40% said
television is too violent, 28% said television is too racy, and 8% said
television is too tame. 46% said TV needs more family fare, 33% said it
needs more adult shows, and 26% said it needs more news and information.

Poll Details: *USA Today* asked readers to describe their viewing habits in an
informal write-in, and more than 2,000 people responded.

Availability: Published in *USA Today*, July 23, 1990, p. 1D, 2D.

AIRLINE SELECTION

Description: Respondents were asked about the factors which are the most important in their selection of an airline.

Results: Pleasure travelers thought that an airline's safety record and ticket price were the most important factors in choosing an airline. Business travelers thought that an airline's safety record and schedule convenience were the most important factors in choosing an airline.

Poll Extracts:

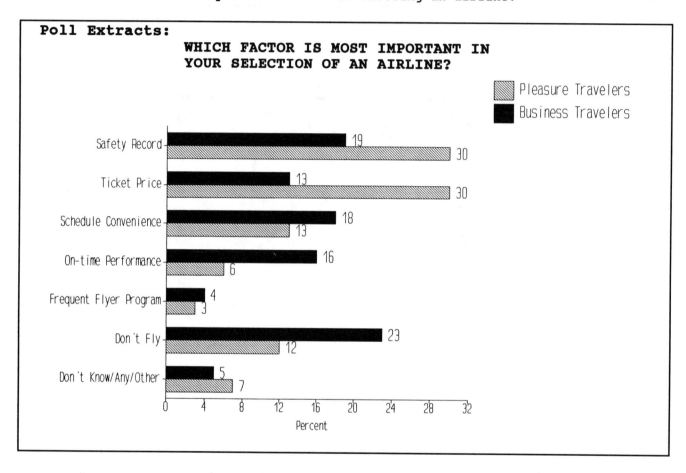

WHICH FACTOR IS MOST IMPORTANT IN YOUR SELECTION OF AN AIRLINE?

Pleasure Travelers
Business Travelers

Safety Record — Business 19, Pleasure 30
Ticket Price — Business 13, Pleasure 30
Schedule Convenience — Business 18, Pleasure 13
On-time Performance — Business 16, Pleasure 6
Frequent Flyer Program — Business 4, Pleasure 3
Don't Fly — Business 23, Pleasure 12
Don't Know/Any/Other — Business 5, Pleasure 7

Percent

Also in Source: "How average consumers form their impressions of an air carrier's safety record is uncertain, however, because this information typically is not a part of airline advertising campaigns."

Poll Details: This Gallup Organization/*Advertising Age* telephone survey involved 1,050 people. The group was composed of 484 men and 566 women.

Availability: Published in *Advertising Age*, November 5, 1990 (volume 61, number 46), p. S-2.

ATLANTA'S ECONOMY

Description: Presents the results of a survey concerning the present state of
the economy of Atlanta, Georgia.

Results: Over 60% of the respondents feel Atlanta's economic condition is good.

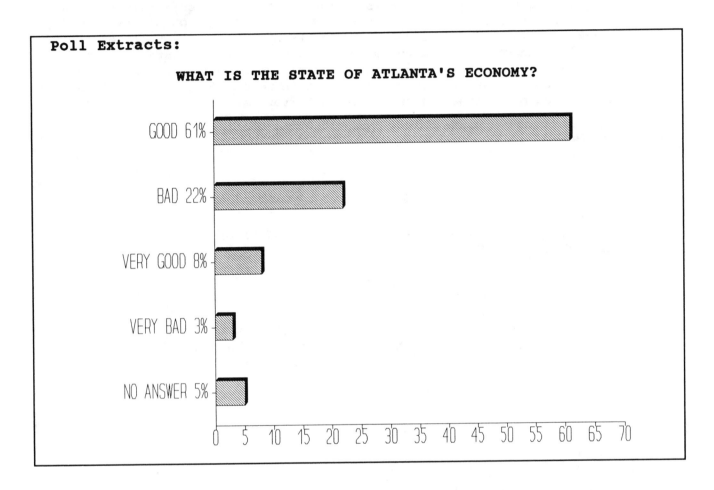

Also in Source: 44% of the respondents will spend the same this year on
holiday shopping as last year, 35% will spend less, and 19% will spend
more. When whites were asked what they thought their household financial
situation would be by next spring compared to today 57% said it would get
better, 26% said it would stay the same, 14% said it would get worse, and
3% had no opinion. When blacks were asked the same question, 69% said it
would get better, 14% said it would stay the same, 9% said it would get
worse, and 8% had no opinion.

Poll Details: Results of *The Atlanta Journal and Constitution* Confidence Poll
are based on telephone interviews with 889 adults in Clyton, Cobb, DeKalb,
Fulton, and Gwinnett counties in Georgia. The margin of error is plus or
minus 3%. The poll was conducted by Voice Information Services Inc., an
operating unit of *The Atlanta Journal and Constitution*.

Availability: Published in *The Atlanta Journal and Constitution*, November 21,
1990, p. A1, A4.

BRIEFCASES WANTED IN 2000 A.D.

Description: This poll asked 1,000 men and women what they'd like to carry in their real leather briefcases in the year 2000.

Results: High on the list of "wants" were:` vision phones, smaller personal computers with increasingly complex capabilities, and entertainment systems (combination AM-FM stereo receiver, VCR, color TV, and CD player). One respondent said, "The briefcase should obviously contain the latest in high-tech gadgetry, but more importantly, the case also acts as a self-defensive tool. The case should be bullet and explosion proof, contain a hidden camera, tape recorder and a built-in weapon device: a knife or gun to protect executives against theft or terrorism."

Poll Extracts:

**WHAT DO YOU WANT TO CARRY IN YOUR BRIEFCASE
IN THE YEAR 2000?**

A highly portable advanced communications system
--a case with a built-in telephone with faxing
capabilities and a collapsible satellite dish 72%

Also in Source: "One wag suggested carrying an instant inflatable lifesize doll so 'I'd never have to dine alone.'"

Poll Details: 1,000 men and women were surveyed by Delsey Luggage.

Availability: Published in the *Chicago Tribune,* February 25, 1990, section 12, p. 2.

BUSINESS TRAVEL COSTS

Description: Presents the results of a survey concerning business travel
       trends and priorities.

Results: Over 50% of the business managers surveyed said their companies have
       taken advantage of special air fares in the past year to hold travel costs
       down. A number of other cost containment measures were also implemented.

Poll Extracts:

COST SAVING POLICIES IMPLEMENTED THIS PAST YEAR:

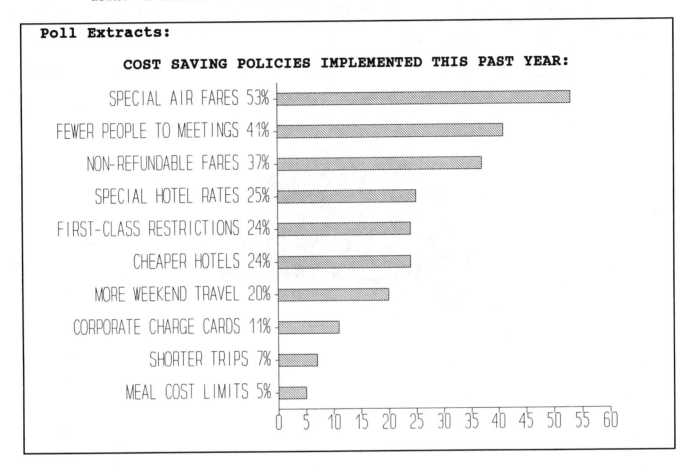

Also in Source: 42% of the respondents said their travel budgets increased
       this past year from one to ten percent. American Airlines was cited as the
       favorite airline and Eastern received the lowest rasting.

Poll Details: *USA Today* conducted an informal survey of 190 corporate travel
       managers at the National Business Travel Association convention.

Availability: Published in *USA Today*, July 7, 1990, p. 1B, 4B.

DETROIT'S IMAGE

Description: This survey asked Detroit-area business leaders about Detroit's image.

Results: Over 80% of the respondents thought that Detroit's image had a negative impact on the business climate of southeast Michigan. Over 88% thought that public safety was the most negative aspect of doing business in Detroit. More than 78% thought public safety was getting worse. "But more than 70% said that quality of life -- recreation and culture -- has a positive impact on business."

Poll Extracts:

IS DETROIT'S IMAGE:

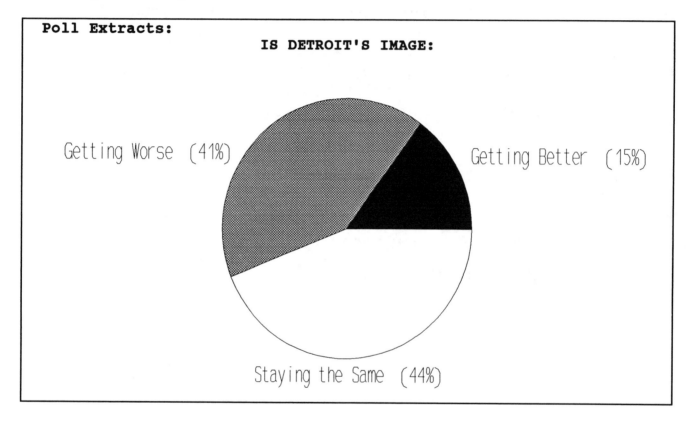

Getting Worse (41%)   Getting Better (15%)

Staying the Same (44%)

Also in Source: The percentage of respondents who thought that the quality of life was getting better, worse, or staying the same. Positive and negative aspects of doing business in southeast Michigan. The percentage of respondents who rated education as a positive factor for business.

Poll Details: This survey by the Greater Detroit Chamber of Commerce queried 650 respondents chosen at random from the chamber's 5,200 members.

Availability: Published in the *Detroit Free Press*, March 29, 1990, p. 1E.

FLYING SAFETY

Description: This reader survey questioned respondents regarding flying
safety.

Results: The fear of flying has increased over the last 2 years. 42% of the
respondents have avoided a specific airline in the last 2 years, in
relation to their concern for personal safety. 46% of respondents feel
least safe on an airplane, when compared to cars, buses, or trains. 54% of
the respondents are worried most about mechanical problems and see
mechanical problems as the most common cause of airplane accidents. 36% of
the respondents believe that the media exaggerates the dangers of air
safety, while 64% believe that the news media have made them more concerned
about air safety.

Poll Extracts:

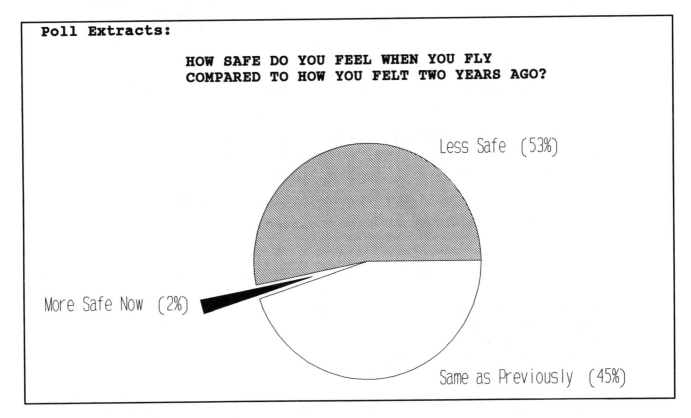

**HOW SAFE DO YOU FEEL WHEN YOU FLY
COMPARED TO HOW YOU FELT TWO YEARS AGO?**

Less Safe (53%)

More Safe Now (2%)

Same as Previously (45%)

Also in Source: Responses to the following questions: "What actions, if any,
have you taken in the past two years that were motivated by your concern
for personal safety?", "If you're concerned about flight safety, what
worries you the most?", "What do you see as the most common cause of
airplane accidents?" and "Is there any time during an airplane flight when
you feel uneasy?"

Poll Details: The responses are to a questionnaire that was published in the
October 1989 issue of *Travel & Leisure.* Participation was voluntary, and
3,100 readers replied. Respondents were evenly divided between male and
female, with 63% of the respondents older than age 44.

Availability: Published in *Travel & Leisure,* February 1990 (volume 20, number
2), p. 71.

FLYING WITH CHILDREN

Description: The results of a readers' survey about flying with children.

Results: Parents flying with children and fliers without children would like to see special accommodations for families flying with children.

Poll Extracts:

Parents who believe children should be over age
12 to fly by themselves .... One-third

Respondents who say travel agents don't really
know the airline rules regarding family travel 45%

Respondents with children under age 12 who would
like a "family class" on flights, which would
include children's meals, restraining safety seats,
and cartoons. 89%

Travelers with children who don't want to pay
extra for a "family class," or wouldn't pay
more than $26 in order to have a "family class." 80%

Respondents without children who support the idea
of having "family sections." 92%

Also in Source: The percentage of respondents who say: their families split up for safety reasons when they fly, in the past they have selected an airline on the basis of its child policies, their children have visited the cockpit, they fly at least once a year with kids under 12, they find playrooms, they find changing tables in men's rooms, and they find stroller rentals at airports. A survey of airlines is mentioned which provides details as to who offers what for families traveling with children.

Poll Details: The results are from a *USA WEEKEND* readers' survey of almost 1,000 fliers. 882 respondents have children under age 12, and 107 respondents do not have children.

Availability: Published in *USA WEEKEND*, March 2-4, 1990, p. 10-12.

GOING TO THE BEACH

Description: Presents the results of a survey concerning the popularity of beach or lake summer vacation activities.

Results: Over 80% of the respondents said that going to the beach was something they like to do or was one of the activities they enjoy most in the summer.

Poll Extracts:

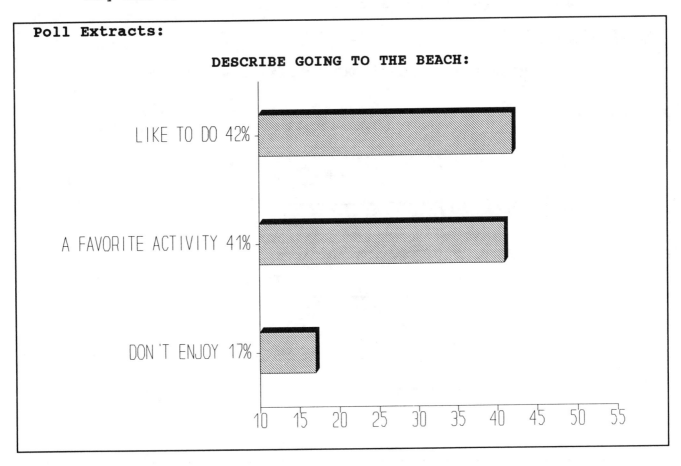

Also in Source: When asked about their appearance in a swimsuit, 4% characterized themselves as real knockouts, 77% said they were presentable, and 15% said they were not presentable. 63% said that relaxing and doing nothing was a favorite beach activity. 58% chose reading, 53% selected picnicking, 40% participated in sports, 38% swam, 29% enjoyed watching attractive people in skimpy outfits, 20% liked getting a tan, and 8% enjoyed showing off their bodies.

Poll Details: This national opinion poll was commissioned by *Parents* magazine.

Availability: Published in *Parents*, August, 1990 (volume 65, number 8), p. 26.

MAKING FLYING MORE COMFORTABLE

Description: Presents the results of a survey concerning possible improvements
which might be implemented to make air travel more comfortable and
enjoyable.

Results: Over half of the respondents said offering a choice of movies would
make their flight more comfortable.

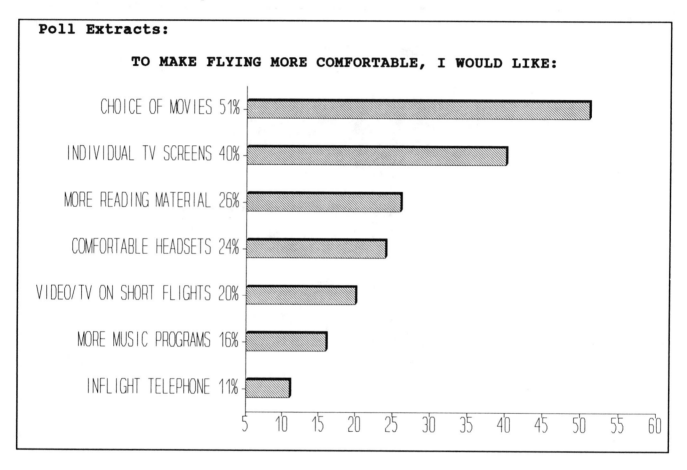

Poll Extracts:

TO MAKE FLYING MORE COMFORTABLE, I WOULD LIKE:

CHOICE OF MOVIES 51%
INDIVIDUAL TV SCREENS 40%
MORE READING MATERIAL 26%
COMFORTABLE HEADSETS 24%
VIDEO/TV ON SHORT FLIGHTS 20%
MORE MUSIC PROGRAMS 16%
INFLIGHT TELEPHONE 11%

5 10 15 20 25 30 35 40 45 50 55 60

Also in Source: A number of issues concerning business travel are included in
the column.

Poll Details: The World Airline Entertainment Association surveyed 4,215
flyers. Those surveyed could select more than one response.

Availability: Published in *USA Today,* November 20, 1990, p. 4B.

NEW YORK'S STANDARD OF LIVING

Description: Presents the results of a survey of New York City residents
concerning the state of their city.

Results: Almost 70% of the respondents said the quality of life in New York
City has worsened in the past five years.

Poll Extracts:

HOW HAS THE QUALITY OF LIFE CHANGED IN NEW YORK CITY?

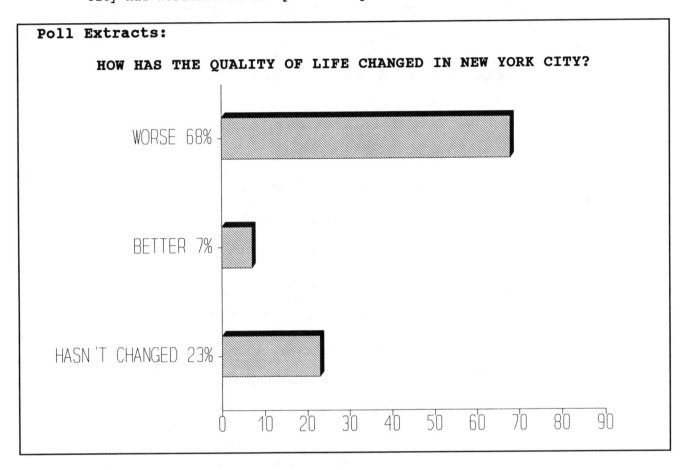

Also in Source: 60% of the respondents worry often or all the time about
crime. 45% think the quality of life will worsen in the next few years.
59% of the respondents would move somewhere else if they could. 78%
described New York as a place that is dirty, 73% described it as a
dangerous place to live, and 54% described New York as a city they like to
live in. 72% said it is getting tougher to live in New York.

Poll Details: The results of the survey were taken from a telephone survey of
1,009 New York City residents for *Time*/CNN on August 2-5, 1990 by
Yankelovich Clancy Shulman. Sampling error was plus or minus 3%.

Availability: Published in *Time*, September 17, 1990 (volume 136, number 12),
p. 36-41, 44.

OBSTACLES TO BUSINESS EXPANSION

Description: Presents the results of a survey concerning factors that may influence a company's attitude toward on-site expansion in the city of Atlanta, Georgia.

Results: Local traffic congestion was cited as the most important improvement factor related to business operations or to the living environment.

```
+----------------------------------------------------------------+
| Poll Extracts:                                                 |
|                                                                |
|              WHAT CEOs WANT IMPROVED IN ATLANTA:               |
|                                                                |
|                                                                |
|         1.   Local traffic congestion                         |
|                                                                |
|         2.   Crime                                            |
|                                                                |
|         3.   Poor public transportation                       |
|                                                                |
|         4.   Harassment by homeless                           |
|                                                                |
|         5.   Poor public schools                              |
|                                                                |
|         6.   Lack of unskilled labor                          |
|                                                                |
|         7.   Quality of unskilled labor                       |
|                                                                |
|         8.   Government bureaucracy                            |
|                                                                |
|         9.   High property taxes                              |
|                                                                |
|        10.   Taxes                                            |
|                                                                |
|                                                                |
+----------------------------------------------------------------+
```

Also in Source: 41% of the CEOs surveyed said they weren't certain if their companies would expand in the next three to five years, 35% said they would, and 24% said they would not expand. The CEOs also rated the Atlanta work force. They like metro Atlanta's managemenmt talent: 79% said it's good to excellent. However, 51% rate the supply of unskilled workers at fair to poor.

Poll Details: The Atlanta Chamber of Commerce surveyed 161 local CEOs in face-to-face interviews.

Availability: Published in *The Atlanta Journal and Constitution,* August 30, 1990, p. C-1.

THE OUTLOOK FOR NEW YORK CITY

Description: This poll asked New Yorkers what they thought the future for New York City would be.

Results: Four years from now, 59% of the respondents would prefer to be living somewhere other than New York City. When asked about their outlook for New York City's economy, 64% of the respondents thought the economy would be getting worse.

Poll Extracts:

IN 10 OR 15 YEARS, RESPONDENTS EXPECTED
NEW YORK CITY TO BE:

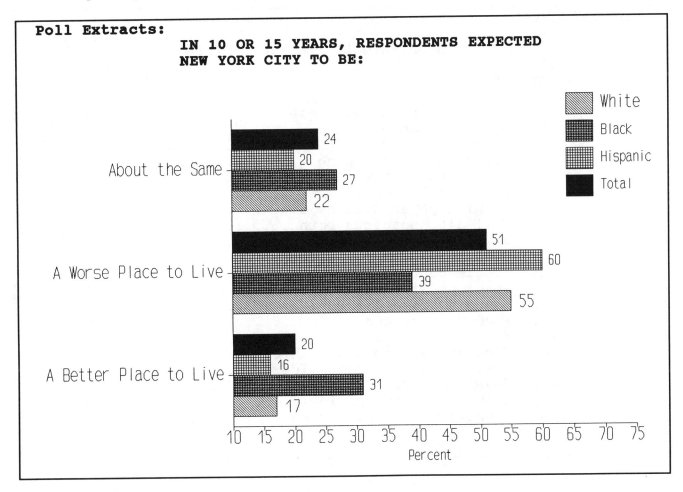

Also in Source: Responses are broken down according to white, black, and Hispanic response. Views on New York City Mayor David N. Dinkins, six months after his inauguration. Views on Mayor Dinkins' handling of race relations. The problems that the respondents thought Mayor Dinkins should concentrate on first.

Poll Details: This *New York Times*/WCBS-TV News Poll conducted June 17-20, 1990, was based on telephone interviews with 1,047 adults. The margin of sampling error is plus or minus 3%. The sampling error for the smaller subgroups is larger. For whites it is 4%, blacks - 5%, and Hispanics - 7%. Further details as to how the the respondents' telephone numbers were selected are provided in the source.

Availability: Published in *The New York Times*, June 26, 1990, p. B1, B2.

PROVIDE A COMFORTABLE BED/MATTRESS

Description: This *Hideaway Report* survey asked readers to list their 10 favorite hotel room amenities.

Results: The overwhelming majority of respondents chose a comfortable bed/mattress over other amenities such as bathroom telephones, jacuzzi tubs, bidets, complimentary toiletries, and a stocked refrigerator/minibar.

Poll Extracts:

FAVORITE GUEST ROOM AMENITIES

Amenity	% Who Mentioned
1. Comfortable bed/mattress	98%
2. Solid soundproofing	89%
3. Abundance of quality towels	80%
4. Thorough housekeeping	74%
5. Quiet, non-drafty air conditioning	73%
6. Comfortable bed pillows	72%
7. Morning paper outside door	71%
8. Well-lit, spacious bath	70%
9. Efficient room service	69%
10. Good reading lamps	62%
11. Remote control TV	53%
12. Spacious sitting area	46%
13. Lounging robe	45%
14. Windows that open	42%
15. In-room safe	38%
16. Stocked refrigerator/minibar	33%
17. Evening turn-down service	30%
18. Generous closet/drawer space	29%
Walkout balcony/patio	29%
20. Complimentary toiletries	27%

Also in Source: A definition of quality bedding, and the care that is required for a mattress and boxspring.

Poll Details: *The Hideaway Report* conducted this readers' survey.

Availability: Originally published in *The Hideaway Report*, September 1990. The information provided is based on an article printed in *Lodging Hospitality*, November 1990 (volume 46, number 11), p. 79-80.

RATING THE WORLD'S AIRLINES

Description: This survey asked 25,000 people to rank the world's airlines with a 0-30 score, indicating poor to excellent; in areas such as comfort, service, timeliness, food, cost and value.

Results: The top ten spots went to international carriers. The Soviet Airline "Aeroflot" was rated as the world's worst airline. Swissair was ranked as the world's best airline for being "on time." Except for timeliness, Singapore Airlines ranked first in all categories.

Poll Extracts:

THE WORLD'S TOP 15 AIRLINES

Rank	Airline	Country	Score
1.	Singapore	Singapore	25.14
2.	Swissair	Switzerland	23.95
3.	JAL	Japan	22.57
4.	SAS	Sweden	22.33
5.	Qantas	Australia	22.08
6.	Lufthansa	W. Germany	22.05
7.	KLM	Netherlands	21.34
8.	British Airways	Great Britain	20.54
9.	Air France	France	20.50
10.	Varig	Brazil	19.94
11.	American	U.S.	18.62
12.	Virgin Atlantic	Great Britain	18.52
13.	Air Canada	Canada	18.39
14.	Delta	U.S.	18.12
15.	Alitalia	Italy	16.74

Also in Source: "Overall, half of all passengers' complaints concerned delays."

Poll Details: This 1990 Zagat Airline Survey was the first for Tim and Nina Zagat. Questionnaires were sent out in Spring 1990 to 25,000 people. The survey includes the opinions of 4,462 business travelers who average almost one night a week on the road. The scoring is as follows: 26-30 indicates excellent; 20-25, very good to excellent; 10-19, good to very good; 0-9, poor to fair.

Availability: Published in the *Chicago Tribune*, September 7, 1990 (section 3), p. 1-2.

TRAVEL-RELATED SERVICES

Description: Business executives were asked who provides the best service in
several travel-related areas.

Results: Respondents rated the following as the best in their particular area:
Domestic Airport -- Atlanta's Hartsfield International Airport-18%,
Domestic Airline -- American-29%, Airline Club -- American's Admiral Club-
21%, Hotel Chain -- Marriott-28%.

Poll Extracts:

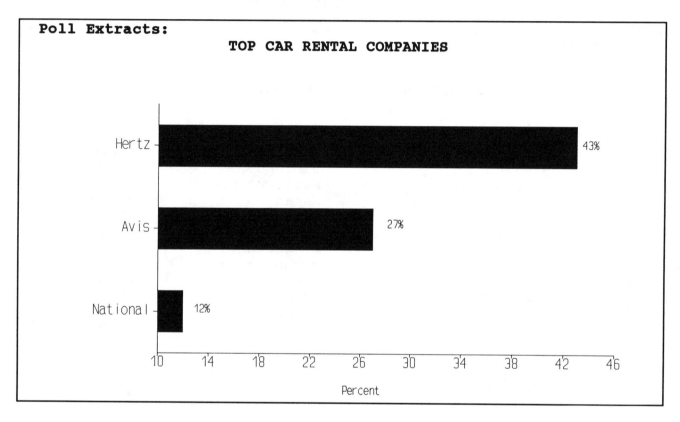

TOP CAR RENTAL COMPANIES

Also in Source: Companies which were ranked best in: overnight delivery
service, long-distance phone service, and credit card service.

Poll Details: Dom Perignon surveyed 1,000 business professionals in 10 cities.

Availability: Published in *The Atlanta Journal and Constitution*, November 2,
1990, p. E-2.

THE VERY BEST HOTELS AND RESORTS

Description: Respondents were asked to list their choices for the best U.S. resort, the best international resort, and the best U.S. city hotel.

Results: The favorite U.S. resort was The Boulders (Arizona), while the best international resort was Jumby Bay (Antigua). The best U.S. city hotel was the Bel-Air (Los Angeles).

Poll Extracts:

The Top 15 U.S. Resorts

1. The Boulders (Arizona)
2. The Greenbrier (West Virginia)
3. Ritz-Carlton Laguna Niguel (California)
4. Mauna Lani Bay (Hawaii)
5. The Cloister (Georgia)
6. Mauna Kea (Hawaii)
7. Lodge at Pebble Creek (California)
8. Ventana (California)
9. Ritz-Carlton Naples (Florida)
10. Auberge du Soliel (California)
11. Hana-Maui (Hawaii)
12. Kapalua Bay (Hawaii)
13. Caneel Bay (U.S. Virgin Islands)
14. The Point (New York)
15. The Halekulani (Hawaii)

Also in Source: The top 10 U.S. city hotels and the top 15 international resorts.

Poll Details: Readers of Andrew Harper's *Hideaway Report* were queried in this annual survey. *Hideaway Report* readers have an average annual income of $309,000 and an average net worth of $2.8 million; their average age is 51.

Availability: The September issue of the *Hideaway Report* listed the results of its annual survey. The information provided is based on an article printed in *The Atlanta Journal and Constitution*, October 7, 1990, p. K-7.

WORST ROADS ACCORDING TO TRUCKERS

Description: Presents the results of an informal survey of truckers identifying the ten worst roads in America.

Results: I-80 in Iowa is considered the worst road in the United States by truckers.

Poll Extracts:

THE 10 WORST ROADS IN AMERICA:

1. I-80 in Iowa

2. I-70 in Kansas

3. I-84 in New York

4. I-40 in Arkansas

5. I-81 in Pennsylvania

6. I-90 in Ohio

7. I-10 in Louisiana

8. I-10 in California

9. I-94 in Illinois

10. I-80 in Pennsylvania

Also in Source: A general discussion of interstate highway accidents and road safety is included in the article.

Poll Details: The ten stretches of interstate highway in the most need of repair were identified by an informal survey conducted in truck stops across the country in August, 1990 by Jay Eger, a 20-year veteran driver and journalist.

Availability: Published in *USA Today*, August 31, 1990, p. 8A.

DAN QUAYLE VERSUS MARILYN QUAYLE

Description: This poll asked the question who is smarter, Dan Quayle or
       Marilyn Quayle.

Results: Approximately half of the respondents felt that Marilyn Quayle is the
       smarter of the two.

Poll Extracts:

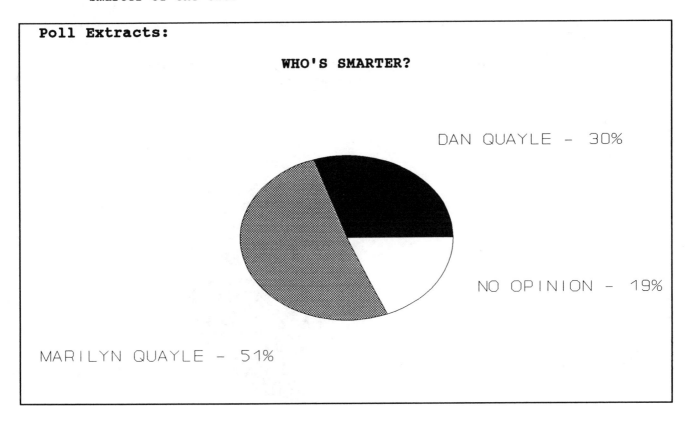

WHO'S SMARTER?

DAN QUAYLE - 30%

NO OPINION - 19%

MARILYN QUAYLE - 51%

Also in Source: The article also includes a number of other questions
       concerning a wide variety of celebrities.

Poll Details: The poll was conducted by Audits & Surveys Inc. for *People
       Weekly*. They contacted 1,000 *People Weekly* readers. This is the
       magazine's 11th annual poll.

Availability: Published in *People Weekly*, January 8, 1990 (volume 33, number
       1), p. 58-68.

PERFORMANCE RATING OF VICE PRESIDENT DAN QUAYLE

Description: This poll surveyed opinions on the performance of Vice President Dan Quayle.

Results: Vice President Dan Quayle's job performance is not rated as highly as President Bush's.

Poll Extracts:

FEELINGS TOWARD VICE PRESIDENT DAN QUAYLE'S JOB PERFORMANCE:

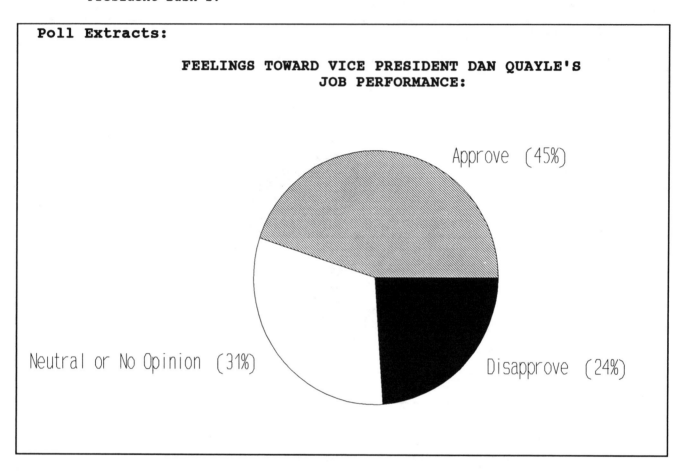

Approve (45%)

Neutral or No Opinion (31%)

Disapprove (24%)

Also in Source: The percentage of respondents who approve, disapprove, or have no opinion toward President Bush's job performance. The percentage of Democratic respondents and black voters who approve of President Bush's performance.

Poll Details: This Ohio Poll was conducted by the University of Cincinnati's Institute for Policy Research for the *Dayton Daily News* and *The Cincinnati Post*. It was a telephone interview of 802 randomly selected people in the State of Ohio, from February 2-12, 1990. The margin of error is 4%.

Availability: Published in the *Dayton Daily News*, March 5, 1990, p. 1-A, 4-A.

BENEFITS VERSUS MORE PAY

Description: Presents the results of a survey concerning the relative importance of employee benefits compared to increased salaries.

Results: Almost 40% of the respondents would need a salary increase of $9,000 or more to select a job with no health insurance over one which offered health insurance.

Poll Extracts:

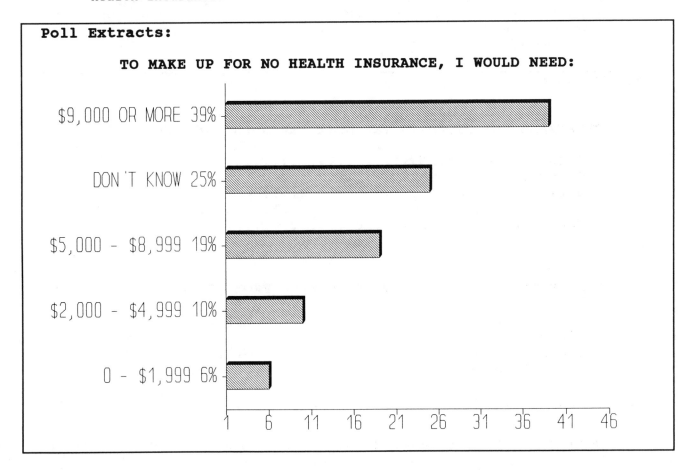

TO MAKE UP FOR NO HEALTH INSURANCE, I WOULD NEED:

$9,000 OR MORE 39%

DON'T KNOW 25%

$5,000 - $8,999 19%

$2,000 - $4,999 10%

0 - $1,999 6%

Also in Source: More than 80% of the respondents consider health and life insurance, pensions, vacations, and sick leave when they decide whether to accept a job offer. 15% of the respondents had changed, quit, or accepted a job based on benefits. 69% said they would not accept a job that did not provide health benefits. 30% of the workers with company health plans had no idea how much their employers contributed to health coverage.

Poll Details: This Gallup survey of 1,000 people was conducted for the Washington-based Employee Benefit Research Institute.

Availability: Published in *The Columbus Dispatch*, September 20, 1990, p. 1F.

COMPUTER HAZARDS

Description: This survey sought opinions on various office environment issues, with computer-related issues as an integral part of the survey.

Results: "Heavy computer users" (workers using a computer for five or more hours a day) are more concerned about eyestrain, and VDT radiation, than their fellow office workers. They also feel a lower level of job satisfaction (37%) than all office workers (41%). Heavy computer users also feel a higher sense of not working at their top productivity than all office workers (46% vs. 49%).

Poll Extracts:

EYESTRAIN WAS CITED AS THE MOST PREVALENT OFFICE HAZARD BY:

Interior Designers	86%
Heavy Computer Users	64%
Office Workers	44%
Facilities Managers	40%
Top Executives	36%

CONCERNED ABOUT RADIATION EMANATING FROM VDT'S:

Heavy Computer Users	49%
Office Workers	27%
Top Managers	22%
Facilities Managers	18%

Also in Source: The percentage of heavy computer users in 1989 as compared to 1988. The percentage of office workers who have a PC at home that they use for office work and, of this group, the percentage that said their PC was provided by their employer.

Poll Details: The report, "Office Environment Index," was developed from a telephone survey of 1,041 full-time office workers, top executives, facilities managers, and interior designers in American companies with 25 or more employees. The survey was conducted from November 1988 to January 1989 by Louis Harris and Associates for Steelcase, Inc., located in Grand Rapids, Michigan.

Availability: Published in *Personal Computing,* May 25, 1990 (volume 14, number 5), p. 34.

DISCRIMINATION IN THE WORKPLACE

Description: Presents the results of a survey concerning the presence of
discrimination in the workplace. The survey addresses several
discrimination issues and remedies.

Results: Almost 80% of the respondents believe some, most, or all employers
practice some form of job discrimination. Over 60% of the people
interviewed said they would be much more willing to take legal action
against an employer now than they would have been five years ago.

Poll Extracts:

HOW WIDESPREAD IS JOB DISCRIMINATION?

Do some, most, or all employers practice
some form of job discrimination?......................Yes...78%

Do most or all employers practice some
form of job discrimination?...........................Yes...51%

Have you personally experienced job discrimination?...Yes...25%

Would you be much more willing to take legal
action against an employer over job discrimination
now than you would have been five years ago?.........Yes...62%

Would you be given a fair shake from the legal
system if you did file suit over discrimination?......No....55%

Would you give up your right to a court hearing
in favor of arbitration on a grievance?...............Yes...53%

Also in Source: 58% said they favored affirmative action in the workplace to
remedy some or all cases of past discrimination, but a breakdown of the
responses by race and sex shows a somewhat different picture. The poll
showed that 67% of blacks favored preferential measures in all cases but
only 44% of whites did. In cases involving women, only 49% of women
favored preferential treatment. 48% said they favored prohibiting all
women able to bear children from working at any job that might be hazardous
to the fetus and 47% were opposed. 53% of the men favored such a policy
while 43% of the women did.

Poll Details: The poll conducted in June, 1990 by Penn & Schoen Associates
involved a random sample of 803 adults, 48% of whom were men. A racial
breakdown showed about 82% were white, 10% black, and 5% Hispanic. Self-
described conservatives edged out liberals, 35% to 34%. The balance
described themselves as moderate.

Availability: Published in *The Washington Post*, July 9, 1990, p. A12.

FIRST JOB PROMOTION

Description: Recent college graduates were polled about their expectations for their first jobs.

Results: A majority of the respondents expected to only spend two years or less in an entry level position before receiving a promotion. Respondents also expected their first job to be composed of "paying your dues" type work, at the following levels: less than 10% -- 10.5% of the respondents, 10 to 50% -- 55.1% of the respondents, 51-75% -- 21.7% of the respondents, and 76% or more -- 8.7% of the respondents.

Poll Extracts:

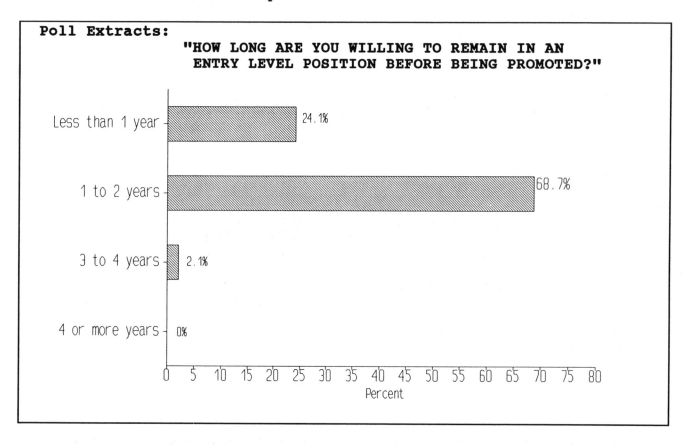

"HOW LONG ARE YOU WILLING TO REMAIN IN AN ENTRY LEVEL POSITION BEFORE BEING PROMOTED?"

Poll Details: Dante Personnel Services surveyed more than 300 college graduates from June to August 1990. 58% of the respondents were women and 42% were men.

Availability: Published in *The Atlanta Journal and Constitution,* October 10, 1990, p. B-2.

IMPACT OF DOWNSIZING

Description: This survey queried employees of companies that had merged with another company or participated in downsizing, as to their perceptions of their companies.

Results: People who have retained their jobs in companies that have merged or downsized are less satisfied with their work and less confident about the future of their company. The percentage of employees who are confident about their company's future: 47% for companies with layoffs, and 71% for companies without layoffs; 48% of companies that have merged or been acquired and 67% for companies that have not merged or been acquired. The percentage of employees who are satisfied or very satisfied with their company: 48% for companies with layoffs, and 66% for companies without layoffs; 49% of companies that have merged or been acquired, and 60% of companies that have not merged or been acquired.

Poll Extracts:

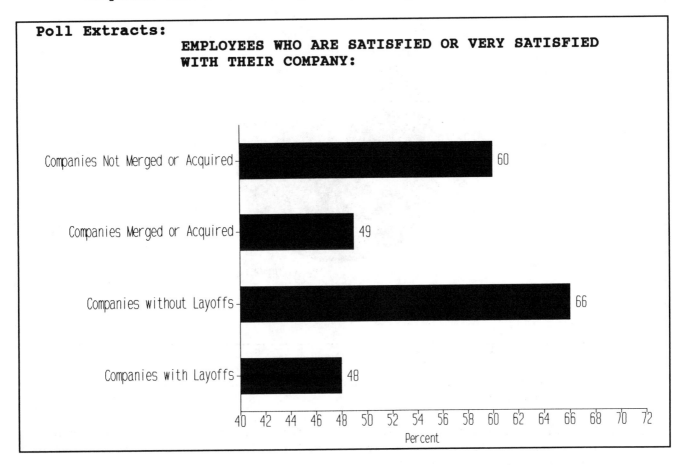

EMPLOYEES WHO ARE SATISFIED OR VERY SATISFIED WITH THEIR COMPANY:

Also in Source: Accompanying article on the devastating impact of downsizing.

Poll Details: The sampling of employee perceptions is based on a nationwide survey of 7,000 Americans by Gantz-Wiley Research Consulting Group Inc. of Minneapolis.

Availability: Published in *The Atlanta Journal and Constitution*, April 23, 1990, p. C-1, C-6.

IMPORTANCE OF A DRESS CODE

Description: Respondents were asked about the importance of a dress code in the workplace.

Results: The majority of workers prefer a dress code. Women favor dress codes more strongly than men. Employees of small businesses rate dress codes more important than do employees of larger firms. People who live on the East Coast prefer dress codes more than those who live on the West Coast.

Poll Extracts:

"HOW IMPORTANT IS A COMPANY DRESS CODE?"

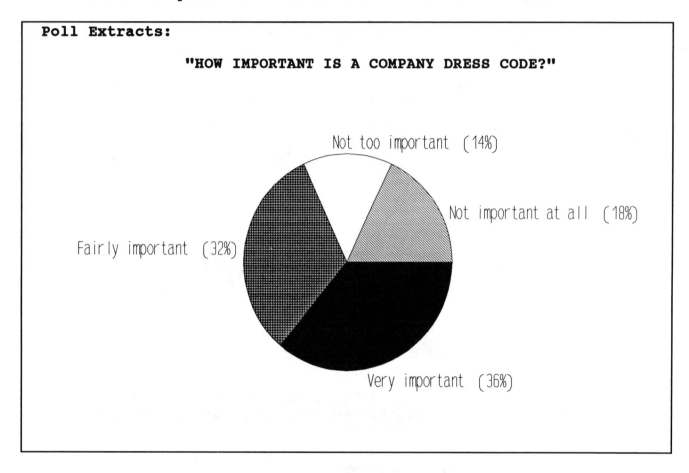

Also in Source: Job satisfaction was thought to have an effect on attitudes toward dress codes.

Poll Details: The Gallup Organization conducted this survey for the Ricoh Corporation. 500 office workers were interviewed by telephone between May 22, and June 3, 1990.

Availability: Published in *The Atlanta Journal and Constitution*, November 21, 1990, p. C-2.

IMPROVING THE WORK FORCE

Description: Respondents were asked what was the most important step American
government or business could take in order to improve the quality of the
U.S. work force, and whether their company was spending more or less money
on educating workers compared to 10 years ago.

Results: 64% of the respondents thought that improving education was the most
important step that American government or business could take in order to
improve the quality of the U.S. work force. The majority of companies is
spending more on education now than it was 10 years ago.

Poll Extracts:

**"IS YOUR COMPANY SPENDING MORE ON EDUCATING
WORKERS THAN IT DID 10 YEARS AGO, SPENDING LESS,
OR SPENDING ABOUT THE SAME AMOUNT?"**

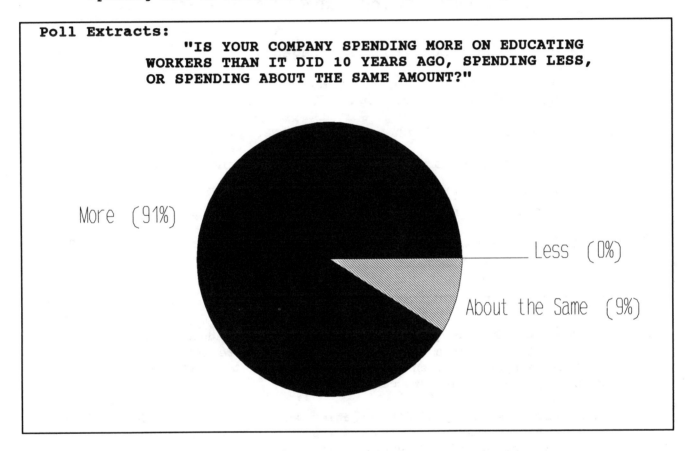

More (91%) Less (0%) About the Same (9%)

Also in Source: What respondents thought about certain proposals for
reforming U.S. public education. Attitudes toward the quality of the U.S.
work force.

Poll Details: This *Fortune* 500 CEO Poll was conducted by Clark Martire &
Bartolomeo. 206 chief executives of Fortune 500 and Service 500
corporations were interviewed between July 31 and August 8, 1990.

Availability: Published in *Fortune*, October 22, 1990 (volume 122, number 10),
p. 75-77.

LABOR AND SKILLS SHORTAGES

Description: Presents the results of a survey concerning the future labor
situation in the United States.

Results: While over 60% of the companies report concern about labor shortages,
only one-third have long-term plans to find and keep employees.

Poll Extracts:

THE LABOR SITUATION - TODAY AND TOMORROW:

Are you concerned about labor shortages?..............Yes...65%

Do you have long-term plans to find and
retain employees?......................................Yes...33%

Are you concerned about the skill gap?...............Yes...42%

Do you have trouble finding technical personnel?......Yes...70%

Do you offer support groups, mentor programs,
language help for women, minorities, and immigrants?..Yes...10%

Is discrimination a problem?..........................Yes...33%

Also in Source: Some companies have taken action to address the situation.
For example, Travelers Corporation has set up a retiree job bank, Days Inn
of America hires homeless and retirees, and the Mariott Corporation plans
to set up on-site day care centers.

Poll Details: The survey of 645 companies was co-sponsored by Towers Perrin
and the Hudson Institute. The results of the survey are included in the
study, *Workplace 2000: Competing in a Sellers Market*.

Availability: Published in *USA Today*, July 20-22, 1990, p. 1A

NOTHING NEW IN OFFICE ROMANCE

Description: Respondents were queried about office romance and dating on the job.

Results: Respondents sounded like their older counterparts who had participated in earlier surveys. It was perceived that more men became involved with a co-worker in order to satisfy their ego (56%). More women became involved with a co-worker for love (61%). Women were more likely to use a romance to advance their careers. 40% of the respondents thought it was okay for married co-workers to work at the same company.

Poll Extracts:

RESPONDENTS BELIEVED THAT:

Office romances have a negative impact
on a company .... 25% -- Yes

Office romances have a positive impact
on a company .... 6% -- Yes

Also in Source: Office romances did not seem to develop extensively from working closely together on the job.

Poll Details: The survey involved business students who had worked five years or less. The survey was conducted by Caroline Fisher (professor at Loyola University in New Orleans) and Claire Anderson (professor at Old Dominion University in Norfolk, Virginia).

Availability: Originally published in the *Orange County Register*. The information provided is based on an article printed in *The Columbus Dispatch*, December 9, 1990, p. 10G.

OFFICE ROMANCE

Description: This study surveyed company policies on marriage and dating between employees.

Results: Companies restrict marriage more than dating. Relationships between employees in different departments worry companies the least. Relationships between bosses and their subordinates worry companies the most. The top reasons cited by employers for restricting relationships are: "possible breaches of confidentiality," "negative effects on performance," and "awkwardness for all concerned."

Poll Extracts:

COMPANIES THAT:

Interfere with office dating relationships (including employees in the same department).................... 85% No

Permit intradepartmental employee marriages.......... 69% No

Restrict marriages between employees in supervisory relationships........................... 88% Yes

Believe restrictions do not fit the family-oriented corporate atmosphere...................... 20% Yes

---

Also in Source: The percentage of respondents who said they needed to hire couples as an incentive to solve a labor shortage.

Poll Details: This study by Philip K. Way, assistant professor of labor and employment relations at the University of Cincinnati, along with members of the Society of Human Resource Managers, surveyed 121 metro Cincinnati business executives.

Availability: Published in *The Cincinnati Enquirer*, March 19, 1990, p. D-4.

OFFICE STRESS

Description: This survey examined managers and their job stress.

Results: The top cause of job stress was lack of information. 28% of managers often bring stress home from the office, but 57% of managers say they rarely bring home stress to work. Fewer managers in the Midwest and West compared with managers in the East said that "overwork" was a cause of stress. Responsibility also caused less stress for older managers than younger managers.

Poll Extracts:

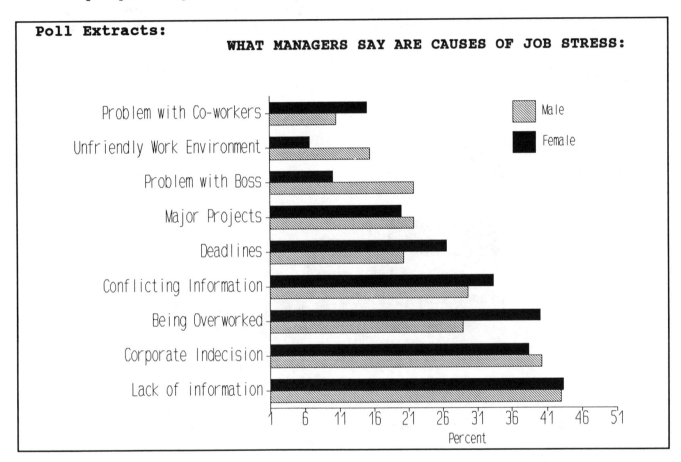

WHAT MANAGERS SAY ARE CAUSES OF JOB STRESS:

Poll Details: This survey by Dunhill Personnel System Inc. surveyed 225 middle managers, including 65 women, at 200 companies.

Availability: Published in *USA Today*, March 15, 1990, p. 8B.

UAW ATTITUDES

Description: This telephone poll gives the perspectives of 150 Detroit-area
            rank-and-file members, as to what is important to United Auto Workers'
            (UAW) members.

Results: 61% of the workers are willing to accept less work to create jobs for
            others. Just over half of the white workers support the idea of reduced
            work time to create jobs, compared to two-thirds of the black workers.
            Only 39% of the respondents think UAW leaders are doing a good job. Only
            31% of the respondents think that Big Three executives are doing a good
            job. Four out of five respondents thought that the union should work
            jointly with the companies to boost quality and output.

Poll Extracts:

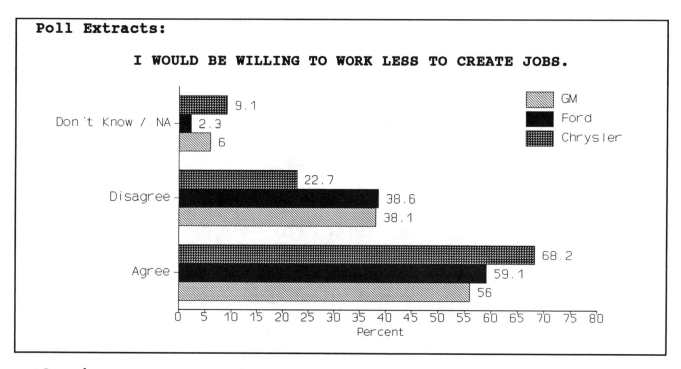

Also in Source: The percentage of respondents who believe that they're
            sharing in the benefits of joint programs to boost productivity. The top
            priorities of respondents for the upcoming contract talks, and the
            willingness of UAW members to strike in 1990. The percentage of
            respondents who thought that their living standards and job security had
            improved in the 1980s, and the percentage of respondents who expected their
            living standards and job security to improve during the 1990s.

Poll Details: The *Detroit Free Press* poll is based on telephone interviews
            conducted by Nordhaus Research Inc. of Southfield, Michigan. The survey
            does not give a scientifically accurate picture of the UAW membership, but
            rather the perspectives of 150 UAW members. The 150 Big Three workers that
            participated were contacted through telephone calls targeting Detroit Area
            counties with large concentrations of blue-collar workers. The interviews
            were conducted between April 30 and May 14, 1990. Demographic
            characteristics of the sample are included in the source. The margin of
            error for the total sample is 7.84 percentage points at the 95% confidence
            level.

Availability: Published in the *Detroit Free Press*, May 18, 1990, p. 1A, 6A.

VALUE OF HEALTH BENEFITS

Description: Respondents were queried on the importance of benefits and how benefits affect the decision to accept or reject a new job.

Results: Health insurance, pensions, vacations, and sick leave are an important factor used by 84% of the respondents in deciding to accept or reject a new job. 61% of the respondents considered health insurance as the most important employer-provided benefit, with 59% of the respondents not accepting a job without health insurance.

Poll Extracts:
AMOUNTS THAT RESPONDENTS SAID THEIR EMPLOYERS WOULD HAVE TO PAY THEM YEARLY IF THEIR EMPLOYER WANTED THEM TO FOREGO HEALTH BENEFITS.

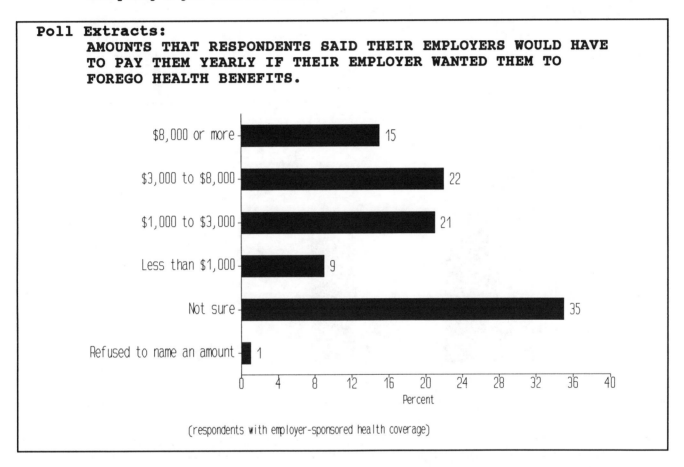

(respondents with employer-sponsored health coverage)

Also in Source: What respondents considered the least important benefit. The amount of money that respondents with employer-sponsored pension coverage wanted to be paid if they were to forego pension coverage.

Poll Details: This survey, *Public Attitudes on the Value of Benefits*, was sponsored by the Employee Benefit Research Institute. The Gallup Organization conducted this telephone poll of 1,000 people in May 1990.

Availability: Published in *Tax Management Financial Planning Journal*, October 16, 1990 (number 21), p. 430-431.

WHO WORKS MORE?

Description: Presents the results of a survey concerning how much time in a
    typical workday is spent on the job versus on breaks or otherwise not
    working.

Results: 75% of the women and 51% of men surveyed said they worked all day.

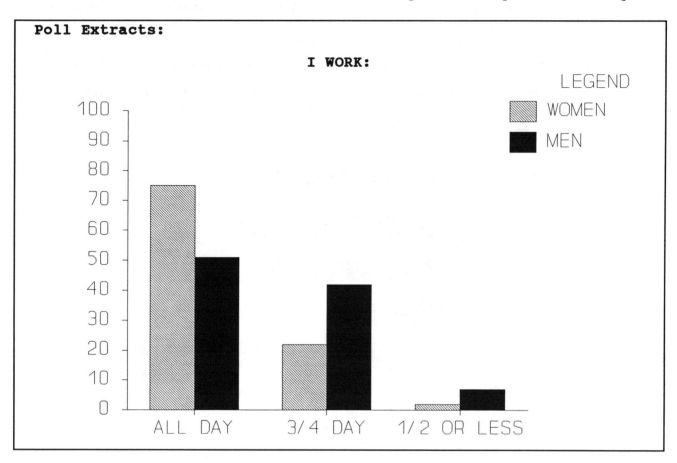

Also in Source: According to the survey, white-collar workers are
    significantly more likely to say all of their work day is productive
    compared to blue-collar workers.

Poll Details: The Gallup Organization conducted a national telephone survey of
    700 adults.

Availability: Published in *The Atlanta Journal and Constitution*, August 14,
    1990, p. C-2.

WOMEN AND CAREERS

Description: This readers' fax poll asked questions relating to women in the workplace.

Results: 64% of the respondents believe the number of women in upper management is "pitifully small." 55% believe that women still need laws to protect themselves in the workplace. 32% believe that discrimination is the main reason women haven't made it to the top of more corporations. 86% of the respondents would have no serious qualms about working for a woman boss. 77% believe that it is fair for women who work fewer hours because of family responsibilities to accept a slower career track. 74% of respondents believe that women do not need to behave more like men to get ahead.

Poll Extracts:

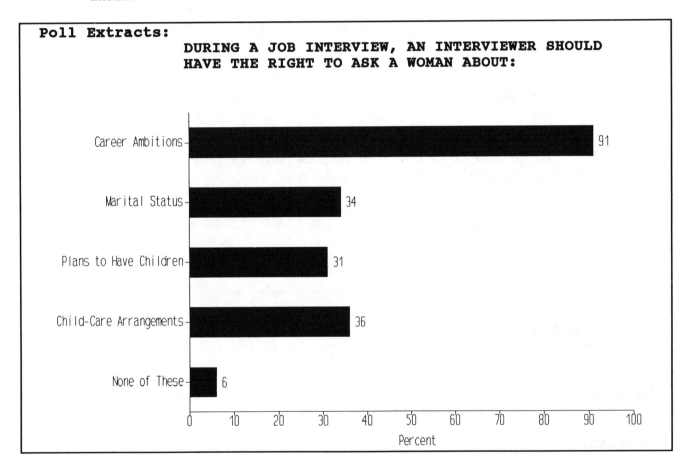

DURING A JOB INTERVIEW, AN INTERVIEWER SHOULD HAVE THE RIGHT TO ASK A WOMAN ABOUT:

Poll Details: This poll was conducted by *Business Month*, which asked readers to fax their responses to seven questions.

Availability: Published in *Business Month*, June 1990 (volume 135, number 6), p. 12-13.

ATTITUDES OF HIGH ACHIEVERS

Description: This survey of high school leaders listed in the 1990 edition of *Who's Who Among American High School Students* queried respondents on a variety of issues.

Results: Respondents chose the Chinese students who protested for democracy in Tiananmen Square as their Number One heroes for 1990. The Chinese student protesters were followed by Mikhail Gorbachev, Mother Teresa, and Nelson Mandela.

Poll Extracts:

RESPONDENTS THOUGHT THAT:

Athletes should be tested for steroids .... Yes -- 83%

Records, tapes, cassettes, and videos that
contain profanity or other objectionable
material should have warning labels .... Yes -- 57%

High schools should dispense contraceptives ... Yes -- 40%

Also in Source: 25% of the respondents said they had engaged in sexual intercourse, and 44% of that group said that their first experience occurred at age 16.

Poll Details: 2,000 students of the 650,000 students listed in *Who's Who Among American High School Students* were surveyed.

Availability: Published in *USA Today*, October 9, 1990, p. 5D.

HISTORY ACCORDING TO PRESCHOOLERS

Description: Presents the results of a survey of children at day care centers on what they know about Independence Day.

Results: When asked from whom the United States gained independence, over 50% of the respondents cited "the King." Only 2% cited the British.

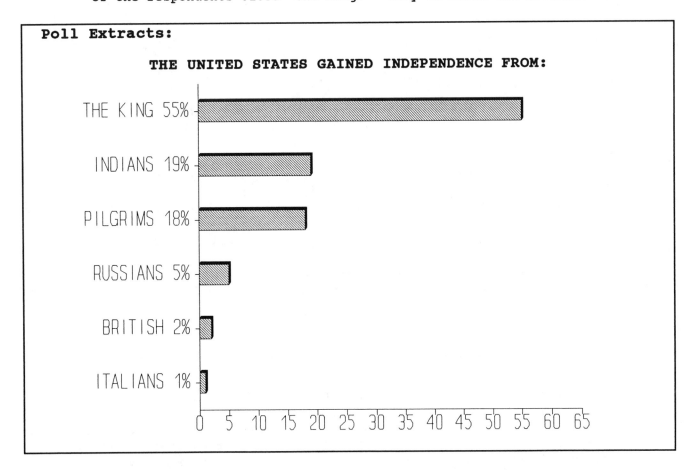

Poll Extracts:

THE UNITED STATES GAINED INDEPENDENCE FROM:

Also in Source: More children age four to six think Mrs. Bush was the American flag's seamstress than Betsy Ross, with 29% casting a vote for the president's wife and 15% going with Ross. 18% of the preschoolers knew the Fourth of July was a holiday but they weren't sure which one. 21% said July 4th had something to do with fireworks. None knew the holiday commemorates the adoption of the Declaration of Independence. 51% knew George Washington had something to do with the presidency and two kids from Atlanta knew he appears on money. One child thought Washington was a statue. 3% said he made the flag. 2% said God made the flag and Debbie Gibson was the guess of 15%.

Poll Details: Playskool Inc. surveyed 151 children, four to six years old, at day care centers in Boston, Atlanta, Cincinnati, Denver, and Los Angeles.

Availability: Published in *The Columbus Dispatch*, July 2, 1990, p. 1A.

MENTORING

Description: This survey examined teen-agers who had an adult mentor.

Results: Students with an adult mentor have improved grades, relationships, and tend to use drugs less. 45% are also more comfortable with, and have more respect for, other races.

Poll Extracts:

STUDENTS SAY THAT A MENTOR HAS HELPED THEM:

Boost Grades........................... 59% Yes

Avoid Drugs........................... 53% Yes

Get Along Better With Teachers........ 57% Yes

Get Along Better At Home............. 46% Yes

Also in Source: A parallel survey of 400 mentors is mentioned.

Poll Details: Louis Harris and Associates Inc. conducted the survey, which was cosponsored by the Commonwealth Fund, the MacArthur Foundation, and the Gannett Foundation. Four hundred teen-agers in the nationwide Career Beginnings program were surveyed.

Availability: Published in *USA Today*, March 28, 1990, p. 1A.

ON THE MINDS OF TEENS

Description: Presents the results of a survey of teenagers concerning a wide
variety of issues.

Results: Over 30% predict that the environment will be the most serious problem
by the time they reach 40. This is followed by drugs, crime, AIDS, and
racism.

Poll Extracts:

WHEN I REACH 40, THE MOST SERIOUS PROBLEMS WILL BE:

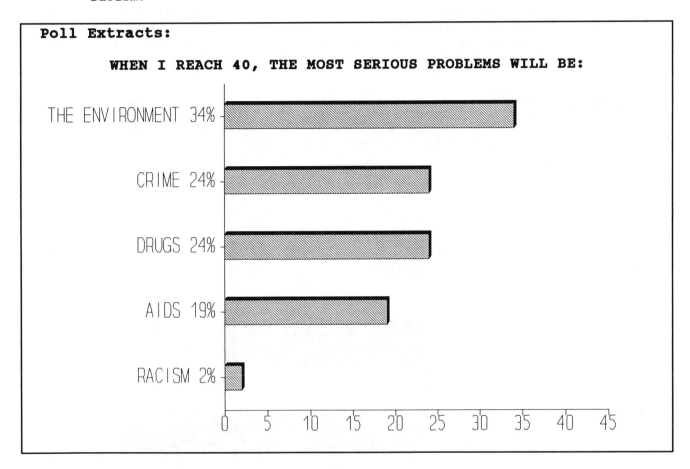

Also in Source: 74% of the respondents are concerned about finding a good job
and 67% worry about supporting a family. 51% worry about dying.
Concerning jobs, 40% rate pay as most important; 37% say job satisfaction;
and 23% cite a job's challenge. 98% want to finish high school and 83%
want a college education. 70% say marriage is in their future and 56% say
divorce is not. 77% expect a black president by the time they reach 40 and
72% overall say a woman will be elected president. 67% want to stay young
forever. Half think you're over the hill at 50. 70% want children. 52%
think the United States will have been at war by the time they reach 40 and
68% think there will be a 52nd state.

Poll Details: 26,946 adolescents responded to a *USA WEEKEND* survey.

Availability: Published in *USA WEEKEND*, August 17-19, 1990, p. 4, 5.

RULES FOR DATING

Description: This poll queried respondents about some of the rituals involved with dating or courtship.

Results: In regards to asking a member of the opposite sex for a date, 49% of the men polled do not agree that men prefer to do the asking. 91% of the respondents thought that women prefer to be asked on a date, rather than to ask. More than two-thirds of the respondents thought that the man should pay for the first-date dinner check. 25% thought that whoever asked for the date should pay. The majority of respondents (76%) preferred to meet people informally in social settings rather than have more formal dating rules.

Poll Extracts:

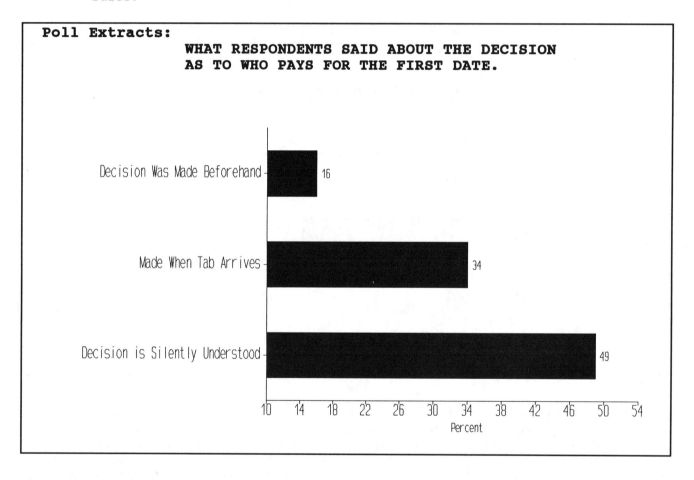

WHAT RESPONDENTS SAID ABOUT THE DECISION
AS TO WHO PAYS FOR THE FIRST DATE.

Also in Source: What men and women respondents said they would do if they saw someone attractive. How students describe what they're doing when they've gone out with someone several times.

Poll Details: R. H. Bruskin Associates compiled the data from a survey of 800 male and female college students on 16 campuses across the country.

Availability: Published in *In View*, May/June 1990 (volume 2, issue 3), p. 16.

TEENAGERS' VIEWS

Description: Presents the results of a survey concerning the views and
opinions of teenagers toward a number of national and international issues.

Results: Almost half of the respondents surveyed identify alcohol as their
school's most serious problem. Student apathy and drugs follow.

Poll Extracts:

SCHOOL'S MOST SERIOUS PROBLEMS ARE:

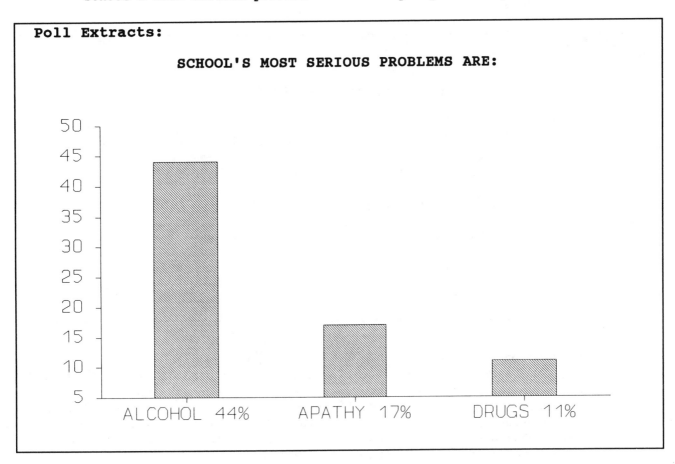

Also in Source: 35% think abortion should be banned. 79% favor the death
penalty. 41% say nuclear weapons are essential while 76% favor gun control
laws. 59% say albums with lewd lyrics should have warning labels but no
sales restrictions. For role models, 29% choose their parents. Also
mentioned: other relatives, 11%; Martin Luther King Jr. and Jesus, 4%; John
F. Kennedy and Nelson Mandela, 3%.

Poll Details: 1,181 student leaders were surveyed by *USA Today*.

Availability: Published in *USA Today*, July 2, 1990, p. 1A.

VACATION HOPES

Description: Presents the results of two surveys concerning childrens' dream vacations. Children were asked what they wanted to do when they travel, who they wanted to travel with, and what they wanted to take along.

Results: Approximately 70% of the respondents would take a book or a Nintendo set on vacation.

Poll Extracts:

ON VACATION, I WOULD TAKE:

A book................71%

Video game or Nintendo set..........68%

Favorite doll or toy...................60%

Swimsuit......................63%

Family pet......................53%

Also in Source: 16% said they wanted to travel with Batman. 45% cited swimming as their favorite vacation activity. A handful of children said they wanted to travel with George Bush, Pee-wee Herman, and ALF. In response to what they would pack, answers included lots of gum, "New Kids on the Block" posters, go-carts, computers, electric guitars, the house, a statue, and a doll house. One child would take "all 27 of my Breyer horses" and another would take a "ceiling fan."

Poll Details: Hyatt Hotels interviewed 250 children, ages five to fourteen, to find out what they want when they travel. Hilton's recent *Survey on Children and Travel* asked 300 children, ages six to twelve, what they would pack for a vacation.

Availability: Published in the *Chicago Tribune*, August 5, 1990, section 12, p. 8.

Appendix

This appendix lists the organizations, centers, or firms (with address and telephone number) that have conducted the polls and surveys included within the issue for the user who wishes to make additional inquiries.

AARP Bulletin
1909 K Street, N.W.
Washington, DC 20049
Tel. 202-872-4700

Advertising Age
Crain Communications Inc.
1400 Woodbridge
Detroit, MI 48207
Tel. 800-992-9970

Advertising Club of Greater St. Louis
440 Mansion House Ctr.
St. Louis, MO 63102
Tel. 314-231-4185

Advocacy Institute
1730 Rhode Island Ave, NW, Suite 600
Washington, DC 20036
Tel. 202-659-8475

Adweek's Marketing Week
ASM Communications, Inc
49 E. 21st St.
New York, NY 10010
Tel. 212-529-5500

AIDS Alert
67 Peachtree Dr., NE,
Atlanta, GA 30309

American Academy of Pediatrics
141 N.W. Point Blvd.
P.O. Box 927
Elk Grove Village, IL 60009
Tel. 312-228-5005

American Association of Retired Persons
1909 K Street, NW
Washington, DC 20049
Tel. 202-872-4700

American Association of School Administrators
1801 N. Moore St.
Arlington, VA 22209
Tel. 703-528-0700

American Banker
One State St. Plaza
New York, NY 10004
Tel. 212-943-6700

American Bar Association
750 N. Lake Shore Dr.
Chicago, IL 60611
Tel. 312-988-5000

American Board of Family Practice
2228 Young Dr.
Lexington, KY 40505
Tel. 606-269-5626

American Broadcasting Companies
1330 Av. of the Americas
New York, NY 10019
Tel. 212-887-7777

American Council on Education
One Dupont Circle, NW
Suite 800
Washington, DC 20036
Tel. 202-939-9300

American Demographics
American Demographics, Inc.
Box 68
Ithaca, NY 14851
Tel. 607-273-6343

American Dietetic Association
216 W. Jackson Blvd
Chicago, IL 60606
Tel. 312-899-4829

American Express Co.
200 Vesey St.
American Express Tower
New York, NY 10285
Tel. 212-640-2000

American Health
80 Fifth Av.
New York, NY 10011
Tel. 212-242-2460

American Medical Association
535 N. Dearborn Street
Chicago, IL 60610
Tel. 312-645-5000

American Resort and Residential Development Association
1220 L Street, NW, Suite 510
Washington, DC, 20005
Tel. 202-371-6700

The American School Board Journal
1680 Duke St.
Alexandria, VA 22314
Tel. 703-838-6722

American Society for Training and Development
Box 1443, 1630 Duke St.
Alexandria, VA 22313
Tel. 703-683-8100

Apparel Merchandising
425 Park Avenue
New York, NY 10022
Tel. 212-371-9400

Apple Computer, Inc.
20525-T Mariani Ave.
Cupertino, CA 95014
Tel. 408-996-1010

Armour Food Company
111 W. Clarendon
Phoenix, AZ   85077
Tel. 602-248-5666

Associated Press
50 Rockefeller Plaza
New York, NY   10020
Tel. 212-621-1500

*The Atlanta Journal
and Constitution*
72 Marietta St., NW
Atlanta, GA   30303
Tel. 404-572-5151

The Baltimore Sun
501 N. Calvert St.
Baltimore, MD   21278
Tel. 301-332-6300

Best's Review
A.M. Company
Ambest Road
Oldwick, NJ   08858
Tel. 201-439-2200

Better Business Bureau
of St. Louis
5100 Oakland
St. Louis, MO   63110
Tel. 314-531-3300

Bishops Committee for
Pastoral Research and
Practices.
National Conference of
Catholic Bishops.
3211 4th St., NE
Washington, DC   20017
Tel. 202-541-3015

Blue Cross and Blue
Shield Association
676 N. St. Clair St.
Chicago, IL   60611
Tel. 312-440-6000

Boston Foundation
60 State
Boston, MA   02109
Tel. 617-723-7415

The Boston Globe
135 Wm T. Morrissey
Blvd.
Boston, MA   02107
Tel. 617-929-2000

Bruskin Associates, R.H.
303 George Street
New Brunswick, NJ   08903
Tel. 212-349-0781

Business and Health
680 Kinderkamack Rd.
Oradell, NJ   07649
Tel. 201-262-3030

Business Month
488 Madison Ave.
New York, NY   10022
Tel. 212-326-2600

Business Week
McGraw-Hill Publications
Co.
1221 Av. of the Americas
New York, NY   10020
Tel. 212-512-2000

Cable News Network
Turner Broadcasting
System
One CNN Center
P.O. Box 105366
Atlanta, GA   30348
Tel. 404-827-1500

California State,
Fullerton
800 North State College
Boulevard
Fullerton, CA 92634
Tel. 714-773-2011

Cambridge Reports Inc.
675 Massachusetts Av.
Cambridge, MA   02139
Tel. 617-661-0110

Campaigns & Elections
1820 Jefferson Place, NW
Washington, DC   20036

Campbell Soup Company
Camden, NJ   08103
Tel. 609-342-4800

Carnegie Foundation for
the Advancement of
Teaching
Five Ivy Lane
Princeton, NJ   08540
Tel. 609-452-1780

CBS Inc.
51 W. 52 St.
New York, NY   10019
Tel. 212-975-4321

CBS News
524 W. 57th Street
New York, NY   10019
Tel. 212-975-5551

CDC Aids Weekly
Box 5528
Atlanta, GA   30307
Tel. 404-377-8895

*Chemical Marketing
Reporter*
80 Broad St.
New York, NY   10004
Tel. 212-248-4177

Chicago Tribune
435 N. Michigan Av.
Chicago, IL   60611
Tel. 312-222-3232

Chilton Research
One Chilton Way
King of Prussia Road
Radnor, PA   19089
Tel. 215-964-4606

*The Christian Science
Monitor*
One Norway Street
Boston, MA   02115

*The Chronicle of
Higher Education*
1255 23rd Street, N.W.
Suite 700
Washington, D.C.   20037
Tel. 202-466-1000

The Cincinnati Enquirer
617 Vine Street
Cincinnati, OH   45202
Tel. 513-721-2700

Cincinnati Post
125 E. Court St.
Cincinnati, OH   45202
Tel. 513-352-2000

Claremont Graduate
School
10th St. & Dartmouth Av.
Claremont, CA 91711
Tel. 714-621-8025

Coalition for the
Homeless
33 Farnsworth
Boston, MA 02210
Tel. 617-451-0707

The Columbus Dispatch
34 South 3rd Street
Columbus, OH 43215
Tel. 614-461-5000

Computerworld
375 Cochituate Road
Box 9171
Framingham, MA 01701
Tel. 617-879-0700

The Conference Board
1755 Mass. Ave., NW
Washington, DC 20036
Tel. 202-483-0580

Consumer Federation
of America
1424 16th St., NW,
Suite 604
Washington, D.C. 20036
Tel. 202-387-6121

Continental Baking
Company
Checkerboard Square
St. Louis, MO 63164
Tel. 314-982-4700

Council for Advancement
and Support of
Education
11 Dupont Circle, N.W.
Suite 400
Wasington, DC 20036
Tel. 202-328-5900

Council for Excellence
in Government
1775 Penn. Ave., N.W.
Suite 750
Washington, DC 20006
Tel. 202-728-0418

The Dallas Morning News
P.O. Box 225237
Communications Center
Dallas, TX 75265
Tel. 214-977-2085

Dayton Daily News
Fourth and Ludlow St.
Dayton, OH 45401
Tel. 513-225-2085

Deloitte & Touche
10 W. Port Road
Wilton, CT 06897
Tel. 203-761-3000

Delsey Luggage
105 40 Riggs Hill Road
Jessup, MD 20794
Tel. 800-558-3344

The Des Moines Register
P.O. Box 957
Des Moines, IA 50304
Tel. 515-284-8000

Design News
275 Washington St.
Newton, MA 02158
Tel. 617-964-3030

Detroit Free Press
321 W. Lafayette Blvd.
Detroit, MI 48231
Tel. 313-222-6400

The Detroit News
615 Lafayette Blvd
Detroit, MI 48231
Tel. 313-222-2300

Down Beat
180 W. Park Ave.
Elmhurst IL 60126
Tel. 708-941-2030

Drug Topics
680 Kinderkamack Rd.
Oradell, NJ 07649
Tel. 201-262-3030

Dun & Bradstreet, Inc.
299 Park Av.
New York, NY 10171
Tel. 212-573-6800

Ebony
820 S. Michigan Ave
Chicago, IL 60605
Tel. 312-322-9200

Education Week
4301 Connecticut Av.,
N.W., Suite 250
Washington, D.C. 20008
Tel. 202-364-4114

Electronic Business
275 Washington St.
Newton, MA 02158
Tel. 617-964-3030

*Electronic Engineering
Times*
600 Community Dr.
Manhasset, NY 11030
Tel. 516-562-5000

Electronic Media
740 Rush St.
Chicago, IL 60611
Tel. 312-649-5200

Employee Benefit
Research Institute
2121 K Street NW #860
Washington, DC 20037
Tel. 202-659-0670

Employers Council on
Flexible Compensation
927 15th Street, NW
Suite 1000
Washington, DC 20005
Tel. 202-659-4300

Ernst & Young
Huntington Building
2000 National City Ctr.
Cleveland, OH 44114
Tel. 216-861-5000

Esquire
1790 Broadway
New York, NY 10019
Tel. 212-459-7500

Family Circle
110 Fifth Av.
New York, NY 10011
Tel. 212-463-1000

Feedstuffs
12400 Whitewater Drive
Suite 160, Box 2400
Minnetonka, MN 55343
Tel. 612-931-0211

Field Institute
234 Front St.
San Francisco, CA 94111
Tel. 415-781-4921

Food Marketing Institute
1750 K St., NW
Suite 700
Washington, DC 20006
Tel. 202-452-8444

Fortune
1271 Av. of the
Americas.
New York, NY 10020
Tel. 212-522-1212

Gallup Poll
The Roper Center for
Public Opinion Research
P.O. Box 440
Storrs, CT 06268
Tel. 203-486-4440

Gannett Company
P.O. Box 7858
Washington, D.C. 20044
Tel. 202-276-5900

Gannett Foundation
1101 Wilson Blvd.
Arlington, VA 22209

Garin-Hart Strategic
Research
1724 Conn. Ave., NW
Washington, DC 20009
Tel. 202-234-5570

Gordon S. Black
Associates
1661 Penfield Road
Rochester, NY 10022
Tel. 716-248-2805

Great Western
Financial Corp.
8484 Wilshire Bl.
Beverly Hills, CA 90211
Tel. 213-852-3411

Greater Detroit Chamber
of Commerce
600 W. Lafayette
Detroit, MI 48226
Tel. 313-964-4000

Greenberg-Lake: The
Analysis Group
515 2nd Street, NE
Washington, DC 20002
Tel. 202-547-5200

Guitar Player
20085 Stevens Creek
Cupertino, CA 95014
Tel. 408-446-1105

Hammond, Phillip E.
Chairman, Dept. of
Religious Studies.
University of California
at Santa Barbara.
Santa Barbara, CA 93106
Tel. 805-961-2311

Harris Survey.
Institute for Social
Research.
The University of North
Carolina at Chapel Hill.
Manning Hall 026A
Chapel Hill, NC 27514
Tel. 919-966-3346

Harte-Hanks Communi-
cations, Inc.
P.O. Box 269
San Antonio, TX 78291
Tel. 512-829-9000

Health Insurance
Association of America
1025 Conn. Ave., NW
Suite 1200
Washington, DC 20036
Tel. 202-223-7780

HFD
HFD-Retailing Home
Furnishings
7 East 12th St.
New York, NY 10003

Hospitals
211 East Chicago Ave.
Suite 700
Chicago, IL 60611
Tel. 312-440-6800

Hudson Institute
5395 Emerson Way
Helman Kahn Center
P.O. Box 26-919
Indianapolis, IN 46226
Tel. 317-545-1000

ICF Inc.
9300 Lee Highway
FairFax, VA 22031
Tel. 703-934-3000

In View
529 Fifth Ave., 11th
Floor
New York, NY 10017
Tel. 615-595-5000

Inc.
488 Madison Ave.
New York, NY 1022
Tel. 212-326-2600

Indiana Department of
Education
100 North Capitol St.
Number 229
Indianapolis, IN 46204
Tel. 317-232-6610

Industry Week
1100 Superior Ave
Cleveland, OH 44114
Tel. 216-696-7000

Institute for Policy
Research.
University of Cincinnati
Clifton Av.
Cincinnati, OH 45221
Tel. 513-475-5028

Institutional Investor
488 Madison Ave
New York, NY 10022
Tel. 212-303-3510

International
Association
for Financial Planning
Two Concourse Pkwy
Suite 800
Atlanta, GA 30328
Tel. 404-395-1605

International
Association
of Chiefs of Police
1110 N. Glebe Road
Suite 200
Arlington, VA 22201
Tel. 703-243-6500

International Food
Information Council
1331 Penn. Ave., NW,
Suite 717
Washington, DC 20004
Tel. 202-662-1280

International Foundation
for Timesharing
1220 L Street, NW,
5th Floor
Washington, DC 20005
Tel. 202-371-6700

J.D. Power & Associates
Agoura Hills, CA
Tel. 818-889-6330

JAMA: The Journal of
the American Medical
Association.
535 North Dearborn St.
Chicago, IL 60610
Tel. 312-645-5000

Johnson Foundation,
Robert Wood
P.O. Box 2316
Princeton, NJ 08543
Tel. 609-452-8701

Korbel Champagne Cellars
River Rd.
Guerneville, CA
Tel. 707-887-2294

KRC Communications
Research
30 Norfolk
Cambridge, MA 02139
Tel. 617-491-8070

Ladies Home Journal
1716 Locust St.
Des Moines, IA 50336
Tel. 515-284-3000

Levi Strauss & Co.
1155-T Battery St.
San Francisco, CA 94106
Tel. 415-544-6000

LEXIS
9393 Springsboro Pike
P.O. Box 933
Dayton, OH 45401
Tel. 513-865-6800

Lilly Endowment
2801 North Meridian St.
P.O. Box 88068
Indianapolis, IN 46208
Tel. 317-924-5471

Lodging Hospitality
1100 Superior Ave
Cleveland, OH 44114
Tel. 216-696-7000

Los Angeles Times
Times Mirror Square
Los Angeles, CA 90053
Tel. 213-972-7972

Louis Harris &
Associates Inc.
630 5th Ave.
New York, NY 10111
Tel. 212-698-9600

MacArthur Foundation,
John D. and Catherine T.
140 South Dearborn St.
Chicago, IL 60603
Tel. 312-726-8000

MacArthur Foundation, J.
Roderick.
9333 North Milwaukee Av.
Niles, IL 60648
Tel. 312-966-0143

Macleans
Magazine Division
Maclean-Hunter Bldg
777 Bay St.
Toronto, Ont.
M5W 1A7, Canada
Tel. 416-596-5000

Market Facts, Inc.
676 N. St. Clair St.
Chicago, IL 60611
Tel. 312-280-9100

Market Opinion Research
243 W. Congress
Detroit, MI 48226
Tel. 313-963-2414

Marriott Corp.
10400 Fernwood Rd.
Bethesda, MD 20058
Tel. 301-897-9000

Mathematica Policy
Research, Inc.
600 Maryland Av., SW
Suite 550
Washington, DC 20024
Tel. 202-484-9220

Mayo Clinic
200 First St., SW
Rochester, MN 55901

McCall's
230 Park Ave.
New York, NY 10169
Tel. 212-916-3411

Media General
333 E. Grace St.
Richmond, VA 23219
Tel. 804-649-6000

Medical Care
E. Washington Square
Philadelphia, PA 19105
Tel. 215-238-4200

Men's Life
News America Publishing
Inc.
1211 Av. of the Americas
New York, NY 10036

Miami University
East High St.
Oxford, OH 45056
Tel. 513-529-2161

Michigan State
University
East Lansing, MI 48824
Tel. 517-355-1855

Monsanto Chemical
Company
800 North Lindbergh
St. Louis, MO 63167
Tel. 800-325-4330

Motor Trend
8490 Sunset Blvd.
Los Angeles, CA 90069
Tel. 213-854-2222

Motor Vehicles Manu-
facturers Association
7430 Second Ave
Suite 300
Detroit, MI 48202
Tel. 313-872-4311

National Association of
Black and White Men
Together
584 Castro St.
Suite 140
San Francisco, CA 94114
Tel. 415-431-1976

National Association of
Chain Drug Stores
P.O. Box 1417-D49
Alexandria, VA 22313
Tel. 703-549-3001

National Association of
Business Economists.
28790 Chagrin Blvd.
Suite 300
Cleveland, OH 44122
Tel. 216-464-7986

National Association of
Elementary School
Principals
1615 Duke St.
Alexandria, VA 22314

National Association
of Realtors
430 N. Michigan Ave.
Chicago, IL 60611
Tel. 312-329-8200

National Business
Travel Association
3255 Wilshire Blvd.
Suite 1514
Los Angeles, CA 90010
Tel. 213-382-3335

National Education
Association
1201 16th St., N.W.
Washington, DC 20036
Tel. 202-833-4000

National Food Processors
Association
1401 New York Ave., NW,
4th Floor
Washington, DC 20005

National Gardening
Association
180 Flynn Ave.
Burlington, VT 05401
Tel. 802-863-1308

National Institute on
Drug Abuse.
Public Health Service
200 Independence Av., SW
Washington, DC 20201
Tel. 301-443-6487

*The National Law
Journal*
111 Eighth Av.
New York, NY 10011
Tel. 212-741-8300

National Research Group
Los Angeles, CA
Tel. 213-856-4400

National Restaurant
Association.
1200 17th St., NW
Washington, DC 20036
Tel. 202-331-5900

National Rifle
Association
1600 Rhode Island Av.,
NW
Washington, DC 20036
Tel. 202-828-6000

National Science
Teachers
Association
1742 Conn. Ave, NW
Washington, DC 20009
Tel. 202-328-5800

National Small Business
United
1155 15th St., N.W.
Suite 710
Washington, DC 44124
Tel. 202-293-8830

National Society of
Professional Engineers.
1420 King Street
Alexandria, VA 22314
Tel. 703-684-2800

National Underwriter
420 East 4th Street
Cincinnati, OH 45202
Tel. 513-721-2140

NBC News
Room 1700
30 Rockefeller Plaza
New York, NY 10036
Tel. 212-664-2593

The NCAA News
Box 1906
Mission, KS 66201
Tel. 913-831-8300

NEA Today
1201 16th St., N.W.
Washington, DC 20036
Tel. 202-822-7200

The New York Times
News Surveys, 6th Floor
229 W. 43rd Street
New York, NY 10036
Tel. 212-556-1234

*New England Journal of
Medicine.*
1440 Main St.
Waltham, MA 02254
Tel. 800-843-6356

NewsWeek
444 Madison Ave
New York, NY 10022
Tel. 212-350-2000

NSTA Reports
1742 Conn. Ave., NW
Washington, DC 20009
Tel. 202-328-5800

Opinion Research Corp.
500 East St., SW
Washington, DC 20024
Tel. 202-484-5992

Parade
750 Third Ave.
New York, NY 10017
Tel. 212-573-7000

Parents
Gruner & Jahr U.S.A.
Publishing
685 Third Ave.
New York, NY 10017
Tel. 212-878-8700

Paul R. Ray & Co.
1 Ravinia Dr.
Atlanta, GA 30346
Tel. 404-399-5809

Penn & Schoen Associates
245 E. 92nd Street
New York, NY 10128
Tel. 212-534-4000

People for the
American Way
2000 M St., NW
Suite 400
Washington, DC 20036
Tel. 202-467-4999

People Weekly
Time, Inc.
Time & Life Building
Rockefeller Center
New York, NY 10020
Tel. 212-522-1212

Personal Computing
999 Riverview Dr.,
Totowa, NJ 07512
Tel. 201-812-1200

Peter D. Hart
Associates
1724 Conn. Ave, N.W.
Washington, DC 20009
Tel. 202-234-5570

Phillip Morris Co.
120 Park Ave.
New York, NY 10017
Tel. 212-880-5000

Playboy
919 N. Michigan Ave
Chicago, IL 60611
Tel. 312-751-8000

Playskool Inc.
4501 West Augusta Blvd.
Chicago, IL 60651
Tel. 312-276-6700

Public Citizen
P.O. Box 19404
Washington, DC 20036
Tel. 312-673-9100

Rand McNally & Company
P.O. Box 7600
Chicago, IL 60680
Tel. 312-673-9100

Redbook
224 W. 57th St.
New York, NY 10019
Tel. 212-649-3450

Research & Development
1350 E. Touhy Ave
Box 5080
Des Plaines, IL 60017
Tel. 708-635-8800

Research & Forecasts
Inc.
301 E. 57th Street
New York, NY 10022

Restaurant Hospitality
1100 Superior Ave
Cleveland, OH 44114
Tel. 216-696-7000

*Restaurants and
Institutions.*
Cahners Plaza
1350 E. Touhy Av.
Des Plaines, IL 60018
Tel. 312-635-8800

Rhode Island Hospital
593 Eddy Street
Providence, RI 02903
Tel. 401-277-4000

Ricoh Corporation
5-T Dedrick Place
W. Caldwell, NJ 07006
Tel. 201-882-2000

The Roper Center for
Public Opinion Research
P.O. Box 440
Storrs, CT 06268
Tel. 203-486-4440

San Francisco Chronicle
925 Mission St.
San Francisco, CA 94103
Tel. 415-777-5700

Scholastic Update
730 Broadway
New York, NY 10003
Tel. 212-505-3000

Science
1333 H. St., NW
Washington, DC 20005
Tel. 202-326-6500

Science World
730 Broadway
New York, NY 10003
Tel. 212-505-3000

Shaklee Corporation
444 Market
San Francisco, CA 94111
Tel. 415-954-3000

Society for Information
Management.
One Illinois Center
111 E. Wacker Drive
Suite 600
Chicago, IL 60601
Tel. 312-644-6610

State University of
New York at Albany
1400 Washington Ave.
Albany, NY 12222
Tel. 518-457-8390

Steelcase Inc.
1120-T
36th Street, SE
Grand Rapids, MI 49508
Tel. 616-247-2710

Supermarket Business
25 West 43rd St.
New York, NY 10036

*Tax Management
Financial Planning
Journal*
1231 25th St., N.W.
Washington, DC 20037
Tel. 202-452-4200

Technology Review
Mass. Institute of
Technology, Alumni
Association. W59-200
Cambridge, MA   02139
Tel. 617-253-8250

Texas A&M University
Public Policy Resources
Laboratory
100 Harrington Tower
College Station,
TX   77843
Tel. 409-845-8800

Texas Women's University
P.O. Box 23925
Denton, TX 76204
Tel. 817-383-1466

Time
Time, Inc
Time & Life Building
New York, NY   10020
Tel. 212-522-1212

Times Mirror Center
Times Mirror Square
Los Angeles, CA   90053
Tel. 213-972-7972

Today's Office
645 Stewart Ave.
Garden City, NY 11530
Tel. 516-227-1300

Travel Weekly
500 Plaza Dr.
Secaucus, NJ   07096
Tel. 201-902-2000

Travel & Leisure
1120 Ave. of the
Americas
New York, NY   10036
Tel. 212-382-5600

U.S. Centers for Disease
Control
1600 Clifton Road, NE
Atlanta, GA   30333
Tel. 404-329-3311

U.S. Dept. of Education
400 Maryland Ave., SW
Washington, DC   20202
Tel. 202-245-3192

U.S. Catholic
205 W. Monroe St.
Chicago, IL   60606
Tel. 312-236-7782

Union of Concerned
Scientists.
26 Church St.
Cambridge, MA   02238
Tel. 617-547-5552

University of Akron
Akron, OH 44325
Tel. 216-375-7111

University of
California, Los Angeles
Higher Education
Research Institute.
Graduate School of
Education.
Los Angeles, CA   90024
Tel. 213-825-1925

University of Michigan
Ann Arbor, MI 48109
Tel. 313-764-1817

University of Virginia
Charlottesville,
Virginia 22903
Tel. 804-924-0311

USA Today
1000 Wilson Blvd.
Arlington, VA   22229
Tel. 703-276-3400

USA Weekend
535 Madison Ave.
New York, NY   10022
Tel. 212-715-2000

The Wall Street Journal
200 Liberty Street
New York, NY   10281
Tel. 800-841-8000

Walt Disney Co.
500 S. Buena Vista St.
Burbank, CA   91521
Tel. 818-560-1000

The Washington Post
1150 15th Street, NW
Washington, DC   20071
Tel. 202-334-6000

The Washingtonian
1828 L. St., N.W.
Suite 200
Washington, DC   20036
Tel. 202-296-3600

Way, Philip K.
University of
Cincinnati, Main Campus
Cincinnati, OH   45221
Tel. 513-556-6000

Wayne State University
Center for Urban Studies
5229 Cass Av.
Detroit, MI   48202
Tel. 313-577-2208

Weekly Reader
245 Long Hill Rd.
Middletown, CT 06457
Tel. 614-771-0006

Weight Watchers
International.
500 North Broadway
Jericho, NY   11753
Tel. 516-939-0400

*Who's Who Among American
High School Students*
Educational
Communications, Inc.
721 N. McKinley Rd.
Lake Forest, IL 60045
Tel. 708-295-6650

Wirthlin Group
1363 Beverly Road
McLean, VA   22101
Tel. 703-556-0001

Working Woman
342 Madison Ave
New York, NY   10173
Tel. 212-309-9800

World Policy Institute
777 United Nations Plaza
New York, NY   10017
Tel. 212-490-0010

Yankelovich Clancy
Shulman
8 Wright Street
Westport, CT   06880
Tel. 203-227-2700

Index